# READINGS IN
# EUROPEAN HISTORY

——

## ABRIDGED EDITION

# READINGS IN

# EUROPEAN HISTORY

*A collection of extracts from the sources chosen with
the purpose of illustrating the progress of
culture in Western Europe since
the German Invasions*

BY

## JAMES HARVEY ROBINSON

PROFESSOR OF HISTORY IN COLUMBIA UNIVERSITY

## ABRIDGED EDITION

IN ONE VOLUME

## GINN AND COMPANY

BOSTON · NEW YORK · CHICAGO · LONDON
ATLANTA · DALLAS · COLUMBUS · SAN FRANCISCO

The Athenæum Press

GINN AND COMPANY · PRO-
PRIETORS · BOSTON · U.S.A.

# PREFACE

It is now generally conceded by teachers that the study of history should consist of something more than plying the text-book, — a method simple, no doubt, and enjoying the sanction of immemorial usage, but painful and on the whole rather fruitless. The text-book is doubtless as essential as ever as a means of supplying the learner with a coherent outline of the subject, but this outline must be given reality and life by recourse to fuller and more vivid accounts of events and persons than can be looked for in even the most carefully constructed manual.

In order to meet this need, so called "source books" have been appearing of late, not only in the United States but in England, France, and Germany. These furnish in a more or less convenient form the very best of all existing material for collateral reading and for discussion, namely, examples of the sources themselves. This is not the place to defend the judicious use of extracts from the sources; indeed, such defense would be superfluous, since few teachers now question the expediency of the newer method, if only the illustrative extracts can be brought into organic relation with the general historical narrative, so that there may be no danger of confusing the student.

It is precisely with a view of obviating this danger that I have arranged my *Readings* so as to follow, chapter by chapter, my *Introduction to the History of Western Europe.* I have, moreover, chosen the extracts with the purpose of reënforcing the main points made in the manual, so that the outline and the source book work together throughout.

I cannot but think that this close interrelation will prove a great convenience.

The present volume is an abridgment of my fuller course of *Readings in European History* occupying two volumes, the first of which relates to the period before the Protestant Revolt, the second to the four centuries which have since elapsed. I regret that there should be any need for this shorter collection of extracts, since the complete edition contains none too much. Yet there are several obvious reasons why teachers, especially in the schools, should find one volume all that they can expect their students to have in hand. I have accordingly reduced the original collection by more than half by omitting many extracts altogether, by cutting down in a few cases those that I retained, and by excising those portions of the bibliographies which had to do with strictly advanced study.

J. H. R.

COLUMBIA UNIVERSITY, NEW YORK,
    January 1, 1906.

# CONTENTS AND LIST OF CITATIONS

## CHAPTER I — THE HISTORICAL POINT OF VIEW

## CHAPTER II — WESTERN EUROPE BEFORE THE BARBARIAN INVASIONS

---

[1] While I have freely availed myself of the assistance offered by translations, I have not hesitated to modify, or even frankly desert in some cases, the renderings which I mention in this list.

## CHAPTER XXII — THE ITALIAN CITIES AND THE RENAISSANCE

## CHAPTER XXIII — EUROPE AT THE OPENING OF THE SIXTEENTH CENTURY

## CHAPTER XXVII — THE PROTESTANT REVOLT IN SWITZERLAND AND ENGLAND

## CHAPTER XXXVI — THE FIRST FRENCH REPUBLIC

## CHAPTER XXXVII — NAPOLEON BONAPARTE

## CHAPTER XLI — EUROPE OF TO-DAY

# READINGS IN
# EUROPEAN HISTORY

## CHAPTER I

### THE HISTORICAL POINT OF VIEW

It is clear that all our information in regard to past events and conditions must be derived from evidence of some kind. This evidence is called the *source*. Sometimes there are a number of good and reliable sources for an event, as, for example, for the decapitation of Charles I, or for the march of Napoleon into Russia. Sometimes there is but a single, unreliable source, as, for instance, in the case of the burial of Alaric in a river bed.[1] For a great many important matters about which we should like to know there are, unfortunately, no written sources at all, and we can only guess how things were. For example, we do not know what the Germans were doing before Cæsar came into contact with them and took the trouble to give a brief account of them. We can learn but little about the bishops of Rome before the time of Constantine, for few references to them have come down to us.

*Primary or original historical sources.*

Few, however, of those who read and study history ever come in contact with the *primary*, or first-hand

*Secondary sources.*

[1] See Vol. I, p. 43, of the unabridged edition of the *Readings*.

sources; they get their information at second hand.   It is much more convenient to read what Gibbon has to say of Constantine than to refer to Eusebius, Eutropius, and other ancient writers from whom he gained his knowledge.   Moreover, Gibbon carefully studied and compared all the primary sources, and it may be urged that he has given a truer, fuller, and more attractive account of the period than can be found in any one of them. His *Decline and Fall of the Roman Empire* is certainly a work of the highest rank; but, nevertheless, it is only a report of others' reports.   It is therefore not a *primary* but a *secondary* source.

Most of the historical knowledge current among us is not, however, derived from even secondary sources, such as Gibbon and similar authoritative writers, but comes from the reading of text-books, encyclopedias, stories, dramas, and magazine articles.   Popular manuals and articles are commonly written by those who know little or nothing of the primary sources; they are consequently at least *third* hand, even when based upon the best secondary accounts.   As a matter of fact, they are usually patched together from older manuals and articles, and may be four, five, or six removes from the original source of knowledge.

It is well known that the oftener a report passes from mouth to mouth the less trustworthy and accurate does it tend to become.   Unimportant details which appeal to the imagination will be magnified, while fundamental considerations are easily forgotten, if they happen to be prosaic and commonplace.   Historians, like other men, are sometimes fond of good stories and may be led astray by some false rumor which, once started into circulation, gets farther and farther from the truth with each repetition.

For example, a distinguished historian of the Church, Cardinal Baronius, writing about 1600, made the statement, upon very insufficient evidence, that, as the year 1000 approached, the people of Europe generally believed that the world was about to come to an end. Robertson, a very popular Scotch historian of the eighteenth century, repeated the statement and went on to describe the terrible panic which seized upon sinful men as the awful year drew on. Succeeding writers, including some very distinguished ones, accepted and even elaborated Robertson's account. About thirty years ago, however, a French scholar pointed out that there was really no adequate basis for this strange tale. To the chroniclers of the time the year 1000 was clearly no more portentous than 997 or 1003. This story of the panic, which passed current as historical fact for some three hundred years, offers an excellent illustration of the danger of relying upon secondary sources.

Sad example of the mythical panic of the year 1000.

One of the first questions then to ask upon taking up an historical work is, Where did the writer obtain his information? Has he simply copied his statements from the more easily accessible works in his own language, however unreliable and out of date they may be ; or has he, dissatisfied with such uncertain sources, familiarized himself with the most recent researches of the distinguished scholars in his field, in whatever language they may have been written; or, still better, has he himself made a personal study of the original evidence which has come down to us of the events and conditions which he discusses?

The importance of the question, Where did the writer obtain his information

For example, a little book or essay on **Charlemagne** might be written after reading Hodgkin's *Charles the Great*, West's *Alcuin*, and one or two other easily accessible books on the subject.   On the other hand, the writer might turn to the great French and German treatises on Charlemagne's reign and acquaint himself with all the articles which have appeared on the subject in historical magazines or in the transactions of learned societies. Every conscientious historian would wish, however, to go still farther and see the evidence with his own eyes and draw his own conclusions.   He would turn to the sources themselves and carefully read the Annals of Lorsch, the life of Charlemagne by his secretary, Einhard, and the valuable Annals which some scholars also attribute to Einhard.   He would also scrutinize all the numerous laws passed in Charlemagne's reign and consult all the writers of the time who refer to the emperor or to public events.   In this way he would master all that the past has handed down to us upon this subject and would know all that is to be known about the matter. The most reliable historian, therefore, is one who examines the sources for himself, but who at the same time takes advantage of the suggestions, criticisms, and explanations which have been made by other scholars who have also studied the original documents.

Advantages of making some use of the primary sources in teaching and studying history.

No improvement in the methods of historical instruction in our high schools and colleges bids fair to produce better results than the plan of bringing the student into contact with the first-hand accounts of events, or, as they are technically termed, the *primary sources*.

This term may perhaps call up in the minds of some the vision of a solitary stoop-shouldered, spectacled enthusiast, engaged in painfully deciphering obscure Latin abbreviations on yellow parchment. But it is a mistake to conclude that the primary sources are always difficult to get at, dull, and hard to read. On the contrary, they are sometimes ready to hand, and are often more vivid and entertaining than even the most striking descriptions by the pen of gifted writers like Gibbon or Macaulay.

The best secondary authorities stand to the sources somewhat as the description of a work of art or of a masterpiece of literature stands to the original. Just as we cannot afford to ignore the picture itself, or the great poem or drama, and confine ourselves to some one else's account of it, so in our historical work we ought to grasp every opportunity of examining for ourselves the foundations upon which history rests.

It may, of course, be urged that the trained historian, after acquainting himself with the men and the circumstances of a particular period, can make better use of the sources than any relatively unskilled student. But, admitting the force of this argument, there is, nevertheless, so much to be learned from a study of the original accounts that cannot be reproduced by the most skilled hand, that no earnest student or reader should content himself with second-hand descriptions when primary sources are available.

The sources are unconsciously molded by the spirit of the time in which they were written. Every line gives some hint of the period in which the author lived and makes an impression upon us which volumes of second-hand accounts can never produce. The mere information, too, comes to us in a form which we do not easily forget. The facts sink into our memory.

*Vividness of the primary sources.*

One who actually talked with Attila, or who witnessed the capture of Jerusalem by the crusaders, is clearly more likely to excite our interest than a writer of our own day, however much he may know of the king of the Huns or of the first crusade. It makes no great impression upon us to be told that the scholars of Dante's time had begun to be interested once more in the ancient learning of the Greeks and Romans; but no one can forget Dante's own poetic account of his kindly reception in the lower regions by the august representatives of pagan literature, — Homer, Horace, Ovid, and Lucan, — people "with eyes slow and grave, of great authority in their looks," who " spake seldom and with soft voices."

A study of the sources cultivates judgment and fair-mindedness. Moreover, the study of the sources enables us to some extent to form our own opinions of the past, so that we need not rely entirely upon mere manuals, which are always one, and generally two or three, removes from the sources themselves. When we get at the sources themselves we no longer merely read and memorize; we begin to consider what may be safely inferred from the statements before us and so develop the all-important faculty of criticism. We are not simply accumulating facts but are attempting to determine their true nature and meaning.

The power to do this is not alone necessary to scholarly work; it is of the utmost importance as well in dealing with the affairs of everyday life. To take a single illustration : one cannot fail to see from a study of the sources that Luther was exceedingly unfair to his enemies and ascribed their conduct to evil motives when they were acting quite consistently and according to what they considered the truth. His opponents, on the other hand, treated him with equal unfairness and proclaimed him a wicked and profligate man because he refused to accept their views.

We meet precisely the same unfairness nowadays, as, for instance, in the case of a municipal election, where each party speaks only evil of the other. It is, however, not so hard to look impartially at the motives and conduct of men who lived long ago as it is to be fair-minded in matters which interest us personally very deeply. By cultivating sympathy and impartiality in dealing with the past we may hope to reach a point where we can view the present coolly and temperately. In this way really thoughtful, historical study serves to develop the very fundamental virtues of sympathy, fairness, and caution in forming our judgments.

Even as lately as a hundred years ago the path to the sources of European history was still a thorny one. The manuscripts of historical importance were often scattered about in innumerable small collections, chiefly in the monasteries. The documents were stacked up in dark rooms, damp cellars, and dusty garrets. They were often carelessly transcribed, full of blunders, and illegible except to those specially versed in the art of deciphering ancient handwriting. There were usually no catalogues and nothing to guide the investigator to the material of which he was in search. He was forced to travel from place to place and turn over masses of worthless or irrelevant matter in the uncertain quest for the little which might be useful to him. *Former difficulties in the way of using manuscript sources.*

But all this is changed. The scholar may now sit at a convenient desk in a comfortable, well-lighted library; he has a clearly printed book before him, the text of *Amenities of modern historical investigation* which has been established by a comparison of all the known manuscripts of the work in question. These have been collated by an expert; errors have been eliminated, and difficult passages annotated. The work has been carefully analyzed and supplied with an index, so that one may discover in a few moments just those paragraphs which have to do with the subject in hand.

How the sources have been printed in convenient collections.

The task of rendering the sources available has been a long and painful one, and has been going on for three or four hundred years. As early as the sixteenth century scholars began to bring together the mediæval chronicles and print them in convenient collections. In the time of Louis XIV a group of Benedictine monks in France won new distinction for their ancient order by publishing several admirable series and by preparing treatises to facilitate historical research.

Progress during the nineteenth century.

The nineteenth century witnessed a development of the critical scientific spirit which has made it necessary to reprint many sources that had appeared previously in a defective form. Moreover, thousands of volumes of precious material hitherto available only in manuscript have been added to our resources.

# CHAPTER II

## WESTERN EUROPE BEFORE THE BARBARIAN INVASIONS

### I. Some Resemblances between Thoughtful Paganism and Christianity

The philosopher and statesman, Seneca (d. A.D. 65), who lived in the time of Nero, in his little book on *Benefits* speaks thus of the bounty of God:

Doth not God bestow all benefits upon us? From whence then hast thou all those things whereof thou art possessed? which thou givest? which thou deniest? which thou keepest? which thou takest unjustly? From whence come the infiniteness of things that delight the eye, affect the ear, and please the understanding? . . . From whence have we so many trees, bearing sundry sorts of savory fruit, so many wholesome herbs, for the maintenance of our health, such variety of meats, strong for all seasons through the whole year, so that an idle sluggard may pick up without effort sufficient sustenance upon the earth to feed and nourish him? . . .

1. Seneca on God's gifts to man.

If a man should give thee money, and fill thy coffer (for that seemeth a great thing in thy sight), thou wouldst term it a benefit. And thinkest thou it no favor, that God hath hidden so many metals in the earth, spread so many rivers on the sands, which floating, discover ingots of massy gold, silver, brass, and iron, which he hath hidden everywhere; that he hath given thee means and knowledge to find it out, by setting marks of his covert riches on the upper face of the earth? If a man should give thee a house enriched with marble pillars, if the cover thereof were resplendent, and painted with gold and goodly colors, thou

9

wouldst highly esteem this present of his : God hath builded thee a great palace, without any danger or fear of falling down, wherein thou seest not little pieces, smaller than the chisel itself wherewith they were carved, but entire huge masses of precious stone, all fastened and fashioned after divers manners, the least piece whereof maketh thee wonder at the beauty of the same : the roof whereof shineth after one sort by day and after another by night : and wilt thou then deny that thou hast received any benefit at all? . . .

It is Nature, saith one, that communicateth and giveth me all these things. But understandest thou not that in speaking after this manner, thou only changest the name of God? For what else is Nature but God, a divine being and reason, which by his searching assistance resideth in the world, and all the parts thereof? . . .

Seneca on un-selfish giving.

To bestow a favor in hope to receive another, is a contemptible and base usury. How badly soever thy former favors have fallen out, yet persevere thou in bestowing others. They are best hoarded in the hands of the ungrateful, whom either shame, or occasion, or imitation, may at length fashion to be grateful. Persevere continually, and cease not to be bountiful : accomplish that good work which thou hast begun, and perform the duty of a good man. Relieve this man with thy goods, another with thy credit; that man by thy favor, this with thy good counsels and wholesome precepts.

2. Epictetus.

Some idea of the resemblance between the beliefs of the Stoics and those of the Christians may be obtained from the teachings of Epictetus, a slave who for many years belonged to a member of Nero's household. By some whim of his master's, Epictetus was given a good education, and after his master's death he taught philosophy at Rome. He himself wrote nothing, but a devoted pupil of his — Arrian — has left us a conscientious account of his teachings, which represent the most elevated form of stoicism.

If the things are true which are said by the philosophers about the kinship between God and man, what else remains for men to do than what Socrates did? Never say, in reply to the question, To what country do you belong? that you are an Athenian, or a Corinthian, but that you are a citizen of the world. . . . He who has observed with intelligence the administration of the world, and has learned that the greatest and the supreme and the most comprehensive community is that which is composed of men and God, . . . why should not such a man call himself a citizen of the world, why not a son of God, and why should he be afraid of anything which happens among men? Is kinship with the emperor or with any other of the powerful in Rome sufficient to enable us to live in safety, and above contempt and without any fear at all? But to have God for your maker, and father, and guardian, shall not this release us from our sorrows and fears?

*Like the Christians, Epictetus held that all men were brothers, for all were God's children.*

## II. The Church and the Roman Emperors

In spite of the fact that the Roman emperors permitted the greatest variety of worship within their vast realm and showed no disposition to compel their subjects to think alike upon religious matters, they viewed Christianity with the most cruel suspicion almost from its first appearance. Christians were assumed to be hostile to the government, and were consequently treated with the utmost harshness. Even the wisest and best emperors, such as Trajan and Marcus Aurelius, ordered that any one should be condemned to death who was convicted of bearing the name of Christian.[1]

*3. Edict of Galerius (311), which first granted toleration to the Christians.*

---

[1] Christians were not, however, to be sought out by the government officials and could only be tried when accusation was brought against them by some definite person. A series of extracts illustrating the extent and character of the early persecutions of the Christians is to be found in *Translations and Reprints*, Vol. IV, No. 1.

Christians were first put upon a legal footing with
adherents of the various pagan religions by Emperor
Galerius in the year 311.[1]   His edict reads as follows:

Amongst our other measures for the advantage of the
Empire, we have hitherto endeavored to bring all things
into conformity with the ancient laws and public order of the
Romans.   We have been especially anxious that even the
Christians, who have abandoned the religion of their ancestors, should return to reason.   For they have fallen, we
know not how, into such perversity and folly that, instead
of adhering to those ancient institutions which possibly
their own forefathers established, they have arbitrarily made
laws of their own and collected together various peoples
from various quarters.

After the publication, on our part, of an order commanding the Christians to return to the observance of the ancient
customs, many of them, it is true, submitted in view of the
danger, while many others suffered death.   Nevertheless,
since many of them have continued to persist in their opinions and we see that in the present situation they neither
duly adore and venerate the gods nor yet worship the god
of the Christians, we, with our wonted clemency, have judged
it wise to extend a pardon even to these men and permit
them once more to become Christians and reëstablish their
places of meeting; in such manner, however, that they shall
in no way offend against good order.   We propose to notify
the magistrates in another mandate in regard to the course
that they should pursue.

Wherefore it should be the duty of the Christians, in
view of our clemency, to pray to their god for our welfare,
for that of the Empire, and for their own, so that the Empire

---

[1] A German scholar, Seeck, has pretty conclusively shown that the
so-called Edict of Milan, by which Constantine was long supposed to
have rescued the Christians from persecution, was not really an edict
at all, but a letter addressed by Constantine's colleague, Licinius, to
some government official in the East, commanding him to see that the
edict of Galerius was carried out in a thorough manner.

may remain intact in all its parts, and that they themselves may live safely in their habitations.

When under Theodosius II a collection of the laws of the Roman Empire was published (438), the edicts which had been issued by Constantine and the succeeding emperors in regard to the Christian religion, — the privileges of the clergy, the status of heretics, etc., — were conveniently brought together in the last book of the new code. The very first title, *On the Catholic Faith*, makes it clear that the government would tolerate no one who disagreed with the particular form of Christian belief which the state chose to sanction.

*4. The edicts of Constantine and his successors relating to the Church in the Theodosian Code.*

We desire that all those who are under the sway of our clemency shall adhere to that religion which, according to his own testimony, coming down even to our own day, the blessed apostle Peter delivered to the Romans, namely, the doctrine which the pontiff Damasus [bishop of Rome] and Peter, bishop of Alexandria, a man of apostolic sanctity, accept. According to the teachings of the apostles and of the Gospel we believe in one Godhead of the Father, Son, and Holy Ghost, the blessed Trinity, alike in majesty.

*The Roman government orders every one to accept the view of the Trinity defined by the Council of Nicæa.*

We ordain that the name of Catholic Christians shall apply to all those who obey this present law. All others we judge to be mad and demented ; we declare them guilty of the infamy of holding heretical doctrine ; their assemblies shall not receive the name of churches. They shall first suffer the wrath of God, then the punishment which in accordance with divine judgment we shall inflict [A.D. 380].

The emperors showed themselves ready to exempt the orthodox clergy from the various taxes and other public burdens imposed by the state, but upon condition that only poor men should become clerics. No decurion, that is to say one who was rich enough to assume the heavy responsibilities which the government threw upon the wealthier class in the cities, might join the clergy.

The clergy to be exempted from public burdens; but only the poor in this world's goods to be admitted to the clergy.

Those who exercise the functions of divine worship, that is to say those who are called clerics [*clerici*], shall be exempt from all public burdens, lest otherwise they might be called away from their sacred duties through some one's malicious interference [A.D. 319].

Immunity from public burdens is to be granted neither by custom nor upon any one's plea that he is a clergyman; nor may persons join the order of the clergy easily or in too great numbers. But when a cleric dies another shall be chosen in his stead. He shall not be of decurion rank by descent, nor possess sufficient means easily to bear the public burdens. Should doubt arise between a city and the clergy in regard to any candidate, if justice indicates that he should bear the public burdens and he should appear, either by descent or owing to his patrimony, to be suitable for the rank of decurion, he shall leave the clergy and be turned over to the city. For it is proper that the rich should bear the burdens of the world and that the poor should be supported by the wealth of the Church [A.D. 326].

The government would have the clergy a poor, hereditary class.

From public burdens and from every disquietude of civil office all clerics shall be free, and their sons shall continue in the Church if they are not subject to public responsibilities [A.D. 349].

Exemption from personal taxation.

We decree that all priests, deacons, subdeacons, exorcists, lectors, and doorkeepers, likewise all who are in higher orders, shall be free from personal taxes[1] [A.D. 377].

Bequests to the Church.

Every one shall have the right, when he is dying, to leave so much of his goods as he will to the holy and Catholic Church . . . [A.D. 321].

---

[1] Church lands were, however, by no means to be exempted from the land tax, nor were the clergy to engage in trade on any considerable scale without paying the tax to which lay tradesmen were subject.

It is right that clerics, whether they be bishops, priests, deacons, or those of lower rank, ministers of the Christian law, should be accused only before a bishop — unless there is some reason why the case should be considered elsewhere [A.D. 412].

Minor civil cases and those where church rites were involved were also to be tried by ecclesiastics. These provisions were the beginning of "benefit of clergy" and of the vast jurisdiction of the mediæval Church.

Clerics adhering to the Eunomian or Montanist superstition shall be excluded from all intercourse with any city or town. Should any of these heretics sojourning in the country attempt to gather the people together or collect an assembly, let them be sent into perpetual exile. . . .

We command that their books, which contain the substance of their criminal teachings, be sought out with the utmost care and burnt with fire under the eyes of the magistrates. Should any one perchance be convicted of concealing, through deceit or otherwise, and of failing to produce, any work of this kind, let him know that as the possessor of harmful books written with criminal intent he shall suffer capital punishment [A.D. 398].

III. Comparison between the Lot of those within the Empire and those who lived among Barbarians

It was inevitable that thoughtful observers should be struck with the contrast between the habits and government of the Romans and the customs of the various barbarian peoples. Tacitus, the first to describe the manners and institutions of the Germans with care, is frequently tempted to compare them with those of the Empire, often to the obvious disadvantage of the latter.[1]

[1] The very important little work of Tacitus on Germany, the *Germania*, has been published in *Translations and Reprints*, Vol. VI, No. 3.

5. Salvian's
comparison
of the
Romans
with the
barbarians
(*ca.* 440).

Salvian, a Christian priest, writing about 440, undertook in his book *Of God's Government* to show that the
misfortunes of the time were only the divinely inflicted
punishments which the people of the Empire had brought
upon themselves by their wickedness and corruption.
He contends that the Romans, who had once been virtuous and heroic, had lapsed into a degradation which
rendered them, in spite of their civilization and advantages, far inferior to the untutored but sturdy barbarians.

In what respects can our customs be preferred to those
of the Goths and Vandals, or even compared with them?
And first, to speak of affection and mutual charity (which,
our Lord teaches, is the chief virtue, saying, " By this shall
all men know that ye are my disciples, if ye have love one
to another "), almost all barbarians, at least those who are
of one race and kin, love each other, while the Romans persecute each other. For what citizen does not envy his fellow-
citizen? What citizen shows to his neighbor full charity?

[The Romans oppress each other with exactions] nay,
not each other : it would be quite tolerable, if each suffered what he inflicted. It is worse than that ; for the
many are oppressed by the few, who regard public exactions
as their own peculiar right, who carry on private traffic under
the guise of collecting the taxes. And this is done not only
by nobles, but by men of lowest rank ; not by judges only,
but by judges' subordinates. For where is the city — even
the town or village — which has not as many tyrants as it
has curials? . . . What place is there, therefore, as I have
said, where the substance of widows and orphans, nay even
of the saints, is not devoured by the chief citizens? . . .
None but the great is secure from the devastations of these
plundering brigands, except those who are themselves robbers.

[Nay, the state has fallen upon such evil days that a man
cannot be safe unless he is wicked.] Even those in a position to protest against the iniquity which they see about them

dare not speak lest they make matters worse than before. So the poor are despoiled, the widows sigh, the orphans are oppressed, until many of them, born of families not obscure, and liberally educated, flee to our enemies that they may no longer suffer the oppression of public persecution. They doubtless seek Roman humanity among the barbarians, because they cannot bear barbarian inhumanity among the Romans. And although they differ from the people to whom they flee in manner and in language; although they are unlike as regards the fetid odor of the barbarians' bodies and garments, yet they would rather endure a foreign civilization among the barbarians than cruel injustice among the Romans.

Why Roman subjects prefer to live among the barbarians.

So they migrate to the Goths, or to the Bagaudes, or to some other tribe of the barbarians who are ruling everywhere, and do not regret their exile. For they would rather live *free* under an appearance of slavery than live as captives under an appearance of liberty. The name of Roman citizen, once so highly esteemed and so dearly bought, is now a thing that men repudiate and flee from. . . .

It is urged that if we Romans are wicked and corrupt, that the barbarians commit the same sins, and are not so miserable as we. There is, however, this difference, that if the barbarians commit the same crimes as we, yet we sin more grievously. . . . All the barbarians, as we have already said, are pagans or heretics. The Saxon race is cruel, the Franks are faithless, the Gepidae are inhuman, the Huns are unchaste, — in short, there is vice in the life of all the barbarian peoples. But are their offenses as serious as ours? Is the unchastity of the Hun so criminal as ours? Is the faithlessness of the Frank so blameworthy as ours? Is the intemperance of the Alemanni so base as the intemperance of the Christians? Does the greed of the Alani so merit condemnation as the greed of the Christians? If the Hun or the Gepid cheat, what is there to wonder at, since he does not know that cheating is a crime? If a Frank perjures himself, does he do anything strange, he who regards perjury as a way of speaking, not as a crime?

A.2

## BIBLIOGRAPHY

*A. References.*

The books here mentioned are selected with a view to explaining those conditions in the later Roman Empire some conception of which is essential to an understanding of the Middle Ages. Almost all the accounts of Roman society deal with the period of the later Republic and the early Empire.

**Conditions upon the Eve of the Barbarian Invasions:** For these the best work in English is, DILL, *Roman Society in the Last Century of the Western Empire.* See especially Book II, "Society of the West"; Book III, "The Failure of the Administration and the Ruin of the Middle Class as revealed in the Theodosian Code." See also BRYCE, *The Holy Roman Empire*, Chapter II, "The Roman Empire before the Invasions of the Barbarians."

**Relations between Paganism and Christianity:** DILL, Book I, "The Tenacity of Paganism," and GIBBON, Chapter XXVIII (BURY's edition, Vol. III, pp. 188–215), "The Final Destruction of Paganism."

**Literature and the Text-Books which the Middle Ages inherited from the Later Empire:** DILL, Book V, "Characteristics of Roman Education and Culture in the Fifth Century." See also references to Taylor, in section *B*, below.

**Economic Conditions:** CUNNINGHAM, *Western Civilization*, Vol. I, Book III, Chapter III, "The Roman Empire."

*B. Additional reading in English.*

BURY, *A History of the Later Roman Empire*, A.D. 395–800, Book I, Chapters III–IV, "The Elements of Disintegration within the Roman Empire" and "The Administration of the Empire."

For the religious conditions: HATCH, *The Influence of Greek Thought upon the Christian Church;* RENAN, *The Influence of Rome on the Development of the Catholic Church;* FARRAR, *Seekers after God*, for the teachings of Seneca, Epictetus, and Marcus Aurelius ; BURY, Book I, Chapters I–II, "Christianity and Paganism " and "The Influence of Christianity on Society "; LECKY, *History of European Morals from Augustus to Charlemagne*, Vol. II, Chapter IV (opening) ; TAYLOR, *Classical Heritage of the Middle Ages*, Chapter II, gives an admirable account of the passing of the antique man into the mediæval man.

For the general intellectual and moral transition, see, above all, TAYLOR, Chapters III–V, "Phases of Pagan Decadence," "The Antique Culture," and "Pagan Elements Christianized in Transmission." The bibliographical notes at the end of Taylor's volume are very full and useful in this field. See also GLOVER, *Life and Letters in the Fourth Century*, Cambridge, England, 1901.

# CHAPTER III

## THE GERMAN INVASIONS AND THE BREAK-UP OF THE ROMAN EMPIRE

### I. THE MOVEMENTS OF THE HUNS FORCE THE WEST GOTHS ACROSS THE DANUBE INTO THE ROMAN EMPIRE, A.D. 376

The retired soldier, Ammianus Marcellinus, writing not more than ten or fifteen years after the battle of Adrianople, thus describes the Huns and the passage of the Goths into the Empire.

6. Description by Ammianus Marcellinus of the Huns and of the movements of the Goths

The people called Huns, barely mentioned in ancient records, live beyond the sea of Azof, on the border of the Frozen Ocean, and are a race savage beyond all parallel. At the very moment of birth the cheeks of their infant children are deeply marked by an iron, in order that the hair, instead of growing at the proper season on their faces, may be hindered by the scars; accordingly the Huns grow up without beards, and without any beauty. They all have closely knit and strong limbs and plump necks; they are of great size, and low legged, so that you might fancy them two-legged beasts, or the stout figures which are hewn out in a rude manner with an ax on the posts at the end of bridges.

They are certainly in the shape of men, however uncouth, and are so hardy that they require neither fire nor well flavored food, but live on the roots of such herbs as they get in the fields, or on the half raw flesh of any animal, which they merely warm rapidly by placing it between their own thighs and the backs of their horses.

They never shelter themselves under roofed houses, but avoid them, as people ordinarily avoid sepulchers as things not fit for common use. Nor is there even to be found among them a cabin thatched with reeds; but they wander about, roaming over the mountains and the woods, and accustom themselves to bear frost and hunger and thirst from their very cradles. . . .

There is not a person in the whole nation who cannot remain on his horse day and night. On horseback they buy and sell, they take their meat and drink, and there they recline on the narrow neck of their steed, and yield to sleep so deep as to indulge in every variety of dream.

And when any deliberation is to take place on any weighty matter, they all hold their common council on horseback. They are not under kingly authority,[1] but are contented with the irregular government of their chiefs, and under their lead they force their way through all obstacles. . . .

None of them plow, or even touch a plow handle, for they have no settled abode, but are homeless and lawless, perpetually wandering with their wagons, which they make their homes; in fact, they seem to be people always in flight. . . .

This active and indomitable race, being excited by an unrestrained desire of plundering the possessions of others, went on ravaging and slaughtering all the nations in their neighborhood till they reached the Alani. . . .

The Goths decide to cross the Danube.

[After having harassed the territory of the Alani and having slain many of them and acquired much plunder, the Huns made a treaty of friendship and alliance with those who survived. The allies then attacked the German peoples to the west.] In the meantime a report spread far and wide through the nations of the Goths, that a race of men, hitherto unknown, had suddenly descended like a whirlwind from the lofty mountains, as if they had risen from some secret recess of the earth, and were ravaging and destroying everything which came in their way.

And then the greater part of the population resolved to flee and to seek a home remote from all knowledge of the new

[1] The Huns in Attila's time had a king and appear to have lived in houses and huts. See account given by Priscus below, pp. 25 *sqq.*

barbarians; and after long deliberation as to where to fix their abode, they resolved that a retreat into Thrace was the most suitable for these two reasons : first of all, because it is a district most fertile in grass ; and secondly, because, owing to the great breadth of the Danube, it is wholly separated from the districts exposed to the impending attacks of the invaders.

Accordingly, under the command of their leader Alavivus, they occupied the banks of the Danube, and sent ambassadors to the emperor Valens, humbly entreating to be received by him as his subjects. They promised to live quietly, and to furnish a body of auxiliary troops if necessary.

While these events were taking place abroad, the terrifying rumor reached us that the tribes of the north were planning new and unprecedented attacks upon us ; and that over the whole region which extends from the country of the Marcomanni and Quadi to Pontus, hosts of barbarians composed of various nations, which had suddenly been driven by force from their own countries, were now, with all their families, wandering about in different directions on the banks of the river Danube.

*News of the movements of the Goths reaches the Roman government.*

At first this intelligence was lightly treated by our people, because they were not in the habit of hearing of any wars in those remote districts till they were terminated either by victory or by treaty.

But presently the belief in these occurrences grew stronger and was confirmed by the arrival of ambassadors, who, with prayers and earnest entreaties, begged that their people, thus driven from their homes and now encamped on the other side of the river, might be kindly received by us.

The affair now seemed a cause of joy rather than of fear, according to the skillful flatterers who were always extolling and exaggerating the good fortune of the emperor. They congratulated him that an embassy had come from the farthest corners of the earth, unexpectedly offering him a large body of recruits ; and that, by combining the strength of his own people with these foreign forces, he would have an army absolutely invincible. They observed further that the payment for military reënforcements, which came in every year from the provinces, might now be saved and accumulated in his coffers and form a vast treasure of gold.

With Valens' permission great numbers of Goths pour into the Empire.

Full of this hope, he sent forth several officers to bring this ferocious people and their carts into our territory. And such great pains were taken to gratify this nation which was destined to overthrow the Empire of Rome, that not one was left behind, not even of those who were stricken with mortal disease. Moreover, so soon as they had obtained permission of the emperor to cross the Danube and to cultivate some districts in Thrace, they poured across the stream day and night, without ceasing, embarking in troops on board ships and rafts and on canoes made of the hollow trunks of trees. . . .

In this way, through the turbulent zeal of violent people, the ruin of the Roman Empire was brought about. This, at all events, is neither obscure nor uncertain, that the unhappy officers who were intrusted with the charge of conducting the multitude of the barbarians across the river, though they repeatedly endeavored to calculate their numbers, at last abandoned the attempt as hopeless. The man who would wish to ascertain the number might as well (as the most illustrious of poets says) attempt to count the waves in the African sea, or the grains of sand tossed about by the zephyrs. . . .

The Goths are misused by the Roman officials.

At that period, moreover, the defenses of our provinces were much exposed, and the armies of barbarians spread over them like the lava of Mount Etna. The imminence of our danger manifestly called for generals already illustrious for their past achievements in war ; but nevertheless, as if some unpropitious deity had made the selection, the men who were sought out for the chief military appointments were of tainted character. The chief among them were Lupicinus and Maximus, — the one being count of Thrace, the other a leader notoriously wicked, — both men of great ignorance and rashness.

And their treacherous covetousness was the cause of all our disasters. . . . For when the barbarians who had been conducted across the river were in great distress from want of provisions, those detested generals conceived the idea of a most disgraceful traffic; and having collected dogs from all quarters with the most insatiable rapacity, they exchanged them for an equal number of slaves, among whom were several sons of men of noble birth. . . .

After narrating the events which led up to the battle of Adrianople, and vividly describing the battle itself, Ammianus thus records the death of the emperor Valens:

So now, with rage flashing in their eyes, the barbarians pursued our men, who were in a state of torpor, the warmth of their veins having deserted them. Many were slain without knowing who smote them; some were overwhelmed by the mere weight of the crowd which pressed upon them; and some died of wounds inflicted by their own comrades. The barbarians spared neither those who yielded nor those who resisted. . . .

Just when it first became dark, the emperor, being among a crowd of common soldiers as it was believed, — for no one said either that he had seen him or been near him, — was mortally wounded with an arrow, and, very shortly after, died, though his body was never found. For as some of the enemy loitered for a long time about the field in order to plunder the dead, none of the defeated army or of the inhabitants ventured to go to them.

*Battle of Adrianople and death of Valens.*

The deep impression which the influx of barbarians and the sack of Rome made upon one of the most distinguished scholars of the time is apparent from several passages in the writings of St. Jerome (d. A.D. 420), who gives, however, possibly too dark a picture of the disorder and destruction.

*7. St. Jerome laments the destruction wrought by the barbarians.*

Nations innumerable and most savage have invaded all Gaul. The whole region between the Alps and the Pyrenees, the ocean and the Rhine, has been devastated by the Quadi, the Vandals, the Sarmati, the Alani, the Gepidae,

the hostile Heruli, the Saxons, the Burgundians, the Alemanni, and the Pannonians. O wretched Empire! Mayence,
formerly so noble a city, has been taken and ruined, and in
the church many thousands of men have been massacred.
Worms has been destroyed after a long siege. Rheims, that
powerful city, Amiens, Arras, Speyer, Strasburg,[1] — all have
seen their citizens led away captive into Germany. Aquitaine
and the provinces of Lyons and Narbonne, all save a few
towns, have been depopulated; and these the sword threatens
without, while hunger ravages within. I cannot speak without tears of Toulouse, which the merits of the holy Bishop
Exuperius have prevailed so far to save from destruction.
Spain, even, is in daily terror lest it perish, remembering the
invasion of the Cimbri; and whatsoever the other provinces
have suffered once, they continue to suffer in their fear.

I will keep silence concerning the rest, lest I seem to
despair of the mercy of God. For a long time, from the
Black Sea to the Julian Alps, those things which are ours
have not been ours; and for thirty years, since the Danube
boundary was broken, war has been waged in the very midst
of the Roman Empire. Our tears are dried by old age.
Except a few old men, all were born in captivity and siege,
and do not desire the liberty they never knew. Who could
believe this? How could the whole tale be worthily told?
How Rome has fought within her own bosom not for glory, but
for preservation — nay, how she has not even fought, but with
gold and all her precious things has ransomed her life. . . .

Who could believe [Jerome exclaims in another passage]
that Rome, built upon the conquest of the whole world,
would fall to the ground? that the mother herself would
become the tomb of her peoples? that all the regions of the
East, of Africa and Egypt, once ruled by the queenly city,
would be filled with troops of slaves and handmaidens? that
to-day holy Bethlehem should shelter men and women of noble
birth, who once abounded in wealth and are now beggars?

[1] The names of modern cities here used are not in all cases exact
equivalents for the names of the regions mentioned by Jerome.

## II. ATTILA AND THE HUNS

A description has already been given of the Huns when they first drove the Goths into the Empire.[1] Seventy years after the battle of Adrianople, Priscus, who actually visited the Huns and conversed with Attila, received a very different impression of the people from that given by Ammianus Marcellinus. We may however infer that the Huns had been a good deal changed by their contact with the European peoples.

8. Priscus describes the court of Attila, king of the Huns (448)

Priscus and a companion, Maxim, were sent by the Roman government with messages to Attila in 448. Priscus first tells of their long journey from Constantinople to Scythia, the territory then occupied by the Huns north of the lower Danube. After some difficulty the messengers obtained a first interview with Attila. Then, as the king of the Huns was about to move northward, he and his companion determined to follow him. After describing the incidents of their journey and their arrival at a large village, Priscus continues:

Attila's residence, which was situated here, was said to be more splendid than his houses in other places. It was made of polished boards, and surrounded with wooden inclosures, designed not so much for protection as for appearance' sake. The house of the chieftain Onegesius was second only to the king's in splendor and was also encircled with a wooden inclosure, but it was not adorned with towers like that of the king. Not far from the inclosure was a large bath built by Onegesius, who was the second in power among the Scythians. The stones for this bath had been brought from Pannonia, for the barbarians in this district had no stones or trees, but used imported material. ...

Attila's fine house.

[1] See above, pp. 19 *sqq.*

The next day I entered the inclosure of Attila's palace, bearing gifts to his wife, whose name was Kreka. She had three sons, of whom the eldest governed the Acatiri and the other nations who dwell in Pontic Scythia. Within the inclosures were numerous buildings, some of carved boards beautifully fitted together, others of straight planed beams, without carving, fastened on round wooden blocks which rose to a moderate height from the ground. Attila's wife lived here; and, having been admitted by the barbarians at the door, I found her reclining on a soft couch. The floor of the room was covered with woolen mats for walking on. A number of servants stood round her, and maids sitting on the floor in front of her embroidered with colors linen cloths intended to be placed over the Scythian dress for ornament. Having approached, saluted her, and presented the gifts, I went out and walked to the other houses, where Attila was, and waited for Onegesius, who, as I knew, was with Attila. . . .

A banquet at Attila's.

[We were invited to a banquet with Attila at three o'clock.] When the hour arrived we went to the palace, along with the embassy from the western Romans, and stood on the threshold of the hall in the presence of Attila. The cupbearers gave us a cup, according to the national custom, that we might pray before we sat down. Having tasted the cup, we proceeded to take our seats, all the chairs being ranged along the walls of the room on either side. Attila sat in the middle on a couch; a second couch was set behind him, and from it steps led up to his bed, which was covered with linen sheets and wrought coverlets for ornament, such as Greeks and Romans used to deck bridal beds. The places on the right of Attila were held chief in honor; those on the left, where we sat, were only second. . . .

[First the king and his guests pledged one another with the wine.] When this ceremony was over the cupbearers retired, and tables, large enough for three or four, or even more, to sit at, were placed next the table of Attila, so that each could take of the food on the dishes without leaving his seat. The attendant of Attila first entered with a dish full of meat, and behind him came the other attendants with bread and viands, which they laid on the tables. A luxurious meal, served on silver plate, had been made ready for us and the barbarian guests, but Attila ate nothing but meat on a wooden trencher. In everything else, too, he showed himself temperate ; his cup was of wood, while to the guests were given goblets of gold and silver. His dress, too, was quite simple, affecting only to be clean. The sword he carried at his side, the latchets of his Scythian shoes, the bridle of his horse were not adorned, like those of the other Scythians, with gold or gems or anything costly.

When the viands of the first course had been consumed, we all stood up, and did not resume our seats until each one, in the order before observed, drank to the health of Attila in the goblet of wine presented to him. We then sat down, and a second dish was placed on each table with eatables of another kind. After this course the same ceremony was observed as after the first. When evening fell torches were lit, and two barbarians coming forward in front of Attila sang songs they had composed, celebrating his victories and deeds of valor in war.

### III. CLOVIS AND THE FRANKS

The history of the Franks was written about a century after the time of Clovis by Gregory, bishop of Tours. The following extracts give some notion of this valuable source, upon which a great part of our knowledge of the Merovingian period rests [1] :

9. Gregory of Tours and his history of the Franks.

At this time [A.D. 486] the army of Clovis pillaged many churches, for he was still sunk in the errors of idolatry. The soldiers had borne away from a church, with all the other ornaments of the holy ministry, a vase of marvelous size and beauty. The bishop of this church sent messengers to

The incident of the vase at Soissons.

[1] See p. 60 of the unabridged edition.

the king, begging that if the church might not recover any other of the holy vessels, at least this one might be restored. The king, hearing these things, replied to the messenger: "Follow thou us to Soissons, for there all things that have been acquired are to be divided. If the lot shall give me this vase, I will do what the bishop desires."

When he had reached Soissons, and all the booty had been placed in the midst of the army, the king pointed to this vase, and said: "I ask you, O most valiant warriors, not to refuse to me the vase in addition to my rightful part." Those of discerning mind among his men answered, "O glorious king, all things which we see are thine, and we ourselves are subject to thy power; now do what seems pleasing to thee, for none is strong enough to resist thee." When they had thus spoken one of the soldiers, impetuous, envious, and vain, raised his battle-ax aloft and crushed the vase with it, crying, "Thou shalt receive nothing of this unless a just lot give it to thee." At this all were stupefied.

The king bore his injury with the calmness of patience, and when he had received the crushed vase he gave it to the bishop's messenger; but he cherished a hidden wound in his breast. When a year had passed he ordered the whole army to come fully equipped to the Campus Martius and show their arms in brilliant array. But when he had reviewed them all he came to the breaker of the vase, and said to him, "No one bears his arms so clumsily as thou; for neither thy spear, nor thy sword, nor thy ax is ready for use." And seizing his ax, he cast it on the ground. And when the soldier had bent a little to pick it up the king raised his hands and crushed his head with his own ax. "Thus," he said, "didst thou to the vase at Soissons."

The conversion of Clovis to Christianity.

[Clovis took to wife Clotilde, daughter of the king of the Burgundians. Now Clotilde was a Christian. When her first son was born] she wished to consecrate him by baptism, and begged her husband unceasingly, saying, "The gods whom thou honorest are nothing; they cannot help themselves nor others; for they are carved from stone, or from wood, or from some metal. The names which you have given them were of men, not of gods, — like Saturn, who is said to have escaped by flight, to avoid being deprived of his power by his son; and like Jupiter himself, foul perpetrator of all uncleanness. . . . What power have Mars and Mercury ever had? They are endowed with magical arts rather than divine power.

"The God who should be worshiped is he who by his word created from nothingness the heavens and the earth, the sea and all that in them is; he who made the sun to shine and adorned the sky with stars; who filled the waters with creeping things, the land with animals, the air with winged creatures; by whose bounty the earth is glad with crops, the trees with fruit, the vines with grapes; by whose hand the human race was created; whose bounty has ordained that all things should give homage and service to man, whom he created."

But when the queen had said these things, the mind of Clovis was not stirred to believe. He answered: "By the will of our gods all things are created and produced. Evidently your god can do nothing, and it is not even proved that he belongs to the race of gods."

Meantime the faithful queen presented her son for baptism. She had the church adorned with tapestry, seeking to attract by this splendor him whom her exhortations had not moved. But the child whom they called Ingomer, after he had been born again through baptism, died in his white baptismal robe. Then the king reproached the queen bitterly. "If the child had been consecrated in the name of my gods, he would be alive still. But now, because he is baptized in the name of your god, he cannot live." . . .

After this another son was born to him, and called in baptism Clodomir. He fell very ill. Then the king said: "Because he, like his brother, was baptized in the name of Christ, he must soon die." But his mother prayed, and by God's will the child recovered.

The queen unceasingly urged the king to acknowledge the true God, and forsake idols. But he could not in any wise be brought to believe until a war broke out with the

Alemanni. Then he was by necessity compelled to confess what he had before willfully denied.

It happened that the two armies were in battle, and there was great slaughter. Clovis' army was near to utter destruction. He saw the danger; his heart was stirred; he was moved to tears, and he raised his eyes to heaven, saying : "Jesus Christ, whom Clotilde declares to be the son of the living God, who it is said givest aid to the oppressed, and victory to those who put their hope in thee, I beseech the glory of thy aid. If thou shalt grant me victory over these enemies and I test that power which people consecrated to thy name say they have proved concerning thee, I will believe in thee and be baptized in thy name. For I have called upon my gods, but, as I have proved, they are far removed from my aid. So I believe that they have no power, for they do not succor those who serve them. Now I call upon thee, and I long to believe in thee — all the more that I may escape my enemies."

When he had said these things, the Alemanni turned their backs and began to flee. When they saw that their king was killed, they submitted to the sway of Clovis, saying: "We wish that no more people should perish. Now we are thine." When the king had forbidden further war, and praised his soldiers, he told the queen how he had won the victory by calling on the name of Christ.

Then the queen sent to the blessed Remigius, bishop of the city of Rheims, praying him to bring to the king the gospel of salvation. The priest, little by little and secretly, led him to believe in the true God, maker of heaven and earth, and to forsake idols, which could not help him nor anybody else.

But the king said : "Willingly will I hear thee, O father; but one thing is in the way — that the people who follow me are not content to leave their gods. I will go and speak to them according to thy word."

When he came among them, the power of God went before him, and before he had spoken all the people cried out together: "We cast off mortal gods, O righteous king, and we are ready to follow the God whom Remigius tells us is immortal."

These things were told to the bishop. He was filled with joy, and ordered the font to be prepared. The streets were shaded with embroidered hangings; the churches were adorned with white tapestries, the baptistery was set in order, the odor of balsam spread around, candles gleamed, and all the temple of the baptistery was filled with divine odor. . . . Then the king confessed the God omnipotent in the Trinity, and was baptized in the name of the Father, and of the Son, and of the Holy Ghost, and was anointed with the sacred chrism with the sign of the cross of Christ. Of his army there were baptized more than three thousand.

## BIBLIOGRAPHY

**General Accounts**: ADAMS, *Civilization during the Middle Ages*, pp. 65–88 and 137–146; BRYCE, *Holy Roman Empire*, Chapter III, pp. 14–33; HENDERSON, *Germany in the Middle Ages*, pp. 15–40; DILL, *Roman Society*, Book IV, Chapter I, pp. 285–302, "The General Character of the Invasions"; Chapter II, pp. 303–345, "Roman Feeling about the Invasions"; Chapter III, pp. 342–382, "Relations of the Romans with the Invaders."

**The West Goths**: EMERTON, *Introduction to the Middle Ages*, Chapter III, pp. 22–34; GIBBON, *Decline and Fall of the Roman Empire* (BURY's edition), Vol. III, Chapter XXVI, pp. 69–132, "Crossing of the Eastern Frontier and Battle of Adrianople"; Vol. III, Chapters XXX–XXXI, pp. 240–356, on the Invasion of the West.

**The Huns**: EMERTON, pp. 41–47; GIBBON, Vol. III, Chapters XXXIV–XXXV, pp. 416–479.

**Odoacer**: EMERTON, pp. 48–52; GIBBON, Vol. IV, Chapter XXXVI, pp. 1–56; OMAN, *European History, from 476 to 918*, Chapter I, pp. 1–18.

**The Ostrogoths**: EMERTON, pp. 52–57; GIBBON, Vol. IV, Chapter XXXIX, pp. 170–203; OMAN, Chapter II, pp. 19–32.

**Justinian**: GIBBON, Vol. IV, Chapter XL, pp. 205–267, "Character and Policy"; Vol. IV, Chapters XLI and XLIII, pp. 270–338 and 388–431, on the Conquests in the West; OMAN, Chapters V and VI, pp. 65–110.

**The Lombards**: EMERTON, pp. 57–59; GIBBON, Vol. V, Chapter XLV, first part, pp. 1–30; OMAN, pp. 180–198 and 272–288.

*A. References.*

The Franks: ADAMS, *Growth of the French Nation*, pp. 22–38; EMERTON, pp. 60–72; GIBBON, Vol. IV, Chapter XXXVIII, pp. 98–120; OMAN, pp. 55–64, "Clovis"; pp. 111–127 and 158–180, "The Merovingians"; pp. 256–271, "Mayors of the Palace."

German Laws and Customs: ADAMS, *Civilization*, Chapter V, pp. 89–106; EMERTON, pp. 12–21 and 73–91; GIBBON, Vol. IV, Chapter XXXVIII, pp. 122–140; HENDERSON, *Short History of Germany*, pp. 1–21.

The *Germania* of TACITUS, *Translations and Reprints*, Vol. VI, No. 3. Selections from, in COLBY, *Sources of English History*, pp. 9–11; KENDALL, *Source Book of English History*, pp. 4–11.

The Salic Law: HENDERSON, *Historical Documents of the Middle Ages*, pp. 176–189.

Formulæ for Trials and Ordeals: HENDERSON, *Historical Documents* pp. 314–319; *Translations and Reprints*, Vol. IV, No. 4, pp. 3–22.

---

*B. Additional reading in English.*

HODGKIN, *Italy and her Invaders*, 8 vols. The fullest and most scholarly treatment in English, with many valuable extracts from sources. *Dynasty of Theodosius* and *Theodoric the Goth*. Two useful books by the same author, giving in brief form some of the results reached in his larger work.

VILLARI, *The Barbarian Invasions of Italy*, 2 vols. An animated and graphic narrative of events down to Charlemagne, with extracts from the sources, intended to interest the general reader.

GREGOROVIUS, *History of Rome in the Middle Ages*, Vols. I and II. An able discussion of the period, particularly as regards the city of Rome.

BURY, *History of the Later Roman Empire*, 2 vols. The best survey of conditions in the Empire, especially in the East.

MCCABE, *St. Augustine, His Life and Times*. An attractive and sympathetic sketch of the great church father and his contemporaries.

English versions of the sources.

AMMIANUS MARCELLINUS, *History of Rome*, translated by Yonge (Bohn Library).

ST. AUGUSTINE, *The City of God*.

Examples of the charming letters of Apollinaris Sidonius are given by Hodgkin, Vol. II, pp. 304–373.

*The Letters of Cassiodorus*, translated by Hodgkin, London, 1886.

# CHAPTER IV

## THE RISE OF THE PAPACY

### I. The Bishop of Rome and the Headship of the Church

Leo the Great gives the following clear statement of the nature and grounds of the pope's claim to be head of the whole Church.

... A single person, Peter, is appointed from the whole world as a leader in the calling of all peoples, and is placed above all the other apostles and the fathers of the Church. Although there are many priests among the people of God, and many pastors, Peter should of right rule all of those whom Christ himself rules in the first instance. Great and marvelous, my dear brethren, is the participation in its own power which it has pleased the Divine Excellency to grant to this man. And such powers as it granted to other leaders in common with Peter were granted only through Peter. Our Lord, indeed, asked all the apostles what men said of him, but so long as it was left to all to reply, so long was the hesitation of human ignorance clearly displayed. But when the opinion of the apostles was asked, he who was first in apostolic dignity was the first to reply; who when he had answered, "Thou art the Christ, the Son of the living God," Jesus said to him, "Blessed art thou, Simon Bar-jonah: for flesh and blood hath not revealed it unto thee, but my Father which is in heaven"[1]; — that is to say, thou art blessed for this reason, for my father has taught thee, neither has mere earthly opinion misled thee, but thou art instructed by a heavenly

10. A sermon by Leo the Great on Peter's headship.

[1] Matthew xvi. 16–17.

inspiration. . . .   I am the foundation than which none other
can be established; yet thou too art a rock [*petra*] because
thou art made firm by my strength, so that those things which
I have in virtue of my power thou shalt have in common with
me by participation.   "And upon this rock I will build my
church; and the gates of hell shall not prevail against it." . . .

And he said to the blessed Peter, "I will give unto thee
the keys of the kingdom of heaven: and whatsoever thou
shalt bind on earth shall be bound in heaven: and whatsoever thou shalt loose on earth shall be loosed in heaven."
The right to this power passed also to the other apostles, and
the provisions of this ordinance went forth to all the leaders
of the Church.   Still it was not in vain that what was made
known to all was especially recommended to one.   For this
power was intrusted expressly to Peter, since Peter was
placed as a model before all the rulers of the Church.   Peter's
prerogative remains and everywhere his judgment goes forth
in equity.   For never is severity too great nor forgiveness
too lax where nothing is bound nor loosed except the blessed
Peter bind or loose it.

Just before his passion, which was about to shake the
apostles' constancy, the Lord said to Simon, "Simon, Simon,
behold, Satan asked to have you, that he might sift you as
wheat: but I made supplication for thee, that thy faith fail
not: and do thou, when once thou hast turned again, stablish thy brethren,"[1] that you should not enter into temptation.   The danger of the temptation to yield to fear was
common to all the apostles and all alike needed the aid of
divine protection, since the devil desired to confound and
ruin them all.   Yet the Lord took special care of Peter and
prayed especially that Peter might have faith, as if the state
of the others would be more secure if the mind of their chief
was not overcome.   In Peter, therefore, the strength of all
was confirmed and the aid of divine grace so ordered that
the strength which was granted to Peter by Christ was in
turn transmitted through Peter to the apostles.

[1] Luke xxii. 31–32.

Since, therefore, beloved brethren, we behold this protection divinely appointed to us, we may properly and justly rejoice in the merits and dignity of our leader, sending up thanks to our eternal King and Redeemer, our Lord Jesus Christ, for giving such power to him whom he made the head of the whole Church : so that if anything, even in our own days, is rightly done by us and rightly ordained, it should be properly attributed to the influence and guidance of him to whom it was said, "When once thou hast turned again, stablish thy brethren." To whom, moreover, his Lord, after his resurrection, when Peter had three times professed his eternal love, said mystically three times, "Feed my sheep."[1] Like a faithful shepherd, he has beyond a doubt fulfilled his Lord's command, confirming us by his exhortations, and never ceasing to pray for us that we be not overcome by any temptation. . . .

[Elsewhere Leo says :] Although the priests enjoy a common dignity, they are not all on the same footing, since even among the blessed apostles, who were alike in honor, there was a certain distinction in authority. All were alike chosen, but it was given to one that he should be preëminent among the others. Upon this model the distinction among the bishops is based, and it is salutarily provided that all should not claim the right to do all things, but in each province there should be one who should have the first word among his brethren. Again, in the greater cities others are appointed to greater responsibilities. Through these the oversight of the whole Church is concentrated in one see, that of Peter, and from this head there should never be any dissent.

*Leo on the hierarchy (446).*

The pope's view of the natural superiority of the spiritual over the temporal power finds a clear expression in the following remarkable letter of Gelasius I (494).

. . . There are two powers, august Emperor, by which this world is chiefly ruled, namely, the sacred authority of the

[1] John xxi. 15 *sqq.*

11. Letter
of Pope
Gelasius I
to Emperor
Anastasius
on the
superiority
of the
spiritual
over the
temporal
power (494).

priests and the royal power.  Of these, that of the priests
is the more weighty, since they have to render an account
for even the kings of men in the divine judgment.  You are
also aware, dear son, that while you are permitted honorably
to rule over human kind, yet in things divine you bow your
head humbly before the leaders of the clergy and await from
their hands the means of your salvation.  In the reception
and proper disposition of the heavenly mysteries you recognize that you should be subordinate rather than superior
to the religious order, and that in these matters you depend
on their judgment rather than wish to force them to follow
your will.

If the ministers of religion, recognizing the supremacy
granted you from heaven in matters affecting the public
order, obey your laws, lest otherwise they might obstruct
the course of secular affairs by irrelevant considerations,
with what readiness should you not yield them obedience
to whom is assigned the dispensing of the sacred mysteries
of religion.  Accordingly, just as there is no slight danger
in the case of the priests if they refrain from speaking when
the service of the divinity requires, so there is no little risk
for those who disdain — which God forbid — when they should
obey.  And if it is fitting that the hearts of the faithful should
submit to all priests in general who properly administer divine
affairs, how much the more is obedience due to the bishop
of that see which the Most High ordained to be above all
others, and which is consequently dutifully honored by the
devotion of the whole Church.

## II. Gregory the Great and his Times

12. Sad
state of the
western
world as
depicted in
the letters
of Gregory
the Great.

The calamities of the times, especially the coming
of "the most unspeakable Lombards," as he commonly calls them, convinced Gregory that the end of
the world was near at hand.  In a letter written to a
fellow-bishop shortly after he reluctantly became pope,

he gives a dark picture of the world and of his heavy responsibilities:

*Gregory to Leander, bishop of Seville:*

With all my heart I have wished to answer you better, but the burden of my pastoral calls so overpowers me that I would rather weep than speak, — as your reverence undoubtedly gathers from the very character of my correspondence when I am remiss in addressing one whom I warmly love. In fact, so beaten about am I by the billows in this corner of the world, that I can in no wise bring to harbor the ancient, rolling ship at whose helm I stand through God's mysterious dispensation.

Now the waves break over us from the front, now at the side the foaming mountains of the sea swell high, now in the rear the tempest pursues us. Beset by all these perils, I am forced first to steer directly in the face of the storm, again to swerve the vessel and to receive obliquely the onset of the waters. I groan, because I know that if I am negligent the bilge water of vice is deepening, and that if the storm assails us furiously at that instant the decaying planks forebode shipwreck. Fearful, I remember that I have lost my quiet shore of peace, and sighing I gaze toward the land which, while the wind of circumstances blows contrarily, I cannot gain. So, dearest brother, if you love me, stretch forth the hand of prayer to me amid these floods, and, as you aid me in my troubles, thus as a reward shall you come forth more valiantly from yours. . . .

[Of all the signs described by our Lord as presaging the end of the world], some we see already accomplished; the others we dread as close upon us. For we now see that nation rises against nation, and that they press and weigh upon the land in our own times as never before in the annals of the past. Earthquakes overwhelm countless cities, as we often hear from other parts of the world. Pestilence we endure without interruption. It is true that as yet we do not behold signs in the sun and moon and stars; but that

Signs that the end of the world is at hand. (From one of Gregory's *Sermons.*)

A reference,
perhaps, to
the aurora
borealis.

these are not far off we may infer from the changes in the atmosphere. Before Italy was given over to be desolated by the sword of a heathen foe, we beheld fiery ranks in heaven, and even the streaming blood of the human race as it was afterwards spilt.

13. How a
monk dared
to have gold
in his
possession.
(From
Gregory's
*Dialogues*.)

Gregory's *Dialogues*, a collection of the lives of holy men, was for centuries, probably, the most popular of his works. The incident given below sheds light upon Gregory's life as abbot of a monastery.

There was in my monastery a certain monk, Justus by name, skilled in medicinal arts. . . . When he knew that his end was at hand, he made known to Copiosus, his brother in the flesh, how that he had three gold pieces hidden away. Copiosus, of course, could not conceal this from the brethren. He sought carefully, and examined all his brother's drugs, until he found the three gold pieces hidden away among the medicines. When he told me this great calamity that concerned a brother who had lived in common with us, I could hardly hear it with calmness. For the rule of this our monastery was always that the brothers should live in common and own nothing individually.

Then, stricken with great grief, I began to think what I could do to cleanse the dying man, and how I should make his sins a warning to the living brethren. Accordingly, having summoned Pretiosus, the superintendent of the monastery, I commanded him to see that none of the brothers visited the dying man, who was not to hear any words of consolation. If in the hour of death he asked for the brethren, then his own brother in the flesh was to tell him how he was hated by the brethren because he had concealed money; so that at death remorse for his guilt might pierce his heart and cleanse him from the sin he had committed.

When he was dead his body was not placed with the bodies of the brethren, but a grave was dug in the dung pit, and his body was flung down into it, and the three pieces of gold he had left were cast upon him, while all together cried, "Thy money perish with thee!" . . .

When thirty days had passed after his death, my heart began to have compassion on my dead brother, and to ponder prayers with deep grief, and to seek what remedy there might be for him. Then I called before me Pretiosus, superintendent of the monastery, and said sadly : "It is a long time that our brother who died has been tormented by fire, and we ought to have charity toward him, and aid him so far as we can, that he may be delivered. Go, therefore, and for thirty successive days from this day offer sacrifices for him. See to it that no day is allowed to pass on which the salvation-bringing mass [*hostia*] is not offered up for his absolution." He departed forthwith and obeyed my words.

We, however, were busy with other things, and did not count the days as they rolled by. But lo! the brother who had died appeared by night to a certain brother, even to Copiosus, his brother in the flesh. When Copiosus saw him he asked him, saying, "What is it, brother? How art thou?" To which he answered : "Up to this time I have been in torment; but now all is well with me, because to-day I have received the communion." This Copiosus straightway reported to the brethren in the monastery.

Then the brethren carefully reckoned the days, and it was the very day on which the thirtieth oblation was made for him. Copiosus did not know what the brethren were doing for his dead brother, and the brethren did not know that Copiosus had seen him ; yet at one and the same time he learned what they had done and they learned what he had seen, and the vision and the sacrifice harmonized. So the fact was plainly shown forth how that the brother who had died had escaped punishment through the salvation-giving mass.

How the soul of the sinning monk was saved by the saying of masses.

## BIBLIOGRAPHY

*A. References.*

**General Accounts:** EMERTON, *Introduction*, pp. 93–109; ADAMS, *Civilization*, Chapter IX, pp. 92–113; BÉMONT and MONOD, pp. 115–124.

**Gregory the Great:** GIBBON, Vol. V, Chapter XLV, end, pp. 25–32; OMAN, pp. 198–203.

*B. Additional reading in English.*

NEWMAN, *Manual of Church History*, Vol. I. Covering the whole period before the Protestant Revolt. The most useful recent introduction to the subject, with good bibliographies.

MILMAN, *History of Latin Christianity*. First published in 1856; consequently rather old, but scholarly, readable, and fair-minded, so that it is still deservedly popular as a fuller treatment. For Gregory the Great, see Book III, Chapter VII.

ALZOG, *Manual of Universal Church History*, 3 vols. The most careful and scholarly general account from a Catholic standpoint to be had in English.

HATCH, *Growth of Church Institutions*. A brief but excellent account of the evolution of certain prominent features in church organization.

SCHAFF, *History of the Christian Church*, Vols. I–IV to Gregory VII. Vol. V has never appeared. Vols. VI and VII relate to the Protestant Revolt. A voluminous but well-written treatise, where the student will find special topics fully and interestingly treated. It was written a generation later than Milman's volumes referred to above.

RIVINGTON, LUKE, *The Primitive Church and the See of Peter*. A discussion by a Catholic of the position of the bishops of Rome in the early Church.

MANN, *Lives of the Popes in the Early Middle Ages*, A.D. *590–795*, 2 vols. The most careful and recent treatise on the papacy during this period.

BARNBY, *Gregory the Great*. A condensed account of Gregory's life and times, followed by a summary of his works.

SCHAFF-HERZOG, *A Religious Encyclopædia*, 4 vols., 1891.

ADDIS and ARNOLD, *A Catholic Dictionary, containing some account of the doctrine, discipline, rites, ceremonies, councils, and religious orders of the Catholic Church*, 2d ed., London, 1884. These dictionaries are a great aid to the historical student in looking up special topics and in discovering the exact meaning of technical terms.

# CHAPTER V

## THE MONKS AND THE CONVERSION OF THE GERMANS

### I. The Monastic Attitude of Mind

One of the earliest and most eloquent pleas for monasticism is found in a well-known letter of St. Jerome's, who himself led the life of a monk for many years. He thus urges on a friend, first the duty, then the beauty, of a hermit's existence.

*14. Jerome's plea for the life of solitude (373).*

Though your little nephew twine his arms around your neck; though your mother, with disheveled hair and tearing her robe asunder, point to the breast with which she nourished you; though your father fall down on the threshold before you, pass on over your father's body. Fly with tearful eyes to the banner of the cross. In this matter cruelty is the only piety. . . . Your widowed sister may throw her gentle arms around you. . . . Your father may implore you to wait but a short time to bury those near to you, who will soon be no more. Your weeping mother may recall your childish days, and may point to her shrunken breast and to her wrinkled brow. Those around you may tell you that all the household rests upon you. Such chains as these the love of God and the fear of hell can easily break. You say that Scripture orders you to obey your parents, but he who loves them more than Christ loses his soul. The enemy brandishes a sword to slay me. Shall I think of a mother's tears?

*Family ties and obligations should not stand in the way of the monastic life.*

[When once his friend has cast off the responsibilities of the world he will discover that the desert is full of attractions.] O solitude, whence are brought the stones of the city of the Great King! O wilderness rejoicing close to

*Delights of the hermit.*

41

God! What would you, brother, in the world, — you that are greater than the world? How long are the shades of roofs to oppress you? How long the dungeon of a city's smoke? Believe me, I see more of light! How refreshing to cast off the things that oppress the body and fly away into the pure sparkling ether!

Do you fear poverty? Christ called the poor "blessed." Are you terrified at labor? No athlete without sweat is crowned. Do you think of food? Faith fears not hunger. Do you dread the naked ground for limbs consumed with fasts? The Lord lies with you. Does the thought of unkempt locks disturb you? Your head is Christ. Does the infinite vastness of the desert affright you? In the mind walk abroad in Paradise. So often as you do this there will be no desert. Does your skin roughen without baths? Who is once washed in Christ needs not to wash again. In a word, hear the apostle as he answers: "The sufferings of the present time are not worthy to be compared with the glory which shall be revealed in us!" You are too pleasure-loving, brother, if you wish to rejoice in this world and hereafter to reign with Christ!

## II. The Devil and his Wicked Angels

The following passages give some idea of the religious world in which the monks and missionaries lived, and the views of the next world which they inculcated in the minds of the newly converted barbarians.

**15. St. Gall and the demons. (From the *Life of St. Gall* (630) by an anonymous writer.)**

[St. Columban and St. Gall came, about the year 610, to a village near the Lake of Constance called Bregenz, where they had heard that there might be opportunity to serve God.] There the brethren's hands made ready a dwelling, and the holy Columban fervently prayed to Christ in behalf of that place. The superstitious pagans worshiped three idols of gilded metal, and believed in returning thanks to them rather than to the creator of the world.

So Columban, the man of. God, wished to destroy that superstition, and told Gall to talk to the people, since he himself excelled in Latin, but not in the language of that tribe. The people gathered at the temple for their wonted festival; but they were attracted by the sight of the strangers, not, however, by reverence for the divine religion. When they were assembled, Gall, the elect of God, fed their hearts with honeyed words, exhorting them to turn to their Creator, and to Jesus Christ the Son of God, who opened the gate of heaven for the human race, sunk in indifference and uncleanness.

Then before them all he broke in pieces with stones the enthroned idols, and cast them into the depths of the lake. Then part of the people confessed their sins and believed, but others were angry and enraged, and departed in wrath; and Columban, the man of God, blessed the water and sanctified the place, and remained there with his followers three years. . . .

Some time after, in the silence of the night, Gall, the elect of God, was laying nets in the water, and lo! he heard the demon of the mountain top calling to his fellow who dwelt in the depths of the lake. The demon of the lake answered, "I am here"; he of the mountain returned: "Arise, come to my aid! Behold the aliens come, and thrust me from my temple. Come, come! help me to drive them from our lands." The demon of the lake answered: "One of them is upon the lake, whom I could never harm. For I wished to break his nets, but see, I am vanquished and mourn. The sign of his prayer protects him always, and sleep never overcomes him."

Gall, the elect of God, heard this, and fortified himself on all sides with the sign of the cross, and said to them: "In the name of Jesus Christ, I command you, leave this place, and do not presume to harm any one here." And he hastened to return to the shore, and told his abbot what he had heard.

When Columban, the man of God, heard this, he called the brethren together in the church, and made the accustomed sign (the cross).   Before the brethren could raise their voices, the voice of an unseen being was heard, and wailing and lamentation echoed from the mountain top.   So the malicious demons departed with mourning, and the prayer of the brethren arose as they sent up their supplications to God.

Gregory the Great tells the following tale in his *Dialogues* to illustrate the manner in which the devil was wont to harass those who sought to avoid worldly temptations by seeking solitude :

**16. Martin, a hermit, resists the terrors of the devil. (From Gregory's** *Dialogues.***)** In Campania, upon Mt. Marsicus, a venerable man called Martin lived for many years the solitary life, shut up in a very small cave.   Many of us knew him, and were witnesses of his deeds.   I myself have heard much of him both from Pope Pelagius, my predecessor, and from other religious men who related anecdotes of him.   His first miracle was this: hardly had he established himself in the cleft of the mountain, when from the very rock which was hollowed out to make his narrow cave burst forth a stream of water just sufficient to supply the daily need of the servant of God, and there was never too much or too little. . . .

But the ancient enemy of mankind envied the man's strength, and labored with his wonted skill to drive him forth from the cave.   For he entered into the beast that is his friend — the serpent — and sought to make the monk afraid, and to drive him from his dwelling.   He came at twilight, and stretched himself out before the holy man when he was praying, and lay down with him when he went to rest.

The holy man was entirely unafraid.   He would hold to the serpent's mouth his hand or his foot, and say to him, "If thou hast leave to smite me, I do not say thee nay." After these things had taken place continually for three years, on a certain day the ancient enemy of mankind, vanquished by such great endurance, groaned ; and the serpent let himself glide over the steep mountain side to a precipice.   And the flame that went out from him burned all the trees in that place.  Almighty God constrained him to burn the mountain side, and so compelled him to show forth the great virtue of the man from whom he had departed, conquered.

### III. Purgatory, Hell, and Heaven

At this time [Bede writes] a memorable miracle, and like to those of former days, was wrought in Britain ; for, to the end that the living might be saved from the death of the soul, a certain person, who had been some time dead, rose again to life, and related many remarkable things he had seen; some of which I have thought fit here briefly to take notice of.

17. Description of purgatory, hell, and heaven. (From Bede's *Ecclesiastical History of England*.)

There was a master of a family in that district of the Northumbrians which is called Cunningham, who led a religious life, as did also all that belonged to him.  This man fell sick, and his distemper daily increasing, being brought to extremity, he died in the beginning of the night; but in the morning early he suddenly came to life again, and sat up, upon which all those that sat about the body weeping fled away in a great fright : only his wife, who loved him best, though in a great consternation and trembling, remained with him.  He, comforting her, said, "Fear not, for I am now truly risen from death, and permitted again to live among men; however, I am not to live hereafter as I was wont, but from henceforward after a very different manner."

Then rising immediately, he repaired to the oratory of the little town and, continuing in prayer till day, immediately divided all his substance into three parts, one whereof he gave to his wife, another to his children, and the third, belonging to himself, he instantly distributed among the poor. Not long after he repaired to the monastery of Melrose, which is almost inclosed by the winding of the river Tweed, and having been shaven, went into a private dwelling which the abbot had provided, where he continued till the day of his death in such extraordinary contrition of mind and body that, though his tongue had been silent, his life declared that he had seen many things, either to be dreaded or coveted, which others knew nothing of.

Vision of
purgatory.

Thus he related what he had seen. "He that led me had a shining countenance and a bright garment, and we went on silently, as I thought, towards the northeast. Walking on, we came to a vale of great breadth and depth, but of infinite length; on the left it appeared full of dreadful flames; the other side was no less horrid for violent hail and cold snow flying in all directions; both places were full of men's souls, which seemed by turns to be tossed from one side to the other, as it were by a violent storm; for when the wretches could no longer endure the excess of heat, they leaped into the middle of the cutting cold; and finding no rest there, they leaped back again into the middle of the unquenchable flames.

"Now whereas an innumerable multitude of deformed spirits were thus alternately tormented far and near, as far as could be seen, without any intermission, I began to think that this perhaps might be hell, of whose intolerable flames I had often heard talk. My guide, who went before me, answered to my thought, saying, 'Do not believe so, for this is not hell, as you imagine.'

Vision of the
mouth of hell.

"When he had conducted me, much frightened with that horrid spectacle, by degrees, to the farther end, on a sudden I saw the place begin to grow dusk and filled with darkness. When I came into it, the darkness, by degrees, grew so thick that I could see nothing besides it and the shape and garment of him that led me. As we went on through the shades of night, on a sudden there appeared before us frequent globes of black flames, rising, as it were, out of a great pit, and falling back again into the same.

"When I had been conducted thither, my leader suddenly vanished, and left me alone in the midst of darkness and this horrid vision, whilst those same globes of fire, without intermission, at one time flew up and at another fell back into the bottom of the abyss; and I observed that all the flames, as they ascended, were full of human souls, which, like sparks flying up with smoke, were sometimes thrown on high, and again, when the vapor of the fire ceased, dropped down into the depth below. Moreover, an insufferable

stench came forth with the vapors, and filled all those
dark places.

" Having stood there a long time in much dread, not knowing what to do, which way to turn, or what end I might
expect, on a sudden I heard behind me the noise of a most
hideous and wretched lamentation, and at the same time a
loud laughing, as of a rude multitude insulting captured
enemies. When that noise, growing plainer, came up to me,
I observed a gang of evil spirits dragging the howling and
lamenting souls of men into the midst of the darkness, whilst
they themselves laughed and rejoiced.

"Among those men, as I could discern, there was one shorn
like a clergyman, also a layman, and a woman. The evil
spirits that dragged them went down into the midst of the
burning pit; and as they went down deeper, I could no longer
distinguish between the lamentation of the men and the laughing of the devils, yet I still had a confused sound in my ears.

" In the meantime some of the dark spirits ascended from
that flaming abyss, and, running forward, beset me on all
sides, and much perplexed me with their glaring eyes and
the stifling fire which proceeded from their mouths and
nostrils; and they threatened to lay hold on me with burning tongs, which they had in their hands; yet they durst not
touch me, though they frightened me. Being thus on all
sides inclosed with enemies and darkness, and looking about
on every side for assistance, there appeared behind me, on
the way that I came, as it were, the brightness of a star shining amidst the darkness, which increased by degrees, and
came rapidly towards me: when it drew near, all those evil
spirits that had sought to carry me away with their tongs
dispersed and fled.

" He whose approach put them to flight was the same that
had led me before; who, turning then towards the right,
began to lead me, as it were, towards the southeast, and having soon brought me out of the darkness, conducted me into
an atmosphere of clear light.

" While he thus led me in open light, I saw a vast wall
before us, the length and height of which, in every direction,

seemed to be altogether boundless. I began to wonder why we went up to the wall, seeing no door, window, or path through it. When we came to the wall, we were presently, I know not by what means, on the top of it, and within it was a vast and beautiful field, so full of fragrant flowers that the odor of its delightful sweetness immediately dispelled the stench of the dark furnace, which had penetrated me through and through.

"So great was the light in this place that it seemed to exceed the brightness of the day, or of the sun in its meridian height. In this field were innumerable assemblies of men in white and many companies seated together rejoicing. As he led me through the midst of these happy people, I began to think that this might, perhaps, be the kingdom of heaven, of which I had often heard so much. He answered to my thought, saying, 'This is not the kingdom of heaven, as you imagine.'

Vision of heaven.

"When we had passed those mansions of blessed souls and gone farther on, I discovered before me a much more beautiful light, and heard therein sweet voices of persons singing; and so wonderful a fragrancy proceeded from the place that the other, which I had before thought most delicious, then seemed to me but very indifferent, even as that extraordinary brightness of the flowery field, compared with this, appeared mean and inconsiderable. When I began to hope we should enter that delightful place, my guide on a sudden stood still; and then, turning round, led me back by the way we came.

"When we returned to those joyful mansions of the souls in white, he said to me, 'Do you know what all these things are which you have seen?' I answered that I did not; and then he replied, 'That vale you saw, so dreadful for its consuming flames and cutting cold, is the place in which the souls of those are tried and punished who, delaying to confess and amend their crimes, at length have recourse to repentance at the point of death, and so depart this life; but nevertheless because they, even at their death, confessed and repented, they shall all be received into the kingdom of heaven at the day of judgment by the prayers, alms, and fasting of the living, and more especially by masses.

" 'That fiery and stinking pit which you saw is the mouth of hell, into which whosoever falls shall never be delivered to all eternity. This flowery place, in which you see these most beautiful young people, so bright and gay, is that into which the souls of those are received who depart the body in good works, but who are not so perfect as to deserve to be immediately admitted into the kingdom of heaven; yet they shall all, at the day of judgment, see Christ and partake of the joys of his kingdom; for whoever are perfect in thought, word, and deed, as soon as they depart the body immediately enter into the kingdom of heaven; in the neighborhood whereof that place is, where you heard the sound of sweet singing, with the fragrant odor and bright light.

" 'As for you, who are now to return to your body and live among men again, if you will endeavor nicely to watch your actions, and to direct your speech and behavior in righteousness and simplicity, you shall, after death, have a place of residence among these joyful troops of blessed souls; for when I left you for a while, it was to know how you were to be disposed of.' When he had said this to me I much abhorred returning to my body, being delighted with the sweetness and beauty of the place I beheld and with the company of those I saw in it. However, I durst not ask him any questions; but in the meantime, on a sudden, I found myself alive among men."

## IV. THE CONVERSION OF ENGLAND, AS DESCRIBED BY BEDE

In the year of our Lord 582, Maurice, the fifty-fourth emperor from Augustus, ascended the throne and reigned twenty-one years. In the tenth year of his reign, Gregory, a man renowned for learning and behavior, was promoted to the apostolic see of Rome, and presided over it thirteen years, six months, and ten days. He, being moved by divine inspiration, about the one hundred and fiftieth year

18. The arrival in Kent of the missionaries sent by Gregory the Great (597). (From Bede's *Ecclesiastical History of England*.)

A.4

after the coming of the English into Britain, sent the servant of God, Augustine, and with him several other monks who feared the Lord, to preach the word of God to the English nation. . . .

[Augustine, with his companions, arrived in Britain.] The powerful Ethelbert was at that time king of Kent; he had extended his dominions as far as the great river Humber, by which the southern Saxons are divided from the northern. On the east of Kent is the large Isle of Thanet, containing, according to the English way of reckoning, six hundred families, and divided from the other land by the river Wantsum, which is about three furlongs across and fordable only in two places, for both ends of it run into the sea.

In this island landed the servant of our Lord, Augustine, and his companions, being, as is reported, nearly forty men. They had, by order of the blessed Pope Gregory, brought interpreters of the nation of the Franks, and sending to Ethelbert, signified that they were come from Rome, and brought a joyful message, which most undoubtedly assured to all that took advantage of it everlasting joys in heaven, and a kingdom that would never end with the living and true God.

King Ethelbert meets the Roman missionaries.

The king, having heard this, ordered them to stay in that island where they had landed and that they should be furnished with all necessaries till he should consider what to do with them. For he had heard of the Christian religion, having a Christian wife, of the royal family of the Franks, called Bertha, whom he had received from her parents upon condition that she should be permitted to practice her religion with the bishop, Luidhard, who was sent with her to preserve the faith.

Some days later the king came into the island and, sitting in the open air, ordered Augustine and his companions to be brought into his presence. For he had taken precaution that they should not come to him in any house, lest, according to an ancient superstition, if they practiced any magical arts they might impose upon him, and so get the better of him. But they came furnished with divine, not with magic, power, bearing a silver cross for their banner, and the image of our Lord and Saviour painted on a board; and singing the litany, they offered up their prayers to the Lord for the eternal salvation both of themselves and of those to whom they came.

When Augustine had sat down, pursuant to the king's commands, and preached to him and his attendants there present the word of life, the king answered thus : " Your words and promises are very fair, but they are new to us and of uncertain import, and I cannot approve of them so far as to forsake that which I have so long followed with the whole English nation. But because you are come from far into my kingdom, and, as I conceive, are desirous to impart to us those things which you believe to be true and most beneficial, we will not molest you, but give you favorable entertainment and take care to supply you with the necessary sustenance ; nor do we forbid you to preach and gain as many as you can to your religion."

Accordingly, he permitted them to reside in the city of Canterbury, which was the metropolis of all his dominions, and in accordance with the promise that he had made to them, besides allowing them sustenance, he did not refuse them the liberty to preach. . . .

There was on the east side of the city a church dedicated to St. Martin, built whilst the Romans were still in the island, wherein the queen, who, as has been said before, was a Christian, used to pray. In this they first began to meet, to sing, to pray, to say mass, to preach, and to baptize, till the king, being converted to the faith, allowed them to preach openly and to build or repair churches in all places.

When he among the rest, induced by the unspotted life of these holy men and their delightful promises, which, by many miracles, they proved to be most certain, believed and was baptized, greater numbers began daily to flock together to hear the word and, forsaking their heathen rites, to associate themselves, by believing, to the unity of the Church of Christ.

Augustine founds a monastery at Canterbury.

Augustine preaches to the king.

Bede relates the story of the conversion of Northumbria to the Roman Catholic form of faith, as follows:

19. Bede's account of the conversion of Northumbria.

[Edwin, king of Northumbria, urged by his Christian wife, Ethelberga, and by the bishop Paulinus,] answered that he was both willing and bound to receive the new faith which the bishop taught, but that he wished, nevertheless, to confer about it with his principal friends and counselors, to the end that, if they also were of his opinion, they might all be cleansed together in Christ, the Fountain of Life. Paulinus consenting, the king did as he had said; for, holding a council with the wise men, he asked of every one in particular what he thought of the new doctrine and the new worship that was preached.

To which the chief of his own priests, Coifi, immediately answered: "O king, consider what this is which is now preached to us; for I verily declare to you that the religion which we have hitherto professed has, as far as I can learn, no virtue in it. For none of your people has applied himself more diligently to the worship of our gods than I; and yet there are many who receive greater favors from you, and are more preferred than I, and who are more prosperous in all their undertakings. Now if the gods were good for anything, they would rather forward me, who have been more careful to serve them. It follows, therefore, that if upon examination you find those new doctrines which are now preached to us better and more efficacious, we should immediately receive them without any delay."

Another of the king's chief men, approving of Coifi's words and exhortations, presently added: "The present life of man, O king, seems to me, in comparison with that time which is unknown to us, like to the swift flight of a sparrow through the room wherein you sit at supper in winter amid your officers and ministers, with a good fire in the midst, whilst the storms of rain and snow prevail abroad; the sparrow, I say, flying in at one door and immediately out at another, whilst he is within is safe from the wintry storm; but after a short space of fair weather he immediately vanishes out of your sight into the dark winter from which he has emerged. So this life of man appears for a short space, but of what went before or what is to follow we are utterly ignorant. If, therefore, this new doctrine contains something more certain, it seems justly to deserve to be followed."

The other elders and king's counselors, by divine inspiration, spoke to the same effect. But Coifi added that he wished more attentively to hear Paulinus discourse concerning the God whom he preached. So the bishop having spoken by the king's command at greater length, Coifi, hearing his words, cried out: "I have long since been sensible that there was nothing in that which we worshiped, because the more diligently I sought after truth in that worship, the less I found it. But now I freely confess that such evident truth appears in this preaching as can confer on us the gifts of life, of salvation, and of eternal happiness. For which reason I advise, O king, that we instantly abjure and set fire to those temples and altars which we have consecrated without reaping any benefits from them."

## V. Boniface and the Conversion of Germany

Many of the people of Hesse were converted [by Boniface] to the Catholic faith and confirmed by the grace of the spirit: and they received the laying on of hands. But some there were, not yet strong of soul, who refused to accept wholly the teachings of the true faith. Some men sacrificed secretly, some even openly, to trees and springs. Some secretly practiced divining, soothsaying, and incantations, and some openly. But others, who were of sounder mind, cast aside all heathen profanation and did none of these things; and it was with the advice and consent of these men that Boniface sought to fell a certain tree of great size, at Geismar, and called, in the ancient speech of the region, the oak of Jove [i.e. Thor].

20. How Boniface destroyed the oak of Thor. (From Willibald's *Life of Boniface*, written before 786.)

The man of God was surrounded by the servants of God. When he would cut down the tree, behold a great throng of pagans who were there cursed him bitterly among themselves because he was the enemy of their gods. And when he had cut into the trunk a little way, a breeze sent by God stirred overhead, and suddenly the branching top of the tree was broken off, and the oak in all its huge bulk fell to the ground. And it was broken into four parts, as if by the divine will, so that the trunk was divided into four huge sections without any effort of the brethren who stood by. When the pagans who had cursed did see this, they left off cursing and, believing, blessed God. Then the most holy priest took counsel with the brethren : and he built from the wood of the tree an oratory, and dedicated it to the holy apostle Peter.

The following account of the founding of the famous monastery of Fulda was written by Sturmi's disciple Eigil, who was abbot of Fulda during the years 818 to 822.

**21. How the monastery of Fulda was founded in the German forest.
(From the *Life of St. Sturmi*.)**

[The holy and venerable archbishop Boniface came to Bavaria, and turned many people to the gospel of Christ. Among them a certain boy, Sturmi, son of noble and Christian parents, followed the teaching of Boniface and was ordained priest.] For almost three years he fulfilled the duties of the priesthood, preaching and baptizing among the people. Then by the inspiration of God the purpose came into his soul to chasten himself by the straiter life and the hardships of the wilderness. He sought counsel thereupon from Boniface, — his master in the spirit, — who, when he understood Sturmi, knew that this purpose was inspired of God and rejoiced that God had designed to lead him by his grace. He gave Sturmi two companions, and when he had prayed and blessed them all he said : "Go forth into that solitude which is called Bochonia and seek a place meet for the servants of God to dwell in. For God is able to prepare for his servants a place in the wilderness."

And so those three went forth into the wilderness and entered into places solitary and rough, and saw almost nothing but heaven and earth and great trees; and they prayed Christ fervently that he would direct their feet in the path of peace. On the third day they came to the place which even to this day is called Hersfeld; and when they had seen and explored the region round about, they asked Christ that the place might be blest to the dwellers therein. On the very spot where the monastery now stands they built poor huts of the bark of trees. There they tarried many days, serving God with holy fasts and watching and prayer. . . .

Then after some time spent in holy meditation Sturmi returned to the bishop, and described the lay of the land and the course of the streams, and the hills and valleys. . . . Boniface heard him attentively, and answered: "I fear to have you dwell in this place which ye have found because a barbarous race lives close by, for, as thou knowest, the fell Saxons are near at hand. Wherefore seek a dwelling in the wilderness farther away and higher up the stream, where ye may remain without danger." . . .

So, after resting a little, Sturmi mounted his ass and set forth alone, commending his journey to Christ, who is the way, the truth, and the life. All alone, sitting upon his ass, he began his journey through the vast places of the wilderness. He eagerly explored the region and observed with quick eye the mountains and the hills and the plains, the springs and torrents and rivers. With psalms always upon his lips, he prayed to God with groaning, his soul lifted up to heaven. And wherever night found him, there he rested; and he hewed wood with the sword which he bore in his hand, and laid it in a circle, and set it on fire to protect his ass, lest the wild beasts which were there in great numbers might devour him. For himself, he made on his forehead the sign of the cross of Christ, in the name of God, and rested in safety. . . .

[And Sturmi went on his way till he reached the torrent that even to this day is called Grezzibach.] He observed how the land lay, and what was the nature of the soil, and he tarried there a little space. And then he went back a little way and came to the place already made ready and blessed by God, even the place where the holy monastery [of Fulda] now stands. When he had come thither straightway the holy man Sturmi was filled with exceeding great joy, for he knew

Sturmi starts forth alone to discover a proper site for the monastery.

that through the merits and prayers of the holy bishop Boniface the place had been revealed to him by God.

[This paragraph is condensed.]

Then on the second day the man of God came again to Hersfeld and found his brethren there calling upon God with fervent prayers. He told them of the place he had found and bade them make ready to go thither with him. But Sturmi went straightway to the holy bishop Boniface to tell him how he had found a place for the brethren to dwell in. Together they rejoiced and gave God thanks and held sweet converse about the life and conversation of monks. Then did the bishop let Sturmi go back to his wilderness, while he went to the palace of Carloman, the king, to gain from him a grant of the place Sturmi had chosen.

Boniface procures a charter from King Carloman for Fulda.

When Boniface came before the king, he said to him: "We have found in the wilderness called Bochonia, beside the river named Fulda, a place meet for the servants of God to dwell in, where before us no man has dwelt. It is under your sway, and we do beg of your beneficence to give us this place, so that we may be enabled to serve God under your protection." . . . Then did the king before all the lords of his palace give over to the bishop the place he had asked for, saying, " This place which thou seekest on the bank of the river Fulda I give over whole and entire from my law to the law of God — from that place in all directions in a circle four thousand paces toward east and west and north and south, ye shall hold the region."

Then the king gave command that a charter be written to this end, and he sealed it with his own hand.

The building of the monastery.

In the year of the incarnation of Christ 744, in the first month, the twelfth day of the month, while the brothers Carloman and Pippin were reigning over the Frankish people, did Sturmi arise, in the name of God, and with seven brethren he did go to the place where now the monastery stands. They prayed to the Lord Christ that he would ever protect and defend them by his power; and, serving God in sacred psalms and in fasts, vigils, and prayers by day and by night, they did busy themselves cutting down the forests and clearing the ground by their own labor so far as strength was given them.

## BIBLIOGRAPHY

**The Monks:** ADAMS, *Civilization*, pp. 131–136; EMERTON, *Introduction*, Chapter XI, pp. 135–149; GIBBON, Vol. IV, Chapter XXXVII, pp. 57–75.

**The Benedictine Rule:** Selections in FLING, *European History Studies*, Vol. II, No. 6, pp. 94–99. The most complete translation is in HENDERSON, *Select Documents*, pp. 274–314. Monastery Charters: FLING, pp. 91–94; HENDERSON, pp. 329–333.

**The Conversion of the Saxons:** BÉMONT and MONOD, pp. 124–132; GARDINER, *Student's History of England*, pp. 37–52; GREEN, *Short History of the English People* (larger edition), Chapter I, section 3, pp. 17–36; TERRY, *History of England*, pp. 34–49; GEE and HARDY, *Documents of English Church History*, pp. 2–15; *Old South Leaflets*, No. 113; KENDALL, *Source Book of English History*, pp. 14–16; GREEN, pp. 38–41.

**Missionaries to the Continent:** *Life of St. Columban*, written in the seventh century. *Translations and Reprints*, Vol. II, No. 7. Very valuable and interesting.

A. References.

MONTALEMBERT, *The Monks of the West*, 6 vols. The best and fullest discussion of the subject, attractive on account of the writer's enthusiasm and literary style. See especially Introduction, Chapters II, III, and IV, on the nature of monasticism and its services to Christendom; Books II and III on the precursors of Benedict in the East and West; Book IV on Benedict; Book VII on St. Columban; and Books VIII–XIV on the establishment of the Church in Britain.

SMITH, T. G., *Christian Monasticism from the Fourth to the Ninth Centuries*. A brief survey of the same field.

HARNACK, *Monasticism*. An admirable philosophical comparison of the spirit of eastern and western monasticism.

TAYLOR, *The Classical Heritage of the Middle Ages*, Chapter VII. An eloquent description of the character of monasticism and its founders.

Good general chapters on the origin and spread of monastic institutions are to be found in works already mentioned. NEWMAN, *Manual of Church History*, Chapter III, sections 10 and 11; SCHAFF, *History of the Christian Church*, Vol. IV, Chapter II; MILMAN, *History of Latin Christianity*, Book III, Chapter VI, on Western Monasticism in General; Book IV, Chapters III and IV, Conversion of England; Book IV, Chapter V, Conversion of the Germans.

BEDE, *Ecclesiastical History*, translated by Giles (Latin and English on opposite pages). The great authority for the beginnings of the English Church. A type of the best early mediæval historian.

B. Additional reading in English.

# CHAPTER VI

## CHARLES MARTEL AND PIPPIN

### I. THE KORAN

Singular
origin of the
Koran, the
Bible of the
Mohamme-
dans.

Mohammed apparently suffered from a certain nervous disorder which is often accompanied by hallucinations. When about forty years of age, as he was engaged in meditation upon a solitary mountain near Mecca, the angel Gabriel appeared to him and uttered five verses, — the first of the revelations from heaven which were to compose the Koran. Similar messages came to him from time to time during his periods of nervous excitement. These he revealed to his friends and converts, who committed them to memory and, in some cases, wrote them down. It is probable that the prophet himself could neither read nor write.

At the time of his death no collection had as yet been made of these inspired utterances; they had only been recorded piecemeal on palm leaves, skins, shoulder blades of animals, and, above all, in the hearts of his followers. The early caliphs, realizing that the *Book of God* might otherwise be speedily lost, ordered that a man who had acted as Mohammed's amanuensis should collect and arrange the text. A second and more careful edition, made in 660, was sent to all the chief cities in the Mohammedan empire and has remained the authoritative text among all Mohammedans down to the present day.

The revelations were strung together without regard to the order in which Mohammed received them and with little or no attention to their contents. The longer *surahs* or chapters come first and then the short ones, although chronologically the shorter were the earlier. It is therefore not unnatural that the Koran should be confused and often obscure, and in an English version it is hard to perceive much of the marvelous eloquence which recommends it to the Arab mind.

It is chiefly made up of repeated assertions of God's unity and greatness and of the futility and wickedness of the worship of idols. There are frequent references to the last judgment, to heaven and its delights, to hell and the fate of those who stubbornly refuse to accept the Koran as the word of God, and Mohammed as his prophet. Many episodes from the Old and New Testaments are given here and there, such as the stories of Abraham, of Joseph, of Moses, of the birth of Jesus. Mohammed could hardly have been acquainted with the Bible at first hand, but must have gathered his knowledge of it from the Jews and Christians settled in Arabia. The Koran also embodies popular sayings and favorite legends current among the desert tribes long before the time of Mohammed. Some important rules of conduct are also laid down.

*In the Name of God, the Compassionate, the Merciful*

**22. Passages from the Koran. The opening prayer.**

Praise be to God, the Lord of the Worlds!
The Compassionate, the Merciful!
King of the day of judgment!
Thee we worship, and Thee we ask for help.
Guide us in the straight way,
The way of those to whom Thou art gracious;
Not of those upon whom is Thy wrath, nor of the erring.

*In the Name of God, the Compassionate, the Merciful*

God's beau-
tiful world.

Have we not made the earth as a bed?
And the mountains as tent-pegs?
And created you in pairs,
And made you sleep for rest,
And made the night for a mantle,
And made the day for bread-winning,
And built above you seven firmaments,
And put therein a burning lamp,
And sent down water pouring from the squeezed clouds
To bring forth grain and herb withal,
And gardens thick with trees?

Description
of the bliss
of heaven
and the
pains of hell.

When the earth shall be shaken in a shock,
And the mountains shall be powdered in powder,
And become like flying dust,
And ye shall be three kinds.

Then the people of the right hand — what people of good
　　omen!
And the people of the left hand — what people of ill omen!
And the outstrippers, still outstripping: —
These are the nearest [to God],
In gardens of delight;
A crowd of the men of yore,
And a few of the latter days;
Upon inwrought couches,
Reclining thereon face to face.
Youths ever young shall go unto them round about
With goblets and ewers and a cup of flowing wine, —
Their heads shall not ache with it, neither shall they be
　　confused;
And fruits of their choice,
And flesh of birds to their desire;
And damsels with bright eyes like hidden pearls, —
A reward for what they have wrought.
They shall hear no folly therein, nor any sin,
But only the greeting, "Peace! peace!"

And the people of the right hand — what people of good
    omen !
Amid thornless lote-trees,
And bananas laden with fruit,
And shade outspread,
And water flowing,
And fruit abundant,
Never failing, nor forbidden, . . .
But the people of the left hand — what people of ill omen ! —
Amid burning wind and scalding water,
And a shade of black smoke,
Not cool or grateful !
Verily before that they were prosperous ;
But they persisted in the most grievous sin,
And used to say,
" When we have died, and become dust and bones, shall we
    indeed be raised again,
And our fathers, the men of yore,"
Say : Verily those of yore and of the latter days
Shall surely be gathered to the trysting-place of a day which
    is known.
Then ye, O ye who err and call it a lie,
Shall surely eat of the tree of Zakkum,
And fill your bellies with it,
And drink upon it scalding water, —
Drink like the thirsty camel : —
This shall be their entertainment on the Day of Judgment !


## II. How Pippin, the First of the Carolingian Line, became King of France

The Franks in olden times were wont to choose their kings
from the family of the Merovingians. This royal line is considered to have come to an end in the person of Childeric III,
who was deposed from the throne by command of Stephen,
the Roman pontiff ; his long hair was cut off and he was
thrust into a monastery.

23. The last
Merovingian
kings.
(From Ein-
hard's
*Life of the
Emperor
Charles.)

Although the line of the Merovingians actually ended with Childeric, it had nevertheless for some time previously been so utterly wanting in power that it had displayed no mark of royalty except the empty kingly title.

All the resources and power of the kingdom had passed into the control of the prefects of the palace, who were called the "mayors of the palace,"[1] and who employed the supreme authority. Nothing was left to the king. He had to content himself with his royal title, his flowing locks, and long beard. Seated in a chair of state, he was wont to display an appearance of power by receiving foreign ambassadors on their arrival, and, on their departure, giving them, as if on his own authority, those answers which he had been taught or commanded to give.

Thus, except for his empty title, and an uncertain allowance for his subsistence, which the prefect of the palace used to furnish at his pleasure, there was nothing that the king could call his own, unless it were the income from a single farm, and that a very small one, where he made his home, and where such servants as were needful to wait on him constituted his scanty household. When he went anywhere he traveled in a wagon drawn by a yoke of oxen, with a rustic oxherd for charioteer. In this manner he proceeded to the palace, and to the public assemblies of the people held every year for the dispatch of the business of the kingdom, and he returned home again in the same sort of state. The administration of the kingdom, and every matter which had to be undertaken and carried through, both at home and abroad, was managed by the mayor of the palace.

**24. Pope Zacharius authorizes the coronation of Pippin.** (From *The Lesser Annals of Lorsch.*) In the year of the Incarnation of our Lord, 750,[2] Pippin sent ambassadors to Pope Zacharias to ask his opinion in the matter of the kings of the Franks, who, though of the royal line, and called kings, enjoyed in truth no power in the realm except that official documents were issued in their

[1] Maiores domus.

[2] It appears from other sources that it was in 752 — not 750 — that Pippin received the kingly crown from the hand of Boniface.

name.  Otherwise they were destitute of power, and did only what the mayor of the palace told them.

Only upon the day when the people, according to ancient usage, were wont to bring gifts to their sovereign on the March Field, did the king, surrounded by the army, sit in his chair, the mayor of the palace standing before him, and proclaim such laws as had been established by the Franks. The next day he returned home, and stayed there during the remainder of the year.

Pope Zacharias, therefore, in virtue of apostolic authority, told the ambassadors that he judged it better and more advantageous that he should be king and be called king who had the power rather than he who was falsely called king.

The said pontiff accordingly enjoined the king and the people of the Franks that Pippin, who already exercised the regal power, should be called king and raised to the throne.

And this was done by St. Boniface, the archbishop, who anointed him king in the city of Soissons.  And so it came about that Pippin was called king, while Childeric, falsely called king, was shaven and sent to the monastery.

(753) . . . In this year Pope Stephen [the successor of Zacharias] came to King Pippin in the town which is called Kiersey, to beg protection for himself and the Roman church from the attacks of the Lombards. . . .

(754) Pope Stephen, after King Pippin had assured him that he would defend the Roman church, consecrated him to the honor of the royal dignity, and with him his two sons, Karl and Carloman; and the pope spent that winter in Francia.

25. The coronation of Pippin by the pope. (From Einhard's *Annals*.)

## BIBLIOGRAPHY

**General Discussion of the Work of Charles Martel and Pippin:** ADAMS, *Civilization*, pp. 146–154.

**Charles Martel:** EMERTON, *Introduction*, Chapter X, pp. 114–134; HENDERSON, *Germany in the Middle Ages*, pp. 40–46; OMAN, Chapter XVII, pp. 289–299.

*A. References.*

The Arabs — their Original Character : GIBBON, Vol. V, Chapter L, first part, pp. 311–332.

Mohammed : BÉMONT and MONOD, Chapter X, pp. 135–147 ; GIBBON, Vol. V, Chapter L, latter part, pp. 333–396.

Arab Conquests and Civilization : GIBBON, Vol. V, Chapter LI, pp. 397–494 ; MUNRO, *History of the Middle Ages*, Chapter IX, pp. 86–94.

Pippin : EMERTON, Chapter XII, pp. 150–179 ; HENDERSON, pp. 46–56 ; OMAN, Chapter XIX, pp. 322–334.

---

*B. Additional reading in English.*

GILMAN, *The Saracens* (with an excellent bibliography at the end) ; AMEER ALI, *The Life and Teachings of Mohammed* and *A Short History of the Saracens*. Two recent and interesting studies from the point of view of an enlightened Oriental writer. MUIR, *Life of Mahomet* and *Annals of the Early Caliphate*. The former is the most thorough treatment in English ; the latter deals with the fifty years following Mohammed's death.

MILMAN, Book IV, Chapters I–II.

The whole Koran has been carefully translated by E. H. PALMER, 2 vols., 1880 ; but most readers will derive far more pleasure and profit from the extracts given in STANLEY LANE-POOLE, *Speeches and Table Talk of the Prophet Mohammad*, — a most charming little book, which helps one to feel the beauty of the poetical passages of the Koran.

HODGKIN, *Italy and her Invaders*, Vol. VII, Book VIII, Chapters III–XI.

GREGOROVIUS, Vol. II, Book IV, Chapters I–III.

KITCHIN, *History of France*, Vol. I, Book II, Part I, Chapters I–II.

# CHAPTER VII

## CHARLEMAGNE

### I. Charlemagne, the Man

Charles was large and robust, of commanding stature and excellent proportions, for it appears that he measured in height seven times the length of his own foot. The top of his head was round, his eyes large and animated, his nose somewhat long. He had a fine head of gray hair, and his face was bright and pleasant; so that, whether standing or sitting, he showed great presence and dignity. Although his neck was thick and rather short, and his belly too prominent, still the good proportions of his limbs concealed these defects. His walk was firm, and the whole carriage of his body was manly. His voice was clear, but not so strong as his frame would have led one to expect.

26. Charlemagne's personal appearance and habits. (From Einhard's *Life of Charles.*)

His health was good until the last four years of his life, when he was attacked with frequent fevers, and latterly walked lame on one foot. Even then he relied more on his own judgment than on the advice of physicians, whom he almost hated because they used to recommend him to leave off roasted meats, which he preferred, and to accustom himself to boiled.

He took constant exercise in riding and hunting, which was natural for a Frank, since scarcely any nation can be found to equal them in these pursuits. He also delighted in the natural warm baths, frequently exercising himself by swimming, in which he was very skillful, no one being able to outstrip him. It was on account of the warm baths at Aix-la-Chapelle that he built his palace there and lived there constantly during the last years of his life and until his death. . . .

He wore the dress of his native country, that is, the
Frankish; next his body a linen shirt and linen drawers;
then a tunic with a silken border, and stockings. He bound
his legs with garters and wore shoes on his feet. In the winter he protected his shoulders and chest with a vest made of
the skins of otters and sable. He wore a blue cloak, and
was always girt with his sword, the hilt and belt being of
gold and silver. Sometimes he wore a jeweled sword, but
he did so only on great festivals or when receiving foreign
ambassadors.

He thoroughly disliked the dress of foreigners, however
fine; and he never put it on except at Rome — once at the
request of Pope Adrian, and again, a second time, to please
Adrian's successor, Pope Leo. He then wore a long tunic,
chlamys, and shoes made after the Roman fashion. On
festivals he used to walk in processions clad in a garment
woven with gold, and shoes studded with jewels, his cloak
fastened with a golden clasp, and wearing a crown of gold
set with precious stones. At other times his dress differed
little from that of a private person.

In his eating and drinking he was temperate; more particularly so in his drinking, for he had the greatest abhor-
rence of drunkenness in anybody, but more especially in
himself and his companions. He was unable to abstain
from food for any length of time, and often complained that
fasting was injurious to him. On the other hand, he very
rarely feasted, only on great festive occasions, when there
were very large gatherings. The daily service of his table
consisted of only four dishes in addition to the roast meat,
which the hunters used to bring in on spits, and of which he
partook more freely than of any other food.

While he was dining he listened to music or reading.
History and the deeds of men of old were most often read.
He derived much pleasure from the works of St. Augustine,
especially from his book called *The City of God*. He partook very sparingly of wine and other drinks, rarely taking
at meals more than three draughts. In summer, after the
midday repast, he would take some fruit and one draught,

and then, throwing aside his clothes and shoes as at night, he would repose for two or three hours. He slept at night so lightly that he would break his rest four or five times, not merely by awaking, but even getting up.

While he was dressing and binding on his sandals, he would receive his friends; and also, if the count of the palace announced that there was any case which could only be settled by his decision, the suitors were immediately ordered into his presence, and he heard the case and gave judgment as if sitting in court. And this was not the only business that he used to arrange at that time, for he also gave orders for whatever had to be done on that day by any officer or servant.

He was ready and fluent in speaking, and able to express himself with great clearness. He did not confine himself to his native tongue, but took pains to learn foreign languages, acquiring such knowledge of Latin that he could make an address in that language as well as in his own. Greek he could better understand than speak. Indeed, he was so polished in speech that he might have passed for a learned man. *Charlemagne's knowledge of the ancient languages.*

He was an ardent admirer of the liberal arts, and greatly revered their professors, whom he promoted to high honors. In order to learn grammar, he attended the lectures of the aged Peter of Pisa, a deacon; and for other branches he chose as his preceptor Albinus, otherwise called Alcuin, also a deacon, — a Saxon by race, from Britain, the most learned man of the day, with whom the king spent much time in learning rhetoric and logic, and more especially astronomy. He learned the art of determining the dates upon which the movable festivals of the Church fall, and with deep thought and skill most carefully calculated the courses of the planets. *Alcuin.*

Charles also tried to learn to write, and used to keep his tablets and writing book under the pillow of his couch, that when he had leisure he might practice his hand in forming letters; but he made little progress in this task, too long deferred and begun too late in life. *Charlemagne never learned to write.*

## II. How Charlemagne was made Emperor

A.D. 799

27. Circumstances of Charlemagne's coronation as emperor. (From the so-called *Annals of Einhard*.)

Maltreatment of Pope Leo by the Romans.

As Pope Leo [III] was riding from the Lateran in Rome to service in the church of St. Lawrence, called "the Gridiron," he fell into an ambush which the Romans had set for him in the neighborhood of this church. He was dragged from off his horse and, as some would have it, his eyes put out, his tongue cut off, and he was then left lying in the street, naked and half dead. Afterward the instigators of this deed ordered that he should be taken into the monastery of the holy martyr Erasmus to be cared for. His chamberlain Albinus succeeded, however, in letting him down over the wall at night, whereupon Duke Winigis of Spoleto, who had hurried to Rome on hearing of this deed of sacrilege, took him into his charge and carried him to Spoleto.

When the king [Charlemagne] received news of this occurrence, he gave orders that the Roman pope, the successor of St. Peter, should be brought to him, with all due honor. He did not, however, give up on this account the expedition into Saxony which he had undertaken. He held a general assembly at a place called Lippeham, on the Rhine; he then crossed the river and pushed on with his entire army to Paderborn, where he set up his camp and awaited the pope. In the meantime he sent his son Charles, with a part of the army, to the Elbe to settle certain matters with the Wilzer and Abodrites and to receive into his charge certain of the North Saxons.

Charlemagne reinstates Pope Leo.

While he was awaiting his son's return, the pope arrived, was honorably received, and remained several days with him. After he had laid before the king all the reasons for his coming, he was accompanied back to Rome by the king's ambassadors and reinstated in his authority there.

After the pope's departure, the king remained several days longer and finished his business with Daniel, ambassador of the Patrician Michael of Sicily. He received also the sad news of the undoing of Gerold and Eric ; the one, Gerold, governor of Bavaria, lost his life in a battle with the Huns and was buried in Reichenau; the other, Eric, after many battles and brilliant victories, met his death through the treachery of the inhabitants of Tersat,[1] a town of Liburnia. When affairs in Saxony had been as well ordered as time would permit, the king returned again to Francia.

In the winter, which was spent in Aix-la-Chapelle, came Count Wido, count and governor of the border land of Brittany, who, during this year, and in alliance with other counts, had traversed the whole territory of the Bretons, and now brought to the king the arms of the dukes who had submitted themselves, with their several names inscribed thereon. It appeared at that time as if that whole country was completely subjugated ; and so it would have been had not the fickleness of its faithless people soon changed all this, as usual.

Trophies of victory were also brought which had been taken from Moorish robbers killed on the island of Majorca. The Saracen, Azan, governor of Oska, sent to the king the keys of that city, together with other gifts, and promised to give the town over to him whenever opportunity should offer. Moreover, a monk came from Jerusalem, bringing to the king the blessing of the Patriarch and certain relics from the place of the resurrection of our Lord. The king spent Christmas in his palace at Aix-la-Chapelle. When the monk desired to return home, he gave him, as a companion, Zacharias, a priest of his palace, and sent, besides, pious gifts to the holy places.

A.D. 800

When spring came again, about the middle of March, the king left Aix-la-Chapelle and journeyed toward the coast of Gaul. Off this coast, which was being devastated by the piratical Northmen, he built and manned a fleet. Easter he celebrated in St. Riquier at the shrine of St. Richard. From

[1] Near Fiume.

here he traveled along the coast to the city of Rouen, where he crossed the Seine and betook himself to Tours in order to perform his devotions at the shrine of St. Martin. On account of the illness of his wife, Luitgarda, who died and was buried here, he was forced to remain some days in this place; she died on the 4th of June. From here he returned, by way of Orleans and Paris, to Aix-la-Chapelle; early in August he reached Mayence, where he held a diet and announced his intended journey to Italy.

From Mayence he went with his army to Ravenna, where he stayed only seven days and whence he dispatched his son Pippin, with the army, into the country of Beneventum. He and his son left Ravenna together, but at Ancona they parted company and he betook himself to Rome.

On the very day of his arrival Pope Leo went to meet him at Nomentum. He received the pope with great reverence, and they dined together. Then he remained behind while the pope returned to the city in order that he might be waiting to receive him the next morning on the steps of St. Peter's, together with the bishops and all the clergy.

When he appeared and dismounted from his horse, the pope received him with gratitude and thanksgiving and conducted him into the church, while all the people glorified God in hymns of praise. This was on the 24th day of November. Seven days later, the king publicly proclaimed, in an assembly which he had called together, all the reasons why he had come to Rome, and thenceforth he labored daily to carry out all that he had come to do.

He began with the most serious and difficult matter, namely, the investigation into the offenses of which the pope had been accused. But since no one could be found who was willing to substantiate the charges, the pope, carrying the Gospels in his hand, mounted the pulpit in St. Peter's and before all the people, and in the name of the Holy Trinity, took an oath to clear himself from the crimes imputed to him.

On the same day Zacharias, the priest whom the king had dispatched to Jerusalem, arrived at Rome with two monks sent to the king by the Patriarch. By way of a blessing, they brought with them the keys to the sepulcher of our Lord and to the place of Calvary, together with an ensign. The king received them graciously, kept them as his guests for some days, and when they were ready to return, dismissed them with gifts.

A.D. 801

On the most holy day of the birth of our Lord, the king went to mass at St. Peter's, and as he knelt in prayer before the altar Pope Leo set a crown upon his head, while all the Roman populace cried aloud, "Long life and victory to the mighty Charles, the great and pacific Emperor of the Romans, crowned of God!" After he had been thus acclaimed, the pope did homage to him, as had been the custom with the early rulers, and henceforth he dropped the title of Patrician and was called Emperor and Augustus. . . .

## III. Charlemagne's Ideals of Government

In the elaborate instructions for the *missi* we have the fullest statement of the tasks of government which devolved upon Charlemagne, and of the various offenses which he foresaw and for which he deemed it especially necessary to provide.

The most serene and most Christian lord emperor Charles has chosen from his nobles the wisest and most prudent men, archbishops and some of the other bishops also, together with venerable abbots and pious laymen, and has sent them throughout his whole kingdom; through them he would have all the various classes of persons mentioned in the following sections live strictly in accordance with the law. Moreover, where anything which is not right and just has been enacted in the law, he has ordered them to inquire into this most diligently and to inform him of it; he desires, God granting, to reform it.

28. Extracts from the general capitulary for the *missi* (802).

And let no one, through cunning craft, dare to oppose or thwart the written law, as many are wont to do, or the

judicial sentence passed upon him; or to do injury to the
churches of God, or the poor, or the widows, or the wards,
or any Christian.   But all shall live entirely in accordance
with God's precept, justly and under a just rule, and each
one shall be admonished to live in harmony with his fellows
in his business or profession.   The canonical clergy ought
to observe in every respect a canonical life without heeding
base gain; nuns ought to keep diligent watch over their
lives; laymen and the secular clergy ought rightly to observe
their laws without malicious fraud; and all ought to live in
mutual charity and perfect peace.

General
duties of
the *missi*.
And let the *missi* themselves make a diligent investigation
whenever any man claims that an injustice has been done to
him by any one, just as they desire to deserve the grace of
omnipotent God and to keep their fidelity pledged to him, so
that in all cases, everywhere, they shall, in accordance with
the will and fear of God, administer the law fully and justly
in the case of the holy churches of God and of the poor, of
wards and widows, and of the whole people.   And if there
shall be anything of such a nature that they, together with
the provincial counts, are not able of themselves to correct it
and to do justice concerning it, they shall, without any reservations, refer this, together with their reports, to the judgment
of the emperor.   The straight path of justice shall not be
impeded by any one on account of flattery or gifts, or on
account of any relationship, or from fear of the powerful.

All required
to take an
oath of fidel-
ity to Charle-
magne as
emperor.
Concerning the fidelity to be promised to the lord emperor:
he has commanded that every man in his whole kingdom,
whether ecclesiastic or layman, each according to his vow
and occupation, shall now pledge to him as emperor the
fidelity which he has previously promised to him as king;
and all of those who have not yet taken any oath shall do
likewise, down to those who are twelve years old.

What the
oath to the
emperor
included.
And that it shall be announced to all in public, so that
each one may know, how great and how many things are comprehended in that oath; not merely, as many have thought
hitherto, fidelity to the lord emperor as regards his life, and

not introducing any enemy into his kingdom out of enmity, and not consenting to, or concealing another's faithlessness to him; but that all may know that this oath contains in itself the following meaning:

First, that each one voluntarily shall strive, in accordance with his knowledge and ability, to live entirely in the holy service of God in accordance with the precept of God and in accordance with his own promise, because the lord emperor is unable to give to all individually the necessary care and discipline.

Secondly, that no man, either through perjury or any other wile or fraud, or on account of the flattery or gift of any one, shall refuse to give back or dare to abstract or conceal a serf of the lord emperor, or a district, or land, or anything that belongs to him; and that no one shall presume, through perjury or other wile, to conceal or abstract his fugitive serfs belonging to the fisc, who wrongly and fraudulently claim that they are free.

That no one shall presume to rob or in any way do injury fraudulently to the churches of God, or to widows or orphans or pilgrims; for the lord emperor himself, after God and his saints, has constituted himself their protector and defender.

That no one shall dare to lay waste a benefice of the lord emperor, or to make it his own property.

That no one shall presume to neglect a summons to war from the lord emperor; and that no one of the counts shall be so presumptuous as to dare to excuse any one of those who owe military service, either on account of relationship, or flattery, or gifts from any one.

That no one shall presume to impede in any way a ban or command of the lord emperor, or to dally with his work, or to impede or to lessen or in any way to act contrary to his will or commands. And that no one shall dare to neglect to pay his dues or tax.

That no one, for any reason, shall make a practice in court of defending another unjustly, either from any desire of gain when the cause is weak, or by impeding a just judgment by his skill in reasoning, or by a desire of oppressing when the cause is weak. . . .

The oath to the emperor should include the observance of all those things mentioned above.

Duties of the
prelates.

Bishops and priests shall live according to the canons and shall teach others to do the same.

Bishops, abbots, and abbesses, who are in charge of others, shall strive with the greatest devotion to surpass those subject to them in this diligence and shall not oppress those subject to them with a harsh rule of tyranny, but with sincere love shall carefully guard the flock committed to them with mercy and charity and by the examples of good works. . . .

Duties of
the monks.

The monks shall live sincerely and strictly in accordance with the rule, because we know that any one whose good will is lukewarm is displeasing to God, as John bears witness in the Apocalypse : " I would thou wert cold or hot. So then because thou art lukewarm, and neither cold nor hot, I will spew thee out of my mouth." Let them in no way usurp to themselves secular business. They shall not have leave to go outside of their monastery at all, unless compelled by a very great necessity; but the bishop in whose diocese they are shall take care in every way that they do not get accustomed to wandering outside of the monastery. But if it shall be necessary for a monk to go outside in obedience to a command, this shall be done with the counsel and consent of the bishop. Such persons shall be sent out with a certificate, that there may be no suspicion of evil in them and that no evil report may arise from them.

To manage the property and business outside of the monastery, the abbot, with the permission and counsel of the bishop, shall appoint some person who is not a monk, but another of the faithful. Let the monks wholly shun secular gain or a desire for worldly affairs ; for avarice or a desire for this world ought to be avoided by all Christians, but especially by those who claim to have renounced the world and its lusts. Let no one presume in any way to incite strife or controversies, either within or without the monastery. But if any one shall have presumed to do so, he shall be corrected by the most severe discipline of the rule, and in such a manner that others shall fear to commit such actions. Let them entirely shun drunkenness and feasting, because it is known to all that these give rise to lust. . . .

Let no bishops, abbots, priests, deacons, or other members of the clergy presume to keep dogs for hunting, or hawks, falcons, and sparrow hawks, but each shall observe fully the canons or rule of his order. If any one shall presume to violate this order, let him know that he shall lose his office; and in addition he shall suffer such punishment for his offense that the others will be afraid to appropriate such things for themselves. . . .

*The clergy shall not hunt.*

And we command that no one in our whole kingdom shall dare to deny hospitality either to rich or poor, or to pilgrims; that is, no one shall deny shelter and fire and water to pilgrims traversing our country in God's name, or to any one traveling for the love of God or for the safety of his own soul. If, moreover, any one shall wish to serve them farther, let him expect the best reward from God, who himself said, "And whoso shall receive one such little child in my name receiveth me"; and elsewhere, " I was a stranger, and ye took me in."

*All shall provide for the stranger.*

Concerning messengers coming from the lord emperor: the counts and local judges shall provide most carefully, as they desire the grace of the lord emperor, for the *missi* who are sent out, so that they may go through their provinces without any delay. The emperor commands all, everywhere, to see to it that the *missi* are not hindered anywhere, but are sent forward with the utmost dispatch and provided with such things as they may require. . . .

*The counts to aid the missi.*

In our forests no one shall dare to steal our game. This has already been many times forbidden; we now again strictly forbid it for the future. If one would keep his fidelity pledged to us, let him take heed to his conduct. . . .

*No one to disturb the royal game.*

Finally, we desire that all our commands should be made known throughout our whole realm by means of the *missi*

Various purposes of the orders sent out by the *missi*.

now sent forth, whether these commands be directed to those connected with the Church — bishops, abbots, priests, deacons, canons, monks or nuns — with a view of securing the observance of our ban or decrees, or whether we would duly thank the citizens for their good will, or request them to furnish aid, or to correct some matter. . . .

## IV. CHARLEMAGNE'S ANXIETY TO IMPROVE EDUCATION

Charlemagne's attitude toward the ignorance of many of the churchmen of his time and his appreciation of the advantages of elementary education are most fully expressed in a famous letter written some time between 780 and 800.

29. Charlemagne's letter on the dangers of ignorance.

*Charles, by the grace of God, King of the Franks and Lombards and Patrician of the Romans, to Abbot Baugulf, and to all the congregation, also to the faithful committed to you, we have directed a loving greeting by our messengers in the name of omnipotent God:*

Be it known, therefore, to your Devotion pleasing to God, that we, together with our faithful, have considered it to be expedient that the bishoprics and monasteries intrusted by the favor of Christ to our government, in addition to the rule of monastic life and the intercourse of holy religion, ought to be zealous also in the culture of letters, teaching those who by the gift of God are able to learn, according to the capacity of each individual; so that just as the observance of the monastic rule imparts order and grace to moral conduct, so also zeal in teaching and learning may do the same for the use of words, so that those who desire to please God by living rightly should not neglect to please him also by speaking correctly. For it is written, "Either from thy words thou shalt be justified, or from thy words thou shalt be condemned."

Although it is better to *do* the right than *know* it, nevertheless knowledge should precede action. Therefore, each one ought to study what he would accomplish, so that the mind may the better know what ought to be done, if the tongue utters the praises of omnipotent God without the hindrances of errors. For if errors should be shunned by all men, so much the more ought they to be avoided, as far as possible, by those who are chosen for the very purpose that they may be the servants of truth.

Yet, in recent years, when letters have been written to us from various monasteries to inform us that the brethren who dwelt there were offering up in our behalf holy and pious prayers, we noted in most of these letters correct thoughts but uncouth expressions; for what pious devotion dictated faithfully to the mind, the tongue, uneducated on account of the neglect of study, was not able to express without error. We, therefore, began to fear lest perchance, as the skill in writing was wanting, so also the wisdom for understanding the Holy Scriptures might be much less than it rightly ought to be. And we all know well that, although errors of speech are dangerous, far more dangerous are errors of the understanding.

Therefore, we exhort you not only not to neglect the study of letters, but also with most humble mind, pleasing to God, to pursue it earnestly in order that you may be able more easily and more correctly to penetrate the mysteries of the divine Scriptures. Since, moreover, figures of speech, tropes, and the like are found in the sacred pages, it cannot be doubted that in reading these one will understand the spiritual sense more quickly if previously he shall have been fully instructed in the mastery of letters. Such men truly are to be chosen for this work as have both the will and the ability to learn and a desire to instruct others. And may this be done with a zeal as great as the earnestness with which we command it.

## BIBLIOGRAPHY

*A. References.*

**General Summary of the Work of Charlemagne:** ADAMS, *Civilization*, pp. 154–169.

**The Conquests:** BÉMONT and MONOD, pp. 179; EMERTON, *Introduction*, Chapter XIII, pp. 180–213 and 232–235; HENDERSON, *Germany in the Middle Ages*, pp. 56–70; *Short History of Germany*, pp. 26–30; OMAN, Chapters XX–XXI, pp. 335–360.

**Capitulary for the Saxons:** *Translations and Reprints*, Vol. VI, No. 5, pp. 2–5.

**The Revival of the Empire:** BÉMONT and MONOD, p. 203; BRYCE, *Holy Roman Empire*, Chapters IV–V, pp. 34–75; EMERTON, pp. 214–227; HENDERSON, *Germany in the Middle Ages*, pp. 71–79; *Short History of Germany*, pp. 30–35; MUNRO, *History of the Middle Ages*, pp. 9–18; OMAN, pp. 369–379.

**Division of the Empire in 806:** *Translations and Reprints*, Vol. VI, No. 5, pp. 27–33.

**The Revival of Culture:** BÉMONT and MONOD, pp. 203–206; EMERTON, pp. 227–232; HENDERSON, *Germany in the Middle Ages*, pp. 79–81; *Short History of Germany*, pp. 35–38; OMAN, pp. 379–382.

**Letter of Alcuin on Education:** COLBY, *Sources of English History*, pp. 16–19.

*B. Additional reading in English.*

DAVIS, *Charlemagne*, 1900.

MOMBERT, *A History of Charles the Great*. A scholarly and interesting work, with a good discussion of the sources.

HODGKIN, *Italy and her Invaders*, Vol. VII, Book VIII, Chapters XIII–XIV, and Vol. VIII. A short account by the same author may be found in his *Charles the Great*.

The intellectual conditions are discussed in MULLINGER, *Schools of Charles the Great*, and WEST, *Alcuin*.

EINHARD, *Life of Charlemagne*, translated by Turner. An inexpensive English version of this extraordinary little work.

KITCHIN, *History of France*, Book II, Part II, Chapter III.

GREGOROVIUS, *Rome in the Middle Ages*, Vol. II, Book IV, Chapters IV–VII, and Vol. III, Book V, Chapter I.

MORLEY, *Mediæval Tales*, Parts I and II, furnishes examples of the romances which in later years wove themselves about the name of the great emperor.

# CHAPTER VIII

## THE DISRUPTION OF CHARLEMAGNE'S EMPIRE

### I. STRUGGLES BETWEEN THE SONS OF LOUIS THE PIOUS

(840) Louis [the German], the emperor's son, took possession of the part of the Empire lying beyond the Rhine as if it were his by right. He won the support of many East Franks by his prudent conduct, and marched through Alemannia to Frankfort. The emperor, learning this, was forced to return from Aquitaine, leaving his business there unfinished. He sent his brother Druogo, the archchaplain, Count Albert, and many others before him to guard the west bank of the Rhine; then he himself followed and celebrated Easter at Aix-la-Chapelle. About this time, night after night, a strange glow appeared in the air, in fashion like a beam, in the southeast, and another arising from the northwest. The two joined together and formed a cone and presented an appearance like clotted blood at the zenith.

30. The death of Louis the Pious and the strife between his sons. (From the *Annals of Fulda*.)

After Easter the emperor gathered an army and pursued his son through Thuringia up to the frontiers of the barbarians. He drove him out of the imperial territory and forced him to make a difficult march homeward to Bavaria through the land of the Slavs. The emperor himself set all things in order in that region, and then returned to the royal town of Salz, and celebrated there the Rogation Days and the festival of our Lord's Ascension. On the very day before the Ascension of our Lord, i.e. on the twelfth of May, there was an eclipse of the sun at about the seventh and eighth hour — so completely was the sun obscured that the stars were seen and the color of things on earth was changed.

In these days the emperor fell ill and began to waste away. He was taken on a ship down the Main to Frankfort, and from there after a few days to an island in the Rhine near Ingilenheim. His illness steadily increased upon him, and on the twentieth of June he ended his life. His body was brought to the city of Metz and buried with all due honor in the basilica of St. Arnulf the Confessor.

Lothaire accepted by the Franks as their ruler. Lothaire, who came from Italy too late [to see his father], was accepted by the Franks to rule over them in his father's stead. For men say the dying emperor had designated him as the one who should hold after him the helm of the state, and had sent him the royal insignia — the scepter of the Empire and the crown.

Lothaire's brothers did not agree, however, to this arrangement, and they made ready to rebel against him. He went with his army to the precincts of Mayence, and there his brother Louis marched to meet him with a strong following of East Franks. They, however, agreed together to postpone decisive action until another time; and Lothaire marched northward to meet Charles [the Bald]. Meantime Louis bound to his cause by an oath of fidelity the East Franks, the Alemannians, the Saxons, and the Thuringians.

(841) Meanwhile Lothaire placed garrisons along the Rhine and prepared to secure the east bank against an invasion from the west. He heard, through a messenger, of Louis' hostile measures, and, giving up pursuing Charles, he turned about, and at the beginning of the month of April crossed the Rhine secretly at Worms with all his army. Louis was betrayed by some of his followers and, almost surrounded by the army of Lothaire, he was forced to retreat to Bavaria.

The emperor placed guards whom he believed he could trust in those regions, and then turned his energy and his forces once more against Charles, who had already planned to establish a camp beyond the Maas. Louis was summoned to aid Charles and came by way of Alemannia. There the counts to whom Lothaire had intrusted the defense of that region met Louis with an army. They gave battle on the thirteenth of May. Count Adalbert, who had stirred up the strife, was killed; and with him a countless number of men were laid low.

Louis, victor in this encounter, crossed the Rhine and hastened toward Gaul to aid his brother Charles. The three brothers met in Auxerre, near Fontenay. They could not agree to divide the Empire because Lothaire, who wished to be sole monarch, was opposed to it. So they agreed that the case should be decided by the power of the sword and so proved by the judgment of God. On the twenty-fifth of June a great battle was fought between them, and the blood shed on both sides was so great that the present age remembers no such carnage among the Frankish people before. On the same day Lothaire began a retreat to his city of Aix-la-Chapelle. Louis and Charles seized his camp and collected and buried the bodies of their slain. They then parted; Charles remained in the west and Louis went in the month of August to the royal town Salz.      *Battle of Fontenay (841).*

Lothaire again collected his forces. He went to Mayence and ordered the Saxons, with his little son Lothaire, to meet him at Speyer. He himself crossed the Rhine, intending to pursue his brother Louis to the confines of the outlying nations. He returned to Worms, unsuccessful. He celebrated there the marriage of his daughter, and then marched toward Gaul to subdue Charles. He spent the whole winter in fruitless effort and strife and then returned to Aix. On December 25 a comet appeared in Aquarius.

(843) Lothaire and Louis dwelt each in the confines of his own kingdom and kept the peace. Charles was marching about Aquitaine. . . . In the terrible and increasing calamities of the time and the general devastation, many men in various parts of Gaul were forced to eat a kind of bread made of earth and a little flour. It was an abominable crime that men should be reduced to eat earth, when the horses of those who were devastating the land were plentifully supplied with fodder.      *31. The Northmen at Nantes. (From the Annals of St. Bertin.)*

Pirates of the Northmen's race came to the city of Nantes. They killed the bishop and many of the clergy and laity,

A.6

both men and women, and plundered the city. Then they marched away to lay waste the land of lower Aquitaine. Finally they reached a certain island [Rhé, near Rochelle], and took thither from the mainland materials to build them houses; and they settled there for the winter as if it were a fixed habitation.

*The treaty of Verdun.*

Charles betook himself to a rendezvous with his brothers, and joined them at Verdun; and there they divided the land among them. Louis had as his portion everything beyond the Rhine, and on this side of the Rhine the cities and districts of Speyer, Worms, and Mayence. Lothaire received the territory between the Rhine and the Scheldt to their emptying into the sea, besides Cambria, Hennegau, Lomatschgau, and the provinces on the left bank of the Maas, and further on to the place where the Saône joins the Rhone, and the counties along the Rhone on both banks to the sea. The other lands to the confines of Spain they ceded to Charles. When each had given his oath to the others they parted.

## II. A Melancholy Glimpse of the Conditions in the Ninth Century

The *Annals of Xanten* give us a terrible impression of the disorder and gloom which prevailed in the Frankish kingdoms, owing to the civil wars and the devastations of the Northmen. The portion here given was probably written as the events occurred.

*32. An extract from the Annals of Xanten.*

(844) Pope Gregory departed this world and Pope Sergius followed in his place. Count Bernhard was killed by Charles. Pippin, king of Aquitaine, together with his son and the son of Bernhard, routed the army of Charles, and there fell the abbot Hugo. At the same time King Louis advanced with his army against the Wends, one of whose kings, Gestimus by name, was killed; the rest came to Louis and pledged him their fidelity, which, however, they

broke as soon as he was gone.   Thereafter Lothaire, Louis, and Charles came together for counsel in Diedenhofen, and after a conference they went their several ways in peace.

(845) Twice in the canton of Worms there was an earthquake ; the first in the night following Palm Sunday, the second in the holy night of Christ's Resurrection.   In the same year the heathen broke in upon the Christians at many points, but more than twelve thousand of them were killed by the Frisians.   Another party of invaders devastated Gaul ; of these more than six hundred men perished. Yet owing to his indolence Charles agreed to give them many thousand pounds of gold and silver if they would leave Gaul, and this they did.   Nevertheless the cloisters of most of the saints were destroyed and many of the Christians were led away captive.

After this had taken place King Louis once more led a force against the Wends.   When the heathen had learned this they sent ambassadors, as well as gifts and hostages, to Saxony, and asked for peace.   Louis then granted peace and returned home from Saxony.   Thereafter the robbers were afflicted by a terrible pestilence, during which the chief sinner among them, by the name of Reginheri, who had plundered the Christians and the holy places, was struck down by the hand of God.   They then took counsel and threw lots to determine from which of their gods they should seek safety ; but the lots did not fall out happily, and on the advice of one of their Christian prisoners that they should cast their lot before the God of the Christians, they did so, and the lot fell happily.   Then their king, by the name of Rorik, together with all the heathen people, refrained from meat and drink for fourteen days, when the plague ceased, and they sent back all their Christian prisoners to their country.

(846) According to their custom the Northmen plundered Eastern and Western Frisia and burned the town of Dordrecht, with two other villages, before the eyes of Lothaire, who was then in the castle of Nimwegen, but could not

punish the crime. The Northmen, with their boats filled with immense booty, including both men and goods, returned to their own country.

In the same year Louis sent an expedition from Saxony against the Wends across the Elbe. He personally, however, went with his army against the Bohemians, whom we call Beu-winitha, but with great risk. . . . Charles advanced against the Britons, but accomplished nothing.

At this same time, as no one can mention or hear without great sadness, the mother of all churches, the basilica of the apostle Peter, was taken and plundered by the Moors, or Saracens, who had already occupied the region of Beneventum. The Saracens, moreover, slaughtered all the Christians whom they found outside the walls of Rome, either within or without this church. They also carried men and women away prisoners. They tore down, among many others, the altar of the blessed Peter, and their crimes from day to day bring sorrow to Christians. Pope Sergius departed life this year.

(847) After the death of Sergius no mention of the apostolic see has come in any way to our ears. Rabanus [Maurus], master and abbot of Fulda, was solemnly chosen archbishop as the successor of Bishop Otger, who had died. Moreover the Northmen here and there plundered the Christians and engaged in a battle with the counts Sigir and Liuthar. They continued up the Rhine as far as Dordrecht, and nine miles farther to Meginhard, when they turned back, having taken their booty.

(848) On the fourth of February, towards evening, it lightened and there was thunder heard. The heathen, as was their custom, inflicted injury on the Christians. In the same year King Louis held an assembly of the people near Mayence. At this synod a heresy was brought forward by a few monks in regard to predestination. These were convicted and beaten, to their shame, before all the people. They were sent back to Gaul whence they had come, and, thanks be to God, the condition of the church remained uninjured.

(849) While King Louis was ill his army of Bavaria took its way against the Bohemians. Many of these were killed and the remainder withdrew, much humiliated, into their own country. The heathen from the North wrought havoc in Christendom as usual and grew greater in strength; but it is revolting to say more of this matter.

(850) On January 1st of that season, in the octave of the Lord, towards evening, a great deal of thunder was heard and a mighty flash of lightning seen; and an overflow of water afflicted the human race during this winter. In the following summer an all too great heat of the sun burned the earth. Leo, pope of the apostolic see, an extraordinary man, built a fortification round the church of St. Peter the apostle. The Moors, however, devastated here and there the coast towns in Italy. The Norman Rorik, brother of the above-mentioned younger Heriold, who earlier had fled dishonored from Lothaire, again took Dordrecht and did much evil treacherously to the Christians. In the same year so great a peace existed between the two brothers — Emperor Lothaire and King Louis — that they spent many days together in Osning [Westphalia] and there hunted, so that many were astonished thereat; and they went each his way in peace.

(851) The bodies of certain saints were sent from Rome to Saxony, — that of Alexander, one of seven brethren, and those of Romanus and Emerentiana. In the same year the very noble empress, Irmingard by name, wife of the emperor Lothaire, departed this world. The Normans inflicted much harm in Frisia and about the Rhine. A mighty army of them collected by the river Elbe against the Saxons, and some of the Saxon towns were besieged, others burned, and most terribly did they oppress the Christians. A meeting of our kings took place on the Maas.

(852) The steel of the heathen glistened; excessive heat; a famine followed. There was not fodder enough for the animals. The pasturage for the swine was more than sufficient.

(853) A great famine in Saxony so that many were forced to live on horse meat.

(854) The Normans, in addition to the very many evils which they were everywhere inflicting upon the Christians, burned the church of St. Martin, bishop of Tours, where his body rests.

(855) In the spring Louis, the eastern king, sent his son of the same name to Aquitaine to obtain possession of the heritage of his uncle Pippin.

(856) The Normans again chose a king of the same name as the preceding one, and related to him, and the Danes made a fresh incursion by sea, with renewed forces, against the Christians.

(857) A great sickness, accompanied by swelling of the bladder, prevailed among the people. This produced a terrible foulness, so that the limbs were separated from the body even before death came.

(858) Louis, the eastern king, held an assembly of the people of his territory in Worms.

(859) On the first of January, as the early mass was being said, a single earthquake occurred in Worms and a triple one in Mayence before daybreak.

(860) On the fifth of February thunder was heard. The king returned from Gaul after the whole empire had gone to destruction, and was in no way bettered.

(861) The holy bishop Luitbert piously furnished the cloister which is called the Freckenhorst with many relics of the saints, namely, of the martyrs Boniface and Maximus, and of the confessors Eonius and Antonius, and added a portion of the manger of the Lord and of his grave, and likewise of the dust of the Lord's feet as he ascended to heaven. In this year the winter was long and the above-mentioned

kings again had a secret consultation on the above-mentioned island near Coblenz, and they laid waste everything round about.

## BIBLIOGRAPHY

**General Summary of Events and Conditions :** ADAMS, *Civilization*, pp. 170–179; HENDERSON, *Short History of Germany*, Vol. I, pp. 38–48. *A. References.*

**Louis the Pious :** BÉMONT and MONOD, pp. 211–215; EMERTON, *Mediæval Europe*, pp. 3–24 ; HENDERSON, *Germany in the Middle Ages*, Chapter VI, pp. 82–99 ; OMAN, Chapter XXIII, pp. 383–404.

**The Division of the Empire in 817 :** HENDERSON, *Historical Documents*, pp. 201–206.

**The Process of Disruption :** BÉMONT and MONOD, pp. 215–240; EMERTON, pp. 24–40 ; HENDERSON, *Germany in the Middle Ages*, Chapter VII, pp. 100–116 ; OMAN, Chapters XXIV–XXV, pp. 405–445.

**The Strasburg Oath :** EMERTON, pp. 26–28 ; MUNRO, p. 20.

**The Treaty of Aix :** HENDERSON, *Historical Documents*, pp. 206, 207.

**Arnulf of Carinthia :** EMERTON, pp. 90–94 ; OMAN, Chapter XXVII, pp. 468–472.

**The Norman Invasions :** MUNRO, Chapter IV, pp. 33–39 ; GIBBON, Vol. VI, part of Chapter LVI, pp. 173–193.

------

KEARY, *The Vikings in Western Christendom*. The most complete account of the Norman raids during the period of the later Carolingians. *B. Additional reading in English.*

JOHNSON, *The Normans*. A good general narrative covering the history of all Norman settlements in southern Europe.

There are no books in English dealing especially with the fortunes of the Empire during these years. The reader must turn to chapters in the large works: GREGOROVIUS, *Rome in the Middle Ages*, Vol. III, Book V, Chapters II–VI ; KITCHIN, *History of France*, Vol. I, Book II, Part II, Chapters IV–V; MILMAN, *Latin Christianity*, Vols. II and III, Book V, Chapters II–VII and IX.

POOLE, *Illustrations of Mediæval Thought*, Chapters I and II, furnish an admirable account of certain especially enlightened thinkers and reformers of the ninth century.

# CHAPTER IX

## FEUDALISM

### I. The Granting of Fiefs

**33. Record of a grant made by Abbot Faritius to Robert, a knight.**

Abbot Faritius also granted to Robert, son of William Mauduit, the land of four hides in Weston which his father had held from the former's predecessor, to be held as a fief. And he should do this service for it, to wit: that whenever the church of Abingdon should perform its knight's service he should do the service of half a knight for the same church; that is to say, in castle ward, in military service beyond and on this side the sea, in giving money in proportion to the knights on the capture of the king, and in the rest of the services which the other knights of the church perform. He also did homage to the same abbot. This land previously did the service of three weeks yearly only.

**34. The count of Champagne grants a fief to the bishop of Beauvais (1167).**

In the name of the holy and undivided Trinity, Amen. I, Louis, by the grace of God king of the French, make known to all present as well as to come, that at Mante, in our presence, Count Henry of Champagne conceded the fief of Savigny to Bartholomew, bishop of Beauvais, and his successors. And for that fief the said bishop has made promise and engagement for one knight, and justice and service to Count Henry; and he has also agreed that the bishops who shall come after him will do likewise. In order that this may be understood and known to posterity, we have caused the present charter to be corroborated by our seal.

Done at Mante, in the year of the Incarnate Word 1167; present in our palace those whose names and seals are appended: seal of Count Thiebault, our steward; seal of Guy, the butler; seal of Matthew, the chamberlain; seal of Ralph, the constable. Given by the hand of Hugh, the chancellor.

I, Pons of Mont-Saint-Jean, make known to all, both present and future, that since I have long been the man of my
beloved Lady Blanche, countess of Champagne, for twenty
pounds assigned to the fair at Bar, and since later both the
countess and my dear lord have added other twenty pounds
assigned to the same fair and gave me three hundred pounds
in cash,— I swore by the saints that I would in good faith
aid them and their heirs with my people and fortifications.
If necessary I will fight especially against Erard of Brienne
and Philippa his wife, and against Adelaide, queen of Cyprus,
and her heirs, and against all who would aid them ; except
that should the said countess or count or their people be
against Milo of Noyers, my sister's husband, in his castle of
Noyers or elsewhere in his lands, neither I nor my people
shall be held to go thither. If, however, the said Milo or
his people set upon the countess or the count or their
people, we shall be held to defend them and their lands with
all our might.

It is also to be known that my heir who shall hold Charnia-
cum shall also have the fief above mentioned of forty pounds.

That all this shall be held valid, I corroborate what has
here been written with the impression of my seal. Done in
the year of grace 1219, in the month of June.

## II. Ceremony of doing Homage and swearing Fealty

Through the whole remaining part of the day those who
had been previously enfeoffed by the most pious Count
Charles did homage to the [new] count, taking up now again
their fiefs and offices and whatever they had before rightfully and legitimately obtained. On Thursday, the seventh
of April, homages were again made to the count, being completed in the following order of faith and security.

First they did their homage thus. The count asked the
vassal if he were willing to become completely his man, and
the other replied, "I am willing"; and with hands clasped,
placed between the hands of the count, they were bound

together by a kiss.   Secondly, he who had done homage gave his fealty to the representative of the count in these words, "I promise on my faith that I will in future be faithful to Count William, and will observe my homage to him completely against all persons, in good faith and without deceit." And, thirdly, he took his oath to this upon the relics of the saints.   Afterward the count, with a little rod which he held in his hand, gave investitures to all who by this agreement had given their security and accompanying oath.

**37. Rules for homage and fealty established by St. Louis.** If any one should hold from a lord in fee, he ought to seek his lord within forty days, and if he does not do it within forty days, the lord may and ought to seize his fief for default of homage, and the things which should be found there he should seize without return, and yet the vassal would be obliged to pay to his lord the redemption.

When any one wishes to enter into the fealty of a lord he ought to seek him, as we have said above, and should say as follows: "Sir, I request you, as my lord, to put me in your fealty and in your homage for such and such a thing situated in your fief, which I have obtained."   And he ought to say from what man, and this one ought to be present and in the fealty of the lord ; and he ought to explain whether it is by purchase, or by escheat, or by inheritance; and with his hands joined, to speak as follows: "Sir, I become your man and promise to you fealty for the future as my lord towards all men who may live or die, rendering to you such service as the fief requires, paying to you your relief, as you are the lord."   And he ought to say whether for guardianship, or as an escheat, or as an inheritance, or as a purchase.

The lord should immediately reply to him, "And I receive you and take you as my man, and give you this kiss as a sign of faith, saving my right and that of others," according to the usage of the various districts.

And the lord may take the revenues and the products of the year, if the relief is not paid to him, and also money rents.   But no one makes money payments for a guardianship, or for a dowry, or for a partition, or for a report of the extent of the fief, according to the usages of various districts; except in the one case where the one who holds in guardianship ought to give security to the parties that when the child shall come of age, the one who has the guardianship will do it at his own expense and at his cost and will guarantee the socage tenants for any payments. This in the case of a fief, but in villanage there is no guardianship.

## III. Mutual Duties of Vassal and Lord

*To William, most glorious duke of the Aquitanians, Bishop Fulbert, the favor of his prayers:*

Asked to write something concerning the form of fealty, I have noted briefly for you, on the authority of the books, the things which follow. He who swears fealty to his lord ought always to have these six things in memory: what is harmless, safe, honorable, useful, easy, practicable. *Harmless*, that is to say, that he should not injure his lord in his body; *safe*, that he should not injure him by betraying his secrets or the defenses upon which he relies for safety; *honorable*, that he should not injure him in his justice or in other matters that pertain to his honor; *useful*, that he should not injure him in his possessions; *easy* and *practicable*, that that good which his lord is able to do easily he make not difficult, nor that which is practicable he make not impossible to him.

That the faithful vassal should avoid these injuries is certainly proper, but not for this alone does he deserve his holding; for it is not sufficient to abstain from evil, unless what is good is done also. It remains, therefore, that in the same six things mentioned above he should faithfully counsel and aid his lord, if he wishes to be looked upon as worthy of his benefice and to be safe concerning the fealty which he has sworn.

The lord also ought to act toward his faithful vassal reciprocally in all these things. And if he does not do this, he will be justly considered guilty of bad faith, just as the former,

38. Bishop Fulbert of Chartres explains in a celebrated letter the duties of vassal and lord (1020).

Positive duties of lord and vassal.

if he should be detected in avoiding or consenting to the avoidance of his duties, would be perfidious and perjured.

I would have written to you at greater length, if I had not been occupied with many other things, including the rebuilding of our city and church, which was lately entirely consumed in a terrible fire ; from which loss, though we could not for a while be diverted, yet by the hope of God's comfort and of yours we breathe again.

## IV. FEUDAL MILITARY SERVICE

**39. List of men summoned under Philip III of France to perform military service (1272).** In the year 1272 the bishop of Paris came to Tours at the citation of the lord king and presented himself in the king's house on the second Sunday after Easter, before Ferrario of Verneuil, knight, marshal of France, saying that he had come at the citation of the lord king prepared to fulfill his duty ; who replied to him that he should come again, or send, at the first hour of the next day, because in the meanwhile he could not speak or respond to him, since Gregory of St. Martin of Tours was absent, on account of his weakness, and because, moreover, he was expecting new instructions from the king.

On the next day, and on Tuesday, the aforesaid bishop presented himself before the said marshal, saying that he had come ready for the service of the king with three knights, whose names were John of Marcey, John of Julliaco, and Adam of Blois. He said that if he was held to send more, he was ready to do what he ought; and if he had furnished more than he owed, that this should not bind either him or the church of Paris for the future.

The bishop of Troyes appeared for his see, saying that he owed two knights, whose names were Ralph and Droce of Préaux.

The bishop of Noyon was represented by Theobald of Boesseria, a knight, who acknowledged that the said bishop owed five knights and sent three knights beyond what he owed. The names of the knights are as follows: Ansold of

Rancorolis, Nevelon of Rancorolis, his brother, etc. . . .
They went forth to the service of the king.

The bishop of Bayeux was represented by Thomas of
Semilly, his procurator, who acknowledged that the said
bishop owed ten knights for the service of the king in the
army. These he sent, namely, John of Bellengreville, John
of Caenchy, Richard of Rovancestre, William of Surrain,
and others. . . .

John of Rouvray, a knight, lord of Yneto, appeared for
himself, confessing that he owed, by reason of his holding
of Rouvray, one knight, whom he brought with him, namely,
John of Caim.

Fulco of Bauquancayo, a knight, appeared for the abbot
of St. Ebrulf, and went forth for the said abbot, as he should,
and was held to do.

The archdeacon of Cheuteville did not appear, but sent
one knight, namely, Peter of Maucomble.

Reginaldus Trihan, a knight, appeared and went forth for
himself.

. . . John of Rouvray, a knight, appeared for himself, saying that he owed one knight for his fief of Corbon and its ap-
purtenances. He offered for himself John of Meler, a knight.
What service he owed on his wife's part he did not know.

Robert Bertran, a squire, appeared and said that he owed
the lord king two knights and a half.

. . . The abbot St. Columba at Sens appeared in person,
and said he had never known his monastery to do military
service by furnishing knights. The service was rendered in
money, namely, eight score pounds for the army and the sum
of seventeen Parisian pounds.

Hugh de Conflent, knight, marshal of Champagne, appeared for the king of Navarre, and brought with him sixty
knights, to do the service owed to the king.

Stephanus Mener and Adam Allutarius appeared for the
city of Villeneuve-le-Roi, near Sens, and said they owed no
military service to the king, unless they chose to render
it out of sheer courtesy. And they would do the bidding of
the lord king only on condition that they go only as far from

Villeneuve as they can return thither in one day, during the sunlight or the daylight.

The representative chosen by the abbot of Ferrières appeared in person, and said that he owed no military service with horses and arms, but only the sum of seventeen pounds Parisian, and his followers six score pounds, namely, sixty pounds for Ferrières and sixty for Beausse. . . .

## V. Failure of Feudalism to secure Order. The Truce of God

The general failure of feudalism to secure peace and order, indeed its tendency directly to promote disorder, is illustrated by many of the passages from the chronicles found in the following chapters (see, especially, Chapter X). The provisions of the Truce of God are eloquent of existing conditions.

**40. The Truce of God issued by a synod held at Cologne in 1083.[1]**

Inasmuch as in our own times the Church, through its members, has been extraordinarily afflicted by tribulations and difficulties, so that tranquillity and peace were wholly despaired of, we have endeavored with God's help to come to its aid, in the midst of its sufferings and perils. And by the advice of our faithful subjects we have at length provided this remedy, so that we might to some extent reëstablish, on certain days at least, the peace which, because of our sins, we could not make enduring. Accordingly we have enacted and set forth the following:

Having called together those under us to a legally summoned council, which was held at Cologne, the chief city of our province, in the church of St. Peter, in the 1083d year of our Lord's Incarnation, in the sixth indiction, on the twelfth day before the Kalends of May, after arranging other business, we have caused to be read in public what we

---

[1] This document has been preserved only in this form, in which it was communicated by the archbishop of Cologne to the bishop of Münster.

proposed to do in this matter. After this had been fully discussed by all, both clergy and people with God's aid reached an agreement, and we set forth in what manner and during what parts of the year the peace should be observed, namely:

That from the first day of the Advent of our Lord through Epiphany, and from the beginning of Septuagesima to the eighth day after Pentecost and through that whole day, and throughout the year on every Sunday, Friday, and Saturday, and on the fast days of the four seasons, and on the eve and the day of all the apostles, and on all days canonically set apart — or which shall in future be set apart — for fasts or feasts, this decree of peace shall be observed; so that both those who travel and those who remain at home may enjoy security and the most entire peace, so that no one may commit murder, arson, robbery, or assault, no one may injure another with a sword, club, or any kind of weapon. Let no one, however irritated by wrong, presume to carry arms, shield, sword, or lance, or any kind of armor, from the Advent of our Lord to the eighth day after Epiphany, and from Septuagesima to the eighth day after Pentecost. On the remaining days, indeed, namely, on Sundays, Fridays, apostles' days, and the vigils of the apostles, and on every day set aside, or to be set aside, for fasts or feasts, arms may be carried, but on this condition, that no injury shall be done in any way to any one.

If it shall be necessary for any one, during the period of the peace, — i.e. from the Advent of our Lord to the eighth day after Epiphany, and from Septuagesima to the eighth day after Pentecost, — to go from one bishopric into another in which the peace is not observed, he may bear arms, but on the condition that he shall not injure any one, except in self-defense if he is attacked; and when he returns into our diocese he shall immediately lay aside his arms. If it shall happen that any castle is besieged during the days which are included within the peace, the besiegers shall cease from attack unless they are set upon by the besieged and compelled to beat the latter back.

And in order that this statute of peace should not be violated by any one rashly or with impunity, a penalty was fixed by the common consent of all, namely : If a free man or noble violates it, i.e. commits homicide, or wounds any one, or is at fault in any manner whatever, he shall be expelled from his lands, without any indulgence on account of the payment of money or the intercession of friends ; and his heirs shall take all his property.   If he holds a fief, the lord to whom it belongs shall receive it again.   Moreover, if it appear that his heirs after his expulsion have furnished him any support or aid, and if they are convicted of it, the estate shall be taken from them and revert to the king.   But if they wish to clear themselves of the charge against them, they shall take oath, with twelve who are equally free or equally noble.

If a slave kills a man, he shall be beheaded ; if he wounds a man, he shall lose a hand ; if he does an injury in any other way with his fist or a club, or by striking with a stone, he shall be shorn and flogged.   If, however, he is accused and wishes to prove his innocence, he shall clear himself by the ordeal of cold water, but he must himself be put into the water and no one else in his place.   If, however, fearing the sentence decreed against him, he flees, he shall be under a perpetual excommunication ; and if he is known to be in any place, letters shall be sent thither, in which it shall be announced to all that he is excommunicate, and that it is unlawful for any one to associate with him.   In the case of boys who have not yet completed their twelfth year, the hand ought not to be cut off ; but only in the case of those who are twelve years or more of age.   Nevertheless, if boys fight, they shall be whipped and prevented from fighting.

It is not an infringement of the peace if any one orders his delinquent slave, pupil, or any one in any way under his charge, to be chastised with rods or sticks.   It is also an exception to this constitution of peace if the lord king publicly orders an expedition to attack the enemies of the kingdom, or is pleased to hold a council to judge the enemies of justice.   The peace is not violated if, during the times

specified, a duke, or other counts, magistrates, or their substitutes, hold courts and inflict punishment legally on thieves,
robbers, and other criminals.

The statute of this noble peace is especially enacted for
the safety of those engaged in feuds; but after the end of
the peace they are not to dare to rob and plunder in the
villages and houses, since the laws and penalties enacted
before this peace are still legally valid to restrain them from
crime; moreover robbers and highwaymen are excluded
from this divine peace, and indeed from any peace.

If any one attempt to oppose this pious institution and
is unwilling to promise peace to God with the others, or to
observe it, no priest in our diocese shall say a mass for him,
or take any care for his salvation; if he is sick, no Christian
shall dare to visit him; on his deathbed he shall not receive
the eucharist, unless he repent. The supreme authority of
the peace pledged to God and generally extolled by all will
be so great that it will be observed not only in our times, but
forever among our posterity, because if any one shall presume
to infringe or violate it, either now or ages hence, until the
end of the world, he is irrevocably excommunicated by us.

The responsibility for carrying out the above-mentioned
penalties against the violators of the peace rests no more
with the counts, local judges, or officials than with the whole
people in general. They are to be especially careful not to
show friendship or hatred, nor to do anything contrary to
justice in punishing, nor to conceal crimes, which may be
hidden, but to bring them to light. No one is to receive
money for the release of those taken in fault, or to attempt
to aid the guilty by any favor of any kind, because whoever
does this incurs the intolerable damnation of his soul; and
all the faithful ought to remember that this peace has not
been promised to men, but to God, and therefore must be
observed so much the more rigidly and firmly. Wherefore we
exhort all in Christ to guard inviolably this necessary contract of peace, and if any one hereafter presumes to violate
it, let him be damned by the ban of irrevocable excommunication and by the anathema of eternal perdition. . . .

A.7

## BIBLIOGRAPHY

*A. References.*

**Origins of Feudalism :** ADAMS, *Civilization*, pp. 194–211 ; EMERTON, *Introduction*, Chapter XV, pp. 236–255.

**Feudal Institutions :** EMERTON, *Mediæval Europe*, Chapter XIV, pp. 477–508 ; ADAMS, *Civilization*, pp. 211–226 ; *French Nation*, pp. 63–72 ; BÉMONT and MONOD, pp. 246–257 ; MASSON, *Mediæval France*, pp. 3–13 ; MUNRO, Chapter V, pp. 40–50.

**Life of the Feudal Nobles :** MUNRO, Chapter XIII, pp. 135–147 ; BÉMONT and MONOD, pp. 257–267.

---

*B. Additional reading in English.*

There is no complete and satisfactory treatment in English of the origin and development of feudalism on the continent. Older accounts, like those of Hallam and Guizot, are based, in some instances, upon theories since proved to be erroneous, and are therefore to be avoided. A description of feudal institutions in France, brief but reliable and scientific as far as it goes, may be found in SEIGNOBOS, *The Feudal Régime*, translated by DOW. For a thorough and authoritative analysis of English feudalism, see POLLOCK and MAITLAND, *History of English Law before the Time of Edward I,* 2 vols., especially Book II, " Doctrine of English Law," Chapters I and II.

Suggestive ideas of life in a feudal society may be gathered from the great romances of the eleventh and twelfth centuries, which, though in many cases ascribed by their authors to the time of Charlemagne, in reality depict far more nearly the manners of the age in which they were composed and recited. Two excellent illustrations are Steele's translations of the adventures of Renaud of Montauban and Huon of Bordeaux. See *History of Western Europe,* pp. 254 *sqq.*

# CHAPTER X

## THE DEVELOPMENT OF FRANCE

### I. The Election of Hugh Capet (987)

Louis V, the last of the direct descendants from Charlemagne, died in 987.[1] Many of the great feudal lords assembled to attend his funeral; before they dispersed they held a meeting, at which Duke Hugh (Capet) presided, to consider the general situation. The archbishop of Rheims, Adalbero, urgently recommended that the all-important matter of choosing a king should be postponed until all the great barons could be brought together. He moved that all those present should pledge themselves by an oath to the "great duke" (Hugh) that they would take no steps in the matter until the proposed meeting should be held. This plan was adopted.

Charles of Lorraine, the uncle of the late king, was, however, unwilling to wait for the decision of the barons, and attempted to induce Adalbero to secure the throne for him. The archbishop put him off on the ground that his companions and supporters were evil men, and that in any case nothing could be done without the consent of the great lords.

Meanwhile the nobles of Gaul who had taken the oath came together at the appointed time at Senlis; when they had all taken their places in the assembly, the duke, having made a sign to the archbishop of Rheims, the latter expressed himself as follows: "King Louis, of divine memory, left no

[1] See *History of Western Europe*, pp. 120 *sqq.*

41. The
archbishop
of Rheims
urges the
choice of
Hugh in-
stead of
Charles of
Lorraine.
(From
*Richer.*[1])

children ; we must therefore take counsel as to the choice of a successor, in order that the country shall not come to ruin through neglect and the lack of a pilot. Our deliberations on this subject were recently postponed, by common consent, in order that each one might here voice the sentiments with which God might inspire him, and that from all these individual opinions a general and collective decision might be reached.

" Now that we are once more assembled together, let us endeavor, in all prudence and rectitude, not to sacrifice reason and truth to our personal likes or dislikes. We know that Charles has his partisans, who claim that the throne belongs to him by right of birth. Regarding the question from this point of view, we reply that the throne cannot be acquired by hereditary right. Nor should one be placed upon it who is not distinguished alike by nobility of body and wisdom of mind, and by his good faith and magnanimity. We see in the annals of history rulers of illustrious origin deposed on account of their unworthiness, and replaced by incumbents of equal, or even of inferior, birth.

"And what is there to recommend Charles of Lorraine? He is feeble and without honor, faith, or character; he has not blushed to become the servitor of a foreign king [the emperor], nor to take to wife a girl of only knightly rank. How could the great duke bear that a woman belonging to the lowest rank of his vassals should be queen and rule over him ? How could he give precedence to a woman, when his equals and even his superiors in birth bend the knee before him and place their hands beneath his feet? If you consider this matter carefully, you will see that Charles' fall has been brought about through his own fault rather than that of others.

" Make a choice, therefore, that shall insure the welfare of the state instead of being its ruin. If you wish ill to your

---

[1] Richer, a monk of Rheims, who was living at the time, gives the only good accounts we possess of the revolution which put the Capetians on the throne of France.

country, choose Charles; if you wish to see it prosperous, make Hugh, the glorious duke, king. Do not let yourselves be misled by your sympathy for Charles, nor blinded to the common good by hatred of the duke. For if you blame the good, how can you praise the bad? If 'you praise the bad, how despise the good? Remember the words of the Scripture: 'Woe unto them that call evil good, and good evil; that put darkness for light, and light for darkness.' Choose the duke, therefore; he is the most illustrious among us all by reason of his exploits, his nobility, and his military following. Not only the state, but every individual interest, will find in him a protector. His great-heartedness will render him a father to you all. Who has ever fled to him for aid and been disappointed? Who that has been left in the lurch by his friends has he ever failed to restore to his rights?"

This discourse was received with universal applause, and by unanimous consent the duke was raised to the throne. He was crowned at Noyon on the first of June, by the archbishop and the other bishops, as king of the Gauls, the Bretons, the Danes [= Normans?], the Aquitanians, the Goths, the Spaniards, and the Gascons. Surrounded by the nobles of the kingdom, he issued decrees and made laws according to royal custom, judging and disposing of all matters with success.

## II. How Louis the Fat (1108–1137) began, with Abbot Suger's Aid, to get the Upper Hand of his Vassals

The chief adviser of Louis was Suger, abbot of the great monastery of St. Denis, near Paris, who not only greatly aided the king in his task of strengthening the royal power, but wrote a life of him which is one of the most important of the French historical sources.

A king, when he takes the royal power, vows to put down with his strong right arm insolent tyrants whensoever he

*42. Suger's account of Louis the Fat and his vassals.*

The position
and duties
of a medi-
æval French
king.

sees them vex the state with endless wars, rejoice in rapine,
oppress the poor, destroy the churches, give themselves
over to lawlessness which, and it be not checked, would
flame out into ever greater madness; for the evil spirits
who instigate them are wont cruelly to strike down those
whom they fear to lose, but give free rein to those whom
they hope to hold, while they add fuel to the flames which
are to devour their victims to all eternity.

Such an utterly abandoned man was Thomas of Marle.
While King Louis was busied with many wars, he laid
waste the territories of Laon, Rheims, and Amiens, devouring like a raging wolf. He spared not the clergy — fearing
not the vengeance of the Church — nor the people for humanity's sake. And the devil aided him, for the success of the
foolish does ever lead them to perdition. Slaying all men,
spoiling all things, he seized two manors, exceeding rich,
from the abbey of the nuns of St. John of Laon. He fortified the two exceeding strong castles, Crécy and Nogent,
with a marvelous wall and very high towers, as if they had
been his own; and made them like to a den of dragons and
a cave of robbers, whence he did waste almost the whole
country with fire and pillage; and he had no pity. . . .

How the
king took
the castles
of Crécy and
Nogent.

But the king led an army against him right quickly . . .
and marched straight against the castle of Crécy. Well
fortified was it; yet he took it unprepared because his
soldiers smote with an exceeding strong hand; or rather,
because the hand of the Lord fought for him. He stormed
the strongest tower as if it were the hut of a peasant, and
put to confusion the wicked men and piously destroyed the
impious. Because they had no pity upon other men, he cut
them down without mercy. None could behold the castle
tower flaming like the fires of hell and not exclaim, "The
whole universe will fight for him against these madmen."

After he had won this victory, the king, who was ever
swift to follow up his advantage, pushed forward toward the
other castle, called Nogent. There came to him a man who
said: "Oh, my lord king, it should be known to thy Seren-
ity that in that wicked castle dwell exceeding wicked men

who are worthy to lie in hell, and there only. Those are they who, when thou didst issue commands to destroy the commune of Laon, did burn with fire not only the city of Laon, but the noble church of the Mother of God, and many others beside. And well-nigh all the noble men of the city suffered martyrdom because they were true to their faith and defended their lord the bishop. And these evil men feared not to raise their hands against thy venerable Bishop Gaudin, the anointed of the Lord, defender of the church, but did him most cruelly to death, and exposed his naked body on the open road for beasts and birds of prey to feed upon; but first they cut off his finger with the pontifical ring. And they have agreed together, persuaded by the wicked Thomas, to attack and hold your tower."

The king was doubly animated by these words, and he attacked the wicked castle, broke open the abominable places of confinement, like prisons of hell, and set free the innocent; the guilty he punished with very heavy punishment. He alone avenged the injuries of many. Athirst for justice, he ordained that whatsoever murderous wretches he came upon should be fastened to a gibbet, and left as common food for the greed of kites, crows, and vultures. And this they deserved who had not feared to raise their hand against the Lord's anointed.

## III. Philip Augustus and John of England

In 1201 John, king of England, came to Paris and was received with much honor by King Philip. When he withdrew to his own lands again, he and Philip appeared to be upon the best terms, and the French king was able to turn his attention to a couple of recalcitrant counts who were "persecuting the churches of God and despoiling them of their goods," and who refused to obey his summons to appear at his court. But meanwhile new difficulties arose with King John. These are

43. How Philip Augustus took Normandy from King John. (From Rigord's *Life of Philip Augustus*.)

explained by Rigord — a monk of St. Denis, writing about the year 1200 — as follows:

John of England refuses to do homage to Philip Augustus.

The king of the French summoned John, king of England, as his liegeman, holding from him the counties of Poitou and Anjou and the duchy of Aquitaine, to come two weeks after Easter to Paris to give a satisfactory answer to the charges which Philip made against him. But since the king of England, instead of coming in person on the day indicated, did not even send a satisfactory reply, the king of the French, with the advice of his princes and barons, assembled an army, entered Normandy, and took the little fort of Boutavant, which he destroyed. Orgueil, Mortemer, and all the land which Hugh of Gournay held soon fell into his power. At Gournay he made Arthur [John's brother] a knight and delivered to him the county of Brittany, which had fallen to him by hereditary right. He even added the counties of Anjou and of Poitou, which he had acquired by right of arms. Lastly, he gave him the support of two hundred knights, with a considerable sum of money. Then the king received Arthur as his liegeman. The latter, with the king's permission, left him in July.

A few days later Arthur rashly advanced with a small troop of men into the territory of the king of England, who suddenly came upon him with a vast multitude of armed men, defeated him, and carried him away prisoner with Hugh le Brun, Geoffrey of Lusignan, and several other knights. King Philip, having learned this news, immediately abandoned the siege of the castle of Arques and appeared with his army before Tours, took the town, and set fire to it. The king of England, on his side, arrived, at the head of his troops, after the departure of the king of France and destroyed the same city with its castle.

Perfidious conduct of King John.

A few days after, the king of England took the viscount of Limoges and carried him off with him. Although Hugh le Brun, viscount of Thouars, Geoffrey of Lusignan, and the viscount of Limoges were all liegemen of the king of England, nevertheless they allied themselves with the king of the French, both by oath and through hostages. For King John had perfidiously carried off the wife of Hugh le Brun, daughter of the count of Angoulême, and this outrage, added to other grievances of the same lords of Poitou, alienated their fidelity to King John. The following winter the two kings discontinued their war after having guarded their fortresses, without, however, concluding either peace or a truce. . . .

In the year of our Lord 1202, in the fortnight following Easter, the king of the French had raised an army, entered Aquitaine, and, with the aid of the people of Poitou and of Brittany, had taken several fortresses. It was at this time that the count of Alençon formed an alliance with King Philip and put his whole land under the protection of this prince. The king then returned to Normandy with his army, and took possession of Conques and the island of Andelys and of Vaudreuil. . . .

In the year of our Lord 1203, Philip, king of the French, having assembled his army, entered Normandy on the 2d of May, took Falaise, a very strong castle, Domfront, and a very rich town which the people call Caen. He also brought under his control all the neighboring districts as far as Mont St. Michel. The Normans then came to ask for mercy and delivered up the towns which had been confided to their protection. . . . Of all Normandy there only remained Rouen, — a very rich town, full of noble men, the capital of all Normandy, — and Verneuil and Arques, strong towns well situated and well defended. Returning from Caen, the king, having left garrisons in the various cities and castles, laid siege to Rouen. . . .

*Philip conquers Normandy*

At the feast of St. John, the burghers, having received no aid from the king of England, fulfilled their promise and delivered to the king of the French their city of Rouen, a rich town, the capital of all Normandy, with the two castles of which we have spoken above. Three hundred and sixteen years had elapsed since this city and all Normandy had ceased to belong to the kings of France. The Northman Rollo, who had come with his pagan followers, had taken it by right of arms in the time of Charles the Simple.

## IV. St. Louis

We are particularly fortunate in possessing full and interesting accounts of St. Louis, who was the very ideal of a devout and sagacious mediæval ruler. The most famous of his biographers was the courtly Sire de Joinville, who was brought up at the elegant and refined court of the counts of Champagne. He was born in 1225, and although eleven years younger than the king, he became his friend and companion, and had excellent opportunities to acquaint himself with the king's character and to follow the events of his reign. Joinville was one of the first to desert Latin and write a serious historical work in French.

The following anecdote shows the king's charming courtesy as well as his extreme conscientiousness.

**44. How St. Louis thought people should dress.** (From *Joinville*.)    One day in Pentecost the saintly king was at Corbeil, where there were eighty chevaliers. After dinner the king came down into the courtyard beneath the chapel and was talking in the gateway with the count of Brittany, the father of the present duke, God keep him! Master Robert de Sorbonne [1] came seeking me and, taking me by the hem of my cloak, led me to the king; and all the other gentlemen followed us. So I said to Master Robert, "Master Robert, what do you want with me?" and he said to me, "If the king should seat himself here in the courtyard and you should go and sit above him on the same bench, would you think yourself blameworthy?" And I replied that I should. And he said, "Then you are also blameworthy when you wear finer clothes than the king, for you array yourself in ermine and cloth of green, which the king never does."

"But," I said, "Master Robert, saving your grace, I am not to blame in wearing ermine and cloth of green, for it is

[1] The founder of the college which grew into the famous divinity school at Paris.

the habit of dress that has come down to me from my father and my mother. But you, on the contrary, are much to be blamed, for your father was a villein and your mother was a villein, and you have forsaken the dress of your father and your mother, and wear finer camelot than the king." And I took the skirt of his outer coat and that of the king's and said to him, " Look now, if I do not speak the truth." Then the king set himself to speak in defense of Master Robert with all his might.

Afterward my lord the king called my lord Philip, his son, the father of the present king, and King Thibaut,[1] and, seating himself at the entrance to his oratory, he put his hand on the ground and said to them, " Sit here close by me so that no one can hear us." " O, sire," they said, " we dare not seat ourselves so close to you." Then he said to me, " Seneschal, sit here," which I did, and so close to him that my garments touched his. Then he made them sit down after me and said to them, " You did very wrong, you who are my sons, not to do at once what I commanded ; see that it does not happen again." And they said that it should not.

Then he said to me that he had summoned us in order to confess to me that he had been wrong in defending Master Robert against me. " But," he said, " I saw that he was so thunderstruck that he was in sore need of my aid. However, do not mind anything I may have said in defense of Master Robert ; for, as the seneschal told him, you should always dress neatly and well, for your ladies will love you the better for it, and your servants value you the more. As the philosopher says, one should array oneself, both as to clothing and arms, in such a manner that the men of sense of his generation cannot cry that he dresses too well, nor the young people that he dresses too poorly."

---

[1] Of Navarre, the son-in-law of St. Louis.

## BIBLIOGRAPHY

*A. References.*

**General Narratives:** ADAMS, *Civilization,* pp. 311–321; MUNRO, Chapters VII and XVIII, pp. 64–72 and 204–213.

**Odo and Charles the Simple:** BÉMONT and MONOD, pp. 235–241; EMERTON, *Mediæval Europe,* pp. 405–411; OMAN, pp. 496–505.

**Hugh Capet:** ADAMS, *Growth of the French Nation,* pp. 54–60; BÉMONT and MONOD, pp. 241–245 and 391–393; EMERTON, pp. 413–419; TOUT, *The Empire and the Papacy,* pp. 66–77.

**The Great Fiefs:** TOUT, pp. 82–92.

**Louis the Fat:** ADAMS, *French Nation,* pp. 73–78; BÉMONT and MONOD, pp. 396–401; MASSON, *Mediæval France,* pp. 47–57; TOUT, pp. 274–282.

**Philip Augustus:** ADAMS, *French Nation,* pp. 81–88; BÉMONT and MONOD, pp. 404–413; MASSON, pp. 69–88; TOUT, pp. 290–294 and 393–405.

**St. Louis:** ADAMS, *French Nation,* pp. 89–95; BÉMONT and MONOD, pp. 413–420; MASSON, pp. 90–119; TOUT, pp. 407–427.

**Philip the Fair:** ADAMS, *French Nation,* pp. 96–103; LODGE, *Close of the Middle Ages,* pp. 49–62; MASSON, pp. 139–156.

**Political Institutions under the Capetians:** ADAMS, *Civilization,* pp. 321–331; BÉMONT and MONOD, pp. 421–444; EMERTON, pp. 422–433.

---

*B. Additional reading in English.*

A survey of the whole Capetian period may be obtained from KITCHIN, *History of France,* Vol. I, Book III. This may be advantageously supplemented by recourse to several short biographies or monographs, such as HUTTON, *Philip Augustus,* — a very readable and satisfactory little book; and PERRY, *St. Louis,* — a careful account of the reign of "the most Christian king," with many quotations from the sources. The fullest treatment in English of the struggle between the king of France and the house of Anjou is found in NORGATE, *England under the Angevin Kings,* 2 vols.

One *source* only is available in English; it is, however, one of the most famous historical works of the Middle Ages, — *The Life of St. Louis,* by JOINVILLE, mentioned above. It may be found in the *Chronicles of the Crusades* (Bohn Library).

# CHAPTER XI

## ENGLAND IN THE MIDDLE AGES

### I. The Battle of Hastings : English and Normans

The courageous leaders mutually prepared for battle, each according to his national custom. The English, as we have heard, passed the night without sleep, in drinking and singing, and in the morning proceeded without delay against the enemy. All on foot, armed with battle-axes, and covering themselves in front by the juncture of their shields, they formed an impenetrable body which would assuredly have secured their safety that day had not the Normans, by a feigned flight, induced them to open their ranks, which till that time, according to their custom, had been closely compacted. King Harold himself, on foot, stood with his brothers near the standard in order that, so long as all shared equal danger, none could think of retreating. This same standard William sent, after his victory, to the pope ; it was sumptuously embroidered with gold and precious stones, and represented the figure of a man fighting.

On the other hand, the Normans passed the whole night in confessing their sins, and received the communion of the Lord's body in the morning. Their infantry, with bows and arrows, formed the vanguard, while their cavalry, divided into wings, was placed in the rear. The duke, with serene countenance, declaring aloud that God would favor his as being the righteous side, called for his arms ; and when, through the haste of his attendants, he had put on his hauberk the hind part before, he corrected the mistake with a laugh, saying, "The power of my dukedom shall be turned into a kingdom." Then starting the song of Roland, in order that the warlike example of that hero might stimulate the soldiers, and calling on God for assistance, the

*45. Harold and William prepare for battle. (From William of Malmesbury's History of the English Kings.)*

battle commenced on both sides, and was fought with great ardor, neither side giving ground during the greater part of the day.

The Normans, by a feigned retreat, rout the English.

Observing this, William gave a signal to his troops, that, feigning flight, they should withdraw from the field.   By means of this device the solid phalanx of the English opened for the purpose of cutting down the fleeing enemy and thus brought upon itself swift destruction; for the Normans, facing about, attacked them, thus disordered, and compelled them to fly. In this manner, deceived by a stratagem, they met an honorable death in avenging their country; nor indeed were they at all without their own revenge, for, by frequently making a stand, they slaughtered their pursuers in heaps. Getting possession of an eminence, they drove back the Normans, who in the heat of pursuit were struggling up the slope, into the valley beneath, where, by hurling their javelins and rolling down stones on them as they stood below, the English easily destroyed them to a man.   Besides, by a short passage with which they were acquainted, they avoided a deep ditch and trod underfoot such a multitude of their enemies in that place that the heaps of bodies made the hollow level with the plain.   This alternating victory, first of one side and then of the other, continued so long as Harold lived to check the retreat ; but when he fell, his brain pierced by an arrow, the flight of the English ceased not until night.

The author discreetly declares that the leaders were equally brave.

In the battle both leaders distinguished themselves by their bravery.   Harold, not content with the functions of a general and with exhorting others, eagerly assumed himself the duties of a common soldier.   He was constantly striking down the enemy at close quarters, so that no one could approach him with impunity, for straightway both horse and rider would be felled by a single blow.   So it was at long range, as I have said, that the enemy's deadly arrow brought him to his death.   One of the Norman soldiers gashed his thigh with a sword, as he lay prostrate ; for which shameful and cowardly action he was branded with ignominy by William and expelled from the army.

William, too, was equally ready to encourage his soldiers by his voice and by his presence, and to be the first to rush forward to attack the thickest of the foe. He was everywhere fierce and furious; he lost three choice horses, which were that day killed under him. The dauntless spirit and vigor of the intrepid general, however, still held out. Though often called back by the kind remonstrance of his bodyguard, he still persisted until approaching night crowned him with complete victory. And no doubt the hand of God so protected him that the enemy should draw no blood from his person, though they aimed so many javelins at him.

This was a fatal day to England, and melancholy havoc was wrought in our dear country during the change of its lords. For it had long before adopted the manners of the Angles, which had indeed altered with the times; for in the first years of their arrival they were barbarians in their look and manner, warlike in their usages, heathens in their rites.

*The character and habits of the English.*

After embracing the faith of Christ, by degrees and, in process of time, in consequence of the peace which they enjoyed, they relegated arms to a secondary place and gave their whole attention to religion. I am not speaking of the poor, the meanness of whose fortune often restrains them from overstepping the bounds of justice; I omit, too, men of ecclesiastical rank, whom sometimes respect for their profession and sometimes the fear of shame suffers not to deviate from the true path; I speak of princes, who from the greatness of their power might have full liberty to indulge in pleasure. Some of these in their own country, and others at Rome, changing their habit, obtained a heavenly kingdom and a saintly intercourse. Many others during their whole lives devoted themselves in outward appearance to worldly affairs, but in order that they might exhaust their treasures on the poor or divide them amongst monasteries.

What shall I say of the multitudes of bishops, hermits, and abbots? Does not the whole island blaze with such numerous relics of its own people that you can scarcely pass a village of any consequence but you hear the name of some new saint? And of how many more has all remembrance perished through the want of records?

General intellectual and religious decline before the Norman Conquest.

Nevertheless, the attention to literature and religion had gradually decreased for several years before the arrival of the Normans. The clergy, contented with a little confused learning, could scarcely stammer out the words of the sacraments; and a person who understood grammar was an object of wonder and astonishment. The monks mocked the rule of their order by fine vestments and the use of every kind of food. The nobility, given up to luxury and wantonness, went not to church in the morning after the manner of Christians, but merely, in a careless manner, heard matins and masses from a hurrying priest in their chambers, amid the blandishments of their wives. The commonalty, left unprotected, became a prey to the most powerful, who amassed fortunes, either by seizing on their property or by selling their persons into foreign countries; although it is characteristic of this people to be more inclined to reveling than to the accumulation of wealth. . . .

Manners and customs of the English.

Drinking in parties was an universal practice, in which occupation they passed entire nights as well as days. They consumed their whole substance in mean and despicable houses, unlike the Normans and French, who live frugally in noble and splendid mansions. The vices attendant on drunkenness, which enervate the human mind, followed; hence it came about that when they engaged William, with more rashness and precipitate fury than military skill, they doomed themselves and their country to slavery by a single, and that an easy, victory. For nothing is less effective than rashness; and what begins with violence quickly ceases or is repelled.

The English at that time wore short garments, reaching to the mid-knee; they had their hair cropped, their beards shaven, their arms laden with golden bracelets, their skin adorned with tattooed designs. They were accustomed to eat till they became surfeited, and to drink till they were sick. These latter qualities they imparted to their conquerors; as to the rest, they adopted their manners. I would not, however, have these bad propensities ascribed to the English universally; I know that many of the clergy at that day trod the path of sanctity by a blameless life; I know that many of the laity, of all ranks and conditions, in this nation were well-pleasing to God. Be injustice far from this account; the accusation does not involve the whole, indiscriminately; but as in peace the mercy of God often cherishes the bad and the good together, so, equally, does his severity sometimes include them both in captivity.

The Normans — that I may speak of them also — were at that time, and are even now, exceedingly particular in their dress and delicate in their food, but not so to excess. They are a race inured to war, and can hardly live without it; fierce in rushing against the enemy, and, where force fails of success, ready to use stratagem or to corrupt by bribery. As I have said, they live in spacious houses with economy, envy their superiors, wish to excel their equals, and plunder their subjects, though they defend them from others; they are faithful to their lords, though a slight offense alienates them. They weigh treachery by its chance of success, and change their sentiments for money. The most hospitable, however, of all nations, they esteem strangers worthy of equal honor with themselves; they also intermarry with their vassals. They revived, by their arrival, the rule of religion which had everywhere grown lifeless in England. You might see churches rise in every village, and monasteries in the towns and cities, built after a style unknown before; you might behold the country flourishing with renovated rites; so that each wealthy man accounted that day lost to him which he had neglected to signalize by some munificent action.

*Character of the Normans*

## II. Rule of William the Conqueror

King William was a very wise man, and very powerful, more dignified and strong than any of his predecessors were. He was mild to the good men who loved God, and beyond all measure severe to the men who gainsaid his will. . . .

*46. William the Conqueror's character. (From the Anglo-Saxon Chronicle.)*

A.8

Thrice every year he wore his crown, as oft as he was in England. At Easter he wore it in Winchester ; at Pentecost, in Westminster; at Midwinter, in Gloucester. And then were with him all the great men over all England, archbishops and suffragan bishops, abbots and earls, thanes and knights.

So also was he a very rigid and cruel man, so that no one durst do anything against his will. He had earls in bonds who had acted against his will; bishops he cast from their bishoprics, and abbots from their abbacies, and thanes into prison; and at last he spared not his own brother, named Odo : he was a very rich bishop in Normandy; at Bayeux was his episcopal see ; and he was the foremost man besides the king; and he had an earldom in England, and when the king was in Normandy, then was he the most powerful in this land : and him the king put in prison.

Among other good things is not to be forgotten the good peace that he made in this land ; so that a man who had any confidence in himself might go over his realm, with his bosom full of gold, unhurt. Nor durst any man slay another man had he done ever so great evil to the other. He reigned over England, and by his sagacity so thoroughly surveyed it that there was not a hide of land within England that he knew not who had it, or what it was worth, and afterwards set it in his writ.

Brytland (Wales) was in his power, and therein he built castles, and completely ruled over that race of men. In like manner he also subjected Scotland to him by his great strength. The land of Normandy was naturally his, and over the country which is called Le Maine he reigned; and if he might yet have lived two years he would, by his valor, have won Ireland, and without any weapons.

Certainly in his time men had great hardship and very many injuries. Castles he caused to be made, and poor men to be greatly oppressed. The king was very rigid, and took from his subjects many a mark of gold, and more hundred pounds of silver, all which he took, by right and with great unright, from his people, for little need. He had fallen into covetousness, and altogether loved greediness.

He planted a great preserve for deer, and he laid down laws therewith, that whosoever should slay hart or hind should be blinded. He forbade the harts and also the boars to be killed. As greatly did he love the tall deer as if he were their father. He also ordained concerning the hares that they should go free. His great men bewailed it, and the poor men murmured thereat; but he was so obdurate that he recked not of the hatred of them all; but they must wholly follow the king's will if they would live, or have land, or property, or even his peace. Alas that any man should be so proud, so raise himself up, and account himself above all men! May the Almighty God show mercy to his soul, and grant him forgiveness of his sins!

### III. Principal Provisions of the Great Charter

*John, by the grace of God King of England, Lord of Ireland, Duke of Normandy and Aquitaine, Count of Anjou, to the archbishops, bishops, abbots, earls, barons, justiciars, foresters, sheriffs, reeves, servants, and all bailiffs and to his faithful people, greeting:*

47. Principal provisions of Magna Charta.

Know that by the suggestion of God and for the good of our soul and of those of all our predecessors and of our heirs, to the honor of God and the exaltation of holy Church, and for the improvement of our kingdom, by the advice of our venerable fathers, Stephen, archbishop of Canterbury, primate of all England and cardinal of the holy Roman Church, Henry, archbishop of Dublin, William of London, Peter of Winchester, Jocelyn of Bath and Glastonbury, Hugh of Lincoln, Walter of Worcester, William of Coventry, and Benedict of Rochester, bishops; of Master Pandulf, subdeacon and member of the household of the lord pope, of Brother Aymeric, master of the Knights of the Temple in England; and of the noblemen William Marshall, earl of Pembroke, William, earl of Salisbury, . . . and others of our faithful.

1. In the first place, we have granted to God, and by this our present charter confirmed for us and our heirs forever,

that the English church shall be free, and shall hold its rights entire and its liberties uninjured. . . .

We have granted, moreover, to all free men of our kingdom, for us and our heirs forever, all the liberties written below, to be had and holden by themselves and their heirs from us and our heirs.

2. If any of our earls or barons, or others holding from us in chief by military service, shall have died, and when he has died his heir shall be of full age and owe relief, he shall have his inheritance by the ancient relief. . . .

5. The custodian [of the lands of a minor], moreover, so long as he shall have the custody of the land, must keep up the houses, parks, warrens, fish ponds, mills, and other things pertaining to the land, from the proceeds of the land itself; and he must return to the heir, when he has come to full age, all his land, furnished with plows and implements of husbandry, according as the time of wainage requires and as the proceeds of the land are able reasonably to sustain. . . .

12. No scutage or aid shall be imposed in our kingdom save by the common council of our kingdom, except for the ransoming of our body, for the making of our oldest son a knight, and for once marrying our oldest daughter; and for these purposes it shall be only a reasonable aid; in the same way it shall be done concerning the aids of the city of London.

14. And for holding a common council of the kingdom concerning the assessment of an aid otherwise than in the three cases mentioned above, or concerning the assessment of a scutage, we shall cause to be summoned the archbishops, bishops, abbots, earls, and greater barons by our letters under seal; and, besides, we shall cause to be summoned generally, by our sheriffs and bailiffs, all those who hold from us in chief, for a certain day, at the end of at least forty days, and for a certain place; and in all the letters of that summons we will state the cause of the summons, and when the summons has thus been given the business shall proceed on the appointed day, on the advice of those who shall be present, even if not all of those who were sum- moned have come.

15. We will not grant to any one, moreover, that he shall take an aid from his free men, except for ransoming his body, for making his oldest son a knight, and for once marrying his oldest daughter; and for these purposes only a reasonable aid shall be taken. . . .

20. A free man shall not be fined for a small offense, except in proportion to the gravity of the offense; and for a great offense he shall be fined in proportion to the magnitude of the offense, saving his freehold; and a merchant in the same way, saving his merchandise; and the villein shall be fined in the same way, saving his wainage, if he shall be at our mercy; and none of the above fines shall be imposed except by the oaths of honest men of the neighborhood. . . .

28. No constable or other bailiff of ours shall take any one's grain or other chattels without immediately paying for them in money, unless he is able to obtain a postponement at the good will of the seller.

30. No sheriff or bailiff of ours, or any one else, shall take horses or wagons of any free man, for carrying purposes, except on the permission of that free man.

31. Neither we nor our bailiffs will take the wood of another man for castles, or for anything else which we are doing, except by the permission of him to whom the wood belongs. . . .

39. No free man shall be taken, or imprisoned, or dispossessed, or outlawed, or banished, or in any way injured, nor will we go upon him, nor send upon him, except by the legal judgment of his peers, or by the law of the land.

40. To no one will we sell, to no one will we deny or delay, right or justice.

41. All merchants shall be safe and secure in going out from England and coming into England, and in remaining and going through England, as well by land as by water, for buying and selling, free from all evil tolls, by the ancient and rightful customs. . . .

63. . . . It has been sworn, moreover, as well on our part as on the part of the barons, that all these things spoken of above shall be observed in good faith and without any evil

*Restrictions placed upon the king's officers.*

*No arbitrary imprisonment.*

*Protection o merchants*

intent. Witness the above-named and many others. Given by our hand in the meadow which is called Runnymede, between Windsor and Staines, on the fifteenth day of June, in the seventeenth year of our reign.

## BIBLIOGRAPHY

*A. References.*

**General Summary :** ADAMS, *Civilization*, pp. 339–348 ; BÉMONT and MONOD, pp. 445–466 ; MUNRO, Chapters VIII and XIX, pp. 74–85 and 214–223.

**The Danish Invasions and Alfred :** CHEYNEY, *A Short History of England*, pp. 59–68 ; ANDREWS, *History of England*, pp. 21–33 ; GARDINER, pp. 55–62 ; GREEN, Chapter I, sect. 5, pp. 44–53 ; TERRY, *A History of England to 1901*, Chapter IV, pp. 57–77 ; COLBY, pp. 19–24 ; KENDALL, *Source Book of English History*, pp. 17–24 ; LEE, *Source Book of English History*, pp. 96–99.

**The Danish Conquest and Cnut :** ANDREWS, pp. 53–60 ; GARDINER, pp. 79–85 ; GREEN, Chapter II, sect. 1, pp. 63–67 ; TERRY, pp. 106–123 ; KENDALL, pp. 31–38 ; LEE, pp. 99–107 ; COLBY, pp. 24–27.

**English Institutions before the Norman Conquest :** CHEYNEY, pp. 78–83 ; ANDREWS, Chapter III, pp. 40–52 ; GARDINER, pp. 29–33 and 69–77 ; GREEN, Chapter I, sect. 6, latter part, pp. 58–61 ; LEE, pp. 87–95.

**The Norman Conquest and William I :** CHEYNEY, pp. 85–115 ; ANDREWS, pp. 66–81 ; GARDINER, pp. 91–114 ; GREEN, Chapter II, sects. 3–5 and beginning of sect. 6, pp. 71–89 ; TERRY, pp. 130–183 ; GEE and HARDY, *Documents Illustrative of English Church History*, pp. 56–59.

**Henry II :** CHEYNEY, pp. 145–170 ; ANDREWS, pp. 93–108 ; GARDINER, Chapter X, pp. 138–158 ; GREEN, Chapter II, sect. 8, pp. 104–112 ; TERRY, pp. 211–229 ; KENDALL, pp. 51–58.

**The Quarrel with à Becket :** COLBY, pp. 56–59 ; KENDALL, pp. 59–61 ; LEE, pp. 130–138.

**Henry's Judicial Reforms :** ADAMS and STEPHENS, *Select Documents of English Constitutional History*, pp. 14–18 ; HENDERSON, *Select Historical Documents*, pp. 16–20 ; LEE, pp. 117–119 ; *Translations and Reprints*, Vol. I, No. 6, pp. 22–26.

**Richard the Lion-Hearted :** ANDREWS, pp. 108–112 ; GARDINER, Chapter XI, pp. 159–171 ; GREEN, Chapter II, sect. 9, first part, pp. 112–115 ; TERRY, pp. 230–244 ; COLBY, pp. 68–70.

King John: CHEYNEY, pp. 174–184; ANDREWS, pp. 112–121; GARDINER, Chapter XII, pp. 173–185; GREEN, Chapter II, sect. 9, end, and Chapter III, sects. 2–3, pp. 115–116 and 122–132; TERRY, pp. 245–265; ADAMS and STEPHENS, pp. 34, 35; Magna Charta, full text in ADAMS and STEPHENS, pp. 42–52; HENDERSON, pp. 135–148; LEE, pp. 169–180; *Translations and Reprints*, Vol. I, No. 6, pp. 6–17.

Henry III: ANDREWS, pp. 123–136; GARDINER, Chapter XII, pp. 185–208; GREEN, Chapter III, sects. 5, 7, pp. 141–147 and 152–160; TERRY, pp. 266–296; COLBY, pp. 78–83; KENDALL, pp. 81–87.

Edward I: CHEYNEY, pp. 209–216; ANDREWS, pp. 136–156; GARDINER, pp. 208–224; GREEN, Chapter IV, sects. 1–3 and 5, first part, pp. 161–193 and 201–207; TERRY, pp. 296–333.

----

GREEN, *The Conquest of England*, 2 vols., new ed., 1899. Comes down to 1071.

*B. Additional reading in English.*

RAMSAY, *Foundations of England*, 2 vols., 1898.

NORGATE, *England under the Angevin Kings*, 2 vols., 1887. These cover more satisfactorily than any other works the general history of England to the thirteenth century. They may be supplemented by the following accounts : PLUMMER, *Life and Times of Alfred the Great*, 1902, and CONYBEARE, *Alfred in the Chronicles*, 1900; STUBBS, *The Early Plantagenets;* GREEN, *Henry II*, 1888; NORGATE, *John Lackland*, 1902; RICHARDSON, *The National Movement in the Reign of Henry III*, 1897; MEDLEY, *English Constitutional History* (excellent).

TRAILL, *Social England*, 6 vols., 1894–1897; new, revised, and finely illustrated edition, 1902 *sqq.* This is a sort of encyclopedia of history, made up of special contributions by various writers upon all the various phases of the social and intellectual life. Naturally valuable as a work of reference rather than to be read consecutively. Vols. I and II relate to the Middle Ages.

*History of England*, edited by HUNT and POOLE. A coöperative history in twelve volumes, now in preparation, which promises to prove the best continuous narrative.

*English History from Contemporary Writers*, edited by YORK-POWELL. Little volumes of interesting extracts from the sources, — *Thomas of Canterbury*, 1899; *Crusade of Richard I*, 1889; *Misrule of Henry III*, 1887; *Simon de Montfort*, 1888.

For additional information in regard to the books for England, especially the various series which have appeared, see the admirable bibliographies in ANDREWS, *History of England*, especially pp. 549 *sqq.*

# CHAPTER XII

## GERMANY AND ITALY IN THE TENTH AND ELEVENTH CENTURIES

### I. THE TIMES OF HENRY I AND OTTO THE GREAT

48. Germany in the early tenth century. (From the continuation of Regino's *Chronicle*.) The following account of the events in Germany in the first half of the tenth century was prepared by a monk at Treves in 960–961. He made use, for the earlier part of his narrative, of certain meager annals, some of which have come down to us. The sources all agree in giving a gloomy account of invasion, pillage, and civil war, which even wise and energetic German kings were unable to prevent.

In the year 907 of the Incarnation the Bavarians were defeated with great bloodshed by the Hungarians. Duke Luitbald was killed in this battle, and his son Arnulf succeeded him in the duchy.

In the year 908 of the Incarnation the Hungarians again crossed the borders and devastated Saxony and Thuringia.

In the year 909 of the Incarnation the Hungarians forced their way into Alemannia.

In the year 910 of the Incarnation the Franconians fought on the frontier of Franconia and Bavaria with the Hungarians and were miserably defeated or put to flight. Count Gebhard lost his life in the battle and left behind him two sons, still boys, Udo and Hermann, who were later to become distinguished in Franconia.

In the year 911 of the Incarnation King Louis, the son of Emperor Arnulf, died, and since the royal line was now extinct, he was succeeded by Conrad, son of that Conrad who had been killed by Adalbert.

Death of Louis the Child, who was followed by Conrad.

In the year 912 of the Incarnation the Hungarians again devastated without opposition Franconia and Thuringia. Archbishop Hatto [of Mayence], a very keen and able man, died, and Heriger succeeded him. Otto, duke of Saxony, died.

In the year 913 of the Incarnation there was a very severe winter. The Hungarians wasted the fields of the Alemannians and were defeated by the Bavarians and Alemannians at the river Inn. In the same year Einhard, bishop of Speyer, was blinded by Counts Bernhard and Conrad.

In the year 914 of the Incarnation Otbert, bishop of Strasburg, was killed. Bishop Salomon [of Constance] was taken prisoner.[1]

In the year 915 of the Incarnation the Hungarians wasted all Alemannia with fire and sword; they harried all Thuringia and Saxony and came as far as the abbey of Fulda.

In the year 917 of the Incarnation the Hungarians came through Alemannia into Alsace and to the borders of Lorraine. Erchanger and Berthold were beheaded. Arnulf, duke of Bavaria, revolted against the king.

In the year 918 of the Incarnation King Conrad celebrated the birth of St. John in the cloister of Hersfeld.

In the year 919 of the Incarnation King Conrad died. He was in all respects a man of insight, gentle, and a friend of divine learning. As he perceived that the day of his death was near, he summoned his brethren and relatives, namely the great among the Franconians. He said to them that his

Death of Conrad, who nominates Henry I as his successor.

[1] By Erchanger, duke of Alemannia, as we learn from the annals of the monastery of St. Gall. His execution is mentioned below.

end was near, and exhorted them as a father that there should
be no discord in the realm over the choice of a king to follow
him.   He commanded them to choose Henry, duke of Saxony, a man of energy and a strong friend of peace.   Moreover since he, Conrad, had been unable to find any other
person so well fitted for the position, he sent to Henry
the scepter and crown and other decorations associated with
the kingly dignity, on condition that he should shield and
protect the realm.   He himself passed from this life and was
honorably buried in the monastery of Fulda.   He was worn
out during the few years of his reign by the Bavarians and
Alemannians and Saxons, for they rose against him in many
a battle ; but with God's help before his death he got the
better of them.

In the year 920 of the Incarnation Duke Henry was chosen
king by agreement of the Franconians, Alemannians, Bavarians, Thuringians, and Saxons.[1]   He began his reign by
strictly enforcing the peace ; for many, even among the nobles,
had turned their attention in those days to robbery.[2] . . .

In the year 928 of the Incarnation Henry made a hostile
expedition into the land of the Bohemians, and won the victory over them with God's aid.   At this time a son, William,
was born to Otto, the king's son.   The winter was uncom-
monly cold.   Ruodger, archbishop of Treves, died.   Ruod-
bert succeeded him.

In the year 929 of the Incarnation Duke Gisalbert took
to wife Gerburga, the daughter of King Henry.

In the year 930 of the Incarnation Otto, the son of King
Henry, took to wife Edith, the daughter of the king of the
Angles.

---

[1] The fact that the peoples of the several duchies were viewed as
subnations is clear in this and other references to them.

[2] In his account of the years here omitted, our chronicler tells of
Hungarian raids, and of trouble between King Charles of France and
Henry I over Lorraine, and of its ultimate cession to Henry.

In the year 931 of the Incarnation King Henry induced the king of the Abotrites and the king of the Danes to become Christians. In the same year the king was invited to Franconia by Eberhard and others, — Franconian counts and bishops, — and was honored by each of them, in his house or in his see, with banquets and gifts as befitted a king.

In the year 932 of the Incarnation the Hungarians destroyed many towns in eastern Franconia and Alemannia with fire and sword. They then crossed the Rhine near Worms, wasted Gaul as far as the sea, and then returned by way of Italy.

In the year 934 of the Incarnation King Henry overcame the Hungarians in a great battle and took many of them prisoners. In the same year he attacked the Slavs, who are called Bucranes, conquered them, and made them tributary. The church of St. Maximin was blown down in a storm. Through the king's favor the right of election was given back to the monks; Hugo, who had been prior, was chosen abbot, and the monks who did not live according to the rule were driven out.[1]

In the year 935 of the Incarnation King Henry suffered from a stroke.

In the year 936 of the Incarnation a number of bishops of Thuringia held a synod at Erfurt. King Henry, who had diligently promoted peace and steadily pursued the heathen, reached his life's end on the 2d of July, after he had won many a brave victory and pushed out the bounds of his realm in every direction. His son Otto was chosen his successor by a unanimous vote of all the great of the realm.

The annals of the reign of Henry I are fragmentary and gloomy, but we have much fuller accounts of Otto's difficulties and his manner of surmounting them. Among the historians of his time Widukind, a monk of Corvei, holds a high place.

---

[1] These statements relate to the writer's own monastery at Treves.

49. Election of Otto the Great (936). (From Widukind's *Deeds of the Saxons*.)

When Henry [I], the father of his country and the greatest and best of kings, was dead, all the people of the Franks and Saxons chose as their chief Otto, his son, whom his father had wished to have them choose. They decided to hold the general election at the palace of Aix-la-Chapelle. . . . When they were come thither the dukes and chief counts and soldiers came together in the portico of the basilica of the great Charles, and put the new king on a throne built there, and gave him their hands, promising to be faithful to him, and pledging him their aid against their enemies. So they made him king after their custom.

While these things were done by the dukes and the other magistrates, the chief pontiff [of Germany, i.e. the bishop of Mayence], with all the priests and the people, awaited below in the basilica the coming of the new king. When he came toward them the pontiff met him and touched the king's right hand. Now the bishop was clad in linen and was adorned with a stole and pallium and bore a staff in his right hand; and he went forward among the people and stood at the altar. He then turned toward the people who stood around that all might see him. "Behold," he said, "I present to you Otto, chosen by God, and previously designated by Henry, lord of this realm, and now made king by all the princes. If this choice is pleasing to you, signify it by raising your right hands toward heaven." And all the people raised their right hands on high, and with a mighty voice prayed for the prosperity of their new ruler.

Then the king, clad according to the Frankish custom in a close tunic, marched with the bishop behind an altar on which lay the royal regalia, — the sword with the belt, the mantle and bracelets, the staff with the scepter and diadem. . . . Then Hildebert, bishop of Mayence, came forward to the altar, took the sword and belt, and turning to the king said: "Take this sword, that thou mayst cast out all the adversaries of Christ, all barbarians and false Christians, by the divine authority given to thee, by all the power of the whole empire of the Franks, to the lasting peace of Christendom."

Then he took the mantle and bracelets and put them upon him : "As the border of this mantle flows to the ground, be thou admonished that thou shouldst glow with the zeal of faith and that thou shouldst endure to the end to maintain peace." Then he took the scepter and staff : " By these tokens be thou admonished that thou shouldst reprove thy subjects with fatherly chastisement and that thou shouldst above all things extend the hand of mercy to the ministers of God and to widows and orphans. And may thy head never lack the oil of compassion, that thou mayst be crowned now and hereafter with an eternal reward."

And he was anointed with the holy oil and crowned by the pontiffs, Hildebert and Wicfried [archbishop of Cologne], with a golden crown. When the consecration was accomplished according to the law, the king was led by those same bishops to the throne, which was built between two marble columns and was reached by a winding stairway, whence he could see all and be seen by all.

When the divine praise had been sung and the mass solemnly celebrated, the king descended to the palace. There he drew near a marble table adorned with royal pomp, and seated himself with the bishops and all the people; and the dukes ministered to him.

## BIBLIOGRAPHY

**General Outline :** ADAMS, pp. 227-245; BÉMONT and MONOD, pp. 268-285. *A. References.*

**The Stem Duchies :** EMERTON, pp. 95-100.

**Henry I :** EMERTON, pp. 103-110; HENDERSON, *Germany in the Middle Ages*, pp. 117-122; TOUT, *The Empire and the Papacy*, pp. 12-18.

**Otto I :** BRYCE, Chapter VI, last part, Chapter VIII, and Chapter IX, first part, pp. 80-88 and 122-145 ; EMERTON, pp. 110-114 and 128-145; HENDERSON, *Germany in the Middle Ages*, pp. 123-144 ; *Short History of Germany*, pp. 49-53 ; TOUT, pp. 18-35.

**Liutprand's Report of his Mission to Constantinople :** HENDERSON, *Historical Documents*, pp. 441-477. An interesting and amusing document.

**Theory of the Empire :** BRYCE, Chapter VII, pp. 89-121.

Conrad II : EMERTON, pp. 174–185 ; HENDERSON, *Germany in the Middle Ages*, pp. 166–173 ; TOUT, pp. 50–60.

Henry III : EMERTON, pp. 185–204 ; HENDERSON, *Germany in the Middle Ages*, pp. 174–182 ; *Short History of Germany*, pp. 54–58 ; TOUT, pp. 60–64.

The Papacy under Leo IX and Nicholas II : EMERTON, pp. 204–233 ; TOUT, pp. 96–103 and 108–116.

The Decree of 1059 in Regard to Papal Elections : HENDERSON, *Historical Documents*, pp. 361–365.

---

*B. Additional reading in English.*

HERBERT FISHER, *The Mediæval Empire*, 2 vols. The most recent and best treatment in English. Admirable for this and the two following chapters.

NEWMAN, pp. 437–443 and 495–502.

MILMAN, Vol. III, Book V, Chapters XI–XIV, and Book VI.

GREGOROVIUS, Vol. III, Book VI, and Vol. IV, Book VII, Chapters I–III.

ALICE GREENWOOD, *The Empire and the Papacy in the Middle Ages*, 1902.

DÖLLINGER, *Fables respecting the Popes in the Middle Ages*, 1872. An interesting refutation of some celebrated legends.

MATHEWS, *Select Mediæval Documents*, pp. 19–35. Gives a few important documents for this period in the original Latin.

# CHAPTER XIII

## THE CONFLICT BETWEEN GREGORY VII AND HENRY IV

### I. THE EARLY YEARS OF HENRY IV

The most comprehensive of all the mediæval chronicles covering the history of the world was written by Ekkehard of Aurach.   He exercised great patience and care and repeatedly revised and elaborated his work. He began to write just before the opening of the First Crusade, in which he became greatly interested (see extract below, pp. 150 *sqq.*)   His fair-mindedness is shown in the following account of Henry IV's early troubles.

50. The early part oi Henry IV's reign. (From the *Chronicle* of Ekkehard of Aurach.)

In the year 1057 of the Incarnation of our Lord, and the year 1808 since the founding of the City, Henry IV, son of Emperor Henry, while still a boy, began to reign in the place of his father.   At the time that this book is being written, he is reigning, in his forty-second year, as the eighty-seventh emperor since Augustus. . . .

In the year of our Lord 1058, Frederick, who as pope was called Stephen, died, and Alexander, bishop of Lucca, followed him.   At that time Hildebrand, who later became pope, administered the office of archdeacon in Rome.

In the year of our Lord 1059, Pope Stephen died, and Gerhard followed him under the name of Nicholas (II).[1] Henry, king of France, died, and Philip, his son, reigned in his stead.

[1] Stephen IX died in 1058 and was succeeded by Nicholas II, who was in turn succeeded by Alexander II in 1061.   The confusion of dates by Ekkehard seems rather surprising, but similar mistakes are common in most of the chronicles.

In the year of our Lord 1060, Luitpold, archbishop of Mayence, died and Siegfried, abbot of Fulda, followed him, who later allied himself with others in a conspiracy against his lord the king.

In the year of our Lord 1062, Archbishop Anno of Cologne, with the consent of the leaders of the empire, brought the prince (Henry IV), of whose person he had taken violent possession, under his control, and withdrew from the prince's mother the government of the empire, as if he felt it to be unworthy that the state should be ruled by the empress, who, though a woman, was enabled to exercise power after the manner of a man. After he had given an account before all of what he had done, he again gained the favor of his lord the king, and was again reconciled to the mother through the son. . . .

In the year of our Lord 1063, Pope Nicholas died and was followed by Bishop Alexander of Lucca. . . .

In the year of our Lord 1064, Siegfried, bishop of Mayence, Gunther of Babenberg, and William of Utrecht, along with many other bishops and noblemen, set forth with a great following on a pilgrimage to Jerusalem. Here they suffered much from the attacks of the barbarians, but finally, having happily reached their goal, they returned, greatly reduced in numbers and strength.

In the year of our Lord 1065, Gunther, bishop of Babenberg, died in Pannonia, as he was returning from Jerusalem. His body was brought back to Babenberg and buried there, and Hermann was chosen to succeed him. Count Gozmin, who had usurped the power in the bishopric of Würzburg, was killed by the followers of Bishop Adelberon.

In the year of our Lord 1066, a comet glowed long over the whole earth. In the same year England was terribly desolated by the Norman William and finally subjugated, and he had himself made king. He then drove almost all the bishops of the said kingdom into banishment and had the nobles killed. The commons he gave over in bondage to his knights, and he compelled the wives of the natives to marry the invaders.

In the year of our Lord 1067, King Henry took to wife Bertha, daughter of a certain Otto, an Italian, and of Adelheid; and he celebrated the wedding at Tribur. Conrad, councilor of the church at Cologne, whom King Henry had designated as bishop of Treves, was taken prisoner by Theodoric, count of that city, and was carried into the forest by his followers and thrown down three times from the top of a mountain, but since he still remained unhurt, they dispatched him with a sword.

In the year of our Lord 1068, King Henry, with youthful recklessness, began to reside in Saxony alone of all the Roman Empire, to despise the princes, oppress the nobles, exalt the lowborn, and to devote himself (as was said) to the chase, to gaming and other occupations of this kind, more than to the administration of justice. He married the daughters of the nobles to his favorites of low origin, and, full of distrust against the powerful of the empire, he began to build certain castles. By thus recklessly sowing the seeds of discord it fell out that the number of those who proposed to deprive the king not only of his kingdom but even of his life grew rapidly. However, as he had not yet fully reached the years of maturity, many judged that the responsibility did not fall so much upon him as upon Archbishop Adelbert of Bremen, since everything was done on his advice. *The king's youthful recklessness*

In the year of our Lord 1069, the Empress Agnes, mother of King Henry, through vexation, or better, through divine inspiration, surrendered the duchy of Bavaria, and, discarding the reins of government in her devotion to Christ, betook herself to Rome, where, with marvelous humility, she brought forth the fruits of repentance and after a few years closed this earthly life in the Lord.

In the year of our Lord 1070, Margrave Teti, not without the connivance of the Saxon princes, established a tyranny directed against the king's followers. This was, however, suppressed through the intervention of the heavenly as well as the earthly majesty, for his castles of Beichlingen and Burgsheidungen were destroyed by the king; his son, likewise a warrior, was killed by some of his servants, and he himself soon died a natural death.

How the duchy of Bavaria was taken from Duke Otto.

In the year of our Lord 1071, Duke Otto lost the duchy of Bavaria. He was a Saxon by origin, a man of excellent rank, to whom few could be compared in insight and military power. He enjoyed such respect among all the princes that the king, who was already an object of suspicion and hate to the Saxons, was fearful lest this Otto might, should the king's influence decline, attempt to win the royal throne itself.

A certain Egino, of mean origin and insignificant resources, took advantage of the situation for his evil ends. Although well known for his impudence and shameless conduct, he managed to slip into the court under the protection of certain of the king's adherents. He lied to the king, saying that that great hero, Otto, who in reality had never known him, had conspired with him to murder the king. He offered himself, as was the custom, as a hostage until the truth of what he had said should be settled by a duel between him and the duke. What more need be said? After royal councils had been announced, one at Mayence and the other at Goslar, Otto disdained to fight with Egino, — the duke with the rogue, the prince with the common man, — nevertheless his innocence and Egino's shamelessness remained by no means concealed.

The duchy of Bavaria given to Welf.

So Otto, guilty of leze majesty, lost the duchy of Bavaria, which a certain Welf received, a distinguished, brave, warlike person, a Swabian by birth. From this seed, alas, did great dissension spring, which grew into the wretched fruit of continuous battles, of rebelliousness, robbery, and destruction, division in the Church, heresy, and many deaths.

In the year of our Lord 1072, the king followed Otto everywhere, destroyed as many of his fortresses as he could, wasted his lands, and strove completely to annihilate him, as an enemy of the state. Nevertheless, Otto, with a select following, and with his own stout arm and his heart full of bitter hate, since he might not fight directly with the royal troops, sought to avenge the injury which he had suffered, now by plundering, now by fire, now by the sword, wherever opportunity offered.

Duke Otto rouses the Saxons to revolt.

At his inspiration the Saxon people — of a very violent disposition as they are — ceased not, with one accord, to organize a conspiracy against the king; sent letters full of insulting and unheard-of accusations against the king to the apostolic see, and sought allies by letter and messenger throughout the whole German empire.

In the first place they made friends with Siegfried, the archbishop of Mayence, Adelbert of Worms, Adelberon of Würzburg, Gebhardt of Salzburg, and other bishops, as many as they could, and then through these they gained Pope Alexander. Many assert too that, last and greatest, Anno, archbishop of Cologne, was one of those privy to this conspiracy. Frightened at last by these intrigues, the king left Saxony and conducted the business of the empire in other regions.

In the year of our Lord 1073, the archbishop of Cologne and Hermann of Babenberg were sent to Rome in order to get together the money which was owing the king there. They brought back, on their return, a letter from Pope Alexander, in which the king was ordered to give an account of his heresy, simony, and many other similar matters which called for improvement, rumors of which had reached him in Rome.

Thereupon the Saxons built many strongholds, for up to this time that country had had but few of them. Moreover they completely destroyed the castles which the king had built some time before. Among these they tore down the castle which was called Harzburg, the cathedral and the abbey which stood there, destroying all these in their rage and perversity, down to the very ground. Horrible to say, they took up the bones of the innocent son of the king, who had · been buried there, and scattered them about as an insult to the father.

Hildebrand, the monk, becomes pope as Gregory VII

In the year of our Lord 1074, after Pope Alexander of blessed memory had died, Hildebrand, later called Gregory, followed him; by profession and rank he was a monk and archdeacon. Under him the Roman Empire and the whole Church began to be threatened by new and unheard-of divisions and turmoil. Since Gregory had reached this height of power without the king's permission, simply through the favor of the Romans, some asserted that he was not rightfully chosen, but had seized the papal dignity with his own hand. Therefore he was not recognized by some of the bishops. Gregory repeatedly summoned King Henry through messengers and letters to answer for his deeds before a synod.

In the year of our Lord 1074, Pope Gregory, after holding a synod, condemned the simonists, namely those who bought and sold the gift of the Holy Ghost, and provided that the Nicolaitae, that is to say, the priests who had married, should be removed from the service of the altar, and forbade the laity to attend masses performed by them.

In the year of the Lord 1075, King Henry moved against the Saxons, after he had collected a strong army from Alemannia, Bavaria, and Germania, and from Bohemia. He fought with the Saxons on the river Unstrut and after much blood had been shed on both sides, he finally returned home victorious.

Rudolph, duke of Alemannia and Burgundy, who later usurped the imperial crown, fought bravely there with his followers for the king. Bishop Hermann of Babenberg was deposed, on account of his simoniacal practices, by command of Pope Hildebrand, and Ruotpert was put in his place by the king. In this year died Anno, archbishop of Cologne, rich in merits of piety, and was buried in the cloister of Siegburg, which he himself had built. He was followed by Hildolf.

## II. THE ISSUE BETWEEN POPE AND EMPEROR IN THE
## MATTER OF INVESTITURE

A conference was arranged at Châlons in 1107 between the representatives of the pope and those of the emperor, where the demands of each party might be clearly stated. Although this did not occur until just after the death of Henry IV, it seems best to introduce at this point an account of the arguments advanced by each side, since they serve to show the real nature of the troubles between Henry and Gregory. The report which follows is given by Suger in his *Life of Louis the Fat* (see above, pp. 101 *sqq.*). He was himself present at the conference and evidently neither liked the Germans nor approved of their arguments and point of view.

**51. The conference at Châlons sur Marne in regard to the question of investiture (1107).(From Suger's *Life of Louis the Fat*.)**

The pope (Paschal II) having spent some time in Châlons, the representatives of the emperor, men void of humility, hard and rebellious, betook themselves according to agreement to the place of meeting, with much display and a numerous escort, all richly appareled. These envoys were the archbishop of Treves, the bishops of Halberstadt and of Münster, several counts, and Duke Welf, who had his sword carried before him. The latter was a man of great corpulence, truly astonishing in the length and breadth of his surface, and a loud-mouthed fellow withal. These turbulent men seemed to have been dispatched with a view to terrify those they met rather than to discuss matters in a rational way.

We should make a single exception of the archbishop of Treves: he was an agreeable person, of good manners, well educated, a good speaker, and with a touch of French polish. He made a clever speech, saluting the lord pope and the assembly in the name of his master, and offering the emperor's services, saving always the rights of the imperial throne.

Then, reaching the real object of their mission, he continued as follows:

"This is the reason that the emperor has sent us hither.
It is well known that in the time of our predecessors it was
recognized by holy and truly apostolic men, like Gregory the
Great and others, that, according to the law of the empire,
in every election the following method should be observed.
First, the election was brought to the emperor's attention
before it was publicly announced.  Before deciding the
matter measures were taken to learn whether he approved
of the candidate proposed, and his sanction was obtained.
Then, following the canons,[1] the election was proclaimed
in a general meeting, as having been carried out by the
clergy with the ratification of the people and the assent of
the distributor of honors.  The person chosen, freely elected
without simony in the manner above described, should then
present himself to the emperor to be invested with the
regalia by the ring and the staff, to pledge his fidelity and
to do homage.  Nor is it any wonder that there should be
no other way by which one should be able to get possession
of towns, castles, markets, tolls, and other things associated
with the imperial dignity.  If the lord pope will recognize
this, the throne and the Church will be united, to the glory
of God, in a firm and advantageous peace."

To all this the lord pope replied judiciously, by the mouth
of the bishop of Piacenza, a distinguished orator, as follows:
"The Church, redeemed and made free by the precious blood
of Jesus Christ, may in no way become a slave again.  Now
if the Church cannot choose a prelate without the permission of the emperor, she is subject to him, and Christ's death
is made of no avail.  To invest with the ring and the staff,
since these belong to the altar, is to usurp the powers of
God himself.  For a priest to place his hands, sanctified by
the body and blood of the Lord, in the blood-stained hands
of a layman, as a pledge, is to dishonor his order and holy
consecration."

---

[1] See *History of Western Europe*, p. 155.

### III. Formal Settlement of the Question of Investiture

The final compromise between the emperor and pope in regard to investitures, called the "Concordat of Worms," reads as follows :

52. Concordat of Worms (September 23, 1122). (*a*) The pope's agreement.

I, Bishop Calixtus, servant of the servants of God, do grant to thee, beloved son Henry, by the grace of God emperor august of the Romans, permission to hold the elections of the bishops and abbots of the German realm who belong to the kingdom, in thy presence, without simony or show of violence ; with the understanding that, should any discord arise among those concerned, thou, by the counsel and judgment of the metropolitan and the suffragan bishops, shalt give support and aid to the party which appears to have the better case. Moreover the one elected may receive the regalia from thee through the scepter, subject to no exactions ; and he shall perform his lawful duties to thee for them. He who is consecrated in other parts of the empire [i.e. in Burgundy or Italy] shall, within six months and subject to no exactions, receive the regalia from thee through the scepter, and shall perform his lawful duties for them, saving all rights which are known to pertain to the Roman Church. In whatever cases thou shalt make complaint to me and ask my help, I, as my office requires, will furnish thee aid. I grant, moreover, to thee, and to all those who are or have been of thy party during this conflict, a true peace.

In the name of the holy and indivisible Trinity, I, Henry, by the grace of God emperor august of the Romans, for the love of God and of the holy Roman Church and of our lord, Pope Calixtus, and for the cleansing of my soul, do surrender to God and to the holy apostles of God, Peter and Paul, and to the holy Catholic Church, all investiture through the ring and the staff ; and do agree that in all churches throughout my kingdom and empire there shall be canonical elections and free consecration.

(*b*) Edict of Henry V.

All the property and regalia of St. Peter which have been seized upon from the beginning of this conflict until this day and which I now hold I restore to that same holy Roman Church ; and will faithfully aid in the restoration of that which is not in my own hands. The goods also of all other churches and princes and of every one, whether lay or ecclesiastical, which have been lost in the struggle, I will restore, as far as I hold them, according to the counsel of the princes and the behests of justice. I will also faithfully promote the restoration of that which I do not hold.

And I grant a true peace to our master, Pope Calixtus, and to the holy Roman Church, and to all those who are or have been on its side. In matters where the holy Roman Church shall seek assistance, I will faithfully render it, and whensoever it shall appeal to me I will see that justice is done.

All this has been done by the consent and counsel of the princes, whose names are here added : Adalbert, archbishop of Mayence ; F., archbishop of Cologne; H., bishop of Ratisbon; O., bishop of Bamberg ; B., bishop of Speyer ; H., of Augsburg; G., of Utrecht; Ou., of Constance ; E., abbot of Fulda ; Henry, duke ; Frederick, duke ; S., duke ; Bertolf, duke ; Margrave Teipold ; Margrave Engelbert ; Godfrey, count palatine ; Otto, count palatine ; Berengar, count.

I, Frederick, archbishop of Cologne and archchancellor, have ratified this.

## BIBLIOGRAPHY

*A. References.*

**General Outline:** BÉMONT and MONOD, pp. 286–300 ; BRYCE, Chapter X, pp. 153–166; HENDERSON, *Short History of Germany*, pp. 58–75.

**Gregory's Character and Views:** EMERTON, pp. 239–246; TOUT, pp. 124–127.

**Gregory's Letter to William the Conqueror:** COLBY, pp. 36–38.

**Minority of Henry IV:** EMERTON, pp. 232–239 ; HENDERSON, *Germany in the Middle Ages*, pp. 183–189 ; TOUT, pp. 120–124.

**The Struggle between Pope and Emperor:** EMERTON, pp. 246–259; HENDERSON, *Germany in the Middle Ages*, pp. 189–210; TOUT, pp. 127–136.

**Henry IV's Last Years:** EMERTON, pp. 260–266; HENDERSON, *Germany in the Middle Ages*, pp. 211–217 ; TOUT, pp. 136–141.

**Henry V:** EMERTON, pp. 266–269 ; HENDERSON, *Germany in the Middle Ages*, pp. 217–227 ; TOUT, pp. 141–150.

---

MONTALEMBERT, *Monks of the West*, Vols. V and VII.

STEPHENS, *Hildebrand and his Times*. (Epochs of Church History Series.)

GREGOROVIUS, Vol. IV, Book VII, Chapters IV–VII ; Book VIII, Chapters I–II.

MILMAN, Vol. III, Book VII, Chapters I–V ; Vol. IV, Book VIII, Chapters I–III.

HENDERSON, *Select Documents*. Contains some documents not included in the present chapter.

MATHEWS, *Select Mediæval Documents*, pp. 35–68. Examples of the documents in the original Latin.

See also references to FISHER, GREENWOOD, DÖLLINGER, under section *B* in Chapter XII, above.

*B. Additional reading in English.*

# CHAPTER XIV

## THE HOHENSTAUFEN EMPERORS AND THE POPES

### I. The German Cities begin to take a Hand in Politics

The German towns first become conspicuous in political affairs in the twelfth century. We find them participating in the struggles of the time, fighting their bishops or neighboring lords, or even the emperor himself. They begin also to have their own annals, in which the local events are given a prominent place.

No German town was more important than Cologne, with its great commerce and its influential archbishop. The following passages from *The Greater Annals of Cologne*, the first part of which was probably written in the form in which we have it about 1175, give a vivid picture of the pride of the burghers and their dubious relations with the emperor.

**53. How the people of Cologne fought Emperor Henry V in 1114. (From the *Annals of Cologne*.)**

Remembering his dislike for the people of Cologne, the emperor got together a great army of Alemannians and Bavarians and of Saxons, under their duke Lothaire, with the purpose of reducing to shame and insignificance this most flourishing among the cities of France and Germany. He first attempted to take and destroy the fortified town of Deutz, so that by stationing a garrison at this point he could cut off the people of Cologne from receiving anything by water. As soon as the people of Cologne heard of this, they called together under their standard great numbers of their most valiant young men, crossed the

Rhine with a strong force of bowmen, and, drawing themselves up in battle array, awaited the attack of the emperor
with stout hearts. When the emperor observed their
bravery he took counsel with his followers and determined
to draw out the battle until evening, when the enemy, supposing his troops to be worn out, would begin to withdraw
and so be the more easily overcome.

In the meanwhile the cavaliers of both sides had a free
field and rode against one another as if they were taking
part in a spectacle; but when a great cloud of arrows
came showering in from the side of the Cologne people the
knights of the enemy fell dead or wounded. There was in
the emperor's army a corps whose armor was made of horn
and so could not be pierced by iron. When these removed
their armor, however, in order to get a little air, for it was
very hot, they were immediately covered with arrows, and
all but six fell on the spot.

When the emperor saw that the enemy did not give way
but steadily held its own, he decided that he would yield
the field, since the position proved ill chosen, and accordingly retreated that night behind the Wagenburg. The next
day he directed his army against Bonn and Jülich, two fortified places belonging to Cologne, and plundered and burned
everything within reach.

On his return, Archbishop Frederick, Duke Gottfried of
Lorraine, Henry of Zutphen, and Count Theodoric of Are
intercepted him with great bravery, but in vain, for some of
the most distinguished on their side — Count Gerhard of
Jülich and Lambert of Mulenarke — were taken prisoners,
and Eberhard of Gandernol, a valorous man, was killed. But
when Count Frederick of Westphalia and his brother Henry
came up with heavy reënforcements the emperor was forced
to give way and barely escaped the pursuing enemy by
flight.

For the third time the combatants met in a great engagement on the plain of Andernach, nine miles from Cologne,
and here the people of Cologne won the victory, as is their
wont. The emperor had under his standard a very strong

force, footmen as well as cavalry, made up of Saxons, Franconians, Alemannians, and Bavarians, as well as valorous knights from Burgundy. He appeared before Andernach with this mighty host, but proposed to fight the battle with the help of his dukes, for he himself took no part, but awaited the outcome of the conflict at a little distance.

Then appeared the ranks of Cologne in battle array, far fewer in number but nowise inferior in bravery, under the leadership of their duke and archbishop, Frederick, and of the former Duke Henry of Lorraine, Count Theodoric of Are, Count Henry of Kessel, and others equally valorous and well versed in war. In the first onset Duke Henry, with a small detachment, rushed upon a far superior mass of the enemy, but was forced to retreat to his camp.

Then amid a frightful din of trumpets both armies, eager for the conflict, set upon each other, and for a long time the struggle remained undecided. At last the chosen youth of Cologne, in a wild rage, resolved either to conquer or die, and began to slash about them with fearful effect, so that the enemy was compelled to flee. Then Count Theodoric, a brave knight to whom the victory was chiefly due, since he had pressed forward with his followers against the enemy like a lion, began a fearful slaughter on all sides.

Many free men of knightly rank were killed or taken prisoners. Duke Bertolf of Carinthia, a faithful adherent of the emperor, was captured and taken in charge by Count Theodoric himself. None of the leaders on the side of Cologne were either killed or captured except Count Henry of Kessel, an excellent man, who, through the turpitude of his followers, fell under the horses' hoofs and perished. He was honorably buried in Cologne near the cathedral of St. Peter.

## II. Otto of Freising's Account of the Italian Cities

Otto, bishop of Freising and uncle of Frederick Barbarossa, may be safely assigned the highest rank among the historians of the twelfth century. In his great *Chronicle,* or History of the World, he exhibits a good deal of critical ability at times and shows really remarkable philosophical insight in some of his reflections. It would tax the skill of a modern historian better to state the conditions in Italy at the advent of Frederick Barbarossa than does Otto in the passage given below. This is taken from his *Deeds of Frederick,* which he undertook after the completion of his *Chronicle;* but he lived only long enough to present the first four years of his nephew's reign.

The Italian cities already exhibited in the twelfth century, as Otto's account shows, many of the traits which distinguished them in later times. Of their bad habits none is more striking than their readiness to call in foreigners to aid them in settling their perpetual broils. Milan, it will be noted, had already begun the career of conquest, which was later to make her one of the most important states of Italy.

[The Lombards after their arrival in Italy] gradually laid aside their fierce barbarian customs and intermarried with the natives. Thus their children have derived from the mothers' race, and from the character of the country and the climate, something of Roman culture and civilization, and retain the elegance and refinement of Latin speech and manner.

54. The towns of Lombardy. (From Otto of Freising's *Deeds of Frederick.*)

In the government of the cities and in the management of civil affairs they also imitate the skill of the ancient Romans. Furthermore they love liberty so well that, to guard against the abuse of power, they choose to be ruled by the authority of consuls rather than by princes. They are divided into three classes, namely, "captains," vavasors, and the people. To prevent the growth of class pride, the consuls are chosen from each class in turn, and, for fear that they may yield to the lust of power, they are changed nearly every year.

Democratic institutions

Reasons for
the wealth
and inde-
pendence of
the Lombard
towns.

It has come to pass that almost the whole country belongs to the cities, each of which forces the inhabitants of her territory to submit to her sway.   One can hardly find, within a wide circuit, a man of rank or importance who does not recognize the authority of his city. . . .   In order that there shall be no lack of forces for tyrannizing over their neighbors, the cities stoop to bestow the sword-belt and honorable rank upon youths of inferior station, or even upon laborers in despised and mechanical trades, who, among other peoples, are shunned like the pest by those who follow the higher pursuits.   To this practice it is due that they surpass all other cities of the world in riches and power; and the long-continued absence of their ruler across the Alps has further contributed to their independence.

Attitude of
the towns
toward their
emperor.

In one respect they are unmindful of their ancient nobility and betray their barbarian origin ; for, although they boast of living under law, they do not obey the law.   They rarely or never receive their ruler submissively, although it is their duty to show him willing and respectful obedience. They do not obey the decrees that he issues by virtue of his legal powers, unless they are made to feel his authority by the presence of his great army.   Although, in a civilized state, the citizens should submit to law, and only an enemy should be coerced by force, yet they often greet with hostility him whom they ought to receive as their own gracious prince, when he comes to demand his own.

This situation brings double evil on the state.   The prince's attention is occupied with gathering together an army to subdue the townsmen, and the citizens, though forced to obey the prince, waste their resources in the struggle.   The fault, in such a case, lies wholly in the insolence of the people; the prince, who has acted under necessity, should be absolved before God and man.

Greatness of
Milan.

Among all these cities Milan has become the leading one. . . .   It must be regarded as more powerful than any of the others, in the first place, on account of its size and its multitude of brave men, and, secondly, because it has brought the two neighboring cities of Como and Lodi under its sway.

Led on by Fortune's smiles, as is the way of this fleeting world, Milan has become so puffed up with pride that she has dared not only to incur the enmity of all her neighbors, but, fearing not even the majesty of the emperor himself, she has recently courted his anger. How this came about I shall presently relate. But first I wish to say something of the prerogatives of the empire.

There is an ancient custom, which has existed ever since the Roman power devolved upon the Franks and has endured until our own day, that when the kings wish to visit Italy they should send officials of their household ahead to go through the various cities and towns and demand what is due to the royal treasury, called by the inhabitants *fodrum*. The usual result is that when the ruler himself arrives, most of those cities, towns, and castles which have ventured either to refuse to pay the tax altogether, or have paid it only in part, are razed to the ground as a warning to posterity.

*Collection of the fodrum.*

Another right which is said to be derived from ancient custom is that when the emperor enters Italy all magistracies and offices are suspended and all things are regulated according to his will and the decisions of men skilled in the law. Even the Italian judges are said to recognize his supreme jurisdiction, to the extent of assigning to him for his own use and that of his army all that he needs of whatsoever the land produces, scarcely excepting the oxen and seed necessary for the cultivation of the land.

*The emperor's rights.*

The emperor camped for five days, it is said, on the plain of Roncaglia and held an assembly there, to which came princes, consuls, and notables from all the cities. Many matters came up for discussion in consequence of the complaints that were made from this quarter and from that. The bishop of Asti and William, marquis of Monteferrat, — a noble and great man and almost the only baron in Italy that has kept himself independent of the cities, — both made grave complaints of the insolence of the people of Asti, and the marquis complained also of the people of Chieri.

*The emperor holds an assembly in the plain of Roncaglia (December, 1154).*

The consuls from Como and Lodi also gave accounts calculated to draw tears of their long-endured sufferings under

Milan's oppression, and this in the presence of the consuls from Milan, Obert de Orto and Gerard Niger.  The emperor, who wished to visit the region of northern Italy and look into these matters, kept these two consuls with him to conduct him through the Milanese territory and help in the choice of convenient places to camp.  There came also to this assembly ambassadors from the Genoese, who had recently returned laden with the spoils of the Saracens from Spain, where they had conquered the well-known cities of Almeria and Lisbon, famed for the manufacture of silk stuffs.  They brought to the emperor lions, ostriches, parrots, and other valuable gifts.

Frederick's ire aroused against Milan.Frederick, wishing, as we have said, to see something of northern Italy, led his troops forth from Roncaglia and set up his camp in the territory of Milan.  The Milanese consuls aforementioned led him about, however, through arid regions where provisions were neither to be found nor procured at any price, and the emperor was thereby so angered that he determined to turn his arms against Milan, first ordering the consuls to return home.  The whole army, distressed by great floods of rain, was so exasperated by the double discomfort of hunger and bad weather that they did everything in their power to increase the emperor's irritation against the consuls aforesaid.  Another thing which contributed not a little to his indignation was the fact that the Milanese not only refused to permit the towns that Milan had destroyed to be rebuilt, but they insulted his noble and upright character by offering him money to bribe him to condone their villany.

## BIBLIOGRAPHY

*A. References.***General Summary:** ADAMS, *Civilization*, pp. 247–257; MUNRO, pp. 184–202.

**Conditions in Germany under the Hohenstaufens:** BÉMONT and MONOD, pp. 479–487.

**Frederick Barbarossa:** BÉMONT and MONOD, pp. 301–317; BRYCE, Chapter XI, pp. 167–181; EMERTON, pp. 282–312; HENDERSON,

*Germany in the Middle Ages*, pp. 246–290 ; *Short History of Germany*, pp. 78–90 ; TOUT, pp. 245–273.

**Peace of Venice :** HENDERSON, *Historical Documents*, pp. 425–430.

**Henry VI :** BÉMONT and MONOD, pp. 319–321 ; BRYCE, Chapter XIII, first part, pp. 205–207 ; EMERTON, pp. 314–316 ; HENDERSON, *Germany in the Middle Ages*, pp. 291–317 ; *Short History of Germany*, pp. 90–92 ; TOUT, pp. 304–312.

**Innocent III and the Imperial Election :** BÉMONT and MONOD, pp. 321–325 ; EMERTON, pp. 316–332 ; HENDERSON, *Germany in the Middle Ages*, pp. 318–337 ; TOUT, pp. 313–335.

**The Dispute with King John :** COLBY, pp. 72–73 ; HENDERSON, *Historical Documents*, pp. 430–432 ; LEE, pp. 155–164.

**Frederick II :** BÉMONT and MONOD, pp. 325–335 ; BRYCE, Chapter XIII, latter part, pp. 207–211 ; EMERTON, pp. 343–352 ; HENDERSON, *Germany in the Middle Ages*, pp. 337–401 ; *Short History of Germany*, pp. 92–101 ; TOUT, pp. 358–392.

**The Imperial Claims of the Hohenstaufens :** BRYCE, Chapter XII, pp. 182–203.

--------

BALZANI, *The Popes and the Hohenstaufens* (Epochs of Church History).

KINGTON-OLIPHANT, *History of Frederick II*, 2 vols. Rather old, but the most complete account in English.

FISHER, *Mediæval Empire*, referred to above ; also GREGOROVIUS, Vol. IV, Book VII, Chapters III–VII ; Vol. V, Book IX, Chapters I–VI ; MILMAN, Vol. IV, Book VII, Chapters VII and IX ; Book IX, Chapters I–V ; Vol. V, Book X ; NEWMAN, pp. 511–518 ; and MATHEWS, pp. 68–163, for some of the documents.

*B. Additional reading in English.*

# CHAPTER XV

## THE CRUSADES

### I. Pope Urban's Address at Clermont

We have four reports of Urban's address, which were drawn up by those who were apparently actually present at the Council of Clermont. One of the most interesting of these is that given by Robert the Monk, of Rheims, in the opening chapters of his history of the First Crusade. This was written toward twenty-five years after Urban's visit to France and does not claim to give more than a general idea of the pope's arguments.

**55. Urban's speech at Clermont as reported by Robert the Monk.** In the year of our Lord's Incarnation one thousand and ninety-five, a great council was celebrated within the bounds of Gaul, in Auvergne, in the city which is called Clermont. Over this Pope Urban II presided, with the Roman bishops and cardinals. This council was a famous one on account of the concourse of both French and German bishops, and of princes as well. Having arranged the matters relating to the Church, the lord pope went forth into a certain spacious plain, for no building was large enough to hold all the people. The pope then, with sweet and persuasive eloquence, addressed those present in words something like the following, saying :

" Oh, race of Franks, race from across the mountains, race beloved and chosen by God, — as is clear from many of your works, — set apart from all other nations by the situation of your country as well as by your Catholic faith and the honor which you render to the holy Church : to you our discourse is addressed, and for you our exhortations are intended. We wish you to know what a grievous cause has led us to your country, for it is the imminent peril threatening you and all the faithful which has brought us hither.

" From the confines of Jerusalem and from the city of Constantinople a grievous report has gone forth and has repeatedly been brought to our ears ; namely, that a race from the kingdom of the Persians, an accursed race, a race wholly alienated from God, 'a generation that set not their heart aright, and whose spirit was not steadfast with God,' has violently invaded the lands of those Christians and has depopulated them by pillage and fire. They have led away a part of the captives into their own country, and a part they have killed by cruel tortures. They have either destroyed the churches of God or appropriated them for the rites of their own religion. They destroy the altars, after having defiled them with their uncleanness. . . . The kingdom of the Greeks is now dismembered by them and has been deprived of territory so vast in extent that it could not be traversed in two months' time.

" On whom, therefore, is the labor of avenging these wrongs and of recovering this territory incumbent, if not upon you, — you, upon whom, above all other nations, God has conferred remarkable glory in arms, great courage, bodily activity, and strength to humble the heads of those who resist you ? Let the deeds of your ancestors encourage you and incite your minds to manly achievements : — the glory and greatness of King Charlemagne, and of his son Louis, and of your other monarchs, who have destroyed the kingdoms of the Turks and have extended the sway of the holy Church over lands previously pagan. Let the holy sepulcher of our Lord and Saviour, which is possessed by the unclean nations, especially arouse you, and the holy places which are now treated with ignominy and irreverently polluted with the filth of the unclean. Oh, most valiant soldiers and descendants of invincible ancestors, do not degenerate, but recall the valor of your progenitors.

The French
urged to find
an outlet for
excessive
population.

" But if you are hindered by love of children, parents, or wife, remember what the Lord says in the Gospel, ' He that loveth father or mother more than me is not worthy of me.' ' Every one that hath forsaken houses, or brethren, or sisters, or father, or mother, or wife, or children, or lands, for my name's sake, shall receive an hundredfold, and shall inherit everlasting life.' Let none of your possessions retain you, nor solicitude for your family affairs. For this land which you inhabit, shut in on all sides by the seas and surrounded by the mountain peaks, is too narrow for your large population; nor does it abound in wealth; and it furnishes scarcely food enough for its cultivators. Hence it is that you murder and devour one another, that you wage war, and that very many among you perish in intestine strife.

" Let hatred therefore depart from among you, let your quarrels end, let wars cease, and let all dissensions and controversies slumber. Enter upon the road to the Holy Sepulcher; wrest that land from the wicked race, and subject it to yourselves. That land which, as the Scripture says, ' floweth with milk and honey' was given by God into the power of the children of Israel. Jerusalem is the center of the earth ; the land is fruitful above all others, like another paradise of delights. This spot the Redeemer of mankind has made illustrious by his advent, has beautified by his sojourn, has consecrated by his passion, has redeemed by his death, has glorified by his burial.

" This royal city, however, situated at the center of the earth, is now held by the enemies of Christ and is subjected, by those who do not know God, to the worship of the heathen. She longs, therefore, to be liberated and ceases not to implore you to come to her aid. From you especially she asks succor, because, as we have already said, God has conferred upon you above all other nations great glory in arms. Accordingly, undertake this journey eagerly for the remission of your sins, with the assurance of the reward of imperishable glory in the kingdom of heaven."

When Pope Urban had urbanely said these and very many similar things, he so centered in one purpose the desires of all who were present that all cried out, " It is the will of God! It is the will of God!" When the venerable Roman pontiff heard that, with eyes uplifted to heaven, he gave thanks to God and, commanding silence with his hand, said:

" Most beloved brethren, to-day is manifest in you what the Lord says in the Gospel, 'Where two or three are gathered together in my name, there am I in the midst of them'; for unless God had been present in your spirits, all of you would not have uttered the same cry; since, although the cry issued from numerous mouths, yet the origin of the cry was one. Therefore I say to you that God, who implanted this in your breasts, has drawn it forth from you. Let that then be your war cry in combats, because it is given to you by God. When an armed attack is made upon the enemy, let this one cry be raised by all the soldiers of God: 'It is the will of God! It is the will of God!' [*Deus vult! Deus vult!*]

" And we neither command nor advise that the old or feeble, or those incapable of bearing arms, undertake this journey. Nor ought women to set out at all without their husbands, or brothers, or legal guardians. For such are more of a hindrance than aid, more of a burden than an advantage. Let the rich aid the needy; and according to their wealth let them take with them experienced soldiers. The priests and other clerks, whether secular or regular, are not to go without the consent of their bishop; for this journey would profit them nothing if they went without permission. Also, it is not fitting that laymen should enter upon the pilgrimage without the blessing of their priests.

" Whoever, therefore, shall determine upon this holy pilgrimage, and shall make his vow to God to that effect, and shall offer himself to him for sacrifice, as a living victim, holy and acceptable to God, shall wear the sign of the cross of the Lord on his forehead or on his breast. When, indeed, he shall return from his journey, having fulfilled his vow, let him place the cross on his back between his shoulders. Thus shall ye, indeed, by this twofold action, fulfill the precept of the Lord, as he commands in the Gospel, ' He that taketh not his cross, and followeth after me, is not worthy of me.'"

## II. The First Crusade

56. Ekke-
hard of
Aurach on
the opening
of the First
Crusade.

Ekkehard, a well-known German historian (see above, pp. 127 *sqq.*), had completed a history of the world in the year 1101 when he determined to make a pilgrimage to Jerusalem. On his return he entirely rewrote the particulars of his history relating to the First Crusade, and finally issued it as a little separate volume called *Hierosolymita*. His work is regarded by historical scholars as remarkably painstaking and temperate.

After mentioning the capture of Jerusalem by Godfrey of Bouillon and his fellow-crusaders in 1099, Ekkehard continues :

Here I am very anxious to add certain details concerning these military undertakings, which are due to divine rather than human inspiration. This I do for the especial purpose of refuting those imprudent — or, better, impudent — critics, who, bound by prejudice, take it upon themselves with insolent lips to blame this novel enterprise, so necessary to a world that is growing old and nearing its end. They, like the Epicureans, prefer the broad way of pleasure to the narrow way of God's service. To them love of the world is wisdom and those who despise it are fools. . . . I, however, since I trust in the Lord and strive not for present but for future things, would, although only as an idle spectator yet a kindly well-wisher, exalt the glorious men of our time who have overcome the kingdoms of this world and who, for the sake of the blessed Shepherd who sought the hundredth sheep that was lost, have left wife and child, principalities and riches, and have taken their lives in their hands. . . .

[After Urban had aroused the spirits of all by the promise of forgiveness to those who undertook the expedition with single-hearted devotion,] toward one hundred thousand men were appointed to the immediate service of God from Aquitaine and Normandy, England, Scotland, Ireland, Brittany,

Galicia, Gascony, France, Flanders, Lorraine, and from other Christian peoples, whose names I no longer retain. It was truly an army of "crusaders," for they bore the sign of the cross on their garments as a reminder that they should mortify the flesh, and in the hope that they would in this way triumph over the enemies of the cross of Christ, as it had once come to pass in the case of the great Constantine. Thus, through the marvelous and unexampled working of divine dispensation, all these members of Christ, so different in speech, origin, and nationality, were suddenly brought together as one body through their love of Christ.

While they were all under one king, Christ, the several peoples nevertheless were led by their several leaders, namely Godfrey of Lorraine and his brothers Baldwin and Eustace, Robert of Flanders, Robert of Normandy, Count Regimund of St. Gilles, Hugh, brother of King Philip of France, and other warriors of similar energy, rank, and bravery. Over all of these the above-mentioned pope placed Bishop Hademar, a man of venerable holiness and wisdom. To him the pope granted the right to exercise in his stead the power transmitted by St. Peter to the Roman see of binding and loosing. . . .

The West Franks were easily induced to leave their fields, since France had, during several years, been terribly visited now by civil war, now by famine, and again by sickness. . . . Among the other nations, the common people, as well as those of higher rank, related that, aside from the apostolic summons, they had in some instances been called to the land of promise by certain prophets who had appeared among them, or through heavenly signs and revelations. Others confessed that they had been induced to pledge themselves by some misfortune. A great part of them started forth with wife and child and laden with their entire household equipment.

The summons, however, failed altogether to reach the East Franks, Saxons, Thuringians, Bavarians, and Alemannians. This was due especially to the division between the civil government and the priesthood, which from the time of Pope Alexander [II] to the present day has, alas, made us as

The Germans at first regard the crusaders as madmen.

hated and offensive to the Romans as the Romans are to us. So it came about that almost the whole German people were, at the beginning of the expedition, quite unacquainted with the reasons for it. Consequently the many legions of horsemen who passed through their land, the hosts of people on foot, the crowds of country people, women and children, were viewed by them with contempt as persons who had altogether lost their wits.

Those bound for the Holy Land seemed to them to be leaving the land of their birth and sacrificing what they already had for a vain hope. The promised land offered no certainty but danger, yet they deserted their own possessions in a greedy struggle for those of others. Nevertheless, although our people are far more arrogant than others, the fury of the Teutons finally gave way in view of the divine mercy, and after they had thoroughly discussed the matter with the multitude of pilgrims, they too inclined their hearts.

Prodigies
announce the
coming
crusade.

Moreover the signs in the sun and the wonders which appeared, both in the air and on the earth, aroused many who had previously been indifferent. It seems to us useful to interweave an account of a few of these signs, although it would carry us too far to enumerate them all. For example, we beheld a comet on the 7th of October to the south, and its brilliancy slanting down seemed like a sword. . . . A few years ago a priest of honorable reputation, by the name of Suigger, about the ninth hour of the day beheld two knights, who met one another in the air and fought long, until one, who carried a great cross with which he struck the other, finally overcame his enemy. . . .

Many, moreover, displayed, either on their clothing, or upon their forehead, or elsewhere on their body, the sign of the cross, which had been divinely imprinted, and they believed themselves on this account to have been destined to the service of God. Others likewise were induced, through some sudden change of spirit or some nocturnal vision, to sell all their property and possessions and to sew the sign of mortification on their mantles. . . .

While through these and similar signs the whole creation seemed to offer its services to the Creator, the watchful enemy, who takes occasion when others sleep to sow his tares amongst the good seed, raised up also false prophets and mixed false brethren and degraded women among the Lord's host under the appearance of religion. In this way the armies of Christ were defiled not only through hypocrisy and lies but through shameless uncleanness, so that the prophecy of the Good Shepherd might be fulfilled, that even the elect may be led astray.

Bad men and women join the crusaders.

Among the sources for the First Crusade there is a history of the eastern emperor, Alexis, written by his daughter, Anna Comnena. After speaking of the kindly but sagacious way in which her father treated the inconvenient and often disorderly troops of crusaders when they reached Constantinople, she gives the following example of their bad manners.

57. A Greek princess describes the bad manners of a crusading prince.

When the Franks had all come together and had taken an oath to the emperor, there was one count who had the boldness to sit down upon the throne. The emperor, well knowing the pride of the Latins, kept silent, but Baldwin approached the Frankish count and taking him by the hand said, "You ought not to sit there; that is an honor which the emperor permits to no one. Now that you are in this country, why do you not observe its customs?" The insolent count made no reply to Baldwin, but said in his barbarous language, as if talking to himself, "This must be a rude fellow who would alone remain seated when so many brave warriors are standing up." Alexis noted the movement of the man's lips and called an interpreter in order to learn what he had said; but when the interpreter had told him he did not complain to the Franks, although he did not forget the matter.

When the counts came to take leave of the emperor he retained this haughty knight and asked him who he was.

"I am a Frank," he replied, " of the most high and ancient nobility. I know but one thing, and that is that there is in my country a church built at the crossroads where all those betake themselves who hope to show their valor in single combat, and there make their prayer to God while they await an enemy; I remained there a long time without anybody daring to measure swords with me."

Alexis was on his guard against accepting this challenge. " If you then waited without being able to show your bravery," he said to him, "you now have a chance to fight; and if I may give you a word of advice, it will be not to put yourself either at the head nor rear of the army but in the middle. The experience which I have had of the way in which the Turks make war has convinced me that that is the best place." [1]

## III. A GLIMPSE OF THE COURT OF THE EASTERN EMPEROR

When the crusaders reached Constantinople they saw about them evidences of an elaborate civilization, of which they could have had little conception in their dreary and uncomfortable castles. It is, no doubt, in the general broadening effects of travel that the chief influence of the crusades on the western peoples is to be found. A hundred and fifty years before the First Crusade, when western Europe was still in the midst of the gloomiest period of the early Middle Ages, Liutprand, an historian of the age of Otto the Great, visited Constantinople. He gives the following account of his reception as ambassador of Berengar, king of Italy.

[1] Anna remarks later in her history with satisfaction that the insolent knight was killed. An eminent scholar believes that he was probably no less a person than Count Robert of Paris. This is but one instance among many which served to arouse hostility between the emperor and the crusaders.

Adjoining the imperial palace in Constantinople there is a hall of extraordinary size and beauty. . . . The Emperor Constantine [VII] had this hall arranged in the following manner for the reception of the recently arrived Spanish ambassador, as well as of Liutfrid [ambassador of Otto I] and myself. In front of the emperor's throne stood a tree of gilded iron, whose branches were filled with birds of various kinds, made of iron and gilded, which gave forth the different sorts of birds' notes. The throne itself was so cunningly constructed that at one instant it looked low, the next, higher, and a moment later had risen to a great elevation. It was guarded on either side by huge lions, I know not whether of metal or wood, but covered with gold, which lashed their tails on the floor and, with open mouth and moving tongue, roared aloud.

58. Liut-prand's account of his reception in Constantinople (949).

In this hall, and accompanied by two eunuchs, I was brought before the emperor. At my entrance the lions roared and the birds sang, each after his kind; but I was neither frightened nor even astonished, since I had taken pains to learn beforehand about these things from those who knew about them. When I raised my head, after prostrating myself before the emperor for the third time, I beheld him, whom before I had seen seated at a moderate height above me, elevated almost to the roof of the hall and clad in different garments. How this was managed I do not know, unless by means of something like the screw of a press. All this time the emperor spoke no word; indeed, even had he wished to do so, it would have been undignified from so great a height. He inquired, however, through his chamberlain, after Berengar's health and pursuits. After I had replied in a fitting manner I retired, at a sign from the interpreter, and was conducted to the inn where quarters had been assigned me.

[Liutprand then tells of his humiliation on discovering that the other ambassadors had brought costly gifts to the emperor from their masters, while the parsimonious Berengar had sent nothing but a letter, " and that full of lies ! " So he determined to give the emperor the presents which his stepfather had sent, as if they had been sent by the Italian king, "piecing out the small gift as well as I could with fine words."]

This plan having accordingly been carried out, the emperor, at the end of three days, sent for me to come to the palace, conversed with me with his own mouth, invited me to dine with him, and, after the meal, honored me and my following with appropriate gifts. . . .

In a hall of extraordinary height and magnificence nineteen tables are spread on the anniversary of the Incarnation of our Lord Jesus Christ; around these the emperor and his guests, instead of sitting as usual, recline to eat. On this day, moreover, only golden dishes are used instead of the usual silver ones. After dinner fruit was served in three golden vessels of such enormous weight that they could not be carried by men but were brought in on little carts decked with purple coverings. They were placed on the table in the following manner. Through openings in the ceiling three ropes of gilded leather were let down, on the ends of which were fastened golden rings; these were attached to hooks rising from the golden vessels, which were then lifted on to the table by means of a windlass above the ceiling, while four or more men lent their aid from below. Later they were removed in the same way.

It would take too long to describe all the performances which followed, but I must mention one of them, for it was quite too wonderful. There was a man who carried on his forehead, without touching it with his hands, a pole at least twenty-four feet long, on which, an ell from the top, a crosspiece two ells long was fastened. Then two little boys, naked except for loin cloths, were brought in. They climbed up the pole, performed all sorts of gymnastic feats upon it, and came down again, headforemost, without the pole moving any more than if it had been rooted in the ground.

Then after one boy had climbed down, the other one stayed up alone and went through his tricks, which threw me into still greater astonishment. For as long as they both were performing on the pole the thing seemed, after a fashion, explicable, since by their equal weight, though to be sure with marvelous skill, they had kept the pole perpendicular. That one by himself, however, should be able to preserve the equilibrium so as to perform his antics and come down again unhurt, — this threw me into such a state of wonder that my amazement attracted the attention of the emperor. He called an interpreter and had him ask me which I admired the more, the boy, who had managed his movements with such care as to leave the pole unmoved; or the man, who had held it so skillfully on his forehead that neither the boy's weight nor his movements had caused the pole to swerve one whit from its position. And when I said I knew not which was most to be admired, the emperor laughed and said that he did not know either.

## BIBLIOGRAPHY

**General Account**: ADAMS, *Civilization*, pp. 258–270; MASSON, pp. 22–33; MUNRO, pp. 106–117.

**The Eastern Situation**: BÉMONT and MONOD, pp. 336–347; GIBBON, Vol. VI, Chapter LVII, pp. 224–258; MUNRO, pp. 86–104; TOUT, pp. 151–176.

**The First Crusade**: BÉMONT and MONOD, pp. 348–356; EMERTON, pp. 357–366; GIBBON, Vol. VI, Chapter LVIII, pp. 259–312; TOUT, pp. 177–184.

**The Kingdom of Jerusalem**: BÉMONT and MONOD, pp. 359–363; EMERTON, pp. 366–374; GIBBON, Vol. VI, Chapter LVIII, pp. 312–321; TOUT, pp. 184–191.

**The Second Crusade**: BÉMONT and MONOD, pp. 356–359; EMERTON, pp. 374–377; GIBBON, Vol. VI, Chapter LIX, pp. 322–347; TOUT, pp. 191–197.

**Documents**: HENDERSON, *Historical Documents*, pp. 333–336; *Translations and Reprints*, Vol. I, No. 2, p. 13; Vol. I, No. 4, pp. 12–16.

**The Third Crusade**: BÉMONT and MONOD, pp. 363–366; EMERTON, pp. 377–379; GIBBON, Vol. VI, Chapter LIX, pp. 347 354; TOUT, pp. 295–304.

**Documents**: COLBY, pp. 68–70; HENDERSON, p. 135; *Translations and Reprints*, Vol. I, No. 2, pp. 13–15; Vol. I, No. 4, pp. 16–20.

**The Fourth Crusade**: BÉMONT and MONOD, pp. 366–368; EMERTON, pp. 379–383; TOUT, pp. 342–355.

Contemporary Records : *Translations and Reprints*, Vol. III, No. 1, pp. 2–20.

The Last Crusades : BÉMONT and MONOD, pp. 368–374 ; EMERTON, pp. 383–388 ; GIBBON, Vol. VI, Chapter LIX, pp. 354–365 ; TOUT, pp. 450–463.

Documents : HENDERSON, pp. 337–344 ; *Translations and Reprints*, Vol. I, No. 2, pp. 16–19 ; Vol. I, No. 4, pp. 20–34.

Results of the Crusades : ADAMS, pp. 270–276 ; EMERTON, pp. 388–397 ; HENDERSON, *Short History of Germany*, pp. 102–108 ; MUNRO, pp. 117–121.

*B. Additional reading in English.*

ARCHER and KINGSFORD, *The Crusades* (Story of the Nations). Perhaps the best short treatment in English.

CONDOR, *The Latin Kingdom of Jerusalem* (1099–1291), London, 1897.

OMAN, *The Byzantine Empire.*

*Essays on the Crusades* by MUNRO, PRUTZ, and DIEHL, published by the " International Quarterly," New York. Very interesting and useful.

OMAN, *A History of the Art of War*, Vol. II, " The Middle Ages," 1898. Contains a good sketch of the military operations of the crusaders.

AMEER ALI, *A Short History of the Saracens.*

MILMAN, *History of Latin Christianity*, Book VII, Chapter VI, for the First Crusade ; Book VII, Chapters IV and VI, last part, for the Second ; Book IX, Chapter VII, for the Third and Fourth ; Book X, Chapter III, for that of Frederick II. For the later period of the crusades, see LANE-POOLE, *Saladin and the Fall of the Kingdom of Jerusalem* (Heroes of the Nations), 1898, and PEARS, *The Fall of Constantinople* (1202–1204).

Sources in English.

For an account of the sources of the first crusade, see SYBEL, *The History and Literature of the Crusades*, edited by Lady Duff Gordon.

Some of the sources may be found translated into English in the *Chronicles of the Crusades* in the Bohn Library, — for example, an account of the Third Crusade by RICHARD OF DEVIZES, and JOINVILLE'S famous Life of St. Louis (see above, p. 106). Material is also available in ARCHER, *The Crusade of Richard I* (English History from Contemporary Sources).

The Chronicles of ROGER OF HOVEDEN, ROGER OF WENDOVER, MATTHEW OF PARIS, and that ascribed to MATTHEW OF WESTMINSTER all contain information relating to the crusades and are all to be had in the Bohn Library.

# CHAPTER XVI

## THE MEDIÆVAL CHURCH AT ITS HEIGHT

### I. THE SEVEN SACRAMENTS

We have drawn up in the briefest form a statement of the truth concerning the seven sacraments, so that the Armenians, now and in future generations, may more easily be instructed therein.

59. An account of the seven sacraments, written for the Armenians by Pope Eugene IV (1438).

There are seven sacraments under the new law: that is to say, baptism, confirmation, the mass, penance, extreme unction, ordination, and matrimony. These differ essentially from the sacraments of the old law; for the latter do not confer grace, but only typify that grace which can be given by the passion of Christ alone. But these our sacraments both contain grace and confer it upon all who receive them worthily.

The first five sacraments are intended to secure the spiritual perfection of every man individually; the two last are ordained for the governance and increase of the Church. For through baptism we are born again of the spirit; through confirmation we grow in grace and are strengthened in the faith; and when we have been born again and strengthened we are fed by the divine food of the mass; but if, through sin, we bring sickness upon our souls, we are made spiritually whole by penance; and by extreme unction we are healed, both spiritually and corporeally, according as our souls have need; by ordination the Church is governed and multiplied spiritually; by matrimony it is materially increased.

To effect these sacraments three things are necessary: the things [or symbols], that is, the "material"; the words, that is, the "form"; and the person of the "ministrant," who administers the sacrament with the intention of carrying out what the Church effects through him. If any of these things be lacking, the sacrament is not accomplished.

The indelible characters.

Three of these sacraments — baptism, confirmation, and ordination — impress indelibly upon the soul a character, a certain spiritual sign, distinct from all others; so they are not repeated for the same person. The other four do not imprint a character upon the soul, and admit of repetition.

Baptism.

Holy baptism holds the first place among all the sacraments because it is the gate of spiritual life; for by it we are made members of Christ and of the body of the Church. Since through the first man death entered into the world, unless we are born again of water, and of the spirit, we cannot, so saith Truth, enter into the kingdom of heaven. The material of this sacrament is water, real and natural — it matters nothing whether it be cold or warm. Now the form is: "I baptize thee in the name of the Father, and of the Son, and of the Holy Ghost." . . .[1]

The ministrant of this sacrament is the priest, for baptism belongs to his office. But in case of necessity not only a priest or deacon may baptize, but a layman or a woman — nay, even a pagan or a heretic, provided he use the form of the Church and intend to do what the Church effects. The efficacy of this sacrament is the remission of all sin, original sin and actual, and of all penalties incurred through this guilt. Therefore no satisfaction for past sin should be imposed on those who are baptized; but if they die before they commit any sin, they shall straightway attain the kingdom of heaven and the sight of God.

Confirmation.

The second sacrament is confirmation. The material is the chrism made from oil, which signifies purity of conscience, and from balsam, which signifies the odor of fair fame; and it must be blessed by the bishop. The form is: "I sign thee with the sign of the cross and confirm thee with the chrism of salvation. in the name of the Father, and of the

---

[1] Certain variations in the words used do not necessarily vitiate the sacrament.

Son, and of the Holy Ghost." The proper ministrant of this sacrament is the bishop. . . .

In this sacrament the Holy Ghost is given to strengthen us, as it was given to the apostles on the day of Pentecost, that the Christian may confess boldly the name of Christ. And therefore he is confirmed upon the brow, the seat of shame, that he may never blush to confess the name of Christ and especially his cross, which is a stumbling-block to the Jews and foolishness to the Gentiles, according to the apostle. Therefore he is signed with the sign of the cross.

The third sacrament is the eucharist. The material is wheaten bread and wine of the grape, which before consecration should be mixed very sparingly with water; because, according to the testimony of the holy fathers and doctors of the Church set forth in former times in disputation, it is believed that the Lord himself instituted this sacrament with wine mixed with water, and also because this corresponds with the accounts of our Lord's passion. For the holy Pope Alexander, fifth from the blessed Peter, says, " In the offerings of sacred things made to God during the solemnization of the mass, only bread and wine mixed with water are offered up. Neither wine alone nor water alone may be offered up in the cup of the Lord, but both mixed, since it is written that both blood and water flowed from Christ's side." . . . *The holy eucharist.*

The form of this sacrament is furnished by the words of the Saviour when he instituted it, and the priest, speaking in the person of Christ, consummates this sacrament. By virtue of these words, the substance of the bread is turned into the body of Christ and the substance of the wine into his blood. This is accomplished in such wise that the whole Christ is altogether present under the semblance of the bread and altogether under the semblance of the wine. Moreover, after the consecrated host and the consecrated wine have been divided, the whole Christ is present in any part of them. The benefit effected by this sacrament in the souls of those who receive it worthily is the union of man with Christ. And since, through grace, man *Transubstantiation of the bread and the wine.*

is made one body with Christ and united in his members, it follows that through this sacrament grace is increased in those who partake of it worthily. Every effect of material food and drink upon the physical life, in nourishment, growth, and pleasure, is wrought by this sacrament for the spiritual life. By it we recall the beloved memory of our Saviour; by it we are withheld from evil, and strengthened in good, and go forward to renewed growth in virtues and graces.

Penance and its three parts.

The fourth sacrament is penance. The material, as we may say, consists in the acts of penitence, which are divided into three parts. The first of these is contrition of the heart, wherein the sinner must grieve for the sins he has committed, with the resolve to commit no further sins. Second comes confession with the mouth, to which it pertains that the sinner should make confession to his priest of all the sins he holds in his memory. The third is satisfaction for sins according to the judgment of the priest, and this is made chiefly by prayer, fasting, and almsgiving. The form of this sacrament consists in the words of absolution which the priest speaks when he says, " I absolve thee," etc. ; and the minister of this sacrament is the priest, who has authority to absolve either regularly or by the commission of a superior. The benefit of this sacrament is absolution from sins.

Extreme unction.

The fifth sacrament is extreme unction, and the material is oil of the olive, blessed by a bishop. This sacrament shall not be given to any except the sick who are in fear of death. They shall be anointed in the following places : the eyes on account of the sight, the ears on account of the hearing, the nostrils on account of smell, the mouth on account of taste and speech, the hands on account of touch, the feet on account of walking, and the loins as the seat of pleasure. . . . The minister of this sacrament is a priest. The benefit is even the healing of the mind and, so far as is expedient, of the body also.

Ordination.

The sixth sacrament is ordination. The material for the priesthood is the cup with the wine, and the paten with the bread ; for the deaconate, the books of the Gospel ; for the subdeaconate, an empty cup placed upon an empty paten; and in like manner, other offices are conferred by giving to the candidates those things which pertain to their secular ministrations. The form for priests is this : "Receive the power to offer sacrifice in the Church for the living and the dead, in the name of the Father, and of the Son, and of the Holy Ghost." And so for each order the proper form shall be used, as fully stated in the Roman pontifical. The regular minister of this sacrament is a bishop; the benefit, growth in grace, to the end that whosoever is ordained may be a worthy minister.

The seventh sacrament is matrimony, the type of the union of Christ and the Church, according to the apostle, who saith, "This is a great mystery; but I speak concerning Christ and the church." The efficient cause of marriage is regularly the mutual consent uttered aloud on the spot. These advantages are to be ascribed to marriage : first, the begetting of children and their bringing up in the worship of the Lord; secondly, the fidelity that husband and wife should each maintain toward the other; thirdly, the indissoluble character of marriage, for this typifies the indissoluble union of Christ and the Church. Although for the cause of adultery separation is permissible, for no other cause may marriage be infringed, since the bond of marriage once legitimately contracted is perpetual.

*Matrimony*

## II. Tale illustrating the Miraculous Power of the Sacraments

There were many tales current in the twelfth and thirteenth centuries which were used by preachers and writers to show the wondrous workings of the sacraments. The following story is taken from the anecdotes or apologues of Stephen of Bourbon, a Dominican inquisitor (d. 1261), a man of wide experience and much sagacity.

60. Bees
construct a
church for
the host.
(From
Stephen of
*Bourbon.*)

I have heard that a certain rustic, wishing to become wealthy and having many hives of bees, asked certain evil men how he could get rich and increase the number of his bees. He was told by some one that if he retained the sacred host on Easter and placed it in some one of his hives, he would entice away all of his neighbor's bees, which, leaving their own hives, would come to the place where the body of our Lord was and there would make honey. So he did this.

Then all the bees came to the hive where the body of Christ was, and just as if they felt sorrow for the irreverence done to it, by their labor they began to construct a little church and to erect foundations, and bases, and columns, and an altar; then with the greatest reverence they placed the body of our Lord upon the altar. And within their little beehive they formed the little church with wonderful and most beautiful workmanship. The bees of the vicinity, leaving their hives, came to that one; and over that work they sang in their own manner certain wonderful melodies like hymns.

The rustic, hearing this, marveled. But waiting until the fitting time for collecting the honey, he found nothing in his hives. Finding himself impoverished through the means by which he had expected to be enriched, he went to the hive where he had placed the host, and where he saw the bees had come together. But when he approached, just as if they wished to vindicate the insult to our Saviour, the bees rushed upon the rustic and stung him so severely that he escaped with difficulty and in great agony. Going to the priest, he related all that he had done, and what the bees had done.

The priest, by the advice of the bishop, collected his parishioners and made a procession to that place. Then the bees, leaving the hive, rose in the air, making sweet melody. Raising the hive, they found inside the noble structure of that little church and the body of our Lord placed upon the altar. Then, returning thanks, they bore to their own church that little church of the bees, constructed with such skill and elegance, and placed it on the altar.

By this deed those who do not reverence, but offer insult instead, to the sacred body of Christ, or the sacred place where it is, ought to be put to great confusion.

### III. How the Churches and Monasteries were Supported

The following statement indicates how numerous and complicated were the sources of revenue which even a parish church might claim as its rightful means of support.

I, Hugh, dean of Gyé, hereby inform the present generation, and those to come, that, according as I have heard and learned from my predecessors of blessed memory and have myself seen in my time, the church of St. Mary of Châtillon in my parish of Gyé possesses the following revenue: namely, one sixth of the tithe of grain and wine and one half of the offerings, bequests and alms, — provided they are paid in money, — and one half of the small tithe.[1] From Neuilly, one eighteenth of the tithe of grain, one sixth of the tithe of wine, and one half of the small tithes, offerings, and legacies. From C——, on behalf of the allodial lands, two parts of the tithe of grain, one sixth of the tithe of wine, one half of the legacies and offerings, and the whole of the small tithe, except twelve pence, which the parish priest by virtue of his office has been wont to receive as fish money. From the monastery of C——, two parts of the tithe of grain and wine and of the small tithes, one third of the offerings at Christmas, Pentecost, and All Saints. Of the other offerings, however, made there during the year the church of Châtillon receives nothing whatever. Of the legacies up-

61. The revenue of a parish church (1237).

---

[1] That is, the tithe of other than the staple crops, — for example, of pigs, lambs, flax, etc.

ward of twelve pence it receives one third, but of those below that sum it receives by custom nothing at all.

Describing with pride the foundation (1089) and history of his monastery of Zwifalt in Swabia, the monk Ortlieb gives the following account of "our family" (*nostra familia*).

62. Ortlieb's account of those who lived under the jurisdiction of the monastery of Zwifalt (1135).

Now this our monastery church possesses many persons who, because of the oppression of their former lords and of the burdens which weighed them down, have come under our jurisdiction in order to have peace. Some of these are tillers of the soil, some vinedressers; others are bakers, cobblers, artisans, merchants, and those who follow various trades and callings. Some of those who pay their dues to the monastery are on a different footing from others. Even among those who belong directly to the monastery some pay money yearly, while others contribute wax towards making a certain great candle. What all these pay in dues to the monastery is all handed over to the custodian of the church.

Some of those under our jurisdiction belong to the people's church across the river, some to St. Stephen's church at Tigerfeld, or to the church of St. Blasius at Derendingen, or to other churches under our control. While these pay their dues to the particular church to which they are known to belong, they are all, nevertheless, like the others, numbered among the members of our monastery family, and they should obey our decrees, no matter if they pay dues to some other church or monastery.

And it is to be noted that the people of Tigerfeld and those who pay their dues to that church are to be judged, at appointed times, by the advocate of that place in the presence of the provost of our monastery. If any one should be convicted of any rash act, or of failure to pay his dues, one part of the fine exacted shall go to the advocate and two parts to our community. . . .

Among our men some owe service of this kind, namely: when the lord abbot, prior, provost, or others among the brethren would travel anywhither, these men with their horses, do accompany the brethren and minister unto them obediently. And in order that this service may be rightfully required of them they are granted certain benefices. They assuredly rejoice to be honored by this distinction because they have the right to have under them men we call clients, or *ministeriales*. Yet in spite of this, no man of ours has ever become so perverse or haughty that he presumed to ride with us in military array, or refused to carry the wallet of any of our monks upon his pack horse. The founders of our monastery did not intend to give us such men, and we have not consented to receive any one who might prove troublesome to us or to our successors.

The retainers of the monastery required to demean themselves humbly.

## IV. Tale illustrating the Mediæval Attitude towards Heretics

The popular horror in which heresy was held in the twelfth and thirteenth centuries is well shown in the following account.

From the lips of the same brother Elias, a venerable man, I learned that when certain heretics were scattering the virulent seeds of error in parts of Burgundy, both the Preaching Friars and the Minorites drew the two-edged sword of God's word against these same heretics, opposing them valiantly, until they were finally taken by the magistrate of the district. He sent them to the stake, as they merited, in order that these workers of iniquity should perish in their wickedness as a wholesome lesson to others.

63. The body of a burned heretic turns into toads. (From *Luke, bishop of Tuy,* thirteenth century.)

Quantities of wood having been supplied in plenty to feed the flames, suddenly a toad of wonderful size appeared, and without being driven, betook itself of its own accord into the midst of the flames. One of the heretics, who was reported to be their bishop, had fallen on his back in the fire. The toad took his place on this man's face and in the sight of all ate out the heretic's tongue.

By the next day his whole body, except his bones, had been turned into disgusting toads, which could not be counted for their great number. The inhabitants, seeing the miracle, glorified God and praised him in his servants, the Preaching Friars, because the Lord had, in his mercy, delivered them from the horror of such pollution.

Consummate guilt of heresy.

God omnipotent surely wished to show through the most unseemly and filthiest of animals, how foul and infamous are the teachings of heretics, so that all might thereafter carefully shun the heretic as they would the poisonous toad. Just as among four-footed creatures the toad is held the foulest, so the teachings of the heretic are more debased and filthy than those of any other religious sect. The blindness of heresy justifies the perfidy of the Jews. Its pollution makes the madness of the Mohammedans a pure thing in contrast. The licentiousness of the heretics would leave Sodom and Gomorrah stainless. What is held most enormous in crime becomes most holy when compared with the shame and ignominy of heresy. Therefore, dear Christian, flee this unspeakable evil, in comparison with which all other crimes are as trifles.

## BIBLIOGRAPHY

A. References.

Unfortunately the Church has received such slight attention in the manuals most commonly used that there is little in them to supplement the account given in Chapter XVI of the *History of Western Europe*.

**General Review :** BÉMONT and MONOD, pp. 488–502 ; EMERTON, pp. 541–555, — especially good for the development of the canon law ; MUNRO, pp. 169–175.

Interesting examples of the formulæ for excommunication and the interdict will be found in *Translations and Reprints*, Vol. IV, No. 4, pp. 22–33.

B. Additional reading in English.

CUTTS, *Parish Priests and their People*, 1898.

LEA, *Studies in Church History*. Contains essays on " The Rise of Temporal Power," " Benefit of Clergy," and a very full account of " Excommunication."

MAITLAND, S. M., *The Dark Ages*. Essays written some sixty years ago with a view of defending mediæval thought and institutions from the aspersions of certain Protestant writers. The gloomier aspects of the subject will be found in :

LEA, *History of the Inquisition in the Middle Ages*, Vol. I, Chapter I. A startling arraignment of the vices of the mediæval clergy, which makes no claim to describe the normal and salutary activities of the Church.

JESSOPP, *The Coming of the Friars*. Contains several essays on the Church.

Somewhat more systematic accounts of the organization and beliefs of the Church will be found in the histories of the Church, especially in MILMAN, Book XIV, Chapters I–III, and in NEWMAN, pp. 449–457.

# CHAPTER XVII

## HERESY AND THE FRIARS

### I. The Waldensian and Albigensian Heretics

**64. Waldo of Lyons, the founder of the Waldensians. (From an anonymous chronicle written about 1218.)**

And during the same year, that is the 1173d since the Lord's Incarnation, there was at Lyons in France a certain citizen, Waldo by name, who had made himself much money by wicked usury. One Sunday, when he had joined a crowd which he saw gathered around a troubadour, he was smitten by his words and, taking him to his house, he took care to hear him at length. The passage he was reciting was how the holy Alexis died a blessed death in his father's house. When morning had come the prudent citizen hurried to the schools of theology to seek counsel for his soul, and when he was taught many ways of going to God, he asked the master what way was more certain and more perfect than all others. The master answered him with this text: "If thou wilt be perfect, go and sell all that thou hast," etc.

Then Waldo went to his wife and gave her the choice of keeping his personal property or his real estate, namely, what he had in ponds, groves and fields, houses, rents, vineyards, mills, and fishing rights. She was much displeased at having to make this choice, but she kept the real estate. From his personal property he made restitution to those whom he had treated unjustly; a great part of it he gave to his two little daughters, who, without their mother's knowledge, he placed in the convent of Font Evrard; but the greatest part of his money he spent for the poor. A very great famine was then oppressing France and Germany. The prudent citizen, Waldo, gave bread, with vegetables and meat, to every one who came to him for three days in every week from Pentecost to the feast of St. Peter's bonds.

At the Assumption of the blessed Virgin, casting some money among the village poor, he cried, "No man can serve two masters, God and mammon." Then his fellow-citizens ran up, thinking he had lost his mind. But going on to a higher place, he said: "My fellow-citizens and friends, I am not insane, as you think, but I am avenging myself on my enemies, who made me a slave, so that I was always more careful of money than of God, and served the creature rather than the Creator. I know that many will blame me that I act thus openly. But I do it both on my own account and on yours; on my own, so that those who see me henceforth possessing any money may say that I am mad, and on yours, that you may learn to place hope in God and not in riches."

On the next day, coming from the church, he asked a certain citizen, once his comrade, to give him something to eat, for God's sake. His friend, leading him to his house, said, "I will give you whatever you need as long as I live." When this came to the ears of his wife, she was not a little troubled, and as though she had lost her mind, she ran to the archbishop of the city and implored him not to let her husband beg bread from any one but her. This moved all present to tears.

[Waldo was accordingly conducted into the presence of the bishop.] And the woman, seizing her husband by the coat, said, "Is it not better, husband, that I should redeem my sins by giving you alms than that strangers should do so?" And from that time he was not allowed to take food from any one in that city except from his wife.

An experienced inquisitor thus describes the Albigenses:

65. Description of the Albigenses (From the *Inquisitor's Guide* of Bernard of Gui, early fourteenth century.)

It would take too long to describe in detail the manner in which these same Manichæan heretics preach and teach their followers, but it must be briefly considered here.

In the first place, they usually say of themselves that they are good Christians, who do not swear, or lie, or speak evil of others; that they do not kill any man or animal, nor anything having the breath of life, and that they hold the faith of the Lord Jesus Christ and his gospel as Christ and his apostles taught. They assert that they occupy the place of the apostles, and that, on account of the above-mentioned things, they of the Roman Church, namely the prelates, clerks, and monks, and especially the inquisitors of heresy, persecute them and call them heretics, although they are good men and good Christians, and that they are persecuted just as Christ and his apostles were by the Pharisees.

Moreover they talk to the laity of the evil lives of the clerks and prelates of the Roman Church, pointing out and setting forth their pride, cupidity, avarice, and uncleanness of life, and such other evils as they know. They invoke, with their own interpretation and according to their abilities, the authority of the Gospels and the Epistles against the condition of the prelates, churchmen, and monks, whom they call Pharisees and false prophets, who say, but do not.

Then they attack and vituperate, in turn, all the sacraments of the Church, especially the sacrament of the eucharist. . . .

Of baptism, they assert that water is material and corruptible, and is therefore the creation of the evil power and cannot sanctify the soul, but that the churchmen sell this water out of avarice, just as they sell earth for the burial of the dead, and oil to the sick when they anoint them, and as they sell the confession of sins as made to the priests.

Albigenses deny the efficacy of the sacraments in polluted hands.

Hence they claim that confession made to the priests of the Roman Church is useless, and that, since the priests may be sinners, they cannot loose nor bind, and, being unclean themselves, cannot make others clean. They assert, moreover, that the cross of Christ should not be adored or venerated, because, as they urge, no one would venerate or adore the gallows upon which a father, relative, or friend had been hung. They urge, further, that they who adore the cross ought, for similar reasons, to worship all thorns and lances, because as Christ's body was on the cross during the passion, so was the crown of thorns on his head and the soldier's lance in his side. They proclaim many other scandalous things in regard to the sacraments.

Moreover they read from the Gospels and the Epistles in the vulgar tongue, applying and expounding them in their favor and against the condition of the Roman Church in a manner which it would take too long to describe in detail; but all that relates to this subject may be read more fully in the books they have written and infected, and may be learned from the confessions of such of their followers as have been converted.

## II. Attitude of the Civil Government toward Heretics

The following document is a good example of the cordial manner in which the temporal rulers coöperated with the Church in the detection and punishment of heresy, which was universally regarded as the most horrible of crimes (see above, pp. 167 *sq.*) It is taken from the laws of the enlightened Frederick II of Hohenstaufen.[1]

The heretics endeavor to rend the seamless garment of our Lord, and in accordance with their vicious name, which means division, they would destroy the unity of that same indivisible faith. They would withdraw the sheep from Peter's guardianship, to which they were intrusted by the Good Shepherd. They are ravening wolves within, but feign a love for the flock, until they shall have crept into the Lord's fold. They are bad angels, sons of perversity, appointed by the father of lies and deception to mislead the simple-minded. They are serpents who deceive the doves. Like serpents they creep stealthily abroad; with honeyed sweetness they vomit forth their virus. While they pretend

66. Concerning heretics. (From the laws issued by Frederick II of Hohenstaufen, for Sicily, about 1235.)

[1] Extracts from the laws in France and Germany relating to heretics will be found in *Translations and Reprints*, Vol. III, No. 6.

to offer life-giving food they strike with their tail, and prepare a deadly draught, as with some dire poison.

These sects do not assume the old names lest they should be recognized, but, what is perhaps more heinous, not content like the Arians, who took their name from Arius, or the Nestorians, from Nestorius, and others of the same class, they must imitate the example of the martyrs who suffered death for the Catholic faith. They call themselves Patarins, as if they, too, were sufferers.[1] . . .

Against these, who offend alike against God, themselves, and their fellow-men, we cannot restrain ourselves, and must draw forth the sword of merited retribution. . . .

We decree, in the first place, that the crime of heresy and of reprehensible teaching, of whatever kind, by whatever name its adherents may be known, shall, as provided by the older laws, be included among the recognized crimes. (For should not what is recognized to be an offense against the Divine Majesty be judged more terrible than the crime of leze majesty directed against ourself, although in the eyes of the law one is not graver than the other?) As the crime of treason deprives the guilty of life and property, and even blackens the memory of the dead, so in the aforesaid crimes of which the Patarins are guilty, we wish the same rules to be observed in all respects.

And in order that the wickedness of those who walk in darkness, since they do not follow God, should be thoroughly exterminated, we desire that those who practice this class of crimes should, like other malefactors, be diligently sought for and hunted out by our officers. If such be discovered, even if there be only the slightest suspicion of their guilt, we command that they shall be examined by churchmen and prelates. If they shall be found by these to have deviated from the Catholic faith, even in a single respect, and if, when admonished by such churchmen in their function of pastors, they refuse by leaving the wiles of the devil to

[1] The name Patarin, which seems here to be derived from the Latin word *patior*, to suffer, appears to have been given to the Cathari of Milan because they lived among the ragpickers (*patari*).

recognize the God of light, and stubbornly adhere to their error, we command, by this our present edict, that such condemned Patarins shall suffer the death they court; that, condemned to the sentence of the flames, they shall be burned alive in the sight of the people. Nor are we loath to satisfy their cravings in this respect, for they only suffer the penalty of their crime and reap no further gain. No one shall dare to intercede with us for any such, and should any one presume to do this, we shall properly direct the darts of our indignation against him, too. . . .

All who shall receive, trust, aid, or abet the Patarins in any way, seeking to shield others from a penalty which they rashly do not fear for themselves, shall be deprived of all their goods and banished forever. Their sons shall thereafter be excluded from all honors whatsoever and shall be branded with perpetual disgrace. They shall not be permitted to act as witnesses in any case, but shall be rejected as infamous.

Penalties for those who harbor or aid heretics.

But if any one of the sons of such harborers or fautors shall point out a Patarin, whose guilt shall be thus proven, he shall, by the imperial clemency, be freed from the opprobrium and restored to his full rights, in view of the good faith which he has shown.

Premium on delation.

## III. Life and Character of St. Francis

Until his twentieth year Francis wretchedly wasted his days. He astonished every one, for he sought to exceed all others in pomp and vain display. He was full of jests, quips, and light words; he dressed in soft flowing garments, for he was very rich; yet he was not avaricious, only prodigal, and squandered instead of saving his money. He was withal a man of gentle manner, friendly and very courteous.

In the midst of the joys and sins of his youth suddenly the divine vengeance, or grace, came upon him, which began to recall him to the right way by bringing anguish to his

67. How St. Francis came to undertake his mission. (From the first *Life of St. Francis,* by Thomas of Celano, written in 1228; condensed.)

mind and suffering to his body. When he had long been afflicted by bodily sickness — as the sinful man merits, since he will not amend his ways except by punishment — he began to turn his thoughts to other things than had been his wont.

When he had somewhat mended, he once more wandered about the house, supported by a staff, in order to hasten his recovery. One day he went out of doors and looked thoughtfully over the neighboring plain; but the beauty of the fields and their pleasantness, and all things whatsoever that are lovely to the sight, in no way delighted him. He marveled at the sudden change in himself, and those who still loved the things that he had formerly loved seemed to him most foolish.

From that day it came to pass that he seemed worthless in his own sight, and did hold in a certain contempt those things that he was used to hold in admiration and love. He would fain conform his will to the divine will, and so he withdrew himself for a season from worldly business and tumult and sought to store away Jesus Christ within his soul. . . .

On a certain day when he had most earnestly besought the mercy of God, it was made known to him by the Lord what he should do. Therefore he was filled with so great gladness that he could not keep from rejoicing inwardly, and yet he would not make known unto men anything concerning this joy. But so great was the love kindled within him that he could not be wholly silent, so he spoke somewhat cautiously and in parables and told his companions how that he would do noble and mighty deeds. They asked him, saying, " Wilt thou marry a wife, Francis ? " Who, answering, saith, " I will marry a wife more noble and fairer than ever ye saw, and this spotless bride is the true religion of God."

Ever had he been the benefactor of the poor, but from this time he resolved more firmly in his heart to deny no poor man anything who asked of him in the name of the Lord. Thenceforth whensoever he walked abroad and a beggar asked alms of him, if he had money he gave it to him.

If he had no money, then he went apart into some hidden place and took off his shirt and sent it to the beggar secretly.

[Now Francis, from this time, did long to give all things that he had to the Lord;] so this blessed servant of the Most High took some pieces of cloth that he might sell them, and went forth mounted upon his horse and arrived straightway at the city called Foligno. There did the happy merchant sell all the goods that he had, and did even part with his horse when a price was offered for him. Then he took his way toward Assisi, and he passed by the way the church of St. Damian. The new soldier of Christ straightway entered the church and sought out a certain poor priest, and with reverence did kiss his hands and then offered to him all the money that he had. . . .

[Rejoicing in the Lord, he lingered in the church of St. Damian.] His father, hearing of these things, gathered together his friends and neighbors and made all speed possible to the place where the servant of God was abiding. Then he, because he was but a new champion of Christ, when he heard the threats of vengeance, did hide himself in a certain secret cave and there did lie concealed for a month. Fasting and praying, he did entreat the mercy of the Saviour; and though he lay in a pit and in the shadow of death, yet was he filled with a certain unutterable joy, unhoped for until now. All aglow with this gladness, he left the cave and exposed himself openly to the abuses of his persecutors. . . . Armed with the shield of faith and the armor of trust, he took his way to the city. All who knew him did deride him and called him insane and a madman, and pelted him with the mud of the streets and with stones.

The father of the blessed Francis, when he learned that his son was ridiculed in the open streets, first strove by abuse to turn him from his chosen way. When he could not thus prevail over him, he desired the servant of God to renounce all his inheritance. That this might be done, he brought the blessed Francis before the bishop of Assisi. At this Francis did greatly rejoice and hastened with a willing heart to fulfill his father's demands.

When he had come before the bishop he did not delay, nor did he suffer others to hinder him. Indeed, he waited not to be told what he should do, but straightway did take off his garments and cast them away and gave them back to his father; and he stood all naked before the people. But the bishop took heed of his spirit and was filled with exceeding great wonder at his zeal and steadfastness; so he gathered him in his arms and covered him with the cloak which he wore. Behold now had he cast aside all things which are of this world.

The holy one, lover of all humility, did then betake himself to the lepers and abode with them most tenderly for the love of God. He washed away all the putrid matter from them, and even cleansed the blood and all that came forth from the ulcers, as he himself spake in his will: "When I was yet in my sins it did seem to me too bitter to look upon the lepers, but the Lord himself did lead me among them and I had compassion upon them."

Now upon a certain day, in the church of Santa Maria Portiuncula, the gospel was read — how that the Lord sent forth his disciples to preach. It was while they did celebrate the solemn mystery of the mass, and the blessed one of God stood by and would fain understand the sacred words. So he did humbly ask the priest that the gospel might be expounded unto him. Then the priest set it forth plainly to him, and the blessed Francis heard how the disciples were to have neither gold, nor silver, nor money, nor purse, nor script, nor bread, not to carry any staff upon the road, not to have shoes nor two coats, but to preach repentance and the spirit of God, rejoicing always in the spirit of God.

Then said the blessed Francis, "This is what I long for, this is what I seek, this is what I desire to do from the bottom of my heart." And he was exceeding rich in joy, and did hasten to fulfill the blessed words that he had heard. He did not suffer any hindrance to delay him, but did earnestly begin to do that which he had heard. Forthwith he did loose the shoes from his feet, and did lay down the staff from out his hands, and was content with one tunic, and changed his girdle for a rope. Then with great fervor of spirit and joy of mind he began to preach repentance to all men. He used simple speech, yet by his noble heart did he strengthen those who heard him. His word was as a flaming fire, and found a way into the depths of all hearts.

The most blessed Father Francis once made his way through the valley of Spoleto, and he came to a place near Bevagna where birds of divers kinds had gathered together in a great multitude, — crows, doves, and others which are called, in the vulgar tongue, bullfinches. Now Francis, most blessed servant of God, was a man full of zeal and moved to tenderness and gentleness toward all creatures, even those that be lowly and without reason. So when he had seen the birds he did run to them quickly, leaving his companions upon the way.

68. St. Francis' sermon to the birds. (From *Thomas of Celano*.)

When he had come near to them he saw that they awaited him, and he made salutation, as he was wont to do. Wondering not a little that they did not take flight, as is the habit of birds, he begged them humbly, yet with great joy, that they would hear the word of God. And among many things which he said unto them was this which follows : " My brother birds, greatly should ye praise your Creator and always serve him, because he gave you feathers to wear, wings to fly, and whatsoever ye needed. He exalted you among his creatures and made for you a mansion in the pure air. Although ye sow not, neither reap, none the less he protects you and guides you, and ye have not any care."

At this the birdlings — so one said who was with him — began to stretch out their necks and raise their wings, to open their mouths, and to look upon him. He went and came, passing through the midst of them, and his tunic touched their heads and bodies. Then he blessed them, and made the sign of the cross, and gave them leave to fly to other places.

## BIBLIOGRAPHY

*A. References.*

**Monastic Orders:** EMERTON, pp. 555–577; MUNRO, pp. 122–134; TOUT, pp. 198–209.

**The Spread of Heresy:** BÉMONT and MONOD, pp. 512–514; EMERTON, pp. 333–338; MUNRO, pp. 175–178; TOUT, pp. 214–217.

**The Albigensian Crusade:** BÉMONT and MONOD, pp. 506–511; EMERTON, pp. 339–342.

**The Mendicant Friars:** EMERTON, pp. 578–581; MUNRO, pp. 178–180; TOUT, pp. 434–444.

**The Rule of St. Francis:** HENDERSON, *Historical Documents*, pp. 344–349.

*B. Additional reading in English*

LEA, *History of the Inquisition in the Middle Ages*, Vol. I: Chapters II–V deal very fully with the development of the Waldensian and Albigensian heresies and the early attempts to suppress them; Chapter VI takes up both the Franciscan and Dominican orders; while in Chapters VII–XIV there is by far the fullest and best account in English of the origin of the papal Inquisition, its organization and methods. This is one of the most scholarly works ever produced in the United States.

SABATIER, *Life of St. Francis of Assisi*, translated from the French of the Protestant scholar who has done most to clear up the problems connected with the sources for the saint's life and teachings. A charming book, with a very full and scholarly discussion of the sources.

ABBÉ LÉON LE MONNIER, *History of St. Francis of Assisi*, 1894. From the French edition of 1890. The work of a Catholic, written before the appearance of Sabatier's.

JESSOPP, *The Coming of the Friars.*

DRANE, AUGUSTA, *History of St. Dominic, Founder of the Friars Preachers*, 1891.

The oldest and most authentic life of St. Francis, BROTHER LEO'S *Mirror of Perfection* (see below), is to be had in English (Temple Classics). It was written almost immediately after the death of Francis by one who was anxious that the friars should carefully adhere to the ideas of their founder as they are expressed in his will.

*The Life of Francis* by THE THREE COMPANIONS, written in 1246, is also in the Temple Classics.

*The Little Flowers of St. Francis* is a charming collection of anecdotes about him, which was probably written in the fourteenth century.

# CHAPTER XVIII

## THE PEOPLE IN COUNTRY AND TOWN

### I. THE MANOR AND ITS PEOPLE[1]

The following official account of an English manor and its people gives a good idea of the condition of the serfs in general.

Extent of the manor of Bernehorne, made on Wednesday following the feast of St. Gregory the pope, in the thirty-fifth year of the reign of King Edward, in the presence of Brother Thomas, keeper of Marley, John de la More, and Adam de Thruhlegh, clerks, on the oath of William de Gocecoumbe, Walter le Parker, Richard le Knyst, Richard the son of the latter, Andrew of Estone, Stephen Morsprich, Thomas Brembel, William of Swynham, John Pollard, Roger le Glede, John Syward, and John de Lillingewist, who say that there are all the following holdings: . . .

John Pollard holds a half acre in Aldithewisse and owes 18d. at the four terms, and owes for it relief and heriot.

John Suthinton holds a house and 40 acres of land and owes 3s. 6d. at Easter and Michaelmas.

William of Swynham holds 1 acre of meadow in the thicket of Swynham and owes 1d. at the feast of Michaelmas.

Ralph of Leybourne holds a cottage and 1 acre of land in Pinden and owes 3s. at Easter and Michaelmas, and attendance at the court in the manor every three weeks, also relief and heriot.

[1] I am indebted for the illustrations used in this section on the manor and in the one which follows on the towns, to Professor Cheyney's admirable selection of documents in the *Translations and Reprints*, Vol. II, No. 1, and Vol. III, No. 5.

Richard Knyst of Swynham holds 2 acres and a half of land and owes yearly 4s.

William of Knelle holds 2 acres of land in Aldithewisse and owes yearly 4s.

Roger le Glede holds a cottage and 3 roods of land and owes 2s. 6d. at Easter and Michaelmas.

Alexander Hamound holds a little piece of land near Aldewisse and owes 1 goose of the value of 2d.

The sum of the whole rent of the free tenants, with the value of the goose, is 18s. 9d.

Complicated services rendered for a house and 30 acres of land.

They say, moreover, that John of Cayworth holds a house and 30 acres of land, and owes yearly 2s. at Easter and Michaelmas; and he owes a cock and two hens at Christmas of the value of 4d.

And he ought to harrow for 2 days at the Lenten sowing with one man and his own horse and his own harrow, the value of the work being 4d.; and he is to receive from the lord on each day 3 meals, of the value of 5d., and then the lord will be at a loss of 1d. Thus his harrowing is of no value to the service of the lord.

And he ought to carry the manure of the lord for 2 days with 1 cart, with his own 2 oxen, the value of the work being 8d.; and he is to receive from the lord each day 3 meals as above. And thus the service is worth 3d. clear.

And he shall find one man for 2 days, for mowing the meadow of the lord, who can mow, by estimation, 1 acre and a half, the value of the mowing of an acre being 6d. : the sum is therefore 9d. And he is to receive each day 3 meals of the value given above. And thus that mowing is worth 4d. clear.

And he ought to gather and carry that same hay which he has cut, the price of the work being 3d.

And he shall have from the lord 2 meals for 1 man, of the value of 1½d. Thus the work will be worth 1½d. clear.

And he ought to carry the hay of the lord for 1 day with a cart and 3 animals of his own, the price of the work being 6d. And he shall have from the lord 3 meals of the value of 2½d. And thus the work is worth 3½d. clear.

And he ought to carry in autumn beans or oats for 2 days
with a cart and 3 animals of his own, the value of the work
being 12d.   And he shall receive from the lord each day 3
meals of the value given above.   And thus the work is worth
7d. clear.

And he ought to carry wood from the woods of the lord
as far as the manor, for two days in summer, with a cart and
3 animals of his own, the value of the work being 9d.   And
he shall receive from the lord each day 3 meals of the price
given above.   And thus the work is worth 4d. clear.

And he ought to find 1 man for 2 days to cut heath, the
value of the work being 4d., and he shall have 3 meals each
day of the value given above : and thus the lord will lose,
if he receives the service, 3d.   Thus that mowing is worth
nothing to the service of the lord.

And he ought to carry the heath which he has cut, the
value of the work being 5d.   And he shall receive from the
lord 3 meals at the price of 2½d.   And thus the work will
be worth 2½d. clear.

And he ought to carry to Battle, twice in the summer
season, each time half a load of grain, the value of the
service being 4d.   And he shall receive in the manor each
time 1 meal of the value of 2d.   And thus the work is worth
2d. clear.

The totals of the rents, with the value of the hens, is 2s. 4d.

The total of the value of the works is 2s. 3½d., owed
from the said John yearly.

William of Cayworth holds a house and 30 acres of land
and owes at Easter and Michaelmas 2s. rent.   And he shall
do all customs just as the aforesaid John of Cayworth.

William atte Grene holds a house and 30 acres of land and
owes in all things the same as the said John. . . .

And it is to be noted that none of the above-named villeins can give their daughters in marriage, nor cause their
sons to be tonsured, nor can they cut down timber growing
on the lands they hold, without license of the bailiff or ser-
geant of the lord, and then for building purposes and not
otherwise.   And after the death of any one of the aforesaid

Nature of
heriot.

Amount of
relief fixed.

villeins, the lord shall have as a heriot his best animal, if he
had any; if, however, he have no living beast, the lord shall
have no heriot, as they say.   The sons or daughters of the
aforesaid villeins shall give, for entrance into the holding after
the death of their predecessors, as much as they give of rent
per year.

Sylvester, the priest, holds 1 acre of meadow adjacent to
his house and owes yearly 3s. . . .

## II. The Mediæval Town

As the towns grew up, certain local *customs* came
into existence.   These were nothing more than the
rules which the townspeople recognized as necessary to
maintain order and prevent misunderstandings.   They
were not necessarily written down, as every one was
supposed to be familiar with them.   The commissioners
of William the Conqueror judged it wise, however, to
include in Domesday Book some forty of the town customs which involved the king's financial interests.   The
following provisions occur among those of Chester.

70. Cus-
toms of the
town of
Chester.
(From
Domesday
Book.)

If any free man of the king broke the peace which had
been granted, and killed a man in his house, all his land and
money came to the king, and he himself became an outlaw.

He who shed blood between Monday morning and the ninth
hour of Saturday compounded for it with ten shillings.   From
the ninth hour of Saturday to Monday morning bloodshed
was compounded for with twenty shillings.   Similarly any
one paid twenty shillings who shed blood in the twelve
days after Christmas, on the day of the Purification of the
Blessed Mary, on the first day after Easter, the first day of
Pentecost, Ascension day, on the Assumption or Nativity
of the Blessed Mary, and on the day of All Saints.

He who killed a man on these holy days compounded
for it with four pounds; but on other days, with forty

shillings. Similarly he who committed burglary or assault on those feast days or on Sunday, four pounds; on other days, forty shillings.

Any one setting prisoners free in the city gave ten shillings. But if the reeve of the king or of the earl committed this offense, he compounded for it with twenty shillings.

He who committed theft or robbery, or exercised violence upon a woman in a house, compounded for each of these with forty shillings.

He who in the city seized upon the land of another and was not able to prove it to be his was fined forty shillings. Similarly also he who made claim upon it, if he was not able to prove it to be his.

He who did not pay the tax at the period at which he owed it compounded for it with ten shillings.

If fire burned the city, he from whose house it started compounded for it with three oras of pennies, and gave to his next neighbor two shillings. Of all these forfeitures, two parts belonged to the king and the third to the earl.

A man or a woman making false measure in the city, and being arrested, compounded for it with four shillings. Similarly a person making bad ale was either placed in the ducking stool or gave four shillings to the reeve. This forfeiture the officer of the king and of the earl received in the city, in whosesoever land it has been done, either of the bishop or of another man. Similarly also, if any one held the toll back beyond three nights, he compounded for it with forty shillings. . . .

The lists of rules established by the craft guilds, an example of which is given below, cast much light on the industrial conditions and the habits of the mediæval artisans.

In honour of God, of our Lady, and of All Saints, and for the nurture of tranquillity and peace among the good folk, the Megucers, called white-tawyers,[1] the folk of the same

**71. Rules of the guild of white-tawyers.**

---

[1] Those who dressed leather in such a way as to give it a white surface.

trade have, by assent of Richard Lacer, mayor, and of the Aldermen, ordained the points underwritten.

In the first place, they have ordained that they will furnish a wax candle, to burn before our Lady, in the church of All-hallows, near London wall.

Also, that each person of the said trade shall put in the box such sum as he shall think fit, in aid of maintaining the said candle.

Also, if by chance any of the said trade shall fall into poverty, whether through old age or because he cannot labor or work, and shall have nothing with which to keep himself, he shall have every week from the said box seven pence for his support, if he be a man of good repute. And after his decease, if he have a wife, a woman of good repute, she shall have weekly for her support seven pence from the said box, so long as she shall behave herself well and keep single.

And that no stranger shall work in the said trade, or keep a house for the same in the city, if he be not an apprentice, or a man admitted to the franchise of the said city.

And that no one shall take the serving man of another to work with him, during his term, unless it be with the permission of his master.

And if any one of the said trade shall have work in his house that he cannot complete, or if for want of assistance such work shall be in danger of being lost, those of the said trade shall aid him, that so the said work be not lost.

And if any one of the said trade shall depart this life, and have not withal to be buried, he shall be buried at the expense of their common box. And when any one of the said trade shall die, all those of the said trade shall go to the vigil, and make offering on the morrow. . . .


### III. Knights, Burghers, and Farmers

Although the various contracts and other legal documents, examples of which have been given, contain the most accurate information available in regard to the condition of the farmers and townspeople in the Middle Ages, we may get a livelier, and in some ways better, idea of the general situation from the fiction of the period. While this cannot be taken as history, such tales as those given below seem to give an essentially true and living picture of the attitude of the various classes of society toward one another.

Wolfram von Eschenbach (d. *ca.* 1225), the famous German minnesinger, narrates the adventures of William, count of Orange and margrave of Aquitaine, who, although he really lived in the eighth century, fares in Wolfram's tale as any knight might have done at the opening of the thirteenth, when Wolfram wrote.

William had to defend his possessions in southern France against the Saracens. Having carried off a Saracen princess, he was attacked by the infidels, defeated, and forced to hasten to the court of King Louis of France for assistance.

72. Knights and burghers in the early thirteenth century. (From Wolfram von Eschenbach's *William of Orange,* condensed.)

After some days — I know not how many — the bold hero came to Orleans. . . . In the morning he left his inn and fared forth into the city. Now there was in the town a man of power who held his head high because he wielded authority in the king's name. He tried to wreak causeless spite upon the margrave; but the knight gave him as good as he sent. "I go scot free of toll!" he cried. "There are no merchants' mares nor pack horses at my back. I am a knight, as you see. If you can ferret out no harm I have done to the land here, let that stand to my credit. I did not ride out of the road upon the harvest field; I kept to the beaten track, which is free to all the world. What I had need of to feed myself and my horse I have paid for."

But the magistrate and his men sternly ordered him to halt, and at the burgher's behest forthwith the people of the town came flocking from all sides. The magistrate cried, "This traveler must pay to the full a tax as great as the harm he has done." In sooth it was a shame that they did not let him go free. The magistrate called to his people, "Seize his bridle rein!" He answered: "My horse carries no load but only me and this shield. I've had enough of this." Out flashed his sword, and the magistrate grew shorter by a head. Then the margrave hewed out a way through the crowd for man and steed, so hastily that soon the street was wide. The alarm bell began to sound.

Arnalt, son of the count of Narbonne, heard in his castle the doleful cries that rang through all the streets. Soon the magistrate's wife came to him and fell down on the ground before him. She made her moan: "The king is put to shame and I am undone. My husband lies in the market place, slain by one who travels without retinue. He fought off all our people, and has gone hence unhindered. Woe is me! He has left us a grim trophy for toll on the king's highway."

To whom Count Arnalt: "Who can this be whose might has done ye this ill? Were he a merchant, woman, he must needs have a train and pay toll for his wares." Those who had come with the woman bore witness: "He carries a shield, his banner is flecked with rust, yet in all Frankland know we no knight whose armor is so costly and beautiful, like the sun's beam to look upon — and eke his doublet and his shield. As he put us to rout he cried wildly, 'Monjoie!'"

The count cried: "Cowards all! Did ye not even know it is not seemly to treat a knight like a tradesman? What should a knight give for toll? Ye durst not murmur if he took all your lives. Yet for the king's sake, whose crown my sister wears, I must after him."

With his knights, he armed and hastened after the margrave. A little way from the town they overtook him, and the count gave him battle. Both bore themselves bravely. They did not give over fighting until the count became aware that the stranger knight was his own brother. After a parley, Arnalt let William ride on to seek the king. Then the burghers clamored to know why he was suffered to go free. To whom the count: "It is William, the margrave; I can in no wise suffer him to be killed here on French ground. The burghers of Orleans have borne themselves like clumsy boors. Ye dolts! How could my brother pay toll like a merchant? Even he who knows but ill the just dues of knights knows that he goes free of tax."

Meanwhile William rode on his way, and in due time reached Moulon. A great crowd was gathered there for a royal festival, and the knight could find no place to lodge. At last he went forth from the town. He took off his helmet and stretched himself on the grass beside the road. Then came a merchant from the town and begged him most courteously to do honor to all merchants by going to lodge with him. The merchant's name was Wimar, and he was born of knightly blood. He said, "If ye will but grant me this boon to-day, all my fellows will tell afterward of the great honor that was done me." The margrave answered: "What ye ask I grant right gladly. I will requite ye as I can. And now lead on; I follow you."

The merchant then said courteously: "You should ride, and I must walk; else will I stand here the week through." The margrave replied: "I know friendship's tie but ill if I suffer ye to be my servant. Let me show courtesy like your own. I will follow you on foot; for I would be your good comrade."

Wimar led his guest to his house. There the knight suffered them to disarm him, for he had no fear. And now the host bade his servants lay mattress and pillow and rich coverlid on the carpet. Then Wimar ordered that many viands, dainty and fresh, be brought to be cooked and roasted, — meat of all sorts and fish besides. All was daintily prepared. They set a little table for the margrave alone; and when he had washed his hands, his host served him right deftly. There were dishes manifold, and an emperor would not have disdained the liquors. The roast peacock was served with the best sauce the host knew; and there were capon, pheasant, partridge, and lamprey served in jelly.

The knight rested at the merchant's house until the next day and then went to seek the king.

## BIBLIOGRAPHY

*A. References.*

**The Serfs and Peasants:** CHEYNEY, *Industrial and Social History of England*, Chapter II, pp. 31–56; EMERTON, pp. 509–520; MUNRO, pp. 148–153.

**The Growth of Commerce and the Towns:** CHEYNEY, Chapter III, " Town Life and Organization," pp. 57–73, and Chapter IV, " Trade and Commerce," pp. 75–94; ADAMS, *Civilization*, pp. 279–310; BÉMONT and MONOD, pp. 375–390; EMERTON, pp. 520–540; HENDERSON, *Germany in the Middle Ages*, pp. 417–422; MUNRO, pp. 153–159.

**London in the Twelfth Century:** COLBY, pp. 63–66; KENDALL, pp. 65–78.

**The Hanseatic League:** HENDERSON, *Short History of Germany*, pp. 181–202; LODGE, *Close of the Middle Ages*, pp. 419–451.

A number of important documents relating to the manor and the towns may be found in *Translations and Reprints*, Vol. II, No. 1, and Vol. III, No. 5. The extracts from the manor court rolls, which Professor Cheyney gives there — Vol. III, No. 5, pp. 20 *sqq.* — are particularly important.

*B. Additional reading in English.*

BATESON, MARY, *Mediæval England, English Feudal Society from the Norman Conquest to the Middle of the Fourteenth Century*, 1904 (Story of the Nations).

JESSOPP, *Coming of the Friars*, second essay on " Village Life Six Hundred Years Ago."

BARNARD, *Companion to English History* (Middle Ages), Oxford, 1902, containing essays by a number of scholars on social conditions, trade, commerce, architecture, monasticism, etc. Very useful.

GIBBINS, *History of Commerce in Europe*. The best short account, with good maps of the trade routes. Also by the same writer, *The Industrial History of England*, and a more elaborate treatise, *Industry in England*.

INGRAM, *History of Slavery and Serfdom*, 1895, especially Chapters IV and V.

CUNNINGHAM, *Outlines of English Industrial History*, and his fuller *Growth of English Industry and Commerce during the Middle Ages*. All these give good descriptions of the manor, the guilds, the fairs, etc.

JUSSERAND, *English Wayfaring Life in the Middle Ages* (fourteenth century), translated from the French by Lucy Smith, 1887. Very interesting and instructive, with good illustrations.

ZIMMERN, HELEN, *The Hansa* (Story of the Nations). Interesting, with good illustrations.

# CHAPTER XIX

## THE CULTURE OF THE MIDDLE AGES

### I. MEDIÆVAL NATURAL SCIENCE

Mediæval books on science differ greatly, as might be expected, from the scientific manuals of our own age. In the first place, they are usually devoted to things in general and are called *On the Nature of Things, On the Properties of Things, Things that can be Known, Mirror of the World*, etc. A writer did not hesitate to huddle together into a short treatise matters which we should regard as properly belonging to a dozen distinct sciences, such as zoölogy, mineralogy, botany, chemistry, physics, meteorology, anatomy, physiology, ethics, theology, law, and medicine. In the second place, important scientific observations are mixed with what seem to us the most preposterous legends and irrelevant anecdotes. Lastly, writers were rarely satisfied when they had described a particular kind of bird, fish, or mineral unless they could add a moral, or illustrate the truths of Scripture.

Among the more worthy and serious of these mediæval writers is Alexander Neckam in his work entitled *On the Natures of Things*. He was an Englishman, a contemporary of Richard the Lion-Hearted, and for a time a professor in the University of Paris. In a single fair-sized volume he takes up in turn the world and the heavenly bodies ; fire, air, and the various birds ; water and the fishes ; the earth, metals, gems, plants, and animals, with their respective virtues and properties; man, the vanity of his pursuits, his domesticated animals, — the dog, horse, sheep, mule, silkworm; scholastic learning, the universities, Virgil's necromancy, court life, dice, chess, and the vices of envy and arrogance.

**73. The birds and their lesson. (From Neckam,** *On the Natures of Things.***)**

The eagle, [Neckam tells us] on account of its great heat, mixeth very cold stones with its eggs when it sitteth on them, so that the heat shall not destroy them. In the same way our words, when we speak with undue heat, should later be tempered with discretion, so that we may conciliate in the end those whom we offended by the beginning of our speech.

The wren.

The wren is but a little bird, yet it glories in the number of its progeny. Who has not wondered to hear a note of such volume proceeding from so trifling a body? The smaller the body, indeed, the greater the sound, it would seem. By such things we are taught that the virtues of little things should not be scorned. . . . They say, moreover, that when the body of the wren is put upon the spit and placed before the fire it need not be turned, for the wren will turn itself, not forgetful of its royal dignity.

The stratagem by which, according to a fabulous story, it gained the royal power among birds is well known. The birds had agreed among themselves that the glory of the supreme power should be allotted to the one who should excel all others by flying highest. The wren seized its opportunity and hid itself under the eagle's wing. When the eagle, who attains nearest to Jove's gates, would have claimed the supremacy among its fellows, the little wren sallied forth and perching on the eagle's head declared itself the victor. And so it obtained its name of Regulus (i.e. "ruler").

This fable touches those who enter upon the works of others and presumptuously appropriate the credit due elsewhere. As the philosopher says, "We are all like dwarfs standing upon giants' shoulders." We should therefore be careful to ascribe to our predecessors those things which we ought not to claim for our own glory, and not follow the example of that wren which, with little or no effort of its own, claimed to have outdone the eagle.

In contrast with these tales and moralizings, Neckam gives many true and useful facts. For example, the habits and cultivation of the silkworm are clearly and correctly described, and the use of the compass is explained.

The sailors, as they sail over the sea, when in cloudy weather they can no longer profit by the light of the sun, or when the world is wrapped in the darkness of night, and they are ignorant whither the ship's course is directed, touch a needle to the magnet; the needle will then whirl around in a circle until, when its motion ceases, its point is directed to the north.

*The magnetic needle*

A little Anglo-Saxon manual of the tenth century thus describes the heavenly bodies.

On the second day God made the heaven, which is called the firmament, which is visible and corporeal; and yet we may never see it, on account of its great elevation and the thickness of the clouds, and on account of the weakness of our eyes. The heaven incloses in its bosom all the world, and it ever turns about us, swifter than any mill-wheel, all as deep under this earth as it is above. It is all round and entire and studded with stars.

*74. The earth and the stars. (From a little Anglo-Saxon treatise: somewhat condensed.)*

Truly the sun goes by God's command between heaven and earth, by day above and by night under the earth. She is ever running about the earth, and so light shines under the earth by night as it does above our heads by day. . . . The sun is very great: as broad she is, from what books say, as the whole compass of the earth; but she appears to us very small, because she is very far from our sight. Everything, the further it is, the less it seems. . . . The moon and all the stars receive light from the great sun. The sun is typical of our Saviour, Christ, who is the sun of right-eousness, as the bright stars are typical of the believers in God's congregation, who shine in good converse. . . . No one of us has any light of goodness except by the grace of Christ, who is called the sun of true righteousness. . . .

Truly the moon's orb is always whole and perfect, although it does not always shine quite equally. Every day the moon's light is waxing or waning four points through the sun's light. . . . We speak of new moon according to the custom of men, but the moon is always the same, though its light often varies. . . . It happens sometimes when the moon runs on the same track that the sun runs, that its orb intercepts the sun's, so that the sun is all darkened and the stars appear as by night. This happens seldom, and never but at new moons. By this it is clear that the moon is very large, since it thus darkens the sun.

Eclipse of the sun.

Meteors.

Some men say stars fall from heaven, but it is not stars that fall, but it is fire from the sky, which flies down from the heavenly bodies as sparks do from fire. Certainly there are still as many stars in the heavens as there were at the beginning, when God made them. They are almost all fixed in the firmament, and will not fall thence while this world endures. The sun, and the moon, and the evening star, and morning star, and three other stars are not fast in the firmament, but they have their own course severally. These seven stars are called planets.

The planets.

Comets.

Those stars are called comets which appear suddenly and unusually, and which are rayed so that the ray goes from them like a sunbeam. They are not seen for any long time, and as oft as they appear they foreshadow something new toward the people over whom they shine.

A writer of the thirteenth century, Bartholomew Anglicus, in his treatise on *The Properties of Things* gives the following brief and pertinent description of the domestic cat.

75. A description of the cat. (From Bartholomew Anglicus.)

The cat is a full lecherous beast in youth, swift, pliant, and merry, and leapeth and runneth on everything that is to fore him : and is led by a straw, and playeth therewith : and is a right heavy beast in age and full sleepy, and lieth slyly in wait for mice: and is aware where they be, more by smell than by sight, and hunteth and runneth on them in privy places; and when he taketh a mouse, he playeth therewith, and eateth him after the play. In time of love is hard fighting for wives, and one scratcheth and rendeth the other grievously with biting and with claws. And he maketh a ruthful noise and ghastful, when one proffereth to fight with another: nor is he hurt when he is thrown down off an high place. And when he hath a fair skin, he is, as it were, proud thereof, and goeth fast about; and when his skin is burnt, then he bideth at home; and he is oft, for his fair skin, taken of the skinner, and slain and flayed.

## II. Abelard and the Universities

While Abelard was not the first teacher to attract students to Paris, his great gifts and his remarkable popularity served to arouse such enthusiasm for learning that it was not long after his death that the teachers and students became so numerous that they organized themselves into guilds, or corporations, which formed the basis of the later university.

It is not difficult to understand the charm of Abelard's teaching. Three qualities are assigned to it by the writers of the period, some of whom studied at his feet: clearness, richness in imagery, and lightness of touch are said to have been the chief characteristics of his teaching. Clearness is, indeed, a quality of his written works, though they do not, naturally, convey an impression of his oral power. His splendid gifts and versatility, supported by a rich voice, a charming personality, a ready and sympathetic use of human literature, and a freedom from excessive piety, gave him an immeasurable advantage over all the teachers of the day. Beside most of them, he was as a butterfly to an elephant. A most industrious study of the Roman classics that were

76. Abelard's popularity as a teacher. (From McCabe's *Abelard*.)

available, a retentive memory, an ease in manipulating his knowledge, a clear, penetrating mind, with a corresponding clearness of expression, a ready and productive fancy, a great knowledge of men, a warmer interest in things human than in things divine, a laughing contempt for authority, a handsome presence, and a musical delivery, — these were his gifts.

77. An account of the lectures at Paris. (From McCabe's *Abelard*.)

A modern writer gives the following picture of student life at Paris in Abelard's time.

At five or six o'clock each morning the great cathedral bell would ring out the summons to work. From the neighboring houses of the canons, from the cottages of the townsfolk, from the taverns, and hospices, and boarding-houses, the stream of the industrious would pour into the enclosure beside the cathedral. The master's beadle, who levied a precarious tax on the mob, would strew the floor of the lecture hall with hay or straw, according·to the season, bring the master's text-book, with the notes of the lecture between lines or on the margin, to the solitary desk, and then retire to secure silence in the adjoining street. Sitting on their haunches in the hay, the right knee raised to serve as a desk for the waxed tablets, the scholars would take notes during the long hours of lecture (about six or seven), then hurry home — if they were industrious — to commit them to parchment while the light lasted.

The lecture over, the stream would flow back over the Little Bridge, filling the taverns and hospices, and pouring out over the great playing meadow, that stretched from the island to the present Champ de Mars. All the games of Europe were exhibited on that international play-ground : running, jumping, wrestling, hurling, fishing and swimming in the Seine, tossing and thumping the inflated ball — a game on which some minor poet of the day has left us an enthusiastic lyric — and especially the great game of war, in its earlier and less civilized form. The nations were not yet systematically grouped, and long and frequent were the dangerous conflicts.

### III. Roger Bacon and the Beginning of Modern Experimental Science

The following passage makes clear Bacon's attitude toward investigation, and also shows that he was not the only one who was turning his attention to experiment, which was to prove so fruitful in the following centuries.

One man I know, and one only, who can be praised for his achievements in experimental science.[1] Of discourses and battles of words he takes no heed: he pursues the works of wisdom and in them finds satisfaction. What others strive to see dimly and blindly, like bats blinking at the sun in the twilight, he gazes at in the full light of day, because he is a master of experiment. Through experiment he gains knowledge of natural things, medical, chemical, indeed of everything in the heavens and on earth.

He is ashamed that things should be known to laymen, old women, soldiers, plowmen, of which he is ignorant. Therefore he has looked closely into the doings of those who melt metals and who work in gold and silver and other metals and in minerals of all sorts; he knows everything relating to the art of war, the making of weapons, and the chase; he has looked carefully into agriculture, mensuration, and farming work; he has even taken note of remedies, lot casting, and charms used by old women and by wizards and magicians, and of the devices and deceptions of conjurers, so that nothing which deserves investigation should escape him, and in order that he might be able to expose the impostures of the magicians.

If philosophy is to be carried to its perfection and is to be handled with certainty and advantage, his aid is indispensable. As for reward, he neither receives it nor looks for it. If he frequented the courts of kings and princes he would easily find those who would bestow upon him both

*78. Roger Bacon's eulogy of one who devoted himself to experimental science.*

[1] Of Peter of Maricourt, to whom Bacon refers, very little is known.

honor and wealth. Or if he would show the results of his researches in Paris the whole world would follow him. But since either of these courses would hinder him from pursuing the great experiments in which he takes delight, he puts honor and wealth aside, knowing well that his knowledge would secure him wealth whenever he chose. For the last three years he has been working at the invention of a mirror which should produce combustion at a fixed distance, and he will, with God's aid, soon reach his end.

In a curious letter " On the hidden workings of nature and art and the emptyness of magic," Bacon forecasts the wonderful achievements which he believed would come with the progress of applied science.

**79. Bacon foresees marvelous progress in inventions. (Slightly condensed.)**

I will now enumerate the marvelous results of art and nature which will make all kinds of magic appear trivial and unworthy. Instruments for navigation can be made which will do away with the necessity of rowers, so that great vessels, both in rivers and on the sea, shall be borne about with only a single man to guide them and with greater speed than if they were full of men. And carriages can be constructed to move without animals to draw them, and with incredible velocity. Machines for flying can be made in which a man sits and turns an ingenious device by which skillfully contrived wings are made to strike the air in the manner of a flying bird. Then arrangements can be devised, compact in themselves, for raising and lowering weights indefinitely great. . . . Bridges can be constructed ingeniously so as to span rivers without any supports.

## BIBLIOGRAPHY

*A. References.*

**Popular Literature :** BÉMONT and MONOD, pp. 527–534 ; EMERTON, pp. 471–476 ; HENDERSON, *Germany in the Middle Ages*, pp. 427–437 ; MASSON, *Mediæval France*, pp. 36–46.

**Chivalry :** HENDERSON, *Short History of Germany*, pp. 111–121 ; MASSON, pp. 33–36. The making of a knight, and a fourteenth-century tourney : FLING, *Studies*, Vol. II, No. 4.

**Architecture:** BÉMONT and MONOD, pp. 536–544. The burning and rebuilding of Canterbury Cathedral: COLBY, pp. 59–63.

**Rise of the Universities:** BÉMONT and MONOD, pp. 515–527; EMERTON, pp. 465–471; MUNRO, pp. 160–168; TOUT, pp. 428–434 and 444–449. University charters and privileges: HENDERSON, *Select Documents*, pp. 262–266. Course of study at Paris: *Translations and Reprints*, Vol. II, No. 3.

**Scholasticism:** EMERTON, pp. 446–464; TOUT, 209–214. Roger Bacon's account of his own difficulties: COLBY, pp. 83–87.

---

SAINTSBURY, *The Flourishing of Romance*. The best short account of the state of literature in the twelfth and thirteenth centuries.

LOUNSBURY, *History of the English Language*. Short and good.

TEN BRINK, *Early English Literature to Wiclif* (Bohn Library). Excellent.

*Specimens of Early English*, edited by MORRIS and SKEAT, 2 vols. (Clarendon Press), with vocabularies and notes.

SMITH, JUSTIN H., *The Troubadours at Home*. An excellent popular description of the life in Provence and the poems of the troubadours by one who has made a careful study of them and their country.

GAUTIER, LÉON, *Chivalry*. The standard work.

CORNISH, *Chivalry*. Shorter and more recent than Gautier.

PUTNAM, GEORGE HAVEN, *Books and their Makers during the Middle Ages*, 2 vols., 1896–1897. Vol. I deals with the Middle Ages. An interesting work by an experienced publisher.

RASHDALL, *History of the Universities of Europe in the Middle Ages*, 3 vols., 1895. This is by far the best general account of the mediæval universities in any language. It has an excellent index, and may be consulted with advantage upon most topics connected with mediæval higher education. Earlier works on the subject in English should be avoided, as they all rest upon very insufficient investigation.

McCABE, *Abelard*. A model biography.

UEBERWEG, *History of Philosophy*, Vol. I. Contains a good account of the scholastic philosophy.

MOORE, C. H., *The Development and Character of Gothic Architecture*. Excellent. The general history of art is treated in the rather arid review given by LÜBKE, *Outlines of the History of Art*, 2 vols.

Among the few examples of mediæval popular literature to be had in English, the following are especially good and available:

SYMONDS, J. A., *Wine, Women and Song*. (Selections from this in *Latin Students' Songs*, published by Mosher in his Bibelot Series.)

*B. Additional reading in English.*

*The Carmina Burana.*

In this little volume Symonds has translated, with an excellent and scholarly introduction, some of the *Carmina Burana*, a strange collec-ion of verses in Latin, or Latin mixed with German, discovered in the monastery of Benediktbeuren, Bavaria, — hence the name, " Burana." The collection was made apparently in the thirteenth century, and contains the greatest variety of pieces, ranging from love and drinking songs, through satirical attacks on the clergy [1] and parodies of the church service, to poems showing genuine religious and poetic feeling. Few sources give one so vivid a notion of the variety and range of sentiment in the Middle Ages as the *Carmina Burana*.

*The Song of Roland* has been translated into spirited English verse by O'HAGEN.

*Aucassin and Nicolette.*   A most charming tale of the twelfth century.

MALLORY, *Mort d'Arthur* (Temple Classics).   A collection of the stories of King Arthur, made in the fifteenth century for English readers.

WOLFRAM OF ESCHENBACH, *Parzifal*, translated by Jessie L. Weston, 2 vols., London, 1894; and GODFREY OF STRASBURG, *Tristan and Iseult*, translated by the same, New York, 1902.

*The Romance of the Rose.*   A famous production of the thirteenth century, in the Temple Classics.

*Huon of Bordeaux, Renaud of Montauban,* and *The Story of Alexander* (Allen, London).   These three romances have been excellently prepared for English readers by MR. STEELE.

*Mediæval Tales*, edited by HENRY MORLEY in his Universal Library.

For the general mediæval knowledge of the world, the following are especially good :

*The Travels of Sir John Mandeville* (The Macmillan Company, 1900).   This is not only a good edition of the story of travel falsely attributed to Mandeville, but contains the original accounts upon which it was based.

STEELE, *Mediæval Lore.*   Selections from a very early English version, printed at the end of the fifteenth century, of the famous popular encyclopedia of Bartholomew Anglicus, compiled in the thirteenth century.

---

[1] One of these satires, " The Gospel according to the Marks of Silver," is translated by Emerton, *Mediæval Europe*, p. 475.

## CHAPTER XX

### THE HUNDRED YEARS' WAR

#### I. How King John of France was taken Prisoner by the English at Poitiers

Ofttimes the adventures of amours and of war are more fortunate and marvelous than any man can think or wish. Truly this battle, the which was near to Poitiers in the fields of Beauvoir and Maupertuis, was right great and perilous, and many deeds of arms there were done the which all came not to knowledge. The fighters on both sides endured much pain. King John with his own hands did that day marvels in arms. He had an ax in his hands wherewith he defended himself and fought in the breaking of the press. . . .

The pursuit endured to the gates of Poitiers. There were many slain and beaten down, horse and man, for they of Poitiers closed their gates and would suffer none to enter; wherefore in the street before the gate was horrible murder, men hurt and beaten down. The Frenchmen yielded themselves as far as they might know an Englishman: there were divers English archers that had four, five, six prisoners. . . .

Then there was a great press to take the king, and such as knew him cried, " Sir, yield you, or else ye are but dead." [A French knight in the service of the English king made his way through the press] and said in good French, " Sir, yield you." The king beheld the knight and said, " To whom shall I yield me? Where is my cousin, the prince of Wales? If I might see him, I would speak with him." The knight answered and said, " Sir, he is not here ; but yield you to me and I shall bring you to him." " Who be you ? " quoth the king. " Sir," quoth he, " I am Denis of Morbeke, a knight of Artois ; but I serve the king of England because I am

80. Capture of King John (1356). (From Froissart's *Chronicles*.)

banished from the realm of France and have forfeited all that I had there." Then the king gave him his right gauntlet, saying, "I yield me to you."

The prince of Wales, who was courageous and cruel as a lion, took that day great pleasure to fight and chase his enemies. The lord John Chandos, who was with him, all that day never left him nor never took heed of taking any prisoner. Then at the end of the battle he said to the prince, "Sir, it were good that you rested here and set your banner a-high in this bush, that your people may draw hither, for they be sore spread abroad, nor can I see no more banners nor pennons of the French party. Wherefore, sir, rest and refresh you, for ye be sore chafed."

[Then the prince sent two lords to get news of the French king.] These two lords took their horses and departed from the prince and rode up a little hill to look about them. Then they perceived a flock of men-at-arms coming together right slowly, and there was the French king afoot in great peril, for the Englishmen and Gascons were his masters. They had taken him from Sir Denis Morbeke perforce, and such as were most of force said, "I have taken him"; "Nay," quoth another, "I have taken him." So they strave which should have him. Then the French king, to eschew that peril, said, "Sirs, strive not: lead me courteously, and my son, to my cousin the prince, and strive not for my taking, for I am so great a lord as to make you all rich." The king's words somewhat appeased them. Howbeit, ever as they went they made riot and brawled for the taking of the king.

When the two aforesaid lords saw and heard that noise and strife among them, they came to them and said, "Sirs, what is the matter that ye strive for?" "Sirs," said one of them, "it is for the French king, who is here taken prisoner, and there be more than ten knights and squires that challenge the taking of him and of his son." Then the two lords entered into the press and caused every man to draw back, and commanded them in the prince's name, on pain of their heads, to make no more noise nor to approach the king no nearer without they were commanded. Then every man gave room to the lords, and they alighted and did their reverence to the king, and so brought him and his son in peace to the prince of Wales. . . .

The same day of the battle at night the prince made a supper in his lodging to the French king and to the most of the great lords that were prisoners. The prince made the king and his son, the lord James of Bourbon, the lord John of Artois, the earl of Tancreville, the earl of Estampes, the earl Dammartin, the earl Joinville, and the lord of Partenay, to sit all at one board, and the other lords, knights, and squires at other tables. And always the prince served before the king as humbly as he could, and would not sit at the king's board for any desire that the king could make, for he said he was not sufficient to sit at the table with so great a prince as the king was.

Then he said to the king: "Sir, for God's sake, make none evil nor heavy cheer, though God this day did not consent to follow your will; for, sir, surely the king, my father, shall bear you as much honor and amity as he may do, and shall accord with you so reasonably that ye shall ever be friends together after. And, sir, methink ye ought to rejoice, though the expedition be not as ye would have had it, for this day ye have won the high renown of prowess and have surpassed this day in valiantness all other of your party. Sir, I say not this to mock you, for all that be of our party, that saw every man's deeds, are plainly accorded by true sentence to give you the prize and chaplet."

*How the Black Prince received the French king with knightly courtesy.*

## II. Charles the Bold of Burgundy and the Swiss

What ease or what pleasure did Charles, duke of Burgundy, enjoy more than our master, King Louis? In his youth, indeed, he had less trouble, for he did not begin to enter upon any action till nearly the two-and-thirtieth year of his age; so that before that time he lived in great ease and quiet. . . . From the time Duke Charles undertook his war to recover the towns in Picardy (which our master

*81. Charles the Bold and the Swiss. (From the Memoires of Commines.)*

had redeemed from Duke Philip), and joined himself with the lords of the kingdom in the war called the Public Good, what pleasure, what tranquillity had he? He had continual trouble and labor, without the least cessation or refreshment, either to his body or mind; for ambition got entire possession of his heart and constantly spurred him on to attempt new conquests.

Arduous life of Charles the Bold. He was always in the field during summer, exposing his person to the greatest danger, taking the care and command of the whole army upon himself; and yet he thought his work too little. He was the first that rose and the last that went to bed in the camp; and he slept in his clothes, like the poorest foot soldier in the army. In winter, when the campaign was over, he was busily employed about raising money; six hours every morning he set apart for conferences, and for giving audience to ambassadors. And in this perpetual hurry of affairs he ended his days, and was killed by the Swiss in the battle of Nancy; so that it cannot be said that he enjoyed one happy day from the time of his beginning to aggrandize himself to the hour of his death. And then what were the fruits of all his pains and labor? Or what necessity was there of his so doing? — since he was a rich prince, and already had towns and territories large enough to have made him happy, if he could have been contented with them.

How the Swiss defeated Charles the Bold at Granson (1476). All hopes of an accommodation with the Swiss being entirely vanished, their ambassadors returned to acquaint their masters with the duke of Burgundy's absolute refusal of their propositions, and to make preparations for their defense. . . .

The duke, contrary to the advice of his officers, resolved to advance and meet the enemy at the foot of the mountains, to his great disadvantage; for he was already posted in a place much more proper for an engagement, being fortified on one side with his artillery and on the other by a lake, so that to all appearance there was no fear of his being injured by the enemy. He had detached a hundred of his archers to secure a certain pass at the entrance of the mountains, and was advancing forward himself, when the Swiss attacked him, while the greatest part of his army was still in the plain.

The foremost troops designed to fall back; but the infantry that were behind, supposing they were running away, retreated toward their camp, and some of them behaved themselves handsomely enough; but, in the end, when they arrived in their camp, they wanted courage to make a stand and defend themselves, and they all fled, and the Swiss possessed themselves of their camp, in which were all their artillery and a vast number of tents and pavilions, besides a great deal of valuable plunder, for they saved nothing but their lives.

The duke lost all his finest rings, but of men, not above seven men-at-arms; the rest fled, and the duke with them. It may more properly be said of him, "that he lost his honor and his wealth in one day," than it was of King John of France, who, after a brave defense, was taken prisoner at the battle of Poitiers. . . .

The poor Swiss were mightily enriched by the plunder of the duke's camp. At first they did not understand the value of the treasure they were masters of, especially the common soldiers. One of the richest and most magnificent tents in the world was cut into pieces. There were some of them that sold quantities of dishes and plates of silver for about two sous of our money, supposing they had been pewter.

How the poor Swiss mountaineers misunderstood the treasure that fell into their hands.

His great diamond (perhaps the largest and finest jewel in Christendom), with a large pearl fixed to it, was taken up by a Swiss, put up again into the case, thrown under a wagon, taken up again by the same soldier, and after all offered to a priest for a florin, who bought it and sent it to the magistrates of that country, who returned him three francs as a sufficient reward. They took also three very rich jewels, called the Three Brothers, another large ruby called La Hatte, and another called the Ball of Flanders, which were the fairest and richest in the world; besides a prodigious quantity of other goods, which has since taught them what fine things may be purchased for money; inasmuch as their victories, the esteem the king had of their service afterwards, and the presents he made them, have enriched them prodigiously.

### III. Louis XI of France

82. Character and troublous death of Louis XI. (From the *Memoires* of Commines.)

Small hopes and comfort ought poor and inferior people to have in this world, considering what so great a king suffered and underwent, and how he was at last forced to leave all, and could not, with all his care and diligence, protract his life one single hour. I knew him, and was entertained in his service in the flower of his age and at the height of his prosperity, yet I never saw him free from labor and care.

The king's laborious interest in the chase.

Of all diversions he loved hunting and hawking in their seasons, but his chief delight was in dogs. . . . In hunting, his eagerness and pain were equal to his pleasure, for his chase was the stag, which he always ran down. He rose very early in the morning, rode sometimes a great distance, and would not leave his sport, let the weather be never so bad. And when he came home at night he was often very weary and generally in a violent passion with some of his courtiers or huntsmen; for hunting is a sport not always to be managed according to the master's direction; yet, in the opinion of most people, he understood it as well as any prince of his time. He was continually at these sports, lodging in the country villages to which his recreations led him, till he was interrupted by business; for during the most part of the summer there was constantly war between him and Charles, duke of Burgundy, while in the winter they made truces. . . .

When his body was at rest his mind was at work, for he had affairs in several places at once, and would concern himself as much in those of his neighbors as in his own, putting officers of his own over all the great families, and endeavoring to divide their authority as much as possible. When he was at war he labored for a peace or a truce, and when he had obtained it he was impatient for war again.

He troubled himself with many trifles in his government which he had better have let alone; but it was his temper, and he could not help it. Besides, he had a prodigious memory, and he forgot nothing, but knew everybody, as well in other countries as in his own. . . .

The king had ordered several cruel prisons to be made: some were cages of iron, and some of wood, but all were covered with iron plates both within and without, with terrible locks, about eight feet wide and seven high. The first contriver of them was the bishop of Verdun, who was immediately put in the first of them that was made, where he continued fourteen years. Many bitter curses he has had since for his invention, and some from me as I lay in one of them eight months together in the minority of our present king. He also ordered heavy and terrible fetters to be made in Germany, and particularly a certain ring for the feet, which was extremely hard to be opened, and fitted like an iron collar, with a thick weighty chain, and a great globe of iron at the end of it, most unreasonably heavy, which contrivances were called the king's nets. However, I have seen many eminent and deserving persons in these prisons, with these nets about their legs, who afterwards came forth with great joy and honor, and received great rewards from the king.

This by way of digression. But to return to my principal design. As in his time this barbarous variety of prisons was invented, so before he died he himself was in greater torment and more terrible apprehension than those whom he had imprisoned; which I look upon as a great mercy toward him, and as part of his purgatory. And I have mentioned it here to show that there is no person, of what station or dignity soever, but suffers some time or other, either publicly or privately, especially if he has caused other people to suffer.

The king, toward the latter end of his days, caused his castle of Plessis-les-Tours to be encompassed with great bars of iron in the form of thick grating, and at the four corners of the house four sparrow nests of iron, strong, massy, and

*(margin note)* Louis XI's ideas of prison reform.

*(margin note)* Apprehensions and precautions of the dying Louis.

thick, were built. The grates were without the wall, on the farther side of the ditch, and sank to the bottom of it. Several spikes of iron were fastened into the wall, set as thick by one another as was possible, and each furnished with three or four points. He likewise placed ten bowmen in the ditches, to shoot at any man that durst approach the castle before the opening of the gates; and he ordered that they should lie in the ditches, but retire to the sparrow nests upon occasion.

He was sensible enough that this fortification was too weak to keep out an army or any great body of men, but he had no fear of such an attack; his great apprehension was that some of the nobility of his kingdom, having intelligence within, might attempt to make themselves masters of the castle by night and, having possessed themselves of it, partly by favor and partly by force, might deprive him of the regal authority, and take upon themselves the administration of public affairs, upon pretense that he was incapable of business and no longer fit to govern.

The gate of the castle was never opened, nor the drawbridge let down, before eight o'clock in the morning, at which time the officers were let in, and the captains ordered their guards to their several posts, with pickets of archers in the middle of the court, as in a town upon the frontiers that is closely guarded: nor was any person admitted to enter except by the wicket, and with the king's knowledge, unless it were the steward of his household and such persons as were not admitted into the royal presence.

Is it possible then to keep a prince (with any regard to his quality) in a closer prison than he kept himself? The cages which were made for other people were about eight feet square; and he (though so great a monarch) had but a small court of the castle to walk in, and seldom made use of that, but generally kept himself in the gallery, out of which he went into the chambers on his way to mass, but never passed through the court. Who can deny that he was a sufferer as well as his neighbors, considering how he was locked up and guarded, afraid of his own children and relations, and changing every day those very servants whom he had brought up and advanced ; and though they owed all their preferment to him, yet he durst not trust any of them, but shut himself up in those strange chains and enclosures. If the place where he confined himself was larger than a common prison, he also was much greater than common prisoners.

## BIBLIOGRAPHY

**Conquest of Wales :** GREEN, *Short History*, pp. 161–169.

**Scottish Wars :** CHEYNEY, *Short History of England*, pp. 220–226.

**France during the Hundred Years' War :** ADAMS, *Growth of the French Nation*, Chapter IX, pp. 108–135; LODGE, Chapter IV, pp. 66–97.

**Black Death and Peasants' Rebellion :** CHEYNEY, *Industrial and Economic History*, pp. 96–134 ; *Short History*, pp. 243–250; Statutes of Laborers, in *Translations and Reprints*, Vol. II, No. 5.

**Constitutional Progress in England :** ADAMS, *Civilization*, pp. 347–363.

**Wars of the Roses :** GREEN, Chapter VI, sect. 2.

**Tudor Despotism :** GREEN, Chapter VI, opening of sect. 3, on the "New Monarchy." CHEYNEY, *Short History*, pp. 278–284.

**Breaking up of the Feudal System :** CHEYNEY, *Industrial and Economic History*, pp. 136–161.

**Joan of Arc :** GREEN, pp. 274–281. Official report of her trial: COLBY, pp. 113–117.

**Louis XI and Charles the Bold :** ADAMS, *Growth of the French Nation*, pp. 136–143; LODGE, Chapter XVI, pp. 349–393.

*A. References.*

---

The following are the best special treatments of English history in the fourteenth and fifteenth centuries :

TREVELYAN, *England in the Age of Wycliffe*, 1899.

LONGMAN, *The Life and Times of Edward III*, 1869. Still the best work for the period.

GASQUET, *The Great Pestilence, 1348–1349*, 1893.

RAMSAY, *Lancaster and York, 1399–1485*, 2 vols., 1892.

WYLIE, *History of England under Henry IV*, 4 vols., 1884–1898. Very detailed and exhaustive.

BUSCH, *England under the Tudors*, Vol. I.

LOWELL, *Joan of Arc*.

*B. Additional reading in English.*

GREEN, MRS. J. R., *Town Life in England in the Fifteenth Century*, 2 vols.

KIRK, *Charles the Bold*.    Rather antiquated and rhetorical but based upon careful research.

*The Chronicles of Froissart*, edited by MACAULAY (Globe edition), carefully condensed into one volume.

*The Chronicles of Commines*, 2 vols. (Bohn Library).

*The Paston Letters*, edited by GAIRDNER, 1875. These "are the first instance in England of a family correspondence, and throw great light on the social history of the time " (Green).

FRAZER, *English History illustrated from the Original Sources, 1307-1399.*    This contains a great variety of extracts.

Compare excellent bibliographies given by ANDREWS, *History of England*, pp. 196-197 and 229-230, and CHEYNEY, *Short History*, pp. 262-263 and 276-277.

# CHAPTER XXI

## THE POPES AND THE COUNCILS

### I. Wycliffe's Attack upon the Pope, Clergy, and Monks

Wycliffe wrote many treatises, pamphlets, and sermons, in both Latin and English. In his sermons, which are generally very brief, he often refers to the evil life and what he regarded as the perverse teachings of the clergy, especially of the mendicant friars, most of whom seemed to him to be the servants of Antichrist. The following extract illustrates his spirit :[1]

[We should put on the armor of Christ, for Antichrist has turned] hise clerkes to coveitise and worldli love, and so blindid the peple and derkid the lawe of Crist, that hise servantis ben thikke, and fewe ben on Cristis side. And algatis [= always] thei dispisen that men shulden knowe Cristis liif, for bi his liif and his loore shulde help rise on his side, and prestis shulden shame of her lyves, and speciali thes highe prestis, for thei reversen Crist bothe in word and dede.

> 83. Wycliffe on the evil state of the clergy.

And herfore oo greet Bishop of Engelond, as men seien, is yvel paied [= pleased] that Goddis lawe is writun in Englis, to lewide men [= laymen]; and he pursueth a preest, for that he writith to men this Englishe, and somonith him and traveilith him, that it is hard to him to rowte. And thus he pursueth another preest by the helpe of Phariseis, for he prechide Cristis gospel freeli withouten fablis.

> The opposition of the Primate of England to the translating of the Scriptures into English

[1] It seemed a pity to modernize the ancient spelling; it, of course, somewhat impedes the inexperienced reader, but does not prevent his coming at the full sense of the passage.

O men that ben on Cristis half, helpe ye now agens Anti-crist! for the perilous tyme is comen that Crist and Poul telden bifore.   Butt oo confort is of knygttis, that thei savoren myche the gospel and han wille to rede in Englishe the gospel of Cristis liif.   For aftirward, if God wole, this lordship shal be taken from preestis; and so the staaff that makith hem hardi agens Crist and his lawe.   For three sectis figten here, agens Cristene mennis secte.   The firste is the pope and cardinals, bi fals lawe that thei han made; the secounde is emperours [and] bishopis, whiche dispisen Cristis lawe; the thridde is thes Pharisees possessioners and beg-geris.   Alle thes three, Goddis enemyes, traveilen in ypoc-risie, and in worldli coveitise, and idilnesse in Goddis lawe. Crist helpe his Chirche from these fendis, for thei figten perilously.

*Three chief enemies of Christ's law, namely, the pope and cardinals, bad bishops and rulers, and the mendicant friars.*

## II. The Origin of the Great Schism

Froissart, in his famous *Chronicles,* gives the following account of Pope Gregory XI's return to Rome and of the opening of the Great Schism due to the election of Clement VII.

**84. The beginning of schism in holy Church.** (From Froissart's *Chronicles.*)

Ye have heard herebefore how Pope Gregory, the eleventh of that name, was in the city of Avignon.   And when he saw that he could find no manner of peace to be had between the kings of England and France, wherewith he was in great displeasure, for he had greatly travailed thereabout and had made his cardinals to do the same, then he advised himself and had a devotion to go and revisit Rome and the see apos-tolic, the which St. Peter and St. Paul had edified.   He had made promise before that, if ever he came to the degree to be pope, he would never keep his see but there where St. Peter kept his and ordained it.

*How Gregory XI resolved to return from Avignon to Rome.*

This pope was a man of feeble complexion and sickly, and endured much pain, more than any other.   And he thus being in Avignon was sore let with the business of France, and so sore travailed with the king and his brethren that with much pain he had any leisure to take heed anything to himself or to his Church. Then he said to himself that he would go farther off from them to be more at rest, . . . and then he said to his cardinals, " Sirs, make you ready, for I will go to Rome."

Of that motion his cardinals were sore abashed and displeased, for they loved not the Romans, and so they would fain have turned his purpose, but they could not. And when the French king heard thereof he was sore displeased, for he thought that he had the pope nearer at hand there than at any other place. Then the king wrote incontinent to his brother, the duke of Anjou, who was at Toulouse, signifying him that after he had received his letter he should go to Avignon to the pope and break his voyage to Rome, if it were possible. The duke did as the king commanded him, and so came to Avignon, where the cardinals received him with great joy, and so he was lodged in the pope's palace, the ofter thereby to speak with the pope.

Ye may know well that he spoke with the pope and showed him divers reasons to have broken his purpose; but the pope would in no wise consent thereto nor take any heed of any business on this side of the mountains. . . . When the duke saw that he could not come to his intent for no reason nor fair words that he could show, he took leave of the pope, and said at his parting, " Holy father, ye go into a country among such people where ye be but little beloved, and ye will leave the fountain of faith and the realm where holy Church hath most faith and excellence of all the world. And, sir, by your deed the Church may fall into great tribulation. For if ye die there, the which is right likely, and so say the physicians, then the Romans, who be malicious and traitors, shall be lords and masters of all the cardinals and shall make a pope at their own will."

*How the king of France sought to dissuade the pope.*

Howbeit, for all these words and many others, the pope never rested till he was on his way. . . . The Romans were right joyful of his coming, and all the chief men of Rome mounted on their horses and so brought him into Rome with great triumph and lodged him in St. Peter's palace.

And ofttimes he visited a church called Our Lady the Great [Santa Maria Maggiore] within Rome, wherein he had great pleasure and did make therein many costly works. And within a while after his coming to Rome he died and was buried in the said church, and there his obsequy was made, as to a pope appertained.[1]

Of the orgulous words that the Romans said at the election of a new pope.

[When the cardinals had entered the conclave] the Romans assembled themselves before the conclave and made semblance to break it up and slay them all if they did not choose a pope according to their minds, and cried to the cardinals and said, " Sirs, advise you well.  If ye deliver us a Roman pope, we be content; else we will make your heads redder than your hats be."  Such words and menaces greatly abashed the cardinals, for they would rather a died confessors than martyrs.  Then to bring themselves out of that danger and peril they made a pope.  But he was none of the college of cardinals : he was the archbishop of Bari, a great clerk, who greatly had travailed for the wealth of holy Church.

With this promotion to the papality the Romans were appeased, for the cardinal of Genoa put out his head at a window of the conclave and said on high to the people of Rome, " Sirs, appease you, for you have a Roman pope, and that is Bartholomew des Aigles, archbishop of Bari."  The people answered all with one voice, " Then we be content." The same archbishop was not then at Rome ; I think he was in Naples.  Then he was incontinent sent for, of the which tidings he was right glad; and so came to Rome.  And at his coming there was a great feast made to him, and so he had all the rights that pertained to the papality and was called Urban, the sixth of that name.

[1] Here Froissart inserts a fabulous story of the election of a pope one hundred years of age, who straightway died, worn out by the celebration which the enthusiastic Romans prepared in his honor.  His account of the election of Urban VI and Clement VII, given below, is, however, essentially correct, except that, with a view to justifying the desertion of Urban by the cardinals, he exaggerates the disorder which attended his election and which formed the only possible excuse for a new election.

The Romans had great joy. His creation was signified to all the churches of Christendom, and also to emperors, kings, dukes, and earls, and the cardinals sent word to all their friends that he was chosen by a good and true election. Howbeit some of them repented them after that they had spoken so largely of the matter.[1] . . .

The intention of divers of the cardinals was that when they might see a better hour and time they would return again to their election, because this pope was not profitable for them, nor also for the Church, for he was a fumish man and melancholious, so that when he saw himself in prosperity and in puissance of the papality, and that divers Christian kings were joined to him and wrote to him and did put them under his obedience, he waxed proud and headstrong, and would have taken from the cardinals divers of their rights and old customs, the which greatly displeased them. And so they spake together and imagined how he was not well worthy to govern the world; wherefore they purposed to choose another pope, sage and discreet, by whom the Church should be well governed. . . .

The cardinals desert Urban and choose a new pope, Clement VII.

[Accordingly when they left Rome for the summer] all of one accord assembled together and their voices rested on Sir Robert of Geneva, son to the earl of Geneva. He was first bishop of Therouanne and later of Cambrai, and was called cardinal of Geneva. At his election were most of the cardinals, and he was called Clement [VII]. . . .

And when the French king who as then reigned was certified thereof, he had great marvel, and sent for his brother and for all the nobles and prelates of his realm and for the rector and master doctors of the university of Paris, to know of them which election, whether the first or the second, he should hold unto. This matter was not shortly determined, for divers clerks varied, but finally all the prelates of France

Decisive action of the French king in declaring for Clement

---

[1] There appears to be no doubt that Urban was admitted by all at the time to have been regularly elected, and that the plea that the cardinals had been intimidated by the Roman populace was trumped up later, when Urban had made himself hated by his rudeness and austerity.

inclined to Clement, and so did the king's brethren and the most part of the university of Paris; and so the king was informed by all the great clerks of his realm; and so he obeyed the pope Clement and held him for the true pope, and made a special commandment throughout his realm that every man should take and repute Clement for pope and that every man should obey him as God on earth. The king of Spain was of the same opinion and so was the earl of Savoy, the duke of Milan, and the queen of Naples.

The believing thus of the French king upon Clement greatly strengthened his cause, for the realm of France was reputed to be the chief fountain of belief of the Christian faith, because of the noble churches and prelacies that be therein. . . . The Christian realms were in variation and the churches in great difference because of the popes. Urban had the greater part, but to speak of the most profitable revenues and plain obedience, Clement had it. And so Clement, by consent of the cardinals, sent to Avignon to make ready the palace there for him, for his intent was to go thither as soon as he might.

### III. The Council of Constance

**85. The decree *Sacrosancta* passed by the Council of Constance (April 6, 1415).**

The two most interesting acts, historically, passed by the Council of Constance were the decree *Sacrosancta*, in which it declared that as a general council of Christendom it had the right to reform even the papacy; and, secondly, the decree *Frequens*, which provided that general councils should thereafter be assembled regularly and so form a sort of parliament which, with the pope, should govern the Church.

*In the name of the Holy and Indivisible Trinity, of the Father, Son, and Holy Ghost. Amen.*

This holy synod of Constance, constituting a general council for the extirpation of the present schism and the union and reformation of the Church of God in head and members, legitimately assembled in the Holy Ghost, to the praise of omnipotent God, in order that it may the more easily, safely, effectively, and freely bring about the union and reformation of the Church of God, hereby determines, decrees, ordains, and declares what follows:

It first declares that this same council, legitimately assembled in the Holy Ghost, forming a general council and representing the Catholic Church militant, has its power immediately from Christ, and every one, whatever his position or rank, even if it be the papal dignity itself, is bound to obey it in all those things which pertain to the faith, to the healing of the schism, and to the general reformation of the Church of God in head and members.

It further declares that any one, whatever his position, station, or rank, even if it be the papal, who shall contumaciously refuse to obey the mandates, decrees, ordinances, or instructions which have been, or shall be, issued by this holy council, or by any other general council legitimately summoned, which concern, or in any way relate to, the above-mentioned objects, shall, unless he repudiate his conduct, be subjected to condign penance and be suitably punished, having recourse, if necessary, to the resources of the law. . . .

A frequent celebration of general councils is an especial means for cultivating the field of the Lord and effecting the destruction of briers, thorns, and thistles, to wit, heresies, errors, and schism, and of bringing forth a most abundant harvest. The neglect to summon these fosters and develops all these evils, as may be plainly seen from a recollection of the past and a consideration of existing conditions. Therefore, by a perpetual edict, we sanction, decree, establish, and ordain that general councils shall be celebrated in the following manner, so that the next one shall follow the close of this present council at the end of five years. The second shall follow the close of that, at the end of seven years, and councils shall thereafter be celebrated every ten years in such places as the pope shall be required to designate and assign, with the consent and approbation of the council, one

86. The decree *Frequens* passed by the Council of Constance (October, 1417).

month before the close of the council in question, or which, in his absence, the council itself shall designate. Thus, with a certain continuity, a council will always be either in session, or be expected at the expiration of a definite time.

This term may, however, be shortened on account of emergencies, by the supreme pontiff, with the counsel of his brethren, the cardinals of the holy Roman Church, but it may not be hereafter lengthened. The place, moreover, designated for the future council may not be altered without evident necessity. . . .

## BIBLIOGRAPHY

*A. References.*

**The Papacy in the Fourteenth and Fifteenth Centuries :** ADAMS, *Civilization,* Chapter XVI, pp. 392–415; LODGE, pp. 196–201 ; WALKER, *Reformation,* Chapter I.

**Wycliffe :** GREEN, *Short History,* pp. 235–244. Documents in *Translations and Reprints,* Vol. II, No. 5. For treatment of the Lollards, see LEE, pp. 209–223.

**Council of Constance :** LODGE, pp. 206–221.

*B. Additional reading in English.*

CREIGHTON, *History of the Papacy from the Schism to the Sack of Rome,* 6 vols. The first volume of this great work is far the best account in English of the Great Schism, and of the Council of Constance, with a good review of Wycliffe's doctrines.

PASTOR, *History of the Popes,* Vol. I. Gives a brief but excellent review of the effects of the Great Schism and of the results of the council from the standpoint of a learned Catholic.

POOLE, *Illustrations of Mediæval Thought.* Has good chapters on Marsiglio of Padua and Wycliffe.

VAN DYKE, *The Age of Renascence.* A sketch of the papacy (1377–1527).

*Cambridge Modern History,* Vol. I, Chapter XVIII.

LEA, *History of the Inquisition,* Vol. II, Chapter VII. Deals with the trial of Huss.

# CHAPTER XXII

## THE ITALIAN CITIES AND THE RENAISSANCE

### I. THE ITALIAN DESPOTS

No one better understood the Italian despot and the peculiarities of his position than did Machiavelli. The following passage is from *The Prince*, his little handbook for despots.

87. Machiavelli's advice to despots. (From *The Prince*.)

That prince who founds the duration of his government upon his mercenary forces will never be firm or secure; for they are divided, ambitious, undisciplined, unfaithful; insolent to their friends, abject to their enemies, without fear of God or faith to men; so the ruin of that person who trusts to them is no longer protracted than the attempt is deferred. In time of peace they plunder you, in time of war they desert you; and the reason is because it is not love nor any principle of honor that keeps them in the field, but only their pay, and that is not a consideration strong enough to prevail with them to die for you. Whilst you have no service to employ them in, they are excellent soldiers; but tell them of an engagement and they will either disband before, or run away during the battle. . . .

Unreliable character of the *condottiere* and their mercenary troops.

The great officers of these mercenaries [i.e. the *condottiere*] are either men of great courage, or otherwise; if the first, you can never be safe, for they always aspire to make themselves great, either by supplanting you who are their master, or by oppressing other people whom you desire to have protected. On the other hand, if the commanders be not courageous, you are still ruined. If it should be urged that all generals will do the same, whether mercenaries or others, I would answer, that all war is managed either by a prince or a

219

republic. The prince ought to go in person, and perform the office of general himself; the republic should depute some one of her choice citizens, who may be changed if he carries himself ill; if he behaves himself well he may be continued, but so straitened and circumscribed by his commission that he may not transgress. . . .

Of the danger of mercenary forces we have an ancient example in the Carthaginians, who, after the end of their first war with the Romans, had like to have been ruined and overrun by their own mercenaries, though their own citizens commanded them. [In modern times] upon the death of Duke Filippo,[1] the Milanese employed Francesco Sforza against the Venetians, and Francesco, having worsted the enemy at Caravaggio, joined himself with them, with design to have mastered his masters. Francesco's father was formerly in the service of Joan, queen of Naples, and on a sudden marched away from her with his army and left her utterly destitute, so that she was constrained to throw herself under the protection of the king of Aragon.

Example of Sforza making himself master of Milan.

Though both the Venetians and Florentines have lately enlarged their dominion by employing these forces, and their generals have rather advanced than enslaved them, I answer that the Florentines may impute it to their good fortune, because, of such of their generals as they might rationally have feared, some had no victories to encourage them, others were obstructed, and others turned their ambition another way.

## II. HUMANISM

88. Dante and the great writers of Greece and Rome. (From the *Divine Comedy*.)

Dante was not a humanist in the later sense of the term, but he clearly appreciated the distinction and worth of the ancient writers. The following passage from the *Divine Comedy* is his poetic conception of the fate of the famous pagans who lived worthily. He is passing through limbo, the uppermost region of hell,

[1] The last of the Visconti.

with Virgil for his guide. As they proceed he sees
a fire that conquered a hemisphere of darkness.[1]

We were still a little distant from it, yet not so far that
I could not partially discern that honorable folk possessed
that place. " O thou that honorest both science and art,
these, who are they, that have such honor that from the
condition of the others it sets them apart?" And he to me,
" The honorable fame of them which resounds above in thy
life wins grace in heaven that so advances them." At this
a voice was heard by me, " Honor the loftiest Poet! his
shade returns that was departed." When the voice had
ceased and was quiet, I saw four great shades coming to
us : they had a semblance neither sad nor glad. The good
Master [Virgil] began to say, " Look at him with that sword
in hand who cometh before the three, even as lord. He is
Homer, the sovereign poet; the next who comes is Horace,
the satirist; Ovid is the third, and the last is Lucan. Since
each shares with me the name that the solitary voice sounded,
they do me honor, and in that do well."

Thus I saw assembled the fair school of that Lord of the
loftiest song which above the others as an eagle flies. After
they had discoursed somewhat together, they turned to me
with sign of salutation ; and my Master smiled thereat.
And far more of honor yet they did me, for they made me
of their band, so that I was the sixth amid so much wit.
Thus we went on as far as the light, speaking things concerning which silence is becoming, even as was speech there
where I was.

We came to the foot of a noble castle, seven times circled
by high walls, defended roundabout by a fair streamlet.
This we passed as if hard ground ; through seven gates I
entered with these sages ; we came to a meadow of fresh
verdure. People were there with eyes slow and grave, of
great authority in their looks ; they spake seldom and with
soft voices. Thus we drew apart, on one side, into a place

---

[1] I follow Professor Norton's prose version here.

open, luminous, and high, so that they all could be seen. There opposite upon the green enamel were shown to me the great spirits, whom to have seen I inwardly exalt myself.

I saw Electra with many companions, among whom I knew Hector and Æneas, Cæsar in armor, with his ger-falcon eyes; I saw Camilla and Penthesilea on the other side, and I saw the King Latinus, who was seated with Lavinia, his daughter. I saw that Brutus who drove out Tarquin ; Lucretia, Julia, Marcia, and Cornelia; and alone, apart, I saw the Saladin. When I raised my brow a little more, I saw the Master of those who know, seated amid the philosophic family; all regard him, all do him honor. Here I saw both Socrates and Plato, who before the others stand nearest to him; Democritus, who ascribes the world to chance; Diogenes, Anaxagoras, and Thales, Empedocles, Heraclitus, and Zeno; and I saw the good collector of the qualities, Dioscorides, I mean; and I saw Orpheus, Tully, and Linus, and moral Seneca, Euclid the geometer, and Ptolemy, Hippocrates, Avicenna, Galen, and Averroës, who made the great comment. I cannot report of all in full, because the long theme so drives me that many times speech comes short of fact.

**89. Dante's sad life. (From the *Convito*.)**

Dante excuses himself for a certain obscurity which he has introduced into his *Banquet,* with the hope of giving it some dignity in the eyes of the many Italians who had seen him during his wanderings, and perhaps had formed a low estimate of him.

Alas ! would that it might have pleased the Dispenser of the Universe that the cause of my excuse might never have been, that others might neither have sinned against me, nor I have suffered punishment unjustly; the punishment, I say, of exile and poverty ! Since it was the pleasure of the citizens of the most beautiful and the most famous daughter of Rome, Florence, to cast me out from her most sweet bosom (wherein I was born and nourished even to the height of my life, and in which, with her good will, I desire with all my heart to repose my weary soul, and to end the time which is given to me), I have gone through almost all the land in which this language lives — a pilgrim, almost a mendicant — showing forth against my will the wound of Fortune, with which the ruined man is often unjustly reproached.

Truly I have been a ship without a sail and without a rudder, borne to divers ports and lands and shores by the dry wind which blows from grievous poverty; and I have appeared vile in the eyes of many, who perhaps through some report may have imaged me in other form. In the sight of whom not only my person became vile, but my work was held to be of less value, both that already done and that which remained still to do.

Petrarch well knew how to describe himself and his aspirations. He writes thus to posterity:

Greeting. — It is possible that some word of me may have come to you, though even this is doubtful, since an insignificant and obscure name will scarcely penetrate far in either time or space. If, however, you should have heard of me, you may desire to know what manner of man I was, or what was the outcome of my labors, especially those of which some description or, at any rate, the bare titles may have reached you.

To begin with myself, then: the utterances of men concerning me will differ widely, since in passing judgment almost every one is influenced not so much by truth as by preference, and good and evil report alike know no bounds. I was, in truth, a poor mortal like yourself, neither very exalted in my origin, nor, on the other hand, of the most humble birth, but belonging, as Augustus Cæsar says of himself, to an ancient family. As to my disposition, I was not naturally perverse or wanting in modesty, however the contagion of evil associations may have corrupted me.

My youth was gone before I realized it; I was carried away by the strength of manhood; but a riper age brought

90. Petrarch's description of himself. (From his *Letter to Posterity*.)

me to my senses and taught me by experience the truth I had long before read in books, that youth and pleasure are vanity, — nay, that the Author of all ages and times permits us miserable mortals, puffed up with emptiness, thus to wander about, until finally, coming to a tardy consciousness of our sins, we shall learn to know ourselves.

In my prime I was blessed with a quick and active body, although not exceptionally strong; and while I do not lay claim to remarkable personal beauty, I was comely enough in my best days. I was possessed of a clear complexion, between light and dark, lively eyes, and for long years a keen vision, which however deserted me, contrary to my hopes, after I reached my sixtieth birthday, and forced me, to my great annoyance, to resort to glasses. Although I had previously enjoyed perfect health, old age brought with it the usual array of discomforts.

My parents were honorable folk, Florentine in their origin, of medium fortune, or, I may as well admit it, in a condition verging upon poverty. They had been expelled from their native city, and consequently I was born in exile, at Arezzo, in the year 1304 of this latter age, which begins with Christ's birth, July the 20th, on a Monday, at dawn. . . . In my familiar associations with kings and princes, and in my friendship with noble personages, my good fortune has been such as to excite envy. But it is the cruel fate of those who are growing old that they can commonly only weep for friends who have passed away. The greatest kings of this age have loved and courted me. They may know why; I certainly do not. With some of them I was on such terms that they seemed in a certain sense my guests rather than I theirs; their lofty position in no way embarrassing me, but, on the contrary, bringing with it many advantages. I fled, however, from many of those to whom I was greatly attached; and such was my innate longing for liberty, that I studiously avoided those whose very name seemed incompatible with the freedom that I loved.

I possessed a well-balanced rather than a keen intellect, — one prone to all kinds of good and wholesome study, but especially inclined to moral philosophy and the art of poetry. The latter, indeed, I neglected as time went on, and took delight in sacred literature. Finding in that a hidden sweetness which I had once esteemed but lightly, I came to regard the works of the poets as only amenities.

Among the many subjects which interested me, I dwelt especially upon antiquity, for our own age has always repelled me, so that, had it not been for the love of those dear to me, I should have preferred to have been born in any other period than our own. In order to forget my own time, I have constantly striven to place myself in spirit in other ages, and consequently I delighted in history. The conflicting statements troubled me, but when in doubt I accepted what appeared most probable, or yielded to the authority of the writer.

Vespasiano, a Florentine bookseller who died in 1498, gives us some very interesting accounts of his distinguished patrons in his *Lives of Illustrious Men*.

91. Founding of the Vatican Library by Nicholas V. (From Vespasiano's *Lives of Illustrious Men*.)

Owing to the jubilee of 1450 a great quantity of money came in by this means to the apostolic see, and with this the pope commenced building in many places, and sent for Greek and Latin books, wherever he was able to find them, without regard to price. He gathered together a large band of writers, the best that he could find, and kept them in constant employment. He also summoned a number of learned men, both for the purpose of composing new works and of translating such existing works as were not already translated, giving them most abundant provision for their needs meanwhile; and when the works were translated and brought to him, he gave the translators large sums of money, in order that they should do more willingly that which they undertook to do.

He made great provision for the needs of learned men. He gathered together great numbers of books upon every subject, both Greek and Latin, to the number of five thousand volumes. So at his death it was found by inventory that never since the time of Ptolemy had half that number of books of every kind been brought together. All books he caused to be copied, without regard to what it cost him, and there were few places where his Holiness had not copiers at work. When he could not procure a book for himself in any way, he had it copied. . . .

**92. How Cosimo, father of Lorenzo de' Medici, founded a library. (From *Vespasiano*.)**

When Cosimo had finished the monastery [near Florence] and a good part of the church, he fell to thinking how he should have the place peopled with honest men of letters; and in this way it occurred to him to found a fine library; and one day when I happened to be present in his chamber, he said to me, " In what way would you furnish this library? " I replied that as for buying the books it would be impossible, for they were not to be had. Then he said, " How is it possible then to furnish it? " I told him that it would be necessary to have the books copied. He asked in reply if I would be willing to undertake the task. I answered him, that I was willing. He told me to commence my work and he would leave everything to me; and as for the money that would be necessary, he would refer the matter to Con Archangel, then prior of the monastery, who would draw bills upon the bank, which should be paid.

The library was commenced at once, for it was his pleasure that it should be done with the utmost possible celerity; and as I did not lack for money, I collected in a short time forty-five writers, and finished two hundred volumes in twenty-two months; in which work we made use of an excellent list, that of the library of Pope Nicholas, which he had given to Cosimo; in the form of a catalogue made out with his own hands . . . and all the other works necessary to a library, of which no one was wanting. And since there were not copies of all these works in Florence, we sent to Milan, to Bologna, and to other places, wherever they might be found.

Cosimo lived to see the library wholly completed, and the cataloguing and the arranging of the books; in all of which he took great pleasure, and the work went forward, as was his custom, with great promptness.

### III. THE ARTISTS OF THE RENAISSANCE

Giorgio Vasari (1512–1574), a painter of some ability himself and an enthusiastic admirer of the great artists of Italy, among whom he considered his friend and contemporary, Michael Angelo, the greatest, wrote a long series of charming biographies of painters, sculptors, and architects, which form the chief source for the lives of the Italian artists from Giotto to Titian.

Vasari writes thus of Raphael's premature death and of his kindly disposition toward his fellow-artists.

93. Kindly disposition of Raphael (From Vasari's *Lives of the Painters.*)

When this noble artist died, well might Painting have departed also, for when he closed his eyes she too was left, as it were, blind. . . . To him of a truth it is that we owe the possession of invention, coloring, and execution, brought alike and together to that perfection for which few could have dared to hope; nor has any man ever aspired to surpass him.

And in addition to the benefits which this great master conferred on art, being as he was its best friend, we have the further obligation to him of having taught us by his life in what manner we should comport ourselves toward great men, as well as toward those of lesser degree, and even toward the lowest; nay, there was among his many extraordinary gifts one of such value and importance that I can never sufficiently admire it and always think thereof with astonishment.

This was the power accorded to him by heaven, of bringing all who approached his presence into harmony, an effect inconceivably surprising in our calling, and contrary to the nature of our artists. Yet all, I do not say of the inferior grades only, but even those who lay claim to be great personages (and of this humor our art produces immense numbers) became as of one mind, once they began to labor in the society of Raphael, continuing in such unity and concord that all harsh feelings and evil dispositions became subdued and disappeared at the sight of him ; every vile and base thought departing from the mind before his influence.

Such harmony prevailed at no other time than his own. And this happened because all were surpassed by him in friendly courtesy as well as in art; all confessed the influence of his sweet and gracious nature, which was so replete with excellence and so perfect in all the charities, that not only was he honored by men but even by the very animals, who would constantly follow his steps and always loved him.

94. Michael Angelo and the popes. (From Vasari's *Lives of the Painters*.)

Several of Michael Angelo's greatest works were undertaken at the order of Pope Julius II (d. 1512), who had the highest appreciation of his genius. But the independence of the artist and the irascible temper of the pontiff occasioned numerous quarrels between them, which invariably resulted in fresh favors from the pope.

The pope's impatience to see the frescoes in the Sistine Chapel completed.

[The pope was very anxious to see the decoration of the Sistine Chapel completed, and constantly inquired when it would be finished.] On one occasion, therefore, Michael Angelo replied, " It will be finished when I shall have done all that I believe is required to satisfy Art." "And we command," rejoined the pontiff, "that you satisfy our wish to have it done quickly," adding that if it were not at once completed, he would have Michael Angelo thrown headlong from the scaffolding. Hearing this, our artist, who feared the fury of the pope, and with good cause, without taking time to add what was wanting, took down the remainder of the scaffolding, to the great satisfaction of the whole city, on All Saints' day, when Pope Julius went into that chapel to sing mass. But Michael Angelo had much desired to retouch some portions of the work *a secco*,[1] as had been done by the older masters who had painted the stories on the

1 That is, after the damp plaster upon which the paint had been originally laid *al fresco* had dried.

walls. He would also have gladly added a little ultramarine to the draperies and gilded other parts, to the end that the whole might have a richer and more striking effect.

The pope, too, hearing that these things were still wanting, and finding that all who beheld the chapel praised it highly, would now fain have had the additions made; but as Michael Angelo thought reconstructing the scaffold too long an affair, the pictures remained as they were, although the pope, who often saw Michael Angelo, would sometimes say, "Let the chapel be enriched with bright colors and gold; it looks poor." When Michael Angelo would reply familiarly, "Holy Father, the men of those days did not adorn themselves with gold; those who are painted here less than any, for they were none too rich; besides which they were holy men, and must have despised riches and ornaments."

[In 1546, San Gallo, who was in charge of the building operations at St. Peter's in Rome, having died, Pope Paul III asked Michael Angelo to undertake the office.] The master at first replied that he would not, architecture not being his vocation; but when entreaties were found useless, the pope commanded him to accept the trust, and to his infinite regret he was compelled to obey. He did not approve of San Gallo's plan. He would often publicly declare that San Gallo had left the building without lights, and had heaped too many ranges of columns one above the other on the outside; adding that, with its innumerable projections, pinnacles, and divisions of members, it was more like a work of the Teutons than of the good antique manner, or of the cheerful and beautiful modern style.[1] He furthermore affirmed that fifty years of time, with more than three hundred thousand crowns in the cost, might very well be spared, while the work might be completed with increased majesty, grandeur, and lightness, to say nothing of better design, greater beauty, and superior convenience.

*Michael Angelo required by the pope to carry on the work of St. Peter's.*

[1] That is, that it resembled the Gothic rather than the Classical or Renaissance style.

He made a model also, to prove the truth of his words, and this was of the form wherein we now see the work to have been carried on; it cost twenty-five crowns and was finished in a fortnight, that of San Gallo having exceeded four thousand and having occupied several years in making. From this and other circumstances, it was indeed easy to see that the church had become an object of traffic and a means of gain rather than a building to be completed, being considered by those who undertook the work as a kind of bargain to be turned to the best account.

Such a state of things could not fail to displease so upright a man as Michael Angelo, and as the pope had made him superintendent against his will, he determined to be rid of them all. He therefore one day told them openly that he knew well that they had done and were doing all they could by means of their friends to prevent him from entering on this office, but that if he were to undertake the charge he would not suffer one of them to remain about the building.

## BIBLIOGRAPHY

**General Review of the Period :** ADAMS, *Civilization*, Chapter XV ; LODGE, *Close of the Middle Ages*, Chapter XXII.

**Political History :** LODGE, Chapter VIII, "Italy in the Fourteenth Century"; Chapter XII, "Milan and Venice in the Fifteenth Century"; Chapter XIV, "Florence under the Medici."

**Florence :** *Cambridge Modern History*, Vol. I, Chapter V, "Savonarola," and Chapter VI, "Machiavelli."

**Venice :** *Cambridge Modern History*, Vol. I, Chapter VIII.

**The Papacy :** *Cambridge Modern History*, Vol. I, Chapter VII.

**Humanism :** *Cambridge Modern History*, Vol. I, Chapter XVI.

**Extracts from the Writers of the Time :** WHITCOMB, *Literary Source-Book of the Italian Renaissance.*

SYMONDS, J. A., *Renaissance in Italy*, 7 vols. This is by far the most extensive treatment in English of the culture of the Renaissance. It is often brilliant but diffuse. Vol. I, "The Age of the Despots," is the best introduction to the general political and social situation ; Vol. II is on "The Revival of Learning"; Vol. III, "The Fine Arts"; Vols.

IV and V, "Italian Literature"; Vols. VI and VII, "The Catholic Reaction," relate to the sixteenth century.

BURCKHARDT, *The Civilization of the Italian Renaissance.* All serious students of the period should be acquainted with this remarkable volume, where the various phases of the Renaissance are treated in a more profound and scholarly spirit than in "The Age of the Despots."

ARMSTRONG, *Lorenzo de' Medici and Florence in the Fifteenth Century* (Heroes of the Nations).

BROWN, HORATIO, *Venice: An Historical Sketch of the Republic.* By one well versed in the subject.

MRS. OLIPHANT, *Makers of Florence.* Popular essays on Dante, Giotto, and Savonarola. Also *Makers of Venice* by the same writer.

Of the writers of the time, there are available in English the following:

DANTE, *Divine Comedy*, translated into English prose by Professor C. E. Norton; and his *Banquet*, a very interesting but uncompleted treatise on a variety of matters, written in Italian for those who did not know Latin. It is well translated by Miss Katharine Hillard. Professor Norton has also translated Dante's charming account of his early experiences, — *The New Life.*

Dante's treatise on government — *De Monarchia* — is translated in CHURCH, *Dante*, pp. 175-308, and portions, in the Old South Leaflets, General Series, No. 123. His work on the mother tongue — *De Vulgari Eloquio* — is translated with notes by Howell, 1890.

Of the vast literature relating to Dante, the historical student will find especially useful: MOORE, EDW., *Studies in Dante*, first series, on his knowledge of books, and WITTE, KARL, *Essays on Dante.*

*Petrarch, the First Modern Scholar and Man of Letters*, a selection from his letters to Boccaccio and his other friends, translated, with an introduction, by ROBINSON and ROLFE. This book was prepared with a view to giving the historical student an idea of Petrarch and his great rôle in the history of culture.

VILLANI, GIOVANNI, *Florentine Chronicle*, coming down to 1348 and relating especially to Dante's and Petrarch's time. It was continued by Giovanni's brother Matteo to 1363. Portions of the earlier part are translated, — *Selections from the first nine books of the Croniche Fiorentine*, edited by WICKSTEED, and coming down to Dante's death, 1321.

BALDASSARE CASTIGLIONE, *The Book of the Courtier*, completed in 1516 by a gentleman at the court of Urbino. This proved a very popular book and was translated into English in 1561. It deals in a charming way with those qualities which a true gentleman should possess. In

"Tudor Translations" ($7.50) and in a new translation by Opdycke (Scribner's, 1903; $10.00), both unfortunately expensive.

MACHIAVELLI, *The Prince*. This famous little work which casts so much light on the political spirit of the time has been several times translated into English. There is a good edition by N. H. Hill (Clarendon Press), another together with Machiavelli's *History of Florence* in the Bohn Library. The latter becomes detailed with the beginnings of the power of the Medici about 1434 and closes about 1525.

VASARI, *Lives of Seventy of the Most Eminent Painters, Sculptors, and Architects*. Translated, complete, by Mrs. Foster in the Bohn Library, 5 vols. Also in the Temple Classics, a new edition of selected Lives by Blashfield and Hopkins, with useful notes.

For Rome and the popes, see CREIGHTON, *History of the Papacy;* PASTOR, *History of the Popes;* and GREGOROVIUS, *History of the City of Rome*, Vol. VII.

For the art: "College Histories of Art," edited by JOHN C. VAN DYKE, including VAN DYKE, *The History of Painting;* HAMLIN, *The History of Architecture;* MARQUAND and FROTHINGHAM, *The History of Sculpture,* — useful manuals. Larger works: FURGUSSON, *History of Modern Architecture;* FLETCHER, *A History of Architecture;* LÜBKE, *History of Sculpture;* WOLTMANN and WOERMANN, *History of Painting*.

DE VINNE, *The Invention of Printing*, by a well-known expert in that art; BLADES, *Pentateuch of Printing*, — very good; and PUTNAM, *Books and their Makers*, Vol. I.

# CHAPTER XXIII

## EUROPE AT THE OPENING OF THE SIXTEENTH CENTURY

### I. The Expedition of Charles VIII into Italy

There could be no more charming introduction to the history of the sixteenth century than the famous memoirs of Philip of Commines.[1] The French, in modern times, have been distinguished for the skill with which they combine their personal reminiscences with a more or less complete account of the history of their own times, in the form of memoirs, which both delight the casual reader and serve the purposes of the serious historian. Of this attractive but too often unreliable kind of history Commines affords a very early and admirable example. He thus describes the attitude of the Italian states toward the French invader.

*The Memoirs of Philip of Commines.*

In the year 1493 the lord Ludovico [il Moro] began to solicit King Charles VIII, then reigning in France, to undertake an expedition into Italy, to conquer the kingdom of Naples, and to supplant and exterminate those who possessed it; for whilst they were in force and authority Ludovico durst not attempt what he did afterwards; for at that time Ferrante, king of Naples, and Alphonso, his son, were both very rich, of great experience in war, and had the reputation of being very valiant princes, though it afterwards appeared otherwise.[2]

95. Attitude of the Italian states toward the French invader.

[1] For Commines' estimate of both Charles the Bold and Louis XI, see above, pp. 203 *sqq.*

[2] Ferrante was king of Naples only, not of Sicily, which belonged to Ferdinand the Catholic, as part of the possessions of the rulers of Aragon. See *History of Western Europe*, p. 360, note (Vol. II, p. 8, note). Ferrante

This Ludovico was a wise man, but very timorous and humble where he was in awe of any one, and false and deceitful when it was for his advantage; and this I do not speak by hearsay, but as one that knew him well, and had many transactions with him. But to proceed: In the year 1493 he began to tickle King Charles, who was but twenty-two years of age, with the vanities and glories of Italy, demonstrating (as is reported) the right which he had to the fine kingdom of Naples, which he knew well enough how to blazon and display. . . .

How Charles VIII entered into negotiations with the wily Venetians.

[Now since the heart of our king, though he was very young, was strangely bent upon this enterprise,] he requested the Venetians to give him their assistance and counsel in his expedition, and they returned this answer: That he should be very welcome in Italy, but that they were wholly incapable of assisting him, upon account of their continual apprehensions of the Turk — though at that time they were at peace with him. As for undertaking to advise so wise a king, who had so grave a council, that would savor too much of presumption on their part; nevertheless they would rather assist than disturb him in his designs.

Now this they believed a very discreet answer, and truly so it was; and I am of opinion that their affairs are managed with more prudence and discretion at this day than the affairs of any other prince or state in the world; — but God will still have us know that the wisdom and policy of man is of no avail where he pleases to interpose, for he ordered the affair quite otherwise than they were anticipating. . . .

Characteristic attitude of an Italian state toward a foreign invader.

In view of all their grudges against the king of Naples, the Venetians thought it would be highly to their advantage if a war should be begun between our king and the house of Aragon[1]; hoping it would not be brought to a conclusion so

---

died just before Charles started on his Italian expedition. He was succeeded by his brutal son, Alphonso, duke of Calabria, who however abdicated in a panic of fear upon the approach of Charles and his army.

[1] Namely, the above-mentioned Ferrante of Naples and his son Alphonso, who belonged to a branch of the reigning house of Aragon.

soon as it was, and that it would only weaken the power of their enemies and not utterly destroy them; and then, let happen what would, one side or the other would give them towns in Apulia, which borders upon their gulf, in order to have their assistance. And even so it fell out, though they had liked to have been mistaken in their reckoning. Besides, they thought that nobody could accuse them of inviting our king into Italy, since they had neither given him counsel nor assistance, as appeared to the world by their answer above.

In the year 1493 the king advanced to Lyons, to examine into his affairs; but nobody ever imagined he would have passed the mountains himself. . . .

[Nevertheless] the king, on the 23d of August, 1494, set out from Vienne, and marched straight toward Asti. At Susa, the lord Galeazzo di St. Severino came post to meet his Majesty, who advanced from thence to Turin, where he borrowed the jewels of Madame of Savoy, daughter to the late William, marquis of Montferrat, and widow to Charles, duke of Savoy. Having pawned them for twelve thousand ducats, he removed a few days after to Casale, the residence of the marchioness of Montferrat, a young and prudent lady, and daughter to the king of Servia. The Turk having overrun her country, the emperor, whose relative she was, took care of her, and procured her a husband. She also lent the king her jewels, and they also were pawned for twelve thousand ducats; by which you may see how unprosperous was the beginning of this war, had not God himself conducted the enterprise. . . .

*How the king of France raised funds on borrowed jewels.*

Something must now be said of the Florentines, who sent two embassies to the king of France before his setting out upon this expedition; but their design was only to dissemble with him. . . . Our demands were only that they should grant us passage for our troops, and furnish us an hundred men at arms, to be paid by them after the Italian rate (which is but ten thousand ducats a year).

*95a. Florence and the Medici.*

The ambassadors replied according to the instructions that were given them by Piero de' Medici, a young man of no extraordinary parts, son of Lorenzo de' Medici, lately deceased, who had been one of the wisest men of his time, had governed the city almost as a prince, and left it to his son. Their house had already existed two generations, during the lives of Piero, the father of this Lorenzo, and of Cosimo, who founded it, a man worthy to be reckoned among the chief of that age. Indeed, in their profession, which was merchandising, I think this family was the greatest that ever was in the world; for their agents had so much reputation on account of this name of Medici that the effect of it in England and Flanders, as I have myself seen, is scarce credible.

I saw one of their agents, Gerard Canisiani, who kept King Edward IV upon his throne, almost upon his own credit, during the time of the great civil wars in that kingdom; for he furnished the king at different times with more than six-score thousand crowns, — little to his master's advantage, though in the end he got his money back again. I knew also another, named Thomas Portinari, who was security between King Edward and Charles, duke of Burgundy, for fifty thousand crowns, and at another time for eighty thousand. I cannot commend merchants for acting thus; but it is highly commendable in a prince to be punctual with them, and keep his promise exactly; for he knows not how soon he may want their assistance, and certainly a little money sometimes does great service.

This family of Medici seem already to be in a declining condition — as happens in all kingdoms and governments — for the authority of his predecessors has been hurtful to Piero, though indeed Cosimo, the first of the family, was mild and gentle in his administration, and behaved himself as he ought in a free city.

Lorenzo, the father of that Piero of whom we are now speaking, upon occasion of the difference, mentioned in a former part of this book, betwixt him and the Pisans, in which several of them were hanged, had a guard of twenty soldiers assigned him, for the security of his person, by an order from the city council, which at that time did whatever he commanded. However, he governed very moderately; for, as I said before, he was a wise man.

His son Piero, on the contrary, thought that a guard was his due, and, what is more, he employed it to the terror and vexation of his people, committing great injuries and insolences by night, and invading the common treasure. His father had indeed done this before him; but he managed it so prudently that the people were almost satisfied with his proceedings. . . .

I had almost forgotten to mention that while I was at Florence, on my way to join the king, I went to pay a visit to a certain Dominican, named Friar Jerome, who, by all reports, was a very holy man, and had lived in a reformed convent fifteen years. There went along with me one Jean François, a prudent person, and steward of the king's household. The occasion of my going to visit Friar Jerome was that he had always preached much in our king's favor, and his words had served to keep the Florentines from turning against us; for never had any preacher enjoyed so much authority in a city.

95b. The memorable preaching of Friar Jerome Savonarola.

In spite of what has been said or written to the contrary, he always affirmed that our king would come into Italy, saying that he was sent by God to chastise the tyranny of princes, and that none would be able to oppose him. He foretold likewise that he would come to Pisa and enter it, and that the state of Florence would be dissolved on that day. And so it fell out; for Piero de' Medici was driven out that very day.

Many other things he presaged long before they came to pass, as, for instance, the death of Lorenzo de' Medici; and he openly declared that he knew it by revelation; as likewise he predicted that the Church would be reformed by the sword. This is not yet accomplished; but it must be said that it very nearly occurred, and he still maintains that it will come to pass. Many persons blamed him for pretending to receive divine revelations, but others believed him; for my part, I think him a good man.

I asked him whether our king would return safe into France, considering the great preparations that the Venetians were making against him, of which he gave a better account than I could, though I had lately come from Venice. He told me he would meet with difficulties by the way, but that he would overcome them all with honor, though he had but a hundred men in his company; for God, who had conducted him thither, would securely guard him on his way back again.

But because he had not applied himself as he ought to the reformation of the Church, and because he had permitted his soldiers to rob and plunder the poor people, — those who had freely opened their gates to him as well as the enemy who had opposed him, — therefore God had pronounced judgment against him, and in a short time he would receive chastisement.

However, he bade me tell the king that if he would have compassion upon the people, and command his soldiers to do them no wrong, and punish them when they did, as it was his office to do, God would then mitigate, if not revoke, his sentence; but that it would not be sufficient for him to plead that he did the people no wrong himself. And he declared that he would meet the king when he came, and tell him so from his own mouth; and so he did, and pressed hard for the restitution of the Florentine towns.

## II. MACHIAVELLI'S DESCRIPTION OF THE TROUBLES IN ITALY AT THE OPENING OF THE SIXTEENTH CENTURY

Machiavelli's
*Prince.*

Machiavelli's little guide for despots, *The Prince*, was written in 1513, at the opening of Leo X's pontificate, and contains many references to important events which were still fresh in his mind. These contemporaneous events and the princes who took part in them are used constantly as illustrations and warnings. Probably no other book gives one so lively a notion as does *The Prince* of the prevailing political spirit at the beginning of the sixteenth century.[1]

Nothing makes a prince so well thought of as to undertake great enterprises and give striking proofs of his capacity.

Among the princes of our time Ferdinand of Aragon, the present king of Spain, may almost be accounted a new prince, since from one of the weakest he has become, for fame and glory, the foremost king in Christendom. And if you consider his achievements, you will find them all great, and some extraordinary.

In the beginning of his reign he made war on Granada, which enterprise was the foundation of his power. At first he carried on the war leisurely, without fear of interruption, and kept the attention and thoughts of the barons of Castile so completely occupied with it that they had no time to think of changes at home. Meanwhile he insensibly acquired reputation among them and authority over them. With the money of the Church and of his subjects he was able to maintain his armies, and during the prolonged contest to lay the foundations of that military discipline which afterwards made him so famous.

Moreover, to enable him to engage in still greater undertakings, always covering himself with the cloak of religion, he had recourse to what may be called "pious cruelty," in driving out and clearing his kingdom of the Moors; than which exploit none could be more wonderful or uncommon. Using the same pretext, he made war on Africa, invaded Italy, and finally attacked France; and being thus constantly busied in planning and executing vast designs, he kept the minds of his subjects in a state of suspense and wonder and occupied with the results of his actions, which arose one out of another in such close succession as left neither time nor opportunity to oppose them. . . .

96. Machiavelli's estimate of Ferdinand of Aragon.

[1] Extracts from *The Prince* describing the spirit and policy of the Italian despots are given above, pp. 219 *sq.*

96a. Whether
it is prudent
for a prince
to keep his
promises.

Every one understands how praiseworthy it is in a prince to keep faith, and to live uprightly and not craftily. Nevertheless we see, from what has taken place in our own days, that princes who have set little store by their word, but have known how to overreach men by their cunning, have accomplished great things, and in the end got the better of those who trusted to honest dealing.

Be it known, then, that there are two ways of contending, — one in accordance with the laws, the other by force ; the first of which is proper to men, the second to beasts. But since the first method is often ineffectual, it becomes necessary to resort to the second. A prince should, therefore, understand how to use well both the man and the beast. . . . But inasmuch as a prince should know how to use the beast's nature wisely, he ought of beasts to choose both the lion and the fox ; for the lion cannot guard himself from the toils, nor the fox from wolves. He must therefore be a fox to discern toils, and a lion to drive off wolves.

A prince
should not
keep his word
when to keep
it would
injure him.

To rely wholly on the lion is unwise ; and for this reason a prudent prince neither can nor ought to keep his word when to keep it is hurtful to him and the causes which led him to pledge it are removed. If all men were good, this would not be good advice, but since they are dishonest and do not keep faith with you, you in return need not keep faith with them ; and no prince was ever at a loss for plausible reasons to cloak a breach of faith. Of this numberless recent instances could be given, and it might be shown how many solemn treaties and engagements have been rendered inoperative and idle through want of faith among princes, and that he who has best known how to play the fox has had the best success.

It is necessary, indeed, to put a good color on this nature, and to be skilled in simulating and dissembling. But men are so simple, and governed so absolutely by their present needs, that he who wishes to deceive will never fail in finding willing dupes.

One recent example I will not omit. Pope Alexander VI had no care or thought but how to deceive, and always found material to work on. No man ever had a more effective manner of asseverating, or made promises with more solemn protestations, or observed them less. And yet, because he understood this side of human nature, his frauds always succeeded. . . .

Policy of Pope Alexander VI.

In his efforts to aggrandize his son, the duke [Cæsar Borgia], Alexander VI had to face many difficulties, both immediate and remote. . . . It was consequently necessary that the existing order of things should be changed, and the states of Italy thrown into confusion, in order that he might safely make himself master of some part of them; and this became easy for him when he found that the Venetians, moved by other causes, were plotting to bring the French once more into Italy. This design he accordingly did not oppose, but furthered by annulling the first marriage of King Louis of France.[1]

The pope's selfish reasons for encouraging Louis XII to invade Italy.

King Louis therefore came into Italy at the instance of the Venetians, and with the consent of Pope Alexander; and no sooner was he in Milan than the pope got troops from him to forward the papal schemes in Romagna, which province, moved by the reputation of the French arms, at once submitted.

Louis XII captures Milan.

But Machiavelli hated the "barbarians," — the French, Germans, and Spaniards, — and in the last chapter of his *Prince* he called upon the nephew of Leo X to free Italy from the foreign invaders and, by putting in practice the principles of conduct previously described, to establish a strong government and bring peace once more to his distracted country.

96b. Machiavelli calls upon the house of Medici to drive out the "barbarians."

If, as I have said, it was necessary in order to display the valor of Moses that the children of Israel should be slaves in Egypt, and to show the greatness and courage

---

[1] Louis XII's desire for a divorce was due to his eagerness to marry the widow of Charles VIII, Anne of Brittany, who would bring to the French crown the important fief of Brittany.

A.16

of Cyrus that the Persians should be oppressed by the Medes, and to illustrate the excellence of Theseus that the Athenians should be scattered and divided, so at this hour, to prove the worth of some Italian hero, it was required that Italy should be brought to her present abject condition, be more a slave than the Hebrew, more oppressed than the Persian, more disunited than the Athenian, without a head, without order, beaten, spoiled, torn in pieces, overrun, and abandoned to destruction in every shape.

But though, heretofore, glimmerings may have been discerned in this man or that, whence it might be conjectured that he was ordained by God for Italy's redemption, nevertheless it has afterwards been seen in the further course of his actions that Fortune has disowned him; so that our country, left almost without life, still waits to know who it is that is to heal her bruises, to put an end to the devastation and plunder of Lombardy and to the exactions and imposts of Naples and Tuscany, and to stanch those wounds of hers which long neglect has changed into running sores.

We see how she prays God to send some one to rescue her from these barbarous cruelties and oppressions. . . .

With what love he would be received in all those provinces which have suffered from the foreign inundation; with what thirst for vengeance, with what firm fidelity, with what devotion and what tears, no words of mine can declare. What gates would be closed against him? What people would refuse him obedience? What jealousy would stand in his way? What Italian but would yield him homage? This barbarian tyranny stinks in all nostrils.

## III. Spain at the Opening of the Sixteenth Century

In 1512 the republic of Florence dispatched one of its most distinguished citizens, the historian Guicciardini, to Spain with orders to learn all that he could of the country and of the character and projects of Ferdinand the Catholic, king of Aragon, who had been interfering for years in Italian matters. Guicciardini remained in Spain for toward two years, and prepared for his government a brief but very careful report, in which he describes the general condition of the country, the temperament of the people, and the court of Ferdinand. If his observations are trustworthy, it is clear that Spain was not in a flourishing condition on the eve of Charles V's accession, and that it is small wonder that, with the perverse policy of its kings in undertaking foreign conquests and in persecuting the industrious Moors at home, the kingdom should have declined rapidly when the money from the American mines began to give out.

Spain is thinly populated, so that towns and burgs are rare, and between one great town and another scarcely a house will be found. In short, the inhabitants are few. There are some fine cities, like Barcelona, Sargossa, Valencia, Granada, and Seville ; but they are few for such an important kingdom and for so great an area of country. Aside from these principal centers, most of the towns are small and have rude buildings, of which the greater part, in many places, are built of mud and are, moreover, full of filth and dirt. *Meager population of Spain.*

The land is fertile and yields abundantly, since more grain is raised than is necessary for use at home. The same may be said of the wine, which is sent by sea to Flanders and England. Oil, too, is exported in great quantities every year to the countries mentioned above and to Alexandria, to the value of more than sixty thousand ducats. The fertility is greatest in the lower parts of Andalusia and Granada, and would be much greater than it is if all the land were brought under cultivation ; but it is worked only in the neighborhood of the towns and there badly ; the rest remains untilled. Much wool is exported annually, amounting, it is said, to two hundred and fifty thousand ducats, as well as the finest silk, especially from the lower regions. From Viscaya come iron and steel in considerable quantity, *Fertility of the land.*

and much grain, leather, alum, and many other products, so that if only this nation were industrious and given to trade it would be rich.

The country is cold in the region of the Pyrenees, very warm in Andalusia and Granada, and more temperate in the central districts.

Haughtiness of the Spaniards. The men of this nation are gloomy of temperament and swarthy of complexion; dark in color and short of stature; they are proud by nature, and it seems to them as if no nation could be compared with theirs. They are prone to boast in their conversation of their own things, and endeavor to make the best possible appearance. They have little love for foreigners and are very uncivil toward them. They are devoted to arms, perhaps more than any other Christian nation, and are very skillful with them, owing to their agile frames and their dexterity. In military matters they are great sticklers for honor, in such wise that rather than sully it they prefer to die. . . .

Unpopularity of trade and industry. The Spaniards are held to be clever and acute, but nevertheless they are not skillful in any of the arts, whether mechanical or liberal. Almost all the artisans at the king's court belong to the French or to some other foreign nation. The natives do not devote themselves to trade, which they look upon as degrading; the pride of the hidalgo goes to his head, and he would rather turn to arms with little chance of gain, or serve a grandee in wretchedness and poverty, or, before the times of the present king, even assault wayfarers, than engage in trade or any other business. Recently, however, some attention is beginning to be given in a few places to trade, and already in parts of Spain cloth and silks are manufactured ; . . . for example, in Valencia, Toledo, and Seville.

But the whole nation is opposed to industry. Accordingly the artisans only work when they are driven to do so by necessity, and then they take their ease until they have spent their earnings; this is the reason why manual labor is so dear. The meanest cultivators of the soil have the same habit. They will not exert themselves except under dire pressure of want, so that they bring much less land under cultivation than they might, and the little they do till is badly cared for. . . .

Aside from a few grandees of the kingdom who display great luxury, it must be remembered that the rest of the people live at home in the utmost straits ; and if they have a little to spend they put it all on their backs or in purchasing a mule, thus making a great show before the world when they have scarce anything at home, where their surroundings are mean in the extreme and where they exercise an economy truly astonishing.

Although they know how to live on little, they are by no means free from cupidity. On the contrary, they are very avaricious, and not having any of the arts to rely upon, they are driven to robbery, so that in earlier times when the kingdom was less orderly it was full of assassins, who were favored by the nature of the country, with its many mountainous regions and its sparse population. . . .

The Spaniards have not turned their attention to books, and neither the nobility nor others have any idea of Latin, except a very few, who know a little of the language. They are outwardly very religious, but not inwardly. They have infinite ceremonies, which they perform with great exactness, and show much humility in speech, the use of titles, and the kissing of hands. Every one is their lord, every one may command them; but this means little, and you can place no faith in them. . . .

*Superficial religion and politeness of the Spaniards.*

This nation down to our own time has been more oppressed and has enjoyed less glory and dominion than any other nation of Europe, for in the most ancient times the peninsula was occupied in great part by the Gauls. . . . Then the Carthaginians took possession of much of it; then the Romans conquered it all several times. Later the Vandals subjugated the region, and from them Andalusia took its name. Lastly the Moors from Africa conquered not only the southern regions, but extended their dominion into Aragon and Castile and even in some instances as far as the Pyrenees. Down to our own time they held Granada.

*Successive conquests of the Spanish peninsula.*

## BIBLIOGRAPHY

*A. Refer-*
*ences.*

**Charles VIII's Italian Expedition**: JOHNSON, *Europe in the Six-teenth Century*, pp. 4–25; *Cambridge Modern History*, Vol. I, pp. 104–118; DYER and HASSALL, *Modern History*, Vol. I, pp. 214–231.

**Louis XII in Italy**: JOHNSON, pp. 33–49.

**Alexander VI**: *Cambridge Modern History*, Vol. I, pp. 225–242.

**League of Cambray**: JOHNSON, pp. 57–78; DYER and HASSALL, Vol. I, pp. 260–286.

**Spain**: JOHNSON, pp. 91–106; *Cambridge Modern History*, Vol. I, Chapter XI, pp. 347–383.

**Savonarola**: JOHNSON, pp. 25–33; *Cambridge Modern History*, Vol. I, Chapter V, pp. 144–189.

**The Papacy at the Opening of the Sixteenth Century**: *Cambridge Modern History*, Vol. II, Chapter I, pp. 1–34 (excellent).

**Francis I in Italy**: DYER and HASSALL, Vol. I, pp. 356–363.

---

*B. Addi-*
*tional read-*
*ing in*
*English.*

CREIGHTON, *History of the Papacy from the Great Schism to the Sack of Rome.* New edition in 6 vols., 1899–1901. Vol. V contains an admirable account of the opening of the sixteenth century, with special reference to the rôle of the popes. For Savonarola and Charles VIII, see Chapters VII–VIII.

PASTOR, *The History of the Popes from the Close of the Middle Ages.* In course of publication; Vols. I to VI, from the original German, 1898. A work of great erudition, by a distinguished Catholic scholar. See Vol. V, pp. 181–226, on Savonarola, and Vol. VI, pp. 1–454, on Italy and the popes, 1492–1512.

SYMONDS, *Age of Despots*, Chapters VII, IX, and X, on Savonarola and Charles VIII.

GREGOROVIUS, *Rome in the Middle Ages*, Vol. VII, Part II, and Vol. VIII, Part I.

BURKE, U. R., *A History of Spain from the Earliest Times to the Death of Ferdinand the Catholic*, 2 vols., 2d ed., 1900, edited by Hume. Vol. II is the best and most recent account of the reign of Ferdinand and Isabella.

PRESCOTT, *History of the Reign of Ferdinand and Isabella*, 3 vols. Fuller than Burke and charming in style, but as it was completed in 1836, under very adverse circumstances, it is antiquated and somewhat wanting in critical exactness.

# CHAPTER XXIV

## GERMANY BEFORE THE PROTESTANT REVOLT

### I. GERMANY IN THE TIME OF MAXIMILIAN I

It would be difficult indeed to give a clearer or more comprehensive account of the conditions in Germany than that submitted by the Venetian ambassador, Quirini, on his return from the court of Maximilian in 1507.[1] Maximilian was just then contemplating an expedition to Italy, and consequently Quirini opens his report to the doge and council as follows :

Since, most serene prince [namely, the doge], and most sage and weighty council, all the discord which is now to be observed among Christian peoples appears to be due to the most serene king of the Romans [namely, Maximilian] and to the Empire, it seemed to me my duty to report to your excellencies concerning affairs in Germany with such fullness as to enable you in the present emergencies and in those which you will have to face from, let us say, to-day the better to reach your wise decisions.

First, to proceed in an orderly fashion, I will endeavor to narrate all that I have been able to learn of the extent of that country, its government and resources, and the customs throughout Germany ; then of the character and resources of his Majesty the emperor, and the relations which have existed and now exist between him and the princes and estates of the Empire, and between him and the Swiss ; lastly, of the disposition of the Empire and the king toward

98. A Venetian ambassador's account of Germany in 1507.

[1] For an account of the reports of the Venetian ambassadors, see unabridged edition of the *Readings*, Vol. II, p. 30.

this republic and the rest of the Christian rulers, and what his Majesty may be able to accomplish at this juncture.

Enumeration of the chief German princes.

This country of Germany is large and populous, full of principalities, towns, cities, burgs, and castles. . . . Among the temporal rulers there are two kings, about thirty dukes and an archduke, four landgraves, and a great number of counts. The chief among these rulers are the kings of Bohemia and of Denmark, the archduke of Austria, two dukes of Saxony, the duke of Brunswick, the duke of Lüneburg, the duke of Pomerania, the duke of Mechlenburg and he of Jülich and Cleves, the duke of Franconia, the dukes of Bavaria and Würtemberg, the count palatine, the landgrave of Alsace, two margraves of Brandenburg and one of Baden.

The ecclesiastical princes.

Of those in Germany who are at once spiritual and temporal princes, there are five archbishops — Mayence, Cologne, Treves, Magdeburg, and Salzburg — and about twenty-five bishops. Of these latter, the chief are Würzburg, Bamberg, Strasburg, Augsburg, Freising, Eichstädt, Liége, Constance, and Trent. Beside these, there are twenty abbots, five masters of religious orders, and fifteen priors, — all princes of the Empire, who combine spiritual and temporal powers like the bishops.

The free towns.

Besides the above-mentioned principalities there are in Germany about a hundred free towns, of which twenty-eight belong to the Swabian League, sixty-two to the great league of Dantzig and Lübeck [namely, the Hanseatic League], while the rest lie in the region of the Rhine. The principal members of the great league are Dantzig, Stolp, Colberg, Lübeck, Limburg, Hamburg, and Stade; of the Swabian League, Nuremberg, Augsburg, Ulm, Memmingen, and Strasburg. The chief of the Rhine district are Cologne, Speyer, Worms, Frankfort, and Constance. And this ends what I have to say about the size of Germany. . . .

Limited power of the emperor.

The authority over the Empire vested in the emperor, or king of the Romans, goes no further than the laws and justice permit, and he cannot despotically force the princes and free towns to obey any particular desire of his unless he first convoke all the Empire to a diet. . . .

The king of the Romans, or emperor, who proposes in the interest of the Empire to have a careful deliberation, sends a summons to each prince, whether ecclesiastical or secular, and to each of the free towns, that they should all within two months, or three, or whatever time may seem good to him, come together in a certain place, either in person or through representatives or substitutes, on business of importance to the Empire. And all those who are summoned are obliged to come within the limit set; and if they do not come, they incur whatever penalty the king shall impose upon them; and if they do not pay the penalty, they may be excommunicated [1] by the emperor, just as one is excommunicated by the pope. In this case it is free to all to rob and kill the person excommunicated. For this reason every one takes care to come to the diet or send a representative, and not to disobey any command of the emperor which is issued with the consent of the Empire. . . .

*How the diet is summoned*

*The ban.*

When all the princes and representatives have presented themselves, either in person or through their substitutes, the diet opens. The king, or emperor, declares the object and cause for the calling of the diet; he then submits a proposal; the princes remain in consultation some days and then make their answer. This the king accepts, and makes another proposition (" *iterum,*" as it is called), and so business proceeds, the diet either taking action or postponing its decision to another time. In this way two and sometimes three months pass.

*Method of procedure in the diet.*

But the princes or their representatives do not spend all their time in deliberating upon the matters for which the diet was summoned, but settle as well a thousand controversies between prince and prince, between free towns and princes, and between one town and another; they make, moreover, divers provisions according as necessity demands.

*Disputes adjusted by the diet.*

In reaching decisions on important matters the diet is wont to have but three votes, or ballots: one is cast by the electors, the second by the princes, and the third by the

---

[1] Namely, put to the ban, i.e. outlawed. For an illustration of the manner in which Luther was outlawed, see below, pp. 278 *sq.*

representatives of the free towns. . . . When the diet is about to come to an end, these three votes are compared, and the decision sanctioned by two of them is regarded as conclusive and established; and each prince of the empire, whether present or absent, and similarly every free town, is obliged to obey that which the diet decides, under heavy penalties, both as to furnishing money and sending troops in the manner prescribed.

The king, or emperor, has full authority, as soon as the diet has dissolved, to order every one to obey its decisions. If, nevertheless, some one ventures to disobey, the whole Empire, in order not to see its commands disregarded, always turns upon the offender, as happened in recent years in the case of the count palatine, who, for his refusal to accede to what was determined upon at the diet of Augsburg, which was especially concerned with the heritage of Duke George of Bavaria, roused the anger of the king and the whole Empire against him, and in a brief space of time was destroyed. For this reason all the princes and free towns are careful to follow the decisions of the diets, nor do they venture to contravene in any way what has been established. Decisions of the diet cannot be changed except by another diet similar to that which first ratified them.

As for the government of the free towns, each one rules itself by its council, to which are admitted citizens, traders who are not citizens, and artisans ; yet not all the members of these classes are included in the council, for the number varies with the size of the place, and changes from time to time. These councils appoint the magistrates, who administer justice for the time being and, moreover, regulate the revenues and public affairs of the town precisely as if it was a free and independent state.

Some of the towns owe their freedom to privileges granted by the emperor for deeds of valor in the struggle of the Empire against the infidels, who were earlier very troublesome. Others gained their freedom by giving a sum of money to the temporal lord or bishop who held them, and who consented accordingly to cede to the town the territory belonging to it.

So many towns have gained their freedom in these two ways during the period that the Germans have enjoyed control of the Empire, that they now number nearly a hundred. In order to maintain their freedom they are accustomed to unite themselves together in leagues for mutual protection and to oppose those princes who would subjugate them. They receive into their leagues those princes of the Empire who wish to join them, whether ecclesiastical or secular. The leagues are temporary and are continued or changed from time to time as suits their members. . . .

The customs and manners of this German nation are as follows : first, there are four kinds of persons, — princes of the Empire, nobles, citizens of the free towns, and, lastly, the common people. The princes are in the habit of remaining in their own territories far from the court, where they support by their income, so far as they can, the nobles [knights] of the region. These princes are almost continually at strife with one another or with some of the free towns. If they are poor, they generally permit their retainers to attack and rob on the highways. They are naturally proud and insolent, and feel resentment toward any one who is able to rival them in any respect. *Character of the princes.*

They heartily hate the free towns, and all republics and free communities in general, especially the Swiss and our most exalted senate, for it seems to them that the Swiss have always shown themselves rebels toward the Empire and that your sublimities, paying little attention to their authority, hold much territory which they claim is not yours and which they believe should rightfully be divided among them.

Moreover the chief temporal princes are in the habit of leaving their principality to the eldest son and then providing for the rest of their children with other territories, bishoprics, or ecclesiastical benefices ; so that if a duke has ten sons, all demand to be dukes like their father. The result is that there are an infinite multitude of counts, dukes, and margraves in Germany, the chief of whom have been mentioned above. Consequently the greater part of the temporal princes are always ready to descend into Italy in order to *Reason for the great number of dukes, counts, etc., in Germany* provide, some their sons, some their brothers or nephews, with principalities. The ecclesiastical princes, on the other hand, and the free towns would prefer to live in peace and not waste their substance. The princes all live in abundance, but give more attention to drinking than anything else. They are miserably dressed, nor do they affect much ceremony in their courts.

I he knights.    The knights are accustomed to live in some castle far from a town, or at the court of some prince, or among the mountains in solitary regions. They live and dress wretchedly, hate the burghers, and are poor, but so proud that nothing in the world would induce them to engage in commerce. They are devoted to fighting; and when that is wanting they have nothing to do but to hunt or set to plundering on the highways. Were it not for severe repression, no one could travel safely in any part of Germany. Even as it is, in Franconia, where there are a great many of these gentlemen, the roads are very insecure; for example, in the region of Nuremburg and in many other places.

The burghers.    The burghers of the free towns are all merchants. They live well but dress ill, although there are some very rich people among them. They maintain justice, desire peace, hate the knights heartily and fear the princes, and for this reason the cities form leagues among themselves. The towns are moreover at enmity each with its bishop on account of his desire to exercise the temporal as well as the spiritual authority over the town. This hostility is increased by the natural ill feeling which exists between the burghers on the one hand and the knights and princes on the other, for the bishops are always chosen from among the knights and princes, since the canons, who have the right to elect the bishop, all belong by descent to the noble classes and not to the burghers.

The common people.    The lower classes, whether subject to the princes or the free towns, are poor, wild by nature, do not fear to endanger their lives, and are very loyal to their lords. They are loath to exert themselves to earn anything, and the little they get they speedily drink up.

## II. ERASMUS' "PRAISE OF FOLLY"

And what shall I say of those who comfortably delude themselves with imaginary pardons for their sins, and who measure the time in purgatory with an hourglass into years, months, days, and hours, with all the precision of a mathematical table? There are plenty, too, who, relying upon certain magical little certificates and prayers, — which some pious impostor devised either in fun or for the benefit of his pocket, — believe that they may procure riches, honor, future happiness, health, perpetual prosperity, long life, a lusty old age, — nay, in the end, a seat at the right hand of Christ in heaven; but as for this last, it matters not how long it be deferred: they will content themselves with the joys of heaven only when they must finally surrender the pleasures of this world, to which they lovingly cling.

99. Extracts from Erasmus' *The Praise of Folly*.

Indulgences.

The trader, the soldier, and the judge think that they can clean up the Augean stable of a lifetime, once for all, by sacrificing a single coin from their ill-gotten gains. They flatter themselves that all sorts of perjury, debauchery, drunkenness, quarrels, bloodshed, imposture, perfidy, and treason can be compounded for by contract and so adjusted that, having paid off their arrears, they can begin a new score.

How foolish, too, for religious bodies each to give preference to its particular guardian saint! Nay, each saint has his particular office allotted to him, and is addressed each in his special way: this one is called upon to alleviate toothache; that, to aid in childbirth; others, to restore a stolen article, bring rescue to the shipwrecked, or protect cattle, — and so on with the rest, who are much too numerous to mention. A few indeed among the saints are good in more than one emergency, especially the Holy Virgin, to whom the common man now attributes almost more than to her Son.

Petitioning the saints.

And for what, after all, do men petition the saints except for foolish things? Look at the votive offerings which cover the walls of certain churches and with which you see even the ceiling filled; do you find any one who expresses his gratitude that he has escaped Folly or because he has become a whit wiser? One perhaps was saved from drowning, another recovered when he had been run through by his enemy; another, while his fellows were fighting, ran away with expedition and success; another, on the point of being hanged, escaped, through the aid of some saintly friend of thieves, and lived to relieve a few more of those whom he believed to be overburdened with their wealth. . . .

These various forms of foolishness so pervade the whole life of Christians that even the priests themselves find no objection to admitting, not to say fostering, them, since they do not fail to perceive how many tidy little sums accrue to them from such sources. But what if some odious philosopher should chime in and say, as is quite true: "You will not die badly if you live well. You are redeeming your sins when you add to the sum that you contribute a hearty detestation of evil doers: then you may spare yourself tears, vigils, invocations, fasts, and all that kind of life. You may rely upon any saint to aid you when once you begin to imitate his life."

The scholastic theologians.

As for the theologians, perhaps the less said the better on this gloomy and dangerous theme, since they are a style of man who show themselves exceeding supercilious and irritable unless they can heap up six hundred conclusions about you and force you to recant; and if you refuse, they promptly brand you as a heretic, — for it is their custom to terrify by their thunderings those whom they dislike. It must be confessed that no other group of fools are so reluctant to acknowledge Folly's benefits toward them, although I have many titles to their gratitude, for I make them so in love with themselves that they seem to be happily exalted to the third heaven, whence they look down with something like pity upon all other mortals, wandering about on the earth like mere cattle.

Scholastic disputations.

Then they hedge themselves about with such an array of magisterial definitions, conclusions, corollaries, propositions explicate and implicate, and do so abound in subterfuges, that chains forged by Vulcan himself could not hold them so firm but that they could escape by one of those distinctions which enable them to cut all knots as easily as with a two-edged ax, so readily do they think up and rattle out new and prodigious terms and expressions.

St. Paul, they admit, was distinguished for his faith, but nevertheless when he said, " Faith is the substance of things hoped for, the evidence of things not seen," he defined it but inaccurately.  He may have excelled in charity, yet he fails to limit and define it with dialectic precision in his first letter to the Corinthians, Chapter xiii.  The disciples administered the eucharist reverently, and yet had they been asked about the *terminus a quo* and the *terminus ad quem* of transubstantiation ; as to how a body can be in two places at the same time ; of the differences which exist between Christ's body in heaven, on the cross, and in the holy wafer ; or at what point does transubstantiation occur, since the prayer through which it is effected is, as a *quantitas discreta*, in a state of flux, — asked of these matters the apostles would not have replied with the acuteness with which the followers of Scotus distinguish and define these subtleties.

The theologians set themselves above St. Paul and the apostles.

The apostles knew the mother of Jesus, but who of them could philosophically prove how she was preserved from the sin of Eve, as do our divines?  Peter received the keys, and from one who would not commit them to unworthy hands, but whether or not he knew how one could have the key of knowledge without knowledge itself, he certainly never discussed the matter.  The apostles baptized, but never taught the formal, material, efficient, or final cause of baptism, nor do they mention delible or indelible characters. . . .  The apostles inculcated grace, but never distinguished between *gratia gratis data* and *gratia gratificans*.  They exhorted to good works, but did not perceive the distinction between *opus operans* and *opus operatum*.  They frequently urge charity upon us without dividing " infused " from " acquired," or explaining whether charity be an accident or a substance, a created or an uncreated thing.

Next to the theologians in their self-satisfaction may be ranked those who are commonly called the religious and the

The monks.

monks, both terms quite wide of the truth, since a good part of them are a long ways from religion, and as for the monks (whose name suggests solitude), they are to be met in every byway. I do not see who could be more miserable than they unless Folly came to their aid in many ways. Although every one so execrates that stripe of man that even a casual meeting with them is regarded as ominous, yet they have a magnificent idea of their own virtues. First they deem it the most exalted piety to have let learning so completely alone that they cannot even read. Then when they bray out the psalms — which they cannot understand — in the churches, they flatter themselves that they are delighting the ears of the saints with their sweet harmonies. Some of them laud their beggary and filth as great virtues and loudly clamor for bread from door to door. They beset the inns, coaches, and ships, not a little to the prejudice of other beggars. . . .

Confidence of the monks in mere ceremonies and externals.

The greater part of the monks exhibit such confidence in ceremonies and trivial human traditions that one would think a single heaven would scarce suffice as a worthy reward for their merits. They little think that Christ will put them off with a "Who hath required these things at your hands?" and will call them to account only for the stewardship of his legacy of love. One will confidently call attention to his paunch, filled with all kinds of fish; another will pour out a hundred bushels of psalms; a third will enumerate his myriad fastings and will tell how a single meal nearly killed him; a fourth will produce as many ceremonies as would fill seven merchant ships; a fifth will plead that for three-score years he never so much as touched money except he fingered it through double thick gloves; a sixth will bring along his hood so old and nasty that no sailor would venture to protect himself with it. . . . But Christ shall interrupt their boastings: "Woe unto you, scribes and Pharisees! I left you one great precept, but of that alone I hear nothing from you. I told you plainly in my gospel, with no disguising parables, that my Father's kingdom was promised, not for cowls, petitions, and fastings, but for deeds of love. I know them not who rely on their own merits." . . . When the monks and friars shall hear these things and shall see simple sailors and carters preferred to them, how shall their faces fall as they look at one another!

## BIBLIOGRAPHY

**Political Conditions in Germany:** JOHNSON, *Europe in the Six-teenth Century*, pp. 106–128; HENDERSON, *Short History of Germany*, Vol. I, Chapter X, pp. 228–250; *Cambridge Modern History*, Vol. I, Chapter IX, pp. 288–328; DYER, *Modern Europe*, Vol. I, pp. 22–33.

**Religious Conditions:** *Cambridge Modern History*, Vol. I, Chapter XIX, pp. 653–692 ("The Eve of the Reformation," by Henry C. Lea).

**Intellectual Conditions:** WHITCOMB, *Source Book of the German Renaissance*. Contains extracts from the writings of the humanists.

*A. References.*

---

CREIGHTON, *History of the Papacy*, Vol. VI, Chapter I, "Humanism in Germany"; Chapter II, "The Reuchlin Struggle."

BEARD, *Martin Luther*, Chapter I, "Political Conditions of the Empire"; Chapter II, "The Religious Life of Germany"; Chapter III, "The Renaissance in Germany."

JANSSEN, *History of the German People*, Vols. I, II, and III (first half). A very suggestive and readable treatment by a famous Catholic scholar.

RANKE, *History of the Reformation in Germany* (an English translation of the first half of the German original), Vol. I, pp. 85–342. A careful account of the attempts to reform the German constitution before Luther's appearance.

EMERTON, *Desiderius Erasmus*. An admirable biography, with many extracts from Erasmus' writings. FROUDE, in his *Life and Letters of Erasmus*, gives a loose paraphrase of a number of Erasmus' letters. NICHOLS, *The Epistles of Erasmus* (1901–1904), 2 vols. An excellent annotated translation of the letters written before 1517.

STRAUSS, D. F., *Ulrich von Hutten, his Life and Times*. Translated from the German (1874); a good account of the whole humanistic movement.

*B. Additional reading in English.*

# CHAPTER XXV

## MARTIN LUTHER AND HIS REVOLT AGAINST THE CHURCH

### I. Luther's Ninety-five Theses concerning Indulgences (1517)

Luther did not intend his theses to be a complete and final declaration of his beliefs in regard to salvation. He had been deeply disturbed by the talk that he heard about indulgences, the importance of which appeared to him to be grossly overrated. The loud praise of them he thought certain to blind the great body of Christians to more fundamental matters. So with the hope of bringing an ill-understood question to the attention of university men, he hastily drafted in Latin certain propositions involving the chief points; these he posted up, as was the custom, where they might catch the eye of those interested.

He was himself by no means certain of his conclusions, for he said later of the theses: "There is much in them concerning which I am doubtful; much else that I do not understand; other things of which I am not persuaded, and nothing that I stubbornly adhere to; for I submit everything to Holy Church and her judgment." Yet there is no doubt that they really expressed his general convictions, which he did not realize at that time were opposed to the teachings of the Catholic Church.

With the desire and purpose of elucidating the truth, a disputation will be held on the underwritten propositions at Wittenberg, under the presidency of the Reverend Father Martin Luther, monk of the order of St. Augustine, Master of Arts and of Sacred Theology, and ordinary lecturer in the same at that place. He asks those who cannot be present and discuss the subject orally to do so by letter in their absence. In the name of our Lord Jesus Christ. Amen.

100. Examples of Luther's ninety-five theses.

1. Our Lord and Master Jesus Christ in saying " Repent ye,"[1] etc., intended that the whole life of believers should be penitence.

Meaning of penitence defined.

2. This word cannot be understood as sacramental penance, that is, the confession and satisfaction which are performed under the ministry of priests.

3. It does not, on the other hand, refer solely to inward penitence ; nay, such inward penitence is naught, unless it outwardly produces various mortifications of the flesh.

4. The penalty [for sin] must thus continue as long as the hatred of self — that is, true inward penitence ; namely, till our entrance into the kingdom of heaven.

5. The pope has neither the will nor the power to remit any penalties except those which he has imposed by his own authority, or by that of the canons.

21. Thus those preachers of indulgences are in error who say that by the indulgences of the pope a man is freed and saved from all punishment.

Wrong notions of the nature of indulgences.

27. They preach man [rather than God] who say that the soul flies out of purgatory as soon as the money rattles in the chest.

28. It is certain that, when the money rattles in the chest, avarice and gain may be increased, but the effect of the intercession of the Church depends on the will of God alone.

---

[1] See explanation of the first three theses in the unabridged edition of the Readings, Vol. II, p. 58 and note.

39. It is a very difficult thing, even for the most learned theologians, to exalt at the same time, in the eyes of the people, the ample effect of pardons and the necessity of true contrition.

40. True contrition seeks and loves punishment, while the ampleness of pardons relaxes it and causes men to hate it, or at least gives occasion for them to do so.

50. Christians should be taught that, if the pope were acquainted with the exactions of the preachers of pardons, he would prefer that the basilica of St. Peter should be burnt to ashes rather than that it should be built up with the skin, flesh, and bones of his sheep.

Keen ques-
tionings of
the laity.

81. This license in the preaching of pardons makes it no easy thing, even for learned men, to protect the reverence due to the pope against the calumnies, or, at all events, the keen questionings of the laity.

82. As, for instance : Why does not the pope empty purgatory for the sake of his most holy charity and of the supreme necessity of souls, — this being the most just of all reasons, — if he redeems an infinite number of souls for the sake of that most fatal thing, money, to be spent on building a basilica, — this being a very slight reason?

86. Again : Why does not the pope, whose riches are at this day more ample than those of Crœsus, build the basilica of St. Peter with his own money rather than with that of poor believers?

88. Again : What greater good could the Church receive than if the pope were to bestow these remissions and participations a hundred times a day, instead of once, as he does now, on any one of the faithful?

90. To repress these scruples and arguments of the laity by force alone, and not to solve them by giving reasons, is to expose the Church and the pope to the ridicule of their enemies, and to make Christian men unhappy.

91. If then pardons were preached according to the spirit and wish of the pope, all these questions would be solved with ease ; nay, would not exist.

## II. The Disputation at Leipzig (1519)

Eck, Luther's opponent in the Leipzig disputation, gives a good brief account of Luther's conduct in the affair in a letter to Hochstraten, the inquisitor general. Toward two years had elapsed since the posting up of the theses, and it will be readily seen from Eck's letter that Luther had made a good deal of progress on his way toward revolt.

It has not escaped you, reverend Father, in what manner I have thus far opposed the rash men of Wittenberg, who despise all the teachers of four hundred years, however saintly and learned, and disseminate many false and erroneous things among the people ; especially the powerful leader in this uproar, who seduces and corrupts the common people through publications in our language. **101. Eck's report to Hochstraten concerning the Leipzig disputation.**

We have recently held a disputation at Leipzig, before a great audience of most learned men, coming together from all parts, by which (praise, honor, and glory to God!) the reputation of the Wittenberg party has been very much lessened even among the common people, while among the learned it is for the most part quite gone. You should have heard the rashness of the men, how blind they are and how undaunted in their wickedness.

Luther denies that Peter was the chief of the apostles ; he declares that ecclesiastical obedience is not of divine right, but that it was brought in by human appointment or that of the emperor. He denies that the Church was built upon Peter : "Upon this rock," etc. And though I quoted to him Augustine, Jerome, Ambrose, Gregory, Cyprian, Chrysostom, Leo and Bernard, with Theophilus, he contradicted them all without a blush ; and said that he would stand alone against a thousand, though supported by no other, because Christ only is the foundation of the Church, for other foundation can no man lay. I demolished that by quoting Revelations xii, about the twelve foundations, whereupon he defended the Greeks and schismatics, saying that even if they are not under obedience to the pope, still they are saved.

Concerning the tenets of the Bohemians, he said that some of their teachings condemned in the Council of Constance are most Christian and evangelical; by which rash error he frightened away and caused to desert him many who before were his supporters.

Among other things, when I pressed upon him, " If the power of the pope is only of human right and by the consent of believers, whence comes your monk's costume that you wear? Whence have you the power of preaching and of hearing the confessions of your parishioners," etc., he replied that he wished there were no order of mendicants. Then he proceeded to give utterance to many other scandalous and absurd things, for example, that a council, because they are men, can err; that it is not proved from Sacred Scripture that there is a purgatory, etc., — all this you will see by reading our disputation, since it was written down by most faithful notaries. . . .

### III. Luther on Good Works

Luther emphasized so constantly and fervently salvation through simple faith in God's promises, and spoke so lightly of " good works," such as fasts, pilgrimages, attendance at masses, alms, gifts to the Church, etc., that his opponents declared that he cared not how a man acted if only he had faith. Luther explains his position very clearly in the following passages from a little treatise *On Good Works*, which he wrote in German early in 1520 and dedicated to his prince, the elector of Saxony.

The first, highest, and noblest of all good works is to believe in Christ, as he himself answered in John, Chapter vi, when the Jews asked him, "What must we do, that we may work the works of God?" "Jesus answered and said unto them, This is the work of God, that ye believe on him whom he hath sent." Now when we hear this, or preach it to others, we run over it lightly, regarding it as a very simple and easy thing, when we should stop long over it and ponder it well; for all works go back to this and receive all their goodness from it, as one might receive a fief from his lord. We must paint this in strong colors if every one is to see it clearly.

102. Luther's idea of good works and justification by faith.

We find many who pray, fast, endow churches and monasteries, and do this, that, and the other, — who, in short, lead a good life before men; who, if you ask them whether they are sure that what they are doing is pleasing to God, say no, they know not, or are doubtful. Among these are some famous and learned men, who claim that it is not necessary to be sure that we are pleasing to God and who do nothing except urge good works. But we must see that the very same works done without faith are altogether dead and as nothing, for as your conscience stands toward God and believes in him, even so shall it be with your works, which proceed from your faith. Now when there is no faith or good conscience toward God, works are headless and have no life or goodness. So it comes about that when I place faith so high and reject such unbelieving works, they accuse me of forbidding good works altogether, although I gladly extol the good works of faith.

If you ask my critics if they regard as good works laboring at one's trade, coming and going, eating, drinking, and sleeping, and all the other acts that help nourish the body or are generally useful, and whether they believe that God is pleased by such works, you will find that they say no, and limit good works so narrowly that they must consist in praying in church, fasting, or giving alms; other things they regard as actions which God does not esteem. By this damnable want of faith they reduce and diminish the

Luther criticises the narrow conception of "good works."

service of God, whom all serve, who believe in him, in all
that they say or think. And this the Preacher teaches, saying, "Go thy way, eat thy bread with joy, and drink thy
wine with a merry heart; for God hath already accepted
thy works. Let thy garments be always white ; and let not
thy head lack ointment. Live joyfully with the wife whom
thou lovest all the days of the life of thy vanity, which he
hath given thee under the sun." [1] To keep our garments
white is to have all our works good, whatever they may be,
without any distinction. And they will be white when we
confidently believe that they are pleasing to God. . . .

We can understand this whole matter by an obvious
human example. When husband and wife are fond of one
another and live together in love and in confidence in one
another, and each believes truly in the other, who shall
teach them how they should act, what they should do or
leave undone, say or not say, think or not think? Their
own insight tells them all that need be, and more too.
There is no distinction in their "works" for one another.
They do the long, hard, and heavy tasks as willingly as the
slight and easy things, and moreover they act with glad,
peaceful, and secure hearts, and are altogether free and
unconstrained. But when doubt comes they begin to ask
what is best, and begin to distinguish between their acts in
order to gain the one the other's favor, and go about with
troubled and heavy hearts, perhaps well-nigh in despair or
driven to downright desperation.

So the Christian who lives in confidence toward God
knows what things he should do, and does all gladly and
freely, not with a view to accumulating merit and good
works, but because it is his great joy to please God and to
serve him without thought of reward, contented if he but
do God's will. On the contrary, he who is not at one with
God, or is in doubt, will begin to be anxious how he may
satisfy God and justify himself by his works. He runs off
on a pilgrimage to St. James of Compostella, to Rome, to
Jerusalem, — here, there, anywhere ; prays to St. Bridget, or

[1] Eccles. ix. 7–9.

some other saint, fasts this day and that, confesses here and confesses there, asks this man and that, but finds no peace.

## IV. ULRICH VON HUTTEN'S APPEAL TO GERMAN PATRIOTISM

Ulrich von Hutten had returned from a sojourn in Italy filled with love and enthusiasm for his own German people and with dislike for the Italians, especially for the Roman curia. He probably knew little about the Leipzig disputation, and had no interest, in any case, in what the monks and theologians, whom he had just been making sport of in the *Letters of Obscure Men*,[1] might be saying about indulgences and purgatory. He busied himself writing witty dialogues in Latin, denouncing the clergy, and attacking the Roman curia in the name of German liberty and independence.

*Ulrich von Hutten attacks the clergy.*

In one of these dialogues, published early in 1520, Hutten meets a friend, Ernhold, in Mayence, and they talk over public affairs. Ernhold asks him what he is irritated about.

*103. Hutten's Vadiscus, or the Roman Trinity.[2]*

*Hutten.* Because five books of the writings of the historian Tacitus were recently printed at Rome, and when I took them to one of our publishers he declared that he dare not reprint them on account of a bull of Leo X which forbade, in the interests of the Roman printer, that any one should issue the work again within ten years.

---

[1] See *History of Western Europe*, pp. 380 *sq.* (Vol. II, pp. 28 *sq.*).

[2] The dialogue secures its name from Hutten's contention that every thing went by threes in Rome. Three things are carried away from Rome: a bad conscience, a weak stomach, and empty words; three things disturb the Romans: harmony among the German princes, intelligence among the people, and a recognition of the frauds the Romans perpetrate; three things very few Romans believe: the immortality of the soul, the communion of saints, and the punishments of hell; etc.

*Ernhold.* Then we Germans cannot read the book for ten years, since works printed in Rome rarely reach Germany?

*Hutten.* This irritates me especially, and I am vexed more and more every day to see how our people refuse to leave their superstitions, and continue to think that such a bull should be noticed, which prevents us from advancing our studies and sharpening our wits. When the printer said that if he did as I wished and pleased the scholars he would be immediately excommunicated, I asked him if, should the pope forbid us Germans, under pain of his curse, to have vineyards or make money, we should drink water and throw away our gold. He said, no. . . . "But you," I said, "are afraid to let the Germans have Tacitus, when he merits our especial gratitude for having spoken more highly of our people than any other of the ancient writers?" I should have persuaded him had not a papal legate, who is about here now, roused his apprehensions, telling him that it would be a terrible sin to print the book and that Leo would be very angry if he did so. I was quite excusably enraged.

*Ernhold.* Naturally ; and I think there are plenty of other things we suffer by : settling for archbishops' palliums, and paying annates, pensions, and six hundred other exactions. When will the Romans moderate their demands? I fear that we Germans will not stand them much longer, for matters are getting worse and worse, and there is no end to their robbery and extortions.

*Hutten.* As you well say, unless they are more reasonable and show some restraint in their mode of life, this nation of ours will at last have its eyes opened. It will see how miserably it has been misled and swindled, and will recognize the deceptions employed to delude a free people and bring into contempt a brave and strong nation with its noble princes. I already notice that many are beginning to talk freely and act as if we were about to cast off this yoke.

*Ernhold.* God grant that we may soon cease to be the victims of foreigners![1]

[1] Extracts from Hutten's dialogue, "The Onlookers," are given by Whitcomb, *Source Book of the German Renaissance*, pp. 62 *sq.*

The above was written probably in 1519, before Hutten had become interested in Luther, and shows how the Germans might have been led to revolt against the papal supremacy on other than religious grounds. Early in 1520 Hutten was attracted by Luther's utterances and wrote a letter to him beginning "Long live liberty," and offering him the protection of the German knights. He then began translating his own earlier dialogues into German, and added others of a more serious nature, in which he introduced Luther. In September, 1520, he appealed to some of the German princes, urging them to reduce the exactions of the curia. His letter to the elector of Saxony is of the greatest interest, and its description of the economic forces then at work in Germany may profitably be compared with Luther's treatment of the same matters in his *Address to the German Nobility*.

Hutten becomes interested in Luther.

. . . We see that there is no gold and almost no silver in our German land. What little may perhaps be left is drawn away daily by the new schemes invented by the council of the most holy members of the Roman curia. What is thus squeezed out of us is put to the most shameful uses. Would you know, dear Germans, what employment I have myself seen that they make at Rome of our money? It does not lie idle!

104. Hutten appeals to the elector of Saxony.

Leo the Tenth gives a part of it to his nephews and relatives (these are so numerous that there is a proverb at Rome, "As thick as Leo's relations"). A portion is consumed by a host of most reverend cardinals (of which the holy father created no less than one and thirty in a single day), as well as in supporting innumerable referendaries, auditors, prothonotaries, abbreviators, apostolic secretaries, chamberlains, and a variety of officials forming the élite of the great head church.

These in turn draw after them, at untold expense, copyists, beadles, messengers, servants, scullions, mule drivers, grooms, and an innumerable army of prostitutes and of the most degraded followers. They maintain dogs, horses, monkeys, long-tailed apes, and many more such creatures for their pleasure. They construct houses all of marble. They have precious stones, are clothed in purple and fine linen, and dine sumptuously, frivolously indulging themselves in every species of luxury. In short, a vast number of the worst of men are supported in Rome in idle indulgence by means of our money. . . .

Does not your Grace now clearly perceive how many bold robbers, how many cunning hypocrites, are engaged constantly in committing the greatest crimes under cover of the monk's cowl, and how many crafty hawks feign the simplicity of doves, and how many ravening wolves simulate the innocence of lambs? And although there be a few truly pious among them, even they cling to superstition, and pervert the law of life which Christ laid down for us.

Now if all these who devastate Germany, and continue to devour everything, might once be driven out, and an end made of the unbridled plundering, swindling, and deception with which the Romans have overwhelmed us, we should again have gold and silver in sufficiency, and should be able to keep it.

And then this money, in such quantities as might be available, might be put to better uses, as, for example: to put on foot great armaments and extend the boundaries of the empire; also to conquer the Turks, if this seems desirable; to enable many who, because of poverty, now steal and rob, to earn honestly their living once more; and to give to those who otherwise must starve contributions from the state to mitigate their need; to help scholars, and to advance the study of the arts and sciences and of good literature; above all, to make it possible that every virtue receive its reward, want be relieved at home, indolence banished, and deceit killed.

Then, too, the Bohemians, when they come to know this, will make common cause with us; for it was material obstacles alone that kept them back, in earlier times, from dealing with the avarice of their priests. The Greeks would do the same, for they, unable to bear the Romish tyranny, have for a long time, at the instigation of the popes, been regarded as heretics.

The Russians would also become Christians and join us, — they who, when recently they proposed to embrace Christianity, were repelled by the demand of his Holiness for a yearly tribute to be levied upon them of four hundred thousand ducats. Even the Turks would thereby hate us less; and no heathen, as formerly, would have occasion to molest us. For up to the present day the shameful lives of the heads of the Church have made the name of Christian hateful to all strangers.

EBERNBURG, September 11, 1520.

## V. LUTHER'S "ADDRESS TO THE GERMAN NOBILITY" (1520)

Not long after the disputation at Leipzig, Luther began, as we have seen, to attract the attention of Hutten and other German knights, especially Franz von Sickingen, who offered to protect him if he was in danger. This led Luther, who heard that the pope was about to excommunicate him for his protests against the current teaching and practices of the Church, to appeal to the German rulers, with the hope that they might carry out the reforms which the pope and prelates seemed bent on opposing. No English translation can do justice to the vigor of Luther's German, but some notion of the contents of the address may be had from the following extracts.

*Luther's Address to the German Nobility.*

*Dr. Martin Luther, to his Most Serene and Mighty Imperial Majesty, and to the Christian Nobility of the German Nation:*
The grace and might of God be with you, Most Serene Majesty! And you, most gracious and well-beloved lords !

105. Luther
defends the
right of the
secular
rulers to
reform the
Church.

It is not out of mere arrogance and perversity that I, one poor, insignificant man, have taken it upon me to address your lordships. The distress and misery which oppress all ranks of Christendom, especially in Germany, have moved not me alone, but everybody, to cry aloud for help; this it is that now compels me to cry out and call upon God to send down his spirit upon some one who shall reach out a hand to this wretched people. Councils have often put forward some remedy, which has always been promptly frustrated by the cunning of certain men, so that the evils have only grown worse; which malice and wickedness I now intend—God helping me!—to expose, so that, being known, they may cease to work such hindrance and injury. God has given us a young and noble sovereign[1] for our leader, thereby awakening fresh hopes in many hearts; it is our part to do what we can to aid him and to make good use of the opportunity and of his gracious favor.

The Romanists have with great dexterity built themselves about with three walls, which hitherto have protected them against reform; and thereby is Christianity fearfully fallen.

In the first place, when the temporal power has pressed them hard, they have affirmed and maintained that *the temporal power has no jurisdiction over them,—that, on the contrary, the spiritual is above the temporal.*

Secondly, when it was proposed to admonish them from the Holy Scriptures they said, "*It beseems no one but the pope to interpret the Scriptures.*"

And, thirdly, when they were threatened with a council, they invented the idea that *no one but the pope can call a council.*

Thus have they secretly stolen our three rods, that they may go unpunished; and intrenched themselves safely behind these three walls in order to carry on all the knavery and wickedness that we now see.

And whenever they have been compelled to call a council, they have made it of no avail, by binding the princes beforehand with an oath to let them alone. Besides this they have

---

[1] Charles V had just been elected emperor. Luther was soon to learn how hopeless it was to appeal to him. See below, pp. 275 *sqq.*

given the pope full power over the ordering of the council, so that it is all one whether we have many councils or no councils, for in any case they deceive us with pretenses and false tricks, so grievously do the Romanists tremble for their skins before a true, free council; and thus they have over-awed kings and princes, so that these believe that they would be offending God if they refused to believe in all their knavish tricks.

Now may God help us, and give us one of those trumpets that overthrew the walls of Jericho, so that we may also blow down these walls of straw and paper, and that we may regain possession of our Christian rods for the chastisement of sin, and expose the craft and deceit of the devil ; thus may we amend ourselves by punishment and again obtain God's favor.

Let us, in the first place, attack the first wall.

It has been discovered that the pope, bishops, priests, and monks should be called the " spiritual estate," while princes, lords, artisans, and peasants form the " temporal estate," — a very fine hypocritical invention.  But let no one be made afraid by it ; and that for this reason : All Christians are truly of the spiritual estate, and there is no difference among us, save of office alone.  As St. Paul says (1 Cor. xii), we are all one body, though each member has its own work to do, whereby it may serve the others.  This is because we have one baptism, one gospel, one faith, and are all Christians alike ; for baptism, gospel, and faith, — these alone make spiritual and Christian folk. . . .

Therefore a priest should be nothing in Christendom but a functionary.  So long as he holds his office he takes pre-cedence ; if he is deprived of it, he is but a peasant or a burgher, like the rest.  Therefore a priest is verily no priest when he is deprived of his office.  But now they have invented their " indelible characters," and pretend that a priest after deprivation is still something different from a simple layman.  They even imagine that a priest can never be anything but a priest, — that is, that he can never become a layman again.  But all this is nothing but mere talk and ordinance of human invention.

We see then that those we call churchmen, be they priests, bishops, or popes, are not set apart from or above other Christians, except in so far as they have to do with the word of God and the sacraments, for that is their calling and office. And moreover the temporal authorities wield the sword and the rod to chastise the wicked and protect the good. A cobbler, a smith, a peasant — every man has his own calling and office, just like the consecrated priests and bishops : and every one in his office or calling must help and serve the rest, so that all may work together for the common good, as the various members of the body all serve each other.

See now what sort of a Christian doctrine is this, — that the temporal power is not above the spiritual, and may not punish it. That is like saying the hand shall do nothing to help, however grievously the eye may suffer. Is it not unnatural, not to say unchristian, that one member may not help another, even to shield it from destruction ? Nay, the nobler the member, the more the others are bound to help it. Therefore I say, forasmuch as the temporal power has been ordained by God for the chastisement of the wicked and the protection of the good, therefore we must let it exercise its functions, unhampered, throughout the whole Christian body without respect of persons, whether it strikes popes, bishops, priests, monks, nuns, or whatever. . . .

It must indeed have been the archfiend himself who said, as we read in the canon law, " Were the pope so perniciously wicked as to be dragging souls in crowds to the devil, yet he could not be deposed." This is the accursed, devilish foundation on which they build at Rome, and think the whole world may go to the devil rather than that they should be opposed in their knavery. If a man were to escape punishment simply because he was above his fellows, then no Christian might punish another, since Christ has commanded that each of us esteem himself the lowest and humblest of all (Matt. xviii. 4 ; Luke ix. 48).

The second wall is even more flimsy and tottering than the first, — namely, the claim that they alone are masters of the Scriptures. Although they learn nothing in them all

their life long, they assume the sole authority, juggle impu-
dently with empty words, saying the pope cannot err, be he
pious or wicked ; albeit they cannot show so much as a
single letter in proof of it. That is why the canon law contains so many heretical and unchristian — nay, unnatural
— laws ; but of them we need not speak at present. For
since the Romanists claim that the Holy Ghost never leaves
them, however wicked and ignorant they may be, they grow
bold enough to decree whatever they like. But were this
true, where were the need or use of the Holy Scriptures ?
Let us burn them and content ourselves instead with the
unlearned gentlemen at Rome in whom dwells the Holy
Ghost, who nevertheless is wont to dwell only in pious souls !
If I had not read about it, I would never have believed that
the devil could do such stupid things in Rome and still find
a following !

The second
wall : the ex-
clusive claim
of the pope
to interpret
Scripture.

But that we fight not with our own words, let us bring
forth the Scriptures. St. Paul says : " If any thing be revealed to another that sitteth by, let the first hold his peace"
(1 Cor. xiv. 30). What would be the use of this commandment if we were to believe him alone who speaks first or sits
in the highest seat ? Christ himself says that all Christians
shall be taught of God (John vi. 45). But it may come to
pass that the pope and his followers are wicked men, without true understanding, neither true Christians nor taught
of God, whereas some common man may have true understanding. Why, then, should we not follow him ? Has not
the pope often been in error ? Who is to help Christianity
when the pope errs if we are not to believe another who has
the Scriptures for him ? . . . In olden times Abraham was
forced to listen to Sarah, though she was far more strictly
subject to him than we are now to any one on earth. Even
so Balaam's ass was wiser than the prophet himself. If God
has spoken against a prophet through an ass, why should he
not still speak through a good man against the pope ?

The third wall falls of itself as soon as the first two have
fallen; for if the pope acts contrary to the Scriptures, we
are bound to stand by the Scriptures and to punish and

The third
wall: the
exclusive
right of the
pope to
summon a
council.

restrain him, in accordance with Christ's commandment
(Matt. xviii. 15). . . . Moreover there is nothing in the Scriptures to show that the pope has the sole right to summon
and confirm a council; the Romanists have nothing but their
own laws, and these hold good only so long as they are not
opposed to Christianity and the laws of God ; but when the
pope deserves punishment these laws cease to exist, since
Christianity would suffer if he were not punished by means
of a council. . . .

And now I hope we have laid the false and lying specter
by means of which the Romanists have kept our timid con-
sciences in subjection. We have shown that they are subject, like all the rest of us, to the temporal sword ; that they
have no authority to interpret the Scriptures by force and
without knowledge; and that they have no right either to
prevent a council, or to pledge and bind it in advance to
suit their pleasure and thus deprive it of its freedom. And
when they do this they are verily of the fellowship of Antichrist and the devil and have nothing from Christ but the
name.

## VI. THE EDICT OF THE DIET OF WORMS (MAY, 1521)

106. Extracts
from the
Edict of
Worms,
condemning
Luther
and his
adherents.

1. We, Charles V, by God's grace Roman emperor elect,
ever august, king of Germany, Spain, the two Sicilies, Jerusalem, Hungary, Dalmatia, Croatia, etc., archduke of Austria, duke of Burgundy, etc., count of Hapsburg, Flanders,
and Tyrol, salute and tender our gracious good wishes to
each and all of the electors, princes, — both spiritual and secular, — prelates, counts, barons, knights, nobles, captains,
governors, burgomasters, councilors, judges, citizens, and
communities, also rectors and officers of all universities, and
all other beloved and faithful subjects of ours, or of the Empire, of whatsoever rank they may be, to whom these our
imperial letters, or a credible copy certified by a spiritual
prelate or a public notary, may come or be announced.

2. Most reverend, honorable, and illustrious friends and
relatives, devoted and loyal: as it pertains to our office of

Roman emperor, not only to enlarge the bounds of the Holy Roman Empire, which our fathers of the German nation founded for the defense of the Holy Roman and Catholic Church, subduing unbelievers by the sword, through the divine grace, with much shedding of blood, but also, adhering to the rule hitherto observed by the Holy Roman Church, to take care that no stain or suspicion of heresy should contaminate our holy faith within the Roman Empire, or, if heresy had already begun, to extirpate it with all necessary diligence, prudence, and discretion, as the case might demand;

Charles V holds it to be his duty to extirpate heresy.

3. Therefore we hold that if it was the duty of any of our ancestors to defend the Christian name, much greater is the obligation on us, inasmuch as the unparalleled goodness of Almighty God has, for the protection and increase of his holy faith, endowed us with more kingdoms and lands and greater power in the Empire than any of our ancestors for many years. Moreover we are also sprung from the paternal stock of the emperors and archdukes of Austria, and dukes of Burgundy, and from the maternal stock of the most faithful kings of Spain, the Sicilies, and Jerusalem, — the memory of whose illustrious deeds, wrought for the Christian faith, will never pass away.

5. Since now without doubt it is plain to you all how far the errors and heresies depart from the Christian way, which a certain Martin Luther, of the Augustinian order, has sought violently and virulently to introduce and disseminate within the Christian religion and its established order, especially in the German nation, which is renowned as a perpetual destroyer of all unbelief and heresy; so that, unless it is speedily prevented, the whole German nation, and later all other nations, will be infected by this same disorder, and mighty dissolution and pitiable downfall of good morals, and of the peace and the Christian faith, will result.

.    .    .    .    .    .    .    .    .    .    .    .

9. And although, after the delivery of the papal bull and final condemnation of Luther, we proclaimed the bull in many places in the German nation, as well as in our Burgundian lands, and especially its execution at Cologne,

Luther's wicked arrogance.

Treves, Mayence, and Liége, nevertheless Martin Luther has taken no account of it, nor lessened nor revoked his errors, nor sought absolution from his Papal Holiness or grace from the holy Christian Church; but like a madman plotting the manifest destruction of the holy Church, he daily scatters abroad much worse fruit and effect of his depraved heart and mind through very numerous books, both in Latin and German, composed by himself, or at least under his name, which are full of heresies and blasphemies, not only new ones but also those formerly condemned by holy councils.

Luther's heresies enumerated.

10. Therein he destroys, overturns, and abuses the number, arrangement, and use of the seven sacraments, received and held for so many centuries by the holy Church, and in astonishing ways shamefully pollutes the indissoluble bonds of holy matrimony; and says also that holy unction is a mere invention. He desires also to adapt our customs and practice in the administration of the most holy sacrament of the holy eucharist to the habit and custom of the condemned Bohemians. And he begins to attack confession, — most wholesome for the hearts that are polluted or laden with sins, — declaring that no profit or consolation can be expected from it. . . .

11. He not only holds the priestly office and order in contempt, but also urges secular and lay persons to bathe their hands in the blood of priests; and he uses scurrilous and shameful words against the chief priest of our Christian faith, the successor of St. Peter and true vicar of Christ on earth, and pursues him with manifold and unprecedented attacks and invectives. He demonstrates also from the heathen poets that there is no free will, because all things are determined by an immutable decree.

12. And he writes that the mass confers no benefit on him for whom it is celebrated. Moreover he overthrows the custom of fasting and prayer, established by the holy Church and hitherto maintained. Especially does he impugn the authority of the holy fathers, as they are received by the Church, and would destroy obedience and authority of every kind. Indeed, he writes nothing which does not arouse and

promote sedition, discord, war, murder, robbery, and arson, and tend toward the complete downfall of the Christian faith. For he teaches a loose, self-willed life, severed from all laws and wholly brutish; and he is a loose, self-willed man, who condemns and rejects all laws; for he has shown no fear or shame in burning publicly the decretals and canon law. And had he feared the secular sword no more than the ban and penalties of the pope, he would have committed much worse offenses against the civil law.

13. He does not blush to speak publicly against holy councils, and to abuse and insult them at will. Especially has he everywhere bitterly attacked the Council of Constance with his foul mouth, and calls it a synagogue of Satan, to the shame and disgrace of the whole Church and of the German nation. . . . And he has fallen into such madness of spirit as to boast that if Huss were a heretic then he is ten times a heretic.

14. But all the other innumerable wickednesses of Luther must, for brevity's sake, remain unreckoned. This fellow appears to be not so much a man as the wicked demon in the form of a man and under a monk's cowl. He has collected many heresies of the worst heretics, long since condemned and forgotten, together with some newly invented ones, in one stinking pool, under pretext of preaching *faith*, which he extols with so great industry in order that he may ruin the true and genuine faith, and under the name and appearance of evangelical doctrine overturn and destroy all evangelical peace and love, as well as all righteous order and the most excellent hierarchy of the Church. . . .

16. And now, particularly on account of these things, we have summoned here to Worms the electors, princes, and estates of this our Holy Empire, and carefully examined the aforesaid matters with great diligence, as evident necessity demands, and with unanimous advice and consent of all, we decree what follows.

*Luther summoned to Worms.*

17. It should be noted, however, that although one so condemned and persisting in his obstinate perversity, separated from the rites of the Christian Church and a manifest

heretic, is denied a hearing under all laws; nevertheless, to prevent all unprofitable dispute, . . . we, through our herald, gave him a safe-conduct to come hither, in order that he might be questioned in our own presence and in that of the electors, princes, and estates of the Empire; whether he had composed the books then laid before his eyes. . . .

18. And as soon as these books were enumerated, he acknowledged them as his own, and moreover declared that he would never deny them.

. . . . . . . . . . . .

Luther put under the ban.

25. Accordingly, in view of all these considerations and the fact that Martin Luther still persists obstinately and perversely in maintaining his heretical opinions, and consequently all pious and God-fearing persons abominate and abhor him as one mad or possessed by a demon, . . . we have declared and made known that the said Martin Luther shall hereafter be held and esteemed by each and all of us as a limb cut off from the Church of God, an obstinate schismatic and manifest heretic. . . .

27. And we publicly attest by these letters that we order and command each and all of you, as you owe fidelity to us and the Holy Empire, and would escape the penalties of the crime of treason, and the ban and over-ban of the Empire, and the forfeiture of all regalia, fiefs, privileges, and immunities, which up to this time you have in any way obtained from our predecessors, ourself, and the Holy Empire;— commanding, we say, in the name of the Roman and imperial majesty, we strictly order that immediately after the expiration of the appointed twenty days, terminating on the fourteenth day of May, you shall refuse to give the aforesaid Martin Luther hospitality, lodging, food, or drink; neither shall any one, by word or deed, secretly or openly, succor or assist him by counsel or help; but in whatever place you meet him, you shall proceed against him; if you have sufficient force, you shall take him prisoner and keep him in close custody; you shall deliver him, or cause him to be delivered, to us or at least let us know where he may be captured. In the meanwhile you shall keep him closely imprisoned until

you receive notice from us what further to do, according to the direction of the laws. And for such holy and pious work we will indemnify you for your trouble and expense.

* 28. In like manner you shall proceed against his friends, adherents, patrons, maintainers, abettors, sympathizers, emulators, and followers. And the property of these, whether personal or real, you shall, in virtue of the sacred ordinances and of our imperial ban and over-ban, treat in this way; namely, you shall attack and overthrow its possessors and wrest their property from them and transfer it to your own custody and uses. . . .

29. Consequently we command you, each and all, under the penalities already prescribed, that henceforth no one shall dare to buy, sell, read, preserve, copy, print, or cause to be copied or printed, any books of the aforesaid Martin Luther, condemned by our holy father the pope as aforesaid, or any other writings in German or Latin hitherto composed by him, since they are foul, harmful, suspected, and published by a notorious and stiffnecked heretic. Neither shall any dare to approve his opinions, nor to proclaim, defend, or assert them, in any other way that human ingenuity can invent, notwithstanding he may have put some good in them to deceive the simple man.

*No one to print, sell, or discuss Luther's writings.*

. . . . . . . . . . .

38. And in order that all this may be done and credit given to this document, we have sealed it with our imperial seal, which has been affixed in our imperial city of Worms, on the eighth day of May, after the birth of Christ 1521, in the second year of our reign over the Roman Empire, and over our other lands the sixth.

By our lord the emperor's own command.

## BIBLIOGRAPHY

**Luther's Early Years**: KÖSTLIN, *Life of Luther*, pp. 10–56; HENDERSON, *Short History of Germany*, Vol. I, pp. 251–273; DYER and HASSALL, *Modern Europe*, Vol. I, pp. 400–415; WALKER, *The Reformation*, pp. 77–108.

*A. References.*

The Theses: KÖSTLIN, pp. 82–107.

The Diet of Worms: HENDERSON, Vol. I, pp. 275–284; KÖSTLIN, pp. 222–245; WALKER, pp. 108–123.

*B. Additional reading in English.*

*Partisan character of the books on the Protestant Revolt.*

The student of the Protestant Revolt must always remember that almost all accounts of the period are partisan ; most of them, especially the older ones, are so biased as to be wholly unreliable. Even apart from religious bias, Luther's character strangely fascinates many writers, but is utterly repellent to others. The works mentioned below are all of them either Protestant or Catholic in sympathy, but they are scholarly and in the main accurate.

SEEBOHM, *The Era of the Protestant Revolution* (Epochs of Modern History), is an admirable little book, which deals briefly with the whole course of the Protestant Revolt in the various countries of western Europe.

BEARD, *Martin Luther*. The best life in English. Chapter IV, " Luther's life prior to his Revolt " ; Chapter VII, " Luther's appeal to the Nation in 1520 " ; Chapter IX, " The Diet of Worms." The work was never completed, owing to the death of the writer. *The Reformation of the Sixteenth Century in its Relation to Modern Thought and Knowledge* (Hibbert Lectures, 1883), by the same author, is very suggestive and valuable.

CREIGHTON, *History of the Papacy*, Vol. VI, Chapter III, " Luther's Life before 1521," and Chapter V, " The Diet of Worms." Excellent.

JANSSEN, *History of the German People*, Vol. III. The most celebrated modern Catholic work in this field. Very valuable, especially to those who know only the traditional Protestant views.

SPALDING (archbishop of Baltimore), *The History of the Protestant Reformation, in a Series of Essays*, 2 vols. This work is not a systematic history, and is chiefly concerned with the alleged misrepresentations and errors of the less judicious Protestant writers.

RANKE, *History of the Reformation*, Vol. I, Book II.

BAX, *German Society at the Close of the Middle Ages*, 1894. A rather slight work, but clear and brief. See especially Chapters I, V, and VII, on the conditions in town and country.

*First Principles of the Reformation, or the Three Primary Works of Dr. Martin Luther*, edited by WACE and BUCHHEIM, Philadelphia, contains a correct, if rather lifeless, translation of Luther's " Theses," his letter of 1520 to Leo X, his " Address to the German Nobility," " Babylonish Captivity of the Church," and " Liberty of the Christian." Very valuable to one who cannot read German and Latin.

LUTHER, *Table Talk*, translated by Hazlitt (Bohn Library).

# CHAPTER XXVI

## COURSE OF THE PROTESTANT REVOLT IN GERMANY
### (1521–1555)

### I. THE PEASANT WAR [1]

The Edict of Worms denounced Luther as an opponent of law and a breeder of sedition. This view was substantiated in the eyes of many by the revolt, first of the knights, and then of the peasants, for in both cases the malcontents had much to say of evangelical truth and liberty. The following manifesto of the peasants, drawn up in 1524, clearly shows the influence of Luther's teachings. Yet the revolt cannot be attributed to him, but rather to the general social and economic conditions which had produced a number of similar disturbances earlier. Much had been said by the popular leaders of "God's justice" and of the vices of the clergy before ever Luther was heard of.

*Peace to the Christian reader and the grace of God through Christ:*

There are many evil writings put forth of late which take occasion, on account of the assembling of the peasants, to cast scorn upon the gospel, saying, "Is this the fruit of the new teaching, that no one should obey but that all should everywhere rise in revolt, and rush together to reform, or perhaps destroy altogether, the authorities, both ecclesiastic

**107. The fundamental and correct chief articles of the peasants, relating to the matters in which they feel themselves aggrieved.**

[1] The fact that this chapter is devoted exclusively to the Peasant War will not seem unreasonable to one who considers how admirably the material here given illustrates the extreme intricacy of the Protestant Revolt considered as a religious, social, economic, and political reform.

and lay?" The articles below shall answer these godless and criminal fault-finders, and serve, in the first place, to remove the reproach from the word of God and, in the second place, to give a Christian excuse for the disobedience or even the revolt of the entire peasantry.

In the first place, the gospel is not the cause of revolt and disorder, since it is the message of Christ, the promised Messiah; the word of life, teaching only love, peace, patience, and concord. Thus all who believe in Christ should learn to be loving, peaceful, long-suffering, and harmonious. This is the foundation of all the articles of the peasants (as will be seen), who accept the gospel and live according to it. How then can the evil reports declare the gospel to be a cause of revolt and disobedience? That the authors of the evil reports and the enemies of the gospel oppose themselves to these demands is due, not to the gospel, but to the devil, the worst enemy of the gospel, who causes this opposition by raising doubts in the minds of his followers, and thus the word of God, which teaches love, peace, and concord, is overcome.

In the second place, it is clear that the peasants demand that this gospel be taught them as a guide in life, and they ought not to be called disobedient or disorderly. Whether God grant the peasants (earnestly wishing to live according to his word) their requests or no, who shall find fault with the will of the Most High? Who shall meddle in his judgments or oppose his majesty? Did he not hear the children of Israel when they called upon him and save them out of the hands of Pharaoh? Can he not save his own to-day? Yea, he will save them and that speedily. Therefore, Christian reader, read the following articles with care and then judge. Here follow the articles :

Pastors to be chosen by the people.

*The First Article.* First, it is our humble petition and desire, as also our will and resolution, that in the future we should have power and authority so that each community should choose and appoint a pastor, and that we should have the right to depose him should he conduct himself improperly. The pastor thus chosen should teach us the gospel pure and simple, without any addition, doctrine, or ordinance of man.

*The Second Article.* According as the just tithe is established by the Old Testament and fulfilled in the New, we are ready and willing to pay the fair tithe of grain. The word of God plainly provides that in giving rightly to God and distributing to his people the services of a pastor are required. We will that for the future our church provost, whomsoever the community may appoint, shall gather and receive this tithe. From this he shall give to the pastor, elected by the whole community, a decent and sufficient maintenance for him and his, as shall seem right to the whole community. What remains over shall be given to the poor of the place, as the circumstances and the general opinion demand. Should anything farther remain, let it be kept, lest any one should have to leave the country from poverty. The small tithes,[1] whether ecclesiastical or lay, we will not pay at all, for the Lord God created cattle for the free use of man. We will not, therefore, pay farther an unseemly tithe which is of man's invention.

The tithe.

*The Third Article.* It has been the custom hitherto for men to hold us as their own property, which is pitiable enough, considering that Christ has delivered and redeemed us all, without exception, by the shedding of his precious blood, the lowly as well as the great. Accordingly it is consistent with Scripture that we should be free and should wish to be so. Not that we would wish to be absolutely free and under no authority. God does not teach us that we should lead a disorderly life in the lusts of the flesh, but that we should love the Lord our God and our neighbor. We would gladly observe all this as God has commanded us in the celebration of the communion. He has not commanded us not to obey the authorities, but rather that we should be humble, not only towards those in authority, but towards every one. We are thus ready to yield obedience according to God's law to our elected and regular authorities

Protest against serfdom.

---

[1] That is, tithes of other products than the staple crops, — for example, tithes of pigs or lambs.

in all proper things becoming to a Christian. We therefore take it for granted that you will release us from serfdom as true Christians, unless it should be shown us from the gospel that we are serfs.

Hunting
and fishing
rights.

*The Fourth Article.* In the fourth place, it has been the custom heretofore that no poor man should be allowed to touch venison or wild fowl, or fish in flowing water, which seems to us quite unseemly and unbrotherly as well as self-ish and not agreeable to the word of God. In some places the authorities preserve the game to our great annoyance and loss, recklessly permitting the unreasoning animals to destroy to no purpose our crops, which God suffers to grow for the use of man; and yet we must submit quietly. This is neither godly nor neighborly; for when God created man he gave him dominion over all the animals, over the birds of the air and over the fish in the water. Accordingly it is our desire, if a man holds possession of waters, that he should prove from satisfactory documents that his right has been unwittingly [*unwissenlich*] acquired by purchase. We do not wish to take it from him by force, but his rights should be exercised in a Christian and brotherly fashion. But whoso-ever cannot produce such evidence should surrender his claim with good grace.

Restrictions
on wood-
cutting.

*The Fifth Article.* In the fifth place, we are aggrieved in the matter of woodcutting, for the noble folk have appropri-ated all the woods to themselves alone. If a poor man requires wood, he must pay two pieces of money for it. It is our opinion in regard to a wood which has fallen into the hands of a lord, whether spiritual or temporal, that unless it was duly purchased it should revert again to the commu-nity. It should, moreover, be free to every member of the community to help himself to such firewood as he needs in his home.

Excessive
services
demanded of
the peasants.

*The Sixth Article.* Our sixth complaint is in regard to the excessive services which are demanded of us and which are increased from day to day. We ask that this matter be properly looked into, so that we shall not continue to be oppressed in this way, but that some gracious consideration be given us, since our forefathers were required only to serve according to the word of God.

*The Seventh Article.*  Seventh, we will not hereafter allow ourselves to be farther oppressed by our lords, but will let them demand only what is just and proper according to the word of the agreement between the lord and the peasant. The lord should no longer try to force more services or other dues from the peasant without payment, but permit the peasant to enjoy his holding in peace and quiet. The peasant should, however, help the lord when it is necessary, and at proper times, when it will not be disadvantageous to the peasant, and for a suitable payment.

*The Eighth Article.*  In the eighth place, we are greatly burdened by holdings which cannot support the rent exacted from them. The peasants suffer loss in this way and are ruined; and we ask that the lords may appoint persons of honor to inspect these holdings, and fix a rent in accordance with justice, so that the peasant shall not work for nothing, since the laborer is worthy of his hire.  *[Readjustment of rents]*

*The Ninth Article.*  In the ninth place, we are burdened with a great evil in the constant making of new laws. We are not judged according to the offense, but sometimes with great ill-will, and sometimes much too leniently. In our opinion, we should be judged according to the old written law, so that the case shall be decided according to its merits, and not with partiality.  *[Protest against the new Roman law then being introduced into Germany.]*

*The Tenth Article.*  In the tenth place, we are aggrieved by the appropriation by individuals of meadows and fields which at one time belonged to a community. These we will take again into our own hands. It may, however, happen that the land was rightfully purchased. When, however, the land has unfortunately been purchased in this way, some brotherly arrangement should be made according to circumstances.  *[Loss of common land]*

*The Eleventh Article.*  In the eleventh place, we will entirely abolish the due called "heriot," and will no longer endure it, nor allow widows and orphans to be thus shamefully robbed against God's will.  *[The heriot.]*

*Conclusion.* In the twelfth place, it is our conclusion and final resolution that if any one or more of the articles here set forth should not be in agreement with the word of God, as we think they are, such article we will willingly retract if it is proved really to be against the word of God by a clear explanation of the Scripture. Or if articles should now be conceded to us that are hereafter discovered to be unjust, from that hour they shall be dead and null and without force. Likewise, if more complaints should be discovered which are based upon truth and the Scriptures and relate to offenses against God and our neighbor, we have determined to reserve the right to present these also, and to exercise ourselves in all Christian teaching. For this we shall pray to God, since he can grant our demands, and he alone. The peace of Christ abide with us all.

The demands of the peasants seem moderate and reasonable enough to us, but nearly three hundred years elapsed before they were met by the reforms of the early nineteenth century. Luther's comments on the "Twelve Articles" are very instructive. Article II, on the tithe, he declares to be downright highway robbery, for the peasants would appropriate a source of revenue which belongs to the authorities, not to them. As to Article III, on serfdom, he says :

There should be no serfs, because Christ has freed us all! What is that we hear? That is to make Christian freedom wholly bodily. Did not Abraham and the other patriarchs and prophets have serfs? Read what St. Paul says of servants, who in all times have been serfs. So this article is straight against the gospel, and moreover it is robbery, since each man would take his person from his lord to whom it belongs. A serf can be a good Christian and enjoy Christian liberty, just as a prisoner or a sick man may be a Christian although he is not free. This article would make all men equal and convert the spiritual kingdom of Christ into an external worldly one ; but that is impossible, for a worldly realm cannot stand where there is no inequality ; some must be free, others bond ; some rulers, others subjects. . . .

My counsel would be that a few counts and lords should be chosen from the nobles, and from the towns a few councilors, who should settle the matter peacefully. You lords should unbend your stiff minds a bit, — for you will have to do that sooner or later whether you will or no, — and give up a little of your oppression and tyranny, so that the poor man can have a little space and air. On the other hand, the peasants will have to let a few of their articles go, which are screwed up too high. In this way the matter, even if it cannot be treated in a Christian spirit, can at least be adjusted according to human laws and agreements.

If you will not follow this advice, which God would approve, I must leave you to yourselves. But I am guiltless of your souls, your blood, and your goods. I have told you that you are both wrong and are fighting for the wrong. You nobles are not fighting against Christians, for Christians would not oppose you, but would suffer all. You are fighting against robbers and blasphemers of Christ's name ; those that die among them shall be eternally damned. But neither are the peasants fighting Christians, but tyrants, enemies of God, and persecutors of men, murderers of the Holy Ghost. Those of them who die shall also be eternally damned. And this is God's certain judgment on you both — that I know. Do now what you will so long as you care not to save either your bodies or souls.

The following is a condensation of the account given by Michael Eisenhart, a citizen of Rothenburg on the Tauber, of the conduct of the peasantry during the spring of 1525. The revolt had begun near the lake of Constance, late in the previous December, and had spread from Swabia into Alsace, Franconia, Württemberg, Thuringia, and Saxony. The towns also joined in the movement.

109. The
revolt of the
peasants
and the
artisans.
(From
Eisenhart
of Rothen-
burg; con-
densed.)

Through the preachers here in Rothenburg, — namely, Caspar Cristian, a priest, and Brother Melchoir, who married the blind monk's sister and held the wedding in Schwarzman's house, — also especially through the efforts of Hans Rotfuchs, the blind monk himself, and another fellow who gave himself out for a peasant, and through certain citizens here in Rothenburg who adhere to the heresy of Luther and Carlstadt, it has come about that bad, false teaching has greatly got the upper hand, owing also to the dissimulation and concessions of some of the town authorities. Dr. Andreas Carlstadt has appeared in person, preached here, and asked to be received as a burgher.

On March 21, a Tuesday, thirty or forty peasants got together in a mob in Rothenburg, bought a kettledrum, and marched about the town, a part going to Pretheim and a part toward Orenbach. They got together again on Thursday and on Friday, as many as four hundred.

The working
classes in
Rothenburg
revolt and
form a
provisional
government.

The working classes in the town now begin to revolt. They cease to obey the authorities and form a committee of thirty-six to manage affairs. Cunz Eberhardt and George Bermeter are meanwhile dispatched to learn what the peasants are doing ; but the peasants will give no reply, for they say that they have not all got together yet. A letter is received from Margrave Casimir [of Brandenburg]. This is read to the community. He offers to aid the town authorities and if necessary come in person to reëstablish peace and harmony. The community and their committee of thirty-six treat this scornfully and do not accept the offer.

*March 24.* This evening between five and six o'clock some one knocked off the head of Christ's image on a crucifix and struck off the arms.

*March 25.* The town councils are in great danger and anxiety, for they are oppressed by the community and its committee of thirty-six.

*March 27.* The councilors are forced to pledge their obedience to the community, for they are taken out one by one, guarded by members of the committee of thirty-six. Each thought he was going to be killed, but after taking the pledge he was secretly sent home without his companions' knowledge.

*March 26.* Chrischainz, the baker, knocked the missal out of the priest's hand in the chapel of our Lady and drove away the priest from mass. To-day the peasants let themselves be seen in the field outside the Galgenthor.

The following Monday, while the priest was performing service in the parish church and chanting " Adjuva nos, deus salutaris noster," Ernfried Kumpf addressed him rudely, saying that if he wished to save himself he would better leave the altar. Kumpf then knocked the missal on to the floor and drove the scholars out of the choir.

On Tuesday eight hundred peasants came together. Those who would not join them willingly they forced to do so or took their property, as happened to a peasant at Wettring.

On Friday the peasants all gathered, as many as two thousand strong, and camped near Neusitz. Lorenz Knobloch went out to them, and they promised to make him a captain. The same day some of the peasants were sent into the town to give a report of their demands and plans. Meanwhile representatives of the emperor and of the Swabian League arrive with a hope of making peace, but they ride away without accomplishing anything, as did those from Nuremberg.

On this same day all the artisans were to lay all their complaints and demands before a committee. The taxes, wages, and methods of weighing were discussed. The peasants encamped near Santhof. Friday, April 7, Kueplein, during the sermon, threw the lighted oil lamps about the church. Some of the peasants came into Rothenburg and the neighboring towns, everywhere plundering cupboards and cellars. *Demands of the artisans.*

On Good Friday all services were suspended in the churches of Rothenburg, for there was neither chanting nor preaching except that Dr. John Teuschel preached against emperor, kings, princes, and lords, ecclesiastical and lay, with foul abuse and slander, on the ground that they were hindering God's word. *Religious revolution.*

A.19

On Saturday the blind monk, Hans Rotfuchs, spoke contemptuously of the holy sacrament, calling it idolatry and heresy.

On holy Easter there was neither singing nor preaching. Monday Dr. Andreas Carlstadt again attacked the holy sacrament with abusive words. In the night some millers attacked the church at Cobenzell and threw the pictures and images into the Tauber.

*April 18.* The reforms of the committee are proclaimed. The younger priests may, and should, marry, and may enjoy their benefices for three years. The old priests shall have theirs for life. There is a struggle between Kueplein and his followers, on the one hand, who want to destroy a picture of the Virgin, and the pious old Christians, on the other, who wish to protect it. Some knives are drawn.

Crimes of the peasants

*April 19.* The peasants take three casks of wine from the priest at Scheckenpach and drink it up.

*April 20.* The women here in Rothenburg take eleven measures of grain from the house of Conrad Volemar. George Bermeter [one of the revolutionists] is chosen burgomaster.

On the same day, Thursday after Easter, the women run up and down Hafengasse with forks and sticks, declaring that they will plunder all the priests' houses, but are prevented.

*Friday.* All priests are forced to become citizens, otherwise they would have lost all their goods. They are to take their share of guard duty and work on the fortifications.

On Wednesday (April 26) Lorenz Knobloch was hewn to pieces by the peasants at Ostheim, and then they pelted one another with the fragments. They said he was a traitor and that he wanted to mislead them. Divine retribution! He had said he would not die until he had killed three priests, but, thank God, not one fell into his hands.

*April 30.* The monastery of Anhausen was plundered and burned in the night, also that near Dinkelsbühl. The peasants also attacked the monastery of Schwarzach, and the castle of Reichelsberg was burned.

*May 6.* Early in the morning the great bell rang three times, summoning the people to hear a message from Margrave Casimir, brought by three noblemen, and inviting all to take refuge in Rothenburg under his protection. The greater part refused, and some were noted by the margrave's representative, and afterward lost their heads.

*Monday.* The peasants approach Neuhaus, and next day plunder and burn.

In Rothenburg the citizens are summoned to decide whether, like the neighboring towns of Heilbronn, Dinkelsbühl, and Wimfen, they will aid the peasants. The majority decide to send them guns and pikes, powder and lead.

*May 12.* The clergy forced to take arms like the rest. All monks are compelled to lay aside their cowls and the nuns their veils.

*May 15.* The bell summoned the community. In spite of the protests of the old Christians, they are forced to obey the majority, and Rothenburg that day fell away from the empire and joined the peasants. In the meantime a gallows was erected in the market place as a warning, according to their ideas of brotherhood. Supplies were sent to the camp.

*Rothenburg deserts the empire and joins the peasants.*

*May 15.* The peasants attack the castle of Würzburg and scale the walls, but are all killed. The peasants attempt to get possession of Rothenburg by conspiracy, but are ejected without bloodshed.

*Further attack of the peasants on the castle of Würzburg.*

*May 21.* Certain Hohenlohe peasants burn their lord's castle.

On the next Monday Margrave Casimir proceeds with his forces to subdue and punish the peasants. Hans Krelein the older, priest at Wernitz, was beheaded, with four peasants, at Leutershausen. Seven have their fingers cut off. Likewise at Neuenstat eighteen burghers and peasants are beheaded. At Kitzingen fifty-eight have their eyes put out and are forbidden to enter the town again.

*Casimir's revenge.*

On Friday before Whitsuntide the forces of the Swabian League slay four thousand peasants at Königshofen.

On Monday after Whitsunday eight thousand peasants are slaughtered by the troops of the League near Büttart

*Defeat of the peasants by the Swabian League.*

and Sulzdorf. In all these battles the League lost not over one hundred and fifty men.

On June 6 messengers are sent from Rothenburg to Casimir to ask for pardon. Next day others are sent to the League, but they are told that they must surrender unconditionally.

On Thursday following, after the League had retaken the town of Würzburg, they beheaded sixty-two.

After the League had attacked Bamberg they beheaded twenty-one.

On Friday after Corpus Christi, mass was once more chanted in Rothenburg, as formerly.

*June 17.* Vespers, complines, and matins are once more sung.

On June 23 Dr. John Teuschel and the blind monk Hans are taken and shut up, but several others, including Dr. Andreas Carlstadt, who had done most to stir up trouble, secretly escape.

Entrance of Margrave Casimir into Rothenburg.

On the eve of Peter and Paul's day Margrave Casimir rides into Rothenburg with four hundred horsemen, a thousand footmen, and two hundred wagons full of arms and equipments.

Atrocities of the soldiers.

Next day four hundred foot soldiers belonging to the margrave and the League divide into two parts. One went to the village of Orenbach, which they plundered, and burned the church to the ground. The other went to Pretheim, a fine village. This they plundered, killing a number of people, including the innkeeper, behind a table. They burned the village, including the church, and carried off six hundred head of cattle and thirty carts full of plunder.

*June 30.* The citizens of Rothenburg are summoned to the market place by a herald and surrounded by pikemen. They are accused of deserting the empire and joining the peasants, and are threatened with the vengeance they deserve.

The names of a number of citizens are read off, and they are beheaded on the spot. Their bodies are left on the market place all day. Some got away through the ring of soldiers : Lorenz Diem, the sexton, Joseph Schad, a tanner, Fritz Dalck, a butcher, and others, but were nevertheless executed.

*July 1.* Fifteen more are beheaded in the market place, including the blind monk. All the bodies are left on the market place all day, then buried. All of these died without confession or the last sacrament, and did not even ask for it.

## BIBLIOGRAPHY

**Revolt of the Knights :** HÄUSSER, *Period of the Reformation*, pp. 72–87 ; HENDERSON, *Short History of Germany*, Vol. I, pp. 285–307.

**Peasant War :** HÄUSSER, pp. 92–105 ; HENDERSON, Vol. I, pp. 308–332 ; *Cambridge Modern History*, Vol. II, pp. 174–197 ; KÖSTLIN, *Life of Luther*, pp. 304–324.

**Progress of Protestantism before 1530 :** DYER, *Modern Europe*, Vol. II, pp. 50–67 ; *Cambridge Modern History*, Vol. II, pp. 142–173 and 197–205.

**Diet of Augsburg :** DYER, Vol. II, pp. 92–99 ; KÖSTLIN, pp. 402–426.

**The Schmalkaldic War :** JOHNSON, *Europe in the Sixteenth Century*, pp. 220–252 ; HENDERSON, Vol. I, pp. 363–394 ; *Cambridge Modern History*, Vol. II, pp. 232–279.

*A. References.*

---

JANSSEN, *History of the German People*, Vol. IV, pp. 121–369, " The Social Revolution." Vols. V–VI carry the history of Germany down to the "so-called ' religious peace of Augsburg.' "

RANKE, *History of the Reformation*, Vols. II and III. The German original covers the period to 1555, but the English translation closes with the year 1534.

ARMSTRONG, *History of Charles V*, 2 vols., 1902. Best recent account.

*B. Additional reading in English.*

# CHAPTER XXVII

## THE PROTESTANT REVOLT IN SWITZERLAND AND ENGLAND

### I. CALVIN AND HIS WORK

Three phases of Calvin's work and influence.

Perhaps the three most important phases of Calvin's work are the following: (1) He was ever the ardent defender of the Protestants, refuting the calumnies and criticisms of their opponents, denouncing the papacy, and exhibiting what he believed to be the weaknesses and fallacies of the Roman Catholic teachings and traditions; (2) he furnished the Protestants with a text-book of theology, — his *Institutes of the Christian Religion,* — which for two or three centuries enjoyed unrivaled authority among a large and influential class in France, Scotland, England, and America; (3) lastly, in the ordinances drawn up under his influence for the city of Geneva, he established a system of government, civil and ecclesiastical, which in its spirit became the ideal of the various English Puritan sects, as well as of those who migrated to Holland and New England.

110. Extracts from Calvin's address to Francis I (1536). (Condensed.)

As a preface to the first edition of his *Institutes,* published at Basel shortly after his flight from France, Calvin prepared an address to King Francis I, in which he briefly states the reasons for the Protestant revolt and exposes the slanders heaped upon his party. In this, as in all of Calvin's writings, one is impressed by his cogent and logical manner of arguing, combined as it is with great vigor of expression.

*John Calvin, to the most mighty and noble monarch, Francis, the most Christian king of the French, his sovereign prince and lord, with peace and salvation in the Lord:*

When I did first set my hand to this work [i.e. his *Institutes*] I thought nothing less, most illustrious King, than to write anything to be presented to your Majesty. My mind was to teach certain rudiments whereby they that are touched with some zeal of religion might be instructed to true godliness. And this travail I undertook principally for my countrymen, the French, of whom I understood very many to hunger and thirst for Christ, but few had received so much as any little knowledge of him. That this was my purpose the book itself declareth, being framed to a simple and plain manner of teaching. *[margin: Aim of the Institutes.]*

But when I perceived that the furious rage of certain wicked men hath so far prevailed in your realm that in it there is no room for sound doctrine, I thought I should do a thing worth my travail if in a single work I should give both instruction for them whom I proposed to instruct, and send forth an apology to you, whereby you may learn what manner of doctrine that is against which these furious men burn in so great rage, who at this day trouble your realm with sword and fire. For I shall not fear to confess that I have in this work comprehended in a manner the substance of that selfsame doctrine against which they cry out that it ought to be punished with imprisonment, banishment, proscription and fire. . . . *[margin: Calvin adds to his Institutes an "Apology" for the Protestants.]*

You yourself can bear witness, most noble King, with what lying slanders our teachings are daily accused unto you: as that they tend only to wrest from kings their scepters, to throw down all judges' seats and judgments, to subvert all orders and civil governments, to trouble the peace and quiet of the people, to abolish all laws, to undo all proprieties and possessions; finally to turn all things upside down. And yet you hear but the smallest portion, for they spread among the people horrible things, which if they were true, the whole world might worthily judge our cause, with the maintainers thereof, worthy of a thousand fires and gallows. . . . *[margin: Accusations brought against the Protestants.]*

Wherefore I do not unjustly require, most victorious King, that it may please you to take into your own hands the whole hearing of the cause, which hitherto hath been carelessly tossed about without any order of law, more by outrageous hate than judicial gravity. Nor would I have you think that I here go about to make my own private defense, whereby I may procure to myself a safe return into my native country, to which, while I bear such affection of natural love as becometh me, yet as the case now is I am not miscontent to remain abroad. But I take upon me the common cause of all the godly, yea, and the cause of Christ himself, which at this day, having been by every means torn and trodden down in your kingdom, lieth as it were in despaired case. . . .

Calvin maintains that the Protestant teachings are not new.

[Our detractors call our teaching] new, and lately forged; they cavil that it is doubtful and uncertain ; they demand by what miracle it is confirmed ; they ask whether it be meet that it should prevail against the consent of so many holy fathers and the most ancient customs; they press upon us to confess it to be schismatical, which moveth war against the Church, or that the true Church hath lain dead through the many ages in which no such thing hath been heard of. Last of all, they say that they need no arguments, for (say they) it may be judged by its fruits of what sort it is, which, namely, hath bred so big a heap of sects, so many turmoils of sedition, so great licentiousness of vices. Truly, full easy it is for them to triumph over a forsaken cause among the credulous and ignorant multitude, but if we might also have our turn to speak, verily this sharp haste would soon be cooled wherewith they do, licentiously and with full mouth, foam against us.

First, whereas they call it new, they do great wrong to God, whose holy word deserves not to be accused of newness. To them indeed I nothing doubt that it is new, to whom Christ is new, and his gospel is new. But they that know the preaching of Paul to be old, and that Jesus Christ died for our sins and rose again for our justification, shall find nothing new among us. Secondly, that it hath long lain hidden, unknown, and buried, — that is the fault of the ungodliness of men. Sith it is by the bountifulness of God restored to us, it ought at least, by right of full restitution, to receive the title of anciety.

They may mock at the uncertainty of our teachings, but if they were driven to seal their own doctrine with their own blood and with the loss of their lives, men might see how much they set by it. Far other is our faith, which dreadeth neither the terrors of death nor yet the very judgment seat of God. . . .

As for the dilemma into which they would drive us, to compel us to confess that either the Church hath lain dead a certain time, or that we have controversy against the real Church : truly the Church of Christ hath lived and shall live so long as Christ shall reign at the right hand of the Father. . . . But they err not a little from the truth when they acknowledge no church but that which they see with the present eye, and when they affirm that the form of the Church is always to be seen ; for they set the true form of the Church in the see of Rome and in the order of their prelates. We, on the contrary side, affirm both that the Church may consist of no visible form, and that the form itself is not contained in that outward splendor which they foolishly admire, but hath a far other indication, namely, the pure teaching of the word of God and the right ministration of the sacraments. . . .

Thus, O King, is the venomous injustice of slanders so largely spread abroad that you should not too easily believe their reports. . . . Your mind, though it be now turned away and estranged from us, yea, even inflamed against us, yet we trust that we shall be able to recover the favor thereof. But if the whisperings of the malicious do so possess your ears that there is no place for accused men to speak for themselves ; and if those outrageous furies do still, with your winking at them, exercise cruelty, with prisoning, tormenting, mutilating, and burning, — then shall we indeed, as sheep appointed to the slaughter, be brought to all extremities, yet so that in our patience we shall possess our soul and wait for the strong hand of the Lord, which

*Protestants do not assert that the true Church ceased to exist during the Middle Ages.*

shall without doubt be present in time and stretch forth itself armed, both to deliver the poor out of affliction and to take vengeance on the despisers which now triumph with so great assuredness.

The Lord, the King of kings, establish your throne with righteousness and your seat with equity, most noble King.

At Basel, the tenth day before the Kalends of September [1536].

Under Farel's influence Geneva espouses Protestantism.

It was not Calvin but Farel, another French Protestant, who first won the city of Geneva from the old Church. Farel (1489–1565) was an ardent missionary of the new faith, who had succeeded in converting several towns in French Switzerland before he went to Geneva in 1533. Owing to his preaching, a general assembly of the people proclaimed (May, 1536) that they wished to live according to the "holy law of the gospel and the word of God" and to desert "all masses, papal ceremonies and abuses, images and idols."

111. Protestant intolerance in Geneva before Calvin's arrival.

Just before Calvin's coming we have the following entry in the city council's register (July 24, 1536):

John Ballard was interrogated wherefore he refused to hear the word of God? He replied that he believed in God, who taught him by his spirit. He could not believe our preachers. He said that we could not compel him to go to the sermon against his conscience. . . . We admonished him that he should within three days obey the proclamation or show just cause why he should not. He replied, " I wish to live according to the gospel of God, but I do not wish to adopt the interpretation of certain individuals, but to follow that of the Holy Spirit through the holy mother Church Universal in which I believe." Asked to say whether he would go to the sermon or no, he replied that his conscience would not permit him to go, and that he would not act against its dictates ; for it was directed by a higher authority than that of preachers. Having heard these things, the council ordered that if he did not obey the proclamations, and go to the sermon as established, he and his family should leave the city within ten days.

In August, 1536, Calvin happening to pass through Geneva, expecting to spend but one night there, was seized upon by Farel, who, as Calvin reports, "burning with a marvelous zeal to advance the gospel, made every effort to hold me." Calvin consented to remain.

Calvin's arrival in Geneva (August, 1536).

The town records show that the ministers, Farel, Calvin, and others, were constantly appearing before the town council to denounce sinful practices and suggest reforms. There was, however, a large party in Geneva which disliked Calvin and Farel and their puritanical influences. These "liberals"[1] got the upper hand in the town council, and banished Calvin and Farel (April, 1538) for refusing to administer the communion in the manner favored by the council, and for continuing to preach when forbidden to do so. But in two or three years the liberals became unpopular in their turn, and Calvin, after prolonged negotiations, reluctantly consented to return to Geneva, in September, 1541. He was now in a position to hold his own, in spite of the liberals, who nevertheless continued to give him much trouble for many years.

He immediately submitted his plan of church government, which was adopted. He held that our Lord had established four orders of officers for governing his Church, — namely, pastors, teachers, elders, and deacons. The elders (or presbyters) were laymen appointed to watch over the morals of their fellows, and are so

---

[1] The French historians of the seventeenth century call this party *libertins*, which means nothing worse than "liberals."

conspicuous in Calvin's plan of organization that they have given their name to the Presbyterian Church. He thus describes them :

112. The duties of the elders, or presbyters

The office of the elders is to watch over the conduct of every individual, to admonish lovingly those whom they see doing wrong or leading an irregular life. When there is need, they should lay the matter before the body deputed to inflict paternal discipline [i.e. the consistory], of which they are members. As the Church is organized, it is best that the elders be chosen, two from the small council, four from the council of sixty, and six from the council of two hundred[1]; they should be men of good life and honest, without reproach and beyond suspicion, above all God-fearing and endowed with spiritual prudence. And they should be so chosen that they be distributed in each quarter of the city, so that they can have an eye on everything.[2] . . .

The consistory, or session.

The elders, who have been described, shall assemble once a week with the ministers, namely Thursday morning, to see if there be any disorders in the Church and discuss together such remedies as shall be necessary. . . . If any one shall in contempt refuse to appear before them, it shall be their duty to inform the council, so that it may supply a remedy.

The rules made for the villages under the supremacy of Geneva show the actual scope of the religious control.

113. Extracts from Calvin's regulations for the villages about Geneva.

The whole household shall attend the sermons on Sunday, except when some one shall be left at home to tend the children or cattle.

If there is preaching on week days, all who can must come, — unless there be some good excuse, — so that at least one from each household shall be present. Those who have men-servants or maid-servants shall bring them when

---

[1] This refers to the different bodies which constituted the city government.

[2] It is interesting to compare this conception of excommunication and of government by lay elders with the system of the Catholic Church.

it is possible, so that they shall not live like beasts without instruction. . . . Should any one come after the sermon has begun, let him be warned. If he does not amend, let him pay a fine of three sous. Let the churches be closed except during service, so that no one may enter them at other hours from superstitious motives. If any one be discovered engaged in some superstition within or near the church, let him be admonished. If he will not give up his superstition, let him be punished.

Those who are found to have rosaries or idols to adore, let them be sent before the consistory, and in addition to the reproof they receive there, let them be sent before the council. Let the same be done with those who go on a pilgrimage. Those who observe feasts or papistical fasts shall only be admonished. Those who go to mass shall, besides being admonished, be sent before the council, and it shall consider the propriety of punishing the offenders by imprisonment or special fines, as it judges best.

*Persecution of Catholics*

He who blasphemes, swearing by the body or blood of our Lord, or in like manner, shall kiss the earth for the first offense, pay five sous for the second and ten for the third. He who contradicts the word of God shall be sent before the consistory for reproof, or before the council for punishment, as the case may require. If any one sings indecent, licentious songs, or dances *en virollet* or otherwise, he shall be kept in prison three days and then sent to the council.[1]

## II. Henry VIII, Wolsey, and Queen Catherine

The Venetian ambassador, Giustiniani, thus describes Henry VIII, Queen Catherine, and Wolsey, in 1519:

*114. A Venetian ambassador's description of Henry VIII, Queen Catherine, and Wolsey.*

His Majesty is twenty-nine years old and extremely handsome; nature could not have done more for him. He is much handsomer than any other sovereign in Christendom; a great deal handsomer than the king of France; very fair,

---

[1] There are similar provisions for drunkenness, gambling, quarreling, taking more than five per cent interest, etc.

and his whole frame admirably proportioned. On hearing that Francis I wore a beard, he allowed his own to grow, and, as it is reddish, he has now a beard that looks like gold. He is very accomplished, a good musician, composes well, is a most capital horseman, a fine jouster, speaks good French, Latin, and Spanish ; is very religious, — hears three masses daily when he hunts, and sometimes five on other days. He hears the office every day in the queen's chamber, — that is to say, vespers and compline.

He is very fond of hunting, and never takes his diversion without tiring eight or ten horses, which he causes to be stationed beforehand along the line of country he means to take ; and when one is tired he mounts another, and before he gets home they are all exhausted. He is extremely fond of tennis, at which game it is the prettiest thing in the world to see him play, his fair skin glowing through a shirt of finest texture. He gambles with the French hostages, to the amount occasionally, it is said, of from six thousand to eight thousand ducats in a day.

He is affable and gracious, harms no one, does not covet his neighbor's goods, and is satisfied with his own dominions, having often said to me, " Sir ambassador, we want all potentates to content themselves with their own territories ; we are satisfied with this island of ours." He seems extremely desirous of peace.

He is very rich. His father left him ten millions of ready money in gold, of which he is supposed to have spent one half in the war against France, when he had three armies on foot : one crossed the Channel with him, another was in the field against Scotland, and the third remained with the queen in reserve. . . .

The queen is the sister of the mother of the king of Spain, now styled King of the Romans. She is thirty-five years old and not handsome, though she has a very beautiful complexion. She is religious, and as virtuous as words can express. I have seen her but seldom.

The cardinal of York is of low origin, and has two brothers, one of whom holds an untitled benefice, and the other is pushing his fortune. He rules both the king and the entire kingdom. On my first arrival in England he used to say to me, "His Majesty will do so and so." Subsequently, by degrees, he forgot himself, and commenced saying, "We shall do so and so." At this present he has reached such a pitch that he says, "I shall do so and so." He is about forty-six years old, very handsome, learned, extremely eloquent, of vast ability, and indefatigable. He alone transacts as much business as that which occupies all the magistracies, offices, and councils of Venice, both civil and criminal; and all state affairs likewise are managed by him, let their nature be what it may.

Early in 1527 King Henry VIII determined to obtain a divorce from Catherine, and soon announced to her that they must separate. Wolsey then reluctantly induced Pope Clement VII to send a legate, Cardinal Campeggio, to England, who, with Wolsey, was to hold a court to determine whether the dispensation granted to Henry to marry his brother's widow was sufficient and valid under the circumstances. The trial was begun in May, 1529. When Queen Catherine was called upon in court she rose from her chair and came to the king, and, kneeling down at his feet, said:

Henry VIII proposes to divorce Catherine.

"Sir, in what have I offended you? or what occasion of displeasure have I given you, intending thus to put me from you? I take God to be my judge, I have been to you a true and humble wife, ever conformable to your will and pleasure; never contradicting or gainsaying you in anything; being always contented with all things wherein you had any delight or took any pleasure, without grudge, or countenance of discontent or displeasure. I loved, for your sake, all them whom you loved, whether I had cause or no; whether they were my friends or my enemies.

115. Queen Catherine's protest against Henry's plan to rid himself of her (1529).

"I have been your wife these twenty years or more, and you have had by me divers children; and when you had me first, I take God to be my judge, that I was a maid. Whether it be true or no, I put it to your own conscience. If there be any just cause that you can allege against me, either of dishonesty, or matter lawful to put me from you, I am content to depart, to my shame and confusion; and if there be none, then I pray you to let me have justice at your hands.

"The king, your father, was, in his time, of such an excellent wit, that he was accounted amongst all men for wisdom to be a second Solomon ; and the king of Spain, my father, Ferdinand, was accounted one of the wisest princes that had reigned in Spain for many years. It is not, therefore, to be doubted, but that they had gathered as wise counselors unto them, of every realm, as in their wisdom they thought meet. And I conceive that there were in those days as wise and well-learned men, in both the realms, as be now at this day, who thought the marriage between you and me good and lawful. Therefore it is a wonder to me what new inventions are now invented against me. And now to put me to stand to the order and judgment of this court seems very unreasonable. . . . I humbly pray you to spare me until I may know what counsel my friends in Spain will advise me to take ; and if you will not, then your pleasure be fulfilled." And with that she rose up and departed, nevermore appearing in any court.

Catherine's friends, however, induced the pope to evoke the case to Rome, and so quite removed the whole matter from Wolsey's control. He thereby forfeited the king's favor, and Sir Thomas More was appointed chancellor in his stead. A few months after the trial (October, 1529) we find Wolsey writing piteously to the disappointed monarch.

*Most gracious and merciful Sovereign Lord :*

Though that I, your poor, heavy, and wretched priest, do daily pursue, cry, and call upon your Royal Majesty for grace, mercy, remission, and pardon, yet in most humble wise I beseech your Highness not to think that it proceedeth of any mistrust that I have in your merciful goodness, nor that I would encumber or molest your Majesty by any indiscreet or inopportune suit; but that the same only cometh of an inward and ardent desire that I have continually to declare unto your Highness how that, wot unto God, I neither desire nor covet anything in this world but the attaining of your gracious favor and forgiveness of my trespass.

And for this cause I cannot desist nor forbear, but to be a continual and most lowly suppliant to your benign grace. For surely, most gracious king, the remembrance of my folly, with the sharp word of your Highness' displeasure, hath so penetrated my heart that I cannot but lamentably cry and say, "It is sufficient." Now withhold thy hand, most merciful king. Forgive and ye shall be forgiven. . . .

Your Grace's most prostrate, poor chaplain,
creature, and beadsman,
THOMAS, Cardinal York, most unhappy.

## III. HENRY VIII REPUDIATES THE HEADSHIP OF THE POPE

The pope excommunicated Henry in 1533 for repudiating Catherine. The king replied by extorting from the English bishops, abbots, and priests written acknowledgments that the Roman pontiff had no more authority than any other foreign bishop. In the spring of 1534 Parliament passed an act regulating the succession to the crown. This declared Henry's marriage with Catherine void and against the laws of Almighty God; his marriage with Anne Boleyn was pronounced good and consonant with God's laws. The crown was to descend to Anne's daughter, the Princess Elizabeth, unless she should have sons by the king. Then follows a harsh provision.

*116. Wolsey's piteous appeal to Henry VIII (October, 1529).*

A.20

117. Ex-
tract from
the first
Act of
Succession
(1534).
(Condensed.)

. . . If any person or persons, of what estate, dignity, or condition soever they be, maliciously, by writing, print, deed, or act, procure or do any thing or things to the prejudice, slander, or derogation of the said lawful matrimony solemnized between your Majesty and the said Queen Anne, or to the peril or slander of any of the heirs of your Highness, being limited by this act to inherit the crown of this realm, every such person and persons, and their aiders and abettors, shall be adjudged high traitors, and every such offense shall be adjudged high treason, and the offenders, and their aiders and abettors, being lawfully convicted, shall suffer pain of death, as in cases of high treason.

Treason to
question the
lawfulness
of Henry's
marriage
with Anne.

[All are to be sworn] truly, firmly, and constantly, without fraud or guile, to observe, fulfill, maintain, and keep, to their cunning, wit, and the utmost of their powers, the whole effects and contents of this present act.

The Act of Supremacy, given below in full, was passed by Parliament in November, 1534. It does little more than sum up briefly what had already been done.

118. The
Act of
Supremacy
(November,
1534).

Albeit the king's Majesty justly and rightfully is and ought to be the supreme head of the Church of England, and so is recognized by the clergy of this realm in their convocations, yet nevertheless, for corroboration and confirmation thereof, and for increase of virtue in Christ's religion within this realm of England, and to repress and extirpate all errors, heresies, and other enormities and abuses heretofore used in the same, be it enacted, by authority of this present Parliament, that the king, our sovereign lord, his heirs and successors, kings of this realm, shall be taken, accepted, and reputed the only supreme head in earth of the Church of England, called *Anglicana Ecclesia;* and shall have and enjoy, annexed and united to the imperial crown of this realm, as well the title and style thereof, as all honors, dignities, preëminences, jurisdictions, privileges, authorities, immunities, profits, and commodities to the said dignity of the supreme head of the same Church belonging and appertaining; and that our said sovereign lord, his heirs and successors, kings of this realm, shall have full power and authority from time to time to visit, repress, redress, record, order, correct, restrain, and amend all such errors, heresies, abuses, offenses, contempts, and enormities, whatsoever they be, which by any manner of spiritual authority or jurisdiction ought or may lawfully be reformed, repressed, ordered, redressed, corrected, restrained, or amended, most to the pleasure of Almighty God, the increase of virtue in Christ's religion, and for the conservation of the peace, unity, and tranquillity of this realm; any usage, foreign law, foreign authority, prescription, or any other thing or things to the contrary hereof notwithstanding.

Numbers of conscientious persons were now arrested for declining to swear that the king's first marriage was void, and for refusing to adjure the supremacy of the pope. The most distinguished victims of Henry's harshness were Bishop Fisher, who had supported Catherine, and Sir Thomas More, who refused to pronounce on the matter. Accordingly : 119. Execution of Fisher and More. (From Hall's *Chronicle*.)

The twenty-second day of the same month John Fisher, bishop of Rochester, was beheaded, and his head set upon London Bridge. This bishop was of very many men lamented; for he was reported to be a man of great learning, and a man of very good life, but therein wonderfully deceived, for he maintained the pope to be supreme head of the Church, and very maliciously refused the king's title of supreme head. It was said that the pope, for that he held so manfully with him and stood so stiffly in his cause, did elect him cardinal, and sent the cardinal's hat as far as Calais, but the head it should have stood on was as high as London Bridge before the hat could come to Bishop Fisher. . . . John Fisher beheaded for treason (1535).

Also the sixth day of July was Sir Thomas More beheaded for the like treason before rehearsed, which, as you have heard, was for the denying of the king's Majesty's supremacy. Execution of Sir Thomas More.

This man was also counted learned, and, as you have heard before, he was lord chancellor of England, and in that time a great persecutor of such as detested the supremacy of the bishop of Rome, which he himself so highly favored that he stood to it until he was brought to the scaffold on the Tower Hill, where on a block his head was stricken from his shoulders and had no more harm.

I cannot tell whether I should call him a foolish wise man or a wise foolish man, for undoubtedly he, beside his learning, had a great wit, but it was so mingled with taunting and mocking, that it seemed to them that best knew him that he thought nothing to be well spoken except he had ministered some mock in the communication, insomuch as at his coming to the Tower one of the officers demanded his upper garment for his fee, meaning his gown, and he answered he should have it and took him his cap, saying that it was the uppermost garment that he had. Likewise, even going to his death at the Tower gate, a poor woman called unto him and besought him to declare that he had certain evidence of hers in the time that he was in office (which after he was apprehended she could not come by), and that he would entreat she might have them again, or else she was undone. He answered, " Good woman, have patience a little while, for the king is so good unto me that even within this half hour he will discharge me of all business, and help thee himself." Also when he went up the stair on the scaffold he desired one of the sheriff's officers to give him his hand to help him up, and said, " When I come down again let me shift for myself as well as I can."

Also the hangman kneeled down to him asking him forgiveness of his death (as the manner is), to whom he said, "I forgive thee, but I promise thee that thou shalt never have honesty of the striking of my head, my neck is so short." Also even when he should lay down his head on the block he, having a great gray beard, struck out his beard, and said to the hangman, "I pray you let me lay my beard over the block lest ye should cut it." Thus with a mock he ended his life.

## IV. Church Reforms of Henry VIII

Henry VIII was no Protestant. He cruelly enforced the acceptance by his subjects of the old beliefs of the Roman Catholic Church, except that concerning the supremacy of the pope. Nevertheless, as "supreme head" of the English Church, he introduced some momentous changes : (1) He brought the clergy completely under his despotic control, and even issued ordinances relating to the Church without submitting them to the clergy at all. (2) He approved the reading of the Bible in English, and (3) ordered that the services be conducted in English instead of Latin. (4) Lastly, he did away with all the monasteries, great and small, and appropriated their lands. Thousands of men and women were in consequence cast adrift, and toward a third of all the lands in England are supposed to have been involved.

The following is an extract from an account of the destruction of the monasteries, written about 1591 by one whose father and uncle witnessed the acts of the visitors in some parts. The details here given correspond very closely with the reports sent in to the king by those whom he had commissioned to dissolve the abbeys.

As soon as the visitors [i.e. the king's commissioners] were entered within the gates, they called the abbot and other officers of the house, and caused them to deliver up to them all their keys, and took an inventory of all their goods both within doors and without; for all such beasts, horses, sheep, and such cattle as were abroad in pasture or grange places, the visitors caused to be brought into their presence, and when they had done so, turned the abbot with all his convent and household forth of the doors.

**120. An account of the destruction of the monasteries**

Which thing was not a little grief to the convent, and all the servants of the house departing one from another, and especially such as with their conscience could not break their profession ; for it would have made a heart of flint to have melted and wept to have seen the breaking up of these houses and their sorrowful departing, and the sudden spoil that fell the same day of their departure from the house. And every person had everything good cheap, except the poor monks, friars, and nuns, that had no money to bestow on anything. . . .

Such persons as afterward bought their corn and hay, or such like, found all the doors either open, the locks and shackles plucked away, or the door itself taken away, went in and took what they found, — filched it away. Some took the service books that lied in the church, and laid them upon their waine coppes to piece the same. Some took windows of the hayleith and hid them in their hay ; and likewise they did of many other things, for some pulled forth the iron hooks out of the walls that bought none, when the yeomen and gentlemen of the country had bought the timber of the church. For the church was the first thing that was put to the spoil ; and then the abbott's lodging, dorter, and frater, with the cloister and all the buildings thereabout within the abbey walls. . . . It would have pitied any heart to see what tearing up of lead there was and plucking up of boards and throwing down of the spars ; when the lead was torn off and cast down into the church and the tombs in the church all broken (for in most abbeys were divers noble men and women, — yea, and in some abbeys, kings, whose tombs were regarded no more than the tombs of all other inferior persons ; for to what end should they stand when the church over them was not spared for their cause!), and all things of Christ either spoiled, carped away, or defaced to the uttermost.

The persons that cast the lead into fodders plucked up all the seats in the choir wherein the monks sat when they said service, — which were like to the seats in minsters, — and burned them and melted the lead therewith all, although there was wood plenty within a flight shot of them. . . .

## V. The Catholic Reaction under Queen Mary
### (1553–1558)

The Venetian ambassador, Giovanni Michele, made a report to his government in 1557 on the state of England. He thus describes Queen Mary and her husband, Philip II:

Queen Mary, the daughter of Henry VIII and of his queen Catherine, daughter of Ferdinand the Catholic, king of Aragon, is a princess of great worth. In her youth she was rendered unhappy by the event of her mother's divorce; by the ignominy and threats to which she was exposed after the change of religion in England, she being unwilling to unbend to the new one; and by the dangers to which she was exposed by the duke of Northumberland, and the riots among the people when she ascended the throne.

121. A Venetian ambassador's account of Queen Mary (1557).

She is of short stature, well made, thin and delicate, and moderately pretty; her eyes are so lively that she inspires reverence and respect, and even fear, wherever she turns them; nevertheless she is very shortsighted. Her voice is deep, almost like that of a man. She understands five languages, — English, Latin, French, Spanish, and Italian, in which last, however, she does not venture to converse. She is also much skilled in ladies' work, such as producing all sorts of embroidery with the needle. She has a knowledge of music, chiefly on the lute, on which she plays exceedingly well. As to the qualities of her mind, it may be said of her that she is rash, disdainful, and parsimonious rather than liberal. She is endowed with great humility and patience, but withal high-spirited, courageous, and resolute, having during the whole course of her adversity not been guilty of the least approach to meanness of deportment; she is, moreover, devout and stanch in the defense of her religion.

Some personal infirmities under which she labors are the causes to her of both public and private affliction; to remedy these recourse is had to frequent bloodletting, and this is the real cause of her paleness and the general weakness of her frame. These have also given rise to the unfounded rumor that the queen is in a state of pregnancy. The cabal she has been exposed to, the evil disposition of the people toward her, the present poverty and the debt of the crown, and her passion for King Philip, from whom she is doomed to live separate, are so many other causes of the grief with which she is overwhelmed. She is, moreover, a prey to the hatred she bears my Lady Elizabeth, and which has its source in the recollection of the wrongs she experienced on account of her mother, and in the fact that all eyes and hearts are turned towards my Lady Elizabeth as successor to the throne. . . .

Description of Philip II.

King Philip is of short stature, but his person appears to advantage both when armed and in common attire. Though of great affability and politeness, his character is marked with gravity. His understanding is good and his judgment correct. Besides Spanish, he knows Latin, French, and Italian. He is also liberal and religious, but without possessing either the dignity or the ambition of his father. . . . As to his authority in England, your Serene Highness may be assured that in all affairs of importance, whether public or private, he is made to act precisely the same part as if he were the natural king of England, and this on account of the great respect and love with which he is treated by the queen and Cardinal Pole. Sensible, however, that he is new in this kingdom, he modestly, and wisely too, leaves everything to the management of the queen and the cardinal [Pole]. He receives petitions, but more in the character of mediator than as a patron, letting justice take its course in criminal cases, but frequently stepping forward to procure pardon or mitigation of punishment after conviction. . . .

Indifference of the English to religion.

Religion, although thriving in this country, is, I apprehend, in some degree the offspring of dissimulation. The queen is far from being lukewarm; she has already founded ten monasteries, and is about to found more. Generally speaking, your Serene Highness may rest assured that with the English the example and authority of the sovereign is everything, and religion is only so far valued as it inculcates the duty due from the subject to the prince. They live as he lives, they believe as he believes, and they obey his commands, not from any inward moral impulse, but because they fear to incur his displeasure ; and they would be full as zealous followers of the Mohammedan or Jewish religions did the king profess either of them, or command his subjects to do so. In short, they will accommodate themselves to any religious persuasion, but most readily to one that promises to minister to licentiousness and profit.

## BIBLIOGRAPHY

**Zwingli and the Swiss Reform :** HÄUSSER, *Period of the Reformation*, pp. 125–142 ; *Cambridge Modern History*, Vol. II, Chapter X, pp. 305–341 ; WALKER, *The Reformation*, Chapter IV, pp. 147–180.

*A. References.*

**Calvin and the Genevan Reformation :** HÄUSSER, pp. 241–255 ; *Cambridge Modern History*, Vol. II, Chapter XI, pp. 342–376 ; WALKER, Chapter VI, pp. 225–276.

**The English Humanists :** GREEN, *Short History of England*, pp. 303–320 ; *Translations and Reprints*, Vol. I, No. 1.

**Henry VIII :** CHEYNEY, *Short History of England*, pp. 289–310 ; ANDREWS, *History of England*, pp. 245–268 ; GREEN, pp. 320–356 ; *Cambridge Modern History*, Vol. II, Chapter XIII, pp. 416–473 (by James Gairdner ; excellent) ; TERRY, *A History of England*, pp. 512–559.

**Edward VI :** CHEYNEY, pp. 310–319 ; *Cambridge Modern History*, Vol. II, Chapter XIV, pp. 474–512 (by Pollard) ; TERRY, pp. 560–570.

**Mary and the Catholic Reaction :** GREEN, pp. 361–369 ; TERRY, pp. 571–586 ; *Cambridge Modern History*, Vol. II, Chapter XV, pp. 512–459 ; CHEYNEY, pp. 319–328.

---

JACKSON, S. M., *Huldreich Zwingli*, 1901. The best biography of Zwingli in English ; scholarly and well illustrated.

*B. Additional reading in English.*

SCHAFF, PHILIP, *History of the Reformation*. Vol. II (Vol. VII of his *History of the Christian Church*) is devoted to Zwingli and Calvin.

SPALDING, *The History of the Protestant Reformation*. Vol. I, Chapter V (Zwingli) ; Vol. II, Chapter I (Henry VIII and Edward VI) ; Chapter II (Mary and Philip). A suggestive review of the subject by a critic hostile to the Protestant movement.

HENRY, P., *Life and Times of Calvin*, 2 vols., 1849. This is a translation of a German work, and in spite of the fact that it is rather out of date, it is the best life of Calvin to be had in English. A new biography is announced in The Heroes of the Reformation Series, by Professor Williston Walker.

CALVIN, *Works : The Institutes of the Christian Religion* has several times been published in English ; for example, a translation by Beveridge, 3 vols., 1845–1846. Beveridge has also translated some important *Tracts of Calvin relating to the Reformation*, 3 vols., 1844–1851.

BEZA, THEODORE, *Life of Calvin*. This is to be found in Vol. I of Beveridge's translation of Calvin's *Tracts*, mentioned just above. Beza was a co-worker of Calvin's and knew him well.

SEEBOHM, *The Oxford Reformers*. An admirable account of the beginnings of humanism in England.

GASQUET, *The Eve of the Reformation*, 1900. Excellent ; by a learned Benedictine.

MOBERLY, *The Early Tudors*. A general review of the period in the Epoch Series.

POLLARD, *Henry VIII*, 1902, and *Thomas Cranmer*, 1903. Two useful biographies, by a careful writer.

STONE, *The Reign of Mary the First*, 1901. An apology, correcting many common misapprehensions.

GEE AND HARDY, *Documents Illustrative of English Church History*. An admirable collection, particularly full on this period. It may be supplemented by the interesting extracts given in KENDALL, *Source Book of English History* ; COLBY, *Selections from the Sources of English History* ; and LEE, *Source Book of English History*.

CAVENDISH, *Cardinal Wolsey*, in Morley's " Universal Library." Written by one of Wolsey's clerks.

WAKEMAN, *Introduction to the History of the Church of England*, 1898, Chapters XI–XIV.

GAIRDNER, *A History of the English Church from Henry VIII to Mary*, 1904.

# CHAPTER XXVIII

## THE CATHOLIC REFORMATION: PHILIP II

### I. THE DECREES OF THE COUNCIL OF TRENT

The decrees of the Council of Trent constitute the most important monument of the Catholic Reformation. These fall into three groups : (1) those which define and explain the doctrines of the Roman Catholic Church and defend them against the objections raised by the Protestants; (2) those which succinctly and explicitly declare accursed the various heretical (Protestant) beliefs; and (3) lastly, a great number of reform decrees abolishing the various abuses and enforcing a more rigid discipline among the clergy and monks.

The Acts of the Council of Trent.

Of the last group, the following relating to the conduct and teaching of the clergy may be cited.

It is to be desired that those who undertake the office of bishop should understand what their portion is, and comprehend that they are called, not to their own convenience, not to riches or luxury, but to labors and cares, for the glory of God. For it is not to be doubted that the rest of the faithful also will be more easily excited to religion and innocence if they shall see those who are set over them not fixing their thoughts on the things of this world, but on the salvation of souls and on their heavenly country. Wherefore this holy Council, being minded that these things are of the greatest importance toward restoring ecclesiastical discipline, admonishes all bishops that, often meditating thereon, they show themselves conformable to their office by their deeds and the actions of their lives ; which is a kind of

122. Prelates should live frugally as an example to others.

315

perpetual sermon; but, above all, that they so order their whole conversation that others may thence be able to derive examples of frugality, modesty, continency, and of that holy humility which so much commends us to God.

Wherefore, after the example of our fathers in the Council of Carthage, this Council not only orders that bishops be content with modest furniture, and a frugal table and diet, but that they also give heed that in the rest of their manner of living, and in their whole house, there be nothing seen which is alien to this holy institution, and which does not manifest simplicity, zeal toward God, and a contempt of vanities.

Nepotism forbidden.

It strictly forbids them, moreover, to strive to enrich their own kindred or domestics out of the revenues of the Church; seeing that even the canons of the apostles forbid them to give to their kindred the property of the Church, which belongs to God; but if their kindred be poor, let them distribute to them thereof as poor, but not misapply or waste the Church's goods for their sakes: yea, this holy Council, with the utmost earnestness, admonishes them completely to lay aside all this human and carnal affection towards brothers, nephews, and kindred, which is the seed plot of many evils in the Church. And what has been said of bishops, the same is to be observed by all who hold ecclesiastical benefices, whether secular or regular, each according to the nature of his rank. . . .

## II. The Abdication of Charles V (1555)

123. Charles V's address at Brussels (1555).

Although [my councilor] Philibert has just fully explained to you, my friends, the causes which have determined me to surrender the possession and administration of these Belgian provinces and leave them to my son, Don Philip, yet I wish to say certain things with my own mouth. You will remember that upon the 5th of January of this year there had elapsed forty years since my grandfather, the emperor Maximilian, in the same place and at the same hour, declared my majority at the age of fifteen, withdrew me from the guardianship under which I had remained up to that time, and made me master of myself.

The following year, which was my sixteenth, King Ferdinand (my mother's father and my grandfather) died in the kingdom over which I was then forced to begin to reign, owing to the fact that my beloved mother, who has but just died, was left, by reason of the death of my father, with disordered judgment, and never sufficiently recovered her health to be capable of ruling over the possessions which she inherited from her father and mother.

At that time I went to Spain by way of the sea. Soon came the death of my grandfather Maximilian, in my nineteenth year, and although I was still young I sought and obtained the imperial dignity in his stead. I had no inordinate ambition to rule a multitude of kingdoms, but merely desired to secure the welfare and prosperity of Germany, my dear fatherland, and of my other kingdoms, especially of my Belgian provinces; and to encourage and extend as far as in me lay Christian peace and harmony throughout the whole world.

But although such zeal was mine, I was unable to show so much of it as I might have wished, on account of the troubles raised by the heresies of Luther and the other innovators of Germany, and on account of serious war into which the hostility and envy of neighboring princes had driven me, but from which I have safely emerged, thanks to the favor of God. . . .

This is the fourth time that I am setting out for Spain. I wish to say to you that nothing I have ever experienced has given me so much pain or rested so heavily upon my soul as that which I experience in parting from you to-day, without leaving behind me that peace and quiet which I so much desired. My sister Mary, who in my absence has governed you so wisely and defended you so well, has explained to you in the last assembly the reasons for my determination.

I am no longer able to attend to my affairs without great The emperor's bodily fatigue and consequent detriment to the interests of bad health.

the state. The cares which so great a responsibility involves, the extreme dejection which it causes, my health already ruined, — all these leave me no longer the vigor sufficient for governing the states which God has confided to me. The little strength that remains to me is rapidly disappearing. I should long ago have laid down the burden if my son's immaturity and my mother's incapacity had not forced both my spirit and my body to sustain its weight until this hour.

The last time that I went to Germany I had determined to do what you see me do to-day; but I could not bring myself to do it when I saw the wretched condition of the Christian state, a prey to such a multitude of disturbances, of innovations, of singular opinions as to faith, of worse than civil wars, and fallen finally into so many lamentable disorders. I was turned from my purpose because my own ills were not yet so great, and I hoped to make an end of all these things and restore peace. In order that I might not be wanting in my duty, I risked my strength, my goods, my repose, and my life for the safety of Christianity and the defense of my subjects.

From this struggle I emerged with a portion of the things I desired. But the king of France and certain Germans, failing to preserve the peace and amity they had sworn, marched against me. The Germans were upon the point of seizing my person. The king of France took the city of Metz, and I, in the dead of winter, exposed to intense cold, in the midst of snow and blood, advanced with a powerful army raised at my own expense to retake the city and restore the empire. The Germans saw that I had not yet laid aside the imperial crown, and that I had no disposition to allow its majesty to be diminished. . . .

I have carried out what God has permitted, — for the outcome of our efforts depends upon the will of God. We human beings act according to our powers, our strength, our spirit, and God awards the victory or permits defeat. I have ever done what I could, and God has aided me. I — and you, too — should return to him boundless thanks for his aid, for having succored me in my greatest trials and in all my dangers.

To-day I feel so exhausted that I could not help you, as you yourselves see. In my present state of dejection and weakness, I should have to render a serious account to God and man if I did not lay aside authority, as I have resolved to do, since my son, King Philip, is of an age sufficiently advanced to be able to govern you; and he will be, I hope, a good prince to all my beloved subjects.

I am determined then to retire to Spain and to yield to my son Philip the possession of all my Belgian provinces. I particularly commend my son to you, and I ask of you, in remembrance of me, that you extend to him the love which you have always borne towards me; moreover I ask you to preserve among yourselves the same affection and harmony. Be just and zealous in the observance of the laws, preserve respect for all that merits respect, and do not refuse to grant to authority the support of which it stands in need.

Above all, beware of infection from the sects of neighboring lands. Extirpate at once the germs of heresy, should they appear in your midst, for fear lest they may spread abroad and utterly ruin your state, and lest you fall into the direst calamities.

### III. PHILIP II OF SPAIN

**124. An esti mate of Philip II by Suriano, a Venetian ambassador (1159).**

We have several descriptions of Philip II, the most important and impartial of which are those of the Venetian ambassadors. The king's affability, industry, religion, and frail constitution are mentioned by all. In his earlier years, however, he exhibited a Castilian haughtiness which he successfully overcame later.

The Catholic king was born in Spain, in the month of May, 1527, and spent a great part of his youth in that kingdom. Here, in accordance with the customs of the country and the wishes of his father and mother, — who belonged to the house of Portugal, — he was treated with all the deference and respect which seemed due to the son of the greatest emperor whom Christendom had ever had, and to the heir to such a number of realms and to such grandeur. As a result of this education, when the king left Spain for the first time and visited Flanders, passing on his way through Italy and Germany, he everywhere made an impression of haughtiness and severity, so that the Italians liked him but little, the Flemings were quite disgusted with him, and the Germans hated him heartily. But when he had been warned by the cardinal of Trent and Queen Mary [of Hungary, his aunt], and above all by his father, that this haughtiness was not in place in a prince destined to rule over a number of nations so different in manners and sentiment, he altered his manner so completely that on his second journey, when he went to England, he everywhere exhibited such distinguished mildness and affability that no prince has ever surpassed him in these traits.[1] Although his actions display that royal dignity and gravity which are natural and habitual to him, he is none the less agreeable for this; on the contrary, his courtesy toward all seems only the more striking. His pleasing figure, his manly air, and his suavity of speech and manner serve to enhance the pleasing effect. He is slight in stature, but so well built, so admirably proportioned, and dressed with such taste and discernment, that one could hardly imagine anything more perfect. . . .

Contrast between Charles V and Philip II.
Although the king resembles his father in his face and speech, in his attention to his religious duties, and in his habitual kindness and good faith, he nevertheless differs from him in several of those respects in which the greatness of rulers, after all, lies. The emperor was addicted to war, which he well understood; the king knows but little of it and has no love for it. The emperor undertook great enterprises with enthusiasm; his son avoids them. The father was fond of planning great things and would in the end realize his wishes by his skill; his son, on the contrary, pays less attention to augmenting his own greatness than to hindering that of others. The emperor never allowed

---

[1] For another estimate of Philip see above, p. 312.

himself to be influenced by threats or fear, while the king has lost some of his dominions owing to unreasonable apprehensions. The father was guided in all matters by his own opinion; the son follows the opinions of others.

In the king's eyes no nation is superior to the Spaniards. It is among them that he lives, it is they that he consults, and it is they that direct his policy; in all this he is acting quite contrary to the habit of his father. He thinks little of the Italians and Flemish and still less of the Germans. Although he may employ the chief men of all the countries over which he rules, he admits none of them to his secret counsels, but utilizes their services only in military affairs, and then perhaps not so much because he really esteems them, as in the hope that he will in this way prevent his enemies from making use of them.

*Philip's partiality for Spain.*

In the letters which Philip II took great pains to write to his young daughters during a trying campaign in Portugal, we discover no signs of a grim despot bent on compassing the death of thousands of his subjects, but rather of a kindly father with an ear for the nightingale's song and an eye for the early flowers, who noticed even when one of his babies cut a tooth.

LISBON, January 15, 1582.

It is good news for me to learn that you are so well. It seems to me that your little sister is getting her eye teeth pretty early. Perhaps they are in place of the two which I am on the point of losing and which I shall probably no longer have when I get back. But if I had nothing worse to trouble me, that might pass. . . .

We are having terrible weather here; torrents of rain fall, sometimes with fearful claps of thunder and flashes of lightning. I have never seen such weather at this season. It would be a good thing for you, my elder daughter, if you are still afraid of thunder. It is not cold, but it rains continuously, and just now with such violence that you would say that the whole sky was turning into water. There have been

*125. A letter of Philip II to his daughters.*

A.21

some terrible storms, but there were not so many ships lost as Luis Tristan [a servant] wrote to you; indeed, I hardly think any were lost, — nothing except a few little boats. The last courier who had a letter from me for you has probably been delayed, for the Tagus was raging so that he could not leave Tuesday morning as usual, but started Wednesday, so that I doubt if he will arrive before the regular post leaves you.

I am inclined to think that Madeleine[1] is no longer so out of patience with me; but she has been ill for some time. She took some physic, and since has been in a very bad humor. She came here yesterday. She is in a sad state, feeble, old, deaf, — in short, half dead. I believe that all this comes from her drinking, and this is the reason that she is so glad not to have her son-in-law with her. Yesterday she told me that she no longer had any grudge against the person called Mariola about whom she wrote to you, whose real name is Maria Fernandez. I believe her, for I think that she really likes to hear Mariola sing; and she is right, for she sings very well, only she is so fat and big that she can scarcely get through the door.

I am ready to believe that Lady Anna de Mendoza takes as good care of your little brothers as you, my eldest daughter, say that she does.

The other day some one gave me what I have inclosed in this box and said that it was a sweet lime. I think, just the same, that it is only a lemon, but nevertheless wanted to send it to you. If it is really a sweet lime, I have never seen one so big. I do not know if it will still be good when it gets to you. If it is, taste it and let me know what it proves to be, for I cannot believe that a lime ever was so big, and consequently shall be pleased to be enlightened by you. The little lemon which is in the box with it is only to fill up the space.

I am sending you also some roses and an orange flower, just to let you see that we have them here. Calabrés brings

[1] An old servant to whom the king frequently refers in the letters to his daughters.

me bunches of both these flowers every day, and we have had violets for a long time. There are no jonquils here; if there were, they ought to have blossomed by this time, since we have these other flowers. After this rainy time I imagine that you will be having flowers, too, by the time my sister arrives, or soon after. God keep you as I would have him!

## IV. THE REVOLT OF THE NETHERLANDS

In 1580 Philip II decided to declare William the Silent an outlaw and put a price upon his head. In so doing he gives an interesting account of the troubles in the Netherlands from a Spanish standpoint.

*Philip, by the grace of God king of Castile, Leon, Aragon, Navarre, Naples, Sicily, Sardinia, the Indies and terra firma, the Atlantic Ocean; duke of Burgundy, Lorraine, Brabant, Limburg, Luxemburg, Gelderland, Milan; count of Flanders, Artois, Hainault, Holland, Zealand, etc.; to all to whom these presents may come, greeting:*

126. Proclamation outlawing William the Silent (1580). (Condensed.)

It is well known to all how favorably the late emperor, Charles the Fifth, of exalted memory, our father, treated William of Nassau in the matter of the succession to his cousin, the prince of Orange, and how, from William's earliest youth, he promoted his advancement, as we, since the emperor's death, have continued to do, by appointing him lieutenant general of Holland, Zealand, Utrecht, and Burgundy, summoning him to our council of state, and heaping upon him honors and emoluments. By reason of this and the oaths of fidelity and homage taken to us for fiefs and lands held of us in various of our countries and provinces, he was specially bound to us, and under obligation to obey and keep faith with us and safeguard our interests and to do all in his power to secure peace and tranquillity in our several dominions and provinces.

Nevertheless, as every one knows, we had scarcely turned our back on the Netherlands before the said William of

Nassau (who had become, in the manner mentioned above, prince of Orange) began to endeavor, by sinister arts, plots, and intrigues, first to gain over those whom he believed to be malcontents, or haters of justice, or anxious for innovations, and then, above all, those who were suspected in the matter of religion. These he flattered and attracted by fine words and vain promises. He was the instigator and chief author of the first protest which was presented by certain young gentlemen who daily frequented his house and table.

Moreover, with the knowledge, advice, and encouragement of the said Orange, the heretics commenced to destroy the images, altars, and churches in a disorderly manner, and to desecrate all holy and sacred objects, especially the sacraments ordained of God. Yet, by divine grace and the foresight of the duchess of Parma, our very dear sister, matters were remedied, and he was forced to retire from our dominions, breathing out threats of vengeance in his rage. These he hoped to carry out the following year by arms, but he was closely pursued by our army and driven from our said lands, where he could get no foothold.

Philip throws the responsibility for unpopular taxes on Alva.

But when a little later some discontent arose among our subjects in regard to the government of the duke of Alva (who had succeeded the said lady), especially in the provinces of Holland and Zealand, Orange managed to return. Nevertheless he was only received on condition that he would take a solemn oath to the estates of the said provinces and towns, pledging himself to guard the said provinces and towns for us, and in our obedience, and to change nothing in the ancient Catholic and Roman religion. He was, as governor, only to assist them against the duke of Alva should he attempt to coerce and oppress them, as Orange alleged that he proposed to do, — namely, in the matter of the tenth and twentieth penny which the duke wished to collect. Now we had not ordered him to levy this tax, and did not wish to have it levied except with the good will and consent of our good subjects and in place of other impositions from which it was proposed to free them.

Nevertheless, so soon as the said Nassau was received into the said government of the provinces, he began, through his agents and satellites, to introduce heretical preaching where he found it possible, persecuting all the good pastors, preachers, monks, and upright persons, and hunting many of them from the region. Then he had a number massacred; or rather, he tried to avoid the responsibility for a massacre carried on by some of his adherents, until the estates, greatly incensed by this cruelty, demanded an account of the affair, when he pretended that it was displeasing to him. Then he introduced liberty of conscience, or to speak more correctly, confusion of all religion, which soon brought it about that the Catholics were openly persecuted and driven out, and the churches and monasteries, whether of men or women, broken up, ruined, and leveled with the ground.

Although a married man, and although his second wife was still alive, he took to himself a nun, an abbess who had been solemnly sanctified by episcopal authority, and her he still keeps; a most disreputable and infamous thing, not only according to the Christian religion, but the Roman law as well.

Moreover he obtained such a hold upon our poor subjects of Holland and Zealand and brought affairs to such a pass that nearly all the towns, one after the other, have been besieged and taken, either by assault or by capitulation, so that more than once he was on the point of being brought to bay by our arms, when the commander who succeeded the duke of Alva (whom we had recalled to please our subjects) died. Then the said Nassau induced the estates to demand the withdrawal of all the foreign troops in hope of peace, but Nassau continued his machinations and displayed all his craft in plunging our people into war with our brother, whom we had appointed lieutenant general. . . .

Therefore, for all these just reasons, for his evil doings as chief disturber of the public peace and as a public pest, we outlaw him forever and forbid all our subjects to associate with him or communicate with him in public or in secret. We declare him an enemy of the human race, and

Reward offered for the arrest or assassination of William the Silent.

in order the sooner to remove our people from his tyranny
and oppression, we promise, on the word of a king and as
God's servant, that if one of our subjects be found so generous of heart and so desirous of doing us a service and
advantaging the public that he shall find means of executing this decree and of ridding us of the said pest, either by
delivering him to us dead or alive, or by depriving him at
once of life, we will give him and his heirs landed estates
or money, as he will, to the amount of twenty-five thousand
gold crowns. If he has committed any crime, of any kind
whatsoever, we will pardon him. If he be not noble, we will
ennoble him for his valor ; and should he require other persons to assist him, we will reward them according to the service rendered, pardon their crimes, and ennoble them too.

In answer to the charges brought against him the
prince of Orange published his famous " Apology."
This contains a good account of his life and a brief
history of the revolt of the Netherlands, in which he
played so important a part.

**127. Ex-
tracts from
the "Apol-
ogy " of
William the
Silent to
the estates
(1581).**

. . . What could be more gratifying in this world, especially to one engaged in the great and excellent task of
securing liberty for a good people oppressed by evil men,
than to be mortally hated by one's enemies, who are at the
same time enemies of the fatherland, and by their mouths
to receive a sweet testimony to one's fidelity to his people
and to his obstinate opposition to tyrants and disturbers of
the peace? Such is the pleasure that the Spaniards and
their adherents have prepared for me in their anxiety to
disturb me. They have but gratified me by that infamous
proscription by which they sought to ruin me. Not only
do I owe to them this favor, but also the occasion to make
generally known the equity and justice of my enterprises. . . .

[If in reviewing my life I am forced to praise myself and
blame others] kindly attribute this, gentlemen, to the situation in which my enemies have placed me, and throw the
blame upon their impudence and importunity. Remember,

gentlemen, that I am falsely accused of being an ingrate, infidel, heretic, and hypocrite, a new Judas and Cain, a disturber of the peace, a rebel, foreigner, enemy of the human race, a public pest of the Christian commonwealth, a traitor and scoundrel; that I am exposed to be killed like a beast, with a reward for any assassin or poisoner who will undertake the job. It is for you to judge, gentlemen, whether, in order to purge myself from the calumnies heaped upon me, I may not be excused for departing from my usual habits in speaking of myself and others. . . .

My enemies object that I have "established liberty of conscience." I confess that the glow of fires in which so many poor Christians have been tormented is not an agreeable sight to me, although it may rejoice the eyes of the duke of Alva and the Spaniards; and that it has been my opinion that persecutions should cease in the Netherlands. I will confess, too, in order that my enemies may know that they have to do with one who speaks out roundly and without circumlocution, that when the king was leaving Zealand he commanded me to put to death several worthy persons suspected on account of their religion. I did not wish to do this, and I could not with a clear conscience, so I warned them myself, since one must obey God rather than men. Let the Spaniards say what they please, I know several nations and peoples who are quite their equals who will approve and praise my conduct, for they have learned that nothing is to be accomplished by fire and sword. . . .

They denounce me as a hypocrite, which is absurd enough, since I have never resorted to dissimulation. As their friend, I told them quite frankly that they were twisting a rope to hang themselves when they began the barbarous policy of persecution. If their unbounded passion and their contempt for me had not prevented their following my advice, they would never have come out where they did. When later I became their opponent and enemy in the interest of your freedom, I do not see what hypocrisy they could discover in me, unless they call it hypocrisy to wage open war, take cities, chase them out of the country, and inflict upon them, without disguise, all the harm that the law of war permits. But, gentlemen, if you will reread my "Justification," published thirteen years ago, you will find there the letters of a deceitful and hypocritical king, who thought to deceive me by his false and honeyed words, just as now he would stun me by his threats and the thunder of his denunciations. . . .

As for me personally, you see, gentlemen, that it is my head that they are looking for, and that they have vowed my death by offering such a great sum of money. They say that the war can never come to an end so long as I am among you. Might it please God that my perpetual exile, or even my death, should bring you a true deliverance from all the evils and calamities which the Spaniards are preparing for you and which I have so often seen them considering in council and devising in detail! How agreeable to me would be such a banishment! how sweet death itself! . . . Why have I so often endangered my life, what reward shall I expect for my long labors for you, which have extended into old age, and for the loss of my goods, if it be not to obtain and purchase your liberty, even at the cost of my blood if necessary?

If, then, gentlemen, you believe that my exile, or even my death, may serve you, I am ready to obey your behests. Here is my head, over which no prince or monarch has authority save you. Dispose of it as you will for the safety and preservation of our commonwealth. But if you judge that such little experience and energy as I have acquired through long and assiduous labors, if you judge that the remainder of my possessions and of my life can be of service to you, I dedicate them to you and to the fatherland.

## V. The Wars of Religion in France

The statesman and fair-minded historian, De Thou (1553–1617), when a young man witnessed the Massacre of St. Bartholomew, and thus describes it.

So it was determined to exterminate all the Protestants, and the plan was approved by the queen. They discussed for some time whether they should make an exception of the king of Navarre and the prince of Condé. All agreed that the king of Navarre should be spared by reason of the royal dignity and the new alliance. The duke of Guise, who was put in full command of the enterprise, summoned by night several captains of the Catholic Swiss mercenaries from the five little cantons, and some commanders of French companies, and told them that it was the will of the king that, according to God's will, they should take vengeance on the band of rebels while they had the beasts in the toils. Victory was easy and the booty great and to be obtained without danger. The signal to commence the massacre should be given by the bell of the palace, and the marks by which they should recognize each other in the darkness were a bit of white linen tied around the left arm and a white cross on the hat.

Meanwhile Coligny awoke and recognized from the noise that a riot was taking place. Nevertheless he remained assured of the king's good will, being persuaded thereof either by his credulity or by Teligny, his son-in-law: he believed the populace had been stirred up by the Guises, and that quiet would be restored as soon as it was seen that soldiers of the guard, under the command of Cosseins, had been detailed to protect him and guard his property.

But when he perceived that the noise increased and that some one had fired an arquebus in the courtyard of his dwelling, then at length, conjecturing what it might be, but too late, he arose from his bed and having put on his dressing gown he said his prayers, leaning against the wall. Labonne held the key of the house, and when Cosseins commanded him, in the king's name, to open the door he obeyed at once without fear and apprehending nothing. But scarcely had Cosseins entered when Labonne, who stood in his way, was killed with a dagger thrust. The Swiss who were in the courtyard, when they saw this, fled into the house and closed the door, piling against it tables

128. The Massacre of St. Bartholomew and the murder of Coligny, as described by De Thou.

(This paragraph is much condensed.)

and all the furniture they could find. It was in the first scrimmage that a Swiss was killed with a ball from an arquebus fired by one of Cosseins' people. But finally the conspirators broke through the door and mounted the stairway, Cosseins, Attin, Corberan de Cordillac, Seigneur de Sarlabous, first captains of the regiment of the guards, Achilles Petrucci of Siena, all armed with cuirasses, and Besme the German, who had been brought up as a page in the house of Guise; for the duke of Guise was lodged at court, together with the great nobles and others who accompanied him.

After Coligny had said his prayers with Merlin the minister, he said, without any appearance of alarm, to those who were present (and almost all were surgeons, for few of them were of his retinue): "I see clearly that which they seek, and I am ready steadfastly to suffer that death which I have never feared and which for a long time past I have pictured to myself. I consider myself happy in feeling the approach of death and in being ready to die in God, by whose grace I hope for the life everlasting. I have no further need of human succor. Go then from this place, my friends, as quickly as you may, for fear lest you shall be involved in my misfortune, and that some day your wives shall curse me as the author of your loss. For me it is enough that God is here, to whose goodness I commend my soul, which is so soon to issue from my body." After these words they ascended to an upper room, whence they sought safety in flight here and there over the roofs.

Meanwhile the conspirators, having burst through the door of the chamber, entered, and when Besme, sword in hand, had demanded of Coligny, who stood near the door, "Are you Coligny?" Coligny replied, "Yes, I am he," with fearless countenance. " But you, young man, respect these white hairs. What is it you would do? You cannot shorten by many days this life of mine." As he spoke, Besme gave him a sword thrust through the body, and having withdrawn his sword, another thrust in the mouth, by which his face was disfigured. So Coligny fell, killed with many thrusts.

Others have written that Coligny in dying pronounced as though in anger these words: "Would that I might at least die at the hands of a soldier and not of a valet." But Attin, one of the murderers, has reported as I have written, and added that he never saw any one less afraid in so great a peril, nor die more steadfastly.

Then the duke of Guise inquired of Besme from the courtyard if the thing were done, and when Besme answered him that it was, the duke replied that the Chevalier d'Angoulême was unable to believe it unless he saw it; and at the same time that he made the inquiry they threw the body through the window into the courtyard, disfigured as it was with blood. When the Chevalier d'Angoulême, who could scarcely believe his eyes, had wiped away with a cloth the blood which overran the face and finally had recognized him, some say that he spurned the body with his foot. However this may be, when he left the house with his followers he said: "Cheer up, my friends! Let us do thoroughly that which we have begun. The king commands it." He frequently repeated these words, and as soon as they had caused the bell of the palace clock to ring, on every side arose the cry, "To arms!" and the people ran to the house of Coligny. After his body had been treated to all sorts of insults, they threw it into a neighboring stable, and finally cut off his head, which they sent to Rome. They also shamefully mutilated him, and dragged his body through the streets to the bank of the Seine, a thing which he had formerly almost prophesied, although he did not think of anything like this.

As some children were in the act of throwing the body into the river, it was dragged out and placed upon the gibbet of Montfaucon, where it hung by the feet in chains of iron; and then they built a fire beneath, by which he was burned without being consumed; so that he was, so to speak, tortured with all the elements, since he was killed upon the earth, thrown into the water, placed upon the fire, and finally put to hang in the air. After he had served for several days as a spectacle to gratify the hate of many and arouse the just indignation of many others, who reckoned that this fury of the people would cost the king and France many a sorrowful day, François de Montmorency, who was nearly related to the dead man, and still more his friend, and who moreover had escaped the danger in time, had him taken by night from the gibbet by trusty men and carried to Chantilly, where he was buried in the chapel.

## VI. MARY QUEEN OF SCOTS AND ELIZABETH

James Melville, a trusted ambassador of Mary Queen of Scots, tells in his *Memoirs* of an interview with Queen Elizabeth in 1564, when she was thirty-one years of age.

**129. Melville's impressions of Elizabeth in 1564.**

During nine days that I remained at the court it pleased her Majesty to confer with me every day and sometimes thrice in a day, — in the morning, after dinner, and after supper. Sometimes she would say that, seeing she could not meet with the queen [i.e. Mary], her good sister, to confer with her familiarly, she was resolved to open a good part of her inward mind to me, that I might show it again to the queen. . . . [She said,] "I am resolved never to marry if I be not thereto necessitated by the queen, my sister's, harsh behavior toward me." "I know the truth of that, madam," said I; "you need not tell me. Your Majesty thinks if you were married you would be but queen of England; and now you are both king and queen. I know your spirit cannot endure a commander."

She appeared to be so affectionate to the queen, her good sister, that she expressed a great desire to see her; and because their (so much by her desired) meeting could not be so hastily brought to pass she appeared with great delight to look upon her Majesty's picture. . . .

The queen, my mistress, had instructed me to leave matters of gravity sometimes and cast in merry purposes, lest otherwise I should be wearied, she being well informed of that queen's natural temper. Therefore, in declaring my observations of the customs of Dutchland, Poland, and

Italy, the buskins of the women was not forgot, and what country weed [i.e. costume] I thought best becoming gentlewomen. The queen said she had clothes of every sort; which every day thereafter, so long as I was there, she changed. One day she had the English weed, another the French, another the Italian, and so forth. She asked me which of them became her best. I answered, in my judgment, the Italian dress; which answer I found pleased her well, for she delighted to show her golden-colored hair, wearing a caul and bonnet as they do in Italy.

Her hair was more reddish than yellow, curled in appearance naturally. She desired to know of me what color of hair was reputed best, and whether my queen's hair or hers was best, and which of them two was fairest. I answered that the fairness of them both was not their worst faults. But she was earnest with me to declare which of them I judged fairest. I said she was the fairest queen in England and mine the fairest queen in Scotland. Yet she appeared earnest. I answered they were both the fairest ladies in their countries; that her Majesty was whiter, but my queen was very lovesome.

She inquired which of them was of highest stature. I said my queen. "Then," saith she, "she is too high; for I myself am neither too high nor too low." Then she asked what kind of exercises she used. I answered that when I received my dispatch the queen was but lately come from the highland hunting; that when her more serious affairs permitted she was taken up with reading of histories; that she sometimes recreated herself in playing upon the lute and virginals. She asked if she played well. I said, reasonably, for a queen.

## VII. The Latter Part of Elizabeth's Reign

The following letter from John Hawkins, the famous English mariner, who participated in the fight against the Armada, gives a lively notion of the conflict with the Spanish fleet, which was in progress as he wrote.

130. John
Hawkins'
letter about
the fight
with the
Armada
(July, 1588).

My bounden duty humbly remembered unto your good lordship. I have not busied myself to write often to your lordship in this great cause, for that my lord admiral doth continually advertise the manner of all things that doth pass. So do others that do understand the state of all things as well as myself.

We met with this fleet somewhat to the westward of Plymouth upon Sunday in the morning, being the 21st of July, where we had some small fight with them in the afternoon. By the coming aboard one of the other of the Spaniards, a great ship, a Biscayan, spent her foremast and bowsprit, which was left by the fleet in the sea, and so taken up by Sir Francis Drake the next morning. The same Sunday there was, by a fire chancing by a barrel of powder, a great Biscayan spoiled and abandoned, which my lord took up and sent away. The Tuesday following, athwart of Portland, we had a sharp and long fight with them, wherein we spent a great part of our powder and shot, so as it was not thought good to deal with them any more till that was relieved.

The Thursday following, by the occasion of the scattering of one of the great ships from the fleet which we hoped to have cut off, there grew a hot fray, wherein some store of powder was spent; and after that little done until we came near to Calais, where the fleet of Spain anchored, and our fleet by them; and because they should not be in peace there, to refresh their water or to have conference with those of the duke of Parma's party, my lord admiral, with firing of ships, determined to remove them; as he did, and put them to the seas; in which broil the chief galleass spoiled her rudder, and so rode ashore near the town of Calais, where she was possessed of our men, but so aground that she could not be brought away.

That morning being Monday, the 29th of July, we followed the Spaniards, and all that day had with them a long and great fight, wherein there was great valor showed generally by our company. In this battle there was spent very much of our powder and shot; and so the wind began to blow westerly, a fresh gale, and the Spaniards put themselves somewhat to the northward, where we follow and keep company with them. . . .

Our ships, God be thanked, have received little hurt, and are of great force to accompany them, and of such advantage that with some continuance at the seas, and sufficiently provided of shot and powder, we shall be able, with God's favor, to weary them out of the sea and confound them. Yet as I gather certainly, there are amongst them fifty forcible and invincible ships. There are thirty hulks and thirty small ships, whereof little account is to be made. . . .

At their departing from Lisbon the soldiers were twenty thousand, the mariners and others eight thousand ; so as, in all, they were twenty-eight thousand men. Their commission was to confer with the prince of Parma, as I learn, and then proceed to the service that should be there concluded ; and so the duke to return into Spain with these ships and mariners, the soldiers and their furniture being left behind. Now this fleet is here and very forcible, and must be waited upon with all our force, which is little enough. There should be an infinite quantity of powder and shot provided and continually sent abroad ; without the which great hazard may grow to our country ; for this is the greatest and strongest combination, to my understanding, that ever was gathered in Christendom ; therefore I wish it, of all hands, to be mightily and diligently looked into and cared for. . . .

*Destination of the Armada.*

And so, praying to God for a happy deliverance from the malicious and dangerous practice of our enemies, I humbly take my leave. From the sea, aboard the *Victory*, the last of July, 1588.

The Spaniards take their course for Scotland ; my lord doth follow them. I doubt not, with God's favor, but we shall impeach their landing. There must be order for victual and money, powder and shot, to be sent after us.

Your lordship's humbly to command,

JOHN HAWKYNS.

In a letter written shortly after Elizabeth's death by a writer who, although unknown to us, was apparently well acquainted with her court, we have a good description of the character and tastes of this extraordinary queen.

131. Elizabeth's character and tastes. (From an unknown contemporary.)

I will proceed with the description of the queen's disposition and natural gifts of mind and body, wherein she either matched or exceeded all the princes of her time, as being of a great spirit yet tempered with moderation, in adversity never dejected, in prosperity rather joyful than proud; affable to her subjects, but always with due regard to the greatness of her estate, by reason whereof she was both loved and feared.

In her later time, when she showed herself in public, she was always magnificent in apparel; supposing haply thereby that the eyes of her people (being dazzled by the glittering aspect of those her outward ornaments) would not so easily discern the marks of age and decay of natural beauty; and she came abroad the more seldom, to make her presence the more grateful and applauded by the multitude, to whom things rarely seen are in manner as new.

She suffered not, at any time, any suitor to depart discontented from her, and though ofttimes he obtained not that he desired, yet he held himself satisfied with her manner of speech, which gave hope of success in the second attempt. . . .

She was accounted in her latter time to be very near, and oversparing of expense; and yet, if the rewards which she gave of mere motion and grace had been bestowed of merit, with due respect, they had doubtless purchased her the name of a very liberal prince. . . .

She was very rich in jewels, which had been given her by her subjects; for in times of progress there was no person that entertained her in his house but (besides his extraordinary charge in feasting her and her train) he bestowed a jewel upon her; a custom in former times begun by some of her especial favorites that (having in great measure tasted of her bounty) did give her only of her own; though otherwise that kind of giving was not so pleasing to gentlemen of meaner quality.

Touching these commendable qualities whereto, partly by nature and partly by education and industry, she had attained, there were few men that (when time and occasion served) could make better use or more show of them than herself. The Latin, French, and Italian she could speak very elegantly, and she was able in all those languages to answer ambassadors on the sudden. Her manner of writing was somewhat obscure and the style not vulgar, as being either learned by imitation of some author whom she delighted to read, or else affected for difference' sake, that she might not write in such phrases as were commonly used. Of the Greek tongue also she was not altogether ignorant. She took pleasure in reading of the best and wisest histories, and some part of Tacitus' *Annals* she herself turned into English for her private exercise. She also translated Boethius' *De Consolatione Philosophiae*, and a treatise of Plutarch, *De Curiositate*, with divers others. . . .

*Elizabeth's learning.*

She was of nature somewhat hasty, but quickly appeased; ready there to show most kindness where a little before she had been most sharp in reproving. Her greatest grief of mind and body she either patiently endured or politicly dissembled. I have heard it credibly reported that, not long before her death, she was divers times troubled with the gout in her fingers, whereof she would never complain, as seeming better pleased to be thought insensible of the pain than to acknowledge the disease. . . .

It is credibly reported that not long before her death she had a great apprehension of her own age and declination by seeing her face (then lean and full of wrinkles) truly represented to her in a glass, which she a good while very earnestly beheld; perceiving thereby how often she had been abused by flatterers (whom she held in too great estimation) that had informed her the contrary.

A.22

## BIBLIOGRAPHY

*A. Refer-*
*ences.*

**The Catholic Reformation:** WALKER, *The Reformation*, pp. 356–367;
*Cambridge Modern History*, Vol. II, pp. 639–650.

**The Jesuits:** HÄUSSER, *Period of the Reformation*, Chapter XX,
pp. 265–273; WALKER, pp. 367–392; *Cambridge Modern History*,
Vol. II, pp. 651–659.

**Council of Trent:** HÄUSSER, pp. 258–264; *Cambridge Modern History*, Vol. II, pp. 659–689.

**Spain under Philip II:** *Cambridge Modern History*, Vol. III, Chapter XV, pp. 475–525.

**Revolt of the Netherlands:** JOHNSON, *European History, 1494–
1598*, Chapter VIII, pp. 315–386; HÄUSSER, Chapters XXI–XXV,
pp. 276–344; *Cambridge Modern History*, Vol. III, Chapters VI–VII,
pp. 182–259.

**French Wars of Religion:** JOHNSON, Chapter IX, pp. 387–448;
HÄUSSER, Chapter XXV, pp. 345–381; *Cambridge Modern History*,
Vol. III, Chapter I, pp. 1–52.

**Henry IV of France:** HÄUSSER, Chapter XXIX, pp. 382–401; DYER
and HASSALL, Vol. III, Chapter XXVI, pp. 41–75, and Chapters XXVII
and XXIX, *passim*.

**Mary Queen of Scots:** GREEN, *Short History*, pp. 379–392; *Cambridge
Modern History*, Vol. III, Chapter VIII, pp. 260–293.

**Elizabeth:** CHEYNEY, *Short History of England*, Chapter XIII,
pp. 330–381; TERRY, *History of England*, pp. 587–617; ANDREWS,
*History of England*, pp. 286–325; *Cambridge Modern History*, Vol. III,
Chapter X, pp. 328–363.

**The Armada:** GREEN, pp. 413–420; *Cambridge Modern History*,
Vol. III, Chapter IX, pp. 294–327.

**Elizabethan Literature:** GREEN, pp. 420–442; *Cambridge Modern
History*, Vol. III, Chapter XI, pp. 364–382.

---

*B. Addi-*
*tional read-*
*ing in*
*English.*

SYMONDS, JOHN A., *The Catholic Reaction*, Chapter II, "The Council of Trent"; Chapter III, "The Inquisition"; and Chapter IV, "The
Jesuits." Readable but extremely unsympathetic.

WARD, A. W., *The Counter Reformation*, 1889 (in Epochs of Church
History Series).

FROUDE, *Lectures on the Council of Trent*. Especially Chapters
VIII–XIII. A vivacious account by a gifted but inaccurate scholar.

PRESCOTT, *Reign of Philip II*, 3 vols. See above, p. 246.

MOTLEY, *Rise of the Dutch Republic*, 3 vols. The bias and inaccuracy
of this brilliant and celebrated work can best be seen by comparing it

with the painstaking if rather dry work of a modern Dutch historian, namely, BLOK, *A History of the People of the Netherlands*, Vol. III, Chapters I–VII (translated by Ruth Putnam).

PUTNAM, RUTH, *William the Silent*, 2 vols. A scholarly biography, admirably illustrated.

BAIRD, *The Rise of the Huguenots*, 2 vols., and *The Huguenots and Henry of Navarre*, 2 vols. By an ardent partisan of the Huguenots.

RANKE, *History of the Popes*, 3 vols. (Bohn Library). This is a history of the papacy since the opening of the Protestant Revolt. Vol. III is devoted to documents and discussion of the sources.

JACKSON, C. C., *The Last of the Valois*, 2 vols., 1888, and *The First of the Bourbons*, 2 vols., 1890.

HUME, *Philip II of Spain*, 1902.

*The Autobiography of St. Ignatius Loyola*, edited by J. F. X. O'CONOR, S.J., New York, 1900. A translation of the most authentic account of Loyola's life, from data he himself dictated.

*Canons and Decrees of the Council of Trent*, translated by Rev. J. Waterworth; and *Catechism of the Council of Trent*, translated by Rev. J. Donovan. It is scarcely necessary to say that these official utterances of the council deserve the most careful study. The catechism was first issued in 1566. It was drawn up by a commission appointed by the pope, to whom the matter had been delegated by the council.

ARMSTRONG, *The French Wars of Religion*, 1892.

WHITEHEAD, A. W., *Caspard de Coligny, Admiral of France*, 1904.

SULLY, *Memoirs*, 4 vols. (Bohn Library). This is not a translation of the original as dictated by Sully, but of an adaptation made in the eighteenth century to suit the taste of the time.

CREIGHTON, *The Age of Elizabeth* (in the Epochs of Modern History). Also by the same, *Queen Elizabeth*, 1896; cheaper edition, without illustrations, 1899. These excellent volumes may be supplemented by BEESLEY, *Elizabeth*.

LANG, ANDREW, *The Mystery of Mary Stuart*, 1901. A recent review of all the evidence of her guilt in the murder of her husband.

SIMPSON, *Life of Campion*, 1867. An excellent account of one of the Jesuits who suffered martyrdom under Elizabeth.

PAYNE, *Voyages of Elizabethan Seamen*, 2 vols.

STOW (1525–1605), *A Survey of London*, first published in 1598; HARRISON (1534–1593), *Description of England* (convenient edition in the Camelot Series). These are two important and amusing accounts of English habits and dress by contemporaries.

SAINTSBURY, *Elizabethan Literature*, a useful short work on a great subject.

# CHAPTER XXIX

## THE THIRTY YEARS' WAR

### I. THE OPENING OF THE THIRTY YEARS' WAR

An English historian of the time, Rushworth, thus describes the opening of the Thirty Years' War. James I of England was deeply interested in 1618 in negotiating a marriage between his son and heir, Charles, and a Spanish princess.

132. An English view of the opening of the war. (From Rushworth.)

Whilst Spain and England were thus closing, the fire brake out in Germany between the states and princes Protestant and the house of Austria. These commotions involved and drew along the affairs of most Christian princes, especially of the two potent kings now in treaty. The Catholic cause and the lot of the house of Austria engaged the king of Spain, who was the strongest branch of that stock. King James must needs be drawn in, both by common and particular interest: the religion which he professed and the state of his son-in-law, the elector palatine, who became the principal part of those wars and the most unfortunate. It was an high business to the whole Christian world, and the issue of it had main dependence upon the king of England, being the mightiest prince of the Protestant profession. But this king's proceedings were wholly governed by the unhappy Spanish treaty.

The clouds gather thick in the German sky; jealousies and discontents arise between the Catholics and the Evangelics, or Lutherans, of the Confession of Augsburg. Both parties draw into confederacies and hold assemblies; the one seeking by the advantage of power to encroach and get ground, the other to stand their ground and hold their own. The potency of the house of Austria, a house devoted to the persecution of the reformed religion, became formidable. The old emperor Mathias declared his cousin german, the archduke Ferdinand, to be his adopted son and successor, and caused him to be chosen and crowned king of Bohemia and Hungary, yet reserving to himself the sole exercise of kingly power during his life.

The Jesuits triumphed in their hopes of King Ferdinand. The pope exhorted the Catholics to keep a day of jubilee and to implore aid of God for the Church's high occasions. To answer this festival the elector of Saxony called to mind that it was then the hundredth year complete since Martin Luther opposed the papal indulgences, which was the first beginning of the Protestant Reformation. Whereupon he ordained a solemn feast of three days for thanksgiving and for prayer to God to maintain in peace the purity of the Word and the right administration of the sacraments. The professors of the universities of Lipsick and Wittemberg, the imperial towns of Franckford, Worms, and Noremburg, —yea, the Calvinists also,— observed the same days of jubilee against the Romish Church, and much gold and silver was cast abroad in memory of Luther, whom they called blessed. . . .

The Bohemian troubles took their first rise from the breach of the edict of peace concerning religion and the accord made by the emperor Rudolf whereby the Protestants retained the free exercise of their religion, enjoyed their temples, colleges, tithes, patronages, places of burial, and the like, and had liberty to build new temples and power to choose defenders to secure these rights and to regulate what should be the service in their churches. Now the stop of building certain churches on lands within the lordships of the Catholic clergy (in which the Evangelics conceived a right to build) was the special grievance and cause of breach. *The Bohemian troubles.*

On the 23d of May the chief of the Evangelics went armed into the castle of Prague, entered the council chamber, and opened their grievances; but, enraged by opposition, they threw Slabata, the chief justice, and Smesansius, *The Protestants organize a revolution in Prague.*

one of the council, and Fabricius, the secretary, from an high window into the castle ditch; others of the council, temporizing in this tumult and seeming to accord with their demands, were peacefully conducted to their own houses. Hereupon the assembly took advice to settle the towns and castle of Prague with new guards; likewise to appease the people and take the oath of fidelity. They chose directors, governors, councilors provincial to govern affairs of state, and to consult of raising forces against the enemies of God and the king and the edicts of his Imperial Majesty. They banished the Jesuits throughout all Bohemia.

## II. The Intervention of Gustavus Adolphus

Gustavus Adolphus before sailing for Germany bade a touching farewell to the representatives of his people assembled at Stockholm (May, 1630).

**133. Gustavus Adolphus' farewell to the Swedish estates (May, 1630).**

I call on the all-powerful God to witness, by whose providence we are here assembled, that it is not by my own wish, or from any love of war, that I undertake this campaign. On the contrary, I have been now for several years goaded into it by the imperial party, not only through the reception accorded to our emissary to Lübeck, but also by the action of their general in aiding with his army our enemies, the Poles, to our great detriment. We have been urged, moreover, by our harassed brother-in-law [the elector of Brandenburg] to undertake this war, the chief object of which is to free our oppressed brothers in the faith from the clutches of the pope, which, God helping us, we hope to do.

But even as the pitcher that goes daily to the well must sometime break, so will it be with me; for though, for the welfare of the Swedish kingdom, I have already gone through many dangers and seen much shedding of blood, and have come through it all so far — thanks to God's gracious protection — without bodily harm, yet the time will come when all is over for me and I must say farewell to life. Therefore I have desired before my departure to see you all, from far and near, subjects and estates of Sweden, gathered about me, that we may together commend ourselves and each other, in body, soul, and estate, to our all-gracious God, in the hope that it may be his will, after this weary and troublous life, to bring us again together in the heavenly and everlasting life that he has prepared for us.

Especially do I commend you, counselors of the kingdom, to the all-powerful God, desiring that you may never fail in good counsel, that you may uphold your office and rank to the honor of God, that his holy word may remain undefiled to ourselves and our descendants in the fatherland, so that peace and unity may blossom and flourish, and discontent, discord, and dissension be unknown, and that your counsels may ever bring safety, quiet, and peace to the fatherland. Finally, may you strive to bring up your children to respect the laws and in every way to serve and strengthen the government of the kingdom. This is the wish of my whole heart.

You of the knight's estate I likewise ardently commend to the Most High God, with the hope that you may stand by your traditions, and that you and your descendants may regain for yourselves and spread abroad through the whole world the undying renown of the Goths, our forefathers, whose once famous name is now, alas, long forgotten — yea, well-nigh despised — by foreigners, but whose spirit has already, during my reign, shone forth again in your manly behavior, your unfailing courage, your sacrifices of blood and life. May our descendants once more glory in the might of their forefathers, who subjugated various kingdoms and ruled through hundreds of years to the welfare of the fatherland. May their name again win undying fame and be feared by kings and princes, and may you of the noble class gain world-wide renown. This do I hereby wish you.

You of the priestly class I would, in parting, remind of your duty to admonish your hearers (whose hearts are in your keeping) to be faithful and true to their rulers and

perform their duty obediently and cheerfully. Strengthen
your flocks, that they may live together in peace and concord and not be led astray by the counsels of evil men.
But it is not enough that you instruct them in these matters — it is my wish that you should walk before them in
blameless rectitude, offending none, so that not only by
your teaching and preaching, but by your example as well,
they may become a useful and peaceful people.

For you, burghers, I wish that your little cottages may
grow into big stone houses, your little boats into great
ships; and that the oil in your cruses may never fail. This,
for you, is my parting wish.

For the rest, I wish for you all that your fields may wax
green and bring forth fruit a hundredfold; that your chests
may overflow, and your comfort and well-being grow and
increase, so that your duty may be done with joy and not
in sighing. Above all, do I commend you, each and every
one, in soul and body, to God Almighty.

Gustavus lingered in northern Germany for some
months; for the Protestant princes showed themselves
very reluctant to coöperate with their foreign ally, until
finally they were induced to join him by the fall of
Magdeburg and the fearful massacre of its inhabitants
by the imperial troops under Pappenheim and Tilly.
This event is thus described by a writer of the period:

**134. The destruction of Magdeburg (May, 1631).**

So then General Pappenheim collected a number of his
people on the ramparts by the New Town, and brought
them from there into the streets of the city. Von Falcken-
berg[1] was shot, and fires were kindled in different quarters;
then indeed it was all over with the city, and further resistance was useless. Nevertheless some of the soldiers and
citizens did try to make a stand here and there, but the
imperial troops kept bringing on more and more forces

---

[1] The ambassador of Gustavus Adolphus, who had brought some
aid to the beleaguered city.

— cavalry, too — to help them, and finally they got the Kröckenthor open and let in the whole imperial army and the forces of the Catholic League, — Hungarians, Croats, Poles, Walloons, Italians, Spaniards, French, North and South Germans.

Thus it came about that the city and all its inhabitants fell into the hands of the enemy, whose violence and cruelty were due in part to their common hatred of the adherents of the Augsburg Confession, and in part to their being imbittered by the chain shot which had been fired at them and by the derision and insults that the Magdeburgers had heaped upon them from the ramparts.

Then was there naught but beating and burning, plundering, torture, and murder. Most especially was every one of the enemy bent on securing much booty. When a marauding party entered a house, if its master had anything to give he might thereby purchase respite and protection for himself and his family till the next man, who also wanted something, should come along. It was only when everything had been brought forth and there was nothing left to give that the real trouble commenced. Then, what with blows and threats of shooting, stabbing, and hanging, the poor people were so terrified that if they had had anything left they would have brought it forth if it had been buried in the earth or hidden away in a thousand castles. In this frenzied rage, the great and splendid city that had stood like a fair princess in the land was now, in its hour of direst need and unutterable distress and woe, given over to the flames, and thousands of innocent men, women, and children, in the midst of a horrible din of heartrending shrieks and cries, were tortured and put to death in so cruel and shameful a manner that no words would suffice to describe, nor no tears to bewail it. . . .

Thus in a single day this noble and famous city, the pride of the whole country, went up in fire and smoke ; and the remnant of its citizens, with their wives and children, were taken prisoners and driven away by the enemy with a noise of weeping and wailing that could be heard from afar, while the cinders and ashes from the town were carried by the wind to Wanzleben, Egeln, and still more distant places. . . .

In addition to all this, quantities of sumptuous and irreplaceable house furnishings and movable property of all kinds, such as books, manuscripts, paintings, memorials of all sorts, . . . which money could not buy, were either burned or carried away by the soldiers as booty. The most magnificent garments, hangings, silk stuffs, gold and silver lace, linen of all sorts, and other household goods were bought by the army sutlers for a mere song and peddled about by the cart load all through the archbishopric of Magdeburg and in Anhalt and Brunswick. Gold chains and rings, jewels, and every kind of gold and silver utensils were to be bought from the common soldiers for a tenth of their real value. . . .

## III. The Treaty of Westphalia (1648)

The treaties of Westphalia, the one signed at Münster and the other at Osnabrück, are voluminous, and would fill more than a hundred pages of this volume if printed in full. They contain but six or seven really memorable articles,[1] and are for the most part filled with multitudinous provisions regarding the church lands over which Catholics and Protestants had so long been contending, and minor territorial changes among the lesser German states. The treaty concluded at Osnabrück opens as follows[2] :

**135. Opening of the treaty of Osnabrück (October 24, 1648).**

*In the name of the Holy and Indivisible Trinity. To all whom these presents may concern, be it known :*

When the divisions and disorders which began several years ago in the Roman Empire had grown to a point where not only all Germany but some of the neighboring

[1] For these see *History of Western Europe*, p. 473 (Vol. II, p. 121).
[2] The treaty of Münster opens with essentially the same words.

kingdoms as well, especially Sweden and France, found themselves so involved that a long and bitter war resulted, in the first instance between the most serene and powerful prince and lord, Ferdinand II, emperor elect of the Romans, always august, king of Germany, Hungary, Bohemia, Dalmatia, etc., archduke of Austria, duke of Burgundy, Brabant, etc., etc., etc., . . . of glorious memory, his allies and adherents, on the one part, and the most serene and powerful prince and lord, Gustavus Adolphus, king of Sweden, of the Goths and Vandals, grand prince of Finland, duke of Esthonia, etc., also of glorious memory, together with the kingdom of Sweden, its allies and adherents, on the other part; later, after the decease of these aforementioned, between the most serene and powerful lord, Ferdinand III, emperor elect of the Romans, always august, king of Germany, etc., etc., and the most serene and very powerful princess and lady, Christina, queen of Sweden, of the Goths and Vandals, etc.; from which war resulted a great effusion of Christian blood and the desolation of divers provinces, until at last, through the movings of the Divine Goodness, it came about that both parties began to turn their thoughts toward the means of reëstablishing peace, and by a mutual agreement made at Hamburg, December 25 (New Style), or the 15th (Old Style), of the year 1641, between the parties, the date July 11 (New Style) or 1 (Old Style) was fixed for the meeting of the plenipotentiaries at Osnabrück and at Münster in Westphalia. In accordance with this, the ambassadors plenipotentiary duly appointed by both parties appeared at the said time and places named, to wit . . . [here follow the names of the ambassadors and their numerous titles].

After invoking the aid of God and exchanging their credentials, copies of which are inserted word for word in the present treaty, they arranged and agreed upon the articles of peace and amity which follow, to the glory of God and for the welfare of the Christian commonwealth; the electors, princes, and estates of the Holy Roman Empire being present and approving.

## BIBLIOGRAPHY

*A. References.*

**General Account of the Thirty Years' War:** SCHWILL, *Modern Europe*, pp. 141–160.

**Antecedents of the War:** WAKEMAN, *European History, 1598–1715*, Chapter III, pp. 39–52; HÄUSSER, *Period of the Reformation*, pp. 402–414; HENDERSON, *Short History of Germany*, Vol. I, pp. 422–441; DYER and HASSALL, *History of Modern Europe*, Vol. III, pp. 152–157 and 184–193.

**Bohemian and Danish Periods:** HÄUSSER, pp. 415–438; WAKEMAN, pp. 53–77; HENDERSON, Vol. II, pp. 441–462; DYER and HASSALL, Vol. III, pp. 195–208 and 253–262.

**Gustavus Adolphus and Wallenstein:** WAKEMAN, pp. 78–104; HENDERSON, Vol. II, pp. 462–483; DYER and HASSALL, Vol. III, pp. 264–296; HÄUSSER, pp. 438–443, 458–482, and 501–513.

**Intervention of France:** WAKEMAN, pp. 105–128; DYER and HASSALL, Vol. III, pp. 297–311; HÄUSSER, pp. 514–536.

**Peace of Westphalia:** HÄUSSER, pp. 537–559; DYER and HASSALL, Vol. III, pp. 335–352.

**Richelieu:** WAKEMAN, pp. 132–153.

---

*B. Additional readings in English.*

GARDINER, S. R., *The Thirty Years' War*. A good short account in the Epoch Series.

GINDELY, *History of the Thirty Years' War*, 2 vols. Translation of a popular treatment by a well-known scholar in this field.

PERKINS, J. B., *France under Richelieu and Mazarin*. Vol. I relates to Richelieu and the Thirty Years' War. The same historian has written *Richelieu* (1900) for the Heroes of the Nations Series.

FLETCHER, C. R. L., *Gustavus Adolphus and the Struggle of Protestantism for Existence*, 1890 (Heroes of the Nations Series). Best account in English.

# CHAPTER XXX

## STRUGGLE IN ENGLAND FOR CONSTITUTIONAL GOVERNMENT

### I. DIFFERENCE OF OPINION BETWEEN JAMES I AND THE COMMONS

James I gave an interesting summary of his absolutist theory of kings and their rights in his speeches before Parliament in 1609.

The state of monarchy is the supremest thing upon earth; for kings are not only God's lieutenants upon earth, and sit upon God's throne, but even by God himself they are called gods. There be three principal similitudes that illustrate the state of monarchy: one taken out of the word of God; and the two other out of the grounds of policy and philosophy. In the Scriptures kings are called gods, and so their power after a certain relation compared to the divine power. Kings are also compared to fathers of families; for a king is truly *parens patriae*, the politic father of his people. And lastly, kings are compared to the head of this microcosm of the body of man.

Kings are justly called gods, for that they exercise a manner or resemblance of divine power upon earth; for if you will consider the attributes to God, you shall see how they agree in the person of a king. God hath power to create or destroy, make or unmake at his pleasure, to give life or send death, to judge all and to be judged nor accountable to none, to raise low things and to make high things low at his pleasure, and to God are both soul and body due. And the like power have kings: they make and unmake their subjects, they have power of raising and

136. James I proclaims in Parliament the divine right of kings (1609).

casting down, of life and of death, judges over all their subjects and in all causes and yet accountable to none but God only. They have power to exalt low things and abase high things, and make of their subjects, like men at the chess, — a pawn to take a bishop or a knight, — and to cry up or down any of their subjects, as they do their money. And to the king is due both the affection of the soul and the service of the body of his subjects. . . .

## II. The Petition of Right (1628)

Charles I was, from the start, on even worse terms with Parliament than his father had been. The commons had, in addition to the old grievances, serious complaints to make in regard to the character and policy of Charles' chief minister, Buckingham. Two Parliaments were dissolved by the king in anger, and he raised a great storm of opposition by forced loans, arbitrary imprisonment, and other tyrannical acts. When, however, his third Parliament drew up the famous Petition of Right, a sort of second Magna Charta, he was forced to approve it, because he had to have money to carry on the war with France.

*To the king's Most Excellent Majesty:*

137. Opening of the Petition of Right (1628).

We humbly show unto our sovereign lord the king, the lords spiritual and temporal, and commons in Parliament assembled, that whereas it is declared and enacted by a statute made in the time of the reign of King Edward I, commonly called "*Statutum de Tallagio non Concedendo,*" that no tallage or aid shall be laid or levied by the king or his heirs in this realm without the good will and assent of the archbishops, bishops, earls, barons, knights, burgesses, and other the freemen of the commonalty of this realm; and by authority of Parliament holden in the five-and-twentieth year of the reign of King Edward III, it is declared and enacted, that from thenceforth no person should be compelled to make any loans to the king against his will, because such loans were against reason and the franchise of the land; and by other laws of this realm it is provided, that none should be charged by any charge or imposition called a benevolence, nor by any such like charge; by which statutes before mentioned, and other the good laws and statutes of this realm, your subjects have inherited this freedom, that they should not be compelled to contribute to any tax, tallage, aid, or other like charge not set by common consent in Parliament:

II. Yet nevertheless of late divers commissions, directed to sundry commissioners in several counties with instructions, have issued; by means whereof your people have been in divers places assembled and required to lend certain sums of money unto your Majesty, and many of them upon their refusal so to do . . . have been constrained to make appearance before your privy council and in other places, and others of them have been therefore imprisoned, confined, and sundry other ways molested and disquieted. . . .

III. And whereas also, by the statute called "The Great Charter of the liberties of England," it is declared and enacted, that no freeman may be taken or imprisoned or be disseized of his freehold or liberties, or his free customs, or be outlawed or exiled, or in any manner destroyed but by the lawful judgment of his peers, or by the law of the land. . . .

V. Nevertheless, against the tenor of the said statutes, and other the good laws and statutes of your realm, to that end provided, divers of your subjects have of late been imprisoned without any cause showed; . . . and whereas of late great companies of soldiers and mariners have been dispersed into divers counties of this realm, and the inhabitants, against their will, have been compelled to receive them into their houses, and there to suffer them to sojourn, against the laws and customs of this realm, and to the great grievance and vexation of the people. . . .

## III. The Early Acts of the Long Parliament

After a particularly tumultuous scene in the House of Commons on March, 1629, Charles dissolved Parliament and did not reassemble it again for eleven years. But in 1640 he found himself obliged to raise money to carry on the Scotch war. A Scotch army was in the north of England, remaining inactive only on condition that £850 a day was paid them for maintenance. This money Charles could not secure unless he yielded to the demands of Parliament for reform and the redress of grievances. It was thus that the important measures of the Long Parliament during the first months of its existence were accepted under compulsion by the king. The conviction that the king had not surrendered of his own free will produced a deep distrust of his motives and actions, which continued throughout the civil war and until his execution.

**138. Summary of the work of the Long Parliament in 1641.** (From *Memoirs of the Life of Colonel Hutchinson*.)

They [the Parliament] began by throwing down monopolies, and then impeached the earl of Strafford of high treason, who, after a solemn trial and hot disputes on both sides, was at length attainted of treason ; and the king, against his own mind, to serve his ends, gave him up to death. The archbishop of Canterbury was also made prisoner upon an accusation of high treason, for which he after suffered ; Wren, bishop of Norwich, was likewise committed to the Tower ; several other prelatical preachers were questioned for popish and treasonable doctrines ; the Star Chamber, an unjust and arbitrary court, was taken away, and the High Commission Court ; an act was procured for a triennial Parliament, and another for the continuation of this, that it should not be broken up without their own consent. There were great necessities for money by reason of the two armies that were then maintained in England,

and the people would give the king no money without some ease of grievances, which forced him, against his inclination, to grant those bills, with which, after he had granted, he found he had bound up his own hands, and therefore privately encouraged plots that were in those times contrived against the Parliament.

The Grand Remonstrance, which the commons drew up after spending a year in rectifying the abuses of Charles' personal government, contains a gloomy review of his reign and an account of the measures already passed by the Long Parliament with a view of doing away with the abuses. Some notion of this remarkable document may be derived from the following extracts.[1]

139. Extracts from the Grand Remonstrance of the commons, presented to Charles I, December 1, 1641.

The commons in this present Parliament assembled having, with much earnestness and faithfulness of affection and zeal to the public good of this kingdom and his Majesty's honor and service, for the space of twelve months, wrestled with great dangers and fears, the pressing miseries and calamities, the various distempers and disorders which had not only assaulted but even overwhelmed and extinguished the liberty, peace, and prosperity of this kingdom, the comfort and hopes of all his Majesty's good subjects, and exceedingly weakened and undermined the foundation and strength of his own royal throne, do yet find an abounding malignity and opposition in those parties and factions who have been the cause of those evils and do still labor to cast aspersions upon that which hath been done, and to raise many difficulties for the hindrance of that which remains yet undone, and to foment jealousies between the king and Parliament, that so they may deprive him and his people of the fruit of his own gracious intentions, and their humble desires of procuring the public peace, safety, and happiness of this realm.

[1] The full text of the Grand Remonstrance would fill toward thirty pages of this volume. The whole document is given by Gardiner, *Constitutional Documents*, pp. 202–232.

A.23

For the preventing of those miserable effects, which such malicious endeavors may produce, we have thought good to declare the root and the growth of these mischievous designs; the maturity and ripeness to which they have attained before the beginning of the Parliament; the effectual means which have been used for the extirpation of those dangerous evils, and the progress which hath therein been made by his Majesty's goodness and the wisdom of the Parliament; the ways of obstruction and opposition by which that progress hath been interrupted; the courses to be taken for the removing those obstacles, and for the accomplishing of our most dutiful and faithful intentions and endeavors of restoring and establishing the ancient honor, greatness, and security of this crown and nation.

The root of all this mischief we find to be a malignant and pernicious design of subverting the fundamental laws and principles of government, upon which the religion and justice of this kingdom are firmly established. The actors and promoters hereof have been:

1. The Jesuited papists, who hate the laws as the obstacles of that change and subversion of religion which they so much long for.

2. The bishops and the corrupt part of the clergy, who cherish formality and superstition as the natural effects and more probable supports of their own ecclesiastical tyranny and usurpation.

3. Such councilors and courtiers as for private ends have engaged themselves to further the interests of some foreign princes or states to the prejudice of his Majesty and the state at home. . . .

In the beginning of his Majesty's reign, the [Catholic] party began to revive and flourish again, having been somewhat damped by the breach with Spain in the last year of King James, and by his Majesty's marriage with France . . ., the papists of England, having ever been more addicted to Spain than France; yet they still retained a purpose and resolution to weaken the Protestant parties in all parts, and even in France, whereby to make way for

the change of religion which they intended at home. . . .
[The effects and evidence of their recovery have been:]

The Petition of Right, which was granted in full Parliament, blasted with an illegal declaration to make it destructive to itself, to the power of Parliament, to the liberty of the subject, and to that purpose printed with it, and the petition made of no use but to show the bold and presumptuous injustice of such ministers as durst break the laws and suppress the liberties of the kingdom, after they had been so solemnly and evidently declared. . . .

*The Petition of Right rendered nugatory.*

After the breach of the Parliament in the fourth [year] of his Majesty, injustice, oppression, and violence broke in upon us without any restraint or moderation, and yet the first project was the great sums exacted through the whole kingdom for the default of knighthood, which seemed to have some color and shadow of a law, yet if it be rightly examined by that obsolete law which was pretended for it, it will be found to be against all the rules of justice. . . .

## IV. THE CIVIL WAR

On August 22, 1642, the king raised his standard at Nottingham, and the settlement of the deadlock between him and Parliament was intrusted to the fortunes of war. The first stage of the contest lasted until the middle of 1646. During this period the famous battles of Edgehill (1642), Marston Moor (1644), and Naseby (1645) were fought. A devout Puritan thus describes the marvelous manner in which the Lord aided the raw troops in their fight against the king's army at Edgehill.

*140. A Puritan's account of the battle of Edgehill. (From Nehemiah Wallington.)*

1642. October the 23d, being the Lord's day in the forenoon, both the armies met in the midway between Banbury and Stratford-upon-Avon. And they had a very hot skirmish, their ordnance playing very hot from twelve o'clock till three in the afternoon, and made a great slaughter, and then the main forces joined battle, both horse and foot, and had a furious skirmish on both sides, which continued for all that day.

But that which I would take notice of is God's great mercy and providence, which was seen to his poor despised children, that although the enemy came traitorously and suddenly upon them, and unexpectedly, and four of our regiments falling from us, and our soldiers being a company of despised, inexperienced youths, which never used to lie in the fields on the cold ground before the enemy, they being strong, old, experienced soldiers. But herein we see God's great mercy, for all that to give us the victory; for, as I hear, the slaughter was in all five thousand five hundred and seventeen; but ten of the enemy's side were slain to one of ours. And observe God's wonderful works, for those that were slain of our side were mostly of them that ran away; but those that stood most valiantly to it, they were most preserved; so that you may see the Lord stands for them that stand for him.

How God guided the bullets. If I could but relate how admirably the hand of Providence ordered our artillery and bullets for the destruction of the enemy, when a piece of ordnance was shot off, what a lane was made in their army! Oh, how God did guide the bullets [of the enemy also] (as I wrote afore at Southam), that some fell down before them, some grazed along, some bullets went over their heads, and some one side of them! Oh, how seldom or never almost were they hurt that stood valiant to it, by their bullets! You would stand and wonder. . . .

God's mercy toward them in the Parliament's army that were sickly. Again, consider one wonderful work of our God more; which is, that many of our youths that went forth were weakly and sickly, some with the king's evil, some with agues, and some with the toothache, which their parents and friends were in great care and grief for; yet, when they have lain days and nights in the wet and cold fields, which one would think should make a well body sick, much more to increase their misery and pain that were ill, yet they have testified that their pain had left them, and [they were] never better in all their lives.

This is the Lord's doing, and it is marvelous in my eyes.

I did forget to write this remarkable passage, how the king's army shot off thirty pieces of ordnance and killed not passing four of our men ; and the first time we shot we made a lane among them, cutting off two of their colors.

A pamphleteer of the time sees only the horrors and desolation of the civil strife.

The war went on with horrid rage in many places at one time ; and the fire, when once kindled, cast forth, through every corner of the land, not only sparks but devouring flames ; insomuch that the kingdom of England was divided into more seats of war than counties ; nor has she more fields than skirmishes, nor cities than sieges ; and almost all the palaces of lords, and other great houses, were turned everywhere into garrisons of war.  They fought at once by sea and land ; and through all England (who could but lament the miseries of his country !) sad spectacles were seen of plundering and firing villages ; and the fields, otherwise waste and desolate, were rich only and terribly glorious in camps and armies.

**141. The general desolation caused by the civil war. (From a pamphlet of the time.)**

## V. The Execution of Charles I (1649)

Charles I closed a brief address which he made at the last moment before his execution as follows :

[As for the people,] truly I desire their liberty and freedom as much as anybody whomsoever ; but I must tell you that their liberty and freedom consist in having of government, those laws by which their life and their goods may be most their own.  It is not for having share in government, sirs ; that is nothing pertaining to them ; a subject and a sovereign are clear different things.  And therefore until they do that, I mean that you do put the people in that liberty, as I say, certainly they will never enjoy themselves.  Sirs, it was for this that now I am come here.  If I would have given way to an arbitrary way, for to have all

**142. An account of the execution of Charles I.**

laws changed according to the power of the sword, I needed not to have come here; and therefore I tell you (and I pray God it be not laid to your charge) that I am the martyr of the people. . . .

And to the executioner he said, "I shall say but very short prayers, and when I thrust out my hands — "

Then he called to the bishop for his cap, and having put it on, asked the executioner, "Does my hair trouble you?" who desired him to put it all under his cap; which, as he was doing by the help of the bishop and the executioner, he turned to the bishop, and said, "I have a good cause, and a gracious God on my side."

The bishop said, "There is but one stage more, which, though turbulent and troublesome, yet is a very short one. You may consider it will soon carry you a very great way; it will carry you from earth to heaven; and there you shall find to your great joy the prize you hasten to, a crown of glory."

The king adjoins, "I go from a corruptible to an incorruptible crown; where no disturbance can be, no disturbance in the world."

*The bishop.* "You are exchanged from a temporal to an eternal crown, — a good exchange."

Then the king asked the executioner, "Is my hair well?"

And taking off his cloak and George,[1] he delivered his George to the bishop, . . .

Then putting off his doublet and being in his waistcoat, he put on his cloak again, and looking upon the block, said to the executioner, "You must set it fast."

*The executioner.* "It is fast, sir."

*King.* "It might have been a little higher."

*Executioner.* "It can be no higher, sir."

*King.* "When I put out my hands this way, then — "

Then having said a few words to himself, as he stood, with hands and eyes lift up, immediately stooping down

[1] The jeweled pendant of the Order of the Garter, bearing a figure of St. George.

he laid his neck upon the block; and the executioner, again putting his hair under his cap, his Majesty, thinking he had been going to strike, bade him, "Stay for the sign."

*Executioner.* "Yes, I will, an it please your Majesty."

After a very short pause, his Majesty stretching forth his hands, the executioner at one blow severed his head from his body; which, being held up and showed to the people, was with his body put into a coffin covered with black velvet and carried into his lodging.

His blood was taken up by divers persons for different ends: by some as trophies of their villainy; by others as relics of a martyr; and in some hath had the same effect, by the blessing of God, which was often found in his sacred touch when living.

## VI. THE COMMONWEALTH AND CROMWELL

By the spring of 1653 the Long Parliament, which had been in session nearly thirteen years, was reduced to a mere "rump," as its enemies called it. There were only a hundred or so members left. Cromwell was convinced that the members were corrupt and that they meant to keep the power in their hands in spite of their talk of dissolving themselves. He most reluctantly decided that it was his duty to scatter them. The famous scene here described is taken from the journal kept by Sidney, whose son Algernon was one of the most distinguished members of the "rump."

**143. How Cromwell broke up the remnants of the Long Parliament**

*Wednesday, 20th April.* The Parliament sitting as usual, and being on debate upon the bill[1] with amendments, which it was thought would have been passed that day, the Lord General Cromwell came into the House, clad in plain black clothes, with gray stockings, and sat down, as he used to do, in an ordinary place. After a while he

---

[1] To dissolve itself.

rose up, put off his hat, and spake; at first and for a good while he spake to the commendation of the Parliament, for their pains and care of the public good; but afterwards he changed his style, told them of their injustice, delays of justice, self-interest, and other faults. Then he said, " Perhaps you think this is not parliamentary language; I confess it is not, neither are you to expect any such from me."

Then he put on his hat, went out of his place, and walked up and down the stage or floor in the midst of the House, with his hat on his head, and chid them soundly, looking sometimes, and pointing particularly, upon some persons, as Sir R. Whitlock, one of the Commissioners for the Great Seal; Sir Henry Vane, to whom he gave very sharp language, though he named them not, but by his gestures it was well known that he meant them.

After this he said to Colonel Harrison (who was a member of the House), "Call them in." Then Harrison went out, and presently brought in Lieutenant-Colonel Wortley (who commanded the General's own regiment of foot), with five or six files of musketeers, about twenty or thirty with their muskets. Then the General, pointing to the Speaker in his chair, said to Harrison, "Fetch him down." Harrison went to the Speaker and spoke to him to come down, but the Speaker sat still and said nothing. "Take him down," said the General; then Harrison went and pulled the Speaker by the gown, and he came down.

It happened that day that Algernon Sidney sat next to the Speaker on the right hand; the General said to Harrison, "Put him out." Harrison spake to Sidney to go out, but he said he would not go out, and sat still. The General said again, "Put him out." Then Harrison and Wortley put their hands upon Sidney's shoulders, as if they would force him to go out; then he rose and went towards the door.

Then the General went to the table where the mace[1] lay, which used to be carried before the Speaker, and said,

[1] The mace still lies on the table when the House of Commons is sitting.

"Take away these baubles." So the soldiers took away the mace, and all the House went out; and at the going out, they say, the General said to young Henry Vane, calling him by his name, that he might have prevented this extraordinary course, but he was a juggler and had not so much as common honesty. All being gone out, the door of the House was locked, and the key with the mace was carried away, as I heard, by Colonel Otley.

A pamphlet of the time shows how a great part of the English must have felt in 1659 in regard to the expediency of calling back Charles II.

If we take a view of the several pretensions, carried on in the nation apart, we shall find the most considerable to be the Roman Catholic, the Royalist, the Presbyterian, the Anabaptist, the Army, the Protectorian, and that of the Parliament.

**144. Parties in England in 1659, and expediency of calling in Charles II. (From a pamphlet of the time.)**

1. 'Tis the Roman Catholic's aim not only to abrogate the penal laws, and become capable of all employments in the Commonwealth, but to introduce his religion, to restore the rights of the Church, and utterly eradicate all that he esteems heresy.

2. 'Tis the Royalist's desire to bring in the king as a conqueror, to recover their losses in the late war, be rendered capable of civil employments, and have the former government of the Church.

3. 'Tis the Presbyterian's desire to set up his discipline, to have the covenant reënforced, and only such as take it to be employed in church or state; to be indemnified in reference to what they have done, and secured of what they possess.

4. 'Tis the wish of the baptized churches that there might be no ecclesiastical government of any kind, nor ministerial function, or provision for it; and that only persons so minded should be capable of employment; likewise to be indemnified for what they have done.

5. 'Tis the aim of the Army to govern the nation, to keep themselves from being disbanded, or engaged in war, to secure their pay, and to be indemnified for all past action.

6. 'Tis the desire of the family of the late Protector to establish the heir of the house, that they may rule him, and he the nation, and so both preserve and advance themselves.

7. 'Tis the wish of the present Parliament (as far as they have one common design) to continue themselves in absolute power by the specious name of a popular government ; to new-model and divide, and, at last, take down, the Army ; and, finally, under the pretences of a committee of Parliament, or council of state, set up an oligarchy resembling that of the Thirty Tyrants in Athens.

Lastly, 't is the general interest of the nation to establish the ancient fundamental laws, upon which every one's propriety and liberty are built, to settle religion, to procure a general indemnity for all actions past, to revive their languishing and almost dead trade, gain an alliance with our neighbour states ; to put the government in such hands as, besides present force, can plead a legal title to it ; into the hands of such with whose private interest that of the public not only consists, but in which 't is necessarily involved, which likewise does least contradict the aims of particular parties ; lastly, the hands of such whose counsel is fit to direct in matters of deliberation, and courage fit to vindicate the injuries of the nation. . . .

## VII. THE RESTORATION OF THE STUARTS : CHARLES II

It would be difficult to imagine a more satisfactory description than that given of Charles II at the time of his accession by the distinguished historian of the period, Burnet.

**145. A picture of Charles II. (By Gilbert Burnet, in his *History of my own Time*.)**

The king was then thirty years of age, and, as might have been supposed, past the levities of youth and the extravagance of pleasure. He had a very good understanding : he knew well the state of affairs both at home and abroad. He had a softness of temper that charmed all who came near him, till they found out how little they could depend on good looks, kind words, and fair promises, in which he was liberal to excess, because he intended nothing by them but to get rid of importunity and to silence all further pressing upon him.

He seemed to have no sense of religion; both at prayers and sacrament, he, as it were, took care to satisfy people that he was in no sort concerned in that about which he was employed; so that he was very far from being an hypocrite, unless his assisting at those performances was a sort of hypocrisy, as no doubt it was; but he was sure not to increase that by any the least appearance of devotion. He said once to myself, he was no atheist, but he could not think God would make a man miserable only for taking a little pleasure out of the way. He disguised his popery to the last; but when he talked freely he could not help letting himself out against the liberty that under the Reformation all men took of inquiring into matters, for from their inquiring into matters of religion they carried the humor further to inquire into matters of state. He said often he thought government was a much safer and easier thing where the authority was believed infallible, and the faith and submission of the people was implicit; about which I had once much discourse with him.

He was affable and easy, and loved to be made so by all about him. The great art of keeping him long was the being easy and the making everything easy to him. He had made such observations on the French government that he thought a king who might be checked, or have his ministers called into account by a Parliament, was but a king in name. He had a great compass of knowledge, though he was never capable of great application or study. He understood the mechanics and physic, and was a good chemist, and much set on several preparations of mercury, chiefly the fixing it. He understood navigation well; but above all, he knew the architecture of ships so perfectly that in that respect he was exact rather more than became a prince. His apprehension was quick and his memory good, and he was an everlasting talker. He told his stories with a good grace, but they came in his way too often.

He had a very ill opinion both of men and women, and did not think there was either sincerity or chastity in the world out of principle, but that some had either the one or the other out of humor or vanity. He thought that nobody served him out of love; and so he was quits with all the world, and loved others as little as he thought they loved him. He hated business and could not be easily brought to mind any; but when it was necessary, and he was set to it, he would stay as long as his ministers had work for him. The ruin of his reign, and of all his affairs, was occasioned chiefly by his delivering himself up at his first coming over to a mad range of pleasure.

Two remarkable diaries of this period have been preserved, — one by Samuel Pepys (1633–1703), a very active government official under Charles II ; the other by John Evelyn (1620–1706), a gentleman fond of science, letters, and gardening. These diaries are the most delightful sources for the period they cover. The following entries give a picture of the barbarous habits of the time.

146. Savage vengeance taken upon the leaders of the late rebellion. (From *Pepys' Diary*.)

*October 13, 1660.* I went out to Charing Cross to see Major-General Harrison[1] hanged, drawn, and quartered ; which was done there, he looking as cheerful as any man could do in that condition. He was presently cut down, and his head and heart shown to the people, at which there was great shouts of joy. It is said that he said that he was sure to come shortly at the right hand of Christ to judge them that now judged him ; and that his wife do expect his coming again. Thus it was my chance to see the king beheaded at Whitehall, and to see the first blood shed in revenge for the king at Charing Cross.

*October 15, 1660.* This morning Mr. Carew was hanged and quartered at Charing Cross ; but his quarters, by a great favor, are not to be hanged up.

[1] See above, pp. 360.

*October 17, 1660.* Scot, Scroope, Cook, and Jones suffered for the reward of their iniquities at Charing Cross, in sight of the place where they put to death their natural Prince, and in the presence of the King, his son, whom they also sought to kill. I saw not their execution, but met their quarters mangled and cutt and reeking as they were brought from the gallows in baskets on the hurdle. O the miraculous providence of God!

147. Execution of the regicides. (From *Evelyn's Diary.*)

*January 30, 1661.* This day (O the stupendious and inscrutable judgments of God!) were the carcasses of those arch-rebells Cromwell, Bradshaw, the Judge who condemned his Majestie, and Ireton, sonn-in-law to ye Usurper, dragged out of their superb tombs in Westminster among the kings, to Tyburne, and hanged on the gallows from 9 in the morning till 6 at night, and then buried under that fatal and ignominious monument in a deepe pitt; thousands of people who had seene them in all their pride being spectators.

*May 22, 1661.* The Scotch Covenant was burnt by the common hangman in divers places in London. O prodigious change!

## VIII. James II and the Revolution of 1688

Two writers of the time make clear the impression which James II's attempt to restore the Roman Catholic faith in England made upon the Protestants.

*November 20, 1685.* The popish party at this time behaved themselves with an insolence which did them a prejudice. The king of France continued to practice all the cruelties imaginable towards the Protestants in France to make them turn papists, commanding that all extremities should be used but death, — as seizing their lands, razing their temples and houses, taking all their goods, putting them into prisons, quartering dragoons with them to eat up their estates and to watch them that they should not sleep till they changed their religion. Many of them fled into all parts as they could

148. James II, like the French king, seems about to restore the Roman Catholic Church. (From Reresby's *Mémoires.*)

escape, poor and naked ; for their estates were stopped and themselves condemned to the gallows if they were taken attempting to fly.

*March 1, 1686.* Though it could not be said that there was as yet any remarkable invasion upon the rights of the Church of England, yet the king gave all the encouragement he could to the increase of his own, by putting more papists into office, but especially in Ireland ; by causing or allowing popish books to be printed and sold and cried publicly ; by publishing some popish papers found in the late king's closet and the declaration of his dying a papist and the manner of it ; . . . by sending my Lord Castlemain upon a solemn embassy to the pope, and many other such things ; which made all men expect that more would follow of a greater concern.

This chapter on the long struggle between the Stuarts and the English nation as represented in the Parliament may appropriately close with some extracts from the celebrated Declaration of Right presented to William and Mary in February, 1689.[1]

**149. Extracts from the Declaration of Right (February, 1689).** Whereas the lords spiritual and temporal, and commons assembled at Westminster, lawfully, fully, freely representing all the estates of the people of this realm, did upon the thirteenth day of February, in the year of our Lord 1688,[2] present unto their Majesties, then called and known by the names and style of William and Mary, prince and princess of Orange, being present in their proper persons, a certain

[1] This document is commonly known as " The Bill of Rights," for it was under that title that it was reënacted in December of the same year, 1689, and is included in the statutes of the realm in the form here given.

[2] February, 1688, would, according to our habit of beginning the year on January 1, fall in 1689. Until 1751, when Protestant England tardily accepted the salutary reform of the calendar first recommended in 1582 by Gregory XIII, the year was regarded in that country as beginning March 25.

declaration in writing made by the said lords and commons in the words following, viz. :

Whereas the late King James II, by the assistance of diverse evil counselors, judges, and ministers employed by him, did endeavor to subvert and extirpate the Protestant religion and the laws and liberties of this kingdom : Charges against James II

1. By assuming and exercising a power of dispensing with and suspending of laws, and the execution of laws, without consent of Parliament.

2. By committing and prosecuting divers worthy prelates, for humbly petitioning to be excused from concurring to the same assumed power.

3. By issuing and causing to be executed a commission under the Great Seal for erecting a court, called the " Court of Commissioners for Ecclesiastical Causes."

4. By levying money for and to the use of the crown, by pretense of prerogative, for other time and in other manner than the same was granted by Parliament.

5. By raising and keeping a standing army within this kingdom in time of peace, without consent of Parliament, and quartering soldiers contrary to law.

6. By causing several good subjects, being Protestants, to be disarmed, at the same time when papists were both armed and employed contrary to law.

7. By violating the freedom of election of members to serve in Parliament.

8. By prosecutions in the Court of King's Bench, for matters and causes cognizable only in Parliament; and by diverse other arbitrary and illegal courses.

. . . . . . . . . . . .

10. And excessive bail hath been required of persons committed in criminal cases, to elude the benefit of laws made for the liberty of the subjects.

11. And excessive fines have been imposed ; and illegal and cruel punishments inflicted.

12. And several grants and promises made of fines and forfeitures, before any conviction or judgment against the persons upon whom the same were to be levied.

All which are utterly and directly contrary to the known laws and statutes and freedom of this realm.

And whereas the said late King James II having abdicated the government, and the throne being thereby vacant, his Highness the prince of Orange (whom it hath pleased Almighty God to make the glorious instrument of delivering this kingdom from popery and arbitrary power) did (by the advice of the lords spiritual and temporal and divers principal persons of the commons) cause letters to be written to the lords spiritual and temporal, being Protestants; and other letters to the several counties, cities, universities, boroughs [for choosing representatives to a Parliament which might vindicate and assert the ancient rights and liberties of the nation].[1] . . .

Having therefore an entire confidence that his said Highness the prince of Orange will perfect the deliverance so far advanced by him, and will still preserve them [Parliament] from the violation of their rights, which they have here asserted, and from all other attempts upon their religion, rights, and liberties, the said lords spiritual and temporal, and commons assembled at Westminster, do resolve that William and Mary, prince and princess of Orange, be and be declared king and queen of England, France,[2] and Ireland, and the dominions thereunto belonging, to hold the crown and royal dignity of the said kingdoms and dominions to them the said prince and princess during their lives and the life of the survivor of them ; . . . and that the oaths hereafter mentioned be taken by all persons of whom the oaths of allegiance and supremacy might be required by law. . . .

I, A. B., do swear that I do from my heart abhor, detest, and abjure, as impious and heretical, this damnable doctrine and position that princes excommunicated or deprived by the pope, or any authority of the see of Rome, may be

1 Here follows a statement of the rights of the people and their representatives as against the usurpations of James II, enumerated at the opening of the document.

2 The English kings continued to include their long-lost French possessions in the list of their domains.

deposed or murdered by their subjects, or any other what-soever. And I do declare that no foreign prince, person, prelate, state, or potentate has, or ought to have, any juris-diction, power, superiority, preëminence, or authority, eccle-siastical or spiritual, within this realm. So help me God.

Upon which their said Majesties did accept the crown and royal dignity of the kingdoms of England, France, and Ireland, and the dominions thereunto belonging, according to the resolution and desire of the said lords and commons contained in the said declaration. . . .

And whereas, it hath been found by experience that it is inconsistent with the safety and welfare of this Protestant kingdom to be governed by a popish prince or by any king or queen marrying a papist, the said lords spiritual and temporal, and commons, do further pray that it may be enacted that all and every person and persons that is, are, or shall be reconciled to, or shall hold communion with, the see or Church of Rome, or shall profess the popish religion, or shall marry a papist, shall be excluded and be for-ever incapable to inherit, possess, or enjoy the crown and government of this realm. . . .

*Exclusion of Catholics from the throne.*

## BIBLIOGRAPHY

**The Opening of the Constitutional Struggle under James I :** GREEN, *Short History of the English People*, Chapter VIII, sect. 2 ; ANDREWS, *History of England*, pp. 329–343 ; CHEYNEY, *A Short History of Eng-land*, pp. 383–410 ; TERRY, *History of England*, pp. 618–642 ; KENDALL, *Source Book of English History*, pp. 209–219 ; LEE, *Source Book of Eng-lish History*, pp. 335–347 ; COLBY, *Selections from the Sources of English History*, pp. 181–184.

*A. Refer-ences.*

**The Petition of Right :** GREEN, Chapter VIII, sect. 3 ; CHEYNEY, pp. 410–418 ; TERRY, pp. 642–650 ; LEE, pp. 348–352 ; ANDREWS, pp. 343–348.

**Personal Government of Charles I :** GREEN, Chapter VIII, sect. 5 ; ANDREWS, pp. 348–354 ; CHEYNEY, pp. 418–429 ; TERRY, pp. 650–668 ; COLBY, pp. 188–193.

**The Puritans :** GREEN, Chapter VIII, sect. 1 ; ANDREWS, pp. 319–323 ; KENDALL, pp. 225–227.

The Work of the Long Parliament : GREEN, Chapter VIII, sect. 6; ANDREWS, pp. 354–359; CHEYNEY, pp. 431–442 ; TERRY, pp. 669–680; KENDALL, pp. 232–240.

The Civil War and Death of Charles I : GREEN, Chapter VIII, sect. 7; ANDREWS, pp. 359–369; CHEYNEY, pp. 442–453; TERRY, pp. 681–704 ; KENDALL, pp. 240–250 ; COLBY, pp. 193–195.

Commonwealth and Protectorate : GREEN, Chapter VIII, sects. 9 and 10; ANDREWS, pp. 369–382 ; CHEYNEY, pp. 453–465; TERRY, pp. 705–741.

The Restoration and Ecclesiastical Settlement : GREEN, Chapter IX, sect. 2; ANDREWS, pp. 381–387 ; CHEYNEY, pp. 466–478; TERRY, pp. 742–759; KENDALL, pp. 265–267 ; COLBY, pp. 203–205.

Constitutional Struggle under James II : GREEN, Chapter IX, sect. 6; ANDREWS, pp. 398–403 ; CHEYNEY, pp. 498–515; TERRY, pp. 782–804 ; KENDALL, pp. 284–289 ; COLBY, pp. 214–218.

Revolution of 1688 : GREEN, Chapter IX, sect. 7 ; ANDREWS, pp. 404–412; KENDALL, pp. 289–297; COLBY, pp. 219–223.

---

*B. Additional reading in English.*

GARDINER, *The First Two Stuarts and The Puritan Revolution;* AIRY, *The English Restoration and Louis XIV to 1689;* HALE, *Fall of the Stuarts and Western Europe.* These little volumes in the Epochs of Modern History Series form a valuable short history of the Stuart period, with full reference to foreign affairs.

GOOCH, *History of English Democratic Ideas in the Seventeenth Century,* and FIGGIS, *The Theory of the Divine Right of Kings,* are useful summaries of opposing political theories.

FIRTH, *Cromwell,* 1900 (Heroes of the Nations Series). The most scholarly short life of Cromwell. The lives of Cromwell by HARRISON, MORLEY, and ROOSEVELT are sympathetic apologies, but are well worth reading.

TAYLOR, *England under Charles II, 1660–1678,* in English History by Contemporary Writers, edited by Professor F. York Powell ; FIGGIS, *English History Illustrated from Original Sources, 1660–1715* (1902), in the series edited by Warner. Two small source books containing a variety of illustrative materials.

HUTTON, *The English Church from the Accession of Charles I to the Death of Anne, 1903.* A scholarly work, with useful bibliographies attached to each chapter.

For the lives of Pym, Hampden, Laud, Strafford, and other great men of the time, the student should consult the *Dictionary of National Biography,* which gives extensive bibliographies.

# CHAPTER XXXI

## THE ASCENDENCY OF FRANCE UNDER LOUIS XIV

### I. RICHELIEU AND HIS POLICY OF STRENGTHENING THE KINGSHIP

Richelieu was evidently very desirous to leave to posterity a full account of his deeds and a complete justification of his policy. He undertook to collect material for an elaborate history of the reign of Louis XIII, but fearing that his frail constitution would never permit him to complete the work, he conceived it to be his duty to leave some statement, at least, of the most needed reforms, as a guide for the king when his minister should be dead. In this way Richelieu's famous "Political Testament" originated. It opens as follows :

At the time when your Majesty resolved to admit me both to your council and to an important place in your confidence for the direction of your affairs, I may say that the Huguenots shared the state with you; that the nobles conducted themselves as if they were not your subjects, and the most powerful governors of the provinces as if they were sovereign in their offices.

150. Richelieu's account of the condition of France when he became minister in 1624.

I may say that the bad example of all of these was so injurious to this realm that even the best regulated *parlements* [1] were affected by it, and endeavored, in certain cases, to diminish your royal authority as far as they were able in order to stretch their own powers beyond the limits of reason.

I may say that every one measured his own merit by his audacity; that in place of estimating the benefits which they

[1] The higher law courts.

received from your Majesty at their proper worth, all valued them only in so far as they satisfied the extravagant demands of their imagination; that the most arrogant were held to be the wisest, and found themselves the most prosperous.

I may also say that the foreign alliances were unfortunate, individual interests being preferred to those of the public; in a word, the dignity of the royal majesty was so disparaged, and so different from what it should be, owing to the malfeasance of those who conducted your affairs, that it was almost impossible to perceive its existence.

It was impossible, without losing all, to tolerate longer the conduct of those to whom your Majesty had intrusted the helm of state; and, on the other hand, everything could not be changed at once without violating the laws of prudence, which do not permit the abrupt passing from one extreme to another.

The sad state of your affairs seemed to force you to hasty decisions, without permitting a choice of time or of means; and yet it was necessary to make a choice of both, in order to profit by the reforms which the situation absolutely demanded that you should introduce.

Thoughtful observers did not think that it would be possible to escape all the rocks in so tempestuous a period; the court was full of people who censured the temerity of those who wished to undertake a reform; all well knew that princes are quick to impute to those who are near them the bad outcome of the undertakings upon which they have been well advised; few people consequently expected good results from the change which it was announced that I wished to make, and many believed my fall assured even before your Majesty had elevated me.

Notwithstanding these difficulties which I represented to your Majesty, knowing how much kings may do when they make good use of their power, I ventured to promise you, with confidence, that you would soon get control of your state, and that in a short time your prudence, your courage, and the benediction of God would give a new aspect to the realm. . . .

## II. Kings "by the Grace of God"

It is especially difficult with our modern democratic notions to understand the views and sentiments of those who have regarded obedience to the king, however perverse and licentious he might be, as a sacred obligation. Nowhere is the divine nature of the kingly power set forth with more eloquence and ardor than in the work of the distinguished prelate, orator, and theologian, Bossuet, whom Louis XIV chose as the preceptor of his son, the dauphin (1670–1681). His treatise on *Politics drawn from the Very Words of Holy Scripture* was prepared with a view of giving the heir to the French throne a proper idea both of his lofty position and of his heavy responsibilities. No one can read this work without being profoundly impressed with the irresistible appeal which kingship, as Bossuet represents it, must make to a mind that looked to the Scriptures for its theories of government.

The essential characteristics of royalty, Bossuet explains, are, first, that it is sacred; second, paternal; third, absolute; and fourth, subject to reason. He then continues as follows:

We have already seen that all power is of God.[1] The ruler, adds St. Paul, "is the minister of God to thee for good. But if thou do that which is evil, be afraid; for he beareth not the sword in vain: for he is the minister of God, a revenger to execute wrath upon him that doeth evil."[2]

151. Extracts from Bossuet's work on kingship.

---

[1] Referring to St. Paul's words (Romans xiii. 1, 2): "Let every soul be subject unto the higher powers. For there is no power but of God: the powers that be are ordained of God. Whosoever therefore resisteth the power, resisteth the ordinance of God: and they that resist shall receive to themselves damnation."

[2] See Rom. xiii. 1–7.

Rulers then act as the ministers of God and as his lieutenants on earth. It is through them that God exercises his empire. Think ye "to withstand the kingdom of the Lord in the hand of the sons of David"?[1] Consequently, as we have seen, the róyal throne is not the throne of a man, but the throne of God himself. . . .

Kingship a divine institution.

Moreover, that no one may assume that the Israelites were peculiar in having kings over them who were established by God, note what is said in Ecclesiasticus : "God has given to every people its ruler, and Israel is manifestly reserved to him."[2] He therefore governs all peoples and gives them their kings, although he governed Israel in a more intimate and obvious manner.

It appears from all this that the person of the king is sacred, and that to attack him in any way is sacrilege. God has the kings anointed by his prophets with the holy unction in like manner as he has bishops and altars anointed. But even without the external application in thus being anointed, they are by their very office the representatives of the divine majesty deputed by Providence for the execution of his purposes. Accordingly God calls Cyrus his anointed. "Thus saith the Lord to his anointed, to Cyrus, whose right hand I have holden, to subdue nations before him."[3] . . . Kings should be guarded as holy things, and whosoever neglects to protect them is worthy of death. . . .

There is something religious in the respect accorded to a prince. The service of God and the respect for kings are bound together. St. Peter unites these two duties when he says, "Fear God. Honour the king."[4] . . .

Warning to kings to exercise their power in the fear of the Lord.

But kings, although their power comes from on high, as has been said, should not regard themselves as masters of that power to use it at their pleasure ; . . . they must employ it with fear and self-restraint, as a thing coming from God and of which God will demand an account. "Hear, O kings, and take heed, understand, judges of the earth, lend your ears, ye who hold the peoples under your sway, and delight

---

[1] 2 Chron. xiii. 8.
[2] Ecclesiasticus xvii. 14, 15.
[3] Isa. xlv. 1.
[4] 1 Pet. ii. 17.

to see the multitude that surround you. It is God who gives you the power. Your strength comes from the Most High, who will question your works and penetrate the depths of your thoughts, for, being ministers of his kingdom, ye have not given righteous judgments nor have ye walked according to his will. He will straightway appear to you in a terrible manner, for to those who command is the heaviest punishment reserved. The humble and the weak shall receive mercy, but the mighty shall be mightily tormented. For God fears not the power of any one, because he made both great and small and he has care for both." [1] . . .

Kings should tremble then as they use the power God has granted them; and let them think how horrible is the sacrilege if they use for evil a power which comes from God. We behold kings seated upon the throne of the Lord, bearing in their hand the sword which God himself has given them. What profanation, what arrogance, for the unjust king to sit on God's throne to render decrees contrary to his laws and to use the sword which God has put in his hand for deeds of violence and to slay his children! . . .

The royal power is absolute. With the aim of making this truth hateful and insufferable, many writers have tried to confound absolute government with arbitrary government. But no two things could be more unlike, as we shall show when we come to speak of justice. *The royal power is absolute*

The prince need render account of his acts to no one. "I counsel thee to keep the king's commandment, and that in regard of the oath of God. Be not hasty to go out of his sight: stand not on an evil thing for he doeth whatsoever pleaseth him. Where the word of a king is, there is power: and who may say unto him, What doest thou? Whoso keepeth the commandment shall feel no evil thing." [2] Without this absolute authority the king could neither do good nor repress evil. It is necessary that his power be such that no one can hope to escape him, and, finally, the only protection of individuals against the public authority should be their innocence.

[1] Book of Wisdom vi. 2 *sqq.*     [2] Ecclesiasticus viii. 2–5.

### III. The Ascendency of France in 1671

Sir William Temple, an able English diplomat and man of letters, gives a striking picture of the flourishing condition of France during the first half of Louis XIV's reign.

152. Sir
William
Temple's
account of
France
in 1671.

The crown of France, considered in the extent of country, in the number of people, in the riches of commodities, in the revenues of the king, the greatness of the land forces now on foot, and the growth of those at sea (within these two years past), the number and bravery of their officers, the conduct of their ministers, and chiefly in the genius of their present king; a prince of great aspiring thoughts, unwearied application to whatever is in pursuit, severe in the institution and preservation of order and discipline; in the main a manager of his treasure and yet bountiful from his own motions wherever he intends the marks of favour and discerns particular merit; to this, in the flower of his age, at the head of all his armies, and hitherto unfoiled in any of his attempts either at home or abroad: I say, considered in all these circumstances, France may appear to be designed for greater achievements in empires than have been seen in Christendom since that of Charlemagne.

Important
services of
Richelieu
and Mazarin.

The present greatness of this crown may be chiefly derived from the fortune it has had of two great ministers [Richelieu and Mazarin] succeeding one another, between two great kings, Henry IV and this present prince; so as during the course of one unactive life and of a long minority that crown gained a great deal of ground both at home and abroad, instead of losing it, which is the common fate of kingdoms upon those occasions.

The latter greatness of this crown began in the time of Lewis XI by the spoils of the house of Burgundy and the divisions of the princes, which gave that king the heart of attempting to bring the government (as he called it) *hors de page;* [the monarchs] being before controlled by their princes, and restrained by their states,[1] and in point of revenue kept

---

[1] I.e. estates.

within the bounds of the king's desmesnes and the subjects' voluntary contributions.

'Tis not here necessary to observe by what difficulties and dangers to the crown this design of Lewis was pursued by many succeeding kings, — like a great stone forced up a hill, and, upon every slacking of either strength or care, rolling a great way back, often to the very bottom of the hill, and sometimes with the destruction of those that forced it on, — till the time of Cardinal Richelieu. It was in this great minister most to be admired that, finding the regency shaken by the factions of so many great ones within, and awed by the terror of the Spanish greatness without, he durst resolve to look them both in the face, and begin a war by the course of which for so many years (being pursued by Mazarin till the year 1660) the crown of France grew to be powerfully armed; the peasants were accustomed to payments (which could have seemed necessary only by a war, and which none but a successful one could have helped to digest) and grew heartless as they grew poor. The princes were sometimes satisfied with commands of the army, sometimes mortified and suppressed by the absoluteness or addresses of the ministry. The most boiling blood of the nobility and gentry was let out in so long a war, or wasted with age and exercise; at last it ended at the Pyrenees in a peace and the match so advantageous to France as the reputation of them contributed much to the authority of the young king, who was bred up in the councils and served by the tried instruments of the former ministry; but most of all, advantaged by his own personal qualities, fit to make him obeyed, grew absolute master of the factions of the great men, as well as the purses of his people. . . .

If there were any certain height where the flights of power and ambition used to end, one might imagine that the interest of France were but to conserve its present greatness, so feared by its neighbours and so glorious in the world; but besides that the motions and desires of human minds are endless, it may perhaps be necessary for France (from respects within) to have some war or other in pursuit

The common lot in France

abroad which may amuse the nation, and keep them from reflecting upon their condition at home, hard and uneasy to all but such as are in charge or in pay from the court. I do not say miserable (the term usually given it), because no condition is so but to him that esteems it so; and if a *paysan* of France thinks of no more than his coarse bread and his onions, his canvass cloaths, and wooden shoes, labours contentedly on working days, and dances or plays merrily on holy-days; he may, for aught I know, live as well as a boor of Holland, who is either weary of his very ease or whose cares of growing still richer and richer waste his life in toils on land, or dangers at sea, and perhaps fool him so far as to make him enjoy less of all kind in his riches than the other in his poverty.

## IV. Louis XIV and his Court

In 1671, when Louis XIV decided upon war with Holland, he honored his commander, the prince of Condé, by a visit to him at Chantilly, where a grand fête was given in the forest, for which elaborate preparations were made by Vatel, the prince of cooks. The following spirited account of the occasion and of the cook's sad end is from a letter of Madame de Sévigné's, whose charming correspondence with her daughter and friends constitutes an important source for the period and for the life at Louis' court.

**153. How Louis and his court were entertained by the prince of Condé at Chantilly (1671).**

It is Sunday, the 26th of April; this letter will not go till Wednesday. It is not really a letter, but an account, which Moreuil has just given me for your benefit, of what happened at Chantilly concerning Vatel. I wrote you on Friday that he had stabbed himself; here is the story in detail.

The promenade, the collation in a spot carpeted with jonquils, — all was going to perfection. Supper came; the roast failed at one or two tables on account of a number of unexpected guests. This upset Vatel. He said several times,

"My honor is lost; this is a humiliation that I cannot endure." To Gourville he said, "My head is swimming; I have not slept for twelve nights; help me to give my orders." Gourville consoled him as best he could, but the roast which had failed, not at the king's, but at the twenty-fifth table, haunted his mind. Gourville told Monsieur le Prince about it, and Monsieur le Prince went up to Vatel in his own room and said to him, "Vatel, all goes well; there never was anything so beautiful as the king's supper." He answered, "Monseigneur, your goodness overwhelms me. I know that the roast failed at two tables." "Nothing of the sort," said Monsieur le Prince. "Do not disturb yourself, — all is well."

Midnight comes. The fireworks do not succeed on account of a cloud that overspreads them (they cost sixteen thousand francs). At four o'clock in the morning Vatel is wandering about all over the place. Everything is asleep. He meets a small purveyor with two loads of fish and asks him, "Is this all?" "Yes, sir." The man did not know that Vatel had sent to all the seaport towns in France. Vatel waits some time, but the other purveyors do not arrive; he gets excited; he thinks that there will be no more fish. He finds Gourville and says to him, "Sir, I shall not be able to survive this disgrace." Gourville only laughs at him. Then Vatel goes up to his own room, puts his sword against the door, and runs it through his heart, but only at the third thrust, for he gave himself two wounds which were not mortal. He falls dead.

Meanwhile the fish is coming in from every side, and people are seeking for Vatel to distribute it. They go to his room, they knock, they burst open the door, they find him lying bathed in his blood. They send for Monsieur le Prince, who is in utter despair. Monsieur le Duc bursts into tears; it was upon Vatel that his whole journey to Burgundy depended. Monsieur le Prince informed the king, very sadly; they agreed that it all came from Vatel's having his own code of honor, and they praised his courage highly even while they blamed him. The king said that for five years he had delayed his coming because he knew the extreme trouble his visit would cause. He said to Monsieur le Prince that he ought not to have but two tables and not burden himself with the responsibility for everybody, and that he would not permit Monsieur le Prince to do so again; but it was too late for poor Vatel.

Gourville, however, tried to repair the loss of Vatel, and did repair it. The dinner was excellent; so was the luncheon. They supped, they walked, they played, they hunted. The scent of jonquils was everywhere; it was all enchanting.

Saint-Simon, the king of memoir writers, when seventy-two years old, wrote an account of the first three Bourbon kings. The following passage from this work sums up the characteristics of Louis XIV, which are exhibited in greater detail throughout Saint-Simon's famous *Memoirs*.

**154. Saint Simon's portrait of Louis XIV.** The king's great qualities shone more brilliantly by reason of an exterior so unique and incomparable as to lend infinite distinction to his slightest actions; the very figure of a hero, so impregnated with a natural but most imposing majesty that it appeared even in his most insignificant gestures and movements, without arrogance but with simple gravity; proportions such as a sculptor would choose to model; a perfect countenance and the grandest air and mien ever vouchsafed to man; all these advantages enhanced by a natural grace which enveloped all his actions with a singular charm which has never perhaps been equaled. He was as dignified and majestic in his dressing gown as when dressed in robes of state, or on horseback at the head of his troops.

He excelled in all sorts of exercise and liked to have every facility for it. No fatigue nor stress of weather made any impression on that heroic figure and bearing; drenched with rain or snow, pierced with cold, bathed in sweat or covered with dust, he was always the same. I have often observed with admiration that except in the most extreme and exceptional weather nothing prevented his spending considerable time out of doors every day.

A voice whose tones corresponded with the rest of his person ; the ability to speak well and to listen with quick comprehension ; much reserve of manner adjusted with ex-actness to the quality of different persons ; a courtesy always grave, always dignified, always distinguished, and suited to the age, rank, and sex of each individual, and, for the ladies, always an air of natural gallantry. So much for his exterior, which has never been equaled nor even approached.

In whatever did not concern what he believed to be his rightful authority and prerogative, he showed a natural kind-ness of heart and a sense of justice which made one regret the education, the flatteries, the artifice which resulted in preventing him from being his real self except on the rare occasions when he gave way to some natural impulse and showed that, — prerogative aside, which choked and stifled everything, — he loved truth, justice, order, reason, — that he loved even to let himself be vanquished.

Nothing could be regulated with greater exactitude than were his days and hours. In spite of all his variety of places, affairs, and amusements, with an almanac and a watch one might tell, three hundred leagues away, exactly what he was doing. . . . Except at Marly, any man could have an oppor-tunity to speak to him five or six times during the day ; he listened, and almost always replied, " I will see," in order not to accord or decide anything lightly. Never a reply or a speech that would give pain ; patient to the last degree in business and in matters of personal service ; completely master of his face, manner, and bearing ; never giving way to impatience or anger. If he administered reproof, it was rarely, in few words, and never hastily. He did not lose control of himself ten times in his whole life, and then only with inferior persons, and not more than four or five times seriously.

*How Louis spent his day*

Now for the reverse of the picture :

Louis XIV's vanity was without limit or restraint ; it colored everything and convinced him that no one even approached him in military talents, in plans and enterprises, in government. Hence those pictures and inscriptions in the gallery at Versailles which disgust every foreigner; those opera prologues that he himself tried to sing; that flood of prose and verse in his praise for which his appetite was insatiable; those dedications of statues copied from pagan sculpture, and the insipid and sickening compliments that were continually offered to him in person and which he swallowed with unfailing relish; hence his distaste for all merit, intelligence, education, and, most of all, for all independence of character and sentiment in others; his mistakes of judgment in matters of importance; his familiarity and favor reserved entirely for those to whom he felt himself superior in acquirements and ability; and, above everything else, a jealousy of his own authority which determined and took precedence of every other sort of justice, reason, and consideration whatever.

## V. Revocation of the Edict of Nantes (1685)

155. Saint-
Simon's
angry ac-
count of the
revocation
of the Edict
of Nantes.

Opinions in regard to the expediency of the revocation of the Edict of Nantes naturally differed. Madame de Sévigné, the gentlest of women but most devout of Catholics, wrote: " You have doubtless seen the edict by which the king revokes that of Nantes. Nothing could be finer than all its provisions. No king has done or ever will do anything more honorable."[1] Saint-Simon, on the other hand, gives a somewhat lurid account of the criminal stupidity and the fearful results of the revocation.

The revocation of the Edict of Nantes, without the slightest pretext or necessity, and the various proscriptions that followed it, were the fruits of a frightful plot, in which the new spouse was one of the chief conspirators, and which depopulated a quarter of the realm; ruined its commerce; weakened it in every direction; gave it up for a long time to the

---

[1] Letter of October 28, 1685, *Correspondance*, VII, p. 420.

public and avowed pillage of the dragoons; authorized torments and punishments by which many innocent people of both sexes were killed by thousands; ruined a numerous class; tore in pieces a world of families; armed relatives against relatives, so as to seize their property and leave them to die of hunger; banished our manufactures to foreign lands; made those lands flourish and overflow at the expense of France, and enabled them to build new cities; gave to the world the spectacle of a prodigious population proscribed without crime, stripped, fugitive, wandering, and seeking shelter far from their country; sent to the galleys nobles, rich old men, people much esteemed for their piety, learning, and virtue, people carefully nurtured, weak, and delicate; — and all solely on account of religion; in fact, to heap up the measure of horror, filled the realm with perjury and sacrilege, in the midst of the echoed cries of these unfortunate victims of error, while so many others sacrificed their conscience to their wealth and their repose, and purchased both by simulated abjuration, from which without pause they were dragged to adore what they did not believe in, and to receive the divine body of the Most Holy whilst remaining persuaded that they were only eating bread which they ought to abhor!

Such was the general abomination born of flattery and cruelty. From torture to abjuration, and from that to communion, there was often only a space of twenty-four hours; and executioners were the guides of the converts and their witnesses. . . . The king received from all sides detailed news of these conversions. It was by thousands that those who had abjured and taken the communion were counted; ten thousand in one place, six thousand in another, — all at once and instantly. The king congratulated himself on his power and his piety. He believed himself to have brought back the days of the apostles, and attributed to himself all the honor. The bishops wrote panegyrics of him; the Jesuits made the pulpit resound with his praise. All France was filled with horror and confusion; and yet there was never such triumph and joy, such boundless laudation of the king.

## VI. Opening of the War of the Spanish Succession

The marquis of Torcy (1665–1746), who was at the head of foreign affairs during the War of the Spanish Succession, thus describes, in his remarkable memoirs, the opening of the conflict.

**156. How the War of the Spanish Succession came about. (From the memoirs of Torcy.)**

At length the event long foreseen happened.  Charles II (of Spain), sovereign of so many different dominions, died on the 1st of November in the year 1700 ; and his death in a very little time occasioned a general combustion in Europe.

By his will, signed the 2d of October preceding, he acknowledged the right of his sister, the infanta Maria Theresa, queen of France and mother of the dauphin, as also the right of his aunt, Queen Anna,[1] and consequently that of the dauphin, who was therefore his only heir, according to the laws of the kingdom ; but to prevent all Europe from being alarmed at the uniting of such extensive dominions to the crown of France, of which the dauphin was the only presumptive heir, Charles called the duke of Anjou, the dauphin's second son, to the succession, appointing him sole heir to all his kingdoms and lordships, without any exception or partition whatsoever.  He ordered all his subjects and vassals to acknowledge him as their king and natural sovereign.  But till this prince should come to Madrid, and even till he should come of age,[2] his Majesty ordained a council of regency, or

---

[1] Namely, the wife of Louis XIII and so the dauphin's grandmother. The basis of the claims of France and Austria in 1700 may be seen from the following table.

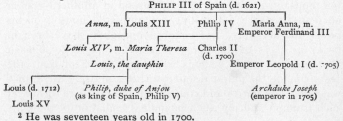

PHILIP III of Spain (d. 1621)

*Anna*, m. Louis XIII        Philip IV        Maria Anna, m. Emperor Ferdinand III

*Louis XIV*, m. *Maria Theresa*    Charles II (d. 1700)

*Louis, the dauphin*        Emperor Leopold I (d. 1705)

Louis (d. 1712)    *Philip, duke of Anjou* (as king of Spain, Philip V)        *Archduke Joseph* (emperor in 1705)

Louis XV

[2] He was seventeen years old in 1700.

junto, for the administration of the state, and nominated the members of which it was to be composed, placing the queen at the head.

Immediately upon the king of Spain's decease, the junto wrote to the king [of France], giving him notice of this event; and the Spanish ambassador had orders to deliver the will to his Majesty, together with the letter signed by the queen and the members of the junto.

As they were in doubt at Madrid whether the king of France would accept the last proposals of his Catholic Majesty, the junto ordered Castel dos Rios, in case of such a refusal, to have the same courier who had been sent from Madrid proceed forthwith to Vienna; the intention of the late king having been to bequeath the entire succession to the archduke, in case his first settlement should not be accepted in France.

The king was then at Fontainebleau. Upon the arrival of the courier, the Spanish ambassador communicated the orders he had just received to that one among the ministers to whom the king confided the department of foreign affairs,[1] and demanded a private audience of his Majesty. The king, before he would fix the hour, was desirous of having the opinion of his council upon an event so unexpected and yet so important to the royal family, to the welfare of the kingdom, and to the general tranquillity of Europe. . . .

It was easier to foresee than to provide for the consequences of the decision in question. His Majesty had engaged to reject every disposition of his realms whatsoever made by the king of Spain in favor of a prince of the line of France, — an engagement that excluded a bequest by will, a donation, or any other form of deed or settlement. By breaking his engagements, he would incur the censure of violating the sacred word of a king, and moreover the consequence of such a violation was inevitable war. His chief aim in hastening the conclusion of the peace signed at Ryswick [1697] was to let his people have time to breathe

---

[1] Namely, the writer himself.

A.25

after a long series of wars, and now, when they had scarce begun to enjoy a little repose, they would be obliged to support a new war, which would immediately become general; for there was not the least reason to expect that the neighboring princes, who were already so greatly alarmed at the power of France, would tamely suffer the king to extend his authority so as to rule, in the name of his grandson, over the dominions subject to the crown of Spain in the Old and New Worlds.

On the other hand, it was to be considered that if the king refused to accept the will, this same act transferred the entire succession to the archduke [Joseph]. The same courier that had been dispatched into France would proceed to Vienna; and the Spanish nation, without any hesitation, would acknowledge the emperor's second son for their king. The house of Austria of course would reunite, between the father and son, the power of Charles V, a power heretofore so fatal to France. And, besides, all security for preserving the peace of Ryswick would cease, the treaty of partition being no longer sufficient to maintain it. . . . The king therefore determined to accept the will.

## BIBLIOGRAPHY

*A. References.*

**Sketch of Louis XIV's Reign:** SCHWILL, *Modern Europe,* pp. 200–214; ADAMS, G. B., *The Growth of the French Nation,* Chapter XIII, pp. 202–233; PERKINS, *France under the Regency,* Chapter V, pp. 129–160.

**Colbert and his Reforms:** PERKINS, Chapter IV, pp. 90–128; WAKEMAN, *European History, 1598–1715,* Chapter IX, pp. 184–205.

**Revocation of the Edict of Nantes:** PERKINS, Chapter VI, pp. 164–207.

**Antecedents of the War of the Spanish Succession:** WAKEMAN, Chapter XIV, pp. 311–339.

**War of the Spanish Succession:** CHEYNEY, *Short History of England,* pp. 529–535; PERKINS, Chapter VIII, pp. 239–292; WAKEMAN, Chapter XV, pp. 340–363.

**Treaty of Utrecht:** WAKEMAN, pp. 363–371; DYER and HASSALL, *Modern Europe,* Vol. IV, pp. 107–116.

HASSALL, *Louis XIV and the Zenith of the French Monarchy*, 1897 (Heroes of the Nations Series).

KITCHIN, *History of France*, Vol. III.

BAIRD, *The Huguenots and the Revocation of the Edict of Nantes*, 2 vols., 1895. A careful and elaborate work by a warm partisan.

SAINT-SIMON, *Memoirs*, 4 vols. A much-abridged translation of the voluminous original.

*Life and Letters of Charlotte Elizabeth, Mother of Philippe d'Orleans*, London, 1889. A selection from the many letters which a German princess, who married Louis XIV's brother, dispatched to her friends.

COMTESSE DE PULIGA, *Madame de Sévigné, her Correspondents and Contemporaries*, 2 vols., London, 1873. Gives some idea of this charming letter writer.

CLAUDE, JEAN, *The Cruel Persecutions of the Protestants in the Kingdom of France*, Boston, 1893. The author, who published his book immediately after the revocation of the Edict of Nantes, was a leading Huguenot and the pastor of the great Protestant church at Charenton, near Paris.

GERARD, *The Peace of Utrecht*, 1885. Really a history of the War of the Spanish Succession.

*B. Additional reading in English.*

# CHAPTER XXXII

## RISE OF RUSSIA AND PRUSSIA

### I. PETER THE GREAT

Peter the Great, in his anxiety to reform Russia and make it a great power, renewed the active intercourse with western Europe which had been fostered to some extent toward a century and a half earlier by Ivan the Terrible. He visited the western regions himself, imported military leaders, artisans, and scientists, and did much to remodel Russian customs. One of the most satisfactory accounts of the tsar's visit to England is given by the sagacious historian, Bishop Burnet.[1]

157. Bishop Burnet's impressions of Peter the Great in 1698.

I mentioned in the relation of the former year [1698] the tsar's coming out of his own country; on which I will now enlarge. He came this winter over to England and stayed some months among us. I waited often on him, and was ordered both by the king and the archbishop and bishops to attend upon him and to offer him such informations of our religion and constitution as he was willing to receive. I had good interpreters, so I had much free discourse with him. He is a man of a very hot temper, soon inflamed and very brutal in his passion. He raises his natural heat by drinking much brandy, which he rectifies himself with great application. He is subject to convulsive motions all over his body, and his head seems to be affected with these. He wants not capacity, and has a larger measure of knowledge than might be expected from his education, which was very indifferent.

[1] See above, p. 362.

A want of judgment, with an instability of temper, appear in him too often and too evidently.

He is mechanically turned, and seems designed by nature rather to be a ship carpenter than a great prince. This was his chief study and exercise while he stayed here. He wrought much with his own hands and made all about him work at the models of ships. He told me he designed a great fleet at Azuph [i.e. Azov] and with it to attack the Turkish empire. But he did not seem capable of conducting so great a design, though his conduct in his wars since this has discovered a greater genius in him than appeared at this time. The tsar's interest in shipbuilding

He was desirous to understand our doctrine, but he did not seem disposed to mend matters in Moscovy. He was, indeed, resolved to encourage learning and to polish his people by sending some of them to travel in other countries and to draw strangers to come and live among them. He seemed apprehensive still [i.e. ever] of his sister's [i.e. the Princess Sophia's] intrigues. There was a mixture both of passion and severity in his temper. He is resolute, but understands little of war, and seemed not at all inquisitive that way.

After I had seen him often, and had conversed much with him, I could not but adore the depth of the providence of God that had raised up such a furious man to so absolute an authority over so great a part of the world. David, considering the great things God had made for the use of man, broke out into the meditation, "What is man, that thou art so mindful of him?" But here there is an occasion for reversing these words, since man seems a very contemptible thing in the sight of God, while such a person as the tsar has such multitudes put, as it were, under his feet, exposed to his restless jealousy and savage temper. Burnet's reflections upon Russian autocracy.

He went from hence to the court of Vienna, where he purposed to have stayed some time, but he was called home sooner than he had intended upon a discovery, or a suspicion, of intrigues managed by his sister. The strangers, to whom he trusted most, were so true to him that those designs Peter's vengeance upon the rebels.

were crushed before he came back. But on this occasion he
let loose his fury on all whom he suspected. Some hundreds
of them were hanged all around Moskow, and it was said
that he cut off many heads with his own hand; and so far
was he from relenting or showing any sort of tenderness
that he seemed delighted with it. How long he is to be the
scourge of that nation God only knows.

A French historical writer of the first half of the
eighteenth century, Jean Rousset de Missy,[1] wrote a
life of Peter the Great. Although the author never
visited Russia, his volumes have some value, since he
appears to have taken pains to get reliable information. He thus describes the reform in dress enforced
by Peter.

**158. How
Peter the
Great forced
his people
to wear
Western
dress.**

The tsar labored at the reform of fashions, or, more properly speaking, of dress. Until that time the Russians had
always worn long beards, which they cherished and preserved with much care, allowing them to hang down on their
bosoms, without even cutting the moustache. With these
long beards they wore the hair very short, except the ecclesiastics, who, to distinguish themselves, wore it very long.
The tsar, in order to reform that custom, ordered that gentlemen, merchants, and other subjects, except priests and
peasants, should each pay a tax of one hundred rubles a year
if they wished to keep their beards; the commoners had to
pay one kopeck each. Officials were stationed at the gates
of the towns to collect that tax, which the Russians regarded
as an enormous sin on the part of the tsar and as a thing
which tended to the abolition of their religion.

These insinuations, which came from the priests, occasioned the publication of many pamphlets in Moscow, where
for that reason alone the tsar was regarded as a tyrant and
a pagan; and there were many old Russians who, after
having their beards shaved off, saved them preciously, in

[1] He wrote under the assumed name Ivan Nestesuranoi.

order to have them placed in their coffins, fearing that they would not be allowed to enter heaven without their beards. As for the young men, they followed the new custom with the more readiness as it made them appear more agreeable to the fair sex.

From the reform in beards we may pass to that of clothes. Their garments, like those of the Orientals, were very long, reaching to the heel. The tsar issued an ordinance abolishing that costume, commanding all the boyars (nobles) and all those who had positions at the court to dress after the French fashion, and likewise to adorn their clothes with gold or silver according to their means.

As for the rest of the people, the following method was employed. A suit of clothes cut according to the new fashion was hung at the gate of the city, with a decree enjoining upon all except peasants to have their clothes made on this model, under penalty of being forced to kneel and have all that part of their garments which fell below the knee cut off, or pay two grives every time they entered the town with clothes in the old style. Since the guards at the gates executed their duty in curtailing the garments in a sportive spirit, the people were amused and readily abandoned their old dress, especially in Moscow and its environs, and in the towns which the tsar oftenest visited.

The dress of the women was changed, too. English hairdressing was substituted for the caps and bonnets hitherto worn; bodices, stays, and skirts, for the former undergarment.[1] . . .

The same ordinance also provided that in the future women, as well as men, should be invited to entertainments, such as weddings, banquets, and the like, where both sexes should mingle in the same hall, as in Holland and England. It was likewise added that these entertainments should conclude with concerts and dances, but that only those should be admitted who were dressed in English costumes. His Majesty set the example in all these changes.

[1] The Russian names of the native garments are omitted here.

## II. Frederick the Great and his Father

159. Instructions of Frederick William I for the education of his son. (Condensed.)

Frederick the Great's father gave the following in-structions for the education of his son.

. . . Above all else, it is important that his character — and it is character which governs all human action — should be, from earliest youth, so formed that he will love and de-light in virtue and feel horror and disgust for vice. Nothing can so greatly contribute to this end as to implant the true fear of God so early in the young heart that it shall take root and bear fruit in the time when there is no longer any guidance or oversight. For other men are guided toward virtue and away from evil by the rewards and punishments dealt out by those who are set above them, but the prince must rely on the fear of God alone, since he is subject to no human law, punishment, or reward.

My son and all his attendants shall say their prayers on their knees both morning and evening, and after prayers shall read a chapter from the Bible.

He shall be kept away from operas, comedies, and other worldly amusements and, as far as possible, be given a dis-taste for them. He must be taught to pay proper respect and submission to his parents, but without slavishness.

His tutors must use every means they can devise to re-strain him from puffed-up pride and insolence and to train him in good management, economy, and modesty. And since nothing is so harmful as flattery, all those who are about the person of my son are forbidden to indulge in it on pain of my extreme displeasure.

As to the further studies that become a prince, his prog-ress must depend upon his years and growth, but it must be looked to that he is taught the most important things first, and all without inspiring distaste or disgust. As this will depend largely on the adroitness of his preceptor, Duhan, the latter must consult from time to time with the head tutor as to the course to be pursued, which must then be presented to me for my approval.

As for the Latin language, he is not to learn it, and I desire that no one shall even speak to me on this subject; but his tutors shall see to it that he acquires a terse and elegant style in writing French as well as German. Arithmetic, mathematics, artillery, and agriculture he must be taught thoroughly, ancient history only superficially, but that of our own time and of the last one hundred and fifty years as accurately as possible. He must have a thorough knowledge of law, of international law, of geography, and of what is most remarkable in each country; and, above all, my son must be carefully taught the history of his own house.

His tutors must take the greatest pains to imbue my son with a sincere love for the soldier's profession and to impress upon him that nothing else in the world can confer upon a prince such fame and honor as the sword, and that he will be despised by all the world if he does not only love it but seek in it his only glory; and his chief tutor shall provide for his being taught the practice of arms as play in his recreation hours.

Nothing is more becoming or more necessary in a prince than the ability to speak well under all circumstances; therefore my son's tutors must look to it that he accustom himself betimes to this art by practice. . . .

The following is a suggestive letter of the crown prince, Frederick, written at the age of sixteen, to his father, Frederick William I.

WUSTERHAUSEN, September 11, 1728.

I have not ventured for a long time to present myself before my dear papa, partly because I was advised against it, but chiefly because I anticipated an even worse reception than usual and feared to vex my dear papa still further by the favor I have now to ask; so I have preferred to put it in writing.

I beg my dear papa that he will be kindly disposed toward me. I do assure him that after long examination of my conscience I do not find the slightest thing with which

160. A youthful letter of Frederick the Great to his father

to reproach myself; but if, against my wish and will, I have vexed my dear papa, I hereby beg most humbly for forgiveness, and hope that my dear papa will give over the fearful hate which has appeared so plainly in his whole behavior and to which I cannot accustom myself. I have always thought hitherto that I had a kind father, but now I see the contrary. However, I will take courage and hope that my dear papa will think this all over and take me again into his favor. Meantime I assure him that I will never, my life long, willingly fail him, and in spite of his disfavor I am still, with most dutiful and childlike respect, my dear papa's

Most obedient and faithful servant and son,

FREDERICK.

Frederick William replied:

**160a. Frederick William's reply.**

A bad, obstinate boy, who does not love his father; for when one does one's best, and especially when one loves one's father, one does what he wishes not only when he is standing by but when he is not there to see. Moreover you know very well that I cannot stand an effeminate fellow who has no manly tastes, who cannot ride or shoot (to his shame be it said!), is untidy about his person, and wears his hair curled like a fool instead of cutting it; and that I have condemned all these things a thousand times, and yet there is no sign of improvement. For the rest, haughty, offish as a country lout, conversing with none but a favored few instead of being affable and popular, grimacing like a fool, and never following my wishes out of love for me but only when forced into it, caring for nothing but to have his own way, and thinking nothing else is of any importance. This is my answer.

FREDERICK WILLIAM.

### III. FREDERICK THE GREAT AND THE SEVEN YEARS' WAR

The Seven Years' War opened disastrously for Frederick the Great. His only ally against all Europe was England. In spite of a victory over the French at

Rossbach (November 5, 1757), his situation, which he describes in the following address to his generals, was a very critical one. But so great was his military skill and the valor of the soldiers, whom he inspired with his own fiery confidence, that on December 5 he won the battle of Leuthen against tremendous odds, — a victory which Napoleon declared would alone have entitled him to rank among the greatest generals.

You are aware, gentlemen, that Prince Karl of Lorraine has succeeded in taking Schweidnitz, defeating the duke of Bevern and making himself master of Breslau, while I was engaged in checking the advance of the French and imperial forces. A part of Schleswig, my capital, and all the military stores it contained, are lost, and I should feel myself in dire straits indeed if it were not for my unbounded confidence in your courage, your constancy, and your love for the fatherland, which you have proved to me on so many occasions in the past. These services to me and to the fatherland have touched the deepest fibers of my heart. There is hardly one among you who has not distinguished himself by some conspicuous deed of valor, wherefore I flatter myself that in the approaching opportunity also you will not fail in any sacrifice that your country may demand of you.

161. Frederick's address to his generals and staff officers, December 3, 1757, before his victory at Leuthen.

And this opportunity is close at hand. I should feel that I had accomplished nothing if Austria were left in possession of Schleswig. Let me tell you then that I propose, in defiance of all the rules of the art of war, to attack the army of Prince Karl, three times as large as ours, wherever I find it. It is here no question of the numbers of the enemy nor of the importance of the positions they have occupied; all this I hope to overcome by the devotion of my troops and the careful carrying out of my plans. I must take this step or all will be lost ; we must defeat the enemy, else we shall all lie buried under his batteries. So I believe — so I shall act.

Communicate my decision to all the officers of the army; prepare the common soldier for the exertions that are to come, and tell him that I feel justified in expecting unquestioning obedience from him. Remember that you are Prussians and you cannot show yourselves unworthy of that distinction. But if there be one or other among you who fears to share with me any and all danger, he shall at once be given his discharge without reproach from me.

The solemn silence with which this speech was received and the glow of enthusiasm reflected in the faces of his hearers convinced Frederick that he had produced the effect he desired. With a gentle smile he continued:

I was convinced that no one of you would wish to leave me; I count then, absolutely, on your faithful help and on certain victory. Should I not return to reward you for your devotion, the fatherland itself must do it. Return now to camp and repeat to your troops what you have heard from me. Then, becoming once more the stern ruler, he announces the punishment that awaits the slightest hesitation in following orders. The regiment of cavalry that does not immediately on the receipt of orders throw itself upon the enemy I will have unmounted immediately after the battle and make it a garrison regiment. The battalion of infantry that even begins to hesitate, no matter what the danger may be, shall lose its flags and its swords and have the gold lace stripped from its uniforms.

And now, gentlemen, farewell; erelong we shall either have defeated the enemy or we shall see each other no more.

Before the end of the long and exhausting war Frederick had met with several crushing reverses, and his resources had dwindled to almost nothing. He writes the following letters, not long before peace was finally concluded, to his trusted French friend, d'Argens.

. . . I am obliged to cover Schweidnitz from all sides against this Daun [an Austrian commander], who keeps a dozen subordinates roaming about trying to defeat our plans. This compels me to give unremitting attention to the movements of the enemy and to procuring information. You may infer, therefore, that my poor head is scarcely equal to poetry. That verse that you criticise shall certainly be corrected, — that is nothing; but I beg you to wait till the end of our siege, which so far goes well. I have not the least vanity, I assure you; and I think chance and my troops are responsible for so large a share in the success of my undertakings that I have no mania for dispatching couriers; nevertheless, if it will give you pleasure, they shall certainly be sent. . . .

162. Letter of Frederick the Great written toward the close of the Seven Years' War (August, 1762).

For the present I am confining my attention to the operation I have undertaken. There is quite enough to keep a young man busy, but what a life for an old man, worn out and broken down like me, whose memory is beginning to fail and who feels his senses weakening and his force of character declining! There is a fitting time of life for all things. At my age, my dear marquis, books, conversation, a comfortable armchair by the fire, — these are all that remain for me, and then in a few moments the grave.

Farewell, my dear marquis; may you live happily and in tranquillity and not forget me.

## IV. The Partition of Poland

Maria Theresa was heartily ashamed of her part in the First Partition of Poland. She writes as follows to Archduke Ferdinand, her son, explaining and excusing her course.

LAXENBURG, September 17, [1772].

. . . Firmian will receive a lengthy document with instructions in regard to our present situation, our engagements toward Russia, Prussia, and the Turks, but particularly in regard to this unfortunate partition of Poland, which is costing me ten years of my life. It will make plain the whole unhappy history of that affair. How many times have

163. Letter of Maria Theresa on the partition of Poland.

I refused to agree to it ! But disaster after disaster heaped
upon us by the Turks; misery, famine, and pestilence at
home; no hope of assistance either from France or England,
and the prospect of being left isolated and threatened with
a war both with Russia and Prussia, — it was all these considerations that finally forced me to accede to that unhappy
proposal, which will remain a blot on my whole reign. God
grant that I be not held responsible for it in the other world !
I confess that I cannot keep from talking about this affair.
I have taken it so to heart that it poisons and imbitters all
my days, which even without that are sad enough. I must
stop writing about it at once, or I shall worry myself into
the blackest melancholy. . . .

## BIBLIOGRAPHY

*A. Refer-
ences.*

**Sketch of Russian History in the 18th Century:** SCHWILL, *Modern
Europe*, pp. 215–229.

**Peter the Great and Charles XII:** WAKEMAN, *European History*,
*1578–1715*, Chapter XIII, pp. 289–310.

**Europe at the Opening of the 18th Century:** HASSALL, *European
History*, *1715–1789*, Chapter I, pp. 1–25.

**Review of Prussian History in the 17th and 18th Centuries:**
SCHWILL, pp. 230–247.

**Frederick the Great and the Seven Years' War:** HENDERSON,
*Short History of Germany*, Vol. II, pp. 148–181 ; HASSALL, Chapter IX,
pp. 244–283.

**Frederick the Great in Peace:** HENDERSON, Vol. II, pp. 182–218.

**First Partition of Poland:** HASSALL, pp. 302–322.

---

*B. Addi-
tional read-
ing in
English.*

RAMBAUD, *History of Russia*, 2 vols. Much the best general account.
It may be supplemented by the same author's little volume on *The
Expansion of Russia*.

SCHUYLER, *Peter the Great*, 1884. The standard life of the tsar in
English.

WALISZEWSKI, *Life of Peter the Great*. From the French. Excellent
and recent.

BAIN, *Charles XII and the Collapse of the Swedish Empire, 1682–
1719*, 1899 (Heroes of the Nations).

STANLEY LANE-POOLE, *Turkey* (Story of the Nations).　By a well-known authority.

CREASY, *History of the Ottoman Turks*.　Based upon the great German work of Von Hammer, which is in 10 volumes.

LONGMAN, *Frederick the Great*, and (more recent) REDDAWAY, *Frederick the Great and the Rise of Prussia*, 1904 (Heroes of the Nations).

CARLYLE, THOMAS, *Frederick the Great*, 3 vols.　A famous work giving many extracts from Frederick's letters and other sources.

PERKINS, *France under Louis XV*, 2 vols.　Excellent for the rôle of France in the middle of the eighteenth century.

BRIGHT, *Maria Theresa*, 1897.　A little volume in the Foreign Statesmen Series.

## CHAPTER XXXIII

### THE EXPANSION OF ENGLAND

### I. How the English got a Foothold in India

At the end of the sixteenth century the English began to turn their attention to India, and in 1601 the East India Company was chartered. In 1614 Sir Thomas Roe was instructed by James I to visit the court of Jehangir, the Mongol emperor of Hindustan. Sir Thomas was to arrange a commercial treaty and to secure for the East India Company sites for commercial agencies, — "factories," as they were called. The English naturally got into trouble immediately with the Dutch traders in the East Indies. There is probably another side to the story which follows.

**164. A Frenchman's account of hostility of the Dutch to English traders (1617).**

*A relation of the Frenchmen which lately arrived into France in a ship of Dieppe out of the East Indies concerning the wrongs and abuses which the Hollanders had lately done to the English there (1617):*

Two English ships coming to Banda, in course of trade and traffic, the Hollanders assaulted with certain of their ships, which English ships in their resistance and defense the said Hollanders took, slew seven or eight of their men (whereof one was a chief factor), chained the captain, merchants, and mariners, and put the mariners into their galleys. All the munition and victuals in the said English ships did the Hollanders take out and carried the same ashore, challenging all to be theirs as their proper inheritance, and therefore will be lords of the same.

400

The Hollanders likewise took an English bark going from Bantam[1] to Jacatra, slew some of her men, wounded many more, chained the captain and mariners, and carried away the said bark at the stern of one of their ships into Bantam Road, and there anchored close by the admiral of the English in most despiteful and daring manner, making their vaunts that they were the chief people of all Europe; and to make a show of the same they advanced their own arms and colors, and under them placed the colors of England and France, and then shot at the said English and French colors in most contemptuous and disdainful manner.

At Bantam the English and Hollanders had great disputes, insomuch as it was verily thought they would have fought together in the road, for the general of the Hollanders had brought thither fourteen great ships, ready to fight, where the English had nine, which they fitted for defense; but they fought not, for the governor of Bantam forbade them to fight in his road, and threatened them that if they did fight contrary to his command he would cut the throats of all their men that he should find upon the land.

The 27th of November the Hollanders proclaimed war against all the English at the Mulluccoes, Banda, and Amboyna, threatening to make one and all prize and to put them to the edge of the sword; which proclamation of theirs they fixed upon the doors of their lodgings at Bantam, challenging all to be theirs as their proper inheritance.

Aurangzeb, who died in 1707, was the last Great Mogul of importance. He saw in his old age that anarchy was likely to come when he was gone, and his farewell to this vain world is sad indeed. He thus writes to a friend :

Health to thee! My heart is near thee. Old age is arrived : weakness subdues me, and strength has forsaken

[1] Bantam was originally the chief settlement of the Dutch in Java, near the Strait of Sunda, somewhat to the west of the present important port of Batavia.

A.26

165. Au-
rangzeb fore-
casts the
dissolution
of the
Mogul's
empire.

all my members. I came a stranger into this world and a stranger I depart. I know nothing of myself, what I am, or for what I am destined. The instant which has passed in power hath left only sorrow behind it. I have not been the guardian and protector of the empire. My valuable time has been passed vainly. I had a patron in my own dwelling (conscience), but his glorious light was unseen by my dim sight.

Life is not lasting; there is no vestige of departed breath, and all hopes from futurity are lost. The fever has left me; but nothing remains of me but skin and bone. . . . The camp and followers, helpless and frightened, are like myself, full of alarms, restless as quicksilver. Separated from their lord, they know not if they have a master or not.

I brought nothing into this world, and, except the infirmities of man, carry nothing out. I have a dread for my salvation, and with what torments I may be punished. Though I have strong reliance on the mercies and bounties of God, yet, regarding my actions, fear will not quit me; but when I am gone reflection will not remain. Come then what may, I have launched my vessel in the waves. Though Providence will protect the camp, yet, regarding appearances, the endeavors of my sons are indispensable. Give my last prayers to my grandson, whom I cannot see, but the desire affects me. The Began [his daughter] appears afflicted; but God is the only judge of hearts. The foolish thoughts of women produce nothing but disappointment. Farewell, farewell, farewell.

The following extract is from a letter written by Clive, in which he describes his famous victory at Plassey, north of Calcutta. This battle completely demonstrated the inability of native armies to cope with Europeans, and marked the beginning of British control in Bengal. According to his account, Clive had only about one thousand Europeans, two thousand Sepoys, and eight pieces of cannon.

At daybreak we discovered the nabob's army moving towards us, consisting, as we since found, of about fifteen thousand horse and thirty-five thousand foot, with upwards of forty pieces of cannon. They approached apace, and by six began to attack with a number of heavy cannon, supported by the whole army, and continued to play on us very briskly for several hours, during which our situation was of the utmost service to us, being lodged in a large grove with good mud banks. To succeed in an attempt on their cannon was next to impossible, as they were planted in a manner round us and at considerable distances from each other. We therefore remained quiet in our post, in expectation of a successful attack upon their camp at night. About noon the enemy drew off their artillery and retired to their camp. . . .

On finding them make no great effort to dislodge us, we proceeded to take possession of one or two more eminences lying very near an angle of their camp, from whence, and an adjacent eminence in their possession, they kept a smart fire of musketry upon us. They made several attempts to bring out their cannon, but our advanced fieldpieces played so warmly and so well upon them that they were always driven back. Their horse exposing themselves a good deal on this occasion, many of them were killed, and among the rest four or five officers of the first distinction; by which the whole army being visibly dispirited and thrown into some confusion, we were encouraged to storm both the eminence and the angle of their camp, which were carried at the same instant, with little or no loss; though the latter was defended (exclusively of blacks) by forty French and two pieces of cannon; and the former by a large body of blacks, both horse and foot.

On this a general rout ensued, and we pursued the enemy six miles, passing upwards of forty pieces of cannon they had abandoned, with an infinite number of hackeries (carts) and carriages filled with baggage of all kinds. . . . It is computed there are killed of the enemy about five hundred. Our loss amounted to only twenty-two killed and fifty wounded, and those chiefly blacks.

166. Clive's own account of his victory at Plassey (June 23, 1757).

## II. The Jesuits in North America

The spirit of the Jesuit explorers is clearly to be seen in Father Marquette's account of his discovery of the Mississippi River in 1673.

167. How Marquette descended the Mississippi River in 1673.

The feast of the Immaculate Conception of the Blessed Virgin — whom I have always invoked since I have been in this country of the Outaouacs to obtain from God the grace of being able to visit the nations who dwell along the Mississippi River — was precisely the day on which Monsieur Joliet arrived with orders to accomplish this discovery with me. . . . We were not long in preparing all our equipment, although we were about to begin a voyage the duration of which we could not foresee. Indian corn, with some smoked meat, constituted all our provisions. With these we embarked — Monsieur Joliet and myself with five men — in two bark canoes, fully resolved to do and suffer everything for so glorious an undertaking.

Accordingly, on the seventeenth day of May, 1673, we started from the mission of St. Ignace at Michilimakinac, where I then was. The joy that we felt at being selected for this expedition animated our courage and rendered the labor of paddling from morning to night agreeable to us. And because we were going to seek unknown countries we took every precaution in our power, so that if our undertaking were hazardous it should not be foolhardy. To that end we obtained all the information that we could from the savages who had frequented those regions; and we even traced out from their reports a map of the whole of that new country. On it we indicated the rivers which we were to navigate, the names of the peoples and of the places through which we were to pass, the course of the Great River, and the direction we were to follow when we reached it. . . .

With all these precautions, we joyfully plied our paddles on a portion of Lake Huron and on that of the Illinois [i.e. Lake Michigan] and on the Bay des Puants [i.e. Green Bay]. The first nation that we came to was that of the " Wild

Oats." I entered their river to go and visit these peoples, to whom we have preached the gospel for several years, — in consequence of which there are several good Christians among them. . . .

We left this bay to enter the river that discharges into it. It is very beautiful at its mouth and flows gently. It is full of bustards, ducks, teal, and other birds, attracted thither by the wild oats, of which they are very fond. But after ascending the river a short distance it becomes very difficult of passage on account of both the currents and the sharp rocks, which cut the canoes and the feet of those who are obliged to drag them, especially when the waters are low. . . . We continued to advance toward the Maskoutens, where we arrived on the 7th of June. . . . *They leave Green Bay for the Wisconsin River*

On the following day, the 10th of June, two Miamis, who were given us as guides, embarked with us in the sight of a great crowd, who could not sufficiently express their astonishment at the sight of seven Frenchmen alone in two canoes daring to undertake so extraordinary and so hazardous an expedition.

We knew that at three leagues from Maskoutens was a river which discharged into the Mississippi. We knew also that the direction we were to follow in order to reach it was west-southwesterly. But the road is broken by so many swamps and small lakes that it is easy to lose one's way, especially as the river leading thither is so full of wild oats that it is difficult to find the channel. For this reason we greatly needed our two guides, who safely conducted us to a portage of twenty-seven hundred paces and helped us to transport our canoes to enter that river. After which they returned home, leaving us alone in this unknown country in the hands of Providence. Thus we left the waters flowing to Quebec, four hundred or five hundred leagues from here, to float on those that would henceforth take us through strange lands. . . .

The river on which we embarked is called the Meskousing [i.e. Wisconsin]. It is very wide. It has a sandy bottom, which forms various shoals that render its navigation very *They reach the Mississippi.*

difficult. . . . After proceeding forty leagues on this same route, we arrived at the mouth of our river, and at 42½ degrees of latitude we safely entered the Mississippi on the 17th of June with a joy that I cannot express.

Here we are, then, on this renowned river, all of whose peculiar features I have endeavored to note carefully. The Mississippi River takes its rise in various lakes in the country of the northern nations. . . . We gently followed its course, which runs toward the south and southeast, as far as the 42d degree of latitude. . . . From time to time we came upon monstrous fish, one of which struck our canoe with such violence that I thought that it was a great tree about to break the canoe in pieces. On another occasion we saw on the water a monster with the head of a tiger, a sharp nose like that of a wild-cat, with whiskers and straight, erect ears. The head was gray and the neck quite black. But we saw no more creatures of this sort. . . . When we reached the parallel of 41 degrees 28 minutes, following the same direction, we found that turkeys had taken the place of game and the pisikious or wild cattle [i.e. buffaloes] that of the other animals.

We call them "wild cattle" because they are very similar to our domestic cattle. They are not longer, but are nearly as large again and more corpulent. When our people killed one, three persons had much difficulty in moving it. . . . Their heavy coat falls off in summer and the skin becomes as soft as velvet. At that season the savages use the hides for making fine robes, which they paint in various colors. . . .

Marquette visits the Illinois.

Finally, on the 25th of June, we perceived on the water's edge soft tracks of men and a narrow and somewhat beaten path leading to a fine prairie. We stopped to examine it, and thinking that it was a road which led to some village of savages, we resolved to go and reconnoiter it. We therefore left our two canoes under the guard of our people, strictly charging them not to allow themselves to be surprised, after which Monsieur Joliet and I undertook this investigation, — a rather hazardous one for two men who exposed themselves

alone to the mercy of a barbarous and unknown people. (Condensed.)
[The savages received us kindly, having probably recognized
us as Frenchmen, especially when they saw our black gowns.]
I spoke to them and asked them who they were. They
replied that they were Illinois, and as a token of peace they
offered us their pipes to smoke. They afterward invited us
to enter their village, where all the people impatiently awaited
us. These pipes for smoking are called in this country
" calumets." This word has come so much into use that in
order to be understood I shall be obliged to use it, as I shall
often have to mention these pipes. . . .

When one speaks the word " Illinois," it is as if one said
in their language " the men," — as if the other savages were
looked upon by them merely as animals. It must also be
admitted that they have an air of humanity which we have
not observed in the other nations that we have seen upon our
route. . . . We take leave of our Illinois at the end of June
about three o'clock in the afternoon. We embark in the sight
of all the people, who admire our little canoes, for they have
never seen any like them. . . .

While skirting some rocks which by their height and
length inspired awe, we saw upon one of them two painted
monsters which at first made us afraid, and upon which the
boldest savages dare not long rest their eyes. They are as
large as a calf; they have horns on their heads like those of
deer, a horrible look, red eyes, a beard like a tiger's, a face
somewhat like a man's, a body covered with scales. . . .

Strange
pictures on
the rocks
near Alton.

While we were conversing about these monsters, sailing
quietly in clear and calm water, we heard the noise of a rapid
into which we were about to run. I have seen nothing more
dreadful. An accumulation of large and entire trees, branches,
and floating islands was issuing from the mouth of the river
Pekitanoui [i.e. Missouri] with such impetuosity that we could
not without great danger risk passing through it. So great
was the agitation that the water was very muddy and could
not become clear. The Pekitanoui is a river of considerable
size coming from the northwest, from a great distance, and
it discharges into the Mississippi. There are many villages

They reach
the mouth of
the Missouri

of savages along this river, and I hope by its means to discover the Vermilion or California Sea. . . .

After escaping as best we could the dangerous rapid, we
proceeded south. After a long journey we reached the large
village of Akamsea [Arkansas]. In the evening the elders
held a secret council in regard to the design entertained by
some to break our heads and rob us; but the chief put a
stop to all these plots. After sending for us he danced the
calumet before us as a token of our entire safety, and to
relieve us of all fear he made me a present of it.

Monsieur Joliet and I held another council to deliberate
upon what we should do, — whether we should push on, or
remain content with the discovery which we had made. After
attentively considering that we were not far from the Gulf of
Mexico, the basin of which is at the latitude of 31 degrees
and 60 minutes, while we were at 33 degrees 40 minutes, we
judged that we could not be more than two or three days'
journey from it, and that beyond a doubt the Mississippi
River discharges into the Florida or Mexican gulf, and not
to the east in Virginia, whose seacoast is at 34 degrees of
latitude, — which we had passed without, however, having as
yet reached the sea, — or to the west in California, because
in that case our route would have been to the west or the
west-southwest, whereas we had always continued it toward
the south. We further considered that we exposed ourselves
to the risk of losing the results of this voyage, of which we
could give no information if we proceeded to fling ourselves
into the hands of the Spaniards, who, without doubt, would
at least have detained us as captives. Moreover we saw
very plainly that we were not in a condition to resist savages
allied to the Europeans, who were numerous and expert in
firing guns, and who continually infested the lower part of
the river. . . .

We therefore reascend the Mississippi, which gives us
much trouble in breasting its currents. It is true that we
leave it at about the 38th degree, which greatly shortens our
road and takes us with but little effort to the lake of the
Illinois. . . . One of the chiefs of this nation, with his

young men, escorted us to the lake of the Illinois, whence at last, at the end of September, we reached the Bay des Puants, from which we had started the beginning of June.

## III. An English View of the Revolt of the American Colonies

The elder Pitt thus spoke in the House of Commons, January 20, 1775, on the growing difficulties between the king and his American colonies.

This resistance to your arbitrary system of taxation might have been foreseen; it was obvious from the nature of things and of mankind, and, above all, from the Whiggish spirit flourishing in that country. The spirit which now resists your taxation in America is the same which formerly opposed loans, benevolences, and ship money in England; the same spirit which called all England on its legs, and by the Bill of Rights vindicated the English constitution; the same spirit which established the great, fundamental, essential maxim of your liberties, that no subject of England shall be taxed but by his own consent.

168. Pitt on the question of withdrawing the English troops from Boston (January, 1775).

This glorious spirit of Whiggism animates three millions in America, who prefer poverty with liberty to gilded chains and sordid affluence, and who will die in the defense of their rights as men, as free men. What shall oppose this spirit, aided by the congenial flame glowing in the breast of every Whig in England, to the amount, I hope, of double the American numbers? Ireland they have to a man. In that country, joined as it is with the cause of the colonies, and placed at their head, the distinction I contend for is and must be observed. This country superintends and controls their trade and navigation, but they tax themselves. And this distinction between external and internal control is sacred and insurmountable; it is involved in the abstract nature of things. Property is private, individual, absolute. Trade is an extended and complicated consideration; it reaches as far as ships can sail or winds can blow; it is a

great and various machine. To regulate the numberless
movements of the several parts, and combine them into effect
for the good of the whole, requires the superintending
wisdom and energy of the supreme power in the empire.
But this supreme power has no effect towards internal taxation, for it does not exist in that relation; there is no such
thing, no such idea in this constitution, as a supreme power
operating upon property. Let this distinction then remain
forever ascertained: taxation is theirs, commercial regulation
is ours. As an American, I would recognize to England her
supreme right of regulating commerce and navigation; as
an Englishman by birth and principle, I recognize to the
Americans their supreme unalienable right in their property,
— a right which they are justified in the defense of to the
last extremity. To maintain this principle is the common
cause of the Whigs on the other side of the Atlantic and on
this. "'Tis liberty to liberty engaged," that they will defend
themselves, their families, and their country. In this great
cause they are immovably allied: it is the alliance of God
and nature, — immovable, eternal, fixed as the firmament
of heaven.

## BIBLIOGRAPHY

*A. Refer-*
*ences.*

**The Union of Scotland and England:** GREEN, *Short History of the
English People*, Chapter IX, sect. 9, pp. 714–715; GARDINER, *A Student's History of England*, pp. 685–686; TERRY, *A History of England*,
pp. 845–849; COLBY, *Selections from the Sources of English History*,
pp. 227–229.

**Walpole's Ministry:** ANDREWS, *History of England*, pp. 437–443;
GREEN, Chapter IX, sect. 10; GARDINER, pp. 712–730; COLBY, pp. 229–
237; KENDALL, *Source Book of English History*, pp. 341–342.

**Balance of Power—Europe at the Opening of the Eighteenth Cen-
tury:** HASSALL, *European History, 1715–1789*, pp. 1–24.

**English Settlements in North America:** GREEN, Chapter VIII,
sect. 4; COLBY, pp. 184–188; KENDALL, pp. 216–219, 222–225.

**Contest between France and England for Colonial Dominion:** GAR-
DINER, pp. 751–767; GREEN, Chapter X, sect. 1; ANDREWS, pp. 445–
454; HASSALL, pp. 241–279; TERRY, pp. 899–910; COLBY, pp. 242–256;
KENDALL, pp. 342–349.

**American Independence:** GREEN, Chapter X, sect. 2; GARDINER, pp. 770–774, 777–798; ANDREWS, pp. 459–467; COLBY, pp. 258–261; KENDALL, pp. 350–360; HASSALL, pp. 332–349.

---

There are several excellent brief accounts of the expansion of England. Perhaps the best introductory outline is WOODWARD, *A Short History of the Expansion of the British Empire*, 2d ed., 1902.

*B. Additional reading in English.*

SEELEY, *Expansion of England*, 1883, is a suggestive but easily overrated book.

MORRIS, *History of Colonization*, 2 vols., 1900. A general sketch of colonization from ancient times. The second volume is largely devoted to England, and is equipped with excellent bibliographies.

Brief general accounts of the expansion of England.

CHEYNEY, *The European Background of American History*, 1904. Especially valuable for the English institutions transplanted in America.

FARRAND, *Basis of American History*, 1904. A critical account of the American world into which the settlers came.

The English in America.

LODGE, *A Short History of the English Colonies in America*, 1881. A useful single-volume work.

THWAITES, *The Colonies, 1492–1750*, 1894, in Epochs of American History. A remarkably compact work, with bibliographies.

EDGAR, *The Struggle for a Continent*, 1902. The best concise history of the Anglo-French contest in America.

LYALL, *The Rise of British Dominion in India*, 1893. The best short account.

British India.

HUNTER, *Brief History of the Indian Peoples*. Especially valuable for native affairs.

There are also useful books by MALLESON: *The Founders of the Indian Empire*, 1882; *History of the French in India*, 1868; and *Final French Struggles in India*, 1878.

There is no satisfactory brief history for the eighteenth century. The great work is that by LECKY, *History of England in the Eighteenth Century*, 8 vols. Not a chronological narrative, but a series of invaluable studies of many aspects of English life.

England in the eighteenth century.

McCARTHY, *The Four Georges*, 2 vols., 1885. May be used in absence of anything better.

SYDNEY, *England in the Eighteenth Century*, 2 vols., 1891. Interesting social history.

MORLEY's *Walpole* and *Burke*, and ROSEBERY's *Pitt* are useful short essays on these statesmen.

# CHAPTER XXXIV

## THE EVE OF THE FRENCH REVOLUTION

### I. THE ANCIEN RÉGIME

The abuses of arbitrary imprisonment by *lettres de cachet* had begun to excite the indignation of the law courts some time before the Revolution, as the following protest of one of them clearly indicates.

*Sire:*

**169. Protest of a French court of law against *lettres de cachet* (1770).**

(Condensed.)

Your Court of Excises,[1] having been impeded in the administration of justice by illegal acts which cannot have emanated from your Majesty personally, have determined that a very humble and very respectful protest should be made to you concerning the matter. . . .

[By means of these arbitrary orders (i.e. the *lettres de cachet*) the most sacred rights are violated, and the victim has no means of learning who is his persecutor. If any one who is able to impose upon your Majesty and procure a *lettre de cachet* is to be shielded from the courts,] how indeed can we be said to live to-day under any laws, sire, since such orders have prodigiously increased of late and are granted for all sorts of reasons and for personal considerations? Formerly they were reserved for affairs of state, and then, sire, it was proper that the courts should respect the necessary secrecy of your administration. Subsequently these orders began to be granted in certain interesting cases, as, for example, when the sovereign was touched by

---

[1] This court (*cour des aides*), as well as the *parlements*, often sent protests to the king, criticising the policy of his ministers and council. The protests were frequently printed, and so served to rouse and cultivate public opinion.

the tears of a family which dreaded disgrace.[1] To-day they are considered necessary every time a common man offers any slight to a person of consideration, — as if persons of quality had not enough advantages already. It is also the usual form of punishment for indiscreet remarks. . . .

These orders signed by your Majesty are often filled in with obscure names of which your Majesty cannot possibly have heard. They are at the disposal of your ministers, and it would appear, in view of the great number which are issued, of their clerks as well. They are confided to officials in both the capital and the provinces, who make use of them in accordance with the suggestions of their subdelegates and other subordinates. They doubtless find their way into many other hands. . . .

The result is, sire, that no citizen in your kingdom can be assured that his liberty will not be sacrificed to a private grudge; for no one is so exalted that he is safe from the ill will of a minister, or so insignificant that he may not incur that of a clerk. The day will come, sire, when the multiplicity of the abuses of the *lettres de cachet* will lead your Majesty to abolish a custom so opposed to the constitution of your kingdom and the liberty which your subjects should enjoy.

Of the hunting rights and royal preserves (*capitaineries*) a celebrated English traveler gives a good account.

The *capitaineries* were a dreadful scourge on all the occupiers of land. By this term is to be understood the paramountship of certain districts granted by the king to princes of the blood, by which they were put in possession of the property of all game, even on lands not belonging to them; and what is very singular, on manors granted long before to individuals; so that the erecting of a district into a *capitainerie* was an annihilation of all manorial rights to game within it. This was a trifling business in comparison to other

170. The hunting preserves in France. (From Arthur Young's *Travels*.)

[1] This refers to the imprisonment of unruly sons or other relatives who were compromising a respectable family by their conduct.

circumstances; for in speaking of the preservation of the game in these *capitaineries* it must be observed that by game must be understood whole droves of wild boars, and herds of deer not confined by any wall or pale, but wandering at pleasure over the whole country, to the destruction of crops, and to the peopling of the galleys by wretched peasants who presumed to kill them in order to save that food which was to support their helpless children.

The game in the *capitainerie* of Montceau, in four parishes only, did mischief to the amount of 184,263 livres per annum. No wonder then that we should find the people asking, "We loudly demand the destruction of all the *capitaineries* and of all the various kinds of game." And what are we to think of demanding as a favor the permission "to thresh their grain, mow their fields, and take away the stubble without regard to the partridge or other game"?[1] Now an English reader will scarcely understand without being told that there were numerous edicts for preserving the game, which prohibited weeding and hoeing lest the young partridges should be disturbed, steeping seed lest it should injure the game, . . . mowing hay, etc., before a certain time so late as to spoil many crops; and taking away the stubble which would deprive the birds of shelter.

## II. Accession of Louis XVI; Marie Antoinette

Louis XV died of smallpox, May 10, 1774. Marie Antoinette, now become queen at eighteen, writes to her mother as follows:

CHOISY, May 14, 1774.

*Madame, my very dear mother:*

Count Mercy[2] has doubtless informed you of the details of our misfortune. Happily his cruel malady left the king

[1] These complaints are from the *cahiers* drawn up for the Estates General in 1789. See *History of Western Europe*, pp. 562 *sq.* (Vol. II, pp. 210 *sq.*). For the abolition of the hunting rights see below, p. 435.

[2] The ambassador of the empire, whom Maria Theresa had selected as the special adviser of her young daughter when she went to France.

fully conscious to the last moment, and his end was very edifying. The new king seems to have gained the heart of the people. Two days before his grandfather's death he had two hundred thousand francs distributed to the poor, which produced a fine effect. Since the late king's death he has worked constantly, and replies with his own hand to the ministers, whom he is not able to see yet, and to many other letters. One thing is certain; he has a taste for economy, and his greatest anxiety is to make his people happy. In short, his eagerness to learn is equal to his need of information, and I trust that God will bless his good will.

171. Marie Antoinette reports to her mother that she is now a queen.

The public are looking for many changes just now. But the king has confined himself to sending away that creature to a convent and driving from court all connected with her. The king owed this example to the people of Versailles, who at the time of the catastrophe attacked Madame de Mazarin, one of the most humble domestics of the favorite. I am often urged to preach clemency to the king toward a number of corrupt souls who have been up to much evil during the last few years. . . .

Madame du Barry sent to a convent.

They have just come to forbid me to visit my Aunt Adelaide, who has a high fever and pain in her loins; they fear smallpox. I tremble and dare not think of the consequences. It is terrible for her to pay so speedily for the sacrifice she has made [in nursing the late king].

I am sincerely delighted that Marshal Lascy was pleased with me. I must confess, my dear mamma, that I was much affected when he came to take leave of me, as I thought how rarely it happened that I saw people of my own country, particularly those who have the additional happiness of approaching you. . . .

The king has left me, as queen, free to fill the vacant positions in my household. I took pleasure in according a mark of attention to the people of Lorraine by selecting Abbé Sabran as my first almoner, — an upright man of exalted birth and already appointed to the bishopric of Nancy, which has just been created.

Although it pleased God to cause me to be born to the station I occupy to-day, I cannot but wonder at the dispensation of Providence, who chose me, the youngest of your children, for the finest kingdom of Europe. I feel more than ever all that I owe to the affection of my august mother, who has been at such pains and trouble to secure this beautiful position for me. I have never so longed to be able to throw myself at her feet, kiss her, show her my whole soul, and let her see how it is filled with respect, love, and gratitude. . . .

[*The king here adds in his own hand:*]

I am very glad to have an opportunity, my dear mamma, to express my love and attachment. I would that I might have your advice in these days which are so full of embarrassment. I should be delighted to be able to satisfy you, and to prove in that way the affection and gratitude that I owe you for granting me your daughter, with whom I could not be better satisfied.

[*The queen then closes:*]

The king would not let my letter go without adding a word for himself. I am sensible that he might have been expected to write a letter of his own, but I beg that my dear mamma will excuse him in view of the great number of things he has to occupy him and also a little on account of his natural timidity and shyness. You can see, dear mamma, by what he says at the end, that while he is fond enough of me he does not spoil me with insipid compliments.

In a letter dated May 15, 1776, Marie Antoinette writes to her mother : "Monsieur de Malesherbes retired from the ministry day before yesterday and was immediately replaced by Monsieur Amelot. Monsieur Turgot was dismissed the same day, and Monsieur de Clugny is to take his place. I confess, dear mamma, that I do not regret the departure of these men, but I had nothing to do with it." Maria Theresa replies with a characteristic warning :

. . . I am very glad that you had nothing to do with the dismissal of the two ministers, who enjoy a high reputation with the public at large and who, in my opinion, have only erred in attempting to do too much at once. You say that you do not regret them. Doubtless you have good reasons; but of late the public no longer praises you as it did, and attributes to you all sorts of little intrigues which would be most unfitting to your station. The king loves you and his ministers should respect you. By asking for nothing contrary to the established order and general welfare, you will make yourself both loved and respected.

172. Maria Theresa warns her daughter of the dangers of levity and dissipation.

My only fear for you (being so young) is an excess of dissipation. You have never cared to read or to apply yourself in any way; this has often troubled me, and accounts for my having tormented you so often with inquiries as to what you were reading. I was so pleased to see you devoting yourself to music. But for a year now there has been no question of either reading or music, and I hear of nothing but racing and hunting, and always without the king and with a lot of ill-chosen young people; all this troubles me very much, loving you, as I do, so dearly. Your sisters-in-law behave very differently, and I must own that all these boisterous diversions in which the king takes no part appear to me unseemly. You will say, " He knows and approves of them." I reply that he is kind and good and that that is all the more reason that you should be circumspect.

### III. The French intervene in the American Revolution

No doubt the influence of the American Revolution upon French affairs has commonly been much exaggerated, since there is every reason to suppose that the example of the colonists did not really modify essentially the trend of affairs in France toward reform. The course of events can be readily explained even if the American war be quite eliminated from consideration.

Yet the embarrassment of the treasury which resulted from France's intervention in the war, and the liberal ideas which it suggested to some of the nobility, may have hastened the French Revolution. The count of Ségur, looking back long years after the events he narrates, thus describes the intervention of France in the struggle of the American colonists.

173. How France became interested in the American Revolution. (From the *Mémoires* of Ségur.)

At this time liberty, which had been hushed in the civilized world for so many centuries, awoke in another hemisphere and engaged in a glorious struggle against an ancient monarchy which enjoyed the most redoubtable power. England, confident of its strength, had subsidized and dispatched forty thousand men to America to stifle this liberty in its cradle; but a whole nation which longs for freedom is scarce to be vanquished.

The bravery of these new republicans won esteem in all parts of Europe and enlisted the sympathies of the friends of justice and humanity. The young men especially, who although brought up in the midst of monarchies had by a singular anomaly been nurtured in admiration for the great writers of antiquity and the heroes of Greece and Rome, carried to the point of enthusiasm the interest which the American insurrection inspired in them.

The French government, which desired the weakening of the power of England, was gradually drawn on by this liberal opinion, which showed itself in so energetic a manner. At first it secretly furnished arms, munitions, and money to the Americans, or permitted supplies to reach them by French ships; but it was too weak to venture to declare itself openly in their favor, affecting on the contrary an appearance of strict neutrality and so far blinding itself as to imagine that its secret measures would not be suspected, and that it might ruin its rival without incurring the danger of meeting it in the open field. Such an illusion could not last long, and the English cabinet was too clear-sighted to let us gain the advantages of a war without incurring any of its risks.

The veil became more and more transparent daily. Soon the American envoys, Silas Deane and Arthur Lee, arrived in Paris, and shortly after the famous Benjamin Franklin joined them. It would be difficult to express the enthusiasm and favor with which they were welcomed in France, into the midst of an old monarchy, — these envoys of a people in insurrection against their king. Nothing could be more striking than the contrast between the luxury of our capital, the elegance of our fashions, the magnificence of Versailles, the polished but haughty arrogance of our nobles, — in short all those living signs of the monarchical pride of Louis XIV, — with the almost rustic dress, the simple if proud demeanor, the frank, direct speech, the plain, unpowdered hair, and, finally, that flavor of antiquity which seemed to bring suddenly within our walls and into the midst of the soft and servile civilization of the seventeenth century these sage contemporaries of Plato, or republicans of Cato's or Fabius' time.

This unexpected sight delighted us the more both because it was novel and because it came at just the period when our literature and philosophy had spread everywhere among us a desire for reform, a leaning toward innovation, and a lively love for liberty. The clash of arms served to excite still more the ardor of war-loving young men, since the deliberate caution of our ministers irritated us, and we were weary of a long peace which had lasted more than ten years. Every one was burning with a desire to repay the affronts of the last war, to fight the English, and to fly to the succor of the Americans. . . .

The young French officers, who breathed nothing but war, hastened to the American envoys, questioned them upon the situation, the resources of Congress, the means of defense, and demanded all the various bits of news which were constantly being received from that great theater where freedom was fighting so valiantly against British tyranny. . . . Silas Deane and Arthur Lee did not disguise the fact that the aid of some well-trained officers would be both agreeable and useful. They even informed us that they were authorized to promise to those who would embrace their cause a rank appropriate to their services.

The American troops already included in their ranks several European volunteers whom the love of glory and independence had attracted. . . . The first three Frenchmen of distinguished rank at court who offered the aid of their service to the Americans were the marquis of Lafayette, the viscount of Noailles, and myself.

## IV. THE PEOPLE OF FRANCE

**174. Extracts from Arthur Young's travels.**

Of all the descriptions that we have of the general condition of the French people upon the eve of the Revolution, the most important and interesting is Arthur Young's account of his travels in France during the years 1787, 1788, and 1789. Young was an honest and observant English gentleman farmer, whose aim was to ascertain "the cultivation, wealth, resources, and national prosperity" of France, which were, as he foresaw, to be fundamentally changed by the Revolution then under way. His book, first published in 1792, met with immediate success, and still fascinates even the casual reader.

In 1787 Arthur Young visited Paris and Versailles, then traveled southward as far as the Pyrenees.

**Young's impressions of Béarn.**

[*August 11.*] Take the road to Lourdes, where is a castle on a rock, garrisoned for the mere purpose of keeping state prisoners sent hither by *lettres de cachet*. Seven or eight are known to be here at present; thirty have been here at a time; and many for life, — torn by the relentless hand of jealous tyranny from the bosom of domestic comfort; from wives, children, friends, and hurried for crimes unknown to themselves — more probably for virtues — to languish in this detested abode of misery, and die of despair. O liberty! liberty! And yet this is the mildest government of any considerable country in Europe, our own excepted. The dispensations of Providence seem to have permitted the human race to exist only as the prey of tyrants, as it has made pigeons for the prey of hawks. . . .

[*The 12th.*] Pau is a considerable town, that has a parliament and a linen manufacture; but it is more famous for being the birthplace of Henry IV. I viewed the castle, and was shown, as all travelers are, the room in which that amiable prince was born, and the cradle — the shell of a tortoise — in which he was nursed. What an effect on posterity have great and distinguished talents! This is a considerable town, but I question whether anything would ever carry a stranger to it but its possessing the cradle of a favorite character.

Take the road to Moneng [Monein] and come presently to a scene which was so new to me in France that I could hardly believe my own eyes. A succession of many well-built, tight, and comfortable farming cottages, built of stone and covered with tiles; each having its little garden, inclosed by clipped thorn hedges, with plenty of peach and other fruit trees, some fine oaks scattered in the hedges, and young trees nursed up with so much care that nothing but the fostering attention of the owner could effect anything like it. To every house belongs a farm, perfectly well inclosed, with grass borders mown and neatly kept around the cornfields, with gates to pass from one inclosure to another. The men are all dressed with red caps, like the highlanders of Scotland. There are some parts of England (where small yeomen still remain) that resemble this country of Béarn; but we have very little that is equal to what I have seen in this ride of twelve miles from Pau to Moneng. It is all in the hands of little proprietors, without the farms being so small as to occasion a vicious and miserable population. An air of neatness, warmth, and comfort breathes over the whole. It is visible in their new-built houses and stables, in their little gardens, in their hedges, in the courts before their doors, even in the coops for their poultry and the sties for their hogs. A peasant does not think of rendering his pig comfortable if his own happiness hangs by the thread of a nine

years' lease. We are now in Béarn, within a few miles of
the cradle of Henry IV. Do they inherit these blessings
from that good prince? The benignant genius of that good
monarch seems to reign still over the country; each peasant
has the fowl in the pot. . . .

[*The 13th.*] The agreeable scene of yesterday continues :
many small properties, and every appearance of rural happiness.

In September, 1788, Young found himself in Brittany.

Brittany.

To Combourg. The country has a savage aspect; husbandry not much further advanced, at least in skill, than
among the Hurons, which appears incredible amidst inclosures. The people almost as wild as their country, and their
town of Combourg one of the most brutal, filthy places that
can be seen ; mud houses, no windows, and a pavement so
broken as to impede all passengers, but ease none. Yet here
is a chateau, and inhabited. Who is this Monsieur de Cha-
teaubriant, the owner, that has nerves strung for a residence
amidst such filth and poverty? . . .

To Montauban. The poor people seem poor indeed ; the
children terribly ragged, — if possible, worse clad than if
with no clothes at all ; as to shoes and stockings, they are
luxuries. A beautiful girl of six or seven years playing with
a stick, and smiling under such a bundle of rags as made
my heart ache to see her. They did not beg, and when I
gave them anything seemed more surprised than obliged.
One third of what I have seen of this province seems uncul-
tivated, and nearly all of it in misery. What have kings,
and ministers, and parliaments, and states to answer for
their prejudices, seeing millions of hands that would be
industrious idle and starving through the execrable maxims
of despotism, or the equally detestable prejudices of a feudal
nobility. Sleep at the *Lion d'Or*, at Montauban, an abominable hole.

Thomas Jefferson was also traveling in France just
before the Revolution. He writes from Nice to a friend,
April 11, 1787 :

In the great cities I go to see what travelers think alone worthy of being seen; but I make a job of it and generally gulp it all down in a day. On the other hand, I am never satiated with rambling through the fields and farms, examining the culture and cultivators with a degree of curiosity which makes some take me for a fool, and others to be much wiser than I am. I have been pleased to find among the people a less degree of physical misery than I had expected. They are generally well clothed and have a plenty of food, — not animal, indeed, but vegetable, which is just as wholesome. Perhaps they are overworked, the excess of the rent required by the landlord obliging them to too many hours of labor in order to produce that and wherewith to feed and clothe themselves. The soil of Burgundy and Champagne I have found more universally good than I had expected; and as I could not help making a comparison with England, I found that comparison more unfavorable to the latter than is generally admitted. The soil, the climate, and the productions are superior to those of England, and the husbandry as good except in one point, that of manure.

175. Jefferson finds less misery in France than he expected.

## V. Voltaire and Rousseau

In his famous *Handy Philosophic Dictionary*, a little volume of essays on a variety of themes, published anonymously in 1764, Voltaire gives under the word "law" his ideas of the reform demanded in church and state. It will be noted that he seems here to have no quarrel with religion, but only with what he regards as the encroachments of the clergy on the rights of the state.

No law made by the Church should ever have the least force unless expressly sanctioned by the government. It was owing to this precaution that Athens and Rome escaped all religious quarrels.

Such religious quarrels are the trait of barbarous nations or such as have become barbarous.

176. Voltaire's views of the relation of church and state.

The civil magistrate alone may permit or prohibit labor on religious festivals, since it is not the function of the priest to forbid men to cultivate their fields.

Civil
marriage.

Everything relating to marriage should depend entirely upon the civil magistrate. The priests should confine themselves to the august function of blessing the union.

The Church's
regulations
regarding
usury.

Lending money at interest should be regulated entirely by the civil law, since trade is governed by civil law.

All ecclesiastics should be subject in every case to the government, since they are subjects of the state.

Payment of
annates to
the pope.

Never should the ridiculous and shameful custom be maintained of paying to a foreign priest the first year's revenue of land given to a priest by his fellow-citizens.

No priest can deprive a citizen of the least of his rights on the ground that the citizen is a sinner, since the priest — himself a sinner — should pray for other sinners, not judge them.

All should
pay taxes.

Officials, laborers, and priests should all alike pay the taxes of the state, since they all alike belong to the state.

Uniformity.

There should be but one standard of weights and measures and one system of law.

Let the punishment of criminals be useful. A man when hanged is good for nothing : a man condemned to hard labor continues to serve his country and furnish a living lesson.

Every law should be clear, uniform, and precise. To interpret law is almost always to corrupt it.

Nothing should be regarded as infamous except vice.

The taxes should never be otherwise than proportional to the resources of him who pays.

Among Rousseau's writings the most permanently influential is his *Émile, or Education*. This opens with his protest against the artificiality of the civilization which he saw about him, and his oft-repeated exhortation to return to nature as the safest guide.

All things are good as their Author made them, but everything degenerates in the hands of man. By man our native soil is forced to nourish plants brought from foreign regions, and one tree is made to bear the fruit of another. Man brings about a general confusion of elements, climates, and seasons; he mutilates his dogs, his horses, and his slaves; he defaces and confounds everything, and seems to delight only in monsters and deformity. He is not content with anything as Nature left it, not even with man, whom he must train for his service like a saddle horse, and twist in his own particular way like a tree in his garden.

177. Rousseau's summons to turn back to nature.

Yet without this interference matters would be still worse than they are, for our species cannot remain half made over. As things now are, a man left to himself from his birth would, in his association with others, prove the most preposterous creature possible. The prejudices, authority, necessity, and example, and, in short, the vicious social institutions in which we find ourselves submerged, would stifle everything natural in him and yet give him nothing in return. He would be like a shrub which has sprung up by accident in the middle of the highway to perish by being thrust this way and that and trampled upon by passers-by. . . .

To form this rare creature, man, what have we to do? Much, doubtless, but chiefly to prevent anything being done. . . . In the natural order of things, all men being equal, their common vocation is manhood, and whoever is well trained for that cannot fulfill any vocation badly which demands manhood. Whether my pupil be destined for the army, the church, or the bar, concerns me but little. Before he is called to the career chosen by his parents, Nature summons him to the duties of human life. To live is the trade I wish to teach him. . . . All our wisdom consists in servile prejudices; all our customs are but suggestion, anxiety, and constraint. Civilized man is born, lives, dies in a state of slavery. At his birth he is sewed in swaddling clothes; at his death he is nailed in a coffin; and as long as he preserves the human form he is fettered by our institutions. It is said that nurses sometimes claim to give the infant's head a better form by kneading it, and we permit them to do this! It would appear that our heads were badly fashioned by the Author of Nature, and that they need to be made over outwardly by the midwife and inwardly by philosophers! The Caribbeans are more fortunate than we by half. . . . Observe Nature and follow the path she traces for you!

## VI. Turgot

Turgot, immediately after learning from Louis XVI that he had been appointed comptroller general, wrote the following instructive and touching letter to that inefficient young monarch, who was so ready to desert him a few months later.

COMPIÈGNE, August 24, 1774.

*Sire :*

**178. Turgot's letter to the king upon assuming office (August, 1774).**

Having just come from the private interview with which your Majesty has honored me, still full of the anxiety produced by the immensity of the duties now imposed upon me, agitated by all the feelings excited by the touching kindness with which you have encouraged me, I hasten to convey to you my respectful gratitude and the devotion of my whole life.

Your Majesty has been good enough to permit me to place on record the engagement you have taken upon you to sustain me in the execution of those plans of economy which are at all times, and to-day more than ever, an indispensable necessity. . . . At this moment, sire, I confine myself to recalling to you these three items :

No bankruptcy.

No increase of taxes.

No loans.

No *bankruptcy*, either avowed or disguised by illegal reductions.

No *increase of taxes;* the reason for this lying in the condition of your people, and, still more, in that of your Majesty's own generous heart.

No *loans;* because every loan always diminishes the free revenue and necessitates, at the end of a certain time, either bankruptcy or the increase of taxes. In times of peace it is permissible to borrow only in order to liquidate old debts, or in order to redeem other loans contracted on less advantageous terms.

To meet these three points there is but one means. It is to reduce expenditure below the revenue, and sufficiently below it to insure each year a saving of twenty millions, to be applied to redemption of the old debts. Without that, the first gunshot will force the state into bankruptcy.

The question will be asked incredulously, "On what can we retrench?" and each one, speaking for his own department, will maintain that nearly every particular item of expense is indispensable. They will be able to allege very good reasons, but these must all yield to the absolute necessity of economy. . . .

These are the matters which I have been permitted to recall to your Majesty. You will not forget that in accepting the place of comptroller general I have felt the full value of the confidence with which you honor me; I have felt that you intrust to me the happiness of your people, and, if it be permitted to me to say so, the care of promoting among your people the love of your person and of your authority.

At the same time I feel all the danger to which I expose myself. I foresee that I shall be alone in fighting against abuses of every kind, against the power of those who profit by these abuses, against the crowd of prejudiced people who oppose themselves to all reform, and who are such powerful instruments in the hands of interested parties for perpetuating the disorder. I shall have to struggle even against the natural goodness and generosity of your Majesty, and of the persons who are most dear to you. I shall be feared, hated even, by nearly all the court, by all who solicit favors. They will impute to me all the refusals; they will describe me as a hard man because I shall have advised your Majesty that you ought not to enrich even those that you love at the expense of your people's subsistence.

*Turgot foresees the danger of opposition to all reforms.*

And this people, for whom I shall sacrifice myself, are so easily deceived that perhaps I shall encounter their hatred by the very measures I take to defend them against exactions.

I shall be calumniated (having, perhaps, appearances against me) in order to deprive me of your Majesty's confidence. I shall not regret losing a place which I never solicited. I am ready to resign it to your Majesty as soon as I can no longer hope to be useful in it. . . .

Your Majesty will remember that it is upon the faith of your promises made to me that I charge myself with a burden perhaps beyond my strength, and it is to yourself personally, to the upright man, the just and good man, rather than to the king, that I give myself.

I venture to repeat here what you have already been kind enough to hear and approve of. The affecting kindness with which you condescended to press my hands within your own, as if sealing my devotion, will never be effaced from my memory. It will sustain my courage. It has forever united my personal happiness with the interest, the glory, and the happiness of your Majesty. It is with these sentiments that I am, sire, etc.

## BIBLIOGRAPHY

*A. References.*

**The Ancien Régime:** MATHEWS, *The French Revolution*, pp. 1–30; LOWELL, *The Eve of the French Revolution*, pp. 4–24; *Cambridge Modern History*, Vol. VIII, pp. 36–65.

**Church and Clergy:** MATHEWS, pp. 42–51; LOWELL, pp. 25–69.

**The Philosophers:** MATHEWS, pp. 52–72; LOWELL, pp. 243–273; *Cambridge Modern History*, Vol. VIII, pp. 1–35. Extracts from the writings of some of the more noted philosophers are given in *Translations and Reprints*, Vol. VI, No. 1.

**Turgot and Necker:** MATHEWS, pp. 91–101; *Cambridge Modern History*, Vol. VIII, pp. 66–78.

**Rousseau:** LOWELL, pp. 274–321.

**Early Years of Louis XVI's Reign:** HASSALL, *Balance of Power* (*European History, 1715–1789*), pp. 401–424; *Cambridge Modern History*, Vol. VIII, pp. 79–98.

_____

*B. Additional reading in English.*

MACLEHOSE, *The Last Days of the French Monarchy.* Well illustrated. This and LOWELL'S *Eve of the French Revolution* are the best general accounts to be had in English of the institutions of the old monarchy.

DE TOCQUEVILLE, *State of Society in France before the Revolution.* A very remarkable philosophical account of the character and policy of the French government. This should be studied with the utmost care by all students of the period. A new edition of the French original, with introduction and notes, Oxford, Clarendon Press, 1904.

TAINE, *The Ancient Régime.* A brilliant work. The chapters on the society, literature, and philosophy of the period are the best; those on the economic conditions are disappointing.

ROCQUAIN, *The Revolutionary Spirit before the Revolution,* 1894. A condensation, omitting the valuable notes of the original French edition. A suggestive account of the various disturbances preceding the disorders of the Revolution itself.

MORLEY, JOHN, *Voltaire,* a brilliant essay; *Rousseau,* 2 vols.; *Diderot and the Encyclopædists,* 2 vols.; *Critical Miscellanies,* 3 vols., containing essays on Turgot and other important persons of the period. Mr. Morley's writings are noteworthy not only for their scholarship and distinguished style but also for the fundamental sympathy between his views and many of those of the eighteenth-century philosophers.

SOREL, *Montesquieu.* A useful little biography.

SAY, LÉON, *Turgot.* Very valuable review of Turgot's work.

VOLTAIRE'S writings (e.g. *The Philosophical Dictionary*), MONTESQUIEU'S *Spirit of Laws* (in the Bohn Library), ROUSSEAU'S *Social Contract* and *Émile* are readily procured in English.   [Sources in English.]

STEPHENS, W. W., *Life and Writings of Turgot.* Contains extracts from the preambles to Turgot's decrees.

YOUNG, ARTHUR, *Travels in France* (Bohn Library). See above, p. 420.

CAMPAN, MADAME DE, *Memoirs.*

*Translations and Reprints,* Vol. VI, No. 1, in which Professor Whitcomb gives some interesting extracts from the writings of the philosophers; the same, Vol. V, No. 2, *Protest of the Cour des Aides of 1775.* A very extraordinary indictment of the *Ancien Régime* presented to the king by his magistrates during Turgot's administration. No single document on the *Ancien Régime* is better worth careful study.

# CHAPTER XXXV

## THE FRENCH REVOLUTION

### I. THE CAHIERS OF 1789

The *cahiers*, drawn up in accordance with an ancient custom by the three orders of the realm, form one of the most extraordinary historical documents of all time. The conditions under which they were drafted were, on the whole, favorable to a frank and general expression on the part of all classes of the French people of their suggestions for reform. A portion of one of the *cahiers* of the third estate, selected somewhat at random, is given below.[1]

**179. *Cahier* of the third estate of Carcassonne.** Cahier *of the grievances, complaints, and protests of the electoral district of Carcassonne, drawn up by the commissioners named by the general assembly of the third estate and based upon the various* cahiers *received from the several communities of the said district:*

. . . In view of the obligation imposed by his Majesty's command that the third estate of this district should confide to his paternal ear the causes of the ills which afflict them and the means by which they may be remedied or moderated, they believe that they are fulfilling the duties of faithful subjects and zealous citizens in submitting to the consideration of the nation, and to the sentiments of justice and affection which his Majesty entertains for his subjects, the following:

[1] A *cahier* of a single order in one electoral district would fill several pages of this volume, and all those prepared to be taken to Versailles occupy together, when printed, six compactly printed quarto volumes. Professor Whitcomb has translated a typical *cahier* of each of the orders in *Translations and Reprints*, Vol. IV, No. 5.

1. Public worship should be confined to the Roman Catholic apostolic religion, to the exclusion of all other forms of worship; its extension should be promoted and the most efficient measures taken to reëstablish the discipline of the Church and increase its prestige.

Roman Catholic religion.

2. Nevertheless the civil rights of those of the king's subjects who are not Catholics should be confirmed, and they should be admitted to positions and offices in the public administration, without however extending this privilege — which reason and humanity alike demand for them — to judicial or police functions or to those of public instruction.

Treatment of non-Catholics.

3. The nation should consider some means of abolishing the annates and all other dues paid to the holy see, to the prejudice and against the protests of the whole French people. . . .

Abolition of papal dues.

[Pluralities should be prohibited, monasteries reduced in numbers, and holidays suppressed or decreased.]

7. The rights which have just been restored to the nation should be consecrated as fundamental principles of the monarchy, and their perpetual and unalterable enjoyment should be assured by a solemn law, which should so define the rights both of the monarch and of the people that their violation shall hereafter be impossible.

8. Among these rights the following should be especially noted: the nation should hereafter be subject only to such laws and taxes as it shall itself freely ratify.

Granting of subsidies.

9. The meetings of the Estates General of the kingdom should be fixed for definite periods, and the subsidies judged necessary for the support of the state and the public service should be voted for no longer a period than to the close of the year in which the next meeting of the Estates General is to occur.

Regular meetings of the Estates General.

10. In order to assure to the third estate the influence to which it is entitled in view of the number of its members, the amount of its contributions to the public treasury, and the manifold interests which it has to defend or promote in the national assemblies, its votes in the assembly should be taken and counted by head.

Vote by head.

No exemptions from taxes.

11. No order, corporation, or individual citizen may lay claim to any pecuniary exemptions. . . . All taxes should be assessed on the same system throughout the nation.

Privileges of the nobility in holding office to be abolished.

12. The due exacted from commoners holding fiefs should be abolished, and also the general or particular regulations which exclude members of the third estate from certain positions, offices, and ranks which have hitherto been bestowed on nobles either for life or hereditarily. A law should be passed declaring members of the third estate qualified to fill all such offices for which they are judged to be personally fitted.

*Lettres de cachet.*

13. Since individual liberty is intimately associated with national liberty, his Majesty is hereby petitioned not to permit that it be hereafter interfered with by arbitrary orders for imprisonment. . . .

Freedom of the press.

14. Freedom should be granted also to the press, which should however be subjected, by means of strict regulations, to the principles of religion, morality, and public decency. . . .

## II. The Opening of the Estates General in 1789

Arthur Young (see above, page 420) arrived in Paris about a month after the Estates had come together. He reports (June 8, 1789):

180. Arthur Young visits the National Assembly (June, 1789).

The king, court, nobility, clergy, army, and parliament [i.e. *parlements*] are nearly in the same situation. All these consider with equal dread the ideas of liberty now afloat, except the first, who, for reasons obvious to those who know his character, troubles himself little, even with circumstances that concern his power the most intimately. . . .

The innumerable pamphlets.

The business going forward at present in the pamphlet shops of Paris is incredible. I went to the Palais Royal to see what new things were published, and to procure a catalogue of all. Every hour produces something new. Thirteen came out to-day, sixteen yesterday, and ninety-two last week. Nineteen twentieths of these productions are in favor of liberty, and commonly violent against the clergy and the nobility. I have to-day bespoke many of this description that have reputation ; but inquiring for such as had appeared on the other side of the question, to my astonishment I find there are but two or three that have merit enough to be known.

But the coffee-houses in the Palais Royal present yet more singular and astonishing spectacles : they are not only crowded within, but other expectant crowds are at the doors and windows, listening *à gorge déployé* to certain orators, who from chairs or tables harangue each his little audience. The eagerness with which they are heard, and the thunder of applause they receive for every sentiment of more than common hardiness or violence against the present government, cannot easily be imagined. I am all amazement at the ministry permitting such nests and hotbeds of sedition and revolt, which disseminate amongst the people every hour principles that by and by must be opposed with vigor; and therefore it seems little short of madness to allow the propagation at present.

*The speakers at the Palais Royal in Paris.*

Everything conspires to render the present period in France critical. The want of bread is terrible; accounts arrive every moment from the provinces of riots and disturbances, and calling in the military to preserve the peace of the markets. . . .

*Scarcity of food.*

*June 15.* This has been a rich day, and such an one as ten years ago none could believe would ever arrive in France ; a very important debate being expected on what, in our House of Commons, would be termed the state of the nation. My friend, Monsieur Lazowski, and myself were at Versailles at eight in the morning. We went immediately to the hall of the states to secure good seats in the gallery ; we found some deputies already there, and a pretty numerous audience collected. The room is too large ; none but stentorian lungs or the finest, clearest voices can be heard. However, the very size of the apartment, which admits two thousand people, gave a dignity to the scene. It was indeed an interesting one. The spectacle of the representatives of twenty-five millions of people, just emerging from the evils of two

*Arthur Young describes the important session of June 15.*

hundred years of arbitrary power, and rising to the blessings of a freer constitution, assembled with open doors under the eye of the public, was framed to call into animated feelings every latent spark, every emotion of a liberal bosom; to banish whatever ideas might intrude of their being a people too often hostile to my own country, and to dwell with pleasure on the glorious idea of happiness to a great nation. . . .

Monsieur l'Abbé Sieyès opened the debate. He is one of the most zealous sticklers for the popular cause, — being in fact a violent republican. . . .

Mirabeau's speech.

Monsieur de Mirabeau spoke without notes for near an hour, with a warmth, animation, and eloquence that entitle him to the reputation of an undoubted orator. He opposed the words "known" and "verified," in the proposition of Abbé Sieyès, with great force of reasoning, and proposed in lieu that they should declare themselves simply *Représentatives du peuple François;* that no *veto* should exist against their resolves in any other assembly; that all [existing] taxes are illegal, but should be granted during the present sessions of the states, and no longer; that the debt of the king should become the debt of the nation, and be secured on funds accordingly. Monsieur de Mirabeau was well heard, and his proposition much applauded.

Disorderly method of procedure in the Assembly.

In regard to their general method of proceeding, there are two circumstances in which they are very deficient. The spectators in the galleries are allowed to interfere in the debates by clapping their hands, and other noisy expressions of approbation : this is grossly indecent; it is also dangerous; for, if they are permitted to express approbation, they are, by parity of reason, allowed expressions of dissent, and they may hiss as well as clap; which it is said they have sometimes done : this would be to overrule the debate and influence the deliberations.

Another circumstance is the want of order among themselves. More than once to-day there were an hundred members on their legs at a time, and Monsieur Bailly absolutely without power to keep order.

## III. The Decree abolishing the Feudal System
### (August 11, 1789)

The abolition of the feudal system, which took place during the famous night session of August 4–5, 1789, was caused by the reading of a report on the misery and disorder which prevailed in the provinces. The report declares that "Letters from all the provinces indicate that property of all kinds is a prey to the most criminal violence; on all sides châteaux are being burned, convents destroyed, and farms abandoned to pillage. The taxes, the feudal dues, all are extinct; the laws are without force, and the magistrates without authority." With the hope of pacifying and encouraging the people, the Assembly, in a fervor of enthusiasm and excitement, straightway abolished many of the ancient abuses. The document here given is the revised decree, completed a week later.

ARTICLE I. The National Assembly hereby completely abolishes the feudal system. It decrees that, among the existing rights and dues, both feudal and *censuel*,[1] all those originating in or representing real or personal serfdom shall be abolished without indemnification. All other dues are declared redeemable, the terms and mode of redemption to be fixed by the National Assembly. Those of the said dues which are not extinguished by this decree shall continue to be collected until indemnification shall take place.

> 181. Decree abolishing the feudal system.

II. The exclusive right to maintain pigeon houses and dovecotes is abolished. The pigeons shall be confined during the seasons fixed by the community. During such periods they shall be looked upon as game, and every one shall have the right to kill them upon his own land.

> Extinction of all hunting rights.

---

[1] This refers to the *cens*, a perpetual due similar to the payments made by English copyholders.

III. The exclusive right to hunt and to maintain un-inclosed warrens is likewise abolished, and every landowner shall have the right to kill, or to have destroyed on his own land, all kinds of game, observing, however, such police regulations as may be established with a view to the safety of the public.

All hunting *capitaineries*,[1] including the royal forests, and all hunting rights under whatever denomination, are likewise abolished. Provision shall be made, however, in a manner compatible with the regard due to property and liberty, for maintaining the personal pleasures of the king.

The president of the Assembly shall be commissioned to ask of the king the recall of those sent to the galleys or exiled, simply for violations of the hunting regulations, as well as for the release of those at present imprisoned for offenses of this kind, and the dismissal of such cases as are now pending.

**Manorial courts suppressed.**

IV. All manorial courts are hereby suppressed without indemnification. But the magistrates of these courts shall continue to perform their functions until such time as the National Assembly shall provide for the establishment of a new judicial system.

**Tithes abolished.**

V. Tithes of every description, . . . are abolished, on condition, however, that some other method be devised to provide for the expenses of divine worship, the support of the officiating clergy, for the assistance of the poor, for repairs and rebuilding of churches and parsonages, and for the maintenance of all institutions, seminaries, schools, academies, asylums, and organizations to which the present funds are devoted. Until such provision shall be made and the former possessors shall enter upon the enjoyment of an income on the new system, the National Assembly decrees that the said tithes shall continue to be collected according to law and in the customary manner.

VI. All perpetual ground rents, payable either in money or in kind, of whatever nature they may be, whatever their

[1] See above, pp. 413 *sq.*

origin and to whomsoever they may be due, . . . shall be redeemable at a rate fixed by the Assembly. No due shall in the future be created which is not redeemable.

VII. The sale of judicial and municipal offices shall be abolished forthwith. Justice shall be dispensed *gratis*. Nevertheless the magistrates at present holding such offices shall continue to exercise their functions and to receive their emoluments until the Assembly shall have made provision for indemnifying them.

*Sale of offices discontinued.*

VIII. The fees of the country priests are abolished, and shall be discontinued so soon as provision shall be made for increasing the minimum salary [*portion congrue*] of the parish priests and the payment to the curates. A regulation shall be drawn up to determine the status of the priests in the towns.

IX. Pecuniary privileges, personal or real, in the payment of taxes are abolished forever. Taxes shall be collected from all the citizens, and from all property, in the same manner and in the same form. Plans shall be considered by which the taxes shall be paid proportionally by all, even for the last six months of the current year.

*Exemptions from taxation abolished.*

X. Inasmuch as a national constitution and public liberty are of more advantage to the provinces than the privileges which some of these enjoy, and inasmuch as the surrender of such privileges is essential to the intimate union of all parts of the realm, it is decreed that all the peculiar privileges, pecuniary or otherwise, of the provinces, principalities, districts, cantons, cities, and communes, are once for all abolished and are absorbed into the law common to all Frenchmen.

*All local differences in the law abolished.*

XI. All citizens, without distinction of birth, are eligible to any office or dignity, whether ecclesiastical, civil, or military; and no profession shall imply any derogation.

XII. Hereafter no remittances shall be made for annates or for any other purpose to the court of Rome, the vice legation at Avignon, or to the nunciature at Lucerne. The clergy of the diocese shall apply to their bishops in regard to the filling of benefices and dispensations, the which shall

*Papal powers reduced*

be granted *gratis* without regard to reservations, expectancies, and papal months, all the churches of France enjoying ᵗhe same freedom.

XIII. [This article abolishes various ecclesiastical dues.]

Pluralities. XIV. Pluralities shall not be permitted hereafter in cases where the revenue from the benefice or benefices held shall exceed the sum of three thousand livres. Nor shall any individual be allowed to enjoy several pensions from benefices, or a pension and a benefice, if the revenue which he already enjoys from such sources exceeds the same sum of three thousand livres.

Pensions. XV. The National Assembly shall consider, in conjunction with the king, the report which is to be submitted to it relating to pensions, favors, and salaries, with a view to suppressing all such as are not deserved, and reducing those which shall prove excessive; and the amount shall be fixed which the king may in the future disburse for this purpose.

XVI. The National Assembly decrees that a medal shall be struck in memory of the recent grave and important deliberations for the welfare of France, and that a Te Deum shall be chanted in gratitude in all the parishes and the churches of France.

XVII. The National Assembly solemnly proclaims the king, Louis XVI, the *Restorer of French Liberty*.

XVIII. The National Assembly shall present itself in a body before the king, in order to submit to him the decrees which have just been passed, to tender to him the tokens of its most respectful gratitude, and to pray him to permit the Te Deum to be chanted in his chapel, and to be present himself at this service.

XIX. The National Assembly shall consider, immediately after the constitution, the drawing up of the laws necessary for the development of the principles which it has laid down in the present decree. The latter shall be transmitted by the deputies without delay to all the provinces, together with the decree of the 10th of this month, in order that it may be printed, published, read from the parish pulpits, and posted up wherever it shall be deemed necessary.

IV. Declaration of the Rights of Man and of the Citizen

A declaration of the rights of man, which had been demanded by many of the *cahiers*, was the part of the new constitution which the Assembly decided (August 4) should be first drawn up. The members recognized that they were imitating an American precedent in doing this. Our first state constitutions, several of which were preceded by elaborate bills of rights, had very early been translated into French.

Almost every one of the articles in the declaration recalls some abuse of the *Ancien Régime*. This document has exercised a great influence upon Europe, and was imitated in many of the constitutions of the nineteenth century.

The representatives of the French people, organized as a National Assembly, believing that the ignorance, neglect, or contempt of the rights of man are the sole cause of public calamities and of the corruption of governments, have determined to set forth in a solemn declaration the natural, inalienable, and sacred rights of man, in order that this declaration, being constantly before all the members of the social body, shall remind them continually of their rights and duties; in order that the acts of the legislative power, as well as those of the executive power, may be compared at any moment with the objects and purposes of all political institutions and may thus be more respected; and, lastly, in order that the grievances of the citizens, based hereafter upon simple and incontestable principles, shall tend to the maintenance of the constitution and redound to the happiness of all. Therefore the National Assembly recognizes and proclaims, in the presence and under the auspices of the Supreme Being, the following rights of man and of the citizen:

182. Declaration of the rights of man.

ARTICLE 1. Men are born and remain free and equal in rights. Social distinctions may be founded only upon the general good.

2. The aim of all political association is the preservation of the natural and imprescriptible rights of man. These rights are liberty, property, security, and resistance to oppression.

3. The principle of all sovereignty resides essentially in the nation. No body nor individual may exercise any authority which does not proceed directly from the nation.

4. Liberty consists in the freedom to do everything which injures no one else; hence the exercise of the natural rights of each man has no limits except those which assure to the other members of the society the enjoyment of the same rights. These limits can only be determined by law.

5. Law can only prohibit such actions as are hurtful to society. Nothing may be prevented which is not forbidden by law, and no one may be forced to do anything not provided for by law.

6. Law is the expression of the general will. Every citizen has a right to participate personally, or through his representative, in its formation. It must be the same for all, whether it protects or punishes. All citizens, being equal in the eyes of the law, are equally eligible to all dignities and to all public positions and occupations, according to their abilities, and without distinction except that of their virtues and talents.

7. No person shall be accused, arrested, or imprisoned except in the cases and according to the forms prescribed by law. Any one soliciting, transmitting, executing, or causing to be executed, any arbitrary order, shall be punished. But any citizen summoned or arrested in virtue of the law shall submit without delay, as resistance constitutes an offense.

8. The law shall provide for such punishments only as are strictly and obviously necessary, and no one shall suffer punishment except it be legally inflicted in virtue of a law passed and promulgated before the commission of the offense.

9. As all persons are held innocent until they shall have been declared guilty, if arrest shall be deemed indispensable, all harshness not essential to the securing of the prisoner's person shall be severely repressed by law.

10. No one shall be disquieted on account of his opinions, including his religious views, provided their manifestation does not disturb the public order established by law.

11. The free communication of ideas and opinions is one of the most precious of the rights of man. Every citizen may, accordingly, speak, write, and print with freedom, but shall be responsible for such abuses of this freedom as shall be defined by law.

12. The security of the rights of man and of the citizen requires public military forces. These forces are, therefore, established for the good of all and not for the personal advantage of those to whom they shall be intrusted.

13. A common contribution is essential for the maintenance of the public forces and for the cost of administration. This should be equitably distributed among all the citizens in proportion to their means.

14. All the citizens have a right to decide, either personally or by their representatives, as to the necessity of the public contribution; to grant this freely; to know to what uses it is put; and to fix the proportion, the mode of assessment and of collection and the duration of the taxes.

15. Society has the right to require of every public agent an account of his administration.

16. A society in which the observance of the law is not assured, nor the separation of powers defined, has no constitution at all.

17. Since property is an inviolable and sacred right, no one shall be deprived thereof except where public necessity, legally determined, shall clearly demand it, and then only on condition that the owner shall have been previously and equitably indemnified.[1]

[1] The permanent importance of the foregoing Declaration may be emphasized by comparing it with the provisions of the Charter of 1815. See below, pp. 512 *sqq*.

## V. Address of the National Assembly to the French People (February 11, 1790)

183. The National Assembly reviews its achievements during the previous six months. (February, 1790.)

The National Assembly, as it progresses in its work, is receiving upon every hand the felicitations of the provinces, cities, and villages, testimonials of the public satisfaction and expressions of grateful appreciation; but murmurs reach it as well, from those who are affected or injured by the blows aimed at so many abuses and prejudices. While occupied with the welfare of all, the Assembly is solicitous in regard to individual ills. It can forgive prejudice, bitterness, and injustice, but it feels it to be one of its duties to warn you against the influence of calumny, and to quiet the empty terrors which some are vainly trying to arouse in you. To what have they not resorted in order to mislead and discourage you? They pretend to be unaware of the good that the National Assembly has accomplished; this we propose to recall to your mind. Objections have been raised against what has been done; these we propose to meet. Doubts and anxiety have been disseminated as to what we propose to do in the future; this we will explain to you.

What has the Assembly accomplished? In the midst of storms, it has, with a firm hand, traced the principles of a constitution which will assure your liberty forever. The rights of man had been misconceived and insulted for centuries; they have been reëstablished for all humanity in that declaration, which shall serve as an everlasting war cry against oppressors and as a law for the legislators themselves. The nation had lost the right to decree both the laws and the taxes; this right has been restored to it, while at the same time the true principles of monarchy have been solemnly established, as well as the inviolability of the august head of the nation and the heredity of the throne in a family so dear to all Frenchmen.

The Estates General converted into a National Assembly.

Formerly you had only the Estates General; now you have a National Assembly of which you can never be again deprived. In the Estates General the several orders, which were necessarily at odds and under the domination of ancient pretensions, dictated the decrees and could check the free action of the national will. These orders no longer exist; all have disappeared before the honorable title of *citizen*. All being citizens alike, you demanded citizen-defenders and, at the first summons, the National Guard arose, which, called together by patriotism and commanded by honor, has everywhere maintained or established order and watches with untiring zeal over the safety of each for the benefit of all.

Privileges without number, irreconcilably at enmity with every good, made up our entire public law. These have been destroyed, and at the word of this Assembly the provinces which were the most jealous of their own privileges applauded their disappearance, feeling that they gained rather than lost thereby. A vexatious feudal system, powerful even in its ruin, covered the whole of France; it has now disappeared, never to return. In the provinces you were subject to a harassing administration; from this you have been freed. Arbitrary commands threatened the liberty of the citizens; they have been done away with. You desired a complete organization of the municipalities; this you have just received, and the creation of these bodies, chosen by your votes, offers, at this moment, a most imposing spectacle. At the same time the National Assembly has finished the task of a new division of the kingdom, which alone might serve to remove the last trace of former prejudices, substitute for provincial selfishness the true love for one's country, and serve as the basis of a just system of representation. . . . *Abolition of privileges*

This, Frenchmen, is our work, or rather yours, for we are only your organ, and you have enlightened, encouraged, and sustained us in our labors. What a glorious period is this which we at last enjoy! How honorable the heritage which you may transmit to your posterity! Raised to the rank of citizens; admissible to every form of employment; enlightened censors of the administration when it is not actually in your hands; certain that all will be done by you and for you; equal before the law; free to act, to speak, to write; owing no account to individuals but always to the common will; — what condition more happy! Is there a single citizen worthy of the name who would dare look back, who would rebuild once more the ruins which surround us, in order again to contemplate the former structure?

The Assembly replies to the accusations made against it.

Yet what has not been said and done to weaken the natural impressions which such advantages should produce upon you? It is urged that we have destroyed everything; everything must, then, be reconstructed. But what is there which need be so much regretted? If we would know, let those be questioned in regard to the objects of reform or destruction who did not profit by them; let even men of good faith be questioned who did profit by them. But let us leave one side those who, in order to ennoble the demands of purely personal interests, now choose as the objects of their commiseration the fate of those to whom they were formerly quite indifferent. We may then judge if each subject of reform does not enjoy the approval of all of those whose opinions should be considered.

Some say that we have acted too precipitately, as many others proclaim that we have been too deliberate. Too much precipitation! Does not every one know that only by attacking and overthrowing all the abuses at the same time can we hope to be freed from them without danger of their return; that then, and then only, every one becomes interested in the reëstablishment of order; that slow and partial reforms have always resulted in no reform at all, and that an abuse preserved becomes the support, and before long the means of restoring all those which we thought to have destroyed?

Our meetings are said to be disorderly; what of that, if the decrees which proceed from them are wise? We are indeed far from wishing to hold up for your admiration the details of all our debates. More than once they have been a source of annoyance to us, but at the same time we have felt that it was very unjust to take advantage of this disorder; and indeed this impetuosity is the almost inevitable effect of the first conflict which has perhaps ever been fought by every right principle against every form of error.

We are accused of having aspired to a chimerical perfection. A curious reproach indeed, which, if one looks at it closely, proves to be only an ill-disguised desire for the perpetuation of the abuses. The National Assembly has not allowed itself to be influenced by motives of servile interest or pusillanimity. It has had the courage, or rather the sense, to believe that useful ideas, essential to the human race, were not destined simply to adorn the pages of a book, and that the Supreme Being, when he granted the attribute of perfectibility to man, did not forbid him to apply this peculiar appanage of his nature to the social organization, which has become the most comprehensive of his interests and almost the most important of his needs.

It is impossible, some say, to regenerate an old and corrupt nation. Let such objectors learn that there is nothing corrupt but those who wish to perpetuate corrupting abuses, and that a nation becomes young again the moment it resolves to be born anew in liberty. Behold the regeneration! How the nation's heart already beats with joy and hope, and how pure, elevated, and patriotic are its sentiments! With what enthusiasm do the people daily solicit the honor of being allowed to take the oath of citizen! — but why consider so despicable a reproach? Shall the National Assembly be reduced to excuse itself for not having rendered the French people desperate?

But we have done nothing for the people, their pretended friends cry on all sides. Yet it is the people's cause which is everywhere triumphant. Nothing done for the people! Does not every abuse which is abolished prepare the way for, and assure to them, relief? Is there an abuse which does not weigh upon the people? They do not complain, — it is because the excess of their ills has stifled complaint. They are now unhappy, — say better that they are still unhappy, — but not for long; that we swear. . . .

These, Frenchmen, are the reproaches which have been directed against your representatives in the mass of culpable writings in which a tone of civic grief is assumed. But their authors flatter themselves in vain that we are to be discouraged. Our courage is redoubled; you will not long wait for the results. . . . We will pursue our laborious task, devoting ourselves to the great work of drawing up the constitution — your work as well as ours. We will complete it, aided by the wisdom of all France.

## BIBLIOGRAPHY

*A. References.*

**The Cahiers:** LOWELL, *Eve of the French Revolution*, Chapters XXI–XXII, pp. 342–376; *Cambridge Modern History*, Vol. VIII, pp. 134–144.

**The Pamphlets:** LOWELL, Chapter XX, pp. 322–341.

**Convocation of the Estates General:** MATHEWS, *The French Revolution*, Chapter VIII, pp. 102–110; STEPHENS, H. MORSE, *History of the French Revolution*, Vol. I, Prologue, and Chapter I, pp. 1–54; *Cambridge Modern History*, Vol. VIII, pp. 96–118.

**Opening of the National Assembly:** MATHEWS, Chapter IX, pp. 111–124; STEPHENS, Chapter II, pp. 55–74; *Cambridge Modern History*, Vol. III, pp. 145–158.

**Fall of the Bastile:** MATHEWS, Chapter X, pp. 125–137; STEPHENS, pp. 128–145; *Cambridge Modern History*, Vol. VIII, pp. 159–169.

**The Country at Large in Summer of 1789:** STEPHENS, Chapter VI, pp. 169–197.

**Abolition of the Ancien Régime:** MATHEWS, Chapters XI–XII, pp. 138–165.

**The Civil Constitution of the Clergy:** STEPHENS, Chapter X, pp. 291–309.

[For the full bibliography of the French Revolution, see close of the following chapter.]

# CHAPTER XXXVI

## THE FIRST FRENCH REPUBLIC

### I. THE FLIGHT OF THE KING AND THE ORIGIN OF A REPUBLICAN PARTY

The National Assembly, which had done so much to reform France, was drawing to a close in the summer of 1791, after two years of arduous labor. It was subjecting the new constitution which it had been drafting to a final revision before it left the task of government to the king and the Legislative Assembly, after carefully defining and restricting the powers of both. The flight of the king toward the eastern frontier, on June 20, 1791, served to show how slight was the chance that the new government would succeed, when the monarch was ready to desert his people in order to put himself in the hands of foreign powers and of the runaway nobles. The impression that the news of the king's flight made upon the people of Paris is described by Prudhomme, a well-known journalist of the time, in his newspaper.

184. How the Parisians viewed the flight of the king (June 20, 1791). (From Prudhomme's *Révolutions de Paris*.)

It was not until ten o'clock in the morning that the municipal government announced, by firing a cannon thrice, the unexpected event of the day. But for three hours the news had already been passing from mouth to mouth and was circulating in all quarters of the city. During these three hours many outrages might have been committed. The king had gone. This news produced a moment of anxiety, and everybody ran in a crowd to the palace of the Tuileries to see if it were true; but every one turned almost immediately

447

to the hall where the National Assembly met, declaring that their king was in there and that Louis XVI might go where he pleased.

Then the people became curious to visit the apartments vacated by the royal family; they traversed them all, and we questioned the sentinels we found there, "Where, and how, could he have escaped? How could this fat royal person, who complained of the meanness of his lodging, manage to make himself invisible to the sentries, — he whose girth would stop up any passage?" The soldiers of the guard had nothing to say to this. We insisted: "This flight is not natural; your commanders must have been in the plot, . . . for while you were at your post Louis XVI left his without your knowing it and yet passing close to you." These reflections, which naturally suggested themselves, account for the reception which made Lafayette pale when he appeared in the Place de Grève and passed along the quays. He took refuge in the National Assembly, where he made some confessions that did little to restore him to popular favor.

Far from being "famished for a glimpse of the king," the people proved, by the way in which they took the escape of Louis XVI, that they were sick of the throne and tired of paying for it. If they had known, moreover, that Louis XVI, in his message, which was just then being read in the National Assembly, complained "that he had not been able to find in the palace of the Tuileries the most simple conveniences of life," the people might have been roused to some excess; but they knew their own strength and did not permit themselves any of those little exhibitions of vengeance which are natural to irritated weakness.

**Conduct of the populace in the royal apartments.** They contented themselves with making sport, in their own way, of royalty and of the man who was invested with it. The portrait of the king was taken down from its place of honor and hung on the door. A fruit woman took possession of Antoinette's bed and used it to display her cherries, saying, "It's the nation's turn now to be comfortable." A young girl refused to let them put the queen's bonnet on her head and trampled on it with indignation and contempt. They had more respect for the dauphin's study, — but we should blush to report the titles of the books which his mother had selected. . . .

The prevailing spirit was apathy in regard to kings in general and contempt for Louis XVI in particular. This showed itself in the least details. On the Place de Grève the people broke up a bust of Louis XVI, which was illuminated by that celebrated lantern which had been a source of terror to the enemies of the Revolution. When will the people execute justice upon all these bronze kings, monuments of our idolatry?

The flight of the king, his arrest at Varennes, and the agitation which accompanied and followed the affair led the queen's brother, the Emperor Leopold, to issue, in concert with the king of Prussia, the Declaration of Pillnitz. This was regarded by the French as an expression of sympathy for the *Émigrés* and as a promise to form a European alliance for the purpose of undoing the Revolution in France. To those who signed the declaration it was, however, scarcely more than an empty threat, which they had little idea of carrying out.

His Majesty the emperor and his Majesty the king of Prussia, having given attention to the wishes and representations of Monsieur [the brother of the king of France], and of Monsieur le Comte d'Artois, jointly declare that they regard the present situation of his Majesty the king of France as a matter of common interest to all the sovereigns of Europe. They trust that this interest will not fail to be recognized by the powers, whose aid is solicited; and that in consequence they will not refuse to employ, in conjunction with their said majesties, the most efficient means, in proportion to their resources, to place the king of France in a position to establish, with the most absolute freedom, the foundations of a monarchical form of government, which

185. The Declaration of Pillnitz (August 27, 1791).

A 29.

shall at once be in harmony with the rights of sovereigns and promote the welfare of the French nation. In that case[1] their said majesties the emperor and the king of Prussia are resolved to act promptly and in common accord with the forces necessary to obtain the desired common end.

In the meantime they will give such orders to their troops as are necessary in order that these may be ready to be called into active service.

LEOPOLD.<br>FREDERICK WILLIAM.

PILLNITZ, August 27, 1791.

## II. ORIGIN OF THE JACOBIN CLUB

The spontaneous origin of the Jacobin Club, which was to play such a conspicuous rôle in the Revolution, is here described by one of its prominent early members, Alexandre de Lameth. The society grew with astonishing rapidity. By December, 1790, there were eleven hundred names enrolled upon the list of Paris members, and by June, 1791, the affiliated clubs throughout the provinces numbered four hundred and six. It must not be supposed that the Jacobins represented a well-defined policy or defended a single set of political opinions. Nor were they by any means always in agreement among themselves. For example, in the winter of 1791–1792 a strong party among them opposed the growing tendency to involve France in a war with Europe. Lameth makes clear the way in which the society supplemented the work of the National Assembly by discussing important matters which were about to come up for consideration.

---

[1] Namely, in case the other powers agreed to join them in checking the Revolution. The signers of the declaration well knew that England would not associate itself with them for such a purpose and that consequently their threat would not be executed.

After the transfer of the Assembly to Paris [October, 1789], the deputies from provinces which were distant from the capital, and who, for the most part, had never visited Paris (for traveling was not so easy then as it is now), experienced a sort of terror at the idea of being alone and, so to speak, lost in the midst of this huge city. They almost all, consequently, endeavored to lodge as near as possible to the Assembly, which then sat near the Feuillants (at the point where the Rue de Rivoli and the Rue Castiglione now intersect), in order that they might be easily found in case of necessity.

186. How the Jacobin Club originated in 1789.

But they were desirous that there should also be a place where they might come together in order to agree upon the attitude that they should take toward public questions. They applied, therefore, for information to residents of the capital in whom they had confidence; a search was then made in the neighborhood of the Assembly, and the refectory of the convent of the Jacobins was leased for two hundred francs a year as a place of meeting. The necessary furniture, which consisted of chairs, together with tables for the committee, was procured for a like sum.

At the first session about one hundred deputies were present, the next day double that number. The Baron de Menou was elected president, and Target, Barnave, Alexandre de Lameth, Le Chapelier, and Adrien du Port were elected secretaries, as well as three others whose names have escaped me.

A committee was chosen to draw up a list of regulations, of which Barnave was the chairman. The society decided on the name Friends of the Constitution. It was determined that all members of the Assembly should be admitted, but only such other persons should be received as had published useful works. The first to be thus received were Condorcet, the Marquis de Casotte, a distinguished economist, the Abbé Lecamus, a mathematician, and a small number of other savants or publicists.

The aim of the Society of the Friends of the Constitution was to discuss questions which were already, or were about to be placed, upon the calendar of the National Assembly. It cannot be denied that, inasmuch as the non-deputies present exercised no restraint upon these discussions, they often had more force and brilliancy than in the Assembly itself, where one found himself hindered by the violent contradictions of the right wing, and often intimidated by a crowd of spectators.

This preliminary consideration shed a great deal of light upon the discussions in the Assembly. The resolve to decide within the society itself, by preliminary ballots, the nominees for president, secretaries, and the committees of the Assembly, proved a great advantage to the popular party; for from that time the elections were almost always carried by the left, although up to that time they had been almost entirely controlled by the right. Camus, an ecclesiastical lawyer, then president and since become a republican, had been elected by the aristocracy.

The number of the deputies who customarily frequented the Society of the Friends of the Constitution quickly rose to nearly four hundred. The number of writers also increased in a marked ratio. But it was not long before the condition of having published a useful book was no longer required for admission to the society, and it was decided that it was sufficient to have been recommended by six members. The organization then grew larger, and no longer possessed the same solidity in its composition. Very soon the place of meeting became insufficient, and permission was obtained from the monks of the convent to meet in their library, and later in their church.

Along in December, 1789, many of the leading inhabitants of the provinces, having come to Paris either on private business or to follow more closely the course of public affairs, had themselves introduced at the society and expressed a desire to establish similar ones in the chief cities of France; for they felt that these associations of citizens intent upon defending the cause of public interest would form an efficient means of counteracting the violent opposition of the aristocracy, a class which had not yet lost the power which it had so long exercised.

### III. The Legislative Assembly and the Enemies of the Revolution

The early months of the Legislative Assembly were mainly occupied with the policy to be pursued toward three classes of opponents to the Revolution,— the run-away nobles, the foreign powers, who seemed ready to aid them, and, at home, the members of the clergy, who refused to support the new constitution. The king was also regarded with the greatest suspicion.

He not unnaturally refused to sanction the edicts which the Assembly directed against the emigrant nobles, but he wrote to his brothers expostulating with them for increasing his unpopularity by their impolitic language and their intrigues with foreign powers.

On October 31, on motion of the Girondist, Isnard, the Assembly bluntly ordered the king's older brother, the count of Provence, to return to France on pain of losing all rights to the regency.

*Louis Stanislas Xavier, Prince of France:*

The National Assembly requires you in virtue of the French constitution, title III, chapter ii, section 3, article 2, to return to the kingdom within a period of two months from to-day, failing which you will, after the expiration of the said period, lose your contingent right to the regency.

**187. The count of Provence summoned back to France; and his impudent reply to the Assembly.**

On December 6 the count published the above order in Coblenz (the *Émigrés'* center of activity), with the following counter-proclamation of his own.

*Members of the French Assembly, calling itself National:*

Sanity requires you, in virtue of title I, chapter i, section 1, article 1, of the imprescriptible laws of common sense, to return to yourselves within a period of two months from to-day, failing which you will, after the expiration of the said period, be regarded as having lost your right to be considered reasonable beings, and will be regarded as madmen, fit for the insane asylum.

Since the opening of the Legislative Assembly most of the Girondists had been warmly advocating war, which they believed would force the king to take a definite stand either with or against the nation. When war was finally declared against Austria on April 20, the Assembly was able to assign a number of plausible reasons for their action.

**188. The French Assembly declares war on Austria.** The National Assembly, deliberating upon the formal proposition of the king, in view of the fact that the court of Vienna, in contempt of treaties, has not ceased to extend open protection to French rebels;

That it has instigated and formed a concert with several of the powers of Europe directed against the independence and safety of the French nation;

**Reasons for war.** That Francis I, king of Hungary and Bohemia, has, by his diplomatic notes of the 18th of March and the 7th of April last, refused to renounce this concert;

That, in spite of the proposition made to him by the note of March 11, 1792, to reduce to a peace basis the troops upon the frontiers, he has continued, and hastened, hostile preparations;

That he has formally attacked the sovereignty of the French nation by declaring his intention of maintaining the claims of the German princes who hold territory in France, whom the French nation has repeatedly offered to indemnify;

That he has endeavored to divide the citizens of France and arm them against one another by holding out to the malcontents the hope of assistance from a concert of the powers;

And that, finally, by his refusal to reply to the last dispatches of the king of France, he leaves no hope of obtaining, by way of friendly negotiation, the redress of these several grievances, — which is equivalent to a declaration of war; — the Assembly decrees that immediate action is urgent.

The National Assembly proclaims that the French nation, faithful to the principles consecrated by its constitution, "not to undertake any war with a view to conquest nor ever to employ its forces against the liberty of any people," only takes up arms for the maintenance of its liberty and independence ; Firm purpose of the French to make no conquests.

That the war which it is forced to prosecute is not a war of nation against nation, but the just defense of a free people against the unjust aggression of a king ;

That the French nation never confuses its brethren with its real enemies ;

That it will neglect nothing which may reduce the curse of war, spare and preserve property, and cause all the unhappiness inseparable from war to fall alone upon those who have conspired against its liberty ;

That it adopts in advance all foreigners who, abjuring the cause of its enemies, shall range themselves under its banners and consecrate their efforts to the defense of liberty ; and that it will promote by all means in its power their settling in France.

Deliberating upon the formal proposition of the king and after having decreed the matter one of urgent importance, the Assembly decrees war against the king of Hungary and of Bohemia.

## IV. The Abolition of Monarchy

The demands for the suspension of Louis XVI, who was believed to be in traitorous correspondence with the Austrians and Prussians, became numerous in the summer of 1792 ; but it remained for the duke of Brunswick to assure the downfall of the monarchy by his proclamation, which became known in Paris, July 28, and seemed to furnish the agitators with an excuse for the revolt which they carried out August 10.

189. The
proclama-
tion of the
duke of
Brunswick
(July 25,
1792).

Their Majesties the emperor and the king of Prussia
having intrusted to me the command of the united armies
which they have collected on the frontiers of France, I
desire to announce to the inhabitants of that kingdom the
motives which have determined the policy of the two sovereigns and the purposes which they have in view.

Accusations
against those
who have
"usurped"
the power in
France.

After arbitrarily violating the rights of the German princes
in Alsace and Lorraine, disturbing and overthrowing good
order and legitimate government in the interior of the
realm, committing against the sacred person of the king
and his august family outrages and brutalities which continue to be renewed daily, those who have usurped the reins
of government have at last completed their work by declaring an unjust war on his Majesty the emperor and attacking
his provinces situated in the Low Countries. . . .

Aims of
the allies.

To these important interests should be added another
matter of solicitude, equally important and very close to the
hearts of the two sovereigns, — namely, to put an end to
the anarchy in the interior of France, to check the attacks
upon the throne and the altar, to reëstablish the legal power,
to restore to the king the security and the liberty of which he
is now deprived and to place him in a position to exercise
once more the legitimate authority which properly belongs
to him.

Convinced that the sane portion of the French nation
abhors the excesses of the faction which dominates it, and
that the majority of the people look forward with impatience
to the time when they may declare themselves openly against
the odious enterprises of their oppressors, his Majesty the
emperor and his Majesty the king of Prussia call upon them
and invite them to return without delay to the path of reason, justice, order, and peace. In accordance with these
views, I, the undersigned, the commander in chief of the
two armies, declare :

The allied
courts medi-
tate no
conquests.

1. That, drawn into this war by irresistible circumstances,
the two allied courts entertain no other objects than the welfare of France, and have no intention of enriching themselves by conquests.

2. That they do not propose to meddle in the internal government of France, and that they merely wish to deliver the king, the queen, and the royal family from their captivity, and procure for his Most Christian Majesty the necessary security to enable him, without danger or hindrance, to make such engagements as he shall see fit, and to work for the welfare of his subjects, according to his pledges. . . .

*They purpose to free the French king.*

7. That the inhabitants of the towns and villages who may dare to defend themselves against the troops of their Imperial and Royal Majesties and fire on them, either in the open country or through windows, doors, and openings in their houses, shall be punished immediately according to the most stringent laws of war, and their houses shall be burned or destroyed. . . .

8. The city of Paris and all its inhabitants without distinction shall be required to submit at once and without delay to the king, to place that prince in full and complete liberty, and to assure to him, as well as to the other royal personages, the inviolability and respect which the law of nature and of nations demands of subjects toward sovereigns. . . . Their said Majesties declare, on their word of honor as emperor and king, that if the château of the Tuileries is entered by force or attacked, if the least violence be offered to their Majesties the king, queen, and royal family, and if their safety and their liberty be not immediately assured, they will inflict an ever memorable vengeance by delivering over the city of Paris to military execution and complete destruction, and the rebels guilty of the said outrages to the punishment that they merit. . . .

*Fate of Paris if it permits the king to come to harm.*

It is for these reasons that I call upon and exhort in the most urgent manner all the inhabitants of the kingdom not to oppose the movements and operations of the troops which I command, but rather, on the contrary, to grant them everywhere a free passage and to assist and aid them with all good will as circumstances shall demand.

Given at the headquarters at Coblenz, July 25, 1792.

CHARLES WILLIAM FERDINAND,
Duke of Brunswick-Lüneburg.

Louis XVI had been suspended August 10 on account of the misgivings which his conduct inspired. The debate carried on six weeks later, during the opening session of the Convention, September 21, 1792, well illustrates the attitude of the new Assembly toward the ancient monarchy and serves to introduce some of the men who were soon to be most active during the Reign of Terror.

**190. The debate during the first session of the Convention.**

The citizens chosen by the French people to form the National Convention having assembled to the number of three hundred and seventy one, and having examined the credentials of the members, declare that the National Convention is organized. . . .

*M. Couthon.* . . . I am not afraid that, in the discussion which is about to take place, any one will dare to speak of royalty again; it is fit only for slaves, and the French would be unworthy of the liberty which they have acquired should they dream of retaining a form of government branded by fourteen centuries of crime. But it is not royalty alone that must be eliminated from our constitution, but every kind of individual power which tends to restrict the rights of the people and violate the principles of equality. . . .

*M. Collot d'Herbois.* . . . There is one question which you cannot postpone until the morrow, or even until this evening, or indeed for a single instant, without being faithless to the wish of the nation, — that is the abolition of royalty. [ *Unanimous applause.* ]

*M. Quinette.* We are not the judges of royalty; that belongs to the people. Our business is to make a concrete government, and the people will then choose between the old form where there was royalty and that which we shall submit to them. . . .

*M. Grégoire.* Assuredly no one of us would ever propose to retain in France the fatal race of kings; we all know but too well that dynasties have never been anything else than rapacious tribes who lived on nothing but human flesh. It is necessary completely to reassure the friends of liberty. We must destroy this talisman, whose magic power is still sufficient to stupefy many a man. I move accordingly that you sanction by a solemn law the abolition of royalty.

The entire Assembly rose by a spontaneous movement and passed the motion of Monsieur Grégoire by acclamation.

*M. Bazire.* I rise to a point of order. . . . It would be a frightful example for the people to see an Assembly commissioned with its dearest interests voting in a moment of enthusiasm. I move that the question be discussed.

*M. Grégoire.* Surely it is quite unnecessary to discuss what everybody agrees on. Kings are in the moral order what monsters are in the physical. Courts are the workshops of crimes, the lair of tyrants. The history of kings is the martyrology of nations. Since we are all convinced of the truth of this, why discuss it? I demand that my motion be put to vote, and that later it be supplied with a formal justification worthy of the solemnity of the decree.

*M. Ducos.* The form of your decree would be only the history of the crimes of Louis XVI, a history already but too well known to the French people. I demand that it be drawn up in the simplest terms. There is no need of explanation after the knowledge which has been spread abroad by the events of August 10.

The discussion was closed. There was a profound silence. The motion of Monsieur Grégoire, put to vote, was adopted amidst the liveliest applause:

"The National Convention decrees that royalty is abolished in France."

The Convention, after ridding France of the institution of monarchy, proposed to make its armies a means of propagating liberty and reform throughout Europe. It accordingly prepared a proclamation to be published in those countries which already were, or should be, occupied by the armies of the new French republic.

191. Proclamation to nations whose tyrants have been driven out by the French republican armies (December 15, 1792).

*The French people to the people of* ; *brothers and friends*:

We have conquered our liberty and we shall maintain it. We offer to bring this inestimable blessing to you, for it has always been rightly ours, and only by a crime have our oppressors robbed us of it. We have driven out your tyrants. Show yourselves free men and we will protect you from their vengeance, their machinations, or their return.

From this moment the French nation proclaims the sovereignty of the people, the suppression of all civil and military authorities which have hitherto governed you and of all the taxes which you bear, under whatever form, the abolition of the tithe, of feudalism, of seigniorial rights and monopolies of every kind, of serfdom, whether real or personal, of hunting and fishing privileges, of the *corvée*, the salt tax, the tolls and local imposts, and, in general, of all the various kinds of taxes with which you have been loaded by your usurpers; it also proclaims the abolition among you of all noble and ecclesiastical corporations and of all prerogatives and privileges opposed to equality. You are, from this moment, brothers and friends; all are citizens, equal in rights, and all are alike called to govern, to serve, and to defend your country.

## V. CAMILLE DESMOULINS AND HIS NEWSPAPER

The most amiable and humorous of the terrorists was Camille Desmoulins. While he was one of the very first to preach republican ideas and to propagate them through his writings, he had little of the relentless and stern fanaticism which blinded Robespierre and Saint-Just to the cruelty of the work in which they were engaged. In the autumn of 1793 Desmoulins, who was a journalist by profession, began to issue a new newspaper, which he called *The Old Cordelier*.[1] The charm

[1] Desmoulins had been from the first a very active member of the club of the Cordeliers, which had been more radical and republican in sentiment than the Jacobins.

of his style, his wit and learning assured his editorials
— and his newspaper was really nothing more than a
periodical editorial — great popularity in Paris, and they
still delight the historical student. In the third issue
(December 15, 1793) he seeks to extenuate the severities
of the Reign of Terror by showing, by skillfully adapted
quotations from Tacitus, that the harsh measures of the
new French republic were as nothing compared with
the atrocities by which the early Roman emperors established their sway.

One difference between monarchy and a republic, which
would alone serve to make every right-hearted man reject monarchy with horror and give preference to a republic, whatever
it may cost to establish it, is that although the people may,
in a democracy, be misled, they always esteem virtue and try
to place only the upright in office, while rogues constitute
the very essence of monarchy. Vice, pillage, and crime are
diseases in republics, but health itself is a disease in monarchies. Cardinal Richelieu admits this in his *Political Testament,*[1] where he makes it a principle that the king should
avoid employing upright men. And before him Sallust said,
" Kings cannot do without scoundrels and, on the contrary,
they must be on their guard against probity." Only in a
republic, then, can the good citizen ever hope to see an end
to the supremacy of intrigue and crime, for in order that
these may disappear it is only necessary that the people
should be enlightened. . . .

And there is another difference between monarchy and
a republic: the reigns of the worst of emperors — Tibe-
rius, Claudius, Nero, Caligula, Domitian — all had happy
beginnings.

It is by reflections such as these that the patriot should
first answer the royalist who is laughing in his sleeve over
the present state of France, as if this violent and terrible

192. Camille
Desmoulins
seeks to
extenuate
the Reign of
Terror by
quotations
from
Tacitus.

[1] See above, pp. 371 *sqq.*

condition was to last. . . . I will begin by fixing the eyes
of my fellow-citizens upon the reigns of the Cæsars, — upon
that river of blood, that sewer of corruption and filth, which
flows perpetually under a monarchy.

For a long time, Tacitus tells us, there had been at
Rome a law which defined the crimes of state and of leze
majesty which were to be punished with death. . . . When
simple remarks had become crimes of state, it was only a
step to view as criminal mere glances, sadness, compassion,
sighs, — silence itself.

Soon it became a crime of leze majesty, or of counter-
revolution, . . . for the journalist, Cremutius Cordus, to have
called Brutus and Cassius the last of the Romans; a crime
of counter-revolution for one of the descendants of Cassius
to possess a portrait of his great-grandfather; a crime of
counter-revolution for Mamercus Scaurus to have composed
a tragedy in which was a line that might have two mean-
ings; a crime of counter-revolution for Torquatus Silanus to
spend his money; a crime of counter-revolution to complain
of the disasters of the time, for this was to criticise the
government. . . .

Everything offended the tyrant. Was a citizen popular?
He was a rival of the prince, who might stir up civil war.
*Studia civium in se verteret et si multi idem audeant, bellum esse.*
Suspect. Did a citizen, on the contrary, avoid popularity and
hug his own fireside? This retired life caused you to gain a
certain respect. *Quanto metu occultior, tanto famae adeptus.*
Suspect. Were you rich? There was danger that the popu-
lace might be corrupted by your largesses. *Auri vim atque
opes Plauti principi infensas.* Suspect. Were you poor?
Ha, invincible emperor! that man must be closely watched.
No one is so enterprising as he who has nothing. *Syllam
inopem, unde praecipuam audaciam.* Suspect.

Were you of a somber and melancholy temperament, or
careless in your dress? You were disgusted that public
affairs were going so well. Suspect. If, on the other hand,
a citizen indulged himself in good times and indigestion, he
was but rejoicing that the emperor had had an attack of

gout. Suspect. . . . Was he virtuous and austere in his habits? Good! a new Brutus, who durst, by his pallid face and Jacobin peruke, to censure the curled and giddy courtier. Suspect.[1]

Now the royalists need not take the trouble to inform me that this description settles nothing, and that the reign of Louis XVI resembled in no way the sway of the Cæsars. If it did not resemble it, it is because with us despotism has long been lulled in the lap of its luxuries and has placed such confidence in the strength of the chains which our fathers have borne for fifteen centuries that it deemed terror no longer necessary. . . . But now that the people have awakened and the sword of the republic has been drawn, let royalty once more set foot in France, and then we shall see that these pictures of tyranny so well drawn by Tacitus will prove the living image of what we shall have to suffer for half a century.

In the succeeding number of his newspaper (issued Decadi, 30th Frimaire, second year of the republic, one and indivisible) Desmoulins no longer extenuates the work of the guillotine but pleads for clemency.

Some persons have expressed their disapproval of my third issue, where, as they allege, I have been pleased to suggest certain comparisons which tend to cast an unfavorable light on the Revolution and the patriots, — they should say the excess of revolution and the professional patriots. My critics think the whole number refuted and everybody justified by the single reflection, "We all know that the present situation is not one of freedom, — but patience! you will be free one of these days."

Such people think apparently that liberty, like infancy, must of necessity pass through a stage of wailing and tears before it reaches maturity. On the contrary, it is of the nature of liberty that, in order to enjoy it, we need only

193. Camille Desmoulins makes a plea for clemency (December 20, 1793).

[1] As Michelet has pointed out, this is rather a satire upon, than a justification of, the Reign of Terror.

desire it. A people is free the moment that it wishes to be so, — you will recollect that this was one of Lafayette's sayings, — and the people has entered upon its full rights since the 14th of July. Liberty has neither infancy nor old age, but is always in the prime of strength and vigor. . . .

Is this liberty that we desire a mere empty name? Is it only an opera actress carried about with a red cap on, or even that statue, forty-six feet high, which David proposes to make? If by liberty you do not understand, as I do, great principles, but only a bit of stone, there never was idolatry more stupid and expensive than ours. Oh, my dear fellow-citizens, have we sunk so low as to prostrate ourselves before such divinities? No, heaven-born liberty is no nymph of the opera, nor a red liberty cap, nor a dirty shirt and rags. Liberty is happiness, reason, equality, justice, the Declaration of Rights, your sublime constitution.

Would you have me recognize this liberty, have me fall at her feet, and shed all my blood for her? Then open the prison doors to the two hundred thousand citizens whom you call suspects, for in the Declaration of Rights no prisons for suspicion are provided for, only places of detention.

Do not think that such a measure would be fatal to the republic. It would, on the contrary, be the most revolutionary that you have adopted. You would exterminate all your enemies by the guillotine! But was there ever greater madness? Can you possibly destroy one enemy on the scaffold without making ten others among his family and friends? . . .

I am of a very different opinion from those who claim that it is necessary to leave the Terror on the order of the day. I am confident, on the contrary, that liberty will be assured and Europe conquered so soon as you have a committee of clemency. This committee will complete the Revolution, for clemency itself is a revolutionary measure, the most efficient of all when it is wisely dealt out.[1]

---

[1] In spite of Desmoulin's eloquent and wise plea for clemency, his friend Robespierre refused to support him, and he was brought to the scaffold, along with Danton, by the party which held that moderation was synonymous with treason to the cause of republican liberty.

## BIBLIOGRAPHY

**End of the National Assembly:** MATHEWS, *French Revolution*, Chapter XIII, pp. 166–181; STEPHENS, *History of the French Revolution*, Vol. I, Chapter XV, pp. 434–470; *Cambridge Modern History*, Vol. VIII, pp. 199–210.

**Opening of the War with Europe:** MATHEWS, pp. 182–195; STEPHENS, Vol. II, pp. 27–44.

**Conditions in Europe in 1792:** FYFFE, *History of Modern Europe*, Chapter I, pp. 1–27.

**Tenth of August and the September Massacres:** STEPHENS, Vol. II, Chapter IV, pp. 107–150; MATHEWS, pp. 195–206; *Cambridge Modern History*, Vol. VIII, pp. 228–244.

**Establishment of the Republic:** MATHEWS, Chapter XV, pp. 207–224; STEPHENS, Vol. II, Chapter V, pp. 151–180.

**Reign of Terror in Paris:** STEPHENS, Vol. II, Chapter X, pp. 321–361; MATHEWS, Chapter XVI, pp. 224–233; *Cambridge Modern History*, Vol. VIII, Chapter XII, pp. 338–371.

**Reign of Terror in the Provinces:** MATHEWS, Chapter XVII, pp. 234–251; STEPHENS, Vol. II, Chapter XI, pp. 362–414.

**Robespierre:** MATHEWS, Chapter XVIII, pp. 252–265.

**Reaction after Thermidor:** MATHEWS, Chapter XIX, pp. 266–285; *Cambridge Modern History*, Vol. VIII, Chapter XIII, pp. 372–397.

**Course of the War to 1795:** FYFFE, Chapter II, pp. 28–73; *Cambridge Modern History*, Chapter XIV, pp. 398–446.

*A. References.*

---

STEPHENS, H. MORSE, *A History of the French Revolution*, 2 vols., 1886–1891 (the third volume, which should bring down the story to the close of the Reign of Terror, has unfortunately never appeared). This is by far the best account to be had in English, perhaps in any language. It is free from both partisanship and sentimentality, and is based on the results of modern French scholarship. Its inaccuracies in detail do not impair its essential value. The same author in his *Europe, 1789–1815*, 1893, furnishes a good summary of the political history of the revolutionary period.

TAINE, *The French Revolution* (from the French), 3 vols. Covers the period 1789 to 1794. A brilliant arraignment of many of the leaders of the Revolution, which the author treats in an unsympathetic spirit. His style, insight, and research, however, serve to give his work both marked originality and value.

*B. Additional reading in English.*

CARLYLE, *The French Revolution*, originally published in 1837 ; new edition with notes by Fletcher and another edition edited by Rose. This famous bit of literature can scarcely be termed a history ; it is a brilliant and erratic commentary on the men and ideas of the times, full of profound observation, not unmixed with highly colored trivialities and inconsequential reflections. Profitable and amusing for one familiar with the actual course of events.

LECKY, *England in the Eighteenth Century*, Chapters XVIII–XX, on the French Revolution. These have been published in a separate volume (Appleton).

SLOANE, *The French Revolution and Religious Reform*. An account of the ecclesiastical legislation and its influence on affairs in France from 1789 to 1804 (1901).

MALLET, B., *Mallet du Pan and the French Revolution*, 1902. A sympathetic account of a well-known journalist.

BELLOC, *Danton*, and by the same writer, *Robespierre*. Two readable biographies.

MORLEY, *Critical Miscellanies* (see above, p. 429). Some of these essays are concerned with the revolutionary leaders and thinkers.

MAHAN, *Influence of Sea Power upon the French Revolution and Empire*, 2 vols. The author aims to explain the successes of Great Britain by its control of the seas.

**The sources in English.** Very few of the sources are to be had in English. The following may be noted.

*The Annual Register* for the period contains some documents.

ANDERSON, *Constitutions and Other Select Documents Illustrative of the History of France, 1789–1901*, gives important state papers.

YOUNG, ARTHUR, *Travels* (see above, p. 420), for the opening of the Estates General.

MORRIS, GOUVERNEUR, *Diary and Letters*, 2 vols., 1888. Observations of an American.

*The Correspondence of William Augustus Miles on the French Revolution, 1789–1817*, 2 vols., 1890.

PASQUIER, *History of my Time, Memoirs*, 1893–1894, Vol. I.

RIGBY, E., *Letters from France in 1789*, 1880.

MALLET DU PAN, *Memoirs and Correspondence*, ed. SAYOUS, 2 vols., 1852.

FERSEN, *Diary and Correspondence relating to the Court of France*, 1892.

# CHAPTER XXXVII

## NAPOLEON BONAPARTE

### I. Boyhood of Napoleon

When nine years old Napoleon Bonaparte and his brother Joseph accompanied their father to France, where the boys were to go to school and learn French. One of their teachers in Autun thus writes of them:

Napoleon brought with him to Autun a somber and pensive character. He never played with any one and ordinarily walked by himself. . . . He had much ability; understood and learned readily. When I was teaching him his lesson he would fix his eyes upon me with his mouth open. If I tried to recapitulate what I had just said, he would not listen to me. If I blamed him for this, he would reply with a cold, not to say imperious, air, "I know that, sir."

I only had him under me for three months. . . . He had by that time learned French so as to make use of it freely in conversation, and could write little themes and make little translations. . . . At the end of three months I sent him off with a certain Monsieur de Champeaux to the military school at Brienne.

Joseph also had much ability: although he took but little interest in study, and knew no French at all when he arrived, he learned it very promptly, as well as the beginnings of Latin. . . . He was as decent and agreeable in his manner as his brother was imperious. His nature was sweet, engaging, and appreciative. He was fond of his companions and protected those whom others annoyed. I never saw in him the least indications of ambition.

*194. How Napoleon and his brother Joseph learned French.*

*Joseph's character*

467

## II. Bonaparte's Italian Campaign (1796–1797)

A writer, Las Cases, who accompanied Napoleon to St. Helena, gathered the following information from the exiled emperor in regard to the circumstances of Bonaparte's first campaign.

195. Circumstances under which Bonaparte undertook the Italian campaign.

During the period of his command at Paris subsequent to the 18th Vendémiaire, Napoleon had to deal with a great dearth of food, which occasioned several popular commotions. One day, when the usual distribution of bread had not taken place, crowds of people collected around the bakers' shops. Napoleon was patrolling the city with a party of his staff to preserve public order. A crowd of persons, chiefly women, assembled around him, loudly calling for bread. The crowd grew, the outcries increased, and the situation of Napoleon and his officers became critical. A woman of monstrously robust appearance was particularly conspicuous by her gestures and exclamations. "Those fine epauleted fellows," said she, pointing to the officers, "laugh at our distress; so long as they can eat and grow fat, they do not care if the poor people die of hunger." Napoleon turned to her and said, "My good woman, look at me ; which is the fatter, you or I ?" Napoleon was at that time extremely thin. " I was merely a slip of parchment," said he. A general burst of laughter disarmed the fury of the populace, and the staff officers continued their round.

Napoleon's memoirs of the campaign in Italy show how he became acquainted with Madame de Beauharnais, and how he contracted the marriage which has been so greatly misrepresented in the accounts of the time. As soon as he

Bonaparte falls in with the former aristocracy.

got himself introduced to Madame de Beauharnais he spent almost every evening at her house, which was frequented by the most agreeable company in Paris. When the majority of the party retired, there usually remained Monsieur de Montesquiou, the father of the grand chamberlain, the duke of Nivernais, so celebrated for the graces of his wit, and a few others. They used to look around to see that the doors were all shut, and then they would say, "Now let us sit down and chat about the old court; let us revisit Versailles once more."

The poverty of the treasury and the scarcity of specie were so great during the republic that on the departure of General Bonaparte to join the army of Italy all his efforts, joined to those of the Directory, only resulted in raising two thousand louis, which he carried with him in his carriage. With this sum he set out to conquer Italy, and to advance toward the empire of the world. The following is a curious fact. An order of the day was issued, signed by Berthier, directing the general in chief, on his arrival at the headquarters at Nice, to distribute to the different generals the sum of four louis in specie to enable them to enter on the campaign. For a considerable time no such thing as specie had been seen. This order of the day displays the circumstances of the time more truly and faithfully than whole volumes written on the subject.

As soon as Napoleon joined the army he proved himself to be a man born to command. From that moment he filled the theater of the world; he occupied all Europe; he was a meteor blazing in the firmament; he centered all eyes on himself, riveted all thoughts, and formed the subject of all conversation. From that time every gazette, every publication, every monument became the record of his deeds. His name was inscribed on every page and in every line, and echoed from every mouth.

His entrance upon the command produced a revolution in his manners, conduct, and language. Decrès has often told me that he was at Toulon when he first heard of Napoleon's appointment to the command of the army of Italy. He had known him well in Paris and thought himself on terms of perfect intimacy with him. "So," said he, "when we learned that the new general was about to pass through the city, I immediately proposed to introduce my comrades to him, and to turn my former connection with him to the best account. I hastened to meet him full of eagerness and joy. The door of the apartment was thrown open, and I was on the point

*Bonaparte alters his friendly manner.*

of rushing toward him with my wonted familiarity; but his attitude, his look, the tone of his voice suddenly deterred me. There was nothing offensive either in his appearance or manner, but the impression he produced was sufficient to prevent me from ever again attempting to encroach upon the distance that separated us."

Bonaparte's freedom from greed.

Napoleon's generalship was characterized by the skill, energy, and purity of his military administration; his constant dislike of peculation of any kind, and his total disregard of his own private interest. " I returned from the campaign in Italy," said he, "with but three hundred thousand francs in my possession. I might easily have carried off ten or twelve millions and have kept it for my own. I never made out any accounts, nor was I ever asked for any. I expected, on my return, to receive some great national reward. It was publicly reported that Chambord was to be given to me, and I should have been very glad to have had the château; but the idea was set aside by the Directory. I had, however, sent back to France at least fifty millions for the service of the state. This I imagine was the first instance in modern history of an army contributing to maintain the country to which it belonged instead of being a burden to it."

The young and rather inexperienced General Bonaparte had to lead his ill-equipped troops against the combined armies of Austria and of the king of Sardinia. His success was, nevertheless, immediate; and after the opening victories in the mountains separating France from Piedmont, he found himself in a position to cheer his troops by the following proclamation:

HEADQUARTERS AT CHERASCO,<br>7th Floréal, Year IV [April 26, 1796].

*Soldiers :*

You have in a fortnight won six victories, taken twenty-one standards, fifty-five pieces of artillery, several strong places, and conquered the richest part of Piedmont; you have made fifteen thousand prisoners and killed or wounded more than ten thousand men. Previously you had fought for sterile crags, which, although you made them famous by your prowess, were useless to your country; to-day your services put you on a footing with the army of Holland or of the Rhine.

Without any resources you have supplied all that was necessary. You have won battles without cannons, passed rivers without bridges, made forced marches without shoes, camped without brandy and often without bread. Only republican phalanxes, soldiers of liberty, would have been able to bear what you have borne. Thanks be to you, soldiers, for this. Your grateful country will owe its prosperity to you. As conquerors at Toulon you but foreshadowed the immortal campaign of 1794; even so your present victories are but harbingers of still greater.

The two armies which but recently attacked you with confidence are fleeing in consternation before you. Those misguided men who laughed at your misery and rejoiced in the thought of the triumph of your enemies have been confounded.

But, soldiers, you have done nothing as yet compared with what there still remains to do. Neither Turin nor Milan yet belongs to you. . . . You were destitute of everything at the opening of the campaign; to-day you are provided abundantly. Numerous stores have been taken from your enemies and siege and field guns have arrived.

Soldiers, your country is justified in expecting great things of you. Will you fulfill its hopes? The greatest obstacles undoubtedly have been overcome, but you have still battles to fight, cities to take, rivers to cross. Is there any one among you whose courage is slackening? Is there any one who would prefer to return across the summits of the Apennines and the Alps and bear patiently the insults of a slavish soldiery? No, there is none such among the conquerors of Montenotte, of Dego, of Mondovi. All of you are burning to extend the glory of the French people. All long to humiliate those haughty kings who dare to contemplate placing us in fetters. All desire to dictate a glorious peace and one which will indemnify our country for the immense sacrifices which it has made; all would wish, as they return to their native villages, to be able to say proudly, " I was with the victorious army of Italy ! "

Stern prohibition of pillage.

Friends, I can promise you this conquest, but there is one condition which you must swear to fulfill. That is to respect the peoples whom you deliver, and repress the horrible pillage which certain rascals, incited by our enemies, commit. Otherwise, you will not be the deliverers of the people but their scourge; you will not do honor to the French people, but will thereby disavow your country. Your victories, your bravery, your success, the blood of our brothers who have died in battle, — all will be lost, even honor and glory. As for me and the generals who have your confidence, we should blush to command an army without discipline and restraint, which recognizes no law but force. . . . Any one who engages in pillage will be shot without mercy.

Peoples of Italy, the French army comes to break your chains; the French people is the friend of all peoples. You may receive them with confidence. Your property, your religion, and your customs will be respected. We are carrying on war as generous enemies, and we have no grudge except against the tyrants who oppress you.

BONAPARTE.

Bourrienne, one of Napoleon's early companions and later his secretary, gives us an account in his memoirs of the motives which led General Bonaparte to sign the Treaty of Campo-Formio.

197. How Bonaparte was led to sign the Treaty of Campo-Formio.

The early appearance of bad weather hastened Napoleon's determination. On the 13th of October, at daybreak, on opening my window I perceived the mountains covered with snow. The previous night had been superb, and the autumn, till then, had promised to be fine and late. I proceeded, as I always did at seven o'clock in the morning, to the general's chamber. I awoke him and told him what I had seen. He feigned at first to disbelieve me, then leaped from his bed, ran to the window, and, convinced of the sudden change, he calmly said, "What! before the middle of October? What a country! Well, we must make peace." While he hastily put on his clothes I read the journals to him, as is my daily custom. He paid but little attention to them.

Shutting himself up with me in his closet, he reviewed with the greatest care all the returns from the different corps of his army. "Here are," said he, "nearly eighty thousand effective men. I feed, I pay them; but I can bring but sixty thousand into the field on the day of battle. I shall gain it, but afterwards my force will be reduced by twenty thousand men, — by killed, wounded, and prisoners. How then shall I oppose all the Austrian forces that will march to the protection of Vienna? It would be a month before the armies could support me, if they should be able to do it at all; and in a fortnight all the roads and passes will be covered deep with snow. It is settled — I will make peace. Venice shall pay for the expense of the war and the boundary of the Rhine; let the Directory and the lawyers say what they like."

He wrote to the Directory in the following words: "The summits of the hills are covered with snow; I cannot, on account of the stipulations agreed to in regard to the recommencement of hostilities, open them again for twenty-five days, and by that time we shall be overwhelmed with snow."

. . . It is well known that by the Treaty of Campo-Formio the two belligerent powers made peace at the expense of the republic of Venice, which had nothing to do with the quarrel in the first instance, and which only interfered at a late period, probably against her own inclination, and impelled by the force of inevitable circumstances. But what has been the result of this great political spoliation? A portion of the Venetian territory was adjudged to the Cisalpine republic; it is now in the possession of Austria. Another considerable portion, including the capital itself, fell to the lot of Austria in compensation for the Belgian provinces and Lombardy, which she ceded to France.

Provisions of the Treat of Campo-Formio.

Destruction of the Venetian republic.

## III. The Egyptian Expedition : the 18th Brumaire

One of Bonaparte's companions in Egypt gives the following remarkable report of a conference between the general and the muftis, or expounders of the Mohammedan laws.

**198. Bonaparte informs the Mohammedans that he is their friend.**

Whilst at Cairo, Bonaparte, on a visit to the pyramids, seated himself on the Soros and held a long conversation with the muftis. "Glory to Allah!" said he; "there is no other God but God. Mohammed is his prophet and I am his friend. Muftis! the divine Koran is the delight of my soul and the object of my contemplation. I love the Prophet, and I hope erelong to see and honor his tomb in the Holy City.

"But my mission is first to exterminate the Mamelukes. If Egypt be their portion, let them show me the lease that God has given them. But the angel of death has breathed upon them: we are come and they have disappeared. The days of regeneration are come. He that hath ears, let him hear. The hour of political resurrection has struck for all who groan under oppression.

"Muftis, imams, mollahs, dervishes, and kalenders: instruct the people of Egypt; encourage them to join in our labors to complete the destruction of the Beys and the Mamelukes. Favor the commerce of the Franks in your country and their endeavors to arrive at the ancient land of Brahma. Let them have storehouses in your ports, and drive far from you the English, accursed among the children of Jesus! Such is the will of Mohammed. The treasures, industry, and friendship of the Franks shall be your lot till you ascend to the seventh heaven and are seated by the side of the black-eyed houris who are endowed with perpetual youth and maidenhood."

**Felicitations of the Mohammedan muftis.**

The Mohammedan muftis in return called him an envoy of God, the favorite of Mohammed, the successor of Iskander [i.e. Alexander the Great] most valiant among the children of Jesus. "May the Prophet," said one of them, "cause thee to sit at his left hand on the day of resurrection, after the third sound of the trumpet." " At length," said another, " the dawn of happiness breaks upon us ; the time destined by God has arrived ; an atmosphere of felicity surrounds us. The resplendent star of victory, which guides the French warriors, has shed upon us its dazzling light ; fame and honor go before them ; good fortune and honor accompany them. The chief who marches at their head is impetuous and terrible ; his name terrifies kings. Princes bow their haughty heads before this invincible Bonaparte." [1]

Madame de Rémusat, whose husband was one of Napoleon's secretaries, gives, in her delightful and important memoirs, a good account of Bonaparte's attitude toward the Egyptian adventure and his return to France. He appears to have explained his motives to her with perfect frankness.

When I returned to France I found public opinion in a lethargic condition. In Paris — and Paris is France — people can never interest themselves in things if they do not care about the persons connected with them. The customs of an old monarchy had taught them to personify everything. This habit of mind is bad for a people who desire liberty seriously; but Frenchmen can no longer desire anything seriously, except perhaps it be equality, and even that they would renounce willingly if every one could flatter himself that he was the first.

199. Bonaparte's attitude toward his Egyptian adventure.

To be equals, with everybody uppermost, is the secret of the vanity of all of you; every man among you must, therefore, be given the hope of rising. The great difficulty that the Directory labored under was that no one cared about them and that people had begun to care a great deal about me.

I do not know what would have happened to me had I not conceived the happy thought of going to Egypt. When

[1] Similar sentiments are expressed in some of Bonaparte's proclamations printed in his correspondence and in the extract from the memoirs of Madame de Rémusat, given below.

I embarked I did not know but that I might be bidding an eternal farewell to France; but I had little doubt that she would recall me. The charm of Oriental conquest drew my thoughts away from Europe more than I should have believed possible. My imagination interfered again this time with my actions; but I think it died out at St. Jean d'Acre. However that may be, I shall never allow it to interfere with me again.

**Bonaparte's dreams of Oriental conquest.**

In Egypt I found myself free from the wearisome restraints of civilization. I dreamed all sorts of things, and I saw how all that I dreamed might be realized. I created a religion. I pictured myself on the road to Asia mounted on an elephant, with a turban on my head, and in my hand a new Koran, which I should compose according to my own ideas. I would have the combined experience of two worlds to set about my enterprise; I was to have ransacked, for my own advantage, the whole domain of history; I was to have attacked the English power in India, and renewed my relations with old Europe by my conquest.

The time which I passed in Egypt was the most delightful part of my life, for it was the most ideal. Fate decided against my dreams; I received letters from France; I saw that there was not a moment to lose. I reverted to the realities of life and I returned to Paris — to Paris, where the gravest interests of the country are discussed during the *entr'acte* of the opera.

**Bonaparte's policy on his return from Egypt**

The Directory trembled at my return. I was very cautious; that is one of the epochs of my life in which I have acted with the soundest judgment. I saw Abbé Sieyès, and promised him that his verbose constitution should be put into effect; I received the chiefs of the Jacobins and the agents of the Bourbons; I listened to advice from everybody, but gave it only in the interest of my own plans. I hid myself from the people, because I knew that when the time came curiosity to see me would make them run after me. Every one was taken in my toils; and, when I became head of the state, there was not a party in France which did not build some special hope upon my success.

General Bonaparte in the following proclamation describes for the benefit of the public his *coup d'état* and endeavors to justify his conduct.

*To the People :*  19th Brumaire, 11 o'clock P.M.

Frenchmen, on my return to France I found division reigning among all the authorities. They agreed only on this single point, that the constitution was half destroyed and was unable to protect liberty.

Each party in turn came to me, confided to me their designs, imparted their secrets, and requested my support. But I refused to be the man of a party.

The Council of Elders appealed to me. I answered their appeal. A plan of general restoration had been concerted by men whom the nation has been accustomed to regard as the defenders of liberty, equality, and property. This plan required calm deliberation, free from all influence and all fear. The Elders therefore resolved upon the removal of the legislative bodies to St. Cloud. They placed at my disposal the force necessary to secure their independence. I was bound, in duty to my fellow-citizens, to the soldiers perishing in our armies, and to the national glory acquired at the cost of so much blood, to accept the command.

The Council assembled at St. Cloud. Republican troops guaranteed their safety from without, but assassins created terror within. Many deputies in the Council of Five Hundred, armed with stilettos and pistols, spread the menace of death around them.

The plans which ought to have been developed were withheld. The majority of the Council was disorganized, the boldest orators were disconcerted, and the futility of submitting any salutary proposition was quite evident.

I proceeded, filled with indignation and chagrin, to the Council of the Elders. I besought them to carry their noble designs into execution. I directed their attention to the evils of the nation, which were their motives for conceiving those designs. They concurred in giving me new proofs of their unanimous good will.

200. Bonaparte's own account of his *coup d'état* of Brumaire.

General Bonaparte favorably received by the Council of the Elders.

Bonaparte
claims that
he was
murderously
assailed in
the Council
of the Five
Hundred.

I presented myself before the Council of the Five Hundred alone, unarmed, my head uncovered, just as the Elders had received and applauded me. My object was to restore to the majority the expression of its will and to secure to it its power.

The stilettos which had menaced the deputies were instantly raised against their deliverer. Twenty assassins rushed upon me and aimed at my breast. The grenadiers of the Legislative Body, whom I had left at the door of the hall, ran forward and placed themselves between me and the assassins. One of these brave grenadiers [Thomé] had his clothes pierced by a stiletto.[1] They bore me out.

At the same moment cries of "Outlaw him!" were raised against the defender of the law. It was the horrid cry of assassins against the power destined to repress them. They crowded around the president [Lucien Bonaparte] uttering threats. With arms in their hands, they commanded him to declare me outlawed. I was informed of this. I ordered him to be rescued from their fury, and six grenadiers of the Legislative Body brought him out. Immediately afterwards some grenadiers of the Legislative Body charged the hall and cleared it.

The seditious, thus intimidated, dispersed and fled. The majority, freed from their assailants, returned freely and peaceably into the hall, listened to the propositions for the public safety, deliberated, and drew up the salutary resolution which will become the new and provisional law of the republic.

Frenchmen, you will doubtless recognize in this conduct the zeal of a soldier of liberty, of a citizen devoted to the republic. Conservative, judicial, and liberal ideas resumed their sway upon the dispersion of those seditious persons who had domineered in the councils and who proved themselves the most odious and contemptible of men.

BONAPARTE.

[1] Thomé had a small part of his coat torn by a deputy who took him by the collar. This constituted, according to Bourrienne, the whole of the attempted assassination of the 19th Brumaire.

## IV. Campaign of Marengo

Bourrienne thus sketches the campaign of Marengo:

It cannot be denied that if, from the 18th Brumaire to the epoch when Bonaparte began the campaign, innumerable improvements had been made in the internal affairs of France, foreign affairs could not be viewed with the same satisfaction. Italy had been lost, and the Austrian camp fires might be seen from the frontiers of Provence. Bonaparte was not ignorant of the difficulties of his position, and it was even on account of these very difficulties that, whatever might be the result of his hazardous enterprise, he wished to have it over as quickly as possible. He cherished no illusions and often said all must be staked to gain all.

The army which the First Consul was preparing to attack, was numerous, well disciplined, and victorious. His own, with the exception of a very small number of troops, was composed of conscripts; but these conscripts were commanded by officers whose ardor was unparalleled. Bonaparte's fortune was now to depend on the winning or losing of a single battle. A battle lost would have dispelled all the dreams of his imagination, and with them would have vanished all his immense schemes for the future of France. . . .

The grand idea of the invasion of Italy by way of the St. Bernard pass emanated exclusively from the First Consul. This miraculous achievement justly excited the admiration of the world. The incredible difficulties it presented did not daunt the courage of Bonaparte's troops, and his generals, accustomed as they had been to brave fatigue and danger, regarded without concern the gigantic enterprise of the modern Hannibal.

A convent, or hospice, which has been established on the mountain for the purpose of affording assistance to solitary travelers, sufficiently attests the dangers of these stormy regions. But the St. Bernard was now to be crossed not by solitary travelers but by an army. Cavalry, baggage, timbers, and artillery were now to wend their way along those narrow paths where the goatherd cautiously picks his

201. The campaign of Marengo as described by Bourrienne.

Situation of Bonaparte after Brumaire.

Crossing of the St. Bernard pass (May, 1800)

footsteps.   On the one hand masses of snow suspended above
our heads threatened every moment to break in avalanches
and sweep us away in their descent; on the other, a false step
was death.   We all passed, men and horses, one by one along
the goat paths.   The artillery was dismounted and the guns
put into hollowed trunks of trees were drawn by ropes. . . .

(Condensed.)    We arrived at Milan on the 2d of June.   But little resistance was offered to our entrance into the capital of Lombardy.   The First Consul passed six days in the city, and the
time approached when all was to be lost or won.   On the 13th
the First Consul slept at Torre di Galifolo.   On the morning
of the 14th General Desaix was sent toward Novi to observe
the road to Genoa, which city had fallen several days before,
in spite of the efforts of its illustrious defender, Masséna.

The battle of     That memorable battle of Marengo, of which the results
Marengo.        were incalculable, has been 'described in various ways.   For
my part, not having had the honor to bear a sword, I can-
not say that I saw any particular movements executed this
way or that; but I may mention here what I heard on the
evening of the battle concerning the hazards of the day.
As to the part which the First Consul took in it, the reader
Bonaparte       is perhaps sufficiently acquainted with his character to
claims all the   account for it.   He did not choose that a result so decisive
glory for
himself.        should be attributed to any other cause than the combina-
tions of his genius; and if I had not known his insatiable
thirst for glory, I should have been surprised at the half
satisfaction evinced at the cause of the success amidst the
joy manifested for the success itself.   It must be confessed
that in this he is very unlike Jourdan, Hoche, Kléber, and
Moreau, who were ever ready to acknowledge the services
of those who had fought under their orders.

Within two hours of the time when the divisions commanded by Desaix left San Giuliano I was joyfully surprised by the triumphant return of the army whose fate,
since the morning, had caused me so much anxiety.   Never
did fortune within so short a time show herself under two
such various faces.   At two o'clock everything indicated the
misery of a defeat with all its fatal consequences; at five,

victory was again faithful to the flag of Arcola. Italy was reconquered at a single blow, and the crown of France appeared in the distance [to the victorious general].

## V. PERSONAL CHARACTERISTICS OF GENERAL BONAPARTE

The son of Madame de Rémusat thus recalls how, when a little boy, he caught a glimpse of the First Consul :

One day my mother came for me (I think she had accompanied Madame Bonaparte into the court of the Tuileries) and took me up a staircase full of soldiers, at whom I stared hard. One of them who was coming down spoke to her; he wore an infantry uniform. "Who was that?" I asked, when he had passed. It was Louis Bonaparte. Then I saw a young man going upstairs in the well-known uniform of the [corps known as the] guides. His name I did not need to ask. Children in those days knew the insignia of every rank and corps in the army, and who did not know that Eugene Beauharnais was colonel of the guides ? *202. Bonaparte's manners when First Consul.*

At last we reached Madame Bonaparte's drawing-room. At first there was no one there but herself, one or two ladies, and my father, wearing his red coat embroidered in silver. I was probably kissed — or, perhaps they thought me grown ; then no one noticed me any further. Soon an officer of the consul's guard entered. He was short, thin, and carried himself badly, or at least carelessly. I was sufficiently drilled in etiquette to observe that he moved about a great deal and made rather free. Among other things I was surprised to see him sit on the arm of a chair. From thence he spoke across a considerable distance to my mother. We were in front of him, and I remarked his thin, almost wan face, with its brown and yellowish tints. We drew near to him while he spoke. When I was within his reach he noticed me ; he took me by my two ears and pulled them rather roughly. He hurt me, and had I not *Careless deportment of Bonaparte.*

been in a palace I should have cried. Then turning to my father, he said, " Is he learning mathematics?" Soon I was taken away. "Who is that soldier?" I asked my mother. "That soldier is the First Consul."

Bonaparte's disregard of others and his insolent attitude toward those who served him are seen in the following incident reported by Madame de Rémusat.

**203. How Bonaparte made others uncomfortable.** Bonaparte dictated with great ease. He never wrote anything with his own hand. His handwriting was bad, and as illegible to himself as to others; and his spelling was very defective. He utterly lacked patience to do anything whatever with his own hands. The extreme activity of his mind and the habitual prompt obedience rendered to him prevented him from practicing any occupation in which the mind must necessarily wait for the action of the body. Those who wrote from his dictation — first Monsieur Bourrienne, then Monsieur Maret, and Méneval, his private secretary — had made a shorthand for themselves in order that their pens might travel as fast as his thoughts.

He dictated while walking to and fro in his cabinet. When he grew angry he would use violent imprecations, which were suppressed in writing and which had, at least, the advantage of giving the writer time to catch up with him. He never repeated anything that he had once said, even if it had not been heard; and this was very hard on the poor secretary, for Bonaparte remembered accurately what he had said and detected every omission. . . .

**Bonaparte's conviction that zeal depends upon disquietude.** He always derived amusement from causing any one uneasiness and distress. His great general principle, which he applied to everything, both great and small, was that there could be no zeal where there was no disquietude.

Bonaparte might freely tease his attendants and secretaries, but, in his early days at least, he took great pains to win the hearts of his soldiers.

Bonaparte's reception by the troops was nothing short of rapturous. It was well worth seeing how he talked to the soldiers, — how he questioned them one after the other respecting their campaigns or their wounds, taking particular interest in the men who had accompanied him to Egypt. I have heard Madame Bonaparte say that her husband was in the constant habit of poring over the list of what are called the *cadres* of the army at night before he slept. He would go to sleep repeating the names of the corps, and even those of some of the individuals who composed them ; he kept these names in a corner of his memory, and this habit came to his aid when he wanted to recognize a soldier and to give him the pleasure of a cheering word from his general. He spoke to the subalterns in a tone of good-fellowship, which delighted them all, as he reminded them of their common feats of arms.

Afterwards when his armies became so numerous and his battles so deadly, he disdained to exercise this kind of fascination. Besides, death had extinguished so many remembrances that in a few years it became difficult for him to find any great number of the companions of his early exploits ; and when he addressed his soldiers before leading them into battle, it was as a perpetually renewed posterity to which the preceding and destroyed army had bequeathed its glory. But even this somber style of encouragement availed for a long time with a nation which believed itself to be fulfilling its destiny while sending its sons year after year to die for Bonaparte.

*203a. How Bonaparte won the hearts of his soldiers. (From Madame de Rémusat's Memoirs.)*

## BIBLIOGRAPHY

**Youth of Bonaparte:** FOURNIER, *Napoleon*, Chaps. I and II, pp. 1–37.
**First Italian Campaign:** FOURNIER, Chapter V, pp. 72–110 ; FYFFE, *History of Modern Europe*, Chapter III, pp. 74 103.
**The Egyptian Expedition:** FOURNIER, Chapter VI, pp. 111–153.
**Overthrow of the Directory and Establishment of the Consulate:** FOURNIER, Chapter VII, pp. 154–187 ; FYFFE, Chapter IV, pp. 104–144.

*A. References.*

[For the general bibliography of the Napoleonic period, see close of the following chapter.]

# CHAPTER XXXVIII

## EUROPE AND NAPOLEON

### I. GENERAL BONAPARTE BECOMES EMPEROR NAPOLEON I

Madame de Rémusat suggests the following reasons why the French people so readily subjected themselves to the despotism of Napoleon.

**204. Why the French people submitted to Bonaparte's rule.** I can understand how it was that men worn out by the turmoil of the Revolution, and afraid of that liberty which had long been associated with death, looked for repose under the dominion of an able ruler on whom fortune was seemingly resolved to smile. I can conceive that they regarded his elevation as a decree of destiny and fondly believed that in the irrevocable they should find peace. I may confidently assert that those persons believed quite sincerely that Bonaparte, whether as consul or emperor, would exert his authority to oppose the intrigues of faction and would save us from the perils of anarchy.

None dared to utter the word "republic," so deeply had the Terror stained that name; and the government of the Directory had perished in the contempt with which its chiefs were regarded. The return of the Bourbons could only be brought about by the aid of a revolution; and the slightest disturbance terrified the French people, in whom enthusiasm of every kind seemed dead. Besides, the men in whom they had trusted had one after the other deceived them; and as, this time, they were yielding to force, they were at least certain that they were not deceiving themselves.

The belief, or rather the error, that only despotism could at that epoch maintain order in France was very widespread. It became the mainstay of Bonaparte; and it is due to him to say that he also believed it. The factions played into his hands by imprudent attempts which he turned to his own advantage. He had some grounds for his belief that he was necessary; France believed it, too; and he even succeeded in persuading foreign sovereigns that he constituted a barrier against republican influences, which, but for him, might spread widely. At the moment when Bonaparte placed the imperial crown upon his head there was not a king in Europe who did not believe that he wore his own crown more securely because of that event. Had the new emperor granted a liberal constitution, the peace of nations and of kings might really have been forever secured.

## II. The Campaign of Austerlitz

After the rupture of the Peace of Amiens, Napoleon collected an army at Boulogne with the declared purpose of making a descent upon England. After some months of preparation and waiting, he suddenly broke up the camp at Boulogne and hurried into Germany. He surrounded and captured the Austrian army at Ulm in October. Six weeks later he defeated the combined forces of the Austrians and Russians in the memorable battle of Austerlitz. After this victory he issued the following proclamation.

Soldiers, I am satisfied with you. In the battle of Austerlitz you have justified what I expected from your intrepidity. You have covered yourselves with eternal glory. An army of one hundred thousand men which was commanded by the emperors of Russia and Austria has been in less than four hours either cut off or dispersed. Those that escaped your swords have thrown themselves into the lakes. Forty stands of colors, the stands of the Russian imperial guard, one hundred and twenty pieces of cannon, twenty generals, and above thirty thousand prisoners are the fruits of this ever-memorable battle. Their

205. Napoleon's proclamation to his soldiers after Austerlitz.

infantry, so celebrated and so superior to you in numbers, has proved unable to resist your charge, and henceforth you have no rivals to fear.

Thus in less than two months the third coalition is conquered and dissolved. Peace cannot be far off; but, as I promised my people before crossing the Rhine, I will conclude it only upon terms consistent with my pledge, which shall secure not only the indemnification, but the reward, of my allies.

Soldiers, when the French people placed the imperial crown upon my head I trusted to you to enable me to maintain it in that splendor of glory which could alone give it value in my estimation. But at that moment our enemies entertained the design of tarnishing and degrading it; and the iron crown, which was gained by the blood of so many Frenchmen, they would have compelled me to place on the head of my bitterest foe, — an extravagant and foolish proposal, which you have brought to naught on the anniversary of your emperor's coronation. You have taught them that it is easier for them to defy and to threaten than to subdue us.

Soldiers, when everything necessary to the security, the happiness, and the prosperity of our country has been achieved, I will return you my thanks in France. Then will you be the objects of my tenderest care. My people will receive you with rapture and joy. To say to me, "I was in the battle of Austerlitz," will be enough to authorize the reply, "That is a brave man."

NAPOLEON.

HEADQUARTERS AT AUSTERLITZ,
December 3, 1805.

### III. DISSOLUTION OF THE HOLY ROMAN EMPIRE

Napoleon's policy in Germany.

In no country of Europe were the effects of Napoleon's policy more striking and permanent than in Germany. The cession of the left bank of the Rhine to France by the Treaty of Lunéville (1801) brought with it a complete reconstruction of the remainder of Germany, since the dispossessed princes were to be indemnified with lands within the empire. Accordingly the ecclesiastical states and the free imperial towns, once so important among the German states, were, with a few exceptions, incorporated into the territories of neighboring secular princes by the great Imperial Recess of 1803. The little holdings of the knights were quietly absorbed by the new "sovereigns" within whose territories they happened to lie. The map of Germany was thus much simplified, and the ancient and hopeless subdivision of Germany greatly diminished.

Napoleon had no desire to unify Germany, but wished to have several independent states, or groups of states, which he could conveniently bring under his control. Consequently, when it came to arranging the Treaty of Pressburg after his great victory at Austerlitz, Napoleon forced the defeated emperor to recognize the rulers of Würtemberg and Bavaria as "kings" and the elector of Baden as enjoying "the plenitude of sovereignty." In short, he proposed that the three most important princes of southern Germany should be as independent as the king of Prussia or the emperor himself, and that, moreover, they should owe their elevation to him. He then formed a union of these new sovereigns and of other German rulers, which was called the Confederation of the Rhine.

After the Treaty of Pressburg and the formation of the Confederation of the Rhine there was really nothing for the emperor to do except to lay down — which he did with some relief — the imperial crown which had belonged to his house with few intermissions since the times of Rudolf of Hapsburg.

206. The
abdication
of the last
Roman
emperor
(August 6,
1806).

*We, Francis the Second, by the grace of God Roman emperor
elect, ever august, hereditary emperor of Austria, etc., king of
Germany, Hungary, Bohemia, Croatia, Dalmatia, Slavonia,
Galicia, Lodomeria, and Jerusalem; archduke of Austria, etc.*

Since the Peace of Pressburg all our care and attention
has been directed towards the scrupulous fulfillment of all
engagements contracted by the said treaty, as well as the
preservation of peace, so essential to the happiness of our
subjects, and the strengthening in every way of the friendly
relations which have been happily reëstablished. We could
but await the outcome of events in order to determine
whether the important changes in the German empire resulting from the terms of the peace would allow us to
fulfill the weighty duties which, in view of the conditions
of our election, devolve upon us as the head of the empire.
But the results of certain articles of the Treaty of Pressburg, which showed themselves immediately after its publication and since that time, as well as the events which,
as is generally known, have taken place in the German
empire, have convinced us that it would be impossible
under these circumstances further to fulfill the duties
which we assumed by the conditions of our election.
Even if the prompt readjustment of existing political complications might produce an alteration in the existing conditions, the convention signed at Paris, July 12, and
approved later by the contracting parties, providing for
the complete separation of several important states of the
empire and their union into a separate confederation,
would utterly destroy any such hope.

Thus convinced of the utter impossibility of longer fulfilling the duties of our imperial office, we owe it to our
principles and to our honor to renounce a crown which
could only retain any value in our eyes so long as we were
in a position to justify the confidence reposed in us by the
electors, princes, estates, and other members of the German
empire, and to fulfill the duties devolving upon us.

We proclaim, accordingly, that we consider the ties which
have hitherto united us to the body politic of the German

empire as hereby dissolved; that we regard the office and
dignity of the imperial headship as extinguished by the
formation of a separate union of the Rhenish states, and
regard ourselves as thereby freed from all our obligations
toward the German empire; herewith laying down the
imperial crown which is associated with these obligations,
and relinquishing the imperial government which we have
hitherto conducted.

We free at the same time the electors, princes, and
estates, and all others belonging to the empire, particularly
the members of the supreme imperial courts and other
magistrates of the empire, from the duties constitutionally
due to us as the lawful head of the empire. Conversely, we
free all our German provinces and imperial lands from all
their obligations of whatever kind toward the German
empire. In uniting these, as emperor of Austria, with the
whole body of the Austrian state we shall strive, with the
restored and existing peaceful relations with all the powers
and neighboring states, to raise them to the height of prosperity and happiness which is our keenest desire and the
aim of our constant and sincerest efforts.

Done at our capital and royal residence, Vienna, August 6, 1806, in the fifteenth year of our reign as emperor
and hereditary ruler of the Austrian lands.

FRANCIS.

## IV. THE CONTINENTAL BLOCKADE

At least as early as 1796 the French government conceived the idea of forcing its English enemy to cry for
peace by ruining her commerce. This became a cherished policy of Napoleon after he gave up the idea of
invading England. After his victory at Jena he felt that
the time had come to attempt to exclude England from
the continent. She had given him an excuse for the Berlin Decree given below by declaring the coast from the
river Elbe to Brest in a state of blockade (May, 1806).

**207. The
Berlin
Decree
(November
21, 1806).
(Extracts.)**

Napoleon, emperor of the French and king of Italy, in consideration of the facts:

1. That England does not recognize the system of international law universally observed by all civilized nations.

2. That she regards as an enemy every individual belonging to the enemy's state, and consequently makes prisoners of war not only of the crews of armed ships of war but of the crews of ships of commerce and merchantmen, and even of commercial agents and of merchants traveling on business.

3. That she extends to the vessels and commercial wares, and to the property of individuals, the right of conquest which is applicable only to the possessions of the belligerent power.

4. That she extends to unfortified towns and commercial ports, to harbors and the mouths of rivers, the right of blockade, which, in accordance with reason and the customs of all civilized nations, is applicable only to strong places. . . . That she has declared districts in a state of blockade which all her united forces would be unable to blockade, such as entire coasts and the whole of an empire.

5. That this monstrous abuse of the right of blockade has no other aim than to prevent communication among the nations and to raise the commerce and the industry of England upon the ruins of that of the continent.

8. That it is a natural right to employ such arms against an enemy as he himself makes use of, and to combat in the same way as he combats. Since England has disregarded all ideas of justice and every high sentiment implied by civilization among mankind, we have resolved to apply to her the usages which she has ratified in her maritime legislation.

The provisions of the present decree shall continue to be looked upon as embodying the fundamental principles of the empire until England shall recognize that the law of war is one and the same on land and on sea, and that the rights of war cannot be extended so as to include private property of any kind or the persons of individuals unconnected with the profession of arms, and that the right of blockade shall be restricted to fortified places actually invested by sufficient forces.

We have consequently decreed and do decree that which follows :

ARTICLE I.  The British Isles are declared to be in a state of blockade.

II.  All commerce and all correspondence with the British Isles is forbidden.  Consequently, letters or packages directed to England, or to an Englishman, or written in the English language, shall not pass through the mails and shall be seized.

III.  Every individual who is an English subject, of whatever state or condition he may be, who shall be discovered in any country occupied by our troops or by those of our allies, shall be made a prisoner of war.

IV.  All warehouses, merchandise, or property of whatever kind belonging to a subject of England shall be regarded as a lawful prize.

V.  Trade in English goods is prohibited, and all goods belonging to England or coming from her factories or her colonies are declared a lawful prize.

VII.  No vessel coming directly from England or from the English colonies, or which shall have visited these since the publication of the present decree, shall be received in any port.

VIII.  Any vessel contravening the above provision by a false declaration shall be seized, and the vessel and cargo shall be confiscated as if it were English property.

X.  The present decree shall be communicated by our minister of foreign affairs to the kings of Spain, of Naples, of Holland, and of Etruria, and to our other allies whose subjects, like ours, are the victims of the unjust and barbarous maritime legislation of England.

(Signed)  NAPOLEON.

Pasquier, in his *Mémoirs*, makes the following admirable criticism of Napoleon's continental system.

208. A contemporary's criticism of Napoleon's continental system.

[Napoleon's unwise severity after the battle of Jena] was nothing compared to a measure adopted in the hour of intoxication of victory, and which, by erecting an insurmountable barrier, so to speak, between France and England, condemned each of these two powers to entertain no hopes of peace and rest until its rival was completely destroyed. . . .

Napoleon flattered himself with the idea of having found the means to deal a blow at his most deadly opponent in the matter nearest his heart. Seeing himself master of the greater part of the European coast, or at least enjoying a domination over the mouths of the principal rivers of Germany, he persuaded himself that it depended on him to close all Europe's markets to England and thus compel her to accept peace from him at his own terms. The conception was no doubt a grand one, and the measure was no more iniquitous than that of England, but the difference lay in the fact that the latter, in her pretensions to a blockade, was not undertaking anything beyond her strength, and did not stand in need of any other nation's coöperation to carry it out.

France, on the contrary, was entering upon an undertaking which could not be put into execution without the voluntary or enforced coöperation of all the European powers. It was therefore sufficient in order to render it fruitless — and the future went to prove this — that a single one of these powers, unable to submit to the privations imposed upon it, should either announce its firm determination not to lend a hand in the matter, or should find ways of eluding it. . . .

Not only was England in a position to supply the continent with the numerous products of her industry, but she also controlled almost the entirety of all colonial wares and provisions. Hence it would become necessary, in the first place, to have recourse to all possible means calculated to make continental industry supply that which English industry would no longer furnish. In the second place, with regard to colonial products, some of which, such as sugar and coffee, were almost indispensable necessaries of life, and others of which were the actual raw material on which depended the manufactures which it was proposed to create, it was necessary to devise a means for allowing them the right of entry, but limited by the strictest necessity. . . .

So it happened that through the most persevering and at times the most ingenious efforts, by the aid of a succession of decrees, and with the help of that strange invention of licenses which were nothing but organized smuggling, continental industry, or rather French industry, backed up with a million bayonets and with an auxiliary force of coast guards, succeeded in meeting a tremendous competition and in deriving large profits.

## V. Napoleon at the Zenith

The following extracts will illustrate the attitude of Napoleon toward his vast empire and the way in which he undertook to shape the destinies of all western Europe. Enraged by the refusal of the Spanish nation to accept his brother as their king, he invaded the peninsula with a large army, occupied Madrid, and in December, 1808, he issued the following proclamations.

Imperial Camp at Madrid, December 7, 1808.

Spaniards, you have been seduced by perfidious men. They have involved you in a mad conflict and induced you to rush to arms. Is there one among you who, if he but reflect a moment upon all that has taken place, will not be convinced that you have been the playthings of the inveterate enemy of the continent, who rejoices as she beholds the shedding of Spanish and French blood? What could be the result of your success even in several campaigns? What but a war without end and prolonged uncertainty in regard to your possessions and your very existence? In a few months you have been subjected to all the horrors of popular faction. The defeat of your armies was the affair of a

**209. Napoleon's proclamation to the Spaniards.**

few marches. I have entered Madrid. The right of war authorizes me to make a terrible example and to wash out with blood the outrages committed against me and my nation. But my only thought is of clemency. A few men only, the authors of your misery, shall suffer. I will speedily expel from the peninsula that English army which has been dispatched to Spain, not to aid you, but to inspire in you a false confidence and to deceive you.

I informed you in my proclamation of June 2 that I wished to be your regenerator. But you have chosen that I should add to the rights ceded to me by your previous dynasty also the right of conquest. But this has not in any way altered my attitude toward you. Indeed, I must praise all that has been generous in your efforts. I would recognize that your true interests have been obscured and that you have been deceived as to the real condition of affairs.

Spaniards, your destiny is in my hands. Refuse the poison which the English have spread abroad among you; let your king be assured of your love and confidence and you will be more powerful, more happy than you have ever been. I have destroyed everything which stands in the way of your prosperity and greatness. I have broken the fetters which hampered the people. I have given you a liberal constitution, and, in the place of an absolute, I have given you a limited and constitutional monarchy. It depends upon you whether this constitution shall continue to govern you. But if all my efforts should prove useless and if you do not respond to my confidence, nothing will remain for me except to treat you as conquered provinces and to place my brother upon another throne. I shall then put the crown of Spain upon my own head and I shall be able to make the wicked respect it, since God has given me the power and the will necessary to surmount all obstacles.

NAPOLEON.

The reforms to which Napoleon alludes had been issued three days before, upon his arrival in Madrid. They furnish an admirable illustration of the way in which the ideas of the French Revolution followed his armies into the conservative countries of western Europe.

IMPERIAL CAMP AT MADRID, December 4, 1808.

To date from the publication of the present decree, feudal rights are abolished in Spain.

All personal obligations, all exclusive fishing rights and other rights of similar nature on the coast or on rivers and streams, all feudal monopolies (*banalités*) of ovens, mills, and inns are suppressed. It shall be free to every one who shall conform to the laws to develop his industry without restraint.

210. Decrees abolishing feudal dues in Spain.

The tribunal of the Inquisition is abolished, as inconsistent with the civil sovereignty and authority.

The property of the Inquisition shall be sequestered and fall to the Spanish state, to serve as security for the bonded debt.

211. Decree abolishing the Inquisition.

Considering that the members of the various monastic orders have increased to an undue degree and that, although a certain number of them are useful in assisting the ministers of the altar in the administration of the sacraments, the existence of too great a number interferes with the prosperity of the state, we have decreed and do decree as follows :

The number of convents now in existence in Spain shall be reduced to a third of their present number. This reduction shall be accomplished by uniting the members of several convents of the same order into one.

From the publication of the present decree, no one shall be admitted to the novitiate or permitted to take the monastic vow until the number of the religious of both sexes has been reduced to one third of that now in existence. . . .

All regular ecclesiastics who desire to renounce the monastic life and live as secular ecclesiastics are at liberty to leave their monasteries. . . .

212. Decree abolishing monastic orders.

In view of the fact that the institution which stands most in the way of the internal prosperity of Spain is that of the customs lines separating the provinces, we have decreed and do decree what follows :

213. Decree abolishing the interior customs lines.

To date from January 1 next, the barriers existing between the provinces shall be suppressed. The custom houses shall be removed to the frontiers and there established.

## VI. The Russian Campaign

214. Napoleon's proclamation at the opening of the Russian campaign (June, 1812).

Before crossing the Russian boundary in June, 1812, Napoleon issued the following proclamation to the Grand Army.

Soldiers, the second war of Poland has commenced. The first was brought to a close at Friedland and Tilsit. At Tilsit, Russia swore eternal alliance with France and war with England. She now violates her oaths, she refuses to give any explanation of her strange conduct, except on condition that the eagles of France shall repass the Rhine, leaving, by such a movement, our allies at her mercy. Russia is dragged along by a fate. Her destinies must be accomplished. Shall she then consider us degenerate? Are we no longer to be looked upon as the soldiers of Austerlitz? She offers us the alternative of dishonor or war. The choice does not admit of hesitation. Let us march forward. Let us pass the Niemen. Let us carry war into her territory. The second war of Poland will be as glorious to the French arms as was the first; but the peace which we shall conclude will be its own guaranty and will put an end to that proud and haughty influence which Russia has for fifty years exercised in the affairs of Europe.

At our Headquarters at Wilkowiszki,
June 22, 1812.

Five months later Napoleon was frantically endeavoring to regain Poland. An eyewitness thus describes the crossing of the Beresina, one of the most tragic episodes in all military history.

On the 25th of November there had been thrown across the river temporary bridges made of beams taken from the

cabins of the Poles. . . . At a little after five in the afternoon the beams gave way, not being sufficiently strong;
and as it was necessary to wait until the next day, the army
again abandoned itself to gloomy forebodings. It was evident that they would have to endure the fire of the enemy
all the next day. But there was no longer any choice; for
it was only at the end of this night of agony and suffering
of every description that the first beams were secured in the
river. It is hard to comprehend how men could submit to
stand, up to their mouths in water filled with ice, rallying all
the strength which nature had given them, added to all that
the energy of devotion furnished, and drive piles several feet
deep into a miry bed, struggling against the most horrible
fatigue, pushing back with their hands enormous blocks of
ice which threatened to submerge and sink them. . . .

215. The
crossing
of the
Beresina.
(From
Constant's
*Memoirs.*)

The emperor awaited daylight in a poor hut, and in the
morning said to Prince Berthier, " Well, Berthier, how can
we get out of this?" He was seated in his room, great
tears flowing down his cheeks, which were paler than usual;
and the prince was seated near him. They exchanged few
words, and the emperor appeared overcome by his grief. I
leave to the imagination what was passing in his soul. . . .

Napoleon
overcome
with grief
and despair.

When the artillery and baggage wagons passed, the bridge
was so overweighted that it fell in. Instantly a backward
movement took place, which crowded together all the multitude of stragglers who were advancing in the rear of
the artillery, like a flock being herded. Another bridge had
been constructed, as if the sad thought had occurred that
the first might give way, but the second was narrow and
without a railing; nevertheless it seemed at first a very valuable makeshift in such a calamity. But how disasters follow one upon another! The stragglers rushed to the second
bridge in crowds. But the artillery, the baggage wagons, — in
a word, all the army supplies, — had been in front on the first
bridge when it broke down. . . . Now, since it was urgent
that the artillery should pass first, it rushed impetuously
toward the only road to safety which remained. No pen
can describe the scene of horror which ensued; for it was

literally over a road of trampled human bodies that conveyances of all sorts reached the bridge. On this occasion one could see how much brutality and cold-blooded ferocity can be produced in human minds by the instinct of self-preservation. . . . As I have said, the bridge had no railing; and crowds of those who forced their way across fell into the river and were engulfed beneath the ice. Others, in their fall, tried to stop themselves by grasping the planks of the bridge, and remained suspended over the abyss until, their hands crushed by the wheels of the vehicles, they lost their grasp and went to join their comrades as the waves closed over them. Entire caissons with drivers and horses were precipitated into the water. . . .

On the 3d of December we arrived at Malodeczno. During the whole day the emperor appeared thoughtful and anxious. He had frequent confidential conversations with the grand equerry, Monsieur de Coulaincourt, and I expected some extraordinary measure. I was not mistaken in my conjectures. At two leagues from Smorghoni the duke of Vicenza summoned me and told me to go on in front and give orders to have the six best horses harnessed to my carriage, which was the lightest of all, and keep them in constant readiness. I reached Smorghoni before the emperor, who did not arrive until the following night. . . . After supper the emperor ordered prince Eugene to read the twenty-ninth bulletin and spoke freely of his plans, saying that his departure was essential in order to send help to the army. . . .

The emperor left in the night. By daybreak the army had learned the news, and the impression it made cannot be depicted. Discouragement was at its height, and many soldiers cursed the emperor and reproached him for abandoning them.

This night, the 6th, the cold increased greatly. Its severity may be imagined, as birds were found on the ground frozen stiff. Soldiers seated themselves with their heads in their hands and bodies bent forward in order thus to feel less the emptiness of their stomachs. . . . Everything had failed us. Long before reaching Wilna, the horses being dead, we received orders to burn our carriages and all their contents.

## VII. The German War of Liberation

By the middle of March, 1813, the timid king of Prussia, encouraged by Napoleon's defeat in Russia, finally decided to throw off the French yoke and lead his country into a war of liberation. He explained his reasons to his people in one of the most famous documents ("*An mein Volk*") in modern German history.

There is no need of explaining to my loyal subjects, or to any German, the reasons for the war which is about to begin. They lie plainly before the eyes of awakened Europe. We succumbed to the superior force of France. The peace which followed deprived me of my people and, far from bringing us blessings, it inflicted upon us deeper wounds than the war itself, sucking out the very marrow of the country. Our principal fortresses remained in the hand of the enemy, and agriculture, as well as the highly developed industries of our towns, was crippled. The freedom of trade was hampered and thereby the sources of commerce and prosperity cut off. The country was left a prey to the ravages of destitution.

216. The king of Prussia rouses his people against Napoleon.

I hoped, by the punctilious fulfillment of the engagements I had entered into, to lighten the burdens of my people, and even to convince the French emperor that it would be to his own advantage to leave Prussia her independence. But the purest and best of intentions on my part were of no avail against insolence and faithlessness, and it became only too plain that the emperor's treaties would gradually ruin us even more surely than his wars. The moment is come when we can no longer harbor the slightest illusion as to our situation.

Brandenburgers, Prussians, Silesians, Pomeranians, Lithuanians! You know what you have borne for the past seven years; you know the sad fate that awaits you if we do not bring this war to an honorable end. Think of the times gone by, — of the Great Elector, the great Frederick! Remember the blessings for which your forefathers fought under their leadership and which they paid for with their blood, — freedom of conscience, national honor, independence, commerce, industry, learning. Look at the great example of our powerful allies, the Russians ; look at the Spaniards, the Portuguese. For such objects as these even weaker peoples have gone forth against mightier enemies and returned in triumph. Witness the heroic Swiss and the people of the Netherlands.

Great sacrifices will be demanded from every class of the people, for our undertaking is a great one, and the number and resources of our enemies far from insignificant. But would you not rather make these sacrifices for the fatherland and for your own rightful king than for a foreign ruler, who, as he has shown by many examples, will use you and your sons and your uttermost farthing for ends which are nothing to you ?

Faith in God, perseverance, and the powerful aid of our allies will bring us victory as the reward of our honest efforts. Whatever sacrifices may be required of us as individuals, they will be outweighed by the sacred rights for which we make them, and for which we must fight to a victorious end unless we are willing to cease to be Prussians or Germans. This is the final, the decisive struggle ; upon it depends our independence, our prosperity, our existence. There are no other alternatives but an honorable peace or a heroic end. You would willingly face even the latter for honor's sake, for without honor no Prussian or German could live.

However, we may confidently await the outcome. God and our own firm purpose will bring victory to our cause and with it an assured and glorious peace and the return of happier times.

FREDERICK WILLIAM.

BRESLAU, March 17, 1813.


Immediately after the great battle of the nations at Leipzig the distinguished Prussian statesman, Stein, writes as follows to his wife :

LEIPZIG, October 21, 1813.

At last, my dear one, we may venture to indulge in a feeling of happiness. Napoleon is beaten and put to flight in disorder. They are driving him over to the left bank of the Rhine and the Austro-Bavarian army will catch up with him before he crosses the river. This is the result of the bloody but glorious battle of the 14th, 16th, 18th, and 19th of October.

217. Stein reports the battle of Leipzig to his wife.

And so that monstrous structure built up by the maddest and most perverse tyranny and cemented by the blood and tears of so many millions now lies in ruins. From one end of Germany to the other men now dare to say that Napoleon is a scoundrel and an enemy of the human race ; that the shameful bonds in which he has held our fatherland are broken, and the humiliation he has heaped upon us is washed out in streams of French blood.

This great event is due to the persistence and noble spirit developed by Emperor Alexander in the important and decisive events of last year, the heroic devotion of his people, and the spirit of justice and moderation which he has shown in all his negotiations with the powers whom he has invited to associate their efforts with his ; to the sacrifices and strength which Prussia has brought to the struggle since she entered it ; to the spirit of opposition and hate toward the oppressor which has shown itself on all sides.

The workings of Providence are at least justified by the terrible judgment which has been meted out to the monster whose obstinacy has led him into political and military follies which have hastened his fall and made him an object of contempt among the people. . . .

These results have been won by two bloody, glorious, and tragic campaigns, and through many costly battles. At Lützen, Bautzen, Teltow, Dresden, Katzbach, Kulm, Dennewitz, Bledin, Leipzig, the seed was sown for this harvest which now awaits us, the fruits of which we should enjoy with a devout and thankful recognition of the hand of Providence, and in all moderation.

The allies have vested in me the whole administration of the territory which they have occupied. Repnin has been made governor of Saxony. I leave in a fortnight, as soon as the army has reached Frankfort.

## VIII. THE DOWNFALL OF NAPOLEON

Six months after the battle of Leipzig Napoleon finally renounced, for himself and his heirs, the thrones of France and Italy (April 11, 1814), and on the same day concluded the Treaty of Fontainebleau with his enemies.

218. Treaty of Fontainebleau, in which Napoleon abdicates (April 11, 1814).

His Majesty the Emperor Napoleon, on the one part, and, on the other, their Majesties the emperor of Austria, the king of Prussia, and the emperor of all the Russias, both in their own names and those of their allies. . . .

1. His Majesty the Emperor Napoleon renounces for himself, his successors and descendants, as well as for all the members of his family, all right of sovereignty and dominion as well in the French empire as in the kingdom of Italy and in every other country.

2. Their Majesties the Emperor Napoleon and the Empress Maria Louisa shall retain their titles and rank, to be enjoyed during their lifetime. The mother, brothers, sisters, nephews, and nieces of the emperor shall retain, wherever they may be, the titles of princes of his family.

3. The island of Elba, adopted by his Majesty the Emperor Napoleon as the place of his residence, shall form during his life a separate principality, which shall be possessed by him in full sovereignty and proprietorship.

There shall be given to the Emperor Napoleon, besides full proprietorship of the island of Elba, an annual revenue of two million francs. . . .

5. The duchies of Parma, Piacenza, and Guastalla shall be given in full proprietorship and sovereignty to her Majesty the Empress Maria Louisa. They shall pass to her son and to his descendants in the direct line. The prince, her son, shall assume from this moment the title of Prince of Parma, Piacenza, and Guastalla. . . .

Eleven months later Napoleon returned from Elba, but was met by a declaration of the allies, who were in conference at Vienna, branding him an enemy and disturber of the world's peace, and a fit object of public vengeance.

In less than two months after his final defeat at Waterloo, the ship bearing him to St. Helena was well on its way. One of the few companions who were permitted to accompany him, the Comte de Las Cases, kept an interesting journal of his experiences, especially of his conversations with Napoleon (see above, p. 468). He makes the following entries in his diary.

*August 10.* This day we cleared the Channel. We had now entered upon the dreary unknown course to which fate had doomed us. Again my agonies were renewed; again the dear connections I had abandoned resumed their sway over my heart. . . . Meanwhile we advanced in our course and were soon to be out of Europe. Thus, in less than six weeks, had the emperor abdicated his throne and placed himself in the hands of the English, who were now hurrying him to a barren rock in the midst of a vast ocean. This is certainly no ordinary instance of the chances of fortune, and no common trial of firmness of mind. . . .

219. Napoleon's exile to St. Helena. (From Las Cases' diary.)

As to the reproach of suffering himself to be transported to St. Helena, it would be a disgrace to answer such a charge.

*August 11–14.* Our course was shaped to cross the Bay of Biscay and to double Cape Finisterre. The wind was fair though light, and the heat excessive. Nothing could be more monotonous than the time we now passed. . . . It is well known that Napoleon was wont to be scarcely more than fifteen minutes at his dinner. Here the two courses alone occupied from an hour to an hour and a half. This was to him a most serious annoyance, though he never mentioned it; his features, gestures, and manner always evinced perfect indifference. Neither the new system of cookery, the difference, or the quality of the dishes ever met with his censure or approbation. . . .

*October 23–24.* The Emperor Napoleon, who but lately possessed such boundless power and disposed of so many crowns, now occupies a wretched hovel, a few feet square, which is perched upon a rock, unprovided with furniture, and without either shutters or curtains to the windows. This place must serve him for bedchamber, dressing room, dining room, study, and sitting room; and he is obliged to go out when it is necessary to have this one apartment cleaned. His meals, consisting of a few wretched dishes, are brought to him from a distance, as though he were a criminal in a dungeon. He is absolutely in want of the necessaries of life: the bread and wine are not only not such as he has been accustomed to, but are so bad that we loathe to touch them; water, coffee, butter, oil, and other articles are either not to be procured or are scarcely fit for use. . . .

We were all assembled around the emperor, and he was recapitulating these facts with warmth: "For what infamous treatment are we reserved!" he exclaimed. "This is the anguish of death. To injustice and violence they now add insult and protracted torment. If I were so hateful to them, why did they not get rid of me? A few musket balls in my heart or my head would have done the business, and there would at least have been some energy in the crime. Were it not for you, and above all for your wives, I would receive nothing from them but the pay of a private soldier. How can the monarchs of Europe permit the sacred character of sovereignty to be violated in my person? Do they not see that they are, with their own hands, working their own destruction at St. Helena? I entered their capitals victorious and, had I cherished such sentiments, what would have become of them? They styled me their brother, and I had become so by the choice of the people, the sanction of victory, the character of religion, and the alliances of their policy and their blood. Do they imagine that the good sense of nations is blind to their conduct? And what do they expect from it? At all events, make your complaints, gentlemen; let indignant Europe hear them. Complaints from me would be beneath my dignity and character; I must either command or be silent."

# BIBLIOGRAPHY

**Napoleon's Reforms in France :** Fournier, *Napoleon*, Chapter IX, pp. 221–241.

**Campaign of Austerlitz :** Fournier, Chapter XI, pp. 283–324; Fyffe, *Modern Europe*, Chapter VI, pp. 179–207.

**Napoleon's Creation of New States :** Fournier, Chapter XII, pp. 325–355.

**Jena and Tilsit :** Fournier, Chapter XIII, pp. 356–390; Fyffe, Chapter VII, pp. 208–246.

**Napoleon's Empire at its Height :** Fournier, Chapter XVI, pp. 493–535; Fyffe, Chapter IX, pp. 271–306.

**Russian Campaign :** Fournier, Chapter XVII, pp. 536–579; Fyffe, Chapter X, pp. 307–329.

**German War of Liberation :** Fournier, Chapter XVIII, pp. 580–642; Fyffe, Chapter XI, pp. 330–367.

**Waterloo :** Fournier, Chapter XX, pp. 694–720.

*A. References.*

---

Fournier, August, *Napoleon the First, A Biography*, 1903; English translation from the German, edited by Professor E. G. Bourne. The best treatment in one volume; scholarly, well written, gives much attention to the general European situation, and is supplied with an extensive and admirable bibliography.

Sloane, William M., *Life of Napoleon Bonaparte*, 4 vols., 4to, magnificently illustrated. A new and cheaper library edition is to be issued. One of the great standard biographies, based upon a long and careful study of the sources. The author confines himself mainly to the personal history of Napoleon, giving much attention to his early years, and makes no attempt to write the history of Europe during the Napoleonic period.

Rose, J. H., *The Life of Napoleon I*, 2 vols., 1902. A careful, up-to-date account, mainly political.

Lanfrey, Pierre, *History of Napoleon*, 4 vols. Translated from the French. This work was interrupted by the author's death, and reaches only to the close of 1811. While the writer makes constant use of the best of sources, Napoleon's own letters, his attitude is unfair, and the motives ascribed for Napoleon's policy are always the lowest. The work forms an excellent antidote to that of Thiers (see below).

Thiers, *History of the Consulate and Empire*. Several editions of the English translation are available. Thiers shows an unmistakable

*B. Additional reading in English.*

tendency, especially in the earlier half of his work, unduly to glorify the Napoleonic régime. The sources relied upon are, moreover, very rarely cited. The work is, nevertheless, important and is probably the most interesting history in twenty volumes ever written.

TAINE, *The French Revolution*, Vol. III (on the Directory). By the same writer, *The Modern Régime*, 2 vols., 1894; especially Vol. I, Book I, in which the author gives in a short space the most brilliant, fascinating, and suggestive analysis of Napoleon's genius ever written. The remainder of the work is a critical estimate of the influence of the institutions established by Napoleon upon the later history of France.

SEELEY, *Life and Times of Stein, or Germany and Prussia in the Napoleonic Age*, 3 vols., 1878.

MAHAN, *Influence of the Sea Power upon the French Revolution and Empire*, 2 vols.

FISHER, H. A. L., *Studies in Napoleonic Statesmanship, Germany*, 1903.

DORMAN, *A History of the British Empire in the Nineteenth Century*, Vol. I (1793–1805), 1902.

OMAN, *History of the Peninsular War*, Vols. I–II, 1903.

BIGELOW, P., *History of the German Struggle for Liberty*.

Some sources available in English.    BINGHAM, *A Selection from the Letters and Despatches of the First Napoleon*, 3 vols., 1884.

ANDERSON, *Constitutions and Documents Illustrative of the History of France, 1789–1901*. Contains translations of many important documents.

*New Letters of Napoleon I* edited by Lecestre (Appleton) (omitted from the great collection of his correspondence).

The *Memoirs* of Napoleon dictated on the island of St. Helena are by no means wholly reliable, but are, nevertheless, very interesting and important. Among the memoirs of his companions on St. Helena to be had in English are LAS CASES, *The Journal of St. Helena* (see above, pp. 468 *sqq.*); MONTHOLON, *History of the Captivity of Napoleon*, 1846; *A Diary of St. Helena* (containing conversations of Napoleon with Sir Malcolm), 1899; GOURGAUD, *Journal*, Chicago, 1903.

Memoirs.    A considerable number of the innumerable memoirs relating to the Napoleonic period have been translated. Among these the most conspicuous are those by MADAME DE RÉMUSAT, relating to the early years of the empire (excellent); BOURRIENNE, very well known and especially valuable for Napoleon's earlier life; MIOT DE MELITO, one of King Joseph's companions (excellent); PASQUIER, SÉGUR, TALLEYRAND, 5 vols.; MÉNEVAL, 3 vols.; MARBOT, 2 vols., etc. *Narrative of Captain Coignet*, translated by Mrs. Carey. A striking account of the life of a simple-minded soldier.

# CHAPTER XXXIX

## EUROPE AFTER THE CONGRESS OF VIENNA

### I. THE CONGRESS OF VIENNA

When the long and bloody struggle of the European powers against Napoleon was finally brought to a successful issue in the spring of 1814, France, who was looked upon as the chief promoter of discord during the previous twenty years, was naturally viewed as the black sheep by the allies. But Louis XVIII was represented at the Congress of Vienna by a well-tried diplomat, Talleyrand, who skillfully took advantage of the divergent interests of the allies and soon restored France to her natural position of importance in the concert of the powers. Early in January, 1815, he was able to write the following complacent letter to Louis XVIII.

*France at first viewed as a black sheep at the Congress of Vienna.*

VIENNA, January 4, 1815.

*Sire:*

I have received the letter of the 23d of last month with which your Majesty deigned to honor me. On the 21st of the present month, the anniversary of a day of horror and eternal mourning,[1] a solemn expiatory service will be celebrated in one of the principal churches of Vienna. . . . Everything in this sad ceremony must be proportioned to the grandeur of its object, the splendor of the crown of France, and the quality of those who are to be present. All the members of the Congress will be invited, and I am sure that they will come. . . .

*220. Talleyrand writes to Louis XVIII describing his successful diplomacy at Vienna.*

[1] The anniversary of the execution of Louis XVI.

Treaty of
Ghent (De-
cember 24,
1814).

The news of the signature of peace between England
and the United States of America was announced to me
on New Year's day by a note from Lord Castlereagh.  I hastened to offer him my congratulations, and I also congratulated myself on the event, feeling that it may influence
both the disposition of the minister and the resolution of
those with whose pretensions we have had to contend
hitherto.  Lord Castlereagh showed me the treaty.  It does
not wound the honor of either of the two parties concerned
and consequently it will satisfy both.

Hostility of
the allies
toward
France.

This happy intelligence was only the precursor of a still
more fortunate event.  The spirit of the coalition, and the
coalition itself, had survived the Peace of Paris.  My correspondence up to the present time has supplied your
Majesty with repeated proofs of this.

If the plans which, on arriving here, I found had been
formed, had been carried into execution, France might have
stood alone in Europe without being in good relations with
any one single power for half a century to come.  All my
efforts were directed to the prevention of so great a misfortune, but my most ardent hopes did not reach the height
of a complete success.

Talleyrand
forms an
alliance
between
France,
England,
Austria, and
lesser powers.

But now, sire, the coalition is dissolved, and forever.
Not only does France no longer stand alone in Europe,
but your Majesty is already in an alliance such as it seemed
that fifty years of negotiation could not have procured
for her.

France is now in concert with two of the greatest powers
and three states of the second order, and will soon be in
concert with all the states which are guided by other than
revolutionary principles and maxims.  Your Majesty will be,
in reality, the head and soul of that union, formed for the
defense of the principles which your Majesty has been the
first to proclaim.

So great and happy a change is only to be attributed to
that special favor of Providence which was so clearly indicated by the restoration of your Majesty to the throne.
Under God, the efficient causes of this change have been :

My letters to Monsieur de Metternich and Lord Castlereagh and the impressions which they have produced;

The suggestions which I gave Lord Castlereagh relative to a union with France and of which I gave your Majesty an account in my last letter;

The pains I have taken to lull his distrust by exhibiting perfect disinterestedness in the name of France;

The peace with America, which, by releasing him from difficulty on that side, has left him more liberty of action and given him greater courage;

Lastly, the pretensions of Russia and Prussia, as set forth in the Russian project of which I have the honor to subjoin a copy; and especially the manner in which those pretensions were advanced and argued in a conference between their plenipotentiaries and those of Austria. The arrogant tone of that insolent and nonsensical document so deeply offended Lord Castlereagh that, departing from his habitual calmness, he declared that the Russians were claiming to lay down the law and that England was not disposed to accept that from anybody.

## II. France after the Restoration

Chancellor Pasquier, with his usual insight, gives in his *Memoirs* the following picture of France on the restoration of the Bourbons.

Vanquished on the 10th of August, 1792, immolated on the 21st of January, 1793, the Bourbon monarchy had returned after twenty-two years, which had seen a republic, a directorial government, a consulate, and an empire. It came back not in a blaze of glory, since not a single victory had been won in the past twenty years either by it or in its name, but bringing with it the blessings of a necessary peace. Peace abroad, peace at home, was all that was expected of it; but for this dual peace to be lasting it must be an honorable one. No longer could any ambitious daydreams be indulged in; we could revel no more in the

221. Difficult position of Louis XVIII and his government.

enjoyment of the brilliant victories which had become so dear to the French heart. Care must be taken the while to respect the memory of them, and to be considerate in the treatment of those who had risen to an illustrious and glorious prominence, all the more precious in that it alone had survived the shipwreck. Yet fate and the force of circumstances rendered these memories, cherished by so large a majority of Frenchmen, a painful subject to the king, the royal family, and almost all those who had returned in their wake.

Strained relations between the returned *Emigrés* and the Napoleonic nobility.

The situation was a delicate one, for hardly any one dared to give frank expression to his natural sentiments. Some there were who, in spite of the caution enjoined by policy, necessarily found their prestige dimmed. Accustomed as they had been for fifteen years to hold first rank both in the army and at court, they now found themselves forced to share their power with men the greater number of whom had hitherto remained unknown to fame, and who suddenly assumed an attitude characterized by a superiority which displayed itself with that ease which usually belongs only to a possession of long date. . .

It not unfrequently occurred that the most illustrious among generals heard people ask in the salons of the Tuileries who they were. These names, which had so often resounded in the bulletins of the *Grande Armée*, were known in Vienna, in Berlin, and in the many capitals through which their bearers had passed as conquerors. On the other hand, those who in their own country, and in its very capital, involuntarily put this slight upon them, were perpetually exasperated at heart by the consideration and respectful treatment which policy dictated should be shown to men of the empire, and which seemed to the returned royalists excessive. . . .

There was an ever-present and ill-concealed feeling of antagonism between the throng of officers who had won their promotion in the wars of the Revolution and the noblemen of all ages who were in so great a hurry to wear their old epaulets once more or to procure fresh ones.

The constitution which Louis XVIII granted to France upon the restoration of the Bourbon dynasty in 1814 is important from two points of view. In the first place, it furnishes an expression of the permanent results of the revolutionary period. Its concessions measure the space which separates the times of Louis XVI from those of his brother, Louis XVIII. In this respect the preamble and the bill of rights are of especial interest. Secondly, no other constitution has as yet ever served France for so long a period, although the present republican constitution bids fair to be as permanent. The Charter, although somewhat modified in 1830 upon the accession of Louis Philippe, was maintained until 1848.

*Louis, by the grace of God king of France and Navarre, to all those to whom these presents come, salutation :*

Divine Providence, in recalling us to our estates after a long absence, has imposed grave responsibilities upon us. Peace was the first necessity of our subjects, and with this we have unceasingly occupied ourselves. That peace so essential to France and to the rest of Europe has been signed.

A Constitutional Charter was demanded by the existing condition of the kingdom; we promised this and now publish it. We have taken into consideration the fact that, although the whole authority in France resides in the person of the king, our predecessors have not hesitated to modify the exercise of this in accordance with the differences of the times. It was thus that the communes owed their enfranchisement to Louis the Fat, the confirmation and extension of their rights to St. Louis and Philip the Fair, and that the judicial system was established and developed by the laws of Louis XI, Henry II, and Charles IX. It was in this way, finally, that Louis XIV regulated almost every portion of the public administration by various ordinances which have never been surpassed in wisdom.

222. Extracts from the French Charter of 1814.

Reasons which led Louis XVIII to grant a constitution.

We, like the kings our predecessors, have had to consider the effects of the ever-increasing progress of knowledge, the new relations which this progress has introduced into society, the direction given to the public mind during half a century, and the serious troubles resulting therefrom. We have perceived that the wish of our subjects for a Constitutional Charter was the expression of a real need. . . .

But while we recognize that the expectations of enlightened Europe ought to be gratified by a free monarchical constitution, we have had to remember that our first duty toward our people was to preserve, for their own interest, the rights and prerogatives of our crown. . . .

For these reasons we have voluntarily, and by the free exercise of our royal authority, granted and do grant, concede, and accord, as well for us as for our successors forever, the Constitutional Charter, as follows.

### Public Rights of the French[1]

Article 1. All Frenchmen are equal before the law, whatever may be their title or rank.

2. They contribute without distinction to the impositions of the state in proportion to their fortune.

3. They are all equally eligible to civil and military positions.

4. Their personal liberty is likewise guaranteed; no one can be prosecuted or arrested except in the cases and in the manner prescribed by law.

5. All may with equal liberty make profession of their religion and enjoy the same protection for their worship.

6. Nevertheless the Roman Catholic and apostolic religion is the religion of the state.

7. The ministers of the Roman Catholic and apostolic religion, and those of other Christian forms of worship only, shall receive subsidies from the royal treasury.

---

[1] To show the permanence of the first achievements of the Revolution this list of rights should be compared with the Declaration of the Rights of Man drawn up in 1789 (see above, pp. 439 *sqq.*).

8. All Frenchmen have the right to publish and cause their opinions to be printed, if they conform to the laws destined to check the abuse of this liberty.

9. All property is inviolable; that known as *national* property forms no exception, since the law recognizes no difference between that and other property.

10. The state may demand the surrender of property in the interest of the public when this is legally certified, but only with previous indemnification.

11. All investigation of opinions expressed or of votes cast previous to the Restoration is prohibited; oblivion of these is imposed upon the courts and upon citizens alike.

12. The conscription is abolished; the method of recruiting both for the army and the navy shall be determined by law.

The unpopularity of Louis XVIII's successor, Charles X, led to the revolution of 1830. After the disorders in Paris on the "July days," the Chamber of Deputies issued the following declaration, August 7, 1830.

The Chamber of Deputies, in view of the imperative necessity resulting from the events of July 26, 27, 28, and 29, and the following days, and the general situation of France due to the violation of the Constitutional Charter;

223. The Chamber of Deputies summons Louis Philippe to the throne.

In view also of the fact that, in consequence of this violation and of the heroic resistance of the citizens of Paris, his Majesty Charles X and his Royal Highness Louis Antoine, the dauphin, and all the members of the older branch of the royal house are at this moment leaving French territory, declares that the throne is vacant in fact and right and that it is indispensable to provide therefor.

The throne declared vacant.

The Chamber of Deputies declares, secondly, that, in accordance with the wish and in the interest of the French people, the preamble of the Constitutional Charter is suppressed as wounding the national dignity, since it appears to *grant* to Frenchmen the rights which are inherently theirs,[1]

---

[1] See preceding page.

A. 33

and that the following articles of the same character must be suppressed or modified in the manner below indicated.

[Here follows a series of modifications in the charter, intended to preclude the illiberal construction which Charles X had placed upon it.]

Louis Philippe invited, under certain conditions, to become king of France.

On condition of the acceptance of these arrangements and propositions, the Chamber of Deputies declares that the general and pressing interest of the French people summons to the throne his Royal Highness Louis Philippe of Orleans, duke of Orleans, lieutenant general of the kingdom, and his descendants forever, from male to male, in order of primogeniture, to the perpetual exclusion of women and their descendants. Accordingly his Royal Highness Louis Philippe of Orleans shall be invited to accept and swear to the clauses and engagements above enumerated, and to the observation of the Constitutional Charter including the modifications indicated, and, after having done this in the presence of the assembled chambers, to take the title of King of the French.

## III. The German Confederation of 1815

The German liberals came out of the struggle against Napoleon with high hopes. They desired that the many German states might be bound together into a really firm national union, under a constitutional government. Prussia favored this plan at Vienna, but Austria opposed it for obvious reasons, and the German Act of Confederation, drawn up by the Congress of Vienna, established a very loose union of sovereign princes, who dealt with one another almost like independent rulers. Nevertheless this constitution lasted Germany from 1815 to 1866, and formed a transition from the ancient Holy Roman Empire, which Napoleon had destroyed, to the present German empire.

*In the name of the Most Holy and Indivisible Trinity:*

The sovereign princes and free towns of Germany, animated by the common desire to carry into effect Article VI of the Peace of Paris of May 30, 1814, and convinced of the advantages which would result for the security and independence of Germany and for the repose and equilibrium of Europe from a firm and lasting union, have agreed to unite themselves in a perpetual confederation, and have for this purpose invested their envoys and deputies at the Congress of Vienna with full powers, viz. :

224. The German Act of Confederation (June 8, 1815).

His Imperial and Royal Apostolic Majesty; the Sieur Clement Wenceslas, Prince of Metternich-Winneburg-Ochsenhausen, Knight of the Golden Fleece, Grand Cross of the Royal Order of St. Stephen of Hungary, Knight of the Order of St. Andrew, of the Order of St. Alexander Newsky and of St. Anne of the First Class; Grand Cordon of the Legion of Honor; Knight of the Order of the Elephant, of the Order of the Annunciation, of the Black Eagle, of the Red Eagle, of the Seraphim, of St. Joseph of Tuscany, of St. Hubert, of the Golden Eagle of Würtemberg, of the Fidelity of Baden, of St. John of Jerusalem, and of several others; Chancellor of the Military Order of Maria Theresa; Curator of the Imperial and Royal Academy of Fine Arts; Chamberlain and Active Privy Councilor of his Majesty the emperor of Austria and king of Hungary and Bohemia; his Majesty's Minister of State and of Conferences, as well as Minister of Foreign Affairs and first plenipotentiary at the Congress, — and the Sieur John Philip, baron of Wessenberg; Grand Cross of the Royal Sardinian Order of St. Mauritius and St. Lazarus, and of the Royal Order of the Crown of Bavaria, etc.; Chamberlain and Active Privy Councilor of his Imperial and Royal Apostolic Majesty, and his Majesty's second plenipotentiary at the Congress.

Metternich's grandeur.

His Royal Majesty of Prussia; the Prince Hardenberg, his Chancellor of State.[1] . . .

[1] It has not been deemed necessary to give the names of all the plenipotentiaries. All the states enumerated in Article IV were represented at the Congress.

## GENERAL PROVISIONS

ARTICLE I. The sovereign princes and free towns of Germany, including their Majesties the emperor of Austria and the kings of Prussia, of Denmark, and of the Netherlands; to wit, the emperor of Austria and the king of Prussia, for all of their possessions formerly belonging to the German empire [1]; the king of Denmark for Holstein; and the king of the Netherlands for the grand duchy of Luxemburg, — unite in a perpetual union which shall be called the German Confederation.

II. The aim of the same shall be the maintenance of the external and internal safety of Germany and of the independence and inviolability of the individual German states.

III. All members of the union have, as such, equal rights. They all engage alike to maintain inviolate the Act of Confederation.

Voting in the Diet.

IV. The affairs of the Confederation shall be confided to a Diet of the Confederation, in which all members of the union shall vote through their plenipotentiaries, either individually or collectively, in the following manner, without prejudice to their rank.

| | VOTES | | | VOTES |
|---|---|---|---|---|
| 1. Austria | 1 | 12. The grand ducal and ducal | | |
| 2. Prussia | 1 | houses of Saxony | | 1 |
| 3. Bavaria | 1 | 13. Brunswick and Nassau | | 1 |
| 4. Saxony | 1 | 14. Mecklenburg-Schwerin and | | |
| 5. Hanover | 1 | Mecklenburg-Strelitz | | 1 |
| 6. Würtemberg | 1 | 15. Holstein-Oldenburg, Anhalt, | | |
| 7. Baden | 1 | and Schwarzburg | | 1 |
| 8. Electoral Hesse | 1 | 16. Hohenzollern, Liechtenstein, | | |
| 9. Grand duchy of Hesse | 1 | Reuss, Schaumburg-Lippe, | | |
| 10. Denmark, for Holstein | 1 | Lippe, and Waldeck | | 1 |
| 11. The Netherlands, for the grand duchy of Luxemburg | 1 | 17. The free towns, Lübeck, Frankfort, Bremen, and Hamburg | | 1 |

Total votes . . . . . . . . . . . . . . . . . . . . . 17

V. Austria shall preside in the Diet of the Confederation. Each member of the union has the right to make

[1] I.e. the Holy Roman Empire.

and support propositions, and the presiding state is bound within a determined period to bring them under deliberation.

VI. Whenever fundamental laws of the Confederation are to be enacted or amended, or measures are to be adopted relative to the Act of Confederation itself or organic institutions of the Confederation, or other arrangements of common interest are under consideration, the Diet shall form itself into a general assembly (*Plenum*), in which the distribution of the votes, based upon the respective extent of the individual states of the union, has been arranged as follows.[1]

System of voting on special occasions.

| | VOTES | | VOTES |
|---|---|---|---|
| 1. Austria | 4 | 20. Mecklenburg-Strelitz | 1 |
| 2. Prussia | 4 | 21. Holstein-Oldenburg | 1 |
| 3. Saxony | 4 | 22. Anhalt-Dessau | 1 |
| 4. Bavaria | 4 | 23. Anhalt-Bernburg | 1 |
| 5. Hanover | 4 | 24. Anhalt-Cöthen | 1 |
| 6. Würtemberg | 4 | 25. Schwarzburg-Sondershausen | 1 |
| 7. Baden | 3 | 26. Schwarzburg-Rudolstadt | 1 |
| 8. Electoral Hesse | 3 | 27. Hohenzollern-Hechingen | 1 |
| 9. Grand duchy of Hesse | 3 | 28. Liechtenstein | 1 |
| 10. Holstein | 3 | 29. Hohenzollern-Sigmaringen | 1 |
| 11. Luxemburg | 3 | 30. Waldeck | 1 |
| 12. Brunswick | 2 | 31. Reuss, Elder Branch | 1 |
| 13. Mecklenburg-Schwerin | 2 | 32. Reuss, Younger Branch | 1 |
| 14. Nassau | 2 | 33. Schaumberg-Lippe | 1 |
| 15. Saxe-Weimar | 1 | 34. Lippe | 1 |
| 16 Saxe-Gotha | 1 | 35. The free town Lübeck | 1 |
| 17. Saxe-Coburg | 1 | 36. The free town Frankfort | 1 |
| 18. Saxe-Meiningen | 1 | 37. The free town Bremen | 1 |
| 19. Saxe-Hildburghausen | 1 | 38. The free town Hamburg | 1 |

Total votes . . . . . . . . . . . . . . . . . . 69

The Diet of the Confederation, in deliberating on the organic laws of the union, shall take into consideration whether the mediatized estates of the former empire shall be granted any collective votes in the *Plenum*. . . .

VIII. When the organic laws shall have been drawn up, the Diet of the Confederation shall take into consideration the future permanent order of voting to be adopted. In so

Reference to the great readjustment of 1803.

[1] The system of voting which now prevails in the Federal Council (*Bundesrath*) of the German empire is based on this plan of 1815.

doing they shall deviate as little as possible from the regulations of the former Diet, especially as based upon the provisions of the Decree of the Imperial Commission of 1803.

IX. The Diet of the Confederation shall sit at Frankfort-on-the-Main. The first meeting is fixed for the 1st of September, 1815.

XI. All members of the Confederation pledge themselves to protect Germany as a whole, as well as every single confederated state, against attack, and mutually guarantee their entire possessions, so far as those are included within the Confederation.

When war is once declared on the part of the Confederation no member shall negotiate separately with the enemy, or conclude an armistice or make peace.

Members reserve the right to form alliances.

XII. The members of the Confederation reserve to themselves the right of forming alliances of all kinds. They pledge themselves, however, to contract no engagement which shall be directed against the safety of the Confederation or that of any individual state within the union.

The members of the Confederation pledge themselves likewise not to make war among themselves upon any pretense, or to follow up their contentions with force, but to submit these to the Diet. It shall devolve upon this body to attempt arbitration by means of a commission. Should this fail and a judicial decision become necessary, the same shall be effected through a well-organized court of arbitration, to the decision of which the conflicting parties shall forthwith submit.

## IV. The Independence of Greece and Belgium

While Metternich and his allies were intervening to check reform in western and southern Europe, the Greeks rose against their masters and declared themselves a free and independent state. This was a source of deep satisfaction to the liberal parties in the West, who had suffered so many disappointments since the opening of the Congress of Vienna. A constitutional assembly was convoked in Greece, which, having completed a provisional constitution, issued the following manifesto.

We, descendants of the wise and noble peoples of Hellas, we who are the contemporaries of the enlightened and civilized nations of Europe, we who behold the advantages which they enjoy under the protection of the impenetrable ægis of the law, find it no longer possible to suffer without cowardice and self-contempt the cruel yoke of the Ottoman power which has weighed upon us for more than four centuries, — a power which does not listen to reason and knows no other law than its own will, which orders and disposes everything despotically and according to its caprice. After this prolonged slavery we have determined to take arms to avenge ourselves and our country against a frightful tyranny, iniquitous in its very essence, — an unexampled despotism to which no other rule can be compared.

225. Proclamation of independence issued by the Greek National Assembly (January 27, 1822).

The war which we are carrying on against the Turk is not that of a faction or the result of sedition. It is not aimed at the advantage of any single part of the Greek people; it is a national war, a holy war, a war the object of which is to reconquer the rights of individual liberty, of property and honor, — rights which the civilized people of Europe, our neighbors, enjoy to-day; rights of which the cruel and unheard-of tyranny of the Ottomans would deprive us — us alone — and the very memory of which they would stifle in our hearts.

Are we, then, less reasonable than other peoples, that we remain deprived of these rights? Are we of a nature so degraded and abject that we should be viewed as unworthy to enjoy them, condemned to remain crushed under a perpetual slavery and subjected, like beasts of burden or mere automatons, to the absurd caprice of a cruel tyrant who, like an infamous brigand, has come from distant regions to invade our borders? Nature has deeply graven these rights in the hearts of all men; laws in harmony with nature have so completely consecrated them that neither three nor four centuries — nor thousands nor millions of centuries — can destroy them. Force and violence have been able to restrict and paralyze them for a season, but force may once more resuscitate them in all the vigor which they formerly enjoyed during many centuries; nor have we ever ceased in Hellas to defend these rights by arms whenever opportunity offered.

Building upon the foundation of our natural rights, and desiring to assimilate ourselves to the rest of the Christians of Europe, our brethren, we have begun a war against the Turks, or rather, uniting all our isolated strength, we have formed ourselves into a single armed body, firmly resolved to attain our end, to govern ourselves by wise laws, or to be altogether annihilated, believing it to be unworthy of us, as descendants of the glorious peoples of Hellas, to live henceforth in a state of slavery fitted rather for unreasoning animals than for rational beings.

Ten months have elapsed since we began this national war; the all-powerful God has succored us; although we were not adequately prepared for so great an enterprise, our arms have everywhere been victorious, despite the powerful obstacles which we have encountered and still encounter everywhere. We have had to contend with a situation bristling with difficulties, and we are still engaged in our efforts to overcome them. It should not, therefore, appear astonishing that we were not able from the very first to proclaim our independence and take rank among the civilized peoples of the earth, marching forward side by side with them. . . .

EPIDAURUS, January $\frac{15}{27}$, 1822:
the First Year of Independence.

The first signal disturbance of the arrangements made by the Congress of Vienna was the revolt of the former Austrian Netherlands from the rule of the king of Holland, to whom the Congress had assigned them. The creation of the present kingdom of Belgium is described in an address read at the opening session of the Belgian congress, November 10, 1830.

In the name of the Belgian people, the provisional government opens an assembly of the representatives of the nation. The nation has confided to these representatives the august mission of founding, on the broad and solid basis of liberty, the edifice of the new social order which will be the beginning and the guarantee of durable happiness to Belgium.

You know, gentlemen, that at the time of our union with Holland a Fundamental Law was presented to an assembly of notables, chosen by the government, not to examine, discuss, modify, and finally to accept it and make it the condition of a compact between the people and the head of the state, but either to submit to it unconditionally, or to reject it altogether. It was rejected, as might have been expected from the good sense and integrity of the Belgians; but by an unparalleled subterfuge it was nevertheless declared to be accepted, and thus it came about that our country was oppressed by a constitution imposed by Holland.

If this Fundamental Law had at least been properly executed in all its provisions, in time, perhaps, and with the aid of the progress which the arbitrary conduct of the ministers compelled us daily to make in the career of constitutional opposition, it might have become the hope of Belgian liberty.

But far from this being the case, freedom of conscience was violated, education fettered, the press condemned to be nothing more than an instrument of the government or forced into silence . . . and the right of petition was disregarded. The despotic imposition of a privileged language, . . . and an enormous debt and expenditure, were the only portion which Holland brought to us at the time of our deplorable union. Add to these grievances taxes, overwhelming by their amount and still more by the manner in which they were apportioned, laws always voted by the Dutch for Holland only and always against Belgium, . . .

and, lastly, the most offensive partiality in the distribution of civil and military appointments by a government in whose eye the name of Belgian was a disgrace; in a word, all Belgium treated as a conquered province, as a colony, — everything rendered a revolution necessary and inevitable and hastened its approach. Such just and real grievances could only lead to one result.

We had risen against despotism to reconquer our rights, and we were treated by tyranny as rebels. Our cities were burned; the most barbarous treatment was inflicted even upon old men and upon women; the rights of humanity, the laws of war, were trampled underfoot. Such conduct testifies to the ferocity of our enemy and calls down blessings on the victory of the people which has cleared our territory of them.

The fruit of this victory has been independence. The people have proclaimed it through us, and have called you together, gentlemen, as the organ of its wishes to establish it forever.

## BIBLIOGRAPHY

*A. References.*

**Congress of Vienna and the Reconstruction of Europe:** Seignobos, *Political History of Europe since 1814,* Chapter I, pp. 1–8; Andrews, *The Historical Development of Modern Europe,* Vol. I, Chapter I, pp. 86–133; Phillips, *Modern Europe from 1815,* Chapter I, pp. 1–13.

**Restoration and July Revolution in France:** Phillips, Chapter II, pp. 22–36; Chapter VIII, pp. 168–185; Andrews, Vol. I, Chapter II, pp. 134–179; Seignobos, Chapter V, pp. 103–132.

**The German Confederation and Metternich's Policy:** Phillips, Chapter III, pp. 37–56; Seignobos, Chapter XII, pp. 374–386; Andrews, Vol. I, Chapter VI, pp. 229–241.

**Struggle for Italian Unity:** Seignobos, Chapter XI, pp. 326–339; Andrews, Vol. I, Chapter V, pp. 180–228.

**Independence of Greece:** Phillips, Chapter VII, pp. 135–167; Seignobos, Chapter XXI, pp. 648–654; Fyffe, *Modern Europe,* Chapter XV, pp. 525–602.

[For the general bibliography of the period since 1815, see the close of the following chapter.]

# CHAPTER XL

## UNIFICATION OF GERMANY AND ITALY

### I. REVOLUTION OF 1848 IN FRANCE: NAPOLEON III

The provisional government established in Paris after
the mob had attacked the Tuileries, February 24, 1848,
immediately issued the following proclamation.

*In the name of the French people:*

A reactionary and oligarchical government has just been
overthrown by the heroism of the people of Paris. That
government has fled, leaving behind it a trail of blood that
forbids it ever to retrace its steps.

The blood of the people has flowed as in July [1830];
but this time this noble people shall not be deceived. It has
won a national and popular government in accord with the
rights, the progress, and the will of this great and generous
nation.

A provisional government, the result of pressing necessity
and ratified by the voice of the people and of the deputies
of the departments, in the session of February 24, is for the
moment invested with the task of assuring and organizing
the national victory. It is composed of Messieurs Dupont
(de l'Eure), Lamartine, Crémieux, Arago (of the Institute),
Ledru-Rollin, Garnier-Pagès, Marie, Armand Marrast, Louis
Blanc, Ferdinand Flocon, and Albert (a workingman).

These citizens have not hesitated a moment to accept the
patriotic commission which is imposed upon them by the
pressure of necessity. With the capital of France on fire,
the justification for the present provisional government must
be sought in the public safety. All France will understand
this and will lend it the support of its patriotism. Under

*227. The
overthrow
of the
Orleanist
monarchy is
proclaimed
by the
provisional
government
(February
24, 1848).*

the popular government which the provisional government proclaims, every citizen is a magistrate.

Frenchmen, it is for you to give to the world the example which Paris has given to France; prepare yourselves by order and by confidence in your destiny for the firm institutions which you are about to be called upon to establish.

Provisional government desires a republic.

The provisional government wishes to establish a republic, — subject, however, to ratification by the people, who shall be immediately consulted.

The unity of the nation (formed henceforth of all the classes of citizens who compose it); the government of the nation by itself; liberty, equality, and fraternity, for fundamental principles, and "the people" for our emblem and watchword: these constitute the democratic government which France owes to itself, and which our efforts shall secure for it.

The workingmen and their leaders played an important part in the February revolution. This fact is emphasized by the decrees in the interest of the laboring classes which were issued by the provisional government on the day following its creation.

228. Decrees of the provisional government relating to the workingmen (February 25, 1848).

The provisional government of the French republic decrees that the Tuileries shall serve hereafter as a home for the veterans of labor.

The provisional government of the French republic pledges itself to guarantee the means of subsistence to the workingman by labor.

It pledges itself to guarantee labor to all citizens.

Labor unions sanctioned.

It recognizes that workingmen ought to enter into associations among themselves in order to insure the advantage of their labor.

Suppression of the civil list.

The provisional government returns to the workingmen, to whom it rightfully belongs, the million which was about to fall due upon the civil list.

The provisional government of the French republic decrees that all articles pledged at the pawn shops since the first of February, consisting of linen, garments, clothes, etc., upon which the loan does not exceed ten francs, shall be given back to those who pledged them. The minister of finance is ordered to meet the payments incidental to the execution of the present edict.

Return of pawned articles.

The provisional government of the republic decrees the immediate establishment of national workshops. The minister of public works is charged with the execution of the present decree.

Establishment of national workshops (February 26).

The formal proclamation of the second French republic is very characteristic of the momentary situation.

*In the name of the French people :*

Citizens : royalty, under whatever form, is abolished ; no more legitimism, no more Bonapartism, no regency.

The provisional government has taken all the measures necessary to render impossible the return of the former dynasty or the advent of a new dynasty.

229. The second French republic is proclaimed (February 26, 1848).

The republic is proclaimed.

The people are united.

All the forts which surround the capital are ours.

The brave garrison of Vincennes is a garrison of brothers.

Let us retain that old republican flag whose three colors made with our fathers the circuit of the globe.

Let us show that this symbol of equality, of liberty, and of fraternity is at the same time the symbol of order — of order the more real, the more durable, since justice is its foundation and the whole people its instrument.

The people have already realized that the provisioning of Paris requires a freer circulation in the streets, and those who have erected the barricades have already in several places made openings large enough for the passage of wagons and carts. Let this example be imitated everywhere. Let Paris reassume its accustomed appearance and trade its activity and confidence. . . .

Louis Napoleon becomes a candidate for the presidency of the new French republic.

Although Louis Napoleon had, after the last of his two early and futile attempts to make himself emperor, been imprisoned, then exiled, he was, after the February revolution, elected a member of the Legislative Body. When it came to choosing a president under the new constitution, he was naturally considered as a candidate, and issued the following campaign manifesto (November, 1848).

*Louis Napoleon to his fellow-citizens:*

230. Louis Napoleon explains his position to the voters of France (November 29, 1848).

In order to recall me from exile, you have elected me a representative of the people; on the eve of choosing a chief magistrate for the republic my name presents itself to you as a symbol of order and security.

Those proofs of so honorable a confidence are, I am well aware, addressed to my name rather than to myself, who, as yet, have done nothing for my country; but the more the memory of the Emperor protects me and inspires your suffrages, the more I feel compelled to acquaint you with my sentiments and principles. There must be no equivocation between us.

I am moved by no ambition which dreams one day of empire and war, the next of the application of subversive theories. Brought up in free countries, disciplined in the school of misfortune, I shall ever remain faithful to the duties which your suffrages and the will of the Assembly impose upon me.

If elected president, I shall shrink from no danger, from no sacrifice, in the defense of society, which has been so outrageously assailed. I shall devote myself wholly and without reservation to the consolidation of the republic, so that it may be wise in its laws, honest in its aims, great and strong in its deeds. My greatest honor would be to hand on to my successor, after four years of office, the public power consolidated, its liberties intact, and a genuine progress assured. . . .

LOUIS NAPOLEON BONAPARTE.

Before the expiration of his four years' term, Louis Napoleon, by the *coup d'état* of December, 1851, secured an extension of his presidency for ten years. He was not satisfied, however, until he had won the title of Emperor. In September, 1852, he undertook a tour through the southern provinces in order to test public opinion. Many suggestions had reached him encouraging him to assume the imperial crown, and frequently on his journey he was received with the cry, "Long live the emperor!" In his speech at Bordeaux, October 9, 1852, he definitely announced his belief that France was ready for the abolition of the second republic.

Louis Napoleon determines to win the imperial title.

The purpose of this journey, as you know, was to see for myself our beautiful provinces of the south and familiarize myself with their needs. It has, however, given rise to a much more important result. Indeed, — and I say it with a candor as far removed from arrogance as from false modesty, — never has a people testified in a manner more direct, spontaneous, and unanimous, the longing to be freed from anxiety as to the future by concentrating in a single person an authority which shall accord with their desires. They realize now both the false hopes with which they have been deluded and the dangers which threaten them. . . .

231. Louis Napoleon's Bordeaux address (October 9, 1852).

France to-day encompasses me with her sympathies because I do not belong to the group of dreamers. In order to benefit the country it is not necessary to resort to new systems, but, above all, to establish confidence in the present and security for the future. This is why France seems to wish to revert to the empire.

There is, nevertheless, one apprehension, and that I shall set at rest. A spirit of distrust leads certain persons to say that the empire means war. I say, the empire means peace. France longs for peace, and if France is satisfied the world is tranquil. Glory is rightly handed down hereditarily, but not war. . . .

Napoleon's policy of peace.

## II. The Revolution of 1848 in Germany and Italy

The February revolution in France was speedily followed by an uprising of the liberal party in Vienna, which, on March 13, forced Metternich to resign the influential position which he had held for so many years. But after a few months' triumph the revolutionary government in Vienna was overthrown by the bombardment and capture of the city, October, 1848, by Windischgrätz, the emperor's general, who had just suppressed the Bohemian revolution. The city had decided to surrender, when it was encouraged to a last futile resistance by the arrival of an army from Hungary ready to forward the revolution. An Englishman, an eyewitness, stationed outside the city, published in the English newspapers the following vivid narrative of the siege and final capitulation of the city.

**232. Vienna retaken by the emperor's troops under Windischgrätz (October 31, 1848).** The beautiful street leading to the Prater [a park] had been the scene of the hardest fighting of all, as it had been fortified by a succession of barricades, built up to the first-floor windows in a half-moon shape, with regular embrasures and planted with cannon. This was strewn with the dead bodies of men and horses; but they, and the pools of blood all about, did not strike us so much as the horrid smell of roast flesh arising from the half-burned bodies of rebels killed in the houses fired by Congreve rockets, which we saw used by the troops with terrible effect. Half of the houses in this beautiful suburb are thus burned down, while the other half are riddled with shot and shell. On every side we may see weeping wives, sisters, and daughters, picking, literally piecemeal, out of the ruins the half-consumed bodies of their relatives.

On Sunday evening, the 29th, the city, dreading a bombardment from the Belvedere, agreed to surrender; but the capitulation was shamefully violated when early the next morning the approach of the Hungarians to raise the siege was signaled from the tower of the cathedral. Then came the real crisis. . . . We were fired upon continually from the ramparts; and I for the first time literally tasted blood, which was dashed over my face and clothes, when a round shot carried off the head of an artilleryman by my side.

All this time the roar of cannon, the whizzing of rockets, and the roll of musketry in our rear told us that the Hungarian army had joined battle; while in our front, from all the ramparts, tops of houses, and churches, the rebels were firing signal guns and waving flags to cheer them on. It was a beautiful clear, sunshiny autumn day; and all felt that there were trembling in the balance not only the fate of the grand old Austrian empire (*an Siegen und an Ehren reich*) — the monarchy of Charles V and Maria Theresa, and so long the bulwark of Christendom against the Turk — but with it the peace and safety of Europe.

At length the firing behind us gradually slackened and then died away; and towards sunset the victorious imperialists marched back from the field of battle, having utterly routed the Hungarians and driven three thousand of them into the Danube, which will roll their bodies down to Pesth, a fearful tiding of their defeat. You may fancy what cheers arose from the imperialists and what yells of despair from the rebels, whose offers of a conditional surrender were now scornfully rejected.

Two months before the overthrow of Metternich and a month before the February revolution in France, it was clear that the Austrian government was likely to have trouble with its subjects in Italy, who had long been discontented with their foreign masters. *Situation in Italy.*

Warned by the demonstrations against Austrian rule which occured in Milan early in January, 1848, Marshal Radetzky, the Austrian commander in Italy, encouraged his troops by the following declaration.

MILAN, January 18, 1848.

**233. Marshal Radetzky encourages his soldiers.**

His Majesty the emperor, being determined according to his rights and duties to defend the Lombardo-Venetian kingdom, as well as every other part of his dominions, against all attacks of an enemy, either from without or from within, has permitted me to make this, his resolve, known to all the troops of the army stationed in Italy. He is persuaded that his intentions will meet with the firmest support in the valor and fidelity of the army.

Soldiers, you have heard the words of the emperor; I am proud to make them known to you. Against your fidelity and your valor the efforts of fanaticism and the infidel spirit of innovation will be broken like brittle glass against solid rock. The sword which I have borne with honor in so many battles during sixty-five years is still eager for action. I shall know how to make use of it to defend the tranquillity of a country a short time since most happy, and which a mad faction now seeks to plunge into misery.

Soldiers, our emperor relies upon you; your old general trusts you : let this suffice. Let them not force us to unfold the banner of the double-headed eagle, for the strength of its talons is yet unimpaired. Let our motto be, Defense and tranquillity to faithful and friendly citizens and destruction to the enemy who shall dare with a treacherous hand to disturb the peace and welfare of nations.

The present order of the day shall be announced to all the corps in their respective languages.

On March 22, 1848, Radetzky, in spite of his boasts, was forced to evacuate Milan, and the provisional government which had been established there appealed to the king of Sardinia for aid.

*Sacred Majesty :*                          MILAN, March 23, 1848.

We have vanquished the enemy who occupied the city. He left the castle last night and marched towards Verona, but he is not yet far from the capital and is marking every step with slaughter and plunder. Our citizens have made heroic efforts, and with very few resources they have repulsed the pride of an enemy confident in his strength. . . .

Although the city is now free, the speedy and potent aid of your Majesty is none the less important. The provisional government therefore implores your Majesty to hasten to assist us by every means. Your Majesty will thus be a benefactor to the sacred cause of Italian independence and brotherhood, and will surely receive the applause and gratitude of this people. We would willingly add more, but our position as a provisional government does not allow us to anticipate the wishes of the nation, which are, without doubt, all directed toward the furtherance of the cause of Italian unity.

234. Milan, after revolting from Austria, appeals to the king of Sardinia for aid (March 23, 1848).

The Austrian government was able, as we have seen, to put down, in October, 1848, the revolt in Vienna, and then had a free hand to reconquer its Italian provinces. The intervention of Charles Albert was unsuccessful, and after his final defeat at Novara, March 23, 1849, his abdication was proclaimed in the following manner.

*Proclamation of Eugene, prince of Savoy-Carignan, lieutenant general of his Majesty:*

I have a sad message to communicate to you. The king, Charles Albert, after having faced with intrepidity the balls of the enemy, would not consent, in view of the reverses of our armies, to bow to ill fortune. He has preferred to crown his life by a new sacrifice. On March 23 he abdicated in favor of the duke of Savoy. The gratitude of his people toward him will know no end, nor our respectful attachment. Let us rally around our new king, in battle a worthy rival of the paternal virtues, and the stanch guardian of the constitutional liberties granted by his august father. Long live the king, Victor Emmanuel!

235. Proclamation of Charles Albert's abdication (March 26, 1849).

TURIN, March 26.

Situation in
Germany.

While Lombardy and Venetia were trying vainly, with
the help of the king of Sardinia, to free themselves
from the yoke of Austria, the Germans were busy at
Frankfort drawing up a new constitution, which they
trusted would at last make a nation out of the various
German states so loosely united by the union of 1815.

But the Frankfort Assembly spent so much time on
its task that conditions became unfavorable to a political
regeneration of Germany. Austria once more regained its
former influence, and when, finally, the Assembly offered
the imperial crown to the timid Frederick William of
Prussia, he naturally declined it. He proposed, nevertheless, that Prussia should join the other German states in
preparing a revision of the constitution drawn up by the
deputies at Frankfort, who had been discredited by the
conduct of the republican factions.

*To my People:*

236. The
king of
Prussia
refuses the
crown ten-
dered him
by the
Frankfort
Assembly
(May 15,
1849).

Taking as a pretense the interests of Germany, the enemies of the fatherland have raised the standard of revolt,
first in the neighboring Saxony, then in several districts of
south Germany. To my deep chagrin, even in parts of our
own land some have permitted themselves to be seduced
into following this standard and attempting, in open rebellion against the legal government, to overturn the order of
things established by both divine and human sanction. In
so serious and dangerous a crisis I am moved publicly to
address a word to my people.

I was not able to return a favorable reply to the offer
of a crown on the part of the German National Assembly,
because the Assembly has not the right, without the consent of the German governments, to bestow the crown, and,
moreover, because they offered it upon condition that I would
accept a constitution which could not be reconciled with the
rights and safety of the German states.

I have exhausted every means to reach an understanding with the German National Assembly. . . . Now the Assembly has broken with Prussia. The majority of its members are no longer those men upon whom Germany looked with pride and confidence. The greater part of the deputies voluntarily left the Assembly when they saw that it was on the road to ruin, and yesterday I ordered all the Prussian deputies who had not already withdrawn to be recalled. The other governments will do the same.

A party now dominates the Assembly which is in league with the terrorists. While they urge the unity of Germany as a pretense, they are really fighting the battle of godlessness, perjury, and robbery, and kindling a war against monarchy; but if monarchy were overthrown it would carry with it the blessings of law, liberty, and property. The horrors committed in Dresden, Breslau, and Elberfeld under the banner of German unity afford a melancholy proof of this. New horrors are occurring and are in prospect.

*Conduct of the republican radicals*

While such crimes have put an end to the hope that the Frankfort Assembly can bring about German unity, I have, with a fidelity and persistence suiting my royal station, never lost hope. My government has taken up with the more important German states the work on the German constitution begun by the Frankfort Assembly.[1] . . .

This is my method. Only madness or deception will dare, in view of these facts, to assert that I have given up the cause of German unity, or that I am untrue to my earlier convictions and assurances. . . .

FREDERICK WILLIAM.

CHARLOTTENBURG, May 15, 1849.

## III. ESTABLISHMENT OF THE KINGDOM OF ITALY

It was left for Cavour and Victor Emmanuel to carry on the work of Italian unification which Charles Albert had begun. Napoleon III, in coming to the aid of the

[1] Prussia's plans were ignominiously given up in the face of Austria's opposition.

Italians, explained his motives to France in a proclamation of May 3, 1859.

237. Napo-
leon III
justifies his
intervention
in Italy.

Frenchmen, Austria in ordering her army to invade the
territory of the king of Sardinia, our ally, has declared war
upon us. She has thus violated treaties and justice, and
threatens our frontiers. All the great powers have protested
against this aggression.

Piedmont having accepted conditions which should have
maintained peace, one cannot but inquire what can be the
reason for this sudden invasion on Austria's part. It is
because Austria has brought matters to such a pass that
either she must dominate as far as the Cottian Alps, or Italy
must be freed to the Adriatic; for every corner of territory
which remains independent in that whole region is a menace
to her authority.

Hitherto moderation has been the rule of my conduct;
now an aggressive policy becomes my duty. Let France
arm herself and say to Europe with determination : " We
do not wish for conquest, but we are resolved to maintain
without flinching our national and traditional policy; we
observe treaties on condition that they shall not be violated
to our disadvantage; we respect the territory and the rights
of neutral powers, but openly avow our sympathy for a people
whose history is bound up with ours, and who groan under
foreign oppression."

France has shown her hatred of anarchy; she has been
pleased to give me an authority strong enough to render
powerless the abettors of disorder and the incorrigible members of former factions who have not hesitated to form
alliances with our enemies ; but she has not, on that account,
abandoned her function as a civilizing power. Her natural
allies have always been those who desire the improvement
of humanity, and when she draws her sword it is not in
order to domineer, but to liberate.

The purpose of this war is, then, to restore Italy to herself, and not simply to change her master ; and we shall have
upon our frontiers a friendly people who will owe their

independence to us. We are not going into Italy to foment disorder, nor to disturb the authority of the Holy Father whom we have replaced upon his throne, but to protect him against that foreign oppression which weighs upon the whole peninsula, and to participate in establishing order there which shall satisfy all legitimate interests. We are, in short, about to enter that classic land rendered illustrious by so many victories. We shall find there traces of our forefathers, of whom God grant we may prove ourselves worthy. . . .

NAPOLEON.

PALACE OF THE TUILERIES, May 3, 1859.

In spite of the fact that, soon after the war began, Napoleon abruptly concluded a truce with Austria, the work of Italian unity went on, and Victor Emmanuel was able to report important progress in his address at the opening of the Sardinian parliament, April 2, 1860.

The last time that I opened this parliament, in the midst of the travails of Italy and dangers to the state, faith in divine justice encouraged me to prophesy a happy issue for us. In a very short space of time an invasion has been repelled ; Lombardy has been freed, thanks to the glorious exploits of our heroes, and central Italy has been delivered, thanks to the remarkable courage of its inhabitants ; and to-day the representatives of right and of the hopes of the nation are assembled about me.

**238. Victor Emmanuel reviews the events of 1859-1860.**

We owe many benefits to a magnanimous ally, to the bravery of his soldiers as well as ours, to the self-abnegation of the volunteers, and to the harmony of the various peoples ; and we render thanks to God, for without superhuman aid these enterprises, memorable not only for our own generation but for ages to come, could not have been achieved.

Out of gratitude to France for the services she has rendered to Italy, and in order to consolidate the union of the two nations, which have a community of origin, of principles, and of destiny, some sacrifice was necessary ; I have made

**Cession of Savoy and Nice to France.**

that one which costs most to my own heart. Subject to the vote of the people and the approbation of the parliament, . . . I have agreed to a treaty providing for the reunion of Savoy and of the district of Nice to France.

We still have many difficulties to overcome, but, sustained by public opinion and by the love of the people, I will not permit any right or liberty to be infringed or diminished.

Victor Emmanuel's attitude toward the Church.

Although I am as consistent in my respect toward the supreme head of our religion as the Catholic rulers, my ancestors, have always shown themselves, nevertheless, should the ecclesiastical authority resort to spiritual arms in support of its temporal interests, I will, relying upon a pure conscience and the traditions of my forefathers, find strength to maintain civil liberty and my authority, for the exercise of which I owe an account only to God and to my people. . . .

On the 18th of February, 1861, after Garibaldi had driven out the Bourbons from southern Italy and thus added the kingdom of the Two Sicilies to the new kingdom of Italy, the first Italian parliament met at Turin in a large hall temporarily built of wood. King Victor Emmanuel opened proceedings with the following review of recent events.

*Senators and Deputies :*

239. Victor Emmanuel's address at the opening session of the Italian parliament (February 18, 1861).

Free and almost entirely united by the wonderful aid of Divine Providence, the harmonious coöperation of the people, and the splendid valor of the army, Italy confides in our uprightness and wisdom. Upon you it devolves to give her uniform institutions and a firm foundation. In extending greater administrative liberty to peoples that have had various usages and institutions, you will take care that political unity, the aspiration of so many centuries, may never be diminished.

The opinion of civilized nations is favorable to us. The just and liberal principles now prevailing in the councils of Europe are favorable to us. Italy herself will in turn become a guarantee of order and peace, and will once more be an efficient instrument of universal civilization.

The emperor of the French, firmly upholding the maxim of non-intervention, — a maxim eminently beneficial to us, — nevertheless deemed it proper to recall his envoy. If this fact was a cause of chagrin to us, it did not change our sentiments of gratitude toward him or diminish our confidence in his affection for the Italian cause. France and Italy, with their common origin, traditions, and customs, formed on the plains of Magenta and Solferino a bond that will prove indissoluble.

The government and people of England, that ancient country of freedom, warmly sanction our right to be the arbiters of our own destinies ; and they have lavishly bestowed upon us their good offices, the grateful remembrances of which will be imperishable.

An illustrious prince having ascended the throne of Prussia, I dispatched to him an ambassador in token of respect for him personally and of sympathy with the noble German nation, which I hope will become more and more secure in the conviction that Italy, having established her natural unity, will not violate the rights of other nations. . . .

*Accession of William as king of Prussia.*

Valiant youths, led on by a captain who has filled with his name the most distant countries, have made it evident that neither servitude nor long misfortune has been able to weaken the fiber of the Italian peoples. These facts have inspired the nation with great confidence in its own destinies. I take pleasure in manifesting to the first parliament of Italy the joy that fills my heart as king and soldier.

*Appreciativ allusion to Garibaldi's band.*

### IV. The Austro-Prussian War and the Founding of the North German Federation

Bismarck availed himself of the complications involved in the disposal of Schleswig-Holstein to put Austria in the wrong. On June 14, 1866, the king of Prussia declared that Austria had violated the principles upon which the union of 1815 was founded, and that the union had, accordingly, ceased to exist. Prussia speedily gained a surprising victory over Austria and her German allies, and Bismarck was able to write to his wife on July 9, three days after the great and decisive battle at Königgrätz, as follows:

HOHENMAUTH, Monday, July 9.

**240. Bismarck writes to his wife about the battle of Königgrätz.**

. . . It goes well with us — at least, if we are not excessive in our demands and do not think that we have conquered the world, we shall achieve a peace that is worth while. But we are as easily elated as we are cast down, and I have the thankless task of pouring water into the intoxicating wine, and making it plain that we do not live alone in Europe but with three neighbors.

The Austrians have taken a stand in Moravia, and we are at present so rash as to propose that to-morrow our headquarters shall be on the spot they now occupy. Prisoners are still coming in, and one hundred and eighty cannon have arrived since the 3d. If they bring on their southern army, we shall, with God's gracious aid, beat that, too. Confidence is everywhere. Our soldiers are dears [*Unsere Leute sind zum Küssen*], — every one of them so heroic, quiet, obedient, and decent, though with empty stomachs, wet clothes, wet camp, little sleep, and no soles to their shoes ! They are friendly to all, with no plundering or burning, but paying what they can, and eating moldy bread. There must be a goodly stock of fear of God among our common men, otherwise things could not be as they are. It is hard to get news of acquaintances; we are scattered miles apart, and do not know where to send, and have no one to send. There are men enough, of course, but no horses. . . .

**Conduct of William in the battle.**

The king exposed himself a great deal on the 3d, and it was a good thing that I was with him, for the warnings of others did not influence him, and no one else would have dared to talk to him as I did the last time, — and it did the job, — when a knot of ten cuirassiers and fifteen horses of the sixth cuirassier regiment were trampling about us in bloody confusion and the shells buzzed around disagreeably near his Majesty. The worst of them happily did not go off. I should, however, rather have had him too venturesome than to have him show himself overprudent. He was delighted with his troops, and with good reason, so that he did not seem to notice the whizzing and din about him. He was as composed as if he were on the Kreuzberg, and kept finding a new battalion to thank and say good-night to, until we were nearly within the firing line again. But so much was said to him of his recklessness that he will be more careful in the future, so your mind may be at rest on that score. I can hardly believe yet that the battle has really taken place. . . .

After the close of the short war between Prussia and Austria, a constitutional convention was summoned to draw up a plan of federation for Prussia and her neighbors north of the river Main. The constitution of the North German Federation was the result. The Assembly did its work so well that when, four years later, the southern states, Bavaria, Baden, and Würtemberg, came into the union after the war with France, the constitution did not have to be materially altered, and still remains that of the present German empire. Sybel, the distinguished historian, was a member of the Assembly in 1867, and well describes in a speech the peculiar difficulties of devising a union which should meet at once the demands of Prussia (a European power) and those of the various German monarchs, who had long regarded themselves as sovereigns and were fearful of being made the subjects of the king of Prussia.

Gentlemen, we must now take up what is obviously the most important and characteristic part of our task. Now that we have sketched out in general the powers which the proposed federal government is to enjoy, we must reach a

241. Three forces provided for in the German federation.

decision in regard to the organization of the union, — perhaps the most difficult question that any statesman has faced during the course of the century, — namely, the formation of a practicable and enduring central authority for Germany, strong enough to fulfill the various functions which devolve upon a modern state, and yet so far limited that the German princes and the individual states will not feel that they have been completely subordinated and mediatized. The central government must also be so far dependent upon the parliament that the political sentiments of the nation at large shall not be violated. Surely no task could be more difficult than ours. . . .

Neither a constitutional monarchy feasible nor a federation as commonly conceived.
The plan of a federation now before us, whatever may be its nature, is in no way a constitutional monarchy, nor is it a federation according to the traditional theories which have been developed in the universities. . . . Indeed, those who have drawn up the plan have unmistakably struck into a path diametrically opposed to that which has been hitherto followed in Germany. They have not taken a treatise upon political theory, I care not how good it may be, and copied out the features of a constitutional state as they are described therein; they have not, after arranging their plan, divided and distorted the real forces in our country in order to fit them into it. On the contrary, they have searched out in the long-standing chaos of German conditions the actually existing forces; they have endeavored to give them a legal basis and a form adjusted to the strength and importance of each; they have supplied each with its proper organ, and defined its scope and activity.

The forces to be considered were, as every one here well knows, the strong, victorious Prussia, whose traditions of a glorious past, whose present might, and, above all, whose future power combine to render her far too big to be fitted into that academic federation of the Göttingen professors. [*Laughter.*] In the situation of Europe at the present moment she necessarily enjoys in some respects a dictatorial power. Then, on the other hand, there are the other German states, who in the war against Prussia certainly won no laurels. Even those who were her allies were thrown sadly into the shade by the gigantic increase of Prussia's power. Yet, in spite of their relation with Prussia, the various German states have exhibited marked vitality and in some instances enjoy a strong support from outside. Moreover, — and that weighed most heavily, — in spite of the efforts of the cultivated class toward unity, the individual states each retains the very real sympathy of its own people on its own soil.

Thirdly and lastly, there was liberal public opinion, — in Prussia, in Germany, in Europe. In Prussia, indeed, it seemed that public opinion had been worsted in the unsuccessful opposition to Bismarck's ministry and had been forced to give up many of its positions. Yet in spite of this, by and large, and in the whole range of European relations, this public opinion has grown stronger and stronger, until not even the strongest of military monarchies can permanently resist the attacks of this spiritual power. . . .

It was necessary, then, to reckon with these three forces, — (1) with the military demands of the great Prussian state, (2) with the various individual German states, the demands of which were supported by local sentiment, and (3) with the strength of public opinion. The draft of the constitution, as it lies before us, provides for an organ for each of these forces : to Prussia — to the crown of Prussia — is assigned the presidency of the federation ; to the smaller states, the Federal Council (*Bundesrath*) ; to public opinion, the Imperial Diet (*Reichstag*).[1]

## V. The Franco-Prussian War and the Founding of the Present German Empire and French Republic

Bismarck, in a letter to his wife written immediately after the battle of Sedan, describes the capture of Napoleon III.

[1] For an account of the peculiarities of the present German federation, especially of the Federal Council, which is a species of *corporate monarch*, in whom the sovereignty is vested, *not in the emperor*, see my pamphlet, *The German Bundesrath*, Philadelphia, 1891.

242. Bismarck describes the surrender of Napoleon III at Sedan.

Day before yesterday before daybreak I left my quarters here; to-day I am returning, and have in the meantime experienced the great battle of Sedan on the 1st; in which we made towards thirty thousand prisoners and forced back the rest of the French army (which we have been pursuing all the way from Bar-le-Duc) into the fortress, where they must surrender themselves along with the emperor. Yesterday at five o'clock in the morning, after I had been discussing until one o'clock in the morning with Moltke and the French generals the terms of the capitulation, General Reille, whom I know, awoke me to tell me that Napoleon wished to speak with me.

I rode, without washing and with no breakfast, towards Sedan, and found the emperor in an open carriage with three officers of high rank and three others on horseback on the highroad near Sedan. I dismounted, greeted him as politely as if we were in the Tuileries, and asked what were his Majesty's commands. He wished to see the king. I told him, as was the truth, that his Majesty had his quarters three miles from there, at the place where I am now writing. On Napoleon's asking whither he should go, I offered him, since I was unfamiliar with the region, my quarters at Donchéry, a little place in the neighborhood close to Sedan. He accepted my invitation, and, accompanied by his six Frenchmen, myself, and Karl,[1] who had in the meantime followed me, drove, in the silence of the morning, toward our forces.

Before we reached the place he began to be apprehensive lest he might encounter a number of people, and he asked me whether he could not get out at a lonely laborer's cottage on the road. I had the place inspected by Karl, who reported that it was miserable and dirty. "*N'importe*," said Napoleon; and I ascended with him a narrow, rickety stairway. In a room ten feet square, with a deal table and two rush-bottomed chairs, we sat an hour, while the others

[1] Bismarck's son.

remained below, — a singular contrast to our last interview in '67 in the Tuileries.

Our negotiations were difficult, unless I consented to touch upon matters which could not but be painful to one who had been so cast down by God's mighty hand. I had summoned officers, through Karl, from the town and had asked Moltke to come. We then sent out one of the former to reconnoiter, and discovered, half a mile away, in Fresnois, a little villa with grounds.

Thither I accompanied the emperor, with an escort from the king's cuirassier regiment, which had been called up in the meantime; and there we concluded, with the French general Wimpffen, the capitulation, according to which forty to sixty thousand French, — I cannot be more accurate at this time, — with all that they had, became our prisoners. Day before yesterday and yesterday cost France one hundred thousand men and an emperor. This morning the latter started with all the members of his court, his horses and carriages, for Wilhelmshöhe, near Cassel.

This has been an event of vast historic importance, — a victory for which we must thank the Lord in humbleness of heart. It decides the conflict, although we must still carry on the war against an emperorless France. . . .

Good-by, my sweetheart. Love to the children.

Your v. B.

The republic was declared in France on September 4, 1870. Jules Favre, the minister of foreign affairs under the new provisional government, two days later issued a remarkable circular to the French diplomatic agents abroad, explaining the situation in France.

243. The French minister of foreign affairs on the downfall of the second empire (September 6, 1870).

Sir, the events which have just taken place in Paris are so well explained by the inexorable logic of facts that it is needless to dwell upon their meaning and bearing. In ceding to an irresistible impulse which had been but too long restrained, the population of Paris has obeyed a necessity superior to that of its own safety. It did not wish to perish with the criminal government which was leading France to her ruin. It has not pronounced the deposition of Napoleon III and of his dynasty; it has simply registered it in the name of right, justice, and public safety; and the sentence was so completely ratified beforehand by the public conscience that no one, even among the most noisy defenders of the power that was falling, raised a voice to uphold it. It collapsed of itself under the weight of its faults and amid the acclamations of the entire nation, without a single drop of blood being shed, without one individual being deprived of his personal liberty.

. . . Rescued from the shame and the danger of a government which has proved a traitor to all its duties, every one now comprehends that the first act of national sovereignty, reconquered at last, must be one of self-control, — the seeking for strength by respecting right. Moreover no time must be lost; our enemies are at our very gates; we have but one thought, — their expulsion from our territory.

But this obligation, which we resolutely accept, we did not impose upon France. She would not have been in her present position if she had listened to our voice. We have energetically defended the policy of peace even at the cost of our popularity. We still maintain the same opinion. We are heartbroken at the sight of these human butcheries consuming the youth of two nations, whom a little good sense and a great deal of liberty would have preserved from such frightful catastrophes. We cannot find any adequate expression of our admiration for our heroic army, sacrificed through the incapacity of its supreme commander, but showing itself greater in defeat than in the most brilliant victory. . . .

I would explain our position in a few words and submit my statement to the judgment of my country and of Europe. We loudly condemned the war, and, while proclaiming our respect for the rights of nations, we asked that Germany should be left mistress of her own destinies. We wished that liberty should be at the same time our common bond and our common protection. We were convinced that these moral forces would forever insure peace. But we claimed arms for all citizens and the right to elect our leaders. Had this been conceded, we should have remained invincible on our own soil. The government of the emperor, which had long since divorced its interests from those of the country, opposed that policy. We revert to it with the hope that, taught by experience, France will have the wisdom to put it into practice.

The king of Prussia has declared that he made war not against France but against the imperial dynasty. The dynasty has fallen. France is free. Does the king of Prussia wish to continue an unholy struggle, which will be at least as fatal to him as to us? Does he wish to give to the nineteenth century the cruel spectacle of two nations destroying one another, and, forgetful of humanity, reason, and culture, heaping corpse upon corpse, and ruin upon ruin? He is free to assume this responsibility in the face of the world and of history.

If it is a challenge, we accept it. We will cede neither an inch of our territory nor a stone of our fortresses. A disgraceful peace would mean a war of extermination at an early date. We will treat only for a permanent peace. In this respect our interest is that of the whole of Europe, and we have reason to hope that, divested of all dynastic considerations, the question will thus present itself to the cabinets of Europe. But even should we stand alone, we shall not yield. We have a resolute army, well-provisioned fortresses, a strong cordon of troops, and, above all, the hearts of three hundred thousand combatants determined to hold out to the bitter end.

The official account of the reëstablishment of the German empire appeared in Berlin, January 24, 1871.

244. How the German empire was proclaimed in Versailles (January 24, 1871).

In the palace of Louis XIV, in that ancient center of a hostile power which for centuries has striven to divide and humiliate Germany, the solemn proclamation of the German empire was made on January 18, exactly one hundred and seventy years after the assumption of the royal dignity by the Prussian sovereigns at Königsberg. Though the German people, owing to the necessities of the times, were represented at the ceremony only by the German army, the eyes of the entire nation were gratefully turned to the place where, surrounded by sovereigns, generals, and soldiers, King William announced to the world the assumption by himself and his heirs of a title for the reëstablishment of which we have been yearning during the sixty long years it has been in abeyance.

As yet the infatuation of the enemy does not permit us to throw aside the weapons we have taken up in self-defense; and as our unity arose out of the first part of the campaign, so will our empire be strengthened by the remaining feats of arms. By the self-sacrificing devotion of all classes of society, the nation has proved that it still possesses that warlike prowess which distinguished our ancestors. It has recovered its ancient position in Europe; and, neither fearing an adversary nor envying any neighbor, discreet and temperate in its acts and aims, it accepts the destiny prophesied for it in the proclamation of its new emperor. This destiny is to add to its power not by conquest but by promoting culture, liberty, and civilization. As far as the German people are concerned, there will be no more wars in Europe after the determination of the present campaign. . . .

Ceremony at Versailles.

Owing to the unfavorable weather the festive procession which was to conduct his Majesty from the prefecture to the palace did not take place. The crown prince, with Lieutenant-General Blumenthal, his chief of staff, and an escort of Prussians, Würtembergers, Badeners, and Bavarians, drove to the palace to receive his royal father at the eastern portal in front of the Princes' Stairway. In the courtyard of the palace a company of the king's own troops was drawn up as a guard of honor. . . .

At a quarter past twelve his Majesty entered the hall, when a choir consisting of men of the Seventh, Forty-Seventh, and Fifty-Eighth regiments intoned the choral, "Let all the world rejoice in the Lord." . . . When the choir ceased, the congregation sang one verse of the choral, " Praise and honor unto the Lord." The ordinary military liturgy was then read by the clergymen and a sermon preached by the Reverend A. Rogge. Alluding to the well-known inscription on the ceiling of the hall, "*Le roi governe par lui-même,*" the preacher observed that the kings of Prussia had risen to greatness by adopting a different and more religious motto, namely, " The kings of the earth reign under me, saith the Lord." The *Te Deum laudamus* closed the service.

The king then walked up to where the colors were displayed, and, standing before them, read the document proclaiming the reëstablishment of the German empire. Count Bismarck having read the king's proclamation to the German nation, the grand duke of Baden stepped forth and exclaimed, " Long live his Majesty the emperor ! " The cheers of the assembly were taken up by the bands playing the national anthem.

## BIBLIOGRAPHY

**Revolution of 1848 in France: Napoleon III:** SEIGNOBOS, *A Political History of Europe since 1814,* Chapter VI, pp. 155–186; PHILLIPS, *Modern Europe, 1815–1899,* Chapter XI, pp. 254–272; Chapter XIV, pp. 332–338; FYFFE, *History of Modern Europe,* Chapter XVIII, pp. 699–706; Chapter XIX, pp. 728–737; Chapter XX, pp. 809–824; ANDREWS, *The Historical Development of Modern Europe,* Vol. I, Chapter VIII, pp. 320–362; Vol. II, Chapter I, pp. 1–41. *A. References.*

**Revolt against Metternich's System:** ANDREWS, Vol. I, Chapters IX–X, pp. 363–448; PHILLIPS, Chapter XI, pp. 232–254; Chapters XII–XIII, pp. 273–331; SEIGNOBOS, Chapter XIII, pp. 401–423.

**Napoleon III and Italian Unity:** ANDREWS, Vol. II, Chapter III, pp. 91–145; SEIGNOBOS, Chapter XI, pp. 336–359; PHILLIPS, Chapter XV, pp. 361–389.

**Bismarck and the North German Federation:** SEIGNOBOS, Chapter XV, pp. 456–476; ANDREWS, Vol. II, Chapters V–VI, pp. 188–260.

**Completion of German Unity:** ANDREWS, Vol. II, Chapter VI, pp. 261–277; PHILLIPS, Chapter XVIII, pp. 449–485; SEIGNOBOS, Chapter XV, pp. 476–484.

The Third French Republic : SEIGNOBOS, Chapter VII, pp. 187–204 ; ANDREWS, Vol. II, Chapter IX, pp. 343–355.

The Eastern Question : ANDREWS, Vol. II, Chapter VIII, pp. 297–342 ; SEIGNOBOS, Chapters XX–XXI, pp. 616–670 ; PHILLIPS, Chapter XIX, pp. 491–523.

*B. Additional reading in English.*

There are at least two satisfactory political histories of the nineteenth century, — those of Andrews and of Seignobos, mentioned above. The English translation of Seignobos is edited by Professor MACVANE and is supplied with extensive and discriminating bibliographies at the close of each chapter. Somewhat briefer and rather journalistic is MÜLLER, *History of Recent Times*, giving especial attention to Germany, 1816–1875. Very recent political developments are treated by Professor ANDREWS in his volume on *Contemporaneous Europe*, the last in the great set, " The History of all Nations," published by Lea Brothers. In due time Vols. X–XII of the *Cambridge Modern History* will appear, and will, it is to be hoped, give a broad view of the general progress of the century.

These general accounts may be supplemented by the following :

ANDERSON, *Constitutions and Other Select Documents Illustrative of the History of France, 1789–1901*, 1904.

MALLESON, *Life of Prince Metternich*.

MUNROE SMITH, *Bismarck and German Unity*. Excellent short account.

SYBEL, *Founding of the German Empire*, Vol. I. Gives an excellent review of German history following 1815.

BISMARCK, *The Man and the Statesman*, 2 vols. Being reflections and reminiscences written and dictated by himself after his retirement.

BUSCH, *Our Chancellor*. Interesting impressions of Bismarck by his secretary.

THAYER, WILLIAM R., *Dawn of Italian Independence*, 2 vols. Scholarly and interesting account up to the revolution of 1848.

COUNTESS CESARESCO, *Liberation of Italy*. This, and STILLMAN, *The Union of Italy, 1815–1895*, are exceptionally good accounts by writers who have lived long in Italy.

HANOTAUX, *Contemporary France*, Vol. I, has appeared, 1903.

COUBERTIN, *The Evolution of France under the Third Republic*.

TRAILL, *Social England*, Vol. VI.

MCCARTHY, *History of Our Own Times*, 4 vols.

HOLLAND, *European Concert in the Eastern Question*.

LOWELL, *Government and Parties in Continental Europe*, 2 vols. Very important.

# CHAPTER XLI

## EUROPE OF TO-DAY

### I. Development of Natural Science

While Roger Bacon had, in the thirteenth century, forecast the methods of modern science, it remained for Francis Bacon, some three centuries later, clearly to enunciate its principles in his famous *Novum Organum*, which he dedicated to James I. In it he harshly criticises the mediæval attitude toward natural science.

The discoveries which have hitherto been made in the sciences are such as lie close to vulgar notions, scarcely beneath the surface. In order to penetrate into the inner and further recesses of nature, it is necessary that both notions and axioms be derived from things by a more sure and guarded way, and that a method of intellectual operation be introduced altogether better and more certain. . . . **245. Francis Bacon proclaims the principles of modern scientific progress.**

There are and can be only two ways of searching into and discovering truth. The one flies from the senses and particulars to the most general axioms, and from these principles, the truth of which it takes for settled and immovable, proceeds to judgment and the discovery of middle axioms. And this way is now in fashion. The other derives axioms from the senses and particulars, rising by a gradual and unbroken ascent, so that it arrives at the most general axioms last of all. This is the true way, but as yet untried. . . .

It is not to be forgotten that in every age natural philosophy has had a troublesome adversary and hard to deal with, — namely, superstition and the blind and immoderate zeal of religion. For we see among the Greeks that those **Religious opposition to science.**

who first proposed to man's uninitiated ears the natural causes for thunder and for storms were thereupon found guilty of impiety. Nor was much more forbearance shown by some of the ancient fathers of the Christian Church to those who, on most convincing grounds (such as no one in his senses would now think of contradicting), maintained that the earth was round and, of consequence, asserted the existence of the antipodes.[1]

**Influence of the scholastic philosophers.**

Moreover, as things now are, to discourse of nature is made harder and more perilous by the summaries and systems of the schoolmen; who, having reduced theology into regular order as well as they were able, and fashioned it into the shape of an art, ended in incorporating the contentious and thorny philosophy of Aristotle, more than was fit, with the body of religion. . . .

**No conflict between science and religion.**

Lastly, some are weakly afraid lest a deeper search into nature should transgress the permitted limits of sober-mindedness; wrongfully wresting and transferring what is said in Holy Writ against those who pry into sacred

[1] Lactantius, a Christian writer of Constantine's time, discussing the idea advanced by the philosophers that there may be "antipodes," that is, men living on the opposite side of the globe, writes: "How can there be any one so absurd as to think that men can have their feet higher than their heads; or that in those parts of the earth instead of resting on the ground things hang down; crops and trees grow downward; rain, snow, and hail fall upward on to the earth? Who indeed can wonder at the hanging gardens which are reckoned as one of the seven wonders when the philosophers would have us believe in hanging fields and cities, seas and mountains? . . .

"If you ask those who maintain these monstrous notions why everything does not fall off into the heavens on that side, they reply that it is of the nature of things that all objects having weight are borne toward the center, and that everything is connected with the center, like the spokes of a wheel; while light things, like clouds, smoke, and fire, are borne away from the center and seek the heavens. I scarce know what to say of such fellows, who when once they have wandered from truth persevere in their foolishness and defend their absurdities by new absurdities. Sometimes I imagine that their philosophizing is all a joke, or that they know the truth well enough and only defend these lies in a perverse attempt to exhibit and exercise their wit." — *Divinae Institutiones*, Lib. iii, sect. 24, Corp. Scrip. Eccl. Lat., XIX, pp. 254 *sq.*

mysteries to the hidden things of nature, which are barred by no prohibition. . . .

But if the matter be truly considered, natural philosophy is, after the word of God, at once the surest medicine against superstition and the most approved nourishment for faith; and therefore she is rightly given to religion as her most faithful handmaid, since the one displays the will of God, the other his power. . . .

. . . Again, in the customs and institutions of schools, academies, colleges, and similar bodies destined for the abode of learned men and the cultivation of learning, everything is found adverse to the progress of science. For the lectures and exercises there are so ordered that to think or speculate on anything out of the common way can hardly occur to any man. And if one or two have the boldness to use any liberty of judgment, they must undertake the task all by themselves; they can have no advantage from the company of others. And if they can endure this also, they will find their industry and largeness of mind no slight hindrance to their fortune. For the studies of men in these places are confined and, as it were, imprisoned in the writings of certain authors, from whom, if any man dissent, he is straightway arraigned as a turbulent person and an innovator. . . .

*Universities opposed to scientific advance.*

In matters of state, change even for the better is distrusted, because it unsettles what is established; these things resting on authority, consent, fame, and opinion, not on demonstration; but arts and sciences should be like mines where the noise of new works and further advances is heard on every side. . . .

No one has yet been found so firm of mind and purpose as resolutely to compel himself to sweep away all theories and common notions and to apply the understanding, thus made fair and even, to a fresh examination of particulars. Thus it happens that human knowledge, as we have it, is a mere medley and ill-digested mass, made up of much credulity and much accident, and also of the childish notions which we at first imbibed.

Great hopes of
experimental
science.
Now if any one of ripe age, unimpaired senses, and well-purged mind apply himself anew to experience and particulars, better hopes may be entertained of that man. In which point I promised to myself a like fortune to that of Alexander the Great, [who, according to Titus Livius,] "had done no more than take courage to despise vain apprehensions." And a like judgment I suppose may be passed on myself in future ages : that I did no great things, but simply made less account of things that were counted great. In the meanwhile, as I have already said, there is no hope except in a new birth of science ; that is, in raising it regularly up from experience and building it afresh; which no one, I think, will say has yet been done or thought of.

## II. APPLIED SCIENCE

While Bacon, Newton, and Laplace were engaged, during the seventeenth and eighteenth centuries, in profound scientific research, practical inventors, like Newcomen, Arkwright, Crompton, Watt, and Cartwright, were availing themselves, often unconsciously, of the great principles of natural law. The result was a series of mechanical devices which were later greatly increased and perfected through the aid of science, and which have served to revolutionize industry and commerce and fundamentally to alter social and political conditions. The central economic facts of this revolution have been the increase in man's productive powers and the vast improvement in the means of transportation.

246. Efficiency of
modern
industrial
methods.
(From C. A.
Beard's
*The Industrial
Revolution.*)
Human progress depends on the ability of mankind to do more work and to accomplish greater tasks ; to supply the necessaries of life with less expenditure of time and strength and thus to secure leisure for thought, invention and artistic development of every kind.

To show the expansion of trade following the new inventions it is necessary to give a few statistics. When machinery was introduced into the textile industries the output of manufactured goods increased by leaps and bounds. In 1764 the cotton imported into England amounted to about 4,000,000 pounds; in 1841 it had increased to nearly 500,000,000 pounds. In 1792 the amount of cotton imported into Lancashire alone from the United States was 138,000 pounds; in 1800 it was 18,000,000 pounds. The wool imported into England in 1766 was only about 2,000,000 pounds; in 1830 the amount had risen to more than 32,000,000 pounds. In 1788 the iron output was 61,000 tons; in 1839 it was over 1,250,000 tons. One hundred years after Crompton invented his spinning mule there were in Lancashire 2655 cotton mills running a total of nearly 38,000,000 spindles and 463,000 power looms; in the twenty-two years from 1793 to 1815 English exports, according to official valuation, rose from £17,000,000 annually to £58,000,000, in spite of the depression caused by the Napoleonic wars.

These figures give an inkling of the industrial transformation which followed the great inventions. Now let us turn to the real increase in the productive capacity of the individual. In other words, let us see whether productive capacity has grown more rapidly than the population. Unfortunately, careful compilations of statistics are only of recent date, but we know that Hargreaves' jenny worked only eight spindles. The number was gradually increased to one hundred and twenty, and by the beginning of the nineteenth century to two hundred. The jenny now has more than a thousand spindles, each revolving at the rate of ten thousand revolutions per minute. A man and two boys can tend two thousand spindles.

The hand-loom weaver used to make from sixty to eighty throws of the shuttle per minute. Fifty years ago the best power loom made only one hundred throws; to-day the highest-grade loom runs at the rate of about four hundred per minute, and along with the increase of the productive capacity of the machine there is a decrease in the amount of human labor required in the operations. Formerly one weaver tended but one loom; now one worker tends from two to ten looms according to the grade of goods. So great has been the increase in the efficiency of textile machinery that a single operative can supply two hundred and fifty persons with the necessary cotton garments, or three hundred persons with woolen clothing.

In every branch of industry attention has been devoted to increasing productive power, until almost marvelous results have been attained. In the continuation of the construction of the Cologne cathedral in 1870, two men with a steam crane lifted as much stone in a day as three hundred and sixty men could have done in the same time in the Middle Ages. The old craftsman produced at best a couple of pairs of shoes per day; the modern worker with machinery can turn out five hundred pairs a day. In one year six English workmen can produce enough bread to supply a thousand people for the same length of time. This includes all the labor from the breaking up of the soil to the delivery of the bread to the consumer.

The extent to which mechanical power can be substituted for hand labor depends upon the ability of man to contrive machinery. Here is the material key to man's spiritual progress. The plowing of a furrow, the sowing of the seed, the reaping of the grain, its transportation from one market to another, the weaving of a fabric, and the making of a coat all represent in the final analysis the application of so much power to matter.

The past achievements of inventors have shown us that there are no limits to the ways in which the exhaustless forces of nature can be applied to do man's work. If we look back, we see man struggling to maintain life by sheer strength of muscle; but if we look forward along the centuries of the future, we see the struggle for existence taking only a small portion of man's energy, leaving all the remainder of his powers of heart and brain free for the enlargement and enriching of life.

The result of the construction and use of compound engines in economizing coal has been illustrated by Sir Lyon Playfair by the statement that "a small cake of coal which would pass through a ring the size of a shilling, when burned in the compound engine of a modern steamboat, would drive a ton of food and its proportion of the ship two miles on its way from a foreign port." Another calculator, says the London *Engineer*, "has computed that half a sheet of note paper will develop sufficient power, when burned in connection with a triple expansion engine, to carry a ton a mile in an Atlantic steamer." How, under such circumstances, the charge for sea freights on articles of comparatively high value has been reduced, is shown by the fact that the ocean transport of fresh meat from New York to Liverpool does not exceed one cent per pound. . . .

247. Improvements in methods of transportation. (From Wells *Economic Changes*.)

Great, however, as has been the revolution in respect to economy and efficiency in the carrying trade upon the ocean, the revolution in the carrying trade on land during the same period has been even greater and more remarkable. Taking the American railroads in general as representative of the railroad system of the world, the average charge for moving one ton of freight per mile has been reduced from about two and one-half cents in 1869 to about a cent in 1887. To grasp fully the meaning and significance of these figures, their method of presentation may be varied by saying that two thousand pounds of coal, iron, wheat, cotton, or other commodities can now be carried on the best-managed railways for a distance of one mile for a sum so small that, outside of China, it would be difficult to find a coin of equivalent value to give to a boy as a reward for carrying an ounce package across the street, even if a man or boy could be found in Europe or the United States willing either to give or accept so small a compensation for such a service.

Transportation on land.

The history of industrial movement would embrace, directly or indirectly, an account of all that chiefly distinguished the nineteenth century from the eighteenth, the old

248. Economic effects of the revolution in the means of communication.
(From *The United States of America,* edited by Professor Shaler.)

régime from the new.  It would include an account of the origin and rise of the factory system of industry, replacing the home work or the small and scattered workshops of the old time by the aggregation of men and machinery at industrial centers.  It would be much concerned with the discovery and perfection of the steam engine, the mighty prime mover in these changes, and after that with the discovery and development of its chief modes of application to the spindle, the weaving frame, the forge, the printing press, the mill, and innumerable other instruments of production; to the railway, the steamship, and other means of transportation and communication.

Aggregation of industries in cities.

But only in its origin is the revolution exclusively industrial, and in the next stage are seen its immediate effects upon human life, of which perhaps the most important spring from the aggregation of industries, and consequently of men, in cities, accompanied by a relative diminution of the number of tillers of the soil, and the separation of producers into two distinct classes, — the capitalists, or organizing and directing class, and the manual laborers. A mind subtle enough might trace a third and more remote series of effects to the same causes.  The thought of our time, whether taking the form of literature, science, the fine arts, or political discussion, is evidently molded in great measure by the spectacle of the industrial revolution and of the phenomena induced by it.

Economic revolution caused by improved transportation.

None of these changes are more characteristic or more indispensable to the state of society that we now see around us than those in the methods of moving men and things from one place to another, and of communication between men in places distant from one another.  The change in industrial organization involves, above all, a greater dependence of each class of men upon other classes, and therefore the necessity for more frequent interchange of goods. The manufacturing class, formerly to a great degree scattered over the country as small handicraftsmen, have now separated entirely from the agricultural class and gathered in factories in the great towns.  Therefore the products of the loom, the mill, and the forge, which formerly, if not actually produced upon the farmer's premises, were to be had near at hand, must now be brought from the more distant towns, and the farm products exchanged for them must traverse the same distance.

One need only visit Mount Vernon to see an illustration of this change. George Washington lived upon his estate, surrounded by small handicraftsmen, and, as regards the commoner needs of daily life, almost entirely independent of transportation. Not only did he raise the foodstuffs for his own consumption and that of his numerous dependents, but blacksmiths, shoemakers, tailors, and carpenters were found among the slaves upon his plantation, and cloth for the coarser sort of garments was spun and woven in his household. Nowadays country gentlemen usually live near a railroad station, and have their supplies sent out every week, or oftener, from the nearest large town, perhaps a hundred miles away.

Still more important to the study of transportation than this withdrawal of the manufacturing classes into towns is the specialization of manufactures by districts, — what has been called the territorial division of labor. The principle that one can accomplish most by concentrating his energies on the thing that he is best fitted to do, has in our time been applied to places as well as to persons. Massachusetts has districts whose people are almost wholly occupied with shoemaking, and others where they are equally engrossed in cotton spinning. Pittsburg and the surrounding country is, roughly speaking, a vast iron furnace, Dakota a wheat field, and so on.

Applied science is by no means confined to the invention of machinery and the facilitating of travel and intercommunication. Science has revolutionized our ideas of animal and plant life and of the treatment of maladies. By means of the most delicately adjusted microscopes it has become possible to discover and study the minute plants known as bacteria, some of which are not over a hundred and fifty thousandth of an inch in diameter.

The study of the life histories of these diminutive plants excites the wonder of those who make observations upon them. It is truly marvelous to know that these bacteria can accomplish, in their short lives of possibly a few hours or days, feats which would baffle the cleverest of chemists if given years of a lifetime to work upon. They give to the farmer the good quality of his crops, to the dairyman superior butter and cheese; they assist in large measure in freeing our rivers and lakes from harmful pollutions. Here it should be strongly emphasized that those bacteria which cause disease are only a few species, all others contributing to our welfare in countless ways.

Quite as astonishing is the discovery that within the root knobs of peas and beans live bacteria which, by splitting up mineral salts containing nitrogen and by absorbing nitrogen from the air, give it over to the plant, so that it is enabled to grow luxuriantly, whereas without their presence the tiller of the soil might fertilize the ground in vain. It is quite possible that not alone peas and beans but all grasses and plants and trees depend upon the presence of such germs for their very existence, which in turn supply man and animals with their means of existence. Hence we see that these nitrifying bacteria, as they are called, if swept out of existence, would be the cause of cessation of all life upon the globe.

The astonishing effects of scientific discovery in promoting the highly practical art of surgery are well described by Dr. Keen in the following passage.

Great theologians, such as a Calvin or a Jonathan Edwards, were they recalled to life, could discourse as learnedly as ever of predestination and free will; great forensic orators, such as a Burke or a Webster, could convince us by the same arguments and arouse us by the same invectives that made our fathers willing captives to their silver tongues. But to-day, so rapid has been our surgical progress that a Velpeau, a Sir William Ferguson, or a Pancoast — all of whom have died within the last thirty years — could not teach modern surgical principles nor perform a modern surgical operation. Even our everyday surgical vocabulary — staphylococcus, streptococcus, infection, immunity, antisepsis and asepsis, toxin and antitoxin — would be unintelligible jargon to him; and our modern operations on the brain, the chest, the abdomen, and the pelvis would make him wonder whether we had all lost our senses, until, seeing the almost uniform and almost painless recoveries, he would thank God for the magnificent progress of the last half century, which had vouchsafed such magical — nay, almost divine — power to the modern surgeon.

## III. Political and Social Democracy

The chief political question of the nineteenth century in all the states of western Europe has been the same, — namely, whether the king should continue to rule in the more or less absolute manner in which he had controlled the government in the previous century, or whether the people should be regarded as the sovereign and rule through their deputies. Everywhere, consequently, though with certain local differences, we find the following four great parties representing four different views of this fundamental question.

251. The chief party issues in western Europe during the nineteenth century. (From Seignobos )

1. The absolutist conservative party, formed by the high officials and landed aristocracy, desired to maintain absolute government, the authority of the Church, and the censorship of the press; it controlled all the central, eastern, and southern states of Europe. It no longer existed in England, for the former absolutist party, the Jacobites, had not survived the century of political liberty.

The constitu-
tional party,
or right
center.

2. The liberal conservative, or constitutional party, sometimes called the Tory, or right center, composed of the
upper middle class and the liberal officeholders, demanded
that the assembly should control the administration of the
government, particularly in financial matters. Its ideal was
personal government by the sovereign, with a parliament of
two houses, one aristocratic, the other elective. It believed
that the electoral body should be limited by a considerable
property qualification, and that the parliament should vote
the annual budget and leave the prince free in the choice
of his ministers and in the direction of general policy.
There should be no censorship of the press, but liberty
should be restricted to the wealthy classes; the nation's
rights should be guaranteed by a constitution. This party
was in power in the states which had constitutions; in the
absolute monarchies it demanded a constitution, a representative assembly, and the abolition of censorship.

The parlia-
mentary
party, or left
center.

3. The parliamentary liberal party, sometimes called the
Whig, or left center, recruited from the middle class, demanded not only control by the elective assembly but its
supremacy over the sovereign, his ministers, and the aristocratic chamber. Its ideal was the parliamentary system, a
ministry chosen from the party in majority in the lower
house, governing in the prince's name, but according to
the will of the elected representatives of the nation. It demanded a constitution which recognized the superior rights
or sovereignty of the people, political liberties (such as liberty
of the press, holding public meetings, and forming associations), and absolute religious liberty. . . . It would admit
only property owners to vote, but tended to lower the qual-
ifications for the franchise in order to include in the voting
body the lower middle class.

The radical
democratic
party.

4. The democratic, or radical party, formed by students,
workingmen, writers, and lawyers, demanded, according to
the motto of the French Revolution, the sovereignty and
political equality of the people. It added to the demands of
the parliamentary party universal suffrage, remuneration
of representatives, abolition of all political privileges of the

wealthy classes, and separation of church and state. Its ideal was a purely representative, democratic, and preferably republican government like that of the French Convention, or even a direct government by the people, in which they should themselves make the constitution. In 1815 this party, so far from being in power in any country, had not even the right to formulate its programme publicly, except in England, Sweden, and Norway.

The two extreme parties, absolutist and democratic, held diametrically opposite conceptions of government and society. The absolutists wanted a society based on hereditary inequality. . . . They also demanded an established religion. The democrats admitted neither political, hereditary, nor ecclesiastical authority.

A country might, however, pass from one of these extremes to the other gradually, for the four parties formed a continuous gradation. The absolutist system became constitutional when the prince consented to grant a constitution, as in the south German states in 1816 to 1819. The constitutional system was insensibly transformed into the parliamentary system as the sovereign took more account of the wishes of the elective chamber, as in England after 1830. The parliamentary system became democratic with the extension of the suffrage and the assembly's acquisition of supremacy over all the other powers, as in Switzerland.

With the revolution of 1848 in France a new party, working for economic as well as political changes, made its appearance, as we have seen.[1] This movement was the outgrowth of the great industrial changes of the preceding half century. The efforts of its adherents were commonly directed towards some socialistic reorganization of society which should secure to the workingman a more generous share of the products of his labor than he could receive under the capitalistic system which had

[1] See above, p. 524.

A.36

grown up. Of the many programmes of reform which have been drawn up by the labor leaders, the following, formulated at a great labor congress at Gotha in 1875, will serve as a statement of their chief economic doctrines.

1. Labor is the source of all wealth, and of all civilization; and since it is only through society that generally productive labor is possible, the whole product of labor, where there is a general obligation to work, belongs to society, — that is, to all its members, by equal right, to each according to his reasonable needs.

In the society of to-day the means of production are a monopoly of the capitalistic class; the dependence of the working classes which results from this is the cause of misery and of servitude in all its forms.

The emancipation of labor requires the conversion of the means of production into the common property of society and the social regulation of all labor and its application for the general good, together with the just distribution of the product of labor.

The emancipation of labor must be the work of the laboring class itself, opposed to which all other classes are reactionary groups.

2. Proceeding from these principles, the socialist labor party of Germany endeavors by every lawful means to bring about a free state and a socialistic society, to effect the destruction of the iron law of wages by doing away with the system of wage labor, to abolish exploitation of every kind, and to extinguish all social and political inequality.

The socialist labor party of Germany, although for the time being confining its activity within national bounds, is fully conscious of the international character of the labor movement, and is resolved to meet all the obligations which this lays upon the laborer, in order to bring the brotherhood of all mankind to a full realization.

The socialist labor party of Germany, in order to prepare the way for the solution of the social question, demands the establishment of socialistic productive associations with the support of the state and under the democratic control of the working people. These productive associations, for both industry and agriculture, are to be created to such an extent that the socialistic organization of all labor may result therefrom.

[In addition to the demand for universal suffrage for all above twenty years of age, secret ballot, freedom of the press, free and compulsory education, etc.,] the socialist labor party of Germany demands the following reforms in the present social organization: (1) the greatest possible extension of political rights and freedom in the sense of the above-mentioned demands; (2) a single progressive income tax, both state and local, instead of all the existing taxes, especially the indirect ones, which weigh heavily upon the people; (3) unlimited right of association; (4) a normal working day corresponding with the needs of society, and the prohibition of work on Sunday; (5) prohibition of child labor and all forms of labor by women which are dangerous to health or morality; (6) laws for the protection of the life and health of workmen, sanitary control of workmen's houses, inspection of mines, factories, workshops, and domestic industries by officials chosen by the workmen themselves, and an effective system of enforcement of the same; (7) regulation of prison labor.

Immediate reforms demanded by the socialists.

A more vigorous denunciation of the present social organization is to be found in the Erfurt programme of October, 1891.

The economic development of industrial society tends inevitably to the ruin of small industries, which are based upon the workman's private ownership of the means of production. It separates him from these means of production and converts him into a destitute member of the proletariat, whilst a comparatively small number of capitalists and great landowners obtain a monopoly of the means of production.

253. Extract from the Erfurt programme of the socialists (October, 1891).

Criticism of
the existing
capitalistic
organization
of society.
Hand in hand with this growing monopoly goes the destruction of these scattered small industries by industries of colossal growth, the development of the tool into the machine, and a gigantic increase in the productiveness of human labor. But all the advantages of this revolution are monopolized by the capitalist and great landowners. To the proletariat and to the rapidly sinking middle classes, the small tradesmen of the towns and the peasants, it brings an increasing uncertainty of existence, increasing misery, oppression, servitude, degradation, and exploitation.

Ever greater grows the mass of the proletariat, ever vaster the army of the unemployed, ever sharper the contrast between oppressors and oppressed, ever fiercer that war of classes between *bourgeoisie* and proletariat which divides modern society into two hostile camps and is the common characteristic of every industrial country.

## IV. IMPERIALISM

An English writer thus briefly indicates the present extent of the colonies of the several European powers.

**254. Present extent of European colonies. (From J. A. Hobson.)**
Since 1884 some three and three-quarter millions of square miles have been added to the British empire. Nor does Great Britain stand alone in this enterprise. The leading characteristic of modern imperialism, the competition of rival empires, is the product of this same period. The close of the Franco-German war marks the beginning of a new colonial policy in France and Germany, destined to take effect in the next decade.

Small extent of German colonies.
It was not unnatural that the newly founded German empire, surrounded by powerful enemies and doubtful allies, and perceiving its more adventurous youth drawn into the United States and other foreign lands, should form the idea of a colonial empire. During the seventies a vigorous literature sprang up in advocacy of the policy, which took shape a little later in the powerful hands of Bismarck. The earliest instance of official aid for the promotion of German

commerce abroad occurred in 1880. But the definite advance of Germany upon its imperialistic career began in 1884 with a policy of African protectorates and annexations of oceanic islands. During the next fifteen years she brought under her colonial sway about a million square miles, with an estimated population of fourteen millions. Almost the whole of this territory is tropical, and the white population forms a total of a few thousands.

Similarly in France a great revival of the old colonial spirit took place in the early eighties. The extension of empire in the Senegal and Sahara in 1880 was followed next year by the annexation of Tunis, and France was soon actively engaged in the scramble for Africa in 1884, while at the same time she was fastening her rule upon Tonquin and Laos in Asia. Her acquisitions since 1880 (exclusive of the extension of New Caledonia and its dependencies) amount to an area of over three and one-half million square miles, with a native population of some thirty-seven million; almost the whole territory is tropical or subtropical, inhabited by lower races, and incapable of colonization. *French colonies.*

Italian aspirations took similar shape from 1880 onwards, though the disastrous experience of the Abyssinian expedition has given a check to Italian imperialism. Her possessions in East Africa are confined to the northern colony of Eritrea and the protectorate of Somaliland. *Italian colonization*

Of the other European states two only, Portugal and Belgium, enter directly into the competition of the new imperialism. Spain may be said to have definitely retired from imperial competition. The large and important possessions of Holland in the East and West Indies, though involving her in imperial politics in some degree, belong to older colonialism; she takes no part in the new expansion.

Russia, the only active expansionist country of the north, stands alone in the character of her imperial growth, which differs from other imperialism in that it has been principally Asiatic in its achievements and has proceeded, by direct extension of imperial boundaries, partaking to a *Russia.*

The United
States.

larger extent than in the other cases of a regular colonial policy of settlement for purposes of agriculture and industry.

The recent entrance of the powerful and progressive nation of the United States of America upon imperialism by the annexation of Hawaii and the taking over of the relics of the ancient Spanish empire, not only adds a new formidable competitor for trade and territory, but changes and complicates the issues. As the focus of political attention and activity shifts more to the Pacific states, and the commercial aspirations of America are more and more set upon trade with the Pacific islands and the Asiatic coast, the same forces which are driving European states along the path of territorial expansion seem likely to act upon the United States, leading her to a virtual abandonment of the principle of American isolation which has hitherto dominated her policy.

## BIBLIOGRAPHY

*A. References.*

**Democracy and Reform in England:** SEIGNOBOS, *Political History of Europe since 1814*, pp. 10–101.

**Socialism in Europe :** SEIGNOBOS, pp. 718–745.

**The Hague Peace Conference :** PHILLIPS, *Modern Europe*, pp. 526–527, 544–546.

**The Partition of Africa :** PHILLIPS, pp. 538–544.

**Europe and Asia :** PHILLIPS, pp. 535–538.

---

*B. Additional reading in English.*

Science.

There are three scholarly and yet popular works on the striking scientific achievements in the nineteenth century : WALLACE, *The Wonderful Century*, 1898 ; WILLIAMS, *Story of Nineteenth Century Science*, 1900 ; and *The Progress of the Century*, 1901. The last contains chapters on literature and religion as well.

Modern
industry.

There is no history of the industrial revolution in Europe as a whole. GIBBINS, *Economic and Industrial Progress of the Century*, 1903, is a popular outline. COCHRANE, *Modern Industrial Progress*, 1904 : a popular description of some of the most striking mechanical inventions of the last century. The best account of English economic history for the first half of the century is to be found in CUNNINGHAM, *Growth of English Industry and Commerce*, edition of 1903, Vol. II, Part II.

MARSHALL, *Principles of Economics*, 1905, Book IV, Chapters VIII–XIII: contains an excellent study of modern industrial organization. McVEY, *Modern Industrialism*, 1905, devotes considerable attention to Great Britain and Germany.

WEBB, *Problems of Modern Industry*, 1898, and ADAMS and SUMNER, *Labor Problems*, 1905, are valuable studies of conditions of labor. INGRAM, *A History of Political Economy*, 1888, Chapters V–VIII: a convenient summary of the theories of the chief modern economists.

For the history of socialism in Europe: ELY, *French and German Socialism*, 1898 ; WEBB, *Socialism in England*, 1901 ; SOMBART, *Socialism and the Social Movement in the Nineteenth Century*, 1898. — Socialism.

LOWELL, *Governments and Parties in Continental Europe*, 2 vols., 1900 : a study of the governmental organizations and the political parties in France, Germany, Italy, and Switzerland. For England : COURTNEY, *The Working Constitution of the United Kingdom*, 1904 ; also ROSE, *Rise of Democracy*, 1897. — Government and politics.

Translations of the constitutions of France, Prussia, Italy, and Belgium are published as supplements to the "Annals of the American Academy of Political and Social Science," 1892–1896. The constitutions of the German empire and Switzerland are to be found in the Wharton School Series (University of Pennsylvania). These are reproduced in LARNED, *History for Ready Reference*, Vol. I, pp. 538 *sqq*. — Translation of constitutions.

*The Statesman's Yearbook*, annually since 1865, is a mine of information on the governments, statistics, and industries of all the countries.

REINSCH, *World Politics at the End of the Nineteenth Century*, 1900 : a suggestive and valuable work on the forces underlying imperialism, the Chinese question, and the reflex influence of Eastern developments on Western politics. By the same, *Colonial Government*, 1902 : an analysis of the economic forces in imperialism and a discussion of the methods of colonial government; useful general and topical bibliographies are given. HOBSON, *Imperialism : a Study*, 1902 : an indictment of British imperial policy on economic grounds. SKRINE, *The Expansion of Russia, 1815–1900*, 1903 : devotes more attention to internal politics than the title implies. RAMBAUD, *The Expansion of Russia*, 1904 : brief and readable account of Russian advance in Europe and Asia. KELTIE, *Partition of Africa*, 1895 : a detailed history of the operations of European powers in Africa. DOUGLAS, *Europe and the Far East*, 1904. — Imperialism.

FOSTER, *Arbitration and The Hague Court*, 1904 : a brief account of the present position of international arbitration. — International arbitration.

# INDEX

This Index should be supplemented by the analytical Table of Contents at the opening of this volume.